FORTY LOST YEARS

This book is given
In honor of
Joshua C. Evans
By
Linda & Bill Evans
May 2001

FORTY LOST YEARS

The apartheid state
and the politics of the National Party
1948 – 1994

Dan O'Meara

Département de science politique
Université du Québec à Montréal

Ravan Press

Ohio University Press
Athens

Published by Ravan Press (Pty) Ltd, P.O. Box 145, Randburg, 2125
South Africa

ISBN: 0 86975 459 9

Published in the United States of America by Ohio University Press,
Scott Quadrangle, Athens, Ohio 45701

ISBN: 0 8214 1173 X

Library of Congress Cataloguing-in-Publication Data available

First published 1996
Second impression 1999

Cover design: Monica Seeber and Centre Court Studio
DTP setting and design: Rob Irvine

Printed by: Kohler Carton & Print, Pinetown

Dedication

Afrikaner nationalism and the Afrikaner people bear a heavy historical responsibility for the monstrous crimes of apartheid.

Yet it should never be forgotten that there were always Afrikaners who found a different way – men and women who stepped out of the narrow *laager* of the nationalist establishment when this was a lonely, difficult and even dangerous thing to do. While insisting that they too were Afrikaners, each in their own way tried to voice the belief that South Africa was not the God-given preserve of the Afrikaner *volk,* but indeed belonged to all who lived in it, black and white.

This small band of Afrikaner dissidents brought honour to their language, to their culture, to their people and to themselves, at a time when the very name 'Afrikaner' or 'Boer' had become a hated synonym for the most despicable forms of racism and political mean-spiritedness. Their example makes it possible that the Afrikaans language and literature may one day receive the international recognition they richly deserve.

I have always been moved by the rare humanity and quiet courage of those Afrikaners who saw the light long before it became politically expedient to do so. Now, in this time of transition in South Africa, faced with the masterful public relations of the suddenly 'reasonable' men anxious for the world – and South Africa's electorate – to forget their historical responsibility for apartheid, it seems to me important to insist that these bearers of the proud tradition of Afrikaner dissent are for better representatives of the authentic soul of Afrikanerdom than the Johnny-come-very-latelies of F W de Klerk's new National Party. As President Nelson Mandela's eulogy for the martyred poet, Ingrid Jonker, made very clear (p. 102 below), these Afrikaner dissidents are also an important part of the reason why a solution became possible in the land of apartheid.

I have been privileged to know a few such Afrikaners, and have admired the work and example of many others. Some are well-known, others have laboured in relative obscurity. A number of these Afrikaners have died, a few have even recanted, or (now that it no longer really matters) have retreated back into a troubled ethnicism. This is far from a monolithic group of people. Among those Afrikaners who swam against the lunatic tide of apartheid are to be found many political tendencies, profound political differences and sometimes sharp personal antipathies. Although I probably agree politically with very few of them, I should like to pay homage to the integrity, the vision and the real patriotism of them all. My purely personal list is far from complete, but includes, in alphabetical order, the following *ware Afrikaners:*

Breyten Breytenbach, André Brink, Ampie Coetzee, Johanna Cornelius, Johan Degenaar, Max du Preez, André du Toit, Betty du Toit, Bram Fischer, Hermann Giliomee, Ingrid Jonker, Hannchen Koornhof, Uys

Krige, Antje Krog, André Letoit, Jansie Lourens, Prof. J S Marais, Gerhard Maré, Johan Maree, Leo Marquard, Beyers Naude, Carl Niehaus, Daantjie Oosthuizen, Helene Perold, Jan Rabie, Ralph Rabie (Johanneskerkorrel), Eddie Roux, Frederik van Zyl Slabbert, Nico Smith, Jan Steytler, Pieter-Dirk Uys, and Charles van Onselen.

This book is dedicated to these and other such Afrikaners, and their dream of a better South Africa.

Contents

Maps, tables and figures xii
Illustrations xiii
Abbreviations and acronyms xv
Acknowledgements xvii
Note on translation and terminology xxi
Glossary xxiii
Dramatis personae xxvii

INTRODUCTION: The politics of democratic transition 3

PART I: A FORT BUILT ON FEAR
    Into the Afrikaner *laager* 17

1 NOT TAKEN AT THE FLOOD
    The 1948 election 19
        The great reverse: The fall of the Smuts government 22
        Too much, too soon: The social conflicts of the 1940s 23
        Irreconcilable interests: The war and capitalist politics 27
        UP the creek: The dilemma of Smuts's party 31
        'Long years afterwards': The meaning of 1948 35

2 SEEK YE FIRST THE POLITICAL KINGDOM!
    The National Party and the politics of Afrikaner nationalism 39
        Afrikaner 'Christian-nationalism' 40
        The organisation, structure and political culture of Afrikaner nationalism   43
            The Afrikaner Broederbond 43
            The National Party 48
        Social bases of the provincial NPs 54
        The NP as political terrain(s) 56

3 AT LAST WE HAVE GOT OUR COUNTRY BACK!
    The National Party in power, 1948–60 59
        No reverse! Reorganising state power 60
        Something better than segregation: Elaborating apartheid 64
        Afrikaner favouritism: Advancing Afrikaner economic interests 74
        How's Hoggenheimer's business? Managing South African capitalism   80

4 ENEMIES ON THIS SIDE OF THE HOUSE
    The struggle for nationalist hegemony, 1948–58 83
        North vs South 85
        A perfectly ordinary person: J G Strydom's leadership 89
        The foreigner who was always right 92

5 OLD BOOKS AND NEW SADDLES
   Sharpeville and the crisis and revival of Afrikaner faith 99
   Now we are going to have big trouble: The Sharpeville crisis 100
   Saddle up! The republican revival and the coming of 'The Rock' . . . 105
   Walls of granite 109

6 BEHIND THE SEALED FOREHEAD
   Internal divisions in the golden age of apartheid 115
   When Verwoerd goes? 116
   Taking the *volk* out of *volkskapitalisme?* The economic struggle . . . 120
   'Wind through a musty house': Afrikaner cultural politics 124
   The Empire strikes back: *Keeromstraat* and the great Afrikaner
   press war 129

PART II: NEW BOTTLE, SOURING WINE
   'Jolly John' Vorster and the crisis of apartheid 133

7 SOME ARE MORE EQUAL
   The changing social composition of the Afrikaner *volk* 135
   Reddingsdaad accomplished: The social impact of NP rule 136
   Richer cream: The Broederbond's changing occupational structure . . 144

8 THE ROCK ... IS GONE!
   The first verligte/verkrampte war 149
   Will the party not split? John Vorster's leadership style 151
   With verligtes like these ...: Defining the terms of the division 155
   Broedertwis: Round one 157
   Volks pyramid vs *volksfront:* The struggle for the Broederbond 159
   The man for the job: John Vorster and Afrikaner unity (i) 164

9 A FUTURE TOO GHASTLY TO CONTEMPLATE
   The crisis of the mid-1970s 169
   Gold, fruit and machines: The limits to growth in the
   apartheid economy 171
   House of cards: The great boom of the 1960s 173
   Winds of change: The recession of the 1970s 176
   Whose backyard? The challenge to domestic and regional hegemony 179
   The reasonable people? The politics of reformed capitalism 182

10 BIDING TIME
   The paralysis of the Vorster government 191
   Too little, too late: The Vorster government and the unfolding crisis . 192
   Divided house: Afrikaner nationalism after Soweto 196
   The cork in the bottle: John Vorster and Afrikaner unity (ii) 203

11 FEAR AND LOATHING IN THE NATIONAL PARTY
The struggle for the succession 209
   The Crown Prince, the General and James Bond vs the Pangaman . . 210
   A *'ligte mistykie':* The first incursion into Angola 219
   The military–industrial complex 224

12 MIGHTY TONGUES TELL MIGHTY LIES
Muldergate: The consolidation and victory of the 'reformists' 229
   People in glass houses 230
   Cats' next exposed: The Information Department scandal 231
   Dogs around a bone: The battle for the Premiership 234
   Rotten apple, rotten house 240

PART III: ADAPT OR DIE!
     The Botha regime, reform and the collapse of
     Afrikaner nationalism 251

13 TO KEEP ALL THAT WE HAVE
The Total Strategy project 253
   Pangaman, organisation man, reformer: The politics of P W Botha . . 254
   French lessons: Strategic reasoning and the art of the possible 259
   American pie: The political art of managing reform 263
   Now we have drum majorettes: Total strategy and reform ideology . . 264

14 NEO-APARTHEID
The Botha reforms 271
   The impossible art: Reforming apartheid 272
   More manageable machinery: Reorganising the South African state . 278

15 I'LL TAKE THE HIGH ROAD!
The end of *volkseenheid* 289
   Le parti, c'est moi: Riding the NP tiger 290
   Open for business: The Total Strategy and South African capitalists . 294
   Broedertwis: Round two 295
   Three little letters: The final break 300

16 BACK TO THE FUTURE
The far right and the collapse of Afrikaner nationalism 305
   Your tortoise or mine? The social base and politics of the far right . . 306
   Nobody for *volkspele*: The end of organised Afrikaner nationalism . . 313

PART IV: STUMBLING TOWARDS THE RUBICON
The terminal crisis of apartheid 317

17 NINETEEN EIGHTY-FOUR
The Total Strategy unravels 319
   The fallacy of (total) strategy (i): Reform and the realm of the possible 321
   Ungovernability: The black reaction to reform 324
   Discontinuous transition: The state and the urban uprising 325
   Take the money and run: Domestic and international capital 328
   Who's the boss? Political struggles inside the state 332

18 THE PURSUIT OF WAR BY OTHER MEANS
The *Groot Krokodil* and the time of the securocrats 339
   Regime consolidation: The 1986 State of Emergency 341
   Making tomorrow happen today: A new counter-revolutionary strategy 344
   L'État c'est moi! P W Botha, the NSMS and NP politics 349

19 ASINAMALI!
The structural crisis of the apartheid economy 353
   The fallacy of strategy (ii): The costs of counter-revolutionary warfare 354
   Power of sanction? The Emergency and the politics of capital 360

20 ON THE ROCKS
The great crisis of Afrikaner faith 367
   Blowing in the wind: Questioning Afrikaner identity 368
   The wind from Helderburg: The verligte challenge 372
   Déjà vu all over again: The political crisis deepens 377

21 CROCODILE TEARS
The fall of P W Botha 383
   Who's next? Line-up in the succession battle 384
   Get your act together! The political reawakening of capital 385
   All the king's horses ... The demise of P W Botha 388

22 THE VIRTUE OF POLITICAL NECESSITY
F W de Klerk's National Party and the art of the possible 395
   Leader without fanfare: The position and politics of F W de Klerk . . 396
   The road not yet taken: The reformist second coming 402
   Man of integrity? NP negotiating strategy 404
   Conclusion: The new National Party and the new South Africa 413

THEORETICAL APPENDIX
Understanding politics in the apartheid state 419
   Introduction 419
   Competing paradigms of politics and change 423
   The debates of the 1980s and 1990s 426
   The security state 427

The regulationists 428
State-centric analyses 431
Discourse analysis 440
Feminism and gender analysis 451
Comparative theories of democratic transition 460
Towards a non-deterministic, materialist theory of politics 466
Historical specificity 468
Structure and state autonomy 472
Agency, power and representation 479
Crisis and change 486

Appendix II: The twelve-point plan 491

Notes 493

Bibliography 537

Index 565

List of maps, tables and figures

Maps

1   South and Southern Africa   2
2   South Africa, provincial and bantustan boundaries,
    1963–1994   72
3   South Africa, provincial boundaries under the
    1994 constitution   413

Tables

1   Position of economically active Afrikaans-speaking white males in
    the occupational structure, 1946–1960   137
2   Occupational position of economically active Afrikaans-speaking
    white females relative to other white females, 1960   138
3   Afrikaner percentage ownership in the private sectors of the South
    African economy, 1938–1975   139
4   Occupational profile of the Broederbond membership, 1952–1977 . .   146

Figure

    Organisational structure of the South African state under the
    National Security Management System   285

List of illustrations

I. PHOTOGRAPHS . . . . *between pages 152 and 153*

A   **The** *hoofleiers*
1   *Volksleier en volksvader:* Dr D F Malan with his wife
2   **In the lion's den:** J G Strijdom opening the 1955 Cape NP congress
3   **The man who was always right:** H F Verwoerd at the 1961 Commonwealth Conference
4   **The man for the job:** B J Vorster receiving Volume I of the History of the National Party
5   **Don't mess with me!:** P W Botha at the October 1971 Cape NP conference
6   **The new style:** President F W de Klerk signs an autograph

B   **The barons**
1   **The old Cape NP inner circle:** Paul Sauer with Dr D F Malan
2   **Transvaal NP heavyweights:** Dr Verwoerd, Ben Schoeman, *et al.*
3   **The men who despised each other:** Hendrik Verwoerd, Eben Dönges and Paul Sauer
4   **'The moment of truth has arrived':** Ben Schoeman opening the 1969 Transvaal NP Congress
5   **The dynasty at mid-term:** Jan de Klerk is sworn in as Acting State President
6   **Reformist rainmaker:** Fanie Botha in 1973
7   **Reformist kingmaker:** Pik Botha, arriving at the 1977 Cape NP congress
8   **National power:** P W Botha with the leaders of the Provincial NPs
9   **North and South:** F W de Klerk, Chris Heunis and Dawie de Villiers

C   **The organisation**
1   **Leadership in opposition:** The NP Federal Council in 1941
2   **They also serve …:** The founder of the *Afrikaner Broederbond*
3   **Cape power:** The Head Council of the Cape NP in 1952
4   **End of an era:** 1954 NP congress bids farewell to Dr Malan
5   **The survivors:** The remaining parliamentarians of the NP's class of 1948
6   **Primrose again:** Dr P Koornhof receiving an NP trophy

D   **The triumphs**
1   **At last we have got our country back:** D F Malan en route to Pretoria in 1948
2   **The Rock and the** *volk:* Hendrik Verwoerd greets a crowd
3   **Making friends:** P W and Elize Botha with the 'Friends of South Africa'
4   **40 Lost Years:** the 40th anniversary of the May 1948 election

E   **Rituals and symbols** . . . . *between pages 344 and 345*
1   **The chosen leader of the chosen** *volk*: D F Malan at Calvinia in 1947
2   *Volkskapitalisme?*: Dr Eben Dönges arriving at an NP rally
3   **The politics of horse and buggy (i):** Paul Sauer and escort
4   **The politics of horse and buggy (ii):** Piet Koornhof and M C Botha
5   **The politics of horse and buggy (iii):** Dr Verwoerd in 1964
6   **'The spirit of the festival':** A float at an anniversary rally

F   **The** *volk*
1   **When will it end?:** A crowd listening to Prime Minister Vorster

G The losers
1 *Trek Verder:* Dr Albert Hertzog arrives in Ermelo
2 **Before the fall:** Dr Connie Mulder at the 1976 Transvaal NP Congress
3 **Who's for dinner?** P W Botha sizes up John Vorster
4 **The BOSS:** General Hendrik van den Bergh and Owen Horwood during Muldergate
5 **Dr No!:** Andries Treurnicht addresses a meeting
6 **There but for Cuito Cuanavale ...?:** Magnus Malan at F W de Klerk's inauguration

> All photographs are reproduced by permission of *Die Burger,* Cape Town.

II. CARTOONS

1 D F Malan's National Party wins a slender majority in the 1948 election, promising, *inter alia,* white bread to replace the wartime brown loaf . 19
2 *Die Doktor* 39
3 Apartheid theory 59
4 The Lion of the North 83
5 Striving for a Republic 99
6 *Die Hollander* 115
7 Afrikaner advancement? 135
8 The many faces of John Vorster 149
9 US Secretary of State visits SA, but fails to persuade Vorster to abandon apartheid 169
10 After Soweto: Bantu Administration Minister M C Botha prohibits blacks from occupying executive positions 191
11 P W Botha: 'Ladies and Gentlemen, there has been a small mistake' . . 209
12 Muldergate: Let the best man win! 229
13 Constructive engagement 253
14 Reformism, Koornhof style 271
15 Power-sharing: The 1984 Constitution 289
16 The politics of the far right 305
17 P W Botha declines to discuss the State of Emergency with Bishop Tutu . 319
18 The PW-mobile 339
19 'We have no money!' 353
20 Heunis to Botha: 'Stop this thing, I want to get off!' 367
21 Cry me a river! 383
22 F W de Klerk and the new National Party 395

> Numbers 1 to 11, 15, 18 and 19 by Abe Berry, from *Act by Act. 40 Years of Nationalist Rule in South Africa. A Cartoon History of Apartheid,* Lowry Publishers, 1989. Reproduced by permission of Mrs Dinah Berry.
>
> Number 12 by Dave Gaskill, from the *Sunday Times,* 1 October 1978. Reproduced by permission of the *Sunday Times.*
>
> Numbers 16, 21 and 22 by Tony Grogan, from *Keep the Funny Side Up. A South African ODDyssey,* Tafelberg Publishers.
>
> Numbers 13, 14, 17 and 20 by Richard Smith. Reproduced by permission of Richard Smith.

List of abbreviations and acronyms

AAC	Anglo American Corporation
AB	*Afrikaner Broederbond* (Brotherhood)
AHI	*Afrikaanse Handelsinstituut* (Afrikaner Commercial Institute)
ANC	African National Congress
AO	*Afrikaner Orde* (Order)
AP	Afrikaner Party
Armscor	Armaments Development and Production Corporation
Assocom	Associated Chambers of Commerce
AV	*Afrikaner Volkswag* (Afrikaner National Guard)
AWB	*Afrikaner Weerstand Beweging* (Afrikaner Resistance Movement)
BCM	Black Consciousness Movement
BLA	Black Local Authority
BOSS	Bureau for State Security
CBM	Consultative Business Movement
CKA	*Christelike Kultuuraksie* (Christian Cultural Action)
CoM	Chamber of Mines
Cosatu	Congress of South African Trade Unions
CRC	Coloureds' Representative Council
DONS	Department of National Security – short-lived new name for BOSS (q.v.)
DP	Democratic Party
EI	*Ekonomiese Instituut* (Economic Institute – of the FAK)
EPG	(Commonwealth) Eminent Persons Group
EVK	*Ekonomiese Volkskongres* (Economic Congress of the *Volk*)
FAK	*Federasie van Afrikaanse Kultuurverenigings* (Federation of Afrikaner Cultural Associations)
FCI	Federated Chamber of Industry
FVB	*Federale Volksbeleggings* (Federal *Volks* Investments)
GK	*Gereformeerde Kerk*
HNP	*Herenigde* (reconstituted) National Party
IDASA	Institute for Democratic Alternatives for South Africa
IFP	Inkatha Freedom Party
IP	Independent Party
JSE	Johannesburg Stock Exchange
JMC(s)	Joint Management Centre(s)
Komkom	*Komunikasie komitee* (Communications committee – of all SCC structures)
KP	*Konserwatiewe Party* (Conservative Party)
LIC	Low intensity conflict
LMC(s)	Local Management Centre(s)
MDM	Mass Democratic Movement
MIS	Military Intelligence Section (of the SADF)
MP	Member of Parliament
MPC	Member of the Provincial Council

MWU	Mine Workers' Union
Nafcoc	National African Federated Chambers of Commerce
NDM	National Democratic Movement
NGK	*Nederduitse Gereformeerde Kerk* (Dutch Reformed Church)
NHK	*Nederduitsch Hervormde Kerk* (Dutch re-Formed Church)
NIS	National Intelligence Service – final name given to old DONS and BOSS (q.v.)
NJMC	National Joint Management Centre
NP	National Party
NRP	New Republic Party
NSMS	National Security Management System
NUM	National Union of Mineworkers
OAU	Organisation of African Unity
OB	*Ossewa Brandwag* (Oxwagon Sentinels)
OFS	Orange Free State
PAC	Pan Africanist Congress of Azania
PFP	Progressive Federal Party
PRP	Progressive Reform Party
Renamo	*Résisténçia Naçional de Moçambique* (Mozambican National Resistance – sometimes also known as MNR)
RSA	Republic of South Africa
RSC	Regional Services Council
SAAF	South African Air Force
SAAU	South African Agricultural Union
SABC	South African Broadcasting Corporation
SACP	South African Communist Party
SADF	South African Defence Force
SALP	(South African) Labour Party – a white parliamentary party which ceased to exist in the 1960s. It should not be confused with the totally separate (Coloured) Labour Party founded in the 1960s
Sanlam	*Suid-Afrikaanse Nasionale Lewensassuransie Maatskappy* (South African National Life Assurance Company)
SAP	South African Police
SASO	South African Students' Organisation (the Black Consciousness founding organisation)
Seifsa	Steel and Engineering Industries Federation of South Africa
Semkom	*Staatkundige, ekonomiese en maatskaplike komitee* (Constitutional, economic and social committee – of all SCC structures)
SISA	State Intelligence and State Security Act (1972)
SP	Security Police
UDF	United Democratic Front
UF	Urban Foundation
UP	United Party
UR	*Uitvoerende Raad* (Executive Council of the Broederbond)
Veikom	*Veiligheidskomitee* (Security Committee – of all SCC structures)

Acknowledgements

Working intermittently on the ideas in this book since 1979, I was able to sustain my commitment to this project only with the encouragement, advice and support of many people.

A request from the ANC Chief Representative in Dar es Salaam, Comrade Reddy Mazimba, to clarify the political implications of 'Muldergate' first gave me the idea for an article which eventually inspired this book. Critical comments on that early piece by Stanley Greenberg, Linzi Manicom, Henry Slater, Joe Slovo and Harold Wolpe helped me clarify the initial argument. The intellectual comradeship, warm friendship and irreverent humour of Rob Davies, Josiah Tshabalala (Sipho Dlamini) and Judith Head carried me through three long and painful years in Maputo. My analysis of the Total Strategy period owes a great deal to this intensely rewarding collaboration, and particularly to Rob Davies.

Shula Marks's encouragement led to an early partial draft on the period 1972–80, while David Lewis, Stephen Gelb and John Saul were responsible for my resuming work on this project. Dave Lewis's incisive comments on this early draft forced me to confront its numerous shortcomings and reformulate much of the argument.

Pierre Beaudet brought me to Quebec and gave me a job when I desperately needed one. Through thirty hectic months, he tactfully but firmly forced me to learn French, instructed me in the vagaries of Quebec nationalism, and shared with me his unique grasp of geopolitics. He also gave me the space to be able to think about South African politics again. He and my other colleagues at *le Centre d'information et de documentation sur le Mozambique et l'Afrique australe* – Paul and Lucie Bélanger, Marie-Hélène Bonin, Stephane Corriveau, Suzanne Dansereau and Salvadora Garcia – together taught me the meaning of international solidarity and reinforced my conviction that pride in one's language and culture does not have to lead to national chauvinism and racism.

John Saul's enthusiasm, insight, comments and friendship helped keep my nose to the grindstone and to refine my analysis. Rob Gordon has shared my fascination with the more arcane details of Afrikaner politics and culture, and his comments, humour and material have been invaluable. Bonnie Campbell facilitated my return to academia, so making it possible for me to resume work on this book.

Mike Morris took the time to make a detailed trenchant critique of the second-to-last draft. With a mixture of great tact and rigour he made me realise that much of the argument was simply inadequate. Since then he generously continued to debate my revised analysis with me at almost every step of the way. I owe him a deep debt of gratitude, not just for his invaluable help, encouragement, friendship – and the visiting fellowship he organised for me at Natal University – but also because the seriousness as well as the humour with which he prodded me to think more deeply about what I was doing were crucial to my developing the confidence that this could be an interesting and worthwhile book.

Duncan Innes' interest in this project obliged me to refine the argument which now comprises chapters 17-22. Gerry Maré and Rachelle Greef generously shared their knowledge of Afrikaans literature, and helped me track down appropriate texts. Raphael de Kadt's comments on the penultimate draft helped me draw out threads in the arguments which were insufficiently developed. Judith Head and Susan Ship made valuable comments on the Theoretical Appendix. John Shingler's editorial eye and knowledge of Afrikaner nationalism were essential aids in the writing and revision of the various drafts. Deborah Posel used all of her considerable generosity and theoretical perspicacity in an effort to save me from my own theoretical errors. Comments on the manuscript by Ravan Press's anonymous readers led me to reshape some of the chapters. Michel Trudel, Murray Shugar, Paul Bergman, Neil Wilson and Ted Hutchinson lent me their ears, their support and their friendship through complicated times. My deepest thanks to them all.

I am grateful to the Students' Visiting Lecturers Trust Fund of Natal University, Durban, for a Visiting Fellowship. My particular thanks go to the Head of the Economic History Department, Bill Freund, for inviting me in the first place and whose expansive but undemanding welcome in his department enabled me to finish the final draft, and to the Departmental Secretary Gail Longano, who cheerfully undertook all sorts of administrative details, so freeing my own time.

Drafts of various chapters were presented at annual conferences of the Canadian Association of African Studies, to workshops of the Canadian Research Consortium on Southern Africa, to Yale University's Southern African Research Program, and to seminars at the following universities: Berkeley, Boston, Cape Town, Carleton, Dar es Salaam, Harvard, McGill, Natal (Durban), Queen's, Saskatchewan, Stanford, Toronto, Trent, UCLA, Universidade Eduardo Mondlane, UQAM, Wilfrid Laurier and York. My thanks to all the participants – and especially Doug Anglin, Bruce Berman, Fred Bienefeld, Barron Boyd, Jeffrey Butler, Halton Cheadle, André du Toit, Linda Freeman, Bill Freund, Magnus Gunther, Jeff Guy, Barbara Harmel, Paul Idahosa, Alan Jeeves, Xoliswa Jozana, Tom Karis, Colin Leys, Alan Mabin, Gerry Maré, Dunbar Moodie, Mike Morris, Jane Parpart, Jenny Robinson, Leonard Thompson, John Saul, John Shingler, Newell Stultz and Paulus Zulu – for their comments and criticisms.

Throughout much of the book's long gestation period I was barred from entering South Africa and struggled to obtain the necessary material. My special thanks to my parents, Tim and Audrey O'Meara, for their long labour of love over the years in sending me all sorts of indispensable resources, without which I would not have been able to continue. No academic could wish for more diligent and selfless research assistants.

Thanks are also due to Jeffrey Butler for the loan of his cuttings on the 1969 split in the National Party; to Lydia and Jonathan Allen; Henry Bernstein, Steve Gelb, Rob Gordon, Mbulelo Mzamane and Nancy Thede for material unavailable in Canada; and (again) to John Shingler for access to his unique collection of rare Afrikaner publications.

I should also like to thank the many Afrikaners who, over the years, have discussed Afrikaner nationalism and the National Party with me. Though most will probably not approve of my conclusions, their generosity with their time and information has been invaluable. I have named in the notes those informants who agreed to go on the record. I have respected the anonymity of those who asked me to do so.

To Lauren and Michele Goldman and Keri O'Meara my gratitude for their long patience with, and understanding of, an irritable and mentally absent parent obsessed with a far-away country. Their easy contempt for the racism with which I grew up gives me great hope.

My deepest thanks go to my wife, Vikki Stark, who, apart from pointing out my numerous typographical errors, has taught me more about myself, the world and politics, than I could ever acknowledge. Without her constant love, support and understanding I should never have completed this study.

Responsibility for any errors of theory, fact or interpretation is mine alone.

Note on translation and terminology

Unless otherwise noted, all translations from Afrikaans and French are my own. Given that one of the subsidiary aims of this book is to communicate something of the emotional feeling of Afrikaner nationalist and other discourses, in translating the frequent excerpts of Afrikaans poems, prose and press, I have generally opted for my own sense of this meaning rather than for literary elegance. My renderings thus often differ from what are now accepted as official translations of some of these works. They also probably exemplify a comment Breyten Breytenbach has made about translations of his own work: all that got lost in translation was the poem. I have taken the liberty of inflicting literary damage in order to bring out the resonance in the Afrikaner political universe of the pieces in question.

My translations of the writings of the French strategist, General André Beaufre, as well as those of Michel Foucault, also occasionally depart from those in the published English versions of their work. In this case I have tried to bring out what seem to me to be important nuances and emphases missing from these official translations.

Afrikaans is a singularly direct language. Its use of compounded words, frequent recourse to the historic present tense and six forms of the diminutive, and occasional deliberatedly bastardised anglicism, all combine to make it a powerfully expressive tool in the cut and thrust of political debate. The blunt, muscular nature of Afrikaner political discourse is seldom apparent in translation into the more subtle English language. Moreover, many key Afrikaner political terms have no direct English equivalent. The word *volk,* for example, is usually translated as either 'people' or 'nation'. However, in the Afrikaner nationalist lexicon, the term conveys both a sense of ethnicity and organic unity absent in either of these paler English terms. Its closest English equivalent would probably be 'ethnic group', yet it does not quite mean this. In this and other cases, therefore, unless the context indicates the narrowest meaning, I have retained these Afrikaner terms in order to convey the wider meaning.

As liberal use is made of Afrikaans terms throughout the text, a glossary is provided to assist the reader. Afrikaans terms appear in *italics,* with the exception of those Afrikaans terms which entered into common usage in South African English, e.g. apartheid not *apartheid,* verligte rather than *verligte.*

The racial/ethnic terminology of South Africa is a political minefield. In terms of the 1950 Population Registration Act – only repealed in 1991 – every individual was classified into one of four racial categories at birth or at entry into the country. This classification could only subsequently be changed by the state itself. In the apartheid hierarchy of racial domination, the position and particular forms of oppression of the three oppressed 'non-white' groups differed. Unfortunately, no analysis of South African politics can avoid using these racist categories – whose very terms have been deeply contested. Thus, for example, at various phases the NP government referred to the African majority as 'Natives', as 'Bantu' or, more recently, as 'Blacks'. The first two terms were always rejected by black activists, while the term 'black' was used by the Black Consciousness Movement to refer collectively to all three racially oppressed groups – Africans, so-called Coloureds and Indians. Except as otherwise indicated in the footnotes, I use the term 'black' in this more inclusive sense, preferring to use the term 'African' for those called 'Blacks' by the apartheid regime.

The official category of 'Coloured' people was likewise widely regarded as racist by members of this group, most of whom refer to themselves as 'so-called Coloureds' – and sometimes, in bitter irony, just as 'so-calleds'. I have retained this clumsy appellation as far as possible.

Finally, Afrikaans is the mother tongue of millions more South Africans than the total number of the white 'Afrikaners' who have given this language such a bad press. A long debate in Afrikaner nationalist circles has grappled with the status of what General Hertzog once called 'brown Afrikaners' – the millions of so-called Coloureds, most of whom are native Afrikaans-speakers. While in the 1990s the National Party suddenly discovered that the so-called Coloureds might be admitted into Afrikaners ranks, I employ the term 'Afrikaners' in the sense as used by the National Party throughout the vast bulk of its existence – as short-hand to indicate those more correctly designated by the clumsy formulation of white Afrikaans-speakers.*

The *Nasionale Party* (National Party – NP) has modified its name at various times during its history. Known simply as the National Party from 1914 to 1934, it split in 1934 when the majority followed NP leader General Hertzog into 'fusion' with General Smuts's South African Party to form the United Party. At fusion the NP rump under Dr D F Malan rechristened itself the *Gesuiwerde Nasionale Party* (Purified National Party). When the Hertzogites eventually rejoined their former comrades at the beginning of World War II, the party adopted the cumbersome title of the *Herenigde Nasionale of Volksparty* (Reunited National or People's Party). This was its official title in 1948, though it was commonly known just as the *Herenigde Nasionale Party* (HNP). When the HNP finally reabsorbed the old Hertzogite rump and *Ossewa Brandwag* renegades in 1951, the party reverted to calling itself the *Nasionale Party* (NP). To avoid clumsy explanations of each of these changes and phases, I refer to the party throughout as the National Party or NP.

The old Sterling-linked South African Pound was replaced by the decimal Rand currency in 1961, at the rate of R2 to £1. Its 2:1 conversion rate with Sterling ended when South Africa declined to follow Britain and devalue its currency in 1967.

---

* For a discussion by a leading Afrikaner nationalist historian of the issue of 'Who and what is an Afrikaner?', see J A van Jaarsveld, *Wie en wat is die Afrikaner?* (Tafelberg, Cape Town, 1981).

Glossary

Afrikaanse Handelsinstituut – Afrikaans Commercial Institute
Afrikaanse Pers – Afrikaner Press. Transvaal Nationalist Press group, publisher of *Die Vaderland* (q.v.) and after 1962, *Dagbreek* (q.v.). Merged with Voortrekker Pers (q.v.) in 1972 to form the Perskor group (q.v.)
Afrikaanse Protestantse Kerk – Afrikaner Protestant Church. Founded 1987 as splinter group from the NGK (q.v.)
Afrikaner Broederbond – Afrikaner Brotherhood
Afrikaner Orde – Afrikaner Order
Akademie vir Wetenskap en Kuns – Academy for Science and Art
Al dra die aap 'n goue ring, bly hy nog steeds 'n lelike ding – even though the ape might wear a golden ring, he still remains an ugly thing – Afrikaans saying
apartheid – 'apart-ness', or the condition of being separate
baas – boss, or master
baasskap – (white) domination
Beeld – Image. Nasionale Pers Transvaal daily, 1977. Not to be confused with its predecessor, *Die Beeld* (q.v.)
Boer(e) – (literally) farmer(s). Term used until the 1960s to describe Afrikaners, now a general term of abuse for whites in South Africa
Bondsraad – Annual conference of the Broederbond
Bring bymekaar wie bymekaar hoort! – Bring together those who belong together (through inner conviction)! Dr D F Malan's injunction to seek *volkseenheid* (q.v.)
broeder(s) – member of the Afrikaner Broederbond
Broederbond – see *Afrikaner Broederbond*
broedertwis – (literally) division between brothers. Term used to describe formal splits in Afrikaner nationalism
broer – (literally) brother – term by which Broederbond members referred to each other in private
bywoner – (white, usually Afrikaner) squatters
Christelike Kultuuraksie – Christian Cultural Action
Dagbreek – Daybreak. A Transvaal pro-NP Sunday weekly. Changed its name to *Dagbreek en Landstem* in 1967. Merged with *Die Beeld* to form *Rapport* (q.v.) in 1970
Die Beeld – The Image. Nasionale Pers Sunday newspaper published in the Transvaal 1965–70
Die Burger – The Citizen. Daily newspaper – organ of the Cape NP, 1915–present
Die Doktor – The Doctor. NP *Hoofleier* (1934–54), Dr D F Malan
Die Hollander – The Dutchman. NP *Hoofleier* (1958–66), Dr H F Verwoerd
Die Man Wat Weet – The Man Who Knows (what's going on)

Die Rots – The Rock. NP *Hoofleier* (1958–66), Dr H F Verwoerd

Die Transvaler – The Transvaler. Daily newspaper – organ of the Transvaal NP, founded in 1937

Die Vaderland – The Fatherland. Originally a 'Hertzogite' daily, it became a pro-NP paper after 1951

die volk daar buite – the *volk* outside of here (parliament)

Die Volksblad – The *Volks* Daily. Organ of the NP of the Orange Free State, published by Nasionale Pers

dominee – (Dutch Reformed Church) minister

dompas – pejorative term to describe the hated 'Reference Book' (pass) under the Influx Control system

eie – (literally) [one's] own – i.e. essential characteristics, essence

Ekonomiese Instituut – Economic Institute (of the FAK)

Ekonomiese Volkskongres – Economic Congress of the *Volk*

Federale Volksbeleggings – Federal *Volks* Investments

Federasie van Afrikaanse Kultuurverenigings – Federation of Afrikaner Cultural Associations

geldmag – finance power

Gereformeerde Kerk – Reformed Church

Groot Krokodil – (The) Great Crocodile – P W Botha's political nickame after 1984

Herenigde Nasionale of Volksparty – Reunited National or People's Party

Herstigte(s) – adherent(s) of the Herstigte Nasionale Party (q.v.)

Herstigte Nasionale Party – Reconstituted National Party

Hoofleier – Leader-in-chief, or National Leader (of the NP)

Hoofstad – Capital city. A conservative nationalist daily newspaper first published in Pretoria in 1968

huisvriende – House friends (i.e. close friends)

Keeromstraat – term to refer to the Nasionale Pers (q.v.) – name of the Cape Town street on which its headquarters were located

koersvastheid – determination to stick to one's course

kultuurpolitiek – the politics of culture

ligte mistykie – a small little mistake. Verligte journalist Schalk Pienaar's ironical use of a corrupted anglicism (*mystykie*) to characterise the first SA incursion into Angola

magsdeling – power-sharing

magsverdeling – division of powers

Mfecane – A period of great violence and social dislocation associated with the slave trade and the rise of the Zulu kingdom in the first two decades of the nineteenth century

Nasionale Pers – National Press. Cape Town-based newspaper group, closely linked to the Cape NP

Nederduitsch Hervormde Kerk – Dutch Re-formed Church

Nederduitse Gereformeerde Kerk – Dutch Reformed Church

Noodhulpliga – First Aid League. The Broerbond-created alternative to the St John Ambulance Brigade

Nuwe Orde – New Order. A fascist splinter group which withdrew from the NP in 1942

Ons – we/us

Oom – Uncle, a term of affectionate respect

oorbeligte(s) – over-enlightened Afrikaner(s)

oorheesing – domination

oorstroming – inundation

Ossewa Brandwag – Ox-wagon Sentinels. A nazi-inclined mass movement in conflict with the NP in the 1940s

oud-smelter(s) – former *smelter(s)* (q.v.)

partypolitiek – party politics

Perskor – Press corp(oration). Giant Transvaal nationalist press group formed out of the 1972 merger of Voortrekker Pers and Afrikaanse Pers (q.v.)

Piet Wapens – Pete Weapons. NP nickname for P W Botha during his tenure as Defence Minister (1966–79)

platteland – (Afrikaner) rural areas/communities (literally, flat country – referring to the Highveld plateau)

Rapport – Report. Pro-NP verligte Sunday newspaper formed by the 1970 merger of *Die Beeld* and *Dagbreek* (q.v.)

Reddingsdaad – act of rescue(ing the Afrikaner *volk*)

Reddingsdaadbeweging – movement for the act of rescue. Name given to the Afrikaner economic movement of the 1940s

Reddingsdaadbond – League for the Act of Rescue

Ruiter(s) – member of the *Ruiterwag* (q.v.)

Ruiterwag – (literally) Mounted guard. Name adopted by the junior wing of the Broederbond

Sestiger(s) – (The) Sixty-ite(s). *Avant-garde* literary group in the 1960s

skeurder – schismatic, splittist

skeuring – split, schism

skinder stories – gossip, slanderous talk

smelter(s) – fusionist(s). Derogatory NP term for those who followed Gen. Hertzog into the United Party in 1934

soutpiele – (literally) 'salt balls'. Derogatory term for English-speaking whites

Suid-Afrikaanse Buro vir Rasse-angeleenthede – South African Bureau for Racial Affairs

Trek Verder – (literally) trek further on. Verkrampte slogan exalting the pursuit of the *volkseie* (q.v.)

tweegatjakkals – (literally) a jackal with two (arse)holes, or a two-faced person

Uitvoerende Komitee – Executive Committee

Uitvoerende Raad – Executive Council (of the Broederbond)

veelvolkigge – (literally) comprised of many *volk*s. Multi-ethnic, multi-national

Veg – (the good) Fight. Short-lived arch-verkrampte journal in the late 1960s

veg organisasie – fighting organisation (the NP caucus)

verkrampte – reactionary (Afrikaner nationalist)

verligte – enlightened (Afrikaner nationalist)

volk – See note on translation (p. xxi)

volksbeweging – *volk*'s movement, people's movement, national movement

volkseie – the essence ('own') of the *volk*

volkseenheid – unity of the *volk*

volksfront – *volk*'s front, people's front

volksgebondenheid – (organic) link to the *volk* (of all Afrikaners)

Volkskongres(se) – Congress(es) of the *volk*

Volksleier – (*Caps.* = supreme) leader of the (entire) *volk*

volkspele – (Afrikaner) folk games and dances

volkstaak – task of the *volk*

volkstaat – (Afrikaner) people's state

volksvreemde – foreign to the *volk*

volksvyand – enemy of the *volk*

Voortrekkers – (literally) those who journeyed ahead. The Broerbond-created alternative to the Boy Scouts/Girl Guides, itself named after the people who undertook 'The Great Trek' in the late 1830s

Voortrekker Pers – Voortrekker (q.v.) Press. Transvaal nationalist press group, publisher of *Die Transvaler* (q.v.). Merged with Afrikaanse Pers (q.v.) in 1972 to form Perskor (q.v.)

vriend – (literally) friend. Term by which Broederbond members referred to each other in public

ware Afrikaners – authentic Afrikaners

Dramatis personae

Given the large list of characters in this book, and the fact that many of the central actors shared the same surname, I include brief potted summaries of their careers. Political nickname(s) appear in brackets. An asterisk indicates that the person in question is also listed in the bibliography

Botha, M C – As Minister of Bantu Administration under Verwoerd and Vorster, was principal Cabinet proponent of hardline implementation of apartheid. Despite reputation as a verkrampte, did not associate himself with the Hertzog group. Defeated by Connie Mulder in 1972 bid for leadership of Transvaal NP. Retired in 1978.

Botha, Pieter Wilhelm (P W, *Piet Wapens*, *Die Groot Krokodil*, *Die Pangaman*) – Longtime key Cape NP figure as first full time organiser 1936 ff, head secretary (1948–58) and leader (1966–86). Appointed Union Information Officer of federal NP 1946. Entered Parliament in 1948, made Deputy Minister (of the Interior) in 1958, promoted to full Cabinet membership in 1961 (Minister of Community Development and of Coloured Affairs), gaining notoriety for the forced removal of the Coloured population from District Six. Appointed Defence Minister in 1966, where he remained until 1980. Key figure in Muldergate, elected NP *Hoofleier* and Prime Minister in 1978. Introduced 'Total Strategy' reforms. Became first executive State President under 1984 constitution. Resigned leadership of NP in early 1989 after a stroke. Forced out of the Presidency by F W de Klerk in August 1989. Resigned from NP in April 1990.

Botha, Roelof Frederik (Pik) – Longtime NP verligte. Served as Pretoria's Ambassador Extraordinary and Plenipotentiary to the USA and Permanent Representative at the United Nations (1975–77). Appointed Foreign Minister in 1977, held this post till 1994, serving under Vorster, P W Botha (no relation) and De Klerk. Key figure in Muldergate, and unsuccessful candidate for the NP *Hoofleier*ship in 1978 and 1989, Pik Botha is currently leader of the Transvaal NP and was appointed Minister of Mineral and Energy Affairs in Nelson Mandela's Government of National Unity.

Botha, Stephanus P ('Fanie', *Fanie Water*) – Held various Cabinet posts under Vorster and P W Botha. As the leading reformist in the latter's Cabinet, presided over crucial labour reforms and became embroiled in a deep enmity with the man who had trounced him in the 1978 election for the leadership of the Transvaal NP, the founder and leader of the Conservative Party, Dr A P Treurnicht. The state of his personal finances forced him to resign in 1983.

Breytenbach, Breyten* – Leading Afrikaans poet and *Sestiger*. Sentenced to nine years' imprisonment in 1976 for subversive activities. Released in 1982 and returned to his exile in Paris.

Brink, André* – Leading *Sestiger* and novelist. Author of first Afrikaans novel banned in South Africa.

Cillié, Pieter J (Piet) – Cape nationalist journalist. Editor of *Die Burger* 1954–77, and author of its influential 'Dawie' column. Leading Cape verligte, and virtual one-man opposition to Dr Verwoerd on 'Coloured' and other questions 1960–62. The principal target of verkrampte Hertzog group. Appointed Chairman of Nasionale Pers, and Professor of Journalism at Stellenbosch University in 1977.

de Klerk, Frederick Willem (F W) – Son of Jan de Klerk and younger brother of Willem. A former University of Potchefstroom law professor, entered Parliament in 1972 and Cabinet in April 1978. Held various Cabinet posts under Vorster and Botha. During internal NP conflict 1978–82 emerged as centrist 'peacemaker'. Supported P W Botha in 1982 split in Transvaal party and elected its leader. His efforts over the next seven years to defend the Transvaal NP from incursions from the right won him the reputation of a conservative. Narrowly elected NP *Hoofleier* in February 1989, Acting State President in August 1989 and State President September 1989–May 1994. Announced release of Nelson Mandela and legalisation of ANC and other banned organisations on 2 February 1990. As leader of the NP, De Klerk was appointed Second Vice-President in Mandela's Government of National Unity in May 1994.

de Klerk, Jan – Brother-in-law of J G Strijdom, and father of Willem and F W de Klerk. As head secretary of Transvaal NP 1948–54, worked closely with Strijdom and Verwoerd to assert the Transvaal dominance over thê Cape NP. Cabinet minister under Strijdom, Verwoerd and Vorster. Founder of job reservation. Narrowly lost NP nomination for State President to Dönges in 1966. President of the Senate (1968–76), served as Acting State President in 1972.

de Klerk, Willem (Wimpie)* – Leading verligte journalist. Son of Jan de Klerk and older brother of F W. While still an academic, coined the terms *verligte* and *verkrampte* in the 1960s. His verligte line saw him fired as editor of *Die Transvaler* in 1982, and De Klerk resigned as editor of *Rapport* in 1987 protesting attempts to make him toe the party line. Active in formation of Democratic Party in 1988–89, and briefly a candidate for its leadership. Returned to NP when his brother became its leader.

du Plessis, Barend Jacobus – Verligte Minister under Botha and De Klerk. Briefly the Mayor of Roodeport, Du Plessis entered Parliament in 1974. As NP Information Officer 1977–81 he had unenviable task of explaining Muldergate. Key figure among Transvaal Young Turks supporting Pik Botha in 1978. Appointed Minister of Education & Training in 1983, and Finance Minister in 1984, where his stewardship of the economy aroused fierce criticism. Surprise main verligte candidate for NP *Hoofleier*ship in 1989, came within 5 votes of beating De Klerk, who made him leader of Transvaal NP. Resigned, pleading 'exhaustion', in 1991.

du Plessis, Professor Lodewicus Johannes ('Wickus) – Professor of Political

Philosophy at Potchefstroom University, and leading theoretician of Christian-nationalism in 1930s. *The* key Broederbond figure 1930–43 (chairman 1930–32; chairman of its 'political commission' 1934–42, named AB "political commissar" in 1934; chairman of its general policy commission 1940–42 which produced infamous 'Draft Republican Constitution'). Member of leadership triumvirate of Transvaal NP 1934–36. Chairman of first and second *Ekonomiese Volkskongresse*. Key *Ossewa Brandwag* intellectual in 1940s. In the 1950s turned into vocal critic of the parochial ethnic outlook of Malan, Strijdom and Verwoerd. Fought vigorously with the latter over the definition of both Afrikaner nationalism and apartheid. Expelled by Verwoerd from NP in 1959. Underwent lobotomy in 1963. Died 1968.

Diederichs, Dr Nicolaas (Nic, Dr Gold) – Professor of Political Philosophy at University of Orange Free State in 1930s and leading Christian-national theoretician. Long-time Broederbond executive member (and chairman 1938–42). *Hoofleier* of *Reddingsdaadbond* 1939–56. Elected to Parliament in 1948. Held various Cabinet economic portfolios under Verwoerd and Vorster. Elected State President in 1975. His death in August 1978 precipitated *dénouement* of Muldergate affair.

Dönges, Dr Theophilus Ebenhaezer (Eben) – Leading Cape Broederbonder and member of its executive in 1940s. Elected to Parliament in 1948 and made Minister of Interior. Held various Cabinet posts under Malan, Strijdom and Verwoerd (1948–66). Succeeded the first as leader of Cape NP in 1953, and deeply disliked by latter two for organising NP's 1947 electoral pact with Havenga's AP. Verwoerd and Strijdom saw this (not incorrectly) as Dönges' attempt to make Havenga next NP leader, forestall a Strijdom succession and then himself succeed Havenga. Despite Dönges' close alliance with Verwoerd in Broederbond executive during wartime NP/*Ossewa Brandwag* war, Verwoerd distrusted Dönges as a 'liberal'. He lost 1958 NP *Hoofleier* election to Verwoerd, but was appointed Finance Minister. Briefly a candidate for NP *Hoofleier*ship in 1966, Dönges withdrew on understanding that Vorster would support him for the Presidency when C R Swart retired. Resigned Cape leadership in 1966 and narrowly beat Jan de Klerk in race for NP nominee as State President. Elected to this post, but fell into coma and died in January 1968 without ever taking office.

Fouché, J J (Jim) – Cabinet Minister under Verwoerd and Vorster, Fouché succeeded C R Swart as leader of the Free State National Party (1961) and – on the death of the never-inaugurated President-elect Dönges – became South Africa's second State President. Was the only one of the six men elected to this position under the 1961 constitution to complete full seven-year term.

Havenga, Nicolaas Christiaan ('Klaas) – Leading Free State nationalist and longtime loyal lieutenant of General Hertzog. Entered Parliament in 1915. Finance Minister in the latter's 'Pact' and United Party administrations 1924–34 and 1934–39, and again under Malan 1948–54. Followed Hertzog into fusion in 1934 and out again in 1939. When Hertzog driven out of the 'reunited' NP in late 1940, Havenga left to form and lead Hertzogite Afrikaner Party. Fought 1948 election in coalition with NP, and led AP back into NP in 1951. Became Malan's deputy and designated successor, but declined to stand in election against Strijdom in October 1954 when he retired from politics.

Hertzog, Dr Albert – Son of General Hertzog. Fell out with his father over fusion. Leading young Broederbonder and member of its executive in 1930s and 1940s. Led 12-year nationalist struggle to take over the (white) Mine Workers' Union. Founded and led highly secret *Afrikaner Orde* until latter forced to disband in 1968. Elected to Parliament in 1948, where he formed his own study group. Cabinet Minister under Verwoerd and Vorster, 1958–68. As Minister of Posts & Telegraphs, refused to introduce television service on grounds that this 'little bioscope' would corrupt nationalists and blacks (the 'English' were already a lôst cause). Leader of verkrampte opposition to Vorster. Fired from Cabinet in 1968, expelled from NP in 1969. Lost his seat in 1970 election and expelled from the Broederbond in 1972. Founder and first leader of the HNP. Retired from politics in 1977.

Hertzog, General James Barry Munnik – South African War Boer general, founder and leader of *Oranje Unie* party in the Free State, and led his party into General Louis Botha's South African Party at Union in 1910. Fell out with Prime Minister Botha over latter's policy of 'reconciliation with imperialism' in 1912, advocating a 'two-stream' (Afrikaner and English) South African nationalism. Founder and *Hoofleier* of the National Party (1914–34), founder and leader of the United Party (1934–39). Won the 1924 election in coalition with the Labour Party which he took into his 'Pact' administration of 1924–33. Prime Minister Hertzog led his National Party into coalition with Jan Smuts's South African Party over the 'Gold Standard Crisis' in 1933. The two parties 'fused' to form the United Party in 1934, with Hertzog as Premier. Hertzog narrowly lost his parliamentary motion to keep South Africa out of World War II. When the Governor-General refused his advice to dissolve Parliament, Hertzog resigned from the Premiership and quit the UP. Led his supporters into 'reunification' with Dr Malan's *Gesuiwerde* National Party in early 1940, and elected *Hoofleier* of the new reunited NP. However was forced out by C R Swart in November 1940 and retired from politics. Died 1942.

Heunis, Jan Christiaan (Chris) – Cabinet Minister under Vorster and Botha. P W Botha's chief political factotum, and his successor as leader of Cape NP 1986. Architect of 'new constitutional dispensation'. Between 1980 and 1986 accumulated ever-greater powers in his 'reformist' empire. Known for convoluted expositions of 'consociational' theory. Lost battle with General Malan for P W Botha's ear in 1986. Further discredited when very narrowly avoided defeat by former Nat MP in 1987 election. Acting State President during P W Botha's illness January–March 1989. Unsuccessfully contested the NP

*Hoofleier*ship in February 1989, retired from politics at end of that year.

Hofmeyr, William Angus ('Willie') – *The* key behind-the-scenes power-broker in the Cape nationalist establishment, and cousin of Smuts's Deputy Premier, J H (Jan) Hofmeyr. Hofmeyr led group of young Western Cape nationalists who founded the Cape NP, *Die Burger*, Santam and Sanlam between 1914 and 1918. Hofmeyr declined offered leadership of Cape NP and invited Dr Malan to leave his pulpit, lead the party and edit *Die Burger*. First chairman of Nasionale Pers 1914–18, and its chief executive officer 1919–32, and chairman again 1948–53. Chairman of Sanlam and Santam 1918–53. First organiser of Cape NP 1914–18. Senator 1929–39, and 1948–53. First chairman of Voortrekker Pers (1937–39). Chairman of NP caucus 1948. Key influence on generations of Cape nationalists (including first three leaders of Cape NP). Died 1953.

Horwood, Professor Owen P F – Controversial Cabinet minister and Natal NP leader under Vorster and Botha. One-time United Party economic strategist, Horwood was Professor of Economics and then Vice-Chancellor of Natal University, where he clashed frequently and bitterly with liberal students. Joining the National Party in the late 1960s, he was appointed to the Senate in 1972, serving in various deputy ministerial positions. Horwood was made Minister of Finance on Dr Diederichs' 1975 accession to the State Presidency. He retired in 1984.

Jansen, Dr E G – Moderate Hertzogite nationalist who remained in reunified NP after Hertzog driven out in November 1940. Minister of Native Affairs under Hertzog (1929–34), and briefly under Malan (1948–49). Leader of Natal NP, though lived in Transvaal and held Transvaal seat. Fought radical 'Draft Republican Constitution'. As Minister of Native Affairs after 1948, aroused ire of radicals for timidity in promoting apartheid. Was replaced by Dr Verwoerd when Jansen became first Afrikaner Governor-General in 1949. Died 1960.

Jonker, Ingrid* – Leading *Sestiger* and poet. Daughter of nationalist MP and censorship advocate, Dr Abraham Jonker. Committed suicide in 1965. Eulogised by President Nelson Mandela in his first Presidential address to Parliament.

Koornhof, Dr Pieter Gerhardus Jacobus (Piet, *Piet Pompies*) – Maverick nationalist and minister under Vorster and Botha. His 1952 Oxford PhD thesis condemned migratory labour, yet Koornhof joined Verwoerd's Department of Bantu Affairs. Appointed secretary of the Broederbond in 1962, and prominent in various of its front organisations. Briefly associated with the verkrampte Hertzog group, Koornhof entered Parliament in 1964 and soon developed a verligte reputation. Appointed to Cabinet in 1972, as Sports Minister, he introduced the first breaches in sports apartheid, earning the hatred of the far right. Koornhof surprisingly nominated the verkrampte Connie Mulder for the NP *Hoofleier*ship in 1978, and succeeded him in the chief apartheid ministry later that year. Though less dogmatic than his predecessors, the 'verligte' Koornhof nevertheless became notorious for his policy of forced removals of thousand of blacks from so-called black spots. His sojourn as one of the key reformers in the Cabinet ended when many of the powers of his ministry were given to his rival Chris Heunis in 1983, and Koornhof was appointed South African Ambassador to Washington in September 1984. His colourful and stormy personal life shocked white South Africa in 1993, and this former chief apartheid minister now describes apartheid as 'barbarous', 'loathsome' and 'inhuman'.

Krige, Uys – Lyrical Afrikaner poet and anti-fascist. Fought in Spain. Encouraged pre-*Sestiger* literary revival. Hated by verkramptes. Denied 1966 Hertzog Prize because considered a 'leftist'.

Kruger, Jimmy ('the Mouth') – Hardline Minister of Police under Vorster. The son of Welsh parents, Kruger was adopted in infancy by an Afrikaner couple. He became notorious for statement that the violent death in police detention of Black Consciousness leader Steve Biko, 'leaves me cold'. After Soweto uprising, Kruger explained that his police had used live rather than rubber bullets, because blacks needed to be made 'tame to the gun'. Kruger seconded Connie Mulder's nomination as NP *Hoofleier* in 1978. Fired by P W Botha, he later supported the Conservative Party.

Leroux, Etienne (real name, Stephen Le Roux) – Leading *Sestiger* and novelist (and son of NP cabinet minister S P Le Roux). Winner of 1964 Hertzog Prize for controversial novel *Sewe Dae by die Silbersteins* which provoked first real cultural split in Afrikaner nationalism.

Louw, Eric H – Former diplomat and leading Cape 'Strijdomite'. Held various portfolios under Malan, Strijdom and Verwoerd, but notorious as strident, undiplomatic Foreign Minister (1955–64). Never member of Broederbond as perennially blackballed by Cape *Keeromstraat* establishment for his 'Transvaal' sympathies. Launched unsuccessful attempt to have P W Botha removed as head secretary of Cape NP in 1955.

Louw, Professor N P van Wyk* – Leading Afrikaner poet and literary critic. Attacked by Verwoerd in 1965 and chief target of verkrampte cultural commissars.

Luyt, Louis – Afrikaner industrial magnate, prominent in Muldergate affair as ostensible owner of the Information Department-funded newpaper, *The Citizen*. Played important role in facilitating formation of Democratic Party in 1989.

Malan, Dr Daniel François (*Die Doktor*)* – Leader of Cape NP from its formation in 1914 to 1953. First editor of *Die Burger* (1915–24). Cabinet Minister under Hertzog 1924–34. Declined to follow the General into fusion in 1934. Formed the *gesuiwerde* NP in 1934, and 'Reunited' with General Hertzog in 1940 following the latter's resignation from the premiership and the United Party over South Africa's involvement in WWII. Took over *Hoofleier*ship of NP from Hertzog in November 1940, and remained leader till his retirement at the age of 84 in 1954. His break with the *Ossewa*

Brandwag in 1941 precipitated great Afrikaner nationalist civil war of 1941–47, ended by Malan's electoral alliance with 'Klaas Havenga's Afrikaner Party in 1947 – over strenuous objections of Transvaal NP leader, J G Strijdom. Led nationalist alliance to narrow victory in 1948 election. Prime Minister 1948–54. Quarrelled with Strijdom over republicanism and tried to prevent the Transvaal leader from succeeding him in on his retirement in October 1954. Died 1959.

Malan, General Magnus André de Merindol* – Professional soldier-politician. Son of Transvaal nationalist MP, Speaker of the House of Assembly and chairman of Volkskas, Dr A I Malan, and brother of Avril, captain of South Africa's then most successful-ever national Rugby team. Malan completed the Regular Command and General Staff Officers' Course run by the US Army in 1962–63. A student of strategy, he served as Officer Commanding the Military Academy. Promoted through various commands, he became the leader of the young cadre of military technocrats whose careers were fostered by Defence Minister P W Botha, rising to Chief of the Army in 1973, and shortly after the debacle in Angola, Chief of the South African Defence Force. A leading advocate of the Total Strategy, he was appointed Minister of Defence when P W Botha relinquished the post in October 1980 – becoming the first-ever serving officer to be appointed to the Cabinet. He was instrumental in persuading Botha to adopt a new counter-revolutionary strategy in June 1986. His presidential ambitions were buried by the failure of the SADF to take the Angolan town of Cuito Cuanavale. In 1991 he lost the post of Defence Minister owing to his implication in the Inkathagate scandal, and was demoted to Minister of Water Affairs.

Marais, Jacobus Albertus (Jaap) – Longtime lieutenant of Albert Hertzog, currently leader of Herstigte Nasionale Party (HNP). Elected to Parliament in 1958, Marais was already a member of Albert Hertzog's right-wing 'Pretoria' group. He led the backbench delegation which persuaded John Vorster to stand for the *Hoofleier*ship in September 1966, but soon fell out with the Prime Minister. Marais led attack on Vorster's new policies and was eventually one of four Hertzogite MPs expelled from NP in September 1969. With Albert Hertzog, formed the HNP. Deputy leader in 1969 and HNP leader on Hertzog's 1977 retirement. Marais and other HNP MPs lost their seats in the 1970 elections. A member of the Broederbond since 1950, Marais, along with all known HNP *broers* was expelled from the Bond in 1972, for which he never forgave its new chairman, erstwhile leading Hertzog group publicist, Dr A P Treurnicht. Unsuccessfully opposed Treurnicht in a number of elections. Following the expulsion of the Treurnichtites from the NP in February 1982, Marais declined to join the latter's new Conservative Party (KP), and gradually saw his HNP eclipsed by the KP.

Meyer, Dr Piet J* – Leading theoretician and intellectual of nationalist far right, was self-confessed 'national socialist' and Nazi supporter. Held position of secretary of virtually every key nationalist organisation in early 1940s.

Leading theoretician and chief propagandist of *Ossewa Brandwag*. Withdrew from politics 1946–58. Rehabilitated by Verwoerd. Chairman of Broederbond 1958–72. Head of SABC 1959–76. Declined to follow Albert Hertzog out of NP in 1969. He presided over the belated introduction of a television service into South Africa in 1976.

Mulder, Dr Cornelius Petrus (Connie) – Cabinet Minister under Vorster and (briefly) Botha. Member of Broederbond Executive 1972–74. A longtime mayor of Randfontein, Mulder entered Parliament in 1958. He was appointed Minister of Information in 1968, and elected leader of the Transvaal NP in 1972. Mulder revamped the Information Department in 1972, appointing Eschel Rhoodie as its secretary and approving his grandiose propaganda strategy. He also worked closely with the head of BOSS, General Hendrik van den Bergh. Known as Vorster's 'Crown Prince', Mulder was the chief victim of Information Scandal. Losing the election as NP *Hoofleier* to P W Botha in September 1978, he was driven out of NP cabinet, caucus and party 1978–79. Mulder founded the National Conservative Party to contest 1981 elections. He joined Andries Treurnicht's Conservative Party in 1982, and was seen by many to be waiting to take over its leadership from the politically naive Treurnicht. Finally re-elected to Parliament as Conservative Party MP in 1989 election, Mulder died before taking his seat.

Muller, S Louwrens – Cabinet Minister under Verwoerd, Vorster and Botha. Deputy leader of the Cape NP in 1978, was widely seen as the NP's consensus candidate for the State Presidency when Dr Diederichs retired. However, when Vorster expressed interest in the post on Diederich's death in 1978, Muller dutifully withdrew his candidacy. The chief organiser of P W Botha's successful bid for NP *Hoofleier*ship, he was appointed Leader of the House by the new Prime Minister. However, Muller had a violent quarrel with his old friend P W Botha over the latter's role in Muller's very narrow loss of the NP nomination for the State Presidency following Vorster's enforced resignation from this post in 1979. Muller resigned from the Cabinet and the caucus, and subsequently the NP. In 1982 he came out in support of Conservative Party.

Olivier, Professor Nicolaas Johannes Jacobus (Nic) – Professor of Bantu Law and Native Administration at Stellenbosch University and key early SABRA theoretician (and vice-chairman). Differed sharply with Dr Verwoerd over the development of 'Native Policy' in the 1950s, was frequently denounced by the latter, and was the principal target and victim of the Verwoerd-organised purge of SABRA in 1961. Later turning his back on 'separate development', Olivier joined Progressive Party. Elected to parliament as a 'Prog' MP in 1974, he served for many years as head of the PFP's research department.

Oppenheimer, Harry – Longtime chairman of dominant South African conglomerate, the Anglo American Corporation and doyen of liberal business. United Party MP in 1950s. Financial backer of Progressive Party throughout 1960s and 1980s. Virtually gave General Mining to a Sanlam subsidiary in 1963 as part of (an eventually highly successful) ploy to moderate Afrikaner nationalism. Founded Urban Foundation with Anton Rupert in 1977.

Pienaar, Schalk* – Leading verligte *Keeromstraat* journalist and wit. Editor of *Die Beeld* 1965–70 and *Beeld* 1974–75. Frequently fell out with Dr Verwoerd and others in the Transvaal NP establishment, and together with his close friend Piet Cillié was one of the chief targets of verkrampte ire. Coined the term '*ligte mistykie*' to describe the SADF's 1975–76 fiasco in Angola. Died 1978.

Rhoodie, Deneys – Brother of Eschel, and Deputy Information Secretary 1972–78.

Rhoodie, Dr Eschel* – (James Bond) Flamboyant Secretary for Information 1972–78 and author of Operation Senekal. Worked closely with his Minister, Dr Connie Mulder, and head of BOSS, Gen. Hendrik van den Bergh. Disgraced and exiled in Muldergate Scandal. Sentenced to 12 years' imprisonment for fraud, but acquitted on appeal. Died in 1993.

Richards, Dirk – Leading Transvaal verligte journalist. As Editor of *Dagbreek* in 1960s was one of the early targets of the Hertzog group.

Rupert, Dr Anton – Most prominent Afrikaner industrialist and cultural patron. Briefly editor of pro-Nazi *Wapenskou* at outbreak of WWII. After a controversial role in the Afrikaner economic movement 1939–43, Rupert founded the Rembrandt Tobacco Corporation in 1947 with strong support from leading members of the Broederbond (including Dr Diederichs and Bond secretary, I M Lombard) . Made large contributions to NP in 1950s, but broke with Verwoerd in 1958 and clashed sharply with him over Sharpeville. As leading verligte influence was one of chief targets of verkramptes. With Harry Oppenheimer founded Urban Foundation in 1977.

Sauer, Paul O – Son of J W Sauer, former Cape Premier and member of Gen. Botha's first Union Cabinet. Prominent Cape wine farmer, longtime key figure in Cape nationalist establishment and chairman of Sauer Commission which wrote NP racial policy for 1948 election. Cabinet minister under Malan, Strijdom and Verwoerd, and intensely disliked by latter two. A close lieutenant of Dr Malan, Sauer entered parliament in 1929, and followed Dr Malan into *Gesuiwerde* NP. He twice recommended Verwoerd for key positions which made latter's career. Strong Cape provincialist, disliked in Transvaal NP. As Acting Prime Minister following April 1960 attempt on Verwoerd's life, Sauer made famous 'book is now closed' speech. Tried to lure Vorster to Cape. Close friend and neighbour of Anton Rupert. Retired 1964.

Schlebusch, Alwyn – Leader of Free State NP for much of 1970s, Cabinet minister under Vorster and Botha, served briefly as only ever Vice-President before 1994 constitution. Headed two commissions which took his name, first against extra-parliamentary liberal opposition, second which recommended new constitution. Leading figure in Muldergate *dénouement*, his rallying of OFS NP for P W Botha assured latter of victory over Mulder.

Schoeman, Beaumont M* – Leading verkrampte journalist, and chief propagandist of Albert Hertzog and HNP. Political correspondent of *Die Vaderland* and deputy editor of *Hoofstad*. Editor of HNP newspaper, *Die Afrikaner*. *Nom de plume*, Louis Naudé*.

Schoeman, Ben J (*Oom Ben*)* – *Oud smelter* Cabinet Minister under Malan, Strijdom, Verwoerd and Vorster (Minister of Transport 1954–72). One-time railway shunter, the self-educated Schoeman was first elected to parliament in 1943. Though key Transvaal NP figure, never got on well with Strijdom and openly opposed Verwoerd in Malan and Strijdom's Cabinet. Withdrew at last minute as NP *Hoofleier* candidate in September 1966, but made Transvaal NP leader by Vorster at that time. Bore brunt of attacks of Hertzog group and eventually initiated action which led to their expulsion from NP in 1969. On retirement in 1972 was longest-serving Cabinet Minister in SA history (his record now surpassed by P W Botha). Supported P W Botha at founding of Conservative Party in 1982, threatening John Vorster with revelations should the latter not refrain from attacks on Botha.

Smuts, Field Marshal Jan Christian (*Oom* Jannie, *Oubaas*) – Cambridge-trained Attorney-General of South African Republic 1896–1900. Boer General in Anglo-Boer War. Political lieutenant to General Louis Botha, with whom formed first *Het Volk* and then South African Party (SAP). Ghost-author of President Reitz's *Eeu van Onreg* (A Century of Wrong), won over to support British Imperial cause 1906–12. Member of Imperial War Cabinet in WWI, earned hatred of all Afrikaner nationalists for refusal even to hear clemency plea before execution of 1914 army rebel, Jopie Fourie. Succeeded Botha as Prime Minister in 1919. Used military to suppress 1922 (white) Miners' Strike (the Rand Revolt), told by Hertzog his 'footsteps are dripping with blood'. Losing 1924 election to NP-led 'Pact' coalition, served as Leader of Opposition 1924–33. Led SAP first into coalition (1933) and then 'fusion' (1934) with Hertzog's NP, serving as Deputy Prime Minister in Hertzog's United Party (UP) government. Increasingly disagreed with Hertzog's pro-German policy 1936–39, and led fight to have South Africa declare war on Germany. Prime Minister 1939–48. Emerged as world statesman and leading proponent of United Nations during WWII. Helped write UN Charter. Lost his own seat in 1948 UP election defeat by Malan's NP. Died 1950.

Strijdom, Johannes Gerhardus (Hans, *Die Leeu van die Noorde*) – Hardline Transvaal NP leader, and leader of NP 'extremists'. Entered Parliament in 1929, was only Transvaal Nationalist MP not to follow General Hertzog into 'fusion' in 1934. Member of Transvaal NP leadership triumvirate 1934–36. Undisputed leader of Transvaal NP 1936–58. Battled Broederbond intellectuals for control of Transvaal nationalist movement 1934–46. His closest ally was Dr Verwoerd. Strijdom opposed 1940 'reunification' with Gen. Hertzog's *smelters* and worked to undermine the General's leadership of reunited NP. Also opposed 1947 electoral pact with Havenga's Afrikaner Party and lost vote in Transvaal NP congress on the issue. Quarrelled with Dr Malan almost immediately after 1948 NP victory as latter would not recognise new predominance of Transvaal NP nor include Verwoerd in his first Cabinet. NP *Hoofleier* and Prime Minister 1954–58. Resolved constitutional crisis over 'Coloured' vote in 1950s by packing the Senate with NP supporters. Declined Verwoerd's resignation and defended him from attack within NP. Died August 1958.

Swart, Charles Robert (Blackie) – Leader of the Free State NP 1940–61. Cabinet Minister under Malan, Strijdom and Verwoerd. Elected to Parliament in 1933, Swart refused to follow his provincial leader, Gen. Hertzog, into 'fusion', beginning long war with Hertzogites. Lost his seat in 1938, returned to Parliament in 1941 by-election. Opposed 'reunification' with Hertzogites in 1940, and leading figure in campaign which drove Hertzog from leadership of 'reunited' NP. Become Free State leader on death of Dr N J van der Merwe. Minister of Justice under Malan, Strijdom and Verwoerd. Supported Strijdom against Havenga in 1954 leadership struggle. Lost 1958 NP *Hoofleier* election to Verwoerd. First State President after South Africa became a republic in May 1961. Retired in 1966.

Treurnicht, Dr Andries Petrus (Dr No) – Verkrampte cleric, editor and politician. As editor of NGK newspaper, *Die Kerkbode*, played key role in Verwoerd's denunciation of 1961 Cottesloe declaration. Appointed first editor of *Hoofstad* newspaper in 1968. Though chief apologist and publicist of Hertzog group, declined to join the HNP in 1969. Elected NP MP in 1971, beating HNP's Jaap Marais for Hans Strijdom's old seat. Elected Broederbond chairman in 1972 and forced by Vorster to supervise expulsion from Bond of his old Hertzog group allies. Made Deputy-Minister of Bantu Administration in 1976, his policy to 'Afrikanerise' African education led to Soweto uprising. Succeeded Connie Mulder as Transvaal NP leader October 1978, trouncing verligte 'Fanie Botha. Made full member of Cabinet in mid-1979. Earned sobriquet of 'Dr No' for opposition to Botha's reforms, though raised little fight in Cabinet. Led the 16 MPs who refused February 1982 vote of confidence in P W Botha's leadership. Lost control of Transvaal NP and expelled from the Party in March 1982. Formed and led Conservative Party in 1982. Opposed F W de Klerk's legalisation of the ANC. Died 1993.

van den Bergh, Hendrik J (*Lang Hendrik*) – Interned as leading member of pro-Nazi *Ossewa Brandwag* during WWII, where struck up friendship with John Vorster. Rose through ranks of SA Police in 1950s. In 1962, appointed head of Security Police by Vorster. Successively founded Republican Intelligence (1963) and Bureau for State Security (1969). John Vorster's *éminence grise* and chief hatchet man, Van den Bergh developed close links with CIA. Led the 'Africa' strategy of late 1960s and 1970s, and came into frequent conflict with Military Intelligence. Strong supporter of Connie Mulder, Van den Bergh was disgraced in Information Scandal. Retired in September 1978.

van Rooyen, Retief – Information Department front man and snitch. Represented state in Biko inquest. Revelations to Pik Botha central in defeat of Connie Mulder in 1978.

Verwoerd, Dr Hendrik Frensch (*Die Hollander, Die Rots*) – Dutch-born nationalist hardliner. A Stellenbosch University academic, Verwoerd first rose to prominence at the 1934 *Volkskongres* on the 'Poor White' question. Appointed editor of the new (Cape-controlled) Transvaal NP organ, *Die Transvaler* in 1937, Verwoerd soon developed close relationship with the embattled Transvaal NP leader J G Strijdom. Lent Strijdom his considerable support in battle against Transvaal Broederbond intellectuals and against Cape NP. His intransigence led Nasionale Pers to withdraw its backing for *Die Transvaler*. Verwoerd opposed 'reunification' with the Hertzogites in 1940. A member of the Broederbond executive throughout this period, he also led the 'party faction' in the struggle against the AB's *Ossewa Brandwag*-aligned intellectuals. Opposed 1947 electoral pact with Havenga's AP. Appointed to Senate in 1948, becoming its President. Malan declined to take this 'Transvaal extremist' into his first Cabinet. However, he appointed Verwoerd Minister of Native Affairs in 1950. Verwoerd set out to develop coherent apartheid policy, turning his department into a super-ministry, making many enemies in Cabinet. Was chief organiser of Strijdom's 1954 successful campaign for NP *Hoofleier*ship. Beat Dönges and Swart for *Hoofleier*ship in September 1958. Prime Minister 1958–66. Survived assassination attempt April 1960. Led campaign to make SA a republic, winning referendum in October 1960. Withdrew SA from Commonwealth in March 1961. Established almost dictatorial control over cabinet, party and entire Afrikaner nationalist movement after 1961, encouraging the rapid elaboration of 'Grand Apartheid'. Assassinated in Parliament, September 1966.

Vorster, Baltazar Johannes (John, Jolly John, the Cork in the Bottle) – NP *Hoofleier* and Prime Minister (1966–78) and State President (1978–79). An *Ossewa Brandwag* General, Vorster was interned for his Nazi sympathies during the war. Nominated the Brakpan candidate of Havenga's Afrikaner Party in 1948, he ran as an independent when editor Verwoerd denounced his candidacy (losing by two votes). He joined the NP in 1951 and entered Parliament in 1953. Henceforth a loyal party man, was made deputy-minister by Verwoerd in 1958, promoted to Minister of Justice in 1961. Working with General van den Bergh, he presided over creation of police state. Despite his junior status, Vorster was the eventually unanimous compromise candidate for NP *Hoofleier* following Verwoerd's assassination in September 1966. Soon began to modify some of the latter's policies, provoking an all-out attack on his leadership and all verligtes by verkrampte Hertzog group. Anxious to preserve party unity, declined to act against them for almost 30 months, but eventually insisted that all disloyal elements be expelled. Following 1970 election triumph enjoyed five calm years as popular white leader, but his haphazard leadership style was principal cause of Angola fiasco (1975–76) and inability of the government to develop coherent policies following Soweto rebellion. Vorster likewise allowed the Information Scandal to get out of hand and resigned the premiership in ill-health in September 1978. Elected the ceremonial State President in October 1978, he was forced out of this post by P W Botha in June 1979. Bitter to the end of his life, Vorster attacked Botha on many occasions and threatened to support the formation of the Conservative Party in 1982. He died in 1983.

Wassenaar, Andries* – Longtime chairman of the Afrikaner conglomerate, Sanlam. Wassenaar was leading light in the business agitation for rapid reforms in the late 1970s, publishing a thinly veiled attack on the management style of the Vorster government.

What an appalling human tragedy apartheid has been. The Afrikaners' Frankenstein: their own creation has degenerated into a monster which now threatens to destroy them. ... How reasonable and intelligent people could have voted for this laughable conception [apartheid], and endorsed it with ever increasing majorities, is one of the great mysteries in the entire history of democracy. I am guilty myself. I voted for it.

It is obvious why apartheid failed. It could never have worked! ... Many people, knowledgable people, sympathetic people, warned us that it would not work. ... But we did not listen. All-knowing and arrogant, we pushed ahead. Do your damnedest! Lost opportunities, lost sympathy, lost insight into each other's aspirations, lost trust in each other's good faith. Forty lost years – years in which Afrikaners rarely confronted the implications of our situation of co-existence with others. Why should we have? The answer was so obvious – apartheid. And the discipline of the National Peoples Movement meant that this answer was not, and could not be questioned.

> Prof. J L Boshoff, 'Veertig verlore jare', *Die Suid-Afrikaan*, 18 Desember 1988/Januarie 1989

Shall we retaliate with bombs and midnight assassinations?
Ruth Slovo!
The Boers are not our teachers

Shall we penetrate deep into their homes
and kill refugees and children?
Matola!
The Boers are not our teachers

Shall we massacre unarmed people whose only crime
is demanding what is rightfully theirs?
Mueda!
They are not our teachers

Remember!
Remember
Kassinga
Remember!
Sharpeville
Remember!
Remember
Remember
They are not our teachers
they are not our teachers
they are not our teachers!

> Abdullah Ibrahim (Dollar Brand), Memorial concert for Ruth First, Maputo, August 1982

Al dra die aap 'n goue ring, bly hy nog steeds 'n lelike ding

> Afrikaans saying (see Glossary)

Map 1: Southern Africa: Capital cities, ports and regional railways

INTRODUCTION

The politics of democratic transition

As Nelson Mandela walked out of Victor Verster prison and into the glare of the world's television cameras on 11 February 1990, the door slammed closed on the heroic age of South African politics. A week earlier, President F W de Klerk had stunned the world when he ended 40 long years of ever-tighter restrictions on political activity by unbanning the African National Congress (ANC) and myriad other illegal organisations.* Following the collapse of communist regimes throughout Eastern Europe, and just two months after the tearing down of the Berlin Wall, the proclaimed end of apartheid seemed but part of the process sweeping away most of the received verities of the post-war world.

In South Africa as in Eastern Europe, the 1990s ushered in a dramatically new but deeply contested order. Here too, initial euphoria at the passing of the hated old system soon gave way to a grim recognition of the real perils, the grubby compromises and the moral ambiguities of a transition to this uncertain future. On-again/off-again negotiations, a free-falling economy and the escalation of political violence into a deadly and seemingly unstoppable blood feud claiming thousands of victims, all did little to end the legacy of apartheid or improve the lot of black South Africans. As the Boiphatong and Bisho massacres joined Sharpeville and Soweto on South Africa's wall of shame, the major political groups retreated into mutual recrimination and hardening positions. Overwhelmed by barbarous civil war in Yugoslavia and unspeakable privation in Somalia, the world seemed to lose interest in South Africa's apparently intractable problems and politicians.

This book tries to grapple with some of those problems and politicians. It does so as South Africa has moved to a new settlement. After nearly four years of fraught negotiations and worsening political violence, Mandela's ANC and De Klerk's National Party finally produced a fragile and contested transitional

---

* The South African Communist Party (SACP) was outlawed in 1950, the ANC and Pan Africanist Congress in April 1960, and the Congress of Democrats in 1962. In 1968, all legal political parties were forbidden to admit members from more than one racial group – leading to the disbandment of the Liberal Party. Eighteen Black Consciousness groups were declared prohibited organisations in 1977, and 19 democratic organisations all but banned in February 1988.

constitution in November 1993. South Africa went into its first non-racial election on 27–28 April 1994 with its collective fingers crossed. Much of the international coverage of the run up to the poll depicted the country as edging implacably towards a place alongside Bosnia, Somalia and Rwanda as one of the horrendous ethnic conflagrations of the 1990s.

In the event, these apocalyptic scenarios were confounded. For once in its benighted history, South Africa seemed to have found favour with the gods of politics. The day before the April election the political violence simply stopped. Despite massive fraud and mind-boggling disorganisation, the long election appeared somehow to have fashioned the essential symbols and experience of a new nationhood. Just over two weeks short of the forty-sixth anniversary of the coming to power of the National Party, Nelson Mandela was inaugurated into the Presidency on 10 May 1994 in a profoundly moving ceremony of grace and reconciliation.

Yet the remarkable and prolonged political honeymoon enjoyed by South Africa's first democratic government cannot last. The country remains transfigured – and ravaged – by the consequences of apartheid. The overriding issue of this entirely new kind of politics is how to overcome this devastating legacy. This question can only be seriously addressed through a correct grasp of the real options available in this new era of negotiated politics. If my assessment in the opening sentence of this Introduction is correct, any attempt to measure the limits and possibilities of transformation in the 'new South Africa' must begin by working out how we got to 2 February 1990 – the political routes travelled and the vehicles used.* Only then will we be in a position to assess which of the proffered political destinations are desirable and/or attainable, and whether in trying to get there it is necessary to repair, to change or even to abandon the existing modes of political transportation.

In attempting to retrace these routes, I make three assumptions. First, it seems clear that the new political direction announced by President F W de Klerk on 2 February 1990 sought to grapple with the unresolved questions posed by the pivotal South African event of the 1980s – the black urban uprising of 1984 to 1986. Turning into *the* international media event of the mid-1980s, this uprising highlighted the abject failure of the regime's celebrated Total Strategy to resolve what I hope to show was the terminal crisis of apartheid. A period of virtual direct military rule from 1986 to 1989 likewise ended in failure, ultimately driving President P W Botha from office. While his successor eventually abandoned Botha's version of 'reform', through four difficult years of negotiations with the ANC, De Klerk's National Party (NP) government clung to a modified notion of 'power-sharing'. Far from accepting genuine non-racial democracy, it sought instead to incorporate the ANC into a political system which would preserve some form of white political veto and most of

---

* 2 February 1990 being the date of De Klerk's historic speech announcing the legalisation of all banned organisations and the liberation of Nelson Mandela.

white privilege.

And to some extent it has succeeded. While the ANC is by far the dominant partner in South Africa's post-election Government of National Unity, Second Vice-President De Klerk still commands formidable political resources. The NP leader is also determined that *he*, rather than State President Mandela, will dictate the pace of the ANC's trumpeted Reconstruction and Development Programme. Those wonderful people who gave us apartheid will still play a central role in shaping the circumstances under which the infant South African democracy will progress to adolescence and maturity.

My second assumption is that the move to negotiations was a direct consequence of a *strategic stalemate* which had set in at the end of the 1980s. The radically new conjuncture after 2 February 1990 grows out of a long and violent impasse in which neither side was able to impose itself decisively on the other. By mid-1987, the apartheid regime had managed to contain the black uprising and overturn the widespread perception that it was about to be swept from power. But, ignoring the strictures of its own counter-revolutionary theoretical guru that compromise with the revolutionaries was the only possible solution to this kind of conflict (see p. 261 below), it proved unable to use this breathing space to construct a political solution capable of re-establishing stability and economic growth.

For its part, by February 1990 the democratic resistance had succeeded in derailing the various political strategies of the Botha regime. It had undone many of the preconditions for ongoing white prosperity and had survived intense repression to begin to mount a new wave of mass resistance. Yet, despite its heady rhetoric of armed struggle and people's war, the ANC proved unable to move beyond the stage of armed propaganda to pose a significant threat to the military underpinnings of the apartheid state – let alone imposing a radical transformation of the structures of power. Moreover, despite the wide potential appeal of its non-racial policies, the ANC's insurrectionist tactics actually prevented it from winning the kind of support from the political middle ground which would have seriously undermined the power-base and legitimacy of the apartheid government.

My final assumption concerns the complex and contradictory effects of this long and violent strategic stalemate. 2 February 1990 marked a fundamental turning point in South African politics. Yet this very absence of a decisive result, of a clear victory or defeat for either the regime or for those who sought to overthrow it, had complex consequences. Once the immediate euphoria following De Klerk's speech had worn off, their combined effect not only enormously complicated the process of negotiations between 1990 and 1994, they continue to resonate through the transition to a new democratic order.

First, the lack of a clear-cut result produced a profound ambiguity and ambivalence at the heart of the negotiation process. On the one hand, the politics of the period after 2 February 1990 has been based on a mutual recognition that neither side was likely to prevail in the short or even medium term. In order to get beyond the violent impasse of the crisis of apartheid each, in some sense, needed the other – each would have to compromise. On the other hand, however, the very fact of the impasse meant that both sides could and did claim not only that they had avoided defeat, but that in some profound sense, they had won.*

This, then, had the contradictory effect of locking both sides into an interdependent relationship in a new process of negotiated transition, while at the same time freezing in place key aspects of their respective political cultures, world views, core values and perceptions of the other. In the apt description of key ANC negotiator and SACP chairman Joe Slovo, the major power centres spent much of the three years following 2 February 1990 trying to 'win at the negotiating table what they had failed to win on the battlefield'.[1]

This tendency to seek to realise major strategic objectives in the negotiation process obviously rendered much more problematic the ability of each side to deal with the political imperatives of the new period. Their dwindling political capabilities were then further complicated by the next consequence of the strategic stalemate – the declining coherence of the coalition of forces making up each of the two major power centres.

In early 1990, both the ruling National Party and the ANC apparently turned their backs on their respective received political wisdoms and undertook to negotiate with the 'enemy' with whom they had so long been locked in mortal moral conflict. Mandela and De Klerk had finally come to recognise that they could not triumph over the forces of evil they had so long depicted the other as representing. But they had not exactly broadcast this realisation to their followers. Most of the rank and file on both sides were still wrapped up in a demonised view of the other, and convinced of the ultimate victory of their own moral cause – whether to bury apartheid or to destroy 'communism'. The rapidity with which both sets of leaders now started negotiating with this enemy thus generated deep unease in their respective political constituencies.† In each of these political coalitions, the leadership came under intense criticism for having betrayed core values, or for having sold out to 'the enemy'.

Negotiations then, infinitely complicated the respective internal politics of the NP and the ANC. Both De Klerk and Mandela had to negotiate with at least one eye on their own fractious and contested constituencies, always bearing in mind

---

* The NP government claimed that the collapse of communism vindicated its long battle against 'the Marxist menace', and that events both in Eastern Europe and in South Africa itself confirmed the NP's insistence on the primary of ethnic factors in political life. The ANC for its part claimed victory in forcing the regime to concede not only the failure of grand apartheid and 40 years of repression, but that in obliging the NP to accept many basic democratic principles, the ANC had vindicated its 30-year armed struggle and confirmed it own status as the incarnation of South Africa's democratic future.

† At Mandela's historic first public address on the day of his release, he described De Klerk as a man of integrity. On the streets of Soweto the next morning, young ANC supporters were seen sporting ANC T-shirts with Mandela's photograph crossed out.

the imperative to preserve their own power-base. Growing disillusionment with their leadership allowed radical critics of the right and the left to make inroads into the traditional constituencies of both the NP and ANC. Yet it also led to a gathering but uneven depoliticisation on both sides – a retreat from the belief that politics can produce viable solutions. These in turn led to moments of intransigence and reinforced the imperative to defend core values and core objectives in negotiations.

Finally, the absence of a clear-cut victory or defeat also profoundly affected the population at large. In the four years following the unbanning of the ANC, South African society experienced no psychological catharsis – no clear and irreversible rupture with, no purging of, the past. As a result, the entire society was forced to grapple with, and struggle over, not just the fundamental fact of the impact and consequences of apartheid, but with myriad unresolved issues of South African history. Literally tens of thousands of people died in the political violence this occasioned. If corrected for its nineteenth-century gender bias, Marx's celebrated observation on the impact of the past on the present reads as an apt description of South Africa in the 1990s:

> Men make their own history, but they do not make it just as they please; they do not make it under circumstances chosen by themselves, but under circumstances directly encountered, given and transmitted from the past. The tradition of all the dead generations weighs like a nightmare on the brain of the living.[2]

As in other regions of the world divided by their histories, South Africa is quite literally haunted by the manifold unresolved issues of its tragic and violent past. The problem, however, is that the collective minds of different groups of South Africans are living the nightmares of different histories. They are thus also haunted by very different fears over what these unresolved pasts mean for their individual and collective futures. The grace period of the April 1994 election and inauguration of the new ANC-dominated Government of National Unity simply held these various nightmares in abeyance for a while. It did not free the country of the need to lay to rest the multiple issues of its conflicted history. Once the honeymoon period of the new government comes to an end, this national obsession with settling the various accounts of different pasts will continue to shape the ways in which both the political organisations as well as the broad sweep of society seek to address the staggering problems of the country's present, and of its possible future.

To put this metaphorically: South Africa seems condemned to live simultaneously through seven distinct historical times. By this I mean that either the entire society or powerful forces within it are trying to deal with the demands of creating a new, post-apartheid democracy while simultaneously confronting residues of unresolved issues of one or other of these historical times. Nelson Mandela's Government of National Unity will have to find ways to come to terms with each.

● Firstly, and perhaps most pressingly, it has to grapple with the dismal political realities of the post-Cold War world of the 1990s – with the limited options available to a semi-peripheral, resource-based economy in an epoch of globalisation, of structural adjustment and of the marginalisation of Africa by the three emerging regional trading blocs – let alone with the terrifying impact of the AIDS pandemic.

• It does so, secondly, while significant forces on all sides of the political spectrum still seem unable to accept the fact of the stalemate of the late 1980s. Trapped in the mindsets of 1976–89, they cling to the belief that political questions can be solved by military means and that decisive victory can still be forced on 'the enemy' if only the opportunistic politics of compromise by discredited leaders were replaced by firm purpose and unwavering commitment to core values.*

• This occurs, thirdly, while the country must address the 1960s and the imperatives and politics of decolonisation and deracialisation. Yet global economic and political prospects are far less propitious than those confronting the rest of Africa during its decolonisation thrust in the 1960s. In particular, the transformation of the world economy over the last twenty-five years has undermined the capacity of even the most powerful states to choose their own economic and social policies.

• In this context of embattled state sovereignty, sections of the NP's former power-base seek, fourthly, to drag South Africa back to 1948 – to the epoch of apartheid and the unrealised dream of ethnic separation and white domination. While the election of May 1994 puts such dreams beyond the realm of hyper-fantasy, the forces which cling to them still possess a capacity to wreak substantial chaos, and possibly undo the fragile glue of the new settlement.

• At yet another level, South Africa is one of the last societies on earth still grappling with the legacy of 1917. In this, the most unequal society on the planet, and the only industrialised economy in Africa, significant and well-organised social forces still cherish the dream of forging 'real' socialism.† The incorporation of key militant labour leaders in the new government is a double-

---

* Thus, following the assassination of the ANC and Communist Party hero Chris Hani, in April 1993, the chairman of the Natal Midlands region of the ANC and member of its National Executive Committee, Harry Gwala, publicly called for the ANC to abandon negotiations and resume the armed struggle. Gwala remained embittered by his failure to secure nomination as the ANC candidate for the KwaZulu/Natal premiership in 1994. The ANC's dismal electoral showing in his Natal Midlands fiefdom somewhat weakened his revolutionary credibility, but the more 'militant' approach represented by Gwala, Winnie Mandela and 'the Young Lions' means that the issue of the ANC's original mission remains front and centre in the post-apartheid era.

† The standard index of measuring the inequalities of wealth is the Gini coefficient. According to this scale, a hypothetical society in which wealth was distributed absolutely equally would have a coefficient of 0, whereas a society whose total wealth was monopolised by a single family would have a coefficient of 1. In 1989 South Africa had the world's highest Gini coefficient, of 0.66. See F Wilson & M Ramphele, *Uprooting Poverty: The South African Challenge* (Norton, New York, 1989), 18ff.

edged sword. It might moderate the worker's demands, but it could also lose these new politicians their support from their old trade union base.

● To complicate matters, the Mandela government must deal, sixthly, with the significant social forces which remain trapped in the legacy of the lost independence of the old Boer Republics during the South African War of 1899–1902. The Afrikaner far right divided into two hostile camps following the fiasco of its March 1994 armed intervention in the Bophutatswana bantustan. Led by steely-eyed General Constand Viljoen, its 'moderate' wing seems to have abandoned the fantasy of somehow preserving apartheid, but insists on the creation of an Afrikaner *Volkstaat* (state of the *volk*) within the borders of South Africa. And the new government has set up a *Volkstaat* Council to investigate this question.

● And finally, as the deadly political violence since 1990 has made clear, other social forces still seem locked in the second decade of the nineteenth century – the great violence of the *mfecane*, associated with the strains imposed on black societies by the slave trade and the rise of the Zulu kingdom under King Shaka. With Chief Mangosuthu Buthelezi's Inkatha Freedom Party now governing the KwaZulu/Natal Province, and determined not to cede any control of this fiefdom to the central government, politics in this region of South Africa remain particularly charged.

If I might now mix my metaphors: this historical simultaneity means that in post-February 1990 South Africa more than a few political taxis are cruising different political routes, trying to attract more or less willing passengers for complicated journeys (at night and without headlights?) to opposing, if still unknown destinations. On the way to the April 1994 elections there were a number of semi-serious collisions, and the country confronted the real possibility of a disastrous multiple pile-up. While the political traffic jam has eased somewhat with the installation of Nelson Mandela's Government of National Unity, these unresolved histories have not yet been laid to rest.

Where does all this leave the political analyst? It seems to me that in this deeply contested and fraught conjuncture, any attempt to gauge South Africa's troubled political future needs to come to terms with the real content of the 'crisis of apartheid' which produced the strategic stalemate of the late 1980s. This is impossible to do without an understanding of the concrete political processes and conflicts in the old apartheid state, and the way in which the various options were conceived of and fought out in that state. In turn, however, both these latter tasks require a clear grasp of the place and role in state politics of the National Party during its forty-plus years in power – years in which its apartheid policies first led to a significant restructuring of South African politics and society, and then became *the* key issue of the 'crisis' in South Africa.

This latter aspect is the central concern of this book. It seeks to explain the internal politics of the National Party and their place in the broader politics of the South African state during these 'forty lost years'. It also attempts to give the reader something of the unique flavour of these Afrikaner nationalist politics, politicians and discourse.

This analytical narrative seeks to redress what I take to be the incomplete and often misleading existing accounts of this doleful period of South African history, and of Afrikaner nationalism and NP rule. Three points are at issue here. First, while a great deal has been written on various aspects of Afrikaner nationalism and the National Party government (see Bibliography, pp. 537-64), much of this extensive literature remains trapped in a negative mirror image of Afrikaner nationalism's ideological assumptions. I have discussed this at length elsewhere and will not repeat myself here.[3] Suffice it to say that by doing so, much of this analysis also implicitly assumes that the only divisions that matter in Afrikaner nationalism are ideological. Afrikaner politicians are treated as a breed apart. Unlike their counterparts in the rest of the world, they are not driven by the struggle for personal position, by interpersonal rivalries and individual greed, but are treated as if they are motivated purely by ideological concerns. This is clearly what these politicians would have liked Afrikaners to believe. In reality, however, the admittedly intensely ideological nature of internal Afrikaner nationalist politics served to *heighten* personality conflicts and power struggles, and then to cover up the growing corruption in the NP and government.

My second point relates to the scope of this literature. To the best of my knowledge, there exists only one study which covers the entire period of NP rule from 1948 to 1994.[4] Superficial and badly written, this inadequate account simply does not understand the dynamics of Afrikaner nationalist politics. My own book seeks to present a more complete picture of the politics of the Afrikaner nationalist government during its long and violent stewardship of the South African state. It questions the still-lingering myth of a long monolithic NP, pointing to the depth of its divisions and the little-discussed personal viciousness of its internal politics.

More particularly, the book is inspired, thirdly, by the profound conviction that the new, 'reformed' and 'post-apartheid' NP of F W de Klerk is a completely inappropriate vehicle in which to travel to the new South Africa – one damaged beyond repair by its own crimes and history. Nevertheless, the NP remains the political vehicle of choice for crucial social groups. Its driver envisages a destination very different from that being considered by most of South African society, and still disposes of formidable means though which to attempt to impose his destination on the country. The April 1994 South African election saw F W de Klerk's 'new' NP emerge as the majority party in one of the new South Africa's nine provinces (the Western Cape), and the second party in the country (with just over 20 percent of the vote compared to the ANC's 62 percent). As Nelson Mandela's Second Vice-President, De Klerk seriously seems to believe that his NP will win the 1999 election. While he is probably dreaming in ultra technicolour, the people who gave the world apartheid will certainly continue to play a significant role in South Africa's post-apartheid politics. Understanding what made them tick – what nightmares weigh on *their* brains – is an essential starting point for any assessment of their present and future role in a democratic South Africa.

This book is in many ways a sequel to my 1983 publication, *Volkskapitalisme: Class, Capital and Ideology in the Development of Afrikaner Nationalism, 1934–1948* (Cambridge University Press). In that earlier book I was concerned to situate the development of Afrikaner nationalism within the context of the broader structures of socio-economic power in South Africa. The book questioned the then conventional wisdom of an Afrikaner nationalist ethnic monolith, pointing to – and seeking to explain – the deep conflicts and tensions inherent in this nationalism since the formation of the National Party in 1914.

In particular, *Volkskapitalisme* grappled with two aspects on which virtually all the then existing analyses of Afrikaner nationalism were silent. The first was the role of class position and class differentiation in the emerging nationalist project. The book dealt, secondly, with what I took to be *the* central element of that project, the quest by a newly urbanised Afrikaner middle class to carve out for itself a share of the economic pie monopolised by English-speaking whites. I argued that the Afrikaner nationalist movement of the 1940s was very far from being a natural, inherent ethnic reflex. Rather, as a response by identifiable elements in the Afrikaans-speaking population to a unique set of historical circumstances, it facilitated the painstaking construction by extremely well-organised groups of petty bourgeois militants of, firstly, a new 'Christian national' ideology and then a broad Afrikaner social and political alliance. And at the heart of this nationalist alliance stood the organised attempt to create an Afrikaner business class.

Most analysts would now acknowledge that both class and the 'economic movement' have to be integrated in any study of the development of Afrikaner nationalism. Yet *Volkskapitalisme* was roundly criticised for what many took to be my 'class reductionism', and/or failure to grapple convincingly with what some critics would call 'ethnicity'.[5] While there were undoubtedly reductionist (and rhetorical) excesses in the book, on the whole I remain persuaded that the fundamental premises underlying my analysis of Afrikaner nationalism were valid.

This present book is based on similar assumptions. In particular, it presumes that none of the many ethnic tensions so characteristic of the 1990s can adequately be explained as simply reflecting the inherent and instinctive primacy of what Clifford Geertz once called 'primordial identities' – those 'congruities of blood, speech, custom and so on, [which] are seen to have an ineffable, and at times overpowering, coerciveness *in and of themselves'*.[6] Contrary to journalistic conventional wisdom about both the post-Cold War conflicts in Eastern and Central Europe, and the still dominant 'ethnic' analyses of South Africa, human beings do *not* always automatically respond in vast numbers to the beating of a nationalist/ ethnic drum by this or that politician. History, even in South Africa, is replete with examples of peoples who have *refused* the invitation to ethnic mobilisation, opting instead for wider, more inclusive forms of identity and political mobilisation. One cannot therefore simply assume that 'ethnicity' is either an instinctive human reflex or that it is in some sense the 'primordial' identity.

This would suggest that social and political identities, and the translation of these identities into social and political action, are infinitely complex and dynamic aspects of human behaviour. I am convinced that to explain such identities and their socio-political mobilisation, the analyst has to situate the particular group of people and socio-political phenomena to be analysed, within the unique set of historico/structural and conjunctural circumstances which shape their (changing) understandings of who they are, of what unites them against other collectivities, of the options open to them and the choices they make.

Such 'circumstances' would include a range of objective and subjective factors. However, this last statement encapsulates perhaps the most controversial question in social science – that of the relationship between structure and agency (or what, in a very different paradigm, used to be called determination and free will) in explaining human social and political behaviour. It seems to me the most fruitful type of social analysis is that which tries to integrate both.

This issue is taken up in the Theoretical Appendix (p. 419 below). Here I would briefly illustrate my own position by again resorting to metaphor. It seems to me that the structural dimensions of analysis delineate the (changing) boundaries, dimensions and topography of the playing field in question. They set out the rules of the game, spell out what kinds of forces are at work, fix the players in their (likewise) changing relationships and roles, define their respective capacities, and establish the broad parameters of possible outcomes. In these terms then, structural dimensions can be considered to be the *conditions of existence,* or in another paradigm, the necessary conditions shaping any process and limiting its possible outcomes.* *On their own, however, they are not sufficient to explain either these processes or their particular outcomes.* Structural conditions do not cause, nor even directly determine, the direction taken by a particular social or political process. While they do establish the limits of what is possible, they do not *directly* account for the collective and individual choices of the actors involved.

In order fully to explain these processes and outcomes it is essential to take into consideration a range of subjective factors which account for these choices and so shape the outcomes. Here I would include: the competing (and constantly evolving) ideologies, belief systems and received cultural values through which conflict is mediated in the society in question; the role of political and other organisations in defining/adapting these values while attempting to secure the exclusive loyalty of target groups for a proffered version of group identity and action; the personal styles, preoccupations, abilities and even personalities of

---

* I take such structural aspects to include: the place of the social formation in question in the international division of economic labour and hierarchy of international conflicts; the overall structure and dynamic of capital accumulation within that social formation; the particular place(s) in this process of the specific social group(s) under study; the socio-economic stratification of these group(s) and the relationship of these strata to each other and to the wider society.

political leaders; the evolving rules, routines and practices of the institutional matrix making up the political system of the society in question.

However, these subjective dimensions of social process spring neither from whim nor from the Heavens. They are not 'independent variables' somehow divorced and freed from the ultimately determining influence of structure. I remain enough of a structuralist to insist that *the boundaries of the possible* are structurally determined; that agency affects causality only within the limits of these structural boundaries of possible outcomes. Nevertheless, the two dimensions are so deeply interpenetrated and overdetermined that the distinction between them is often artificial. It seems to me that the key to coherent analysis which is neither reductionist nor idealist – and which also rejects fashionable post-modernist relativism and inevitable passivity – lies in the extremely difficult task of attempting to penetrate the interaction of the 'structural' and 'subjective' dimensions of social behaviour.

My understanding of these complex theoretical issues is discussed in the Theoretical Appendix. Although this book is a sort of 'son-of-*Volkskapitalisme*', it stands by itself and has a slightly different focus. Given the central role of the National Party in the unfolding drama of democratic transition in South Africa, I am here less directly concerned with the kind of overall sociology of Afrikaner nationalism to be found in the earlier book than with an explanation of its internal politics since the NP came to power in 1948. I nevertheless do try to provide some clues as to such a sociology for those who have not read the earlier work. This necessarily involves some restatement of its central arguments. I hope those who have read that book will not find this too repetitious.

In conclusion, it should be noted that the analyst of Afrikaner nationalism and the NP confronts a series of epistemological, political and stylistic dilemmas. As indicated above, the first of these is discussed in detail in the Theoretical Appendix at the end of the book. However, a comment on the political and stylistic issues involved is in order.

So pervasive and horrifying were the crimes of apartheid that most non-Afrikaners have found it impossible to write about the National Party without expressing their disgust for its policies. Yet this almost universal condemnation is too easy a way out. It obscures the central place of apartheid in the formation and evolution of capitalism in South Africa, reducing apartheid to the simple product of Afrikaner racist paranoia. This simplistic – and false – picture in turn absolves those who should be the co-accused: the foreign governments and investors, the liberal capitalists in South Africa who were all perfectly content to accept the high profits made possible by apartheid. Despite their frequent denunciations of some of apartheid's excesses, these people seemed singularly reluctant to use their overwhelming economic power either to force change on the NP government, or to improve the appalling wages of their black workers. They only began to do so once apartheid was no longer profitable. This curious political bashfulness of capitalism's proponents and agents in apartheid South Africa contrasts markedly with the universal alacrity with which their

13

counterparts acted against *left-wing* governments in other parts of the world. One does not need to be a mechanistic marxist to ask the question why. Nor to believe that the vast *profits* made possible by apartheid had something to do with capital's political reticence.

This means of course, that while Afrikaner nationalism fathered apartheid, as I hope to have shown in *Volkskapitalisme,* the little monster was mothered by South African capitalism. And it was born – legitimately – into and raised by an extended and supportive family much wider than the Afrikaner *volk.* While probing the particular circumstances of its birth, growth and decline, it is crucial to discuss the role of this entire family in the unfolding tragedy of apartheid. At the same time however, it is equally important to come to terms with the profoundly misunderstood, and often ignored, internal dynamics of Afrikaner nationalist politics. Both of these issues have crucial bearing not just on the dynamics of transition in 'the new South Africa' but equally on its capacity to dismantle the terrible legacy of apartheid.

The body of this book sets for itself the ambitious task of explaining not only those historical/structural features which shaped Afrikaner nationalism's hegemony in the South African state, but also of interpreting Afrikaner political culture, Afrikaner nationalist politics and Afrikaner politicians. However, in contrast to *Volkskapitalisme,* my emphasis here is less on structure than on agency. This is more of a stylistic rather than an epistemological choice, made for two reasons. First, in that earlier book I was driven by the urgent need to displace the interpretation of Afrikaner nationalism from the prevailing and smug negative mirror images of its own ideology into radically different channels. To the extent that I believe this succeeded, I can now take the determining effects of structure to some extent as given.

However, an original subsidiary motivation of *Volkskapitalisme* has become more pressing partly as a result of the now broad acceptance that the evolution of Afrikaner nationalism cannot be understood separately from the history of South African capitalism. Ironically, overly structuralist analyses of the state and state politics have tended to reduce it all somehow to the logic of capital. Still reflecting the ethnocentric nature of anglophone social science about South Africa, many on the left who wrote about the South African state in the 1980s failed even to read what the holders of office said and wrote about themselves in their own language – Afrikaans. Much of the research in this area resembles that of an American social scientist wishing to explain French Gaullism by reading only English sources. Such an exercise would not be taken seriously in either French or American universities, but it is somehow deemed acceptable in explaining South Africa.

This then brings me back to my earlier point: a full grasp of the politics of the South African state must come to terms with its dominant political culture and the politics of its ruling party. While I insist that these remain ultimately structurally determined, as I hope to show in the following pages, throughout these 'forty lost years' the 'subjective' aspects of NP politics – including the contrasting personalities of its various leaders – played a central role in shaping crucial policy decisions, in fashioning the overall evolution of the apartheid state.

In these terms, then, this book can be read at three distinct levels. The first is largely narrative. The book tells 'the story' of 'forty lost years' of National Party rule in South Africa. In doing so, it focuses in particular on the internal conflicts within the NP and the broader Afrikaner nationalist movement. It does so because I am convinced that existing accounts are incomplete and do not grasp the real political dynamics at play. And these dynamics (and the party's policy choices) are only fully comprehensible through a grasp of the peculiar political culture of Afrikaner nationalism. In telling this 'story', I have tried to impart something of the flavour and extraordinary intensity of these politics.

While I have relegated to the appendix the overt discussion of the theoretical issues involved, I would like to believe that the concrete analysis in the body of the book is informed by a coherent theoretical position. Thus, secondly, the book can also be read as an implicit intervention in an ongoing theoretical debate over the analysis of the South African state. Finally, the book also seeks to address a series of *political* questions which bear directly on the current situation in South Africa. The first is that of the nature of political power in South Africa after apartheid became official state policy in 1948. This leads, secondly, to the political dimensions of the crisis of apartheid and its attempted resolution in state policy throughout the 1980s. And given the final failure of these policies, the book attempts, thirdly, to assess the prospects for building democracy on the still-standing ruins of apartheid.

The text is divided into four largely chronological parts. Part One explores the construction of the NP project 1948–66, and examines the infighting this occasioned. It does so to set the scene for the crisis of the 1970s. The various levels of this crisis are examined Part Two, which ends with a discussion of the Muldergate affair. Part Three grapples with the attempts by P W Botha's government to reform apartheid between 1978 and 1986, while Part Four seeks to come to terms with reasons for, and the politics of, the collapse of each of the successive reformist strategies. The book concludes with a brief assessment of the transition process.

PART I

A FORT BUILT ON FEAR

Into the Afrikaner *laager*

Gedagtewisseling
Klein donker meidjie, waarheen is die reis
deur kaalboom winterstrate? *Huis, paleis* ...

Waar gaan jy in jou kortmou-flenterrok
noudat dit skemer word? *Pondok, varkhok*
Want ek gaan huis toe, buite is dit koud
maar binne vroetel vlamme aan die hout
staan die gedekte tafel wit en net
en wag die sagte warmte van my bed

Hoe sê jou donker oë dan? Jy wis
dat God die God van blanke kinders is ...?

Blokhuis
Die fondamente van die fort was vrees
haat het die deure een vir een gesluit
Nou loer die bouer deur 'n skietgat uit
en durf die muurskrif agter hom nie lees

Discussion
Small dark maid, where leads your journey
through leafless streets? *House, palace* ...

Where are you going in your tattered shortsleeve dress
now that evening falls? *Hovel, pigsty* ...
Because I am going home, outside is just the cold
but inside flames burrow into wood,
the covered table stands white and fair
and the soft warmth of my bed awaits

How say your dark eyes then? You surely knew
that God is the God of white children ...?

Blockhouse
The foundations of the fort were fear
hatred closed its doors one by one
Now the builder peers through a loophole
and dares not read the writing on the wall

Olga Kirsch, *Blokhuis* (Blockhouse), from *Mure van die Hout*, Afrikaanse Pers Boekhandel, 1948.
Reproduced by permission of Olga Kirsch.

Chapter One

NOT TAKEN AT THE FLOOD

The 1948 election

D F Malan's National Party wins by a slender majority in the 1948 election, promising
inter alia, white bread to replace the wartime brown loaf

The photograph is almost fifty years old, but still the image retains its power to impress. It certainly had a strong emotional impact on many white South Africans when it was splashed over the international and local press.

In the centre sits a slim, goateed, elderly man, dressed in his uniform as a Field Marshal of the Armed Forces of the British Commonwealth. To his left and right, standing respectfully behind him, and clearly impressed with the significance of the occasion, are serious-looking younger men, one in uniform, the others not. On the wall are the flags and the symbol of the United Nations. It is San Francisco in June 1945. The war in Europe has just ended. We are witnessing the South African Prime Minister, Jan Christian Smuts, signing the United Nations Charter which he had helped to draft, and whose prayer-like Preamble he had written. Smuts's signature made South Africa a founder member of the new world body dedicated to peace and economic prosperity.

This photograph well captured South Africa's international standing at the end of World War II. The war brought the country unprecedented prestige and prosperity. Its forces had played a conspicuous part in the liberation of Ethiopia.* A South African contingent had seized Madagascar from the Vichy French. Despite the disaster of General H B Klopper's surrender of Tobruk in June 1942, South African forces also fought valiantly in the North African and Italian campaigns. Pretoria's volunteer – and segregated† – army served under Montgomery's British Eighth Army in North Africa, and Matt Clark's Fifth US Army in Italy. The highest-scoring fighter ace among the Western allies, Squadron Leader M T ('Pat') Pattle, was a South African serving in the Royal Air Force, as was the Battle of Britain hero and the leading tactician in the RAF Fighter Command, Group Captain A G ('Sailor') Malan.‡

---

* The crucial role of the South African Air Force in Ethiopia was underlined by the British Secretary of State for Air as follows: 'When the Italians come to draw up a list of factors which caused them to lose their East African Empire, they will place the SAAF bombers somewhere near the top of the list' – Sir Archibald Sinclair, quoted in *Illustrated History of South Africa: The Real Story* (Reader's Digest, Pleasantville NY & Montreal, 1988), 347.

† Only white troops were assigned to combat units, while so-called Coloured and African volunteer soldiers were confined to unarmed auxiliary units. These black soldiers faced the same dangers as their white counterparts, and those who died in battle were buried in separate burial areas from white soldiers. On demobilisation, white soldiers received £5 in cash and a £25 clothing allowance. The equivalent allowances were £3 and £15 for so-called Coloured soldiers and £2 and a khaki suit worth £2 for Africans.

‡ J L Stokesbury, *A Short History of Air Power* (William Morrow, New York, 1986), 232. Only in the 1970s did the RAF acknowledge Pattle's remarkable feat of downing 41 German and Italian aircraft on the Mediterranean Front – all in the space of just over nine months. The next highest-scoring western allied air ace, US Major Richard Bong took over three years to mark up 40 confirmed 'kills'. What makes Pattle's achievement even more remarkable was the fact that for all but the last two months of his battle career, he flew the outdated Gloster Gladiator biplane fighter. This 'unknown ace' was killed in the final air battle of the Greek campaign on 20 April 1941, leading the RAF's 15 remaining fighter aircraft into an attack on a wave of German bombers escorted by almost 100 fighters – E C R Butler, *The Fighter Aces of the RAF's., 1939–1945* (William Kimber, London, 1962), 148-54. Sailor Malan was himself the RAF's third highest-scoring ace.

World War II had also underlined Prime Minister and Field Marshal Smuts's stature as one of the great icons of the (then) British Commonwealth and a key figure in the birth of the UN. Such was Smuts's international reputation that even today the mention of his country to North Americans of a certain age often spontaneously evokes his name. A confidant of Winston Churchill and King George VI, Smuts's immense prestige and the affection with which he was regarded in Britain were further enhanced when he was inducted as the Chancellor of Cambridge University in 1947. Earlier that year he had played host to the British Royal Family, as cheering (mostly white) crowds welcomed King George to South Africa. Despite the boycott organised by the Official Opposition, the rapturous crowds which greeted the Royal Visit seemed to confirm the popularity with white electorate of their 76-year-old Premier. South Africa was a proud member of what came to be called 'the Free World', and its Premier one of the West's elder statesman.

Beyond the prestige it had conferred on South Africa, World War II also literally transformed the country's sluggish economy, finally dragging it out of the lingering effects of the Great Depression. The government poured millions into the development of the local steel, chemical, textile and armaments industries. As Germany's submarine warfare sharply reduced the flow of imported manufactures, flourishing local industries expanded to take up the slack. This led to a far-ranging extension of South Africa's industrial base. The contribution of private manufacturing to National Income outstripped that of the previously dominant mining sector in 1943, and the industrial share price index more than tripled during the war. Moreover, this burgeoning industrial production was increasingly capital-intensive. The ratio of invested capital per worker in private manufacturing rose from £981 in 1939 to £1 156 in 1946, an increase of some 18 percent.[1] With its industries working at full capacity to meet wartime demand, its ports jammed with allied shipping on one of the world's crucial trade routes, its gold paying for much of the allied war effort, its farmers scrambling to produce the food for its army and for besieged Britain,* South Africa's GNP grew by almost 70 percent in just six years between 1939 and 1945 – a rate of growth higher than that of either Britain or the USA.[2] A founder member of the IMF, South Africa was listed among the world's 10 richest countries at the end of the war.

With the economy transformed, and its Prime Minister and armed forces held in high regard by even the most powerful of nations, at the end of World War II South Africa appeared poised on the cusp of a bright future. Looking at that photograph of Smuts signing the UN Charter in San Francisco, many white South Africans felt an almost American sense of boundless possibilities in 1945. Few realised that their country had reached the pinnacle – that it was soon to enter a

---

* The total gross value of farm products increased by almost 80% during the war. See *Handbook of Agricultural Statistics 1904–1950* (Department of Agriculture, Pretoria, 1961), table 35, 52 & table 70, 69.

period of over forty years as an international pariah, that its government's policies would evoke an international outrage surpassed only by the Nazis, that the United Nations which Smuts had worked so hard to found would denounce South Africa for 'crimes against humanity'. Though the country's fall from grace had already begun, it accelerated precipitously after the general election of 26 May 1948.

The great reverse: The fall of the Smuts government

At first glance, the electoral portents for Smuts's ruling United Party (UP) seemed favourable. The UP enjoyed the support of virtually all sections of South African business, almost all English-speaking white South Africans, and very substantial numbers of Afrikaners. Allied with the small South African Labour Party, the Smuts government went to the polls with a comfortable 50-seat parliamentary majority. The opposition nationalists would have to wrest a minimum 35 seats from the UP if they were to take power. This seemed an unlikely prospect, even to key National Party leaders and organisers. The governing coalition offered a modest programme to reform what was then known as 'Native Policy' in order to speed up post-war economic recovery and ease racial tensions in the cities. Most observers expected the UP government to be returned to power in the 26 May election, albeit with a reduced majority. A pro-government newspaper editorialised as follows:

> It is notorious that the principal opposition, the Nationalists, are at sixes and sevens about leadership, between the Provinces, and about slogans and policies. ... All these things add together: The inevitability of victory for General Smuts.[3]

These cosy expectations were confounded, however. Despite winning a commanding majority of votes cast, the United Party lost 36 seats to the Afrikaner nationalist coalition of the National Party (NP) and the Afrikaner Party (AP). It was swept from office in the greatest electoral upset in South African history, as the NP/AP alliance won a slim parliamentary majority of five seats.* The UP's humiliation was underscored when Field Marshal Smuts himself lost his own Standerton constituency to an NP candidate expelled from the civil service in 1944 for his refusal to resign from the secret Afrikaner Broederbond. Just three years after the end of the War in Europe, world statesman Smuts and the

---

* A total of 1 075 328 votes were cast in an 80,3% poll. The UP/Labour Party together won 547 473 votes (50,9%) to the 443 278 (41,2%) for the NP/AP. Only in the Orange Free State did the NP/AP win more votes than the UP. However, correcting these figures for estimated party support in uncontested constituencies, Heard calculates real UP support at 53,3%, to 39,4% for the NP: *General Elections in South Africa, 1943–1970* (Oxford University Press, London, 1974), tables 17, 18 & 19, 40-1. The NP/AP alliance ended up with eight or more seats than the UP/SALP. However, the three 'Natives Representatives', separately elected by Cape Africans, reduced the nationalist majority to five.

government which had overseen South Africa's impressive war effort were replaced by the parochial and racist National Party which had openly proclaimed support for Nazi Germany. The new Prime Minister was a dour man of decidedly limited vision, Smuts's homeboy and longtime rival, Dr Daniel François Malan.*

The electoral upset of May 1948 stunned most observers. The NP itself had not expected to win and was pinning its hopes on the election due in 1953.[4] Most attempts to explain this surprise result stress three elements: the strong overrepresentation of rural interests which allowed the NP to win a slim majority of seats on a minority of votes;† the NP's trumpeting of its intention to implement apartheid; and the appeal to Afrikaner voters of the NP's radical, ethnically exclusive, version of Afrikaner nationalism.

The NP's successful mobilisation of a new Afrikaner nationalist alliance is addressed in the following chapter. However, here it should be noted that 1948 was more than just an NP victory. It also represented a *defeat* – not only for Smuts's UP, but for a much broader array of key power-brokers in the state and capitalist economy. An understanding of why these powerful political interests suffered such a shattering reverse is essential to grasp the evolution (and eventual dissolution) of the NP's own project after 1948.

With hindsight the outcome of the 1948 election was not very surprising. A combination of far-reaching social change, UP political ineptitude and the demographics of the support for the two major parties created a political opportunity which the Nationalists were quick to seize.

Too much, too soon: The social conflicts of the 1940s

The most important factor in 1948 was the wide-ranging social conflict unleashed by the vast social changes wrought by wartime economic growth. As

---

* Born within four years of each other in the same small northern Cape village of Riebeek-Wes, Malan and Smuts had known and competed with each other for much of their lives. A former Dutch Reformed Church minister, Dr Malan represented his home town in Parliament, and his vision never extended beyond a narrowly Calvinist view of Afrikaner interests (which he believed to be the same as those of his Church). Smuts, on the other hand, was trained in Law and Philosophy at Cambridge University, where he developed a life-long belief in 'holist' philosophy. He had fought as a Boer general against the British in the South African War of 1899–1902, and had ghost-written one of Afrikaner nationalism's earliest and most eloquent tracts *(A Century of Wrong)*. However, after the 1910 unification of the four British Colonies to form the South African state, Smuts was rapidly converted into, first, a leading visionary of the British Empire (and member of the Imperial War Cabinet during WWI) and then a renowned world statesman. With some justice, Afrikaner nationalists depicted Smuts as more concerned with the outside world than with South Africa, let alone the Afrikaans language, people and their church(es). After his defeat in 1948, Smuts said of these charges: '[T]hey ask what I have done for the Afrikaans language – but good heavens, what more work did I have to do?' – G D Scholtz, *Hertzog en Smuts en die Britse Ryk* (Tafelberg, Cape Town, 1975), 152.
† The South African constitution allowed for a weighting of rural votes by as much as 30%.

the country's infrastructure and industrial sector mushroomed, white and black employment grew exponentially. Wartime industrial expansion finally ended the chronic 'poor white problem'. Even more significant were the breaches in the job colour bar which had so long characterised the South African economy. In order to sustain wartime production in the face of severe shortages of (predominantly white) skilled labour, the Smuts government had authorised job 'dilution' – allowing (mainly black) unqualified workers to do skilled work under white supervision in a wide range of industries. This led to rapid wartime wage increases for the burgeoning black industrial labour force. Paradoxically, this also led to a relative reduction in labour costs since these black workers were paid lower absolute wages than were whites doing the same work. State economic planning and administration bodies actively encouraged a process of 'rationalisation' and mechanisation of industry on the basis of low-paid African labour.[5]

An additional 134 000 African workers entered industrial employment between 1939 and 1946, and the ratio of African workers employed in private manufacturing to those employed in mining increased from 187:348 in 1939 to 321:328. The huge wartime influx of Africans to the cities was underscored by the fact that, according to the Fagan Commission, women comprised fully one-third of the soaring urban African population. The commission concluded that the urbanisation of the African population had assumed a permanent and irreversible effect.[6]

This massive influx of black rural migrants to the cities during the war produced acute and growing political uncertainty around the fate and future of the twin essential fictions underlying the system of what was then known as 'segregation'. For over fifty years the segregationist policies of successive governments had rested on the fiction that the black majority was divided into two categories. On the one hand was a relatively small (and unfortunately 'detribalised') urban population whose real purpose, in the words of the 1922 Stallard Commission, was to minister to 'the wants of the white population', and to leave the urban areas when they 'ceased so to minister'. On the other hand, the vast majority of the black population were described as 'tribal natives', deemed to live on the land in the 'Native Reserves' as set out in the 1913 Land Act, and modified under the 1936 Natives Trust and Land Act. The theory of segregation held that each household of 'tribal natives' had access to land in the reserves. From time to time the adult males would leave their land to work as migrant labourers in the cities, while the women and children remained behind and supported themselves on the land.*

This convenient fiction was already crumbling by the early 1930s. It collapsed entirely under the rapid impoverishment of the 'Native Reserves' in the 1930s and 1940s. The Landsdown Commission's detailed inquiry into the ability of the

---

* Hence the male migrant labourer would be paid a wage sufficient only to maintain himself while in the ('white') urban areas, and not to provide subsistence to his family.

reserves to support migrant labour to the mines concluded starkly that by 1943, 'Reserve production [was] but a myth'.[7] This economic collapse of the reserves generated sustained rural conflicts, particularly over the rural land tenure system. The 1936 Natives Trust and Land Act had been designed to give white farmers far greater control over their African labour tenants. However the first attempt to enforce Chapter IV of the Act led to a peasant uprising in Lydenburg against which the government used Air Force bombers. So strong was this black resistance that the responsible minister replied as follows to pressure from farmers to extend the implementation of the 1936 Act: 'I want to live a few more years, not be shot before my time. Lydenburg was the only place where it was applied, and we know what happened there.'[8] Yet the major form of black rural resistance was simple desertion from white farms. By the middle of the war these white farms provided the single largest source of black labour streaming into the industrial centres.[9]

The second fiction underlying segregation had been put in place with the 1923 Urban Areas Act. Resting of the infamous Stallard formula cited above, this presumed that state policy could achieve a perfect numerical correlation between: (a) the number of Africans present in the urban areas; (b) the number of Africans in urban employment; and (c) the number of Africans living in controlled housing. The 1937 Native Laws Amendment Act gave the Minister the right to remove 'surplus Natives' from the urban areas. Local authorities which administered this increasingly complex system had to produce monthly returns of the numbers of Africans employed in their jurisdiction.

This points to a real administrative problem. The overall guidelines of the segregationist 'Native Policy' were set by the Department of Native Affairs. But these policies were administered throughout South Africa by municipalities, which retained wide discretionary powers. By 1937 only 11 local authorities were still implementing the Urban Areas Act, and most were not bothering to collect the necessary statistics.[10] Thus even before the war, significant cracks had opened in the policy of segregation. These were widened to the point of rupture by the massive African migration to the cities during the war. Local authorities were simply overwhelmed by numbers and completely unable to control this influx. Moreover, in most of the major urban centres, and particularly in Johannesburg and its surrounding areas, municipal authorities often proved more susceptible to the blandishments of local business interests – themselves desparate for labour – than to the strictures of the Department of Native Affairs. And the department itself gave in to the inevitable in 1943 when it decreed that the implementation of the pass laws and influx control system should be eased.

The massive influx of (male and female) African migrants to the cities likewise generated escalating urban conflict. An independent and militant African trade union movement mushroomed. By 1945, close to 40 per cent of Africans employed in commerce and industry were at least nominally members of the independent trade unions.[11] These unions fought for minimum wages, for statutory recognition under the Industrial Conciliation Act, and for an end to the migrant labour system. They made frequent resort to the strike weapon. In the years between 1940 and 1948, a total of 409 299 mandays were lost to strikes by 145 522 African workers. This was a dramatic increase over the corresponding figures the entire 1930s – 71 078 mandays lost by 29 251 striking African workers.[12]

Strikes by African workers were outlawed by War Measure 145. However at least 60 illegal strikes by black workers were reported between 1942 and 1944.[13] Despite the 'firm instructions' given to the Department of Labour to prosecute African strikers, the department's 1945 report complained that 'Natives seem to be ignoring War Measure 145'.[14] The increasing demand for black labour, coupled with its growing militancy, produced a 50 percent increase in average real earnings of African workers during the war. For the first time in South African history, average black industrial wages increased more rapidly than did those of white workers.* In 1947, Johannesburg's Director of Native Labour reported:

> During the last two years Native Trade Union activity has increased. There are signs that the dissemination of subversive propaganda has gained ground among the Native population and open defiance of constituted law and order has been manifested at various times.[15]

The high point of these industrial struggles was reached in August 1946. Over 70 000 African mineworkers came out in a strike which was brutally suppressed by the police, leaving 12 miners dead.[16] The massive wartime African urbanisation also led to other intense struggles over a range of issues. The acute housing shortage gave rise to a strong squatters movement, occasionally coming into open conflict with local and national authorities.[17] Periodic outbursts of unrest and protest over pass laws, liquor raids, transport fares and food shortages were common.

The burgeoning urban conflicts between 1942 and 1946 had a profound effect on formal black political opposition. After more than a decade of disorganisation, weak leadership and programmatic confusion, the African National Congress began to revive. For the first time since its formation in 1912 the ANC now demanded 'full citizenship' rights for Africans. Its influential Youth League proclaimed a militant 'Africanist' ideology which fundamentally questioned the gentlemanly liberalism of the mainstream of the ANC leadership. The Youth League also shocked the cautious and elitist constitutionalists of the ANC Old Guard with its advocacy of mass, non-violent struggle to overthrow white supremacy. This challenge from a new, younger generation of African leaders – including the future ANC high command of Nelson Mandela, Walter Sisulu and Oliver Tambo – began to dissipate the ideological hold white liberals

---

* Though they lagged far behind white wages in real terms. See W F J Steenkamp, 'Bantu Wages', *South African Journal of Economics*, 30, 2, 1962, 96.

still exercised over African political organisation, replacing it with a growing stress on independent (and often illegal) militant mass action.

In 1944 the ANC worked with the Communist Party to organise a widely supported campaign against the pass laws. The brutal suppression of the August 1946 strike of African mineworkers catalysed far-reaching changes in the African political opposition. The state's actions during the strike, and particularly the active role played by the leading Cabinet liberal (Acting Prime Minister J H Hofmeyr) in suppressing the strike further detached the middle-class African political leadership from the ideological influence of white liberals pleading moderation. The largely conservative Natives Representative Council angrily suspended sittings – declaring itself to be nothing but a 'toy telephone' – in protest at Hofmeyr's refusal to discuss the strike. In the aftermath of this key event in black politics, the patient expression of grievances in dignified and constitutional councils began to give way to mass action and passive resistance.

The effective economic collapse of the reserves and consequent burgeoning industrial, social and political demands emanating from most strata of the black population led to growing political and ideological conflict throughout white society over all aspects of what was then known as 'Native Policy'. These struggles slowly shattered the ruling 'South Africanist' consensus and its definition of the interests and project of white South Africa.[18] Once the political cement of the need for a united war effort was removed in September 1945, long-simmering policy divisions between the various constituent forces of Smuts's United Party flared into the dominant issue of white politics.

Irreconcilable interests: The war and capitalists politics

The UP had come into being in 1934 as a coalition formed to deal with the 'Gold Standard Crisis' and the economic and social effects of the Great Depression.[19] Its ranks had been depleted at the outbreak of the war in 1939 when then Prime Minister General J B M Hertzog led many Afrikaners in their refusal to support South African involvement in yet another 'British' war. Hertzog was replaced by Smuts, and throughout the duration of the war, the UP was able to retain the support of most of the key sectors which had first joined to form the UP in 1934. Yet the economic effects of the war and rapid black urbanisation widened already deep differences within the party and between the major social forces which supported it.

The almost exclusively anglophone urban manufacturing and commercial capitalists favoured a loosening of segregationist controls over both the labour market in general and urban blacks in particular. The Federated Chambers of Industry had argued during the war for a relaxation of existing controls on the movement of blacks into the cities. Many of its members also favoured recognition of black trade unions. As the Transvaal Chamber of Industry put it:

Whatever progress has been made in the efficiency of our labour in this country ... has been greater where management had a unified and organised body of workers to deal with. And if Natives are to enter industry in ever increasing numbers, it is clear that their being organised and disciplined in proper unions is an indispensable pre-requisite to their development as stable and productive workers.[20]

Manufacturing had emerged as the most dynamic and largest sector of the economy during the war. This meant that the demands of industrial capital now slowly acquired a weight within the economic councils of both state and UP equal to if not greater than those of the traditional dominant sectors in both party and state – mining and agriculture.

For their part, the still-powerful mineowners were terrified of the National Party and its economic programme to nationalise the mining industry. Yet their interests were also in conflict with those of the industrialists with whom they formed a key base of support for the United Party. The mines lost labour to the higher-paying manufacturing sector during the war. By 1943, the mining industry was able to fill only 84 percent of its required labour complement.[21] Faced with the challenge from the African Mineworkers' Union – itself bent on ending the migrant labour system – the Chamber of Mines vigorously opposed any move from a migratory to a stabilised labour force, characterising such proposals as a 'disastrous' policy which would force the closure of most mines.* The Chamber was also totally opposed to granting trade union rights to what it termed 'tribal natives' who would 'fall easy prey to alien interests – often acting from political motives'. In its public relations efforts to discredit the claims of the African Mineworkers' Union in the run-up to the August 1946 strike of African mineworkers, the Transvaal Chamber of Mines announced that such 'tribal natives' were 'not yet sufficiently advanced for trade unionism, nor do they themselves want it'.[22]

The UP's hitherto largest (and overwhelmingly Afrikaner) electoral base lay among the predominantly maize farmers in the Transvaal and Orange Free State provinces. This group had been negatively affected by many of the wartime changes. The government's cheap food policies had kept down the price of maize. While this could be reluctantly swallowed as a necessary cost of the war effort, Transvaal and Free State farmers were increasingly opposed to the government's 'Native policy', or lack of one. The dramatic and rapid black urbanisation during the war drastically aggravated the long-standing labour shortages confronting these farmers, who were unable to compete with the higher wages paid to black workers in industry and commerce. As noted above,

---

* Transvaal Chamber of Mines, *Native Laws Commission of Enquiry: Statements of Evidence Submitted by the Gold Producers' Committee* (Johannesburg, 1947), 46. Here the Chamber advanced the pious argument that: 'Any change from the migratory labour system to stabilised urban communities would have a catastrophic effect on the Natives themselves ... [who] would be the first to oppose it.'

by the middle of the war white farms provided the single largest source of black labour streaming into the industrial heartland of the Witwatersrand.*

The impact of these labour shortages was felt the hardest in the maize-producing areas of the Transvaal and the Free State. Thus while the period 1937–46 produced an increase in the country's farm labour force of just over 20 percent, this was spread highly unevenly. In the Cape Province, white farmers saw their African labour force grow by almost 95 percent.† In Natal, the growth was a more modest but still respectable 16,5 percent. However, Transvaal maize farmers scrambling to keep up with burgeoning wartime demand saw their labour force increase by just 2,3 percent during this period, while the number of African farmworkers in the Orange Free State actually *declined* by 1,8 percent. In 1944 the chairman of the NP caucus study group on racial affairs – future Minister of Bantu Affairs M C ('Daan') de Wet Nel – opposed a Parliamentary motion to abolish the pass system as a hindrance to industrialisation. Nel described the plight of Free State and Transvaal farmers as follows: 'One simply cannot get a Native to work there. The farmers are at their wits' end.'[23]

This huge relative loss of labour suffered by Free State and Transvaal farmers is compounded when the contribution of male to female labour is factored in. While Cape farmers saw the number of African females employed on their farms increase by 43 percent during this period, this pattern was not repeated in any other province. The African female farm labour force decreased by 21 percent in the Free State, with corresponding falls of 32 percent in Natal, and a whopping 46 percent in the Transvaal.[24]

Throughout the 1940s organised agriculture fought for three major policies. The first two of these directly addressed the farm labour crisis. Farmers wanted the full and immediate implementation of Chapter IV of the 1936 Natives Trust and Land Act so as to force their African labour tenants to work as wage labourers. As noted above, the Smuts government dragged its heels on this issue. Secondly, organised agriculture came up with a number of schemes to retain African labour in the rural areas and prevent migration to the cities. In 1944 the South African Agricultural Union (SAAU) proposed that the country's African population be classified into one of two groups – agricultural labourers and industrial workers – and that the state allow no worker to change his or her classification.[25] And, thirdly, organised agriculture strove to persuade the government to implement the 1937 Marketing Act in such a way as would ensure higher prices for agricultural produce.

Yet each of these endeavours ran counter to the thrust of UP wartime policies. The influential 1941 Agricultural and Industrial Requirements Commission had in fact recommended an extensive restructuring of commercial farming to divert African labour from white farms to industry and to reduce the number of

---

* Johannesburg and a ring of mining and industrial towns around it.
† And Cape farmers also had access to so-called Coloured labour – the number of whom working on Cape farms increased by almost 30% during the same period.

individual farmers. The commission also recommended that state subsidies and the pricing mechanism of the Marketing Act should be applied in such a way as to produce fewer but more efficient farmers.[26] In line with such thinking, the Department of Native Affairs declined either to implement Chapter IV of the 1936 Act or to intervene to limit the flow of African labour to the cities. Instead, it outraged farmers by suggesting to them that the most effective way to retain their black labour would be to pay higher wages and improve working conditions. The department went so far to propose state inspection of the upgrading of farm wages and conditions.[27]

To make matters even worse from the Transvaal and Free State farmers' point of view, the application of the pass laws in the major urban centres was eased in 1943. Though it was again tightened up in 1946, the UP government was simply not implementing much of the influx control legislation designed to stem the flow of Africans to the cities. This went to the heart of the interests of white farmers unable to compete with higher urban wages. Any dilution of the pass laws and influx control system was seen as a direct threat to the maintenance of an agricultural labour force. Moreover, the recognition of African trade unions, as advocated by organised industry, together with the various social welfare measures actually extended to African workers in the mid-1940s, were viewed by white (and overwhelmingly Afrikaner) farmers as the state's conceding the permanency of African urbanisation. During these years all proposals to extend the urban rights of Africans were vigorously contested by farming interests.

Government pricing policies were likewise perceived by white farmers to have a negative impact on their own interests. Originally conceived as the principal mechanism to secure higher prices for farm products, during the war the Control Boards set up under the 1937 Marketing Act became the central element of government rationing policies. Their price-fixing powers came to be used to hold down agricultural food prices and to prevent them rising as rapidly as world prices.[28] As the war progressed, the operation of the Control Boards led to fierce conflict within the capitalist class over the very existence of the Marketing Act. Following a series of scandals over the pricing of certain agricultural products, the influential Associated Chambers of Commerce (Assocom) demanded the repeal of the Act in 1944 – on the grounds that it led to 'artificially' high prices and 'diverted labour and capital away from industry'.[29] Assocom also proposed drastic inroads into the statutory privileges – particularly in taxation – enjoyed by the agricultural cooperatives which were central to the operation of much of white agriculture.

In the period of aggravated food shortages immediately following the war, the Control Boards were again used to hold down agricultural prices. Strong pressures from commerce, industry and mining sought to persuade the government to extend this policy. The mineowners had always opposed the Marketing Act on the grounds that it drove up its own costs of feeding its immense labour force, and that this policy was subsidised out of heavy mining taxes. By 1946 the Federated Chambers of Industry, which had originally supported the Act, had joined agriculture's opponents in calling for a drastic revision of the Marketing Act as it lead to 'dear food' and enabled the regulatory boards to encroach on industry's 'legitimate field' by processing agricultural produce.[30]

Generally resentful of the government's failure to implement the anti-squatting provisions of the 1936 Natives Trust and Land Act, Afrikaner farmers now viewed with horror UP proposals to ease state controls on the flow of African labour to the cities. In 1944 the SAAU had launched a concerted campaign to mobilise white farmers around the question of labour and pricing policies. It concluded an agreement with the Broederbond-controlled Afrikaanse Handelsinstituut (Afrikaner Commercial Institute) to work for a revision of the Marketing Act and tighter labour controls.[31] Following the end of the war, Afrikaner farmers were again profoundly alienated by the government's refusal to secure high prices for their maize and other produce in the face of the mineowners' demand for cheap food policies.

UP the creek: The dilemma of Smuts's party

By the beginning of 1948 the ruling UP found itself in an impossible position. On all of the major political issues of the day – black urbanisation, the stabilisation of African labour, pass laws, influx control, social security for urban Africans, black trade unions, black housing, political rights for urban blacks, pricing and taxation policy – its major bases of support not only took mutually exclusive positions, but were engaged in increasingly vigorous conflict with each other. Its Labour Party ally was in even worse disarray. With the white trade union movement under attack by Afrikaner nationalist unions, and burgeoning numbers of African workers effectively undertaking skilled work and joining trade unions, the LP was likewise unable to reconcile the increasingly contradictory demands made on it.[32] Though the LP had withdrawn from the government at the end of the war, it remained in close alliance with the UP on the basis of the latter's 'social security' programme. As this project collapsed between 1946 and 1948, the LP could offer no alternative, and finally split in 1946. Unable to provide a viable political programme to white workers who felt increasingly threatened by the large-scale movement of black workers into semi-skilled work, and unable to resolve the perennial conflicts within the ever more corrupt leadership of many of the white trade unions, the LP was increasingly deserted by the (largely Afrikaner) workers who had voted for it in 1943. Fighting the 1948 election in alliance with the UP, the LP did not even bother to contest many of the seats it had won in 1943.

Faced with the profound divisions between the major capitalist interests which supported it, and unable to provide policies which might have retained the support of white workers, the UP proved unable to come up with an effective project to recast its determinedly 'South Africanist', bilingual, white nationalism in ways which could hold together these divided interests. Part of the problem was leadership. Smuts would turn 78 in 1948, and was unlikely to remain party leader until the following election. His probable successor was the one-time 'boy genius' and super-Minister, the 54-year-old Deputy Prime Minister and Education Minister, J H Hofmeyr.* Despite his extraordinary abilities and administrative capacities, Hofmeyr not well-liked by the white public. Too cerebral and never at ease with the backslapping, macho ways of South African electoral politics, Hofmeyr was widely viewed as far too liberal to carry the white electorate with him. He was held in deep suspicion by many of his UP colleagues, and frankly detested and feared in much of the UP's rural constituency. As Finance Minister until shortly before the election, he took the blame for any negative economic fallout on any one of the UP's constituent groups.

Smuts himself was increasingly out of touch politically. During the war he had devoted most of his own energies to external affairs and defence, delegating parliamentary business to Hofmeyr and party affairs to Louis Esselen. Growing economic shortages at the end of the war generated much ferment against the government, especially among less-well-off whites. A strike of Afrikaner mineworkers in 1947 had signalled the growing strength of the once deeply divided Afrikaner nationalist opposition. Though Smuts toyed with the idea of an electoral pact with 'Klaas Havenga's moderately nationalist Afrikaner Party, he let the opportunity slip and saw the AP won over by D F Malan's nationalists.

But the real problem for the UP lay in the area of what was called 'Colour Policy'. During the war the Smuts government had given many hints that it was reconsidering the overall thrust of segregationist policies. Faced with the 1946 strike of African Mineworkers, Smuts himself remarked that 'our native policy would have to be liberalised at a moderate pace, but public opinion has to be carried with us'.[33] Yet its policy remained contradictory and confused. Its 1946 Asiatic Land Tenure and Indian Representation Act provoked a passive resistance campaign by the Natal and Transvaal Indian Congresses. Smuts's himself failed to persuade the UN General Assembly to reject India's resolution denouncing South African racial policy. The first of many such resolutions to follow, this was 'a humiliating defeat ... that seriously damaged Smuts's reputation back home'.[34] To make matters worse, this Act's provision for limited Indian representation in the Senate and House of Assembly further aggravated the government's woes. The Nationalist opposition whipped up a fever of anti-Indian sentiment, blaming Hofmeyr as the sponsor of the Act. And Smuts's wartime coalition partners, the small South African Labour Party and the Dominion Party, were split from head to toe as a result.

All of this fatally impaired the United Party's efforts to present a coherent project representing the interests of all whites. Smuts's party fought the 1948 election on the mildly reformist but ambiguous proposals of the Native Laws Commission of Inquiry (Fagan Commission) for the 'parallel' development of

---

* Hofmeyr had graduated from high school at the age of 12, and completed a university degree by the time he was 15. At one stage during the war, Hofmeyr simultaneously held five Cabinet portfolios.

white and black interests. The Fagan Report set out to propose a means to repair the vast fissures rapid black urbanisation had opened in the policy of segregation. It was a contradictory document which also tried to be all things to all people. Rejecting the NP notion of apartheid, and basing itself on a detailed investigation of the reserves, the commission argued that African urbanisation was permanent and irreversible. The migration of African labour from white farms was likewise deemed 'inevitable', though it had exceeded 'convenient limits'. The report also strongly defended the need to keep what it called 'a substantial reserve' of African labour in the urban areas and available for 'industrial activities'.[35] While it further recommended that local authorities should no longer be empowered to expel unemployed Africans from the urban areas, it also proposed far-reaching measures to extend and modernise the pass system. Fagan suggested grouping the African population into rural and urban categories, with a system of labour bureaux to channel black labour as required by the various sectors of the economy. Responsibility for the administration of 'Native Policy' would be taken away from local authorities and placed in the hands of the Department of Native Affairs. In general, however, Fagan recommended a policy of 'facilitating the stabilisation' of labour, while arguing that 'migratory labour cannot be prevented by law nor terminated by administrative action'.[36]

These proposals would have significantly extended the power of the state over the African population. Ironically, many of the recommendations of the Fagan Commission of 1946–48 were later echoed by the 1979 report of the Riekert Commission, which was to form the basis of NP policy in 1980–86 (see Chapter 14). Yet depite its heroic efforts to be all things to all (white) people, the Fagan Report was no solution to the political dilemma confronting the UP. Its complex proposals could not be distilled into a single powerful slogan – like 'apartheid' – one which echoed with the gut racial feelings of most whites. Its very complexities made it an object of NP ridicule, simply reinforcing its charge that the UP was confused on 'the colour question', and had no coherent policy.

Since the departure of the Hertzogites in 1939, the United Party had lost many of its key organisers. More importantly still, it had simultaneously shed the priceless political asset it had inherited from General Hertzog's old National Party at 'fusion' in 1934 – a sense of political mission capable of inspiring powerful, mobilised support. After the departure of the Hertzogites in 1939, the UP became a simple electoral machine. Wartime mobilisation and Smuts's charisma had enabled it to swamp the NP in the 1943 election. But just as the war gave Smuts's UP its *raison d'être*, the end of the war left it with little political direction or purpose other than keeping out the Nationalists.

This hobbled it electorally. The UP organisation was no match for that of the highly mobilised NP (see following chapter). Unable to still its internal differences, it ran a lacklustre, directionless campaign. Its tame and over-elaborate electoral manifesto was judged to be 'weary, stale and unprofitable'.[37] Smuts's party seemed collectively incapable of bringing itself to believe that just three years after victory over Germany, traditional UP supporters might support the recently pro-German 'Malanazis', and the UP also neglected to mobilise its supporters in many key areas. It took for granted that those who had supported it in 1943 would do so again, completely underestimating the level of anger against the government among many (largely Afrikaner) social strata. Mired in complacency, the UP seemed oblivious to the impact on its rural supporters of the Agriculture Minister's refusal to increase the maize price. And blinded by the victory of its LP ally in the post-war Johannesburg municipal elections, it simply appeared to forget that the white workers on the rest of the Witwatersrand were mainly Afrikaans-speakers. As the 1947 strike of white mineworkers amply proved, many Afrikaner workers had been now been weaned away from the LP and the largely corrupt trade union bureaucracy on which it was based.

The NP made no such mistakes. Accusing the UP of weakness in its defence of whites against the twin menaces of communism and 'the black sea of South Africa's non-European population', it ran a slick, aggressive campaign.[38] In the context of the mounting tensions of the Cold War, the NP promised to 'purify our state and public services of Communists and Communist influences'. Responding to the deep economic insecurities felt by many Afrikaners, the NP economic programme promised to take hold of the key centres of economic power, nationalise the banks, the land companies and the mines, and create an economic democracy for all Afrikaners.[39]

Yet its major focus was on 'the colour question'. Relentlessly hammering at the theme of what it called the black *oorstroming* (inundation) of the cities, the NP turned the question of 'Native Policy' into the key issue of the election and never allowed the UP to capture the initiative. Its hounding of the 'liberalism' of Smuts's heir apparent, Deputy Prime Minister J H Hofmeyr, was judged by one analyst of South African elections to be 'one of the most concentrated, indeed one of the most scurrilous personal attacks' in South Africa's 'lively political history'.[40] The NP was able to depict the UP as either bent on ending segregation, or worse still, having no real 'Native Policy'. The UP's 'South Africanist' ideology was characterised (and caricatured) as the creature of 'Hoggenheimer', and inimical to all (white) social groups whose language happened to be Afrikaans.* This enabled the NP to portray the UP as the mere tool of an array of anti-Afrikaner interests.

By contrast, as elaborated by its own 'Sauer Commission', the NP's 'apartheid' programme was depicted as offering clear, firm solutions to the growing racial conflict in the cities and urban areas.[41] In reality, the Sauer Report was a vague statement of principles rather than a clear policy programme. Nevertheless, it had much in common with the proposals in the Fagan Report. Both agreed on the need for the central regulation of the movement of Africans so as to maintain racial segregation. Both advocated the establishment of a national labour bureaux

---

* The Semitic-featured caricature of *Die Burger*'s cartoons, 'Hoggenheimer' was a racist symbol for monopoly capital in all its forms. The term was used interchangeably with [British] 'imperialism', but because of its extreme antisemitic connotations, had a deeper impact.

system, the replacement of the numerous existing passes with a single document, and the development of the reserves to maintain the families of migrant labourers. Yet Sauer differed sharply from Fagan on the latter's proposal to ease influx control measures. Their major difference lay over their view of the permanency of African urbanisation. Whereas Fagan had pleaded for state policies which would recognise the irreversibility of African urbanisation and encourage the growth of an urban reserve army of labour, Sauer insisted that employed black workers were to be expelled from the cites and relocated in the urban areas:

> Natives in the urban areas should be regarded as migratory citizens not entitled to political and social rights equal to those of whites. The process of detribalisation [read urbanisation – DO'M] should be arrested. The entire migration of Natives into and from the cities should be *controlled by the state,* which will enlist the cooperation of municipal bodies. Migration into and from the Reserves should likewise be strictly controlled. *Surplus Natives in the urban areas should be returned to their original habitat in the country areas* [i.e. white farms] or the Reserves. Natives from the country areas shall be admitted to the urban areas *only as temporary employees obliged to return to their homes after the expiry of their employment.*[42]

The NP's apartheid proposals are discussed in Chapter 3. Here it should be noted that while 'apartheid' was still little more than a slogan, it had the double advantage of proposing a simple idea, easily grasped by the electorate, and one which found deep resonance with the ingrained racism of most Afrikaners (and other whites). Moreover, while apartheid also clearly meant very different things to Afrikaners of different classes (see below), its very simplicity operated to condense their competing interests into one apparently unified 'Afrikaner' whole.

'Long years afterwards': The meaning of 1948

Almost alone among his complacent party, Jan Smuts himself seemed to have anticipated the significance of the 1948 election. Just over a week before the poll the Prime Minister told a reporter: 'Long years afterwards the effects of this election will be felt here in South Africa.'[43] While Smuts's party won a clear majority of votes cast, decisive Nationalist breakthroughs in two areas were sufficient to sweep the UP from power and plunge South Africa into the 'forty lost years' of apartheid.

First, Transvaal farmers deserted the UP *en masse.* In the previous election in 1943, the UP had captured 15 of the 23 rural Transvaal constituencies. However,

---

* All details in this and the following paragraphs are drawn from Heard, *General Elections in South Africa, 1943–1970,* 38-46. The shock of the rural obliteration of his party, and the loss of his own seat, prompted the former Boer General Smuts to the pathetic compaint; 'My old comrades [of the Anglo-Boer War] have deserted me.' A friend replied: '*Oom* [Uncle] Jannie, how could they have turned against you? They are all dead.' W K Hancock, *Smuts: The Fields of Force, 1919–1950* (Cambridge University Press, Cambridge, 1968), 506.

the UP was driven out of these Transvaal rural areas in May 1948, as the Nationalist coalition swept all such seats.* The second major NP breach of the UP defences occurred in the heartland of the latter's support, the urban areas of the Witwatersrand and Pretoria. After long years of seemingly fruitless struggle, Afrikaner nationalist trade unions had finally captured control of the (white) Mineworkers' Union after the 1947 strike of white mineworkers.[44] They had also made important breakthroughs among workers in the state-owned steel industry in Pretoria. These trade union successes finally paid off electorally in 1948. Whereas in 1943 the LP had been 'uniformly successful in its contests' against the NP,[45] by 1948 it did not even put up candidates in many of its old constituencies. Always identified with the rich and powerful, the UP was hardly able to fill the breach and present itself as a party of the 'working man'. The NP, on the other hand, ran an explicitly anti-capitalist and (Afrikaner) populist platform. For the first time in its history, it now captured eight constituencies in the mining and industrial centres of the Witwatersrand, and a further five seats in the working-class and lower-middle-class areas of Pretoria. It also won two Cape urban seats (in Cape Town and Port Elizabeth) previously held by the government.

This was the *coup de grâce*. Except among the predominantly English-speaking white electorate in Natal, the UP had been all but obliterated as a rural party. To hold on to power it absolutely had to preserve its electoral redoubt in the cities. Had it done so, it would have clung to office despite ceding the virtually all South Africa's rural seats to the Nationalists.* The UP lost power in 1948 because of its overwhelming losses in South Africa's most populous province, the Transvaal. In 1943 Smuts's party had won 53 of the then 64 Transvaal seats. Five years later it held only 30 of the now 66 Transvaal seats.

The Nationalists were further aided by what psephologists have called the 'wasted' UP vote. In South Africa's (then) winner-takes-all electoral system, every vote beyond a majority of one vote is considered wasted in that it does not add to the locally victorious party's national tally of seats won. Whereas the UP tended to win those seats it held on to with decisive majorities, the majorities won by the Nationalist coalition were often much smaller. Heard concludes that the governing coalition 'wasted' 168 559 votes, or 40 000 more votes than those 'wasted' by the NP.[46] Moreover, the UP was further disadvantaged by the constitutional compromise of 1910 in which rural votes were weighted by as much as 30 percent against the urban vote.† Fifty-nine of the Nationalists' 79

---

* Ever since fusion the NP had retained control of most of the Cape rural areas. In 1948 it increased its share of these seats from 19 to 25, leaving the UP in control of just five rural Cape constituencies. As in the previous election, the NP also swept the rural areas of the Orange Free State, leaving the UP with just Bloemfontein City. In rural Natal the UP and NP/AP alliance each took three seats. Thus the UP held only by eight of 71 rural seats in 1948. Yet the NP's dramatic rural gains would not have been sufficient to give it a majority had the UP managed to hold on to the 13 Transvaal and two Cape urban seats it now lost to the Nationalist alliance.

† This meant that rural constituencies could have up to 30% fewer voters than those in urban areas.

seats were won in constituencies with less than 9 000 voters, as opposed to 27 of the UP/LP alliance's 71 seats. Whereas the average number of votes the UP required to win a seat ranged from 5 606 in Natal to 29 544 in the OFS, the corresponding lows and highs for the Nationalist alliance were 4 585 votes in Natal to 5 819 in the Cape. The national average number of votes required to win a seat was 9 124 for the UP/LP and just 5 683 for the Nationalist alliance.[47]

The election of 1948 set South Africa on a course very different from the one it would have taken had the Smuts government clung to power. While I do not for a moment wish to characterise the latter as in any way committed to dismantling segregation, the logic of its acceptance of the irreversibility of African urbanisation would have forced it down a very different road from the doleful path taken by the NP. Moreover, had the UP won in 1948, the effects of the 1950s economic boom, and particularly the Korean War-induced rise in the price of agricultural produce, would have softened the antagonism towards Smuts's party felt by Afrikaner farmers and workers. This would have rendered a Nationalist victory in the following election less likely. While such idle speculation has little point, South African history would have been very different had Smuts but raised the price of maize in early 1948, or moved to address some of the grievances of Afrikaner workers. The 1948 election was not won by the nationalists so much as it was lost by the political ineptitude of a government which had forfeited its *raison d'être,* and was out of touch with its own supporters. Heard's judgement on 1948 is entirely apt: '[R]arely can a country have embarked on a new course on the basis of so indecisive an electoral victory, nor one so little expected.'[48]

Chapter Two

SEEK YE FIRST THE POLITICAL KINGDOM!

The National Party and the politics of Afrikaner nationalism

Dr. D. F. Malan
May 1948 to 1954

Die Doktor

Dr Malan's National Party took power at the end of May 1948 following a turbulent thirty-year history. The NP had been founded in 1914 by the former Boer General, J B M Hertzog. It first came to office in 1924, in a coalition with the Labour Party, and this 'Pact' government ruled South Africa for the following nine years. General Hertzog's NP split in 1934 when the majority followed their leader into 'fusion' with General Smuts's South Africa Party to form the United Party. At fusion the NP rump under Cape NP leader, Dr D F Malan, rechristened itself the *Gesuiwerde Nasionale Party* (Purified National Party) and entered into 14 years of bitter opposition.

General Hertzog resigned as Prime Minister and leader of the United Party in September 1939 when the South African parliament voted narrowly to reject his plea for neutrality and declared war on Germany. Hertzog and his following of now *oud-smelters* (former fusionists) quickly formed themselves into the *Volksparty*, which merged with Dr Malan's *Gesuiwerde* NP in early 1940 as the *Herenigde Nasionale of Volksparty* (Reunited National or People's Party) with Hertzog as its titular head. However, most of Malan's followers never accepted Hertzog's reincarnation as their leader, and the General was manoeuvred into an embittered retirement soon afterwards. The majority of his *oud-smelter* followers soon either followed 'Klaas Havenga out of the HNP to form the minuscule *Afrikaner Party*, or joined Oswald Pirow in the fascist *Nuwe Orde* (New Order), itself driven from the NP in 1942.[1] During most of the World War II, D F Malan's *Herenigde* National Party did furious, occasionally violent, and eventually triumphant battle with the pro-Nazi *Ossewa Brandwag* (Ox-wagon sentinels) for hegemony in the Afrikaner nationalist movement.

Malan's party fought the 1948 election proclaiming itself the true incarnation of 150 years of resistance to Afrikanerdom's double nemesis of British Imperialism and what Afrikaner nationalists still called in the 1980s, the 'uncivilised aboriginal races'.[2] Yet Afrikaner nationalism had been effectively reinvented during the NP's years in the wilderness after fusion. The 'Christian-national' version proclaimed by the NP in 1948 represented a distinct break with earlier brands of Afrikaner nationalism in a number of ways.

Afrikaner 'Christian-nationalism'

The first difference was in its leadership. Most of the rural notables who had dominated the leadership of Hertzog's NP followed the General into fusion in 1934. The NP remained relatively intact only in the Cape Province, and Cape NP leader Dr Malan assumed the national leadership of the now *Gesuiwerde* party. The defection of much of the old NP leadership to the UP in the Transvaal and Orange Free State saw a new cadre of young urban intellectuals emerge to lead the redefinition of *Gesuiwerde* Afrikaner nationalism in the northern provinces. They also dominated the secret *Afrikaner Broederbond* (Afrikaner Brotherhood – see below) and the myriad cultural and other groupings which now came to play a central role in emerging redefined Afrikaner nationalism. Even following the reluctant reabsorption of the Hertzogite *smelters* (fusionists) into the now *Herenigde Nasionale of Volksparty* in 1940, these young Turks remained the pivotal leadership.

The huge 'poor-white problem' of the 1920s and 1930s was the crucible in which was formed the emerging vision of this new urban-oriented elite. Their primary symbolic point of reference was no longer the grim aftermath for most Afrikaners of the Anglo-Boer War nor even the lost Boer republics. Instead, they grappled with the traumatic adaptation by Afrikaners to the tide of urbanisation unleashed by the development of capitalist agriculture and South Africa's industrialisation. The collapse of the old Hertzogite party in 1934 gave this younger generation both the opportunity and the platforms through which to test different approaches to these new problems – problems which the old nationalist leadership of rural notables was not capable of addressing.

This led to raging debates in Afrikaner intellectual and political circles in the 1930s and 1940s. These debates slowly crystallised a cohesive 'Christian-national' reworking of Afrikaner nationalist ideology. At the core of this new nationalist *weltanschauung* stood the notion of *volksgebondenheid* – the belief that ties of blood and *volk* come first,[3] and that the individual existed only in and through the nation. The *volk*, rather than the individual, was the divinely ordained basic unit of social organisation. Individuals could realise their 'true' selves and social potential only in identification with and service to the *volk*. Each *volk*/ethnic group had a divinely allotted role which could only be fulfilled by the vigilant exercise of its right to self-preservation. Each *volk* could best realise and develop this inherent *volkseie* – its essential nature, ideals and calling – within its own community, free of the sense of being endangered by others. South Africa was quite literally conceived as the God-given preserve of a (white) Afrikaner nation, itself divinely charged with the mission of realising its own Calvinistic character in an Afrikaner republic free of all bonds with 'British Imperialism'. This future 'Christian-national' republic would be based on authentic Afrikaner religious and political principles and traditions rather than on the secular and *volksvreemde* (foreign to the *volk*) Westminster model imposed by Britain.*

The elaboration of this new Christian-national ideology of the 1930s and 1940s was an almost purely intellectual affair, conducted in the inner circles of party, press, Broederbond and church. The broad mass of Afrikaans-speakers

---

* I do not wish to be misunderstood here. Important analyses of Afrikaner nationalism underscore its lack of ideological cohesion. See J Lazar, 'Conformity and Conflict: Afrikaner Nationalist Politics in South Africa, 1948–1961' (D Phil dissertation, Oxford University, 1987), and D Posel, *The Making of Apartheid: Conflict and Compromise* (Clarendon Press, Oxford, 1991). However, ideologies seldom take the form of catechism. These nationalist conflicts and different emphases do not vitiate the point that certain broad principles were taken for granted by all factions and strata. To this extent it is legitimate to speak of an ideological *weltanschauung*. The best single source on these ideological struggles remains T D Moodie, *The Rise of Afrikanerdom: Power, Apartheid and the Afrikaner Civil Religion* (University of California Press, Berkeley, 1975).

displayed scant interest in these abstruse philosophical/theological debates.

Neither did they manifest great support for the NP. The majority of Afrikaners voted for General Hertzog's UP in 1938. They did so again in 1943 – despite the trauma of the debate over South Africa's participation in the War and consequent 'reunification' of the *gesuiwerde* and Hertzogite brands of Afrikaner nationalism.

This new Christian-national ideology did not suffice to galvanise Afrikaners' electoral support. Rather, the convoluted formulations of Christian-nationalism had to be translated into concrete issues which could be clearly shown to affect the daily lives of all Afrikaners. The key lay in the economic disadvantages of speaking Afrikaans in an anglophone-controlled economy, under a government little concerned with the fate of the Afrikaans language.

Despite the turbulent and sometimes violent Afrikaner nationalist political divisions of much of the 1940s, the various intersecting networks of the Afrikaner political, cultural, religious and economic elite remained largely united within the nationalist secret society known as the *Afrikaner Broederbond* (Afrikaner Brotherhood – AB or Bond).[4] During these years the AB created a complex range of activities and a vast organisational web designed to enmesh most Afrikaners and mobilise them for Bond efforts to build Afrikaner business (the so-called 'economic movement') and its demand for 'mother-tongue', 'Christian-national' education (as opposed to the bilingual education policy of the Smuts government).[5]

This mobilisation of the different strata of Afrikaans-speakers is examined at great length elsewhere, and will not be repeated here.[6] Suffice it to say that the AB explicitly targeted two groups – nascent Afrikaner business and Afrikaner workers – and systematically set out to advance their specific economic interests and so win them over to a broader 'Afrikaner' national project. Moreover, the economic movement made use of intense nationalist propaganda to mobilise the savings of Afrikaners of all classes and direct this money into the coffers of newly-formed Afrikaner financial undertakings. In a similar fashion, the Christian-national education campaign used the AB's control of virtually all Afrikaner cultural and religious organisations in an effort to convince all Afrikaans-speaking whites that only in the bosom of the *volk* would their interests be protected from the twin perils of British cultural and economic imperialism, and the 'black sea' of South Africa's African majority.

In the end, the AB achieved striking success with its project to reframe the different and often competing interests of various strata of Afrikaners and organise them in terms of the AB's own definition of the interests of 'the Afrikaner'. Once the NP emerged victorious from the wartime intra-nationalist conflicts, it was able to build on this economic, cultural and educational mobilisation of Afrikaners by the Broederbond. This eventually enabled the NP to construct a new nationalist alliance of Afrikaner farmers, labour, the petty bourgeoisie and nascent Afrikaner financial and commercial capital.

The NP mobilised each of these constituent forces on the basis that they were discriminated against and oppressed *as Afrikaners*. Only concerted action by a united Afrikaner *volk* in control of the state could end this historic 'Century of Wrong'. The NP's Christian-nationalism was an overtly exclusivist and ethnic ideology, openly preaching Afrikaner favouritism – well captured in the widely reported comment of one NP supporter after the shock election result that 'at last we have got our country back'.[7] Snatching a tenuous electoral victory on a minority vote, the NP now stood at the head of a burgeoning social movement – the Afrikaner *volksbeweging* (movement of the *volk*).

The organisation, structure and political culture of Afrikaner nationalism

The Afrikaner *volksbeweging* of 1948 was composed of a gamut of political, cultural, economic, religious, labour and educational organisations. Sharing many of the same leaders, this interlocking organisational network generated a broad consensus and common notion of the particularity of Afrikaner identity and Afrikaner culture. Whatever their often ferocious internecine conflicts, all Afrikaner nationalist groups came to share the view that the real purpose of the South African state was to advance Afrikaner interests and realise Afrikaner destiny *(volkseie)*. This conception of the state as the vehicle for Afrikaner advance meant that once the NP arrived in office, each of the constituent elements of the *volksbeweging* had a legitimate claim on the new administration. The social forces and organisations comprising the Afrikaner nationalist social movement each demanded a unique access to the NP government. Each played a role in the definition of the government agenda. Each expected its own conception of its particular interests to be defended in the NP Cabinet and guaranteed by the NP government as an essential element of the interest of the *volk* as a whole.

However, within this web of nationalist organisations some were more equal than others. The three mainstream Afrikaner churches – and especially the biggest of these, the *Nederduitse Gereformeerde Kerk* (Dutch Reformed Church, NGK) – played a crucial role in defining the moral parameters of the discussion around the nationalist agenda. Yet even the churches enjoyed only a certain access to and influence on the NP government. In the end, the programme and politics of Afrikaner nationalism remained under the firm control of two organisations – the Afrikaner Broederbond and the National Party. These were the twin central pillars of the entire nationalist edifice. While there was a great deal of overlap between them, they were distinct organisations whose interests and policies sometimes diverged. A grasp of Afrikaner nationalist politics must begin by clarifying their nature and relationship.

The Afrikaner Broederbond
Formed in Johannesburg in 1918 by a gaggle of clerks, clerics and policemen, and driven by the aim of fostering Afrikaner unity and advancement, the

Broederbond had transformed itself into a secret society in 1920. However, it began to emerge as a real force only when taken over in the late 1920s by younger Transvaal and Free State intellectuals based at the Universities of Potchefstroom, Pretoria and the Orange Free State.[8] The virtual collapse of organised Afrikaner nationalism in these two northern provinces following the break-up of General Hertzog's National Party in 1934 presented this new activist AB leadership with a golden opportunity to fill the sudden political vacuum and take control of the development of now *gesuiwerde* nationalism in the northern provinces.* Anointing themselves the high priests of a new, Christian-national, Afrikaner civil religion, these younger Broederbond intellectuals claimed the exclusive right to define the historic mission and parameters of Afrikaner nationalism. They set out to impose their new Christian-national vision on the entire Afrikaner society.

They did so in four ways. First, the AB aimed to win to its ranks sufficient key Afrikaner professionals to give itself decisive influence in Afrikaner society. Here the Broederbond followed the Masonic model on which it was initially based, and later claimed to despise. Pursuing a deliberate practice of *baantjies vir boeties* (jobs for pals), it turned the Bond into a powerful instrument for the advancement of the careers of its members – while simultaneously placing 'reliable' people in key positions in the civil service and throughout Afrikaner society. This highly ritualistic and profoundly secretive mutual aid function created potent bonds of solidarity among its members and intense collective commitment to the Bond's project to 'Afrikanerise' South Africa.

Secondly, from the end of the 1920s onwards, the new intellectual AB leadership sought to use this strategically placed membership to seize control of all facets of Afrikaans-speaking civil society. In the words of its official history, the Bond set out 'systematically to infiltrate every arena of importance to the continued existence of the Afrikaner and to make the AB's influence felt'. Broederbond branches (called divisions) were instructed to increase their influence in local affairs so that in every district Afrikaners would be aware of a 'moving force, even if its source could not be precisely located'.[9] A 1944 Military Intelligence report to the Prime Minister on the AB quotes 'a leading *Broer*' instructing an annual AB conference as follows:

> The AB must gain control of everything it can lay its hands on in every walk of life in South Africa. Members must help each other gain promotion in the civil service or any other field of activity in which they work, with a view to working themselves up into important administrative positions.[10]

This involved either taking over existing Afrikaner organisations, or, in fields

---

* The *gesuiwerde* Transvaal NP was reduced to just one freshman MP, J G Strijdom. Despite its occasional by-election victory, it was not until the 1943 general election that the Transvaal NP was able to boast more than two MPs elected on its platform. While the OFS *gesuiwerdes* were better represented in parliament, here too a real political vacuum remained.

where these did not exist, establishing new civil organisations to wean Afrikaners from 'imperialistic-oriented' values.* In 1929 the AB formed the *Federasie van Afrikaanse Kultuurverenigings* (Federation of Afrikaner Cultural Associations – FAK). According to the official Broederbond history, the FAK was to be the AB's 'public front', an umbrella body designed to provide 'central organisation' and 'clear direction' to all Afrikaner cultural organisations.[11]

Having established itself as the central organisation of Afrikaner civic life, the Broederbond paid special attention, thirdly, to the reproduction of a politically reliable Afrikaner elite. This meant imposing its iron control over the staffing and curriculum of Afrikaner educational and religious institutions – thereby ensuring both that the next generation was raised in a Broederbond-approved culture and that the AB would be in a position to select likely prospects to be groomed for leadership roles. Educators have always comprised the largest single occupational group within the Broederbond (and almost 60 percent of all its members in the early 1950s, although this had declined to just over 20 percent by the early 1970s). This included not just ordinary school teachers and university lecturers, but the rector of every Afrikaans university and teacher's training college, the directors of provincial education and something like half of the Afrikaans, school principals and inspectors.† The Broederbond junior wing, the *Ruiterwag* ('Mounted guard'), also provided an important proving ground for selected younger future leaders. By the time *Ruiters* graduated into the Broederbond, they had been irrevocably meshed into the interlocking networks of influence which would cultivate their careers and draw on their talents throughout their adult lives.

Finally, having largely succeeded in imposing AB hegemony on the cultural terrain, in 1932 the Bond chairman announced that his organisation would henceforth 'have to devote its attention to the political needs of our people'. Its great opportunity came with the 'betrayal' of Afrikaner nationalism by its historic leader, General Hertzog, in the 1934 'fusion' crisis. A 1934 circular from AB chairman, Professor J C van Rooy, counselled the just over 1 000 *Broeders* during the fusion crisis:

> Let us bear in mind the fact that the main point is for Afrikanerdom to reach its ultimate goal of dominance in South Africa. Brothers, our solution for South Africa's troubles is that the Afrikaner Broederbond must rule South Africa.[12]

Given the weakness of the *gesuiwerde* NP in the north, and particularly in the Transvaal, at least until the short-lived 1940 'reunification' of Hertzog and Malan, Afrikaner civil society represented by the Broederbond effectively dominated the political terrain of the two northern Nationalist Parties.

---

* To mention just two examples, it established the *Voortrekkers* and *Noodhulpliga* in order respectively to organise Afrikaner children and Afrikaner paramedical workers into AB-controlled alternatives to the 'British-oriented' Boy Scouts/Girl Guides and the St John Ambulance Brigade.

† P H Serfontein, *Brotherhood of Power* (Rex Collings, London, 1979), 136.

In all of these regards, the Afrikaner Broederbond developed into one of the most influential and successful organisations of the twentieth century. As a secret society with membership by invitation only, it organised Afrikaner civil, religious and political elites into what effectively became the overall strategy-making, consensus-building and patronage-dispensing body of *gesuiwerde* Afrikaner nationalism. The AB's secret rituals and mode of operation, its rigid self-selection and deep sense of ethnic mission all worked to forge a tight unity and strong sense of group loyalty among its members. Bond membership grew from 160 in 1925 to 1 023 in 1933. Four years into NP rule, 3 520 male Afrikaners had made it into the Broederbond ranks. By the Bond's fiftieth anniversary in 1968 it had 8 154 members, rising to 11 190 ten years later. At the end of the 1980s, Broederbond membership was generally believed to be close to 20 000.[13]

Through the Broederbond these (evolving) urban and rural Afrikaner elites were moulded into a cohesive, consensual socio-cultural movement capable of intervening at any level and in all facets of cultural, economic, political and social life. In tandem with its *Ruiterwag* subsidiary, the Broederbond stood at the centre of an immense organisational web whose influence reached into the nooks and crannies of Afrikaner society and spanned all levels of the state apparatus.

This ultimate old-boy network was also a formidable machine for the individual advancement and collective welfare of its elite membership – whose personal and joint material interests were melded into one 'national' consensus through the AB. Broederbond membership conferred ready access to NP government leaders and a remarkable sense of collective power. While the Bond did not 'run' South Africa, as frequently charged in lurid exposures by the English newspapers, it was one of the essential institutions through which political power was constructed and wielded in the South African state after 1948.

Its relationship with the NP was complex, often conflictual, and changed over time. Many *Broeders* agreed with a longtime AB executive committee member (and later NP Cabinet Minister) that the Broederbond's role in Afrikaner nationalist politics was to 'ensure that the Afrikaner's government always kept to a course which served Afrikaner interests and which ensured the survival of Afrikanerdom'.* The vast majority of the NP leadership were also Broederbonders.† Yet most strongly rejected such AB tutelage of the party and

---

* Albert Hertzog, quoted in B M Schoeman, *Van Malan tot Verwoerd* (Human & Rousseau, Cape Town, 1973), 120. Albert Hertzog was the son of the NP founder and late leader of the *smelters*, General J B M Hertzog.

† However, the list of non-AB National Party leaders includes such significant figures as Paul Sauer, who had 'a strong aversion to secret organisations'(Herman Giliomee, 'Die Afrikaanse Politike Geskiedskrywing', unpublished paper, 1991, 15), and Ben Schoeman and Eric Louw. Schoeman and Louw were consistently blackballed in their attempts to join the Broederbond – Schoeman because of his *smelter* past, and Louw because many fellow Cape nationalists detested both his notorious vulgarity and his long association with Strijdom.

its government. Transvaal NP leader, the so-called 'Lion of the North', J G Strijdom, for example, was a prominent Broederbond 'extremist'. However, before 1948 he worked hard to exclude the Broederbond from what he regarded as the domain of the party. During his premiership (1954–58) he went to even greater lengths to 'keep the Broederbond out of [NP] politics', bluntly instructing its executive committee to confine its organisation to cultural matters and the advancement of Afrikaner business. Strijdom even refused an AB request to discuss the form a future republic might take.[14]

The Broederbond's role in organised Afrikaner nationalism was further complicated by its varying weight in the nationalist politics of what were then South Africa's four provinces. The NP in the Cape Province had been relatively unscathed by fusion, and its leader presided over the *gesuiwerde* NP – as well as its *herenigde* reincarnation after Hertzog's retirement. This meant that in the Cape the Broederbond was always much less important than either the party or *Keeromstraat* core of the Cape nationalist establishment – the leadership of the *Nasionale Pers* (National Press) newspaper group. While many Cape nationalists were loyal *Broeders,* the secret organisation never acquired the same weight and presence in the Cape which it enjoyed in the Transvaal and Orange Free State.

The first decade of NP rule led to something of an identity crisis for the Broederbond. Both Malan and Strijdom were determined to keep the nationalist policy agenda firmly in the party's hands, and the AB was somewhat marginalised for much of the 1950s. This period is characterised in the Bond's official history as one of indecisiveness. The Potchefstroom division informed the *Uitvoerende Raad* (executive council) that because of the tight leash on which the NP kept the Bond, the secret organisation no longer had a task or a vision. Interest among the *Broeders* was waning, and many were bothered by the fact that the party brooked no criticism.[15]

Ironically, the apogee of AB influence was reached during the premiership of Dr H F Verwoerd (1958–66) – himself a long-time AB executive committee member. The irony lies in the fact that during the 1940's war between the NP and the Nazi-inclined *Ossewa Brandwag,* as editor of the *Die Transvaler* organ of the Transvaal NP, Verwoerd had been the OB's most implacable foe and perhaps the man most responsible for its destruction.* As a member of the Broederbond's *Uitvoerende Raad,* during the war Verwoerd had systematically sabotaged all of its attempts to mediate between the party and the OB – earning himself the contempt of a number of fellow UR members destined to serve in his Cabinet.[16]

However, as indicated in Chapters 4 and 5 below, once he had been narrowly elected NP national leader in 1958, Verwoerd sought to shore up his shaky position by advancing former OB members and relying on the Broederbond – whose chairman was now the former OB *éminence grise* and Verwoerd's former *bête noire,* Dr P J Meyer. Premier Verwoerd offered the Broederbond what

---

* So much so that members of the OB's paramilitary wing of *Stormjaërs* once tried to abduct Verwoerd outside of his home, but were harangued into flight by his legendary sharp tongue.

Strijdom had doggedly denied it, 'co-responsibility with the party to prepare the electorate for a republic'.[17] This quickly transformed the AB into a central power-base and think-tank for Verwoerd. The organisation now set up 14 (later 19) 'expert task groups' to cover every facet of political, social and economic policy.[18]

Indeed, so close was Verwoerd's reliance on the Broederbond that during the new internecine NP conflicts following Verwoerd's September 1966 assassination, Bond chairman Meyer claimed the martyred leader's backing for his own belief that the AB had built up *all* four corners of what Meyer called the '*volks* pyramid' of Afrikaner nationalism: the cultural, political, economic and educational. The NP, on the other hand, he declared, was limited to the political realm.* Be that as it may, as indicated in Chapters 7 and 8, by the early 1970s, the Bond's policy-formulating, semi-watchdog role in Afrikaner nationalism was gradually reduced to that of an NP 'support organisation' as Premier Vorster struggled to undermine the political base of the far right.

The AB's genuine hegemony over Afrikaner civil society and civil religion gave it powerful influence over the party. However, while commanding great moral authority, and some power of sanction, the Broederbond was ultimately subject to, and indeed an important constituent of, the secular political power of the National Party, particularly after 1948. The NP was anchored in the terrain of the state. In the end, the relationship between the AB and NP remained true to the *étatiste* world view of Christian-nationalism – the state dominated civil society.

The National Party

For most of the first eighty years of its existence, the NP was a highly mobilised mass political party. Its populist origins and traditions, its tight structure of branch committees, local organisers, regional structures and provincial and federal congresses, all worked to generate lively and sharply contested internal politics. Until the 1980s, the NP leadership generally remained in touch with, and responsive to, its large and active membership, which itself enjoyed some policy input. A system of local and ward organisers strove to keep all members involved in ongoing meetings and campaigns. For much of NP history, most of those voting for the party in provincial and national elections were NP members. Paid-up NP Transvaal membership, for example, equalled 60 percent of its Transvaal vote in 1966.[19]

---

* J P H Serfontein, *Die Verkampte Aanslag* (Human en Rousseau, Cape Town, 1970), 47, *et passim*. Prime Minister Verwoerd's extremely close relationship with the Broederbond partly explains the highly conspiratorial view of the Broederbond in South Africa's English Press–well exemplified by Serfontein's 1979 book on the Bond, *Brotherhood of Power*. See also the posthumous book by the journalist who initiated the round of revelations in the 1960s, C. Bloomberg, *Christian-Nationalism and the rise of the Afrikaner Broederbond in South Africa* (Macmillan, London, 1990) as well as I Wilkens & H Strydom, *The Super Afrikaners* (Jonathan Ball, Johannesburg, 1978). However, this conspiratorial view of the AB dates back to General Hertzog's celebrated 1935 denunciation of the Bond (*Rand Daily Mail*, 8 November 1935), echoed in wartime Military Intelligence reports which present the AB as a Nazi-inspired 'plot' to take over South Africa.

Never a monolithic 'national' party, the NP was in fact a federation of four (and sometimes five) autonomous provincial National Parties.* Since the first NP was formed in 1914, each of these provincial parties had a distinct (and changing) social base, leadership, organisation, membership, congress, constitution, finances, press and political and ideological style and traditions. As a federal party, the NP had a 'national' existence only through five institutions:

(a) The NP *Federal Congress* met only twice between 1941 and 1984 – both times to ratify the stand of the national leader in an internal dispute;

(b) The leadership of each provincial NP was represented in the NP *Federal Council* – supposed to coordinate the actions of, and work out conflicts between, the provincial parties. The Federal Council met infrequently, but had important legitimising powers. On at least one occasion, its decision was decisive in the working out of an internal party conflict (see Chapter 21);

(c) The NP *parliamentary caucus* consisted of all the party's elected Members of Parliament (MPs) and appointed Senators.† The caucus was the parliamentary *'veg organisasie'* (fighting arm), responsible for shaping the NP's parliamentary tactics necessary for the adoption of the government's legislative programme. After some conflict with the Cabinet and Prime Minister after 1948 (see below, p. 51), a situation prevailed in which caucus had no power to formulate policy – though its numerous policy study groups could exert significant pressure on the responsible minister, which now and then did lead to policy modifications. On at least two occasions, however, new and very far-reaching policy was announced to Parliament by the NP leader without even informing the caucus (see below, p. 73 and p. 404).

The caucus traditionally acted as the body representing *die volk daar buite* – the Afrikaner *volk* outside parliament. The fact that each MP represented a single electoral district (constituency), and in the end would have to seek re-election in that constituency, meant that the good politicians in the caucus tended to keep their ear to the political ground back home. It was not unusual for one or more MPs to find themselves in conflict with this or that aspect of government policy. However, given the vast pressures to conform – not the least of which was each caucus member's hopes of political advancement – it was very rare for individuals or groups within the caucus to oppose Cabinet policy openly.‡ On occasion, the caucus could be a fractious body, but (at least till the 1980s) its

---

* The NP of 'South West Africa' (Namibia) was integrated into the NP federal structures from 1949 until the mid-1970s. This reflected the fact that Namibia was effectively governed as South African's fifth province between 1949 and Pretoria's groping towards an 'internal solution' for Namibia in the late 1970s.

† With the abolition of the Senate in January 1981, the caucus was limited to the National Party's MPs.

‡ I can only think of five instances in which this occurred. In two cases, the individual MPs involved were expelled from the caucus (Japie Basson in 1959 and Cas Greyling in 1977). Two other cases led to the eventual expulsion of groups of MPs – four in 1969 and 16 in 1982. In one other case, in 1955, after some caucus debate no disciplinary measures were taken because the offence was much less serious (see footnote, p. 81 below).

lines of cleavage were as often provincial as ideological. Taken as a whole, caucus tended to be seen by Cabinet as a mediated reflection of the overall sentiment among government supporters, and would generally be treated with respect. As Verwoerd put it on being challenged for not having consulted the caucus on a crucial policy shift:

> It would be foolish for the Cabinet to insist on things knowing that it cannot take its own people along on an issue.[20]

(d) the NP *Hoofleier* (leader-in-chief or national leader) was elected by the caucus. Presiding over the NP government (as Prime Minister from 1948 to 1984, and then as the executive State President from September 1984 to May 1994), he (never she) retained enormous powers of patronage within the party and the state. The most important of these was his exclusive prerogative to appoint the Cabinet;

(e) the NP *Cabinet* was responsible for determining and implementing NP government (as opposed to party) policy. To retain the support of the caucus, the Cabinet had to be broadly representative of the various NP factions. Its relationship with the Prime Minister was largely a function both of the latter's leadership style and management practice, as well as the willingness of ministers to take on their leader. In a divided Cabinet, the practice developed of referring the matter in question to a Cabinet committee, charged with reaching consensus.

The triangular relations between *Hoofleier,* Cabinet and caucus could be stormy. The early years of Dr Malan's new government saw some struggle for position between these three levels of the NP government. Barely a year after taking office, Malan told his caucus that while the Cabinet governed in theory, 'in reality all final decisions rest with the Prime Minister'.[21] This comment enraged at least one prominent backbencher. Dr Albert Hertzog inveighed against this 'dictatorial' and 'English' government system:

> It strikes me more and more that the ordinary Member of Parliament actually has no say at all. If he wants to achieve anything, then he must go and speak with the [Cabinet] Ministers and quietly try to influence them, otherwise he will get nothing done. The Prime Minister chose his Ministers before even knowing us ordinary MPs, without first asking our opinion. They make their appointments without taking the slightest notice of us ... Without us the National Party could never have won. But the moment that he had won, together with a few of his old friends, this man whom they call Prime Minister simply decides what they want. They take the whole machinery into their own hands, they accept our loyalty and they make and break us as they see fit.[22]

In the late 1930s at the suggestion of Paul Sauer, the *gesuiwerde* NP had introduced the requirement that its MPs each join three caucus study groups in order to familiarise themselves with the crucial issues of the day.[23] Over the NP's years in opposition, many of these caucus study groups established the practice of working with various of the extra-parliamentary organs of Afrikaner nationalism. This continued after 1948, and in many cases led to a combined parliamentary and extra-parliamentary nationalist offensive to shape the NP government's policies – and, on at least one occasion, to oblige the Prime Minister to get rid of a minister perceived as too weak. So active were the lobbying efforts of the caucus study groups that six years after taking power, Prime Minister Malan attacked them for acting like 'little governments', and for receiving 'submissions from outside bodies'. He again reminded the caucus that its role was not to make policy, but to shape the NP's parliamentary strategy.*

For much of the NP's history, the real locus of power in the party lay in its provincial and local organisations rather than its national structures. The provincial leaders usually commanded greater loyalty and authority within their own province than the *Hoofleier*. At a national level the provincial leaders were great barons, at times wielding as much influence as the *Hoofleier* himself. These provincial NPs have always jealously guarded their interests, prerogatives and identities both from each other and the 'national' institutions of the party.

The sharp 'provincialist' conflicts which always wracked Afrikaner nationalism rested on these four separate party structures. However, this persistent regionalism is more fundamentally explained by the fact that historically each provincial NP had a distinct social base. As separately organised, separately financed and separately led political institutions, each was the institutionalisation of a distinctive social alliance, differing in important respects from those of its partners in the federal party (see below).

The style of politics within the national NP institutions, and particularly within its government, was always baronial. While the *Hoofleier* commanded great prestige and authority throughout Afrikaner society, his real political authority within Cabinet and caucus depended firstly on the strength of his personal political base within his own provincial NP, and secondly on his powers of patronage. Patronage was the key to the *Hoofleier*'s ability to forge alliances with the other provincial barons. It meant that the two most powerful provinces, the Cape and the Transvaal, monopolised the national leadership from 1934, and that the prime potential threat to any *Hoofleier* always lay with the leader of the other major provincial NP.† To avoid outright inter-provincial confrontation, the exercise of the prime ministerial (and from 1984 to 1994, presidential)

---

* Quoted in Schoeman, *Van Malan tot Verwoerd*, 65. The Cabinet ministers replaced under intense pressure from caucus study groups was the NP's first Minister of Native Affairs, Dr E G Jansen. See p. 68 below.

† Between 1934 and 1994, the NP had been led for a total of 31 years by two Cape men (D F Malan and P W Botha) and for 29 years by four Transvalers (J G Strijdom, H F Verwoerd, B J Vorster and F W de Klerk – although the first three of these Transvaal leaders all spent their formative years in the Cape, and P W Botha was born and raised in the Orange Free State). Only once was the NP *Hoofleier* drawn from outside the two major provinces – by NP founder, *Hoofleier* and OFS leader from 1914 to 1934, General J B M Hertzog.

prerogative to make, withhold, reshuffle or terminate Cabinet appointments always had to accommodate the standing of the various barons in party protocol.

The Cabinet was the principal site of political horse-trading and the battle for influence among NP barons. Here the *Hoofleier* had to balance and appease the rival great and lesser barons, to protect his own alliances and frustrate those of pretenders to his leadership. The NP barons owed their power first to their own political fiefdoms in their provincial parties, and secondly to the bureaucratic power-base consequent on attaining a Cabinet portfolio. Particularly powerful political domains came with important ministries such as the old Bantu Affairs Department – and its various successors – as well as Finance, Defence, Justice, Transport, Foreign Affairs, and from the early 1980s, Constitutional Affairs and Development. Strong ministers could occasionally parlay such bureaucratic fiefdoms into a personal power-base from which to claim the next vacant leadership position.* However, given the Broederbond's key role in securing senior public service appointments, a minister seeking power by way of this route had to be well entrenched not only with his senior bureaucrats but also with the Broederbond.†

The NP's structure thus made for a tightly organised party characterised by an active membership – as well as an in-built propensity for intrigue and provincial rivalry. Its close but ambiguous relationship with the Broederbond, and their joint sponsorship of a new kind of Afrikaner nationalism, gradually generated a particular leadership culture which was far more intense, and vicious, than that in the old Hertzog NP.

What Annette Seegers has called the 'peculiarly Afrikaner style of doing things' was characterised by a strong concern with group preservation, consensus, loyalty and deference to authority.[24] Politics was not about position, power, nor even programmes. Rather, it turned around the basic question of *survival*. What was at stake was nothing less than the continued existence of the Afrikaans language and people. This meant that individual leaders and all nationalist politicians saw themselves as the representatives not just of their particular electoral or social constituency, but, in some sense, of *die ganse volk* (the entire Afrikaner people). In the end, they were answerable to the *volk*.

Consensus was thus valued as a means of ensuring that all elements of the *volk* were brought on board. Politicians would hesitate to strike out in new directions, fearing they could not take the *volk* with them. But they also dealt with each other in a particularly fraught way. In situations in which a decision was necessary and consensus proved unattainable, 'the recalcitrants are cast out and crushed'. In such a context, dissidence was dangerous. Because the stakes

---

* The route to the Premiership followed by Verwoerd, Vorster, and, to some extent, P W Botha – who combined both the leadership of the Cape NP and the bureaucratic power-base of the Defence Ministry.

† One reason why Foreign Minister R F (Pik) Botha twice failed to leap from the Foreign Ministry to the NP *Hoofleier*ship.

were so high, internal political differences were redolent with huge personal and social consequences. This tended to exaggerate the weight of political disagreements. Behind the mask of consensus and unity, internal nationalist politics were perennially characterised by particularly nasty forms of intrigue and back-stabbing. The Christian-national reading of what Moodie has called Afrikaner 'sacred history', depicted an endless struggle between 'true' nationalists and opportunists who betrayed their people and trust.[25] This meant that those who disagreed with this or that policy or politician were not just part of a different faction, they were potential *volksveraaiers* (traitors to the *volk*). Afrikaner survival demanded that they too had to be ruthlessly rooted out.

The right kind of political leadership was thus essential to the survival of the *volk*. Here, the broader political culture of nationalist *volksbeweging* was characterised by a real schizophrenia – one reinforced by the organisational forms of *gesuiwerde* Afrikaner nationalism. The Broederbond's elitism and secrecy fetish, together with its pervasive influence on and access to the NP and government leadership, all worked to bolster the centralising, autocratic and *dirigiste* tendencies in the nationalist political culture. In the words of one of the Broederbond's Afrikaner critics:

> Amongst the *volk* the impression was created that the leaders were indeed in control and thus could be trusted with their [i.e. the *volk*'s] future. The *Broederbond* and *Ruiterwag* helped fashion the attitude among many Afrikaners that somewhere there were people who knew better [than they did] and who would take the right decisions. The debates in Afrikaner ranks were thus restricted to a small self-selected group. And because the *Broeders/Ruiters* never tested their viewpoints and debates in public, they became unassailably convinced of the correctness of their own policies and their capacity to carry them out.[26]

The pervasive deference to authority meant that the *volk* generally passively accepted the policies adopted by leadership.* However, this was always tempered by traditional Afrikaner populism which stressed the right of each member of the *volk* to participate in group decisions. As long as the NP represented the *volksbeweging,* the *volk* enjoyed, and insisted upon, the right to be heard. At least until the late 1970s, this meant that the NP's structures of internal democracy and populist political culture often made for lively debate and contested policies.

The policies of the NP government after 1948 directly benefited all elements of its social base. They did so unevenly, however. The unequal returns drawn from NP rule by the various constituent forces of Afrikaner nationalism gave rise to much conflict since 1948, leading to the final collapse of organised Afrikaner nationalism in the mid-1980s. These conflicts centred around competing

---

* Thus, a 1970s study found that 60% of Afrikaners declared they would support the leadership even if they did not understand or approve of what was done. See T Hanf *et al., South Africa: The Prospects for Peaceful Change* (Rex Collings, London, 1981), 400-2.

definitions of Afrikaner nationalism and its hegemonic project – whom should it serve and how, and which of these social forces best personified the Afrikaner *volk* and its history? For much of this period, these internal Afrikaner nationalist conflicts took the predominant form of regionalist or 'provincialist' confrontation. An understanding of the workings and transformation of NP politics must thus begin with an analysis of the different and changing social bases of Afrikaner nationalism in each province.

Social bases of the provincial NPs[27]

The NP triumph of 1948 was due mainly to electoral breakthroughs made in South Africa's then largest province, the Transvaal.* Until the end of World War II, support for the Transvaal NP was largely confined to the considerable Afrikaans-speaking petty bourgeoisie in the state apparatus and the professions, and, emerging out of this latter group, a small class of aspirant commercial and financial capitalists organised in the *Reddingsdaadbeweging* (literally, the 'movement for the act of rescue' – as the so-called Afrikaner economic movement termed itself). As indicated in Chapter 1, in the 1948 election the Transvaal NP finally captured substantial votes from two crucial groups previously loyal to Jan Smuts's governing coalition – Transvaal maize farmers and Afrikaner workers on the Witwatersrand.

The Transvaal had been the principal site of the vicious wartime struggle for hegemony between the NP, the quasi-Nazi *Ossewa Brandwag* and other lesser nationalist organisations. These scars had not healed by 1948. The NP won the 1948 elections in an electoral coalition with 'Klaas Havenga's 'Hertzogite' Afrikaner Party (AP). Most of the excommunicated *Ossewa Brandwag* leadership had been politically resurrected in the AP after the war. Yet when NP *Hoofleier* D F Malan concluded an electoral pact with Havenga in late 1947, he was strongly opposed by the Transvaal NP leader, J G Strijdom. After losing a vote on this issue in the NP Federal Council, Strijdom took the matter to the Transvaal NP congress, where he declared his absolute opposition to the deal. When the Transvaal NP congress finally approved the pact with the AP, Strijdom accepted the decision. However, he wrote to Malan that he 'would not work actively' for the pact in the upcoming election.[28] These persistent NP/OB tensions were responsible for the failure of two future NP prime ministers to secure election in 1948 – Dr Verwoerd lost Alberton by 171 votes because OB-ites could not bring themselves to vote for him, and the Transvaal NP forced OB General John Vorster to stand down as the AP candidate in Brakpan. Vorster then ran as an independent, losing by two votes.

---

* From Union in 1910, till the flowering of the Bantustan scheme in the 1960s, South Africa was divided into four provinces for administrative purposes. Thereafter, the administrative jurisdictions were the four provinces plus the 10 bantustans. The democratic constitution of 1994 eliminated the bantustans and divides South Africa into nine provinces for administrative purposes. See maps, pp. 72 and 413.

The Broederbond had remained largely neutral throughout this prolonged conflict, reinforcing its enormous weight in Transvaal nationalism. With the NP still rebuilding and winning new support from Afrikaner workers and maize farmers, the AB, with its wide network of front organisations, was the primary mechanism through which the Afrikaner petty bourgeoisie exercised ideological dominance over the Transvaal NP and other organs of Transvaal Afrikaner nationalism. It was largely because of the AB's coordinating role that the Transvaal NP in particular came to articulate a rigid 'Christian-national' vision of the Afrikaner *volk*, stressing its 'anti-imperialism' and the interests of the Afrikaner 'small man' against what were seen as the 'imperialist-oriented' monopolies which dominated the economy.

The Transvaal party's thoroughgoing republicanism was a central issue in its fraternal conflicts with the nationalists of South Africa's then second most populous province, the Cape. The social base and content of Cape Afrikaner nationalism were markedly different from those of the Transvaal. The Cape NP had long rested on an economic and political alliance between the wealthier capitalist farmers, particularly of the Western Cape, on the one hand, and a small group of financial capitalists in the Sanlam (and later, Rembrandt) companies on the other. The moving spirits in Sanlam had in fact themselves formed the Cape NP in 1915. They dominated the party machinery and controlled its press. What can be called the nationalist Cape establishment was composed of Sanlam and Nasionale Pers, complemented by the bigger wine farmers and the NP leadership and party machinery.*

The Cape NP was always far more openly capitalist in orientation and sympathies than the Transvaal party. The Cape view of who spoke for the *volk* and 'its' interests was generally uncomfortable with the anti-capitalist rhetoric of the north, instead laying greater emphasis on the conditions to secure stable profit. Significantly, the Broederbond never became an important force in Cape nationalist politics. Indeed, the AB was often characterised as the major opposition force to the *'geldmag'* (financial power) of the Cape – a Transvaal smear phrase for the Cape establishment.

In the Orange Free State (OFS or Free State), a province dominated by agriculture and, later, gold mining, the Afrikaner petty bourgeoisie and rural capitalists were the real base of the NP. This gave the Free State NP a more rural orientation than both the Cape and Transvaal parties. Here too the Broederbond was a significant force. However, the OFS is a small province and its NP was eclipsed by those of the Transvaal and the Cape. Finally, the Afrikaans-speaking population of Natal province was always relatively small, and the Natal NP never developed into a significant force in nationalist politics.

---

* Sometimes collectively and pejoratively referred to by northern nationalists as *Keeromstraat* (U-turn street) – the name of the street on which the offices on Nasionale Pers were long located. Because *Keeromstraat* was also used a pejorative term for Nasionale Pers, to avoid confusion, I use it only in this latter, narrower sense.

The NP as political terrain(s)

Each of these national and provincial NP institutions was the site of widely differing struggles and represented widely varying interests – each was a distinct terrain of political conflict. The structure of the NP as a matrix of cross-cutting terrains is vital to an understanding of how it operated and of the relationship between the NP *qua* party and the NP government.

Since taking office in 1948, the NP was always a multi-headed beast, operating on a number of different levels and terrains of politics. On the one hand, as a mass and populist political party, it organised and mobilised – outside the state apparatus – an alliance of social forces under the banner of Afrikaner nationalism. At this level, the NP was much more than a simple electoral machine, designed to capture votes. As the hegemonic mass organisation of Afrikaner nationalism, it explicitly saw itself as a *volksfront* (*volk*'s or people's front) – the political incarnation of the Afrikaner *volksbeweging*.

On the other hand, however, the NP was also the governing party in South African state between 1948 and 1994. Here it was charged with the governance of the national economy. Responsible for the protection of all South African interests abroad (including those of the hated 'Hoggenheimer'), it was also required to foster a social consensus sufficient for the maintenance of social peace and the efficient operation of the economy. At this level, then, the NP represented within the state apparatus (and particularly through its parliamentary caucus and the Cabinet) the different interests of the social forces from which it drew support. Yet, primarily through the Cabinet and sections of the state bureaucracy, it also operated both to secure favouable conditions of accumulation in the capitalist economy and to maintain the social consensus embodied within its overall hegemonic project.*

The 'National Party' always operated differently at each of these discrete levels of politics. Each level represents a distinct political *terrain* on which intersect a different array of pressures and political struggles. As a political entity, the NP is best seen as a 'set' or matrix of terrains. Each terrain has its own forms of representation, norms and sets of practices and procedures established in past struggles. These specific characteristics of each terrain themselves partially structured the forms of the political conflicts fought out on them. When considering the crucial question of the relationship of NP as a mass party to the NP government and the NP-ruled South African state, each should be seen as a congelation of different terrains of struggle between contending forces.

The significance of this stress on terrain, and the specificity of the forms of politics of each terrain, will become clearer in the following chapters. However, it should be noted here that since the NP assumed office in 1948, its role as the ruling party in the capitalist state and guarantor of the conditions of capital accumulation has significantly shaped its operation as a *volksfront* – the ways in

---

* The concept of hegemonic project is discussed in the Theoretical Appendix, p. 488 (note) below.

which it has sought to represent the interests of the various social forces organised by the party outside the state apparatuses. This in turn has led to vigorous conflicts between the forces organised by the NP on all the political terrains on which it operates. These are explored in the following chapters.

Chapter Three

AT LAST WE HAVE GOT
OUR COUNTRY BACK!

The National Party in power, 1948–60

BANTUSTANS

"Give me the map
there. Know that
we have divided
.....our kingdoms"
— King Lear

Apartheid theory

Dr D F Malan's National Party took power in May 1948 animated by a social project envisaging a radically different South Africa from the one inherited from the United Party government. The NP had fought the election on a self-consciously 'anti-capitalist' programme. This, together with its open sympathy for Nazi Germany during World War II, its profound and proud racism and its expressed intention to fashion a radically authoritarian Christian-national republic, left it widely regarded as a fascist party.[1]

The NP's first 12 years in office produced intense efforts to fashion this 'new South Africa' in three broad areas: (a) reorganising the exercise and culture of state power; (b) elaborating and implementing apartheid; (c) consolidating and advancing the interests of the various constituents of Afrikaner nationalism. These each had a clear impact both on the NP government's overall management of the South African economy and on the emerging pattern of conflicts within Afrikaner nationalism.

No reverse! Reorganising state power

The victory of the National Party-led alliance in 1948 surprised even the NP itself. While expecting to reduce the governing United Party's 50-seat majority, the Nationalists had pinned their hopes for power on the election after 1948. The UP, on the other hand, blamed its defeat on the fact that widespread expectations of a UP landslide deterred many of its supporters from voting. Smuts's party convinced itself that if it could but mobilise all potential UP supporters, it would 'reverse the reverse' and regain power in the following elections. All too conscious of its own narrow parliamentary majority, the new government took such opposition claims very seriously. Its fears were reinforced when the NP lost a 1949 provincial council by-election in the Cape Paarl constituency – a seat it had captured in the parliamentary elections the previous year. The NP's first priority, then, was to consolidate its hold on power.

It did so in three main ways. First, it increased its parliamentary majority in 1949 through the simple expedient of granting parliamentary representation to the white population of the South African-ruled United Nations Mandated Territory then known as South West Africa (now Namibia). The predominantly German- and Afrikaans-speaking 'South Westerners' duly obliged by sweeping the NP to victory in all six seats, giving the Malan government some parliamentary elbow room.

It sought to widen this space in 1951 with legislation to remove 'Cape Coloureds' from the common voters' roll. This led to a prolonged and unseemly battle with the Appeal Court over the constitutionality of this legislation. The NP government finally resorted to increasing the size of the Senate in 1956, in order to secure the two-thirds majority of both Houses of Parliament necessary to override the constitutionally entrenched Coloured voting rights. A prominent Afrikaner NP critic recently concluded that the NP's 'unseemly [*onooglik*] assault on the Coloured vote ... had much more to do with party political interest [the need to deny the UP the Coloured vote] than with racial purity'.*

The second element of the NP government's strategy to consolidate its hold on power focused on the civil service. All politicians were acutely aware of the capacity of senior and middle-level bureaucrats to frustrate the policy initiatives of even the most popular administration. The NP had itself benefited from such a process during the Broederbond's effective wartime 'white-anting' of the civil service.[2] It launched parliamentary investigations in 1948 and 1949 on ways to limit the wide discretionary powers of senior officials, and the Malan government sought to extend an iron grip over the bureaucratic apparatus and culture of government. They relied on the Broederbond to patrol senior and middle-level appointments.

The AB offensive to reserve senior civil service positions exclusively for its own members was based on a careful analysis of how state power was exercised and by whom. A study by a leading academic *Broeder* had shown the upper levels of most state departments still to be staffed largely by 'pro-Imperialist' (and English-speaking) civil servants trained in the hated 'Milner tradition'. They were seen as a powerful potential block to the implementation of future NP government policies.[3] However, medium-to-lower levels of the civil service were overwhelmingly staffed by Afrikaners, most of whom were enthusiastic NP supporters. Shortly after assuming office in 1948, the NP government initiated a systematic purge of senior civil servants and a general reorganisation of the state bureaucracy. Pro-NP bureaucrats were promoted into senior posts, and care was taken to cosset all ranks of an increasingly Afrikanerised civil service as one of the NP's major bases of political support. This occasioned strong complaints from the Public Service Commission, whose protests were simply ignored.

These purges concentrated particularly on three departments central to the implementation of NP apartheid policies – Native Affairs, the police and the military. With the primary responsibility for the elaboration and implementation of the finer details of apartheid, the then 'Department of Native Affairs' could not be left under the control of what the NP saw as the 'liberal' English-speaking bureaucrats who ran it – and who did successfully frustrate many of the policy initiatives of the first NP Minister of Native Affairs (1948–50), Dr E G Jansen.

The two crucial security apparatuses of the state, the police and the military, had likewise to be brought under the firm control, not just of Afrikaners, but of reliable Afrikaners. The number of Afrikaner policemen increased dramatically between 1946 and 1960 – at a rate nearly three times that of English-speakers in the police force (77,7 to 27,8 percent).[4] The NP government inherited a Defence

---

* Giliomee, 'Die Afrikaanse Politieke Geskiedskrywing', 12. This cynical packing of the Senate embarrassed even the most extremist NP supporters – see Schoeman, *Van Malan tot Verwoerd*, 12. The strong memory of the relative ease with which it had overturned constitutional guarantees in the 1950s partly explains the NP's insistence on constitutional vetos rather than guarantees during the negotiations of 1990–93. See my interview with the NP spokesman on Defence, Dr Boy Geldenhuys, *New Era*, 6 (2), June 1991, 9.

Force modelled on British military practices and traditions, and whose senior ranks were overwhelmingly filled by men who had fought in World War II. Many officers were still partly 'infected' by the wartime anti-fascist spirit, regarding the 'Malanazis' as little better than traitors. Led by the Afrikaner wartime fighter ace 'Sailor' Malan, the powerful extra-parliamentary Torch Commando mobilised hundreds of thousands of ex-servicemen and other whites in huge rallies against the NP's attempts to remove Coloured voting rights.

Deeply concerned over the loyalty of the military, Defence Minister Frans Erasmus purged its senior ranks, filling them with pro-government Afrikaners selected through the Broederbond – thereby provoking intense resentment among English-speaking and non-Broederbond Afrikaner officers who saw their promotion barred. Erasmus also began to restructure the Defence Force along the lines of the commando system of the old Boer republics, removing the Crown from military regalia and recasting its traditions along 'national' lines.*

The *étatiste* political culture of Christian-nationalism had never accepted the state-as-arbiter mythology inherited with the British parliamentary model. Rather, the state was seen as an instrument to serve the *volk* (and, occasionally, vice versa), itself embodied in the *volksfront* of the National Party. All public institutions existed to advance government policies. The NP's Afrikanerisation of the South African state entirely jettisoned the Westminster-derived culture of civil service neutrality in party politics. Absolute loyalty to the National Party and to the policies of its government now became the prerequisite of advancement in the civil service:

> English-speakers, those opposed to republicanism and people who had volunteered for service during the Second World War were pressured to leave state service through, for example, being overlooked for promotion and being offered early retirement.[5]

The number of Afrikaners employed in 'public administration' increased by a massive 98,5 percent between 1946 and 1960, while representation by English-speakers declined by 25,2 percent.[6] English-speaking recruits for the public sector virtually disappeared, as the civil service came to be seen by English-speakers as a purely Afrikaner domain – provoking all sorts of uneasy, and usually racist jokes about the supposed incompetence of its functionaries.†

---

* See P H Frankel, *Pretoria's Praetorians* (Cambridge University Press, Cambridge, 1984), chap. 1. The author of perhaps the best existing study of Afrikaner nationalism first began to work in this area partly in order to understand the 'discrimination' which affected his father's army career. See 'Introduction to the Paperback Edition', Moodie, *Rise of Afrikanderdom*, x.

† This was the original thrust of the endemic 'Van der Merwe' jokes. Throughout the 1950s and the 1960s, most English-speaking whites were possessed of profound contempt for (and fear of) Afrikaners, viewing their language, their culture, their Calvinism and their politics as pathetic hangovers from a pre-industrial age. This is reflected in the racist epithets commonly applied to Afrikaners – e.g. 'hairybacks', 'rockspiders', 'dutchies', etc.

All state departments were politicised. While the rhythm of this process varied between ministries, it did lead to a considerable centralisation of ministerial control over the state bureaucracy. In particular, the Department of Native Affairs under Dr H F Verwoerd emerged as a real 'super-ministry' (see below). In this struggle to transform the civil service, the state apparatus itself became yet another terrain, or series of terrains, of ongoing conflict between the social forces organised by the NP. Specific ministries became identified with specific 'regionalist' political lines. Thus under the premiership of Dr D F Malan (1948–54), the Ministries of Finance and of Transport were associated with a 'Cape line'. Transvaal resistance to the 'moderation' of the Cape was waged from the base of Strijdom and Verwoerd in the Ministries of Lands and of Native Affairs respectively.

The NP sought to consolidate its hold on power, thirdly, through measures designed both to narrow the terrain of legal political struggle, and to impose tight state controls over civil society. The 1950 Suppression of Communism Act outlawed the Communist Party, allowed the removal from Parliament of a series of Communist MPs elected to represent Cape 'Natives', and compiled and periodically updated a list of 'named' Communists.

Other new repressive measures were used to restrict or remove from office leading officials of the African National Congress (ANC), including its then President (Chief Albert Luthuli), General-Secretary (Walter Sisulu), and Deputy-President (Nelson Mandela). The Riotous Assemblies Act was amended to end the ANC's 1952 Defiance Campaign and limit other demonstrations. Rejecting the recommendations of its own Botha Commission for a limited recognition of black trade unions,[7] the government used various measures to 'bleed them white' (in the immortal phrase of then Labour Minister Ben Schoeman). This crackdown on the extra-parliamentary opposition led in 1956 to a charge of treason against 156 ANC, trade union and other political activists (all were eventually acquitted).

The space for political opposition was drawn progressively closed throughout the 1950s, culminating in the April 1960 banning of the ANC and the smaller Pan Africanist Congress (PAC). A State of Emergency and draconian legislation introduced by the new Justice Minister, John Vorster, in 1961 in effect outlawed all but parliamentary opposition (see Chapter 5).

These measures considerably strengthened the NP's hold on state power. After the death of Smuts in 1950, the increasingly divided UP proved incapable of mounting a threat to the NP. The one force in white politics which worried the Malan government was hobbled when the UP obliged the Torch Commando leadership to abandon its effective extra-parliamentary opposition and to form an 'anti-fascist united front' to contest the 1953 general elections. Eleven of the more liberal United Party MPs finally jumped ship to form themselves into the Progressive Party (PP or 'Progs') in 1959. The NP won a comfortable parliamentary majority under D F Malan in 1953, and a decisive one under J G ('Hans') Strijdom in 1958 – although it did not win majority support from the now purely white electorate until its narrow victory in the October 1960 referendum over whether South Africa should become a republic.* Its project to 'Afrikanerise' the state culminated in the establishment of a Republic in May 1961 – albeit with a parliamentary form very different from earlier plans for an 'authentic' Christian-national *volks* republic.

From the mid-1950s onwards, the NP established almost absolute control over the South African state, becoming, in popular parlance, virtually synonymous with the state. The only real opposition to its overall project now came from the burgeoning black resistance, led by the ANC. Parliamentary politics dwindled to a legalistic ritual, a side show in the emerging black and white drama of South Africa.

Something better than segregation: Elaborating apartheid

'Apartheid' was the central prop of the NP's 1948 electoral platform. Many observers believed that the 'political slogan' of apartheid won that election for the NP.[8] The literal meaning of the Afrikaans term *apartheid* is 'apart-ness', or the condition of being separate. The word seems to have been invented in 1935 by the Afrikaner historian P van Biljon to indicate an 'all-embracing racial policy essential to replace the old notion of segregation'. It began to be used by the NP in 1943, and inspired a series of pseudo-scientific studies by Broederbond intellectuals.[9] The 1948 report of the NP's Sauer Commission consolidated the findings of many of these studies into an overall statement of the objectives of apartheid.[10]

However, apartheid remained a fairly vague set of principles rather than a fully worked-out programme. While clearly rejecting the 'parallelism' recommended by the Fagan Commission and endorsed by the ruling UP, the NP's 1948 electoral manifesto openly acknowledged that 'apartheid' was still very far from a detailed policy. Instead, it asked the electorate to decide on the 'apartheid principle', promising the later elaboration of this 'scheme'.[11]

In this sense then, this 'apartheid slogan' of 1948 performed a double ideological function. First, it gave expression to a very broad sentiment among most Afrikaners, regardless of social class, that the rapid urbanisation of blacks

---

* Correcting for the probable party political vote in uncontested constituencies, Heard estimates support for the NP in the 1953 general election at 44,5% to 54,7% for the UP-led United Front in an 87,9% poll. However, again largely because of the vast over-representation of rural areas in parliament, the NP took 88 seats to the United Front's 61. *General Elections in South Africa*, table 25, 60. In the 1958 general election the NP took 97 seats to the UP's 53. It now won more of the actual votes cast than did the UP (55,1% to 43,3%). However, again correcting for the probable vote in uncontested constituencies, Heard estimates that the UP was still marginally more popular than the NP (50,1% to 48,5%), table 38, 83, and 88-91. Finally, in the 1960 referendum, on a straight yes-or-no question (no uncontested constituencies), the 90,8% poll of the white electorate gave 52,0% of the vote to the 'Yes' side (NP), to 47,5% to the 'No' (the UP and PP). *General Elections in South Africa*, table 50, 113.

during the 1930s and 1940s – the so-called *oorstroming* (inundation) of the cities – threatened both their precarious places in the urban environment, and their specific interests. *Oorstroming* denied cheap black labour to Afrikaner farmers. As Africans moved into industrial employment in their hundreds of thousands, as their wages rose more rapidly than those of whites during the war, and as industrialists began to contemplate using cheaper African industrial operatives, *oorstroming* also threatened the tenuous hold of Afrikaner workers on relative privilege. Likewise for the Afrikaner petty bourgeoisie and emerging Afrikaner business, heavily dependent for their own advance on agricultural profits, *oorstroming* meant higher wages, militant black trade unions and demands for racial equality.

This 'apartheid principle' thus operated, secondly, to condense into a symbolic whole the divergent interests of each of the class forces within the nationalist alliance. The proposal to ensure the strict control of the movement and employment of African labour could satisfy each of these groups. In the words of the NP's Sauer Commission:

> The entire migration of Natives into and from the cities should be controlled by the state which will enlist the cooperation of municipal bodies. ... Natives from the country areas shall be admitted to the urban areas or towns only as temporary employees, obliged to return to their homes after the expiry of their employment. ... A national system of labour regulation and labour control will be established with a central labour bureau and an effective network throughout the country to allow supply and demand to operate as flexibly as possible and to eliminate the large-scale wastage of labour. A proper survey of the labour force and labour requirements will have to be made *in order effectively to divert labour* into the various channels of agricultural, industrial, mining and urban employment.[12]

While all the social forces mobilised by the NP could agree with these broad prescriptions, 'apartheid' very clearly meant different things to different groups of Afrikaners. While farmers dreamt of secure and cheap black labour, and some of the more visionary intellectuals fantasised about total separation, in its message of congratulations to the victorious NP, the *Afrikaanse Handelsinstituut* (Afrikaans Commercial Institute – AHI) warned that total segregation was a pipe dream:

> No, a person must be practical. It must be acknowledged that the non-white [urban] worker already constitutes an integral part of our economic structure, that he is now so enmeshed in the spheres of our economic life that for the first fifty/hundred years (if not even longer), total segregation is pure wishful thinking. Any government which disregards this irrefutable fact will soon discover that it is no longer in a position to govern.[13]

Yet if the policy content of apartheid remained vague, and if the various constituent forces of Afrikaner nationalism had different interpretations of its meaning, the deep collective wish for apartheid reflected several of the fundamental principles underlying the emerging Christian-nationalist reworking of Afrikaner nationalism in the late 1930s and 1940s. Apartheid was presented as an ethical policy which would grant to other ethnic groups what Afrikaners demanded for themselves. It was the only way to avoid racial conflict in South Africa's *veelvolkigge* (multi-ethnic) situation, since it provided for the survival of Afrikaners (and other whites) while supposedly facilitating the development of other ethnic groups.

All Afrikaner nationalists were convinced that 'the kernel of the native question ... has shifted to the cities'.[14] Apartheid would be won or lost as a battle to control African urbanisation. Deborah Posel has argued that central to the emerging apartheid vision was its desire to develop coherent national policies which would override regional particularities. The locus of control over African urbanisation was to be shifted as far as possible from local authorities to the state. Given the scope of 'the problem', controlling African urbanisation required systematic and coordinated action by a bigger, more centralised and, above all, *rational* state. The NP intention to create a labour bureau system designed 'to allow supply and demand to operate as flexibly as possible' was premised on a simple arithmetic understanding that labour supply and labour demand could be matched and directed. As the above quotation from the Sauer Commission indicates, all of this assumed that the rational state had the capacity to generate precise data on the disposition of the African population on the size of 'the labour force and labour requirements'.*

All of this required enlarging and expanding state institutions, especially the Department of Native Affairs. However, in 1948 these remained but principles and wishes. Christian-national ideologues were firmly convinced of both the morality of their racial assumptions and the rational basis of their apartheid objectives. Yet they were equally aware of the immense work required to elaborate these vague ideas into detailed policy. Just four months after the NP came to power, the Broederbond brought together a large number of Afrikaner intellectuals, churchmen and cultural leaders to launch the *Suid-Afrikaanse Buro vir Rasse-aangeleenthede* (South African Bureau for Racial Affairs – SABRA), dedicated to a solution to the 'colour question' based on 'the scientific study of racial affairs'.[15] The myriad SABRA studies, congresses and other interventions played a key, but complex and contested role in the transformation of what *Die*

---

* Sauer Report. See D Posel, 'Sizing up the Population: Statistics, statecraft and social transformation in South Africa', Keynote address to the 23rd Annual Conference of the Canadian Association of African Studies, Trent University, Peterborough, Ontario, 13 May 1995. Here Posel argues that the NP view of the rational state was well suited to the postwar 'modernist consensus' over the ability of the state to bring about large-scale social transformation. In this view, control depended on the ability to develop knowledge about, and specifically to count the various sectors of the African population. For an outstanding discussion of the elaboration of apartheid policy after 1948, see Posel's book, *The Making of Apartheid: Conflict and compromise* (Clarendon Press, Oxford, 1991).

Transvaler had called 'the apartheid principle' from a generalised impulse for radical racial separation into a fully fledged ideology of independent 'national states'.[16]

While the NP was rock solid behind the *slogan* of apartheid, few of its leading politicians had any idea how to translate this into the rational policies being clamoured for by the ideologues and SABRA experts. Both Malan and Strijdom were concerned that the United Party's meagre attempts to improve conditions for blacks would lead inexorably to the erosion of the colour bar, and eventually to equality.[17] While Strijdom spoke unapologetically of the necessity of perpetual white domination *(baasskap)*, Malan told a delegation of Africans who came to tell him of their fear that under apartheid they would lose their meagre existing rights:

> My government has no intention of depriving you of your rights. *Nothing will be taken from you without giving you something better in its place …* What you want is a rehabilitation of your own national life, not competition and intermixture and equality with the white man in his particular part of the country.*

The implementation of this vision proceeded slowly at first. Interracial sex was banned in 1949, and Native Affairs Minister Dr E G Jansen appointed various commissions to enquire into aspects of projected apartheid policy. However, the NP confronted a real leadership problem on this issue. While the aged Prime Minister Malan was deeply committed to a radical extension of racial separation, his grasp of apartheid theory was at best hazy, and his ability, and willingness, to implement a long-term programme of detailed social engineering was questioned by some Transvalers. His first Minister of Native Affairs was *oud-smelter* and member of the Sauer Commission, Dr Jansen, who had held this portfolio under General Hertzog's last NP Cabinet of 1929 to 1933. Widely regarded as the most courteous and gentle individual in the NP, Jansen was of the old school of rural nationalists. He had little sympathy with SABRA technocrats who believed that the world could be planned down to the second decimal place, and that policy was simply a matter of applying rational planning and management. Jansen was hardly the person to preside over either the development of the bureaucratic rationality or the ruthless measures which would be needed to implement apartheid. Moreover, slack discipline in Malan's Cabinet meant that Minister Jansen was under no pressure from his colleagues to come up with coherent policy.

---

* Quoted in E P Dvorin, *Racial Separation in South Africa: An analysis of apartheid theory* (University of Chicago Press, Chicago, 1952), 95, my emphasis. Malan wrote to an American clergyman about what he saw as the fundamental differences between the white and black groups. The 'difference in colour' was 'merely the physical manifestation of the contrast between two irreconcilable ways of life, between barbarism and civilisation, between overwhelming numerical odds on the one hand and insignificant numbers on the other ' – see L Kuper, *Passive Resistance in South Africa* (Yale University Press, New Haven, 1957), 217-26.

So half-hearted were Jansen's efforts, and so easily seemed he to be waylaid by more liberal senior officials both in his department and in the Native Affairs Commission, that Young Turks in the caucus study group on Native Affairs decided to 'force him into action' in early 1949. Many nationalists were scandalised by Jansen's serious consideration of extending property rights to urban Africans. Growing caucus and Cabinet complaints about the Minister's inability to deal with the 'accumulation of Bantu in the cities, [with] the still growing farm labour shortages and the fact that almost nothing was being done to develop the [Native] reserves' finally obliged Malan to accede to caucus demands.[18] The Prime Minister wanted to replace Jansen with his trusted Cape lieutenant, and Chairman of the NP's commission into 'the colour question', Paul Sauer. However, notorious in the NP for what Dr Malan called his 'laziness', Sauer threatened to resign if *Die Doktor* pushed the issue, suggesting instead that Verwoerd be given the portfolio. This was duly done in 1950.*

Although Verwoerd was surprised at being given this portfolio, this former Professor of Social Work set about taking control of his department with his characteristic zeal and pseudo-scientific conceptions of social engineering. Together with his new Secretary for Native Affairs, Dr W W M Eiselen, Verwoerd initiated an aggressive elaboration of what his own newspaper had called 'the apartheid principle' into detailed policy. In just five years they succeeded in transforming the Department of Native Affairs from a relatively small ministry into a great super-ministry whose tentacles extended into every aspect of government policy – eliciting more than occasional conflict with Cabinet colleagues angry at Verwoerd's growing influence and interference in their own domain.[19] The 1950 Population Registration Act irrevocably assigned every individual on South African soil, every newborn baby and every immigrant and visitor to one of four racial categories – white, 'Bantu' (i.e. Africans), Coloureds and Asiatics. Verwoerd and Eiselen then focused their attention on laying the foundations in four key areas on which their pyramid of 'Grand Apartheid' was to be built: state control over the administration of black people; over the organisation and occupation of urban and rural space; over labour; and over land.

The elected Natives Representative Council set up in 1936 was abolished and the 1951 Bantu Authorities Act imposed government-appointed (and government-paid) 'traditional' chiefs as local administrators in 'tribal areas' (the

---

* D and J de Villiers, *Paul Sauer* (Tafelberg, Cape Town, 1977), 10. Sauer may have had other considerations in mind. Firmly on the 'Cape liberal' wing of the NP (and the son of the man who had fought to have Africans included in the franchise in 1910), Sauer clearly realised that this department was a minefield in which he would be expected to do things which went again the grain. His alternative proposal was the second time that Sauer had pushed Verwoerd into a job which subsequently made *Die Hollander*'s career – the first had been as editor of *Die Transvaler* in 1937. Verwoerd had wanted the Ministry of Transport in 1948, and was incensed when Malan gave it to Sauer. He returned Sauer's favours with cordial loathing, once telling Albert Hertzog that he often wondered why the *bon vivant* Sauer was in the National Party.

reserves). Popular anti-government chiefs, such as the then ANC President, Chief Albert Luthuli, were removed from office. The imposition of these 'Bantu authorities' aroused fierce opposition, eventually provoking revolts in Sekhukhuneland in 1958 and in Pondoland in 1960.

Numerous measures consolidated rigid racial boundaries in the occupation and use of space. The existing racial zoning of residential and business areas was vastly extended. The frequently amended 1950 Group Areas Act imposed countrywide controls on interracial property transfers and over the racial categorisation of business undertakings. It allowed the minister to reserve specific urban residential and business areas for a particular racial group, and oblige other racial groups to vacate such proclaimed 'group areas'. The control over racial space was further extended by the 1951 Prevention of Illegal Squatting Act, empowering the state to resettle in the reserves the 'surplus' peasants still living in so-called 'black spots' in white-zoned land.* A 1954 amendment to the 1936 Natives Trust and Land Act limited the number of labour tenants allowed on white farms (so addressing a key demand of farmers).

Millions of black people were eventually forcibly ejected from 'white' land in terms of these measures.[20] They were usually dumped unceremoniously to 'adapt or die' in remote and primitive 'resettlement areas'. The generally appalling conditions in these 'dumping grounds' regularly produced excruciating poverty, rampant disease and crippling infant mortality. The intense human suffering in places such as Dimbaza, Limehill, Soetwater and hundreds of others provoked international outrage and led to charges of genocide against the NP government.†

These steps to close off separate racial spaces then enabled the state to strengthen the infamous system of 'influx control', and thereby regulate the mobility and employment of black labour, and attempt to manage the pace and thrust of African urbanisation. The 1952 Native Laws Amendment Act and 1955 Natives (Urban Areas) Amendment Act restricted the right of permanent (segregated) urban residence (so-called 'Section 10 rights') to those Africans who could provide documentary proof either of their uninterrupted residence in that city for at least 10 years, or that they had worked uninterruptedly for the same employer for at least 15 years. All other Africans were eventually to be returned to the reserves. In the same year, the Natives (Abolition of Passes and Coordination of Documents) Act scrapped myriad local varieties of passes,

---

* So-called 'black spots' referred to land owned and occupied by blacks in areas set aside for whites.
† At a New York press conference immediately after the announcement of his 1984 Nobel Peace Prize, Archbishop Desmond Tutu labelled apartheid a form of genocide. On being asked where were apartheid's gas chambers, he replied that a policy which removed millions of people at gunpoint and then dumped them in conditions where the policy-makers knew very clearly that thousands had died and that thousands more would die, and which nevertheless continued to be applied without appeal or modification for over twenty years, was, in his mind, nothing less than genocide.

introducing a single standard 'reference book' (the hated *dompas*). All Africans over the age of 16 years were now required to carry a pass at all times. For the first time, this requirement was extended to African women. Until the formal abandonment of influx control in 1986, literally hundreds of thousands of Africans were convicted every year for not having a reference book in their possession.[21] When coupled with the establishment of labour bureaux throughout the country, this enabled the state to begin to control and channel the flow of black labour as required in the various sectors of the economy.

At the core of this central aspect of apartheid – the concern to regulate the flow of black labour – were attempts to control the urbanisation of African women. Women were excluded from the system of influx control until the 1960s. However, as early as the 1930s the NP and other bodies used the massive inflow of African women to the cities, and the growing proportion of females among the urban African population, as the principal index of the permanency of urbanisation. The apartheid effort to control and direct the labour supply rested heavily on reducing the numbers of African women in the cities. Yet this proved to be much more difficult than anticipated. Many attempts to set up a registry of African customary marriage – and hence control over the access of African women to housing in the cities – failed.[22] The extension of passes to women in the late 1950s provoked massive protests and the most sustained resistance hitherto evoked by apartheid – and generated the famous women's slogan: 'Watch-out [Prime Minister] Strijdom! When you strike the women, you strike a rock.'

The development of the 'Native Reserves' was seen as crucial to stemming the flows of black labour to the cities – and particularly of confining African women outside of the urban areas.* Yet this question provoked severe divisions within the ranks of the NP faithful in the mid-1950s. The central finding of the (Jansen-appointed) Tomlinson Commission into the socio-economic development of the reserves held that in order to make total apartheid work, the government would have to invest the then staggering sum of £104 million. If this money was not spent, 'the inevitable consequences of the integration of the Bantu and European populations into a common society must be endured'.† Minister Verwoerd was deeply resentful of the cost of the commission, of the time it took to complete its work and of the fact that his department was obliged to delay its policy initiatives until this creature of his predecesor Jansen deigned

---

* In keeping with the old segregationist notion that the 'labour units' imported to the cities would be African male workers, African women would and should remain in the reserves, working on the land to feed themselves and their children.

† *Summary of the Report of the Commission for the Socio-Economic Development of the Bantu Areas within the Union of South Africa*, UG 61/1955 (Government Printer, Pretoria), 208 and 211. This £104 million equalled approximately US $300 million in 1955 prices. The South African GDP then stood at just under £2 000 million – D H Houghton, *The South African Economy* (OUP, Oxford, 1976), figure 4, 41.

to present its report. The Minister of Native Affairs was also possessed of sharp personal antagonism towards Professor Tomlinson dating from their student days together. Likewise contemptuous of many of Tomlinson's SABRA technical experts, Verwoerd rejected out of hand the commission's finding that white living standards would have to be curtailed in order to make apartheid work.* He refused to consider spending such sums on the development of the reserves. This, he claimed, could be better achieved by establishing 'economic farming units' in the reserves, from which 'full-time stock farmers or agriculturalists' would sell their produce to the 'large non-farming native communities in the native areas' – i.e. to the unemployed.[23]

Verwoerd's summary rejection of the Tomlinson Report devastated its author, and was met with 'disbelief and outrage' by many SABRA intellectuals. It led to a deep and angry polarisation of SABRA on the issue of the nature of 'practical' apartheid and the costs that white South Africa should bear in order to implement a 'morally defensible' apartheid policy. 'Profound clashes of opinion' then marred the 1956 Broederbond-organised *Volkskongres* on racial policy. Some NP politicians went to great lengths to force SABRA delegates to toe Verwoerd's line.[24] Led by SABRA vice-chairman Professor Nic Olivier, the Stellenbosch University wing of SABRA came into ever more frequent confrontation with Verwoerd. At one stage Verwoerd stopped a national tour by the SABRA chairman Willem Landman in which the clergyman was intent on explaining to the *volk* the 'emancipatory possibilities' of apartheid.† The Minister of Native Affairs then ostentatiously resigned his SABRA membership at the organisation's 1958 Congress. These disputes culminated in a Verwoerd-sponsored purge of SABRA in April 1961, the precursor of sharp internal ideological divisions which were to wrack all organisations of Afrikaner nationalism throughout the 1960s.[25]

By the end of the 1950s, the long-existing racial segregation of South African society had been radically extended. The movement and employment of African labour had been brought under strict state control, and all skilled and supervisory jobs reserved for whites. The so-called Coloured franchise and parliamentary representation of Cape Africans had disappeared. Christian-national Education was beginning to take over the schools, and the universities had been segregated. The manifesto of the Broederbond-directed Institute for Christian National Education described Africans as 'cultural infants' whose education should fall under the control and guidance of the state.[26] The 'Bantu Education' system

---

* Verwoerd apparently tried to go behind Tomlinson's back within the commission, and is said at one stage to have accused the Professor of embezzling funds, and blocked his career in the public service thereafter – D Welsh, 'The Executive and the African Population', in R Schire (ed), *Leadership and the Apartheid State: From Malan to De Klerk* (Oxford University Press, Cape Town, 1994), 151.

† S Pienaar, *Getuie van Groot Tye* (Tafelberg, Cape Town, 1978), 60. Pienaar averred that Landman apparently never recovered from the episode.

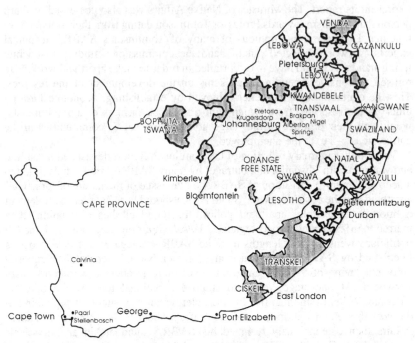

Map 2   Apartheid South Africa: Provinces and Bantustans

introduced by *Broeder* Verwoerd was now teaching African children basic literacy and numeracy skills 'to prepare Natives more effectively for their future occupations' rather than, as Dr Verwoerd so eloquently put it, 'showing him the green pastures of European society in which he is not allowed to graze'.*

However as the conflict between the Cape SABRA-ites and Verwoerd had shown, in an era of rising African nationalism, and massive passive resistance by South African blacks, some Afrikaners were beginning to be troubled by the obvious absence of a moral basis to apartheid. It all smacked too closely of open racism, and a few NP intellectuals found it increasingly difficult to reconcile the supposedly moral policy of apartheid with Prime Minister Strijdom's easy invocation of white *baasskap* (domination/supremacy).

It was in this context that a few months after taking over the premiership following the death of Strijdom in August 1958, Verwoerd and his new Minister

* The first quotation is from the Eiselen Education Commission, cited in F Troup, *Forbidden Pastures: Education under apartheid* (IDAF, 1976), 18, while Verwoerd is cited in ibid, 22. Verwoerd's use of the masculine gender is doubly revealing – African women were simply 'superfluous appendages' to male 'labour units' (as an NP Labour Minister later put it). In this speech Verwoerd announced that the role of black males in white South Africa was to be confined to 'certain forms of labour'.

of Native Affairs, M D C ('Daan') de Wet Nel suddenly announced a new design for apartheid. Without informing the NP caucus, Verwoerd introduced the Promotion of Bantu Self-Government Bill in May 1959, providing the blueprint for what came to be called Grand Apartheid. The new scheme proposed restructuring the Bantu authorities system in the reserves on the basis of eight 'Territorial Authorities' (later expanded to 10, and renamed 'Bantu Homelands' – commonly known as the Bantustans – see map 3, p. 72). Each bantustan was gradually to be given limited self-government as a first step to the eventual independence of these 'national states'. This apparent conversion to the previously despised SABRA line occurred just weeks after the Secretary for Native Affairs announced that the political evolution of the 'homelands' would not extend to sovereignty.[27]

The bantustan scheme rested on the convenient proposition that there was no African majority in South Africa. It held that members of the 'Bantu' population were not even South Africans, but belonged instead to one of 10 'national/ethnic groups' or 'national minorities'. In keeping with Afrikaner nationalism's stress on the realisation of ethnic identity *(volkseie)*, each of these 'national/ethnic minorities' was to be given the right to realise its divinely ordained national calling in its own 'homeland'. In introducing the Bill, Minister de Wet Nel explained to parliament that this new policy of 'separate freedoms' rested on three principles:

> The first is that God has given a divine task and calling to every People [*volk*] in the world, which dare not be denied or destroyed by anyone. The second is that every People in the world of whatever race or colour, just like every individual, has the inherent right to live and develop. Every People is entitled to the right of self-preservation. In the third place, it is our deep conviction that the personal and national ideals of every ethnic group can best be developed within its own national community. Only then will other groups feel they are not being endangered. … This is the philosophical basis of the policy of Apartheid … To our People this is not a mere abstraction which hangs in the air. *It is a divine task which has to be implemented and fulfilled systematically.*[28]

The National Party thus entered the 1960s unselfconsciously claiming the mantle of an 'anti-colonial' party, whose apartheid policy was in fact the realisation of the principle of the right of peoples to self-determination. The fact that Africans were never asked if they agreed to be stripped of their citizenship and assigned to one or other 'tribal' group never seemed to faze Verwoerd's intense conviction of his moral purpose. However, on more than one occasion he conceded that Grand Apartheid was a 'concession' to world opinion and changing circumstances. Referring to his new scheme of eventual bantustan independence, Verwoerd told parliament in 1965:

> We would rather have seen the old position maintained, but in the circumstances of the post-war world that was obviously not possible … I said that we all wished

that these post-Second World War changes had not come about, because then surely the world would have been very comfortable for us. ... But ... in the light of the new spirit and the pressures exerted and the forces which arose after the Second World War it is clear that no country could continue as it did in past years. The old traditional policy of the White man as ruler over the Bantu, who had no rights at all, could not continue.[29]

Afrikaner favouritism: Advancing Afrikaner economic interests

Writing in the mid-1970s, a prominent Afrikaner economist captured the lingering nationalist indignation at the consequences of the urbanisation of Afrikaners in the forty years following the South African War of 1899–1902. Estimating that more than 25 percent Afrikaners were so poor they could not feed or house their families in the early 1930s, he claims that even the remaining 75 percent were

> overwhelmingly oriented towards the rural areas, with only an insignificant number to be found in the high-income sectors of the economy. At the outbreak of World War II, as a group, Afrikaners could have been regarded as underdeveloped. The grandparents and parents of the present generation of English-speakers, which is now so conspicuously pre-occupied with poverty in South Africa, manifestly turned their backs on the poverty of this underdeveloped group. Worse still, they sometimes deliberately blocked its development.[30]

A mid-1940s study of the urban occupational structure by a leading Broederbonder showed Afrikaners to be strikingly disadvantaged relative to their white English-speaking compatriots. Control of all sectors of the economy, except agriculture, was overwhelmingly in the hands of English-speaking whites:

> The overall difference between the place of Afrikaners and non-Afrikaners in urban occupations comes down to the following: Afrikaners are strongly represented in unskilled and less skilled manual labour, in the agricultural trades, amongst the ordinary [white] mine workers, in transport and trafficking and the various branches of the public service, including the teaching professions. On the other hand, there is a greater absence of Afrikaners in the occupations of the well-to-do, in the professions, in most sectors of commerce, amongst clerical workers, in the more attractive engineering trades, in the printing industry and amongst the captains of mining.[31]

A leading Broederbond economist estimated that in 1936 the average annual per capita income of Afrikaans-speaking whites stood at just 60 percent of that of 'other whites'.* According to some data, by 1946 this had risen to 66 percent, while other data in the same source indicates that the proportion of Afrikaner

* Or £86:£142. Professor C G W Schumann, cited in E P du Plessis, *'n Volk Staan Op: Die Ekonomiese Volkskongres en Daarna* (Human en Rousseau, Cape Town, 1964), 235.

income to that of English-speaking whites had *fallen* to under 50 percent.* Despite these discrepancies, however, it is clear that both collectively and individually, Afrikaans-speaking whites were substantially worse off than their English-speaking racial counterparts.

Most Afrikaners probably agreed with an incendiary nationalist tract that their relative economic deprivation was a result of 'pauperisation and domination' by 'the English'.[32] English-speakers stood with one foot in South Africa and one in Britain – 'and their balls hanging in the sea'.† They were slavishly attached to the Afrikaners' 'only foreign enemy' – the British imperialists who had destroyed Boer independence, killed off 25 000 Afrikaner women and children in their concentration camps, and who, under Lord Alfred Milner, had tried to suppress the Afrikaans language.

The economic woes of all strata of Afrikaners were laid at the door of foreign/English/'Imperialist' monopolies – themselves symbolically represented by the mythical nationalist *bête noire* of 'Hoggenheimer'. Thanks to 'Hoggenheimer', the Afrikaners had been reduced to helots, robbed of their birthright, in the land *they* had 'civilised' before 'the English' stole South Africa from them.‡ This presumed 'national dispossession' of Afrikaners is nowhere better expressed than in G A Watermeyer's poem, *Volkshandel III:*

We bled open the very gates
through which trade now richly flows

We hacked wide the open plains
where mine gantries are rooted in reefs;

With Trekker's woe and three-year grief
we measured out the plots

where shopping centres now reach the clouds;
but few of *our* names stand forth

on signboards, or are embossed
in heavy gilt upon the doors;

---

* Basing himself largely on data provided by Stellenbosch economist Sampie Terreblanche, Giliomee at first lists Afrikaner per capita income in 1946 at £266 to £561 for 'English' whites (or 47,4% of 'English' pci) – Adam and Giliomee, *Ethnic Power Mobilized*, table 5, 173. This ratio is confirmed in table 6 on the next page, where the ratio of Afrikaner to 'English' income is given as 68:144 (or 47,2%). However, table 7 (74) lists the ratio of Afrikaner to English income in 1946 as 40:60 (or 66,7%).

† Hence their derogatory designation by Afrikaners as *soutpiele* ('salt balls'). Again, in the macho racial categories of Afrikaner nationalism, *soutie* women were simply lumped in with their partially pickled menfolk.

‡ Generations of schoolchildren were told *ad nauseam* of British perfidy and cupidity, summed up by the President of one of the former Boer Republics, Paul Kruger: 'If the moon were made of gold, the English would try to steal it.'

and when the dividends are declared
in front page columns of *The Star*

we page on – seeking rooms
to be rented from our meagre wage.*

This presumed relative economic deprivation of all Afrikaners, from the chairman of Sanlam to the poorest of 'poor whites', stood at the core of the new Afrikaner nationalism of the 1930s and 1940s. It gave rise to a powerful, Broederbond-organised 'economic movement', designed, in the words of the chairman of the October 1939 Economic *Volkskongres,* 'to mobilise the *volk* to capture control of this foreign [capitalist] system and adapt it to our national character'.[33] And Dr Verwoerd told this congress that taking hold of what he called 'state power' was the best 'weapon' in the Afrikaner struggle to 'assume his legitimate share of commerce and industry'.[34] The Broederbond's envisaged 'Afrikanerisation of economic life' was reflected in the economic programme adopted by the NP in 1944, and which remained a core element of its electoral platform in 1948. Proclaiming 'the Revolution of the Twentieth Century', the NP pledged itself to the expropriation of the great land companies, to 'state control' of the banks and retail monopolies and 'unbridled capitalism', and to slash the numbers of black workers in the cities.[35]

Once in power, the NP set out to address the overall economic position of all Afrikaners and to advance the particular economic interests of all the various social forces organised in the Afrikaner nationalist alliance. Its prime means of doing so was through a particular form of statism. There were a number of aspects to this.

The first was a dramatic increase in the numbers of people – mainly Afrikaners – employed by the state. The period 1950 to 1955 saw the fastest ever growth in state employment (6 percent per annum) in South African history. In the decade after 1950 total state employment increased from 481 518 to 798 545. Afrikaner males were the principal beneficiaries of this increase – their number working in 'public administration' very nearly doubled. By 1970 the total number of state employees stood at 1 105 295 rising to 1 601 158 by 1980. The proportion of whites in state employment rose from 7,45 percent in 1940 to 10,79 percent in 1960, and 13,2 percent in 1980.[36] Between 1946 and 1966, the permanent establishment of the civil service grew almost three times as rapidly as the white population.

NP statism also involved the creation of literally hundreds of new state and semi-state bodies and institutions.[37] As argued above, under NP rule the staffing of official structures was thoroughly Afrikanerised. These state employees were well looked after by the NP government. The predominantly Afrikaner

---

* Watermeyer provoked great mirth among fellow Afrikaner poets with his portrayal of Heaven replete with 'Coloured' servants. J Cope, *The Adversary Within: Dissident writers in Afrikaans* (Humanities Press, New Jersey, 1982), 53.

bureaucrats enjoyed 'security of tenure, cradle-to-the-grave social welfare, and handsome study opportunities'.[38] Over and above the secure employment the NP provided for the predominantly Afrikaner state personnel, its enormous expansion of the size and purview of the various levels of the state apparatus also handed to all levels of the state bureaucracy significant power resources and prestige.

This NP statism not only brought fairly immediate material benefits to most Afrikaners, it also fostered the particular interests of the various social forces organised within the nationalist alliance. The largest of these forces were the Afrikaner farmers whose very name in Afrikaans ('Boers') had become a synonym for the Afrikaner people. The huge influx of Africans to the cities during World War II, coupled with the rapid rise in black industrial wages, had provoked acute farm labour shortages, particularly in the Transvaal and Orange Free State.* Once Verwoerd took over Native Affairs Department in 1950, he moved quickly to deal with this issue.

A policy of strict 'influx control' through rigid pass laws, together with a system of labour bureaux, began to remove the large reserve army of unemployed African workers from the cities and dumped them in the rural reserves. Before any labour bureau could grant rural black workers a permit to work in the cities, it was statutorily obliged to ensure that the labour requirements of farmers in its catchment area had been met. Once the classification 'farm labourer' was stamped in the notorious *dompas* (passbook) of any African worker, it was virtually impossible for him/her legally to change this classification.

These and other measures enabled the state to begin to channel the flow of African labour to all sectors of the economy, and particularly to address the farm labour crisis. Farmers were further assisted by an increase in agricultural subsidies and large-scale state funding for agricultural research. More particularly, the 1937 Agricultural Marketing Act was now implemented in such a way as to secure higher prices for agricultural produce – another major complaint of farmers prior to 1948. Taking 1947–48 agricultural prices as a base of 100, within six years the index of producers' prices had reached 146.[39] Maize producers comprised the largest single group of white farmers, and the key to the NP's new-found political support. Between 1949 and 1952 the government increased the average price of maize by almost 33 percent, and maize production virtually doubled in the first fifteen years of NP rule.[40] However as the senior civil servant in the Department of Agriculture made clear, NP policy explicitly favoured the more efficient and larger farmers, and accepted, in principle at least, the need for a reduction in the number of farming units over the long term.[41] This was to have clear consequences in NP politics by the end of the 1960s (see Chapters 7 and 8).

---

* The *rate of increase* in black industrial wages first surpassed that of white workers during the war. Yet real African wages remained vastly lower than those for whites.

The Broederbond had waged a long campaign in the 1930s and 1940s to 'rescue' Afrikaner workers from the 'claws of the un-national power of the trade unions' and draw them to the bosom of the *volk*.[42] By the late 1940s most white workers had been persuaded that potential competition from cheaper African labour posed a greater threat to their interests than did the bosses. The NP expanded its electoral support among white workers by bestowing on them the benefits of incorporation into the white 'master' race,* and protecting their narrow niche of privilege from competition by black workers. NP labour policy rested on the twin suppositions that white workers should not be replaced by black workers in the same job, and that no black person should ever hold a supervisory position over whites. 'Job reservation' measures now restricted virtually all semi-skilled, skilled and supervisory jobs to white workers only.† The social welfare net available to white workers was significantly widened. White trade unions were coddled, while racially mixed unions were outlawed and black trade unions 'bled white' by the Department of Labour. Taking the real earnings of whites and Africans in private manufacturing and construction in 1947–48 as a base of 100, during the first five years of NP rule the index of real white wages rose by 10 percent while those of Africans fell by 5 percent.[43]

While the NP government thus clearly improved both the living standards and job security of white workers, it conspicuously failed to implement the 'new economic order' it had promised them. Malan's government speedily abandoned its commitment to take a controlling interest in the mines and other strategic industries, to introduce effective state control over banks and other monopolies, and to impose a statutory system of profit sharing. While the NP did expand its electoral base in white labour, it failed to win over the artisan unions or workers in those industrial unions with a history of militant struggle. Growing Afrikaner worker disillusionment with the NP was expressed in the formation of a series of fringe labour parties throughout the 1950s.‡

The redefined Afrikaner nationalism of the late 1930s and 1940s was largely the work of the lawyers, clerics, teachers, intellectuals, civil servants and traders who comprised the urban and rural small town Afrikaner petty bourgeoisie. I have argued elsewhere that, given the central position of such people in rural and urban Afrikaner communities, it was in their daily productive lives that the manifold negative effects of capitalist development on most Afrikaans-speakers were felt most acutely.[44] The Broederbond was the principal organisation through which the interests of this Afrikaner petty bourgeoisie came to be organised and articulated, and through which petty bourgeois nationalists exercised ideological domination over the NP and the other organs of Afrikaner nationalism,

---

* Blacks were expected to address all white males as 'master' or its even more direct Afrikaans equivalent, *baas*.

† The Labour Minister responsible for this legislation was Jan de Klerk – father of F W de Klerk.

‡ The Johannesburg *Sunday Times* library lists 31 'splinter and fringe parties' formed between 1948 and 1969. Seventeen of these 'parties' explicitly sought to foster the interests of white labour, said to be 'ignored in the NP'.

particularly in the northern provinces. It was they who inspired and led the economic movement which stood at the core of this new Afrikaner nationalism.

The bulk of the NP leadership was also drawn from this social stratum.[45] Almost all NP Cabinet ministers, and the vast majority of its MPs were Broederbond members. Once in power in 1948, the NP fostered the interests of the Afrikaner petty bourgeoisie and 'its' economic movement by what a former Broederbond insider and leading Afrikaner economist has termed a sustained policy of 'Afrikaner favouritism'.[46]

Numerous segregationist measures eased the deep fear of the Afrikaner middle class of competition from and contact with a black petty bourgeoisie. The 1950 Group Areas Act was used to drive Indian traders out of the cities, to be replaced in many cases by emerging Afrikaner merchants.* The Broederbond-supervised Afrikanerisation of the civil service also vastly improved both the job opportunities and career prospects of part of this petty bourgeoisie. The fourfold growth in state employment during the first 30 years of NP rule significantly enhanced the position and status of an important section of the Afrikaner population.

Under the NP government, 'the aim of uplifting Afrikaners shifted from helping the poorest to assisting Afrikaner business'.[47] There were two mutually reinforcing dimensions to this central NP project to foster Afrikaner business. On the one hand state capitalism was greatly extended. The public sector share of the economy almost doubled in the first 25 years of NP rule. New parastatals were established and the power and penetration of existing ones were extended. Between 1946 and 1973, the share of state corporations in gross fixed investment in the South African economy rose from 6,2 percent to 11,5 percent, while that of the private sector declined from 63,5 percent to 53 percent – this during a period a rapid real economic growth.[48] Afrikaner businessmen were appointed to key positions on state economic boards and to senior management positions in state industries and key public corporations such as SAR&H, Eskom, Iscor and Sasol.† After a decade of NP rule, just as in the public service, the middle and upper echelons of the wide network a parastatal organisations were virtually monopolised by Afrikaners.

The chairman of the most powerful Afrikaner finance company later wrote that the NP government 'fostered the establishment of state-owned corporations as Afrikanerdom's answer to the somewhat overwhelmingly non-Afrikaner interests in mining and industry' and used the state-owned Industrial Development Corporation in particular 'to strengthen Afrikaner participation in the industrial progress of the country … [and] as a bulwark against the Anglo American Corporation'.[49]

NP rule provided the Afrikaanse Handelsinstituut 'with privileged personal

---

* *Volkshandel,* September 1950. This organ of the Afrikaanse Handelsinstituut was particularly obsessed with the 'menace' of Indian traders, monitoring the number of trading licences issued to Indians. See O'Meara, *Volkskapitalisme,* 167-70.

† Respectively the South African Railways and Harbours, the Electricity Supply Commission, the Iron and Steel Corporation, and the huge oil-from coal parastatal.

access to government and, presumably, some leverage in shaping the economic aspects of apartheid'.[50] The policy of 'Afrikaner favouritism' also included direct assistance to private Afrikaner companies. Interlocking directorships with state corporations gave many Afrikaner undertakings a crucial inside edge. Government and local authority accounts were switched to Afrikaner finance companies, and plum government contracts were awarded to Afrikaner firms. The allocation of fishing quotas and mining concessions promoted the development particularly of *Federale Volksbeleggings* (Federated *Volks* Investments) – the 'official' Afrikaner investment corporation set up at the 1939 AB-organised *Ekonomiese Volkskongres*. A prominent Afrikaner economist has described these measures as 'the redress of imbalance'.[51]

In short, various forms of state support to Afrikaner capital after 1948 ensured its integration on favourable terms into emerging corporate capitalism. In many ways this class force was the major beneficiary of NP rule. In 1948 there existed few Afrikaner business undertakings worth talking about.[52] By 1970, the Cape finance company Sanlam was second only to the Anglo American Corporation as the biggest concentration of non-state economic power in the country, while two other Afrikaner undertakings, Rembrandt and Volkskas, had joined the small group of conglomerates which dominated the private sector of the South African economy. Largely as a consequence of NP policies, Afrikaner control of private industry rose from 6 percent in 1948 to 21 percent in 1975. If the state corporations are included, industrial output under 'control' of Afrikaans-speakers was calculated to have risen to 45 percent of the total by 1975.*

How's Hoggenheimer's business? Managing South African capitalism

The NP came to power in 1948 on an 'anti-capitalist' platform, whose proclaimed apartheid policy promised drastic state intervention in the functioning of the labour and other markets, and the strict state regulation of all sectors of the economy. Given the NP's overt intention to promote purely Afrikaner interests against the then predominant economic power centres, its accession to office struck pure terror in the hearts of most anglophone businessmen. The Johannesburg Chamber of Commerce spoke for all organised business with its 1949 declaration that the NP programme, policies and overall orientation tolled the 'death knell' of the 'free enterprise system'.[53]

However, to the surprise of many of its business opponents, even NP 'extremists' like Native Affairs Minister Verwoerd proved remarkably amenable to the requirements of non-Afrikaner business.[54] The overall effect of NP policies

---

* Adam & Giliomee, *Ethnic Power Mobilized*, 170-1. The assets controlled by Sanlam rose from R60 million to over R19 000 million between 1948 and 1981. Those of Rembrandt and Volkskas respectively rose from R6 million to R6 000 million and R30 million to R5 000 million in the same period. R Davies, D O'Meara and S Dlamini, *The Struggle for South Africa: A guide to movements, organisations & institutions* (Zed Books, London, 1984), vol. 1, pp. 23-4, 70-5, 79-80, 82-5.

was exactly the opposite of that feared by the Chambers of Commerce. Under the governance of this 'anti-capitalist' regime, the South African economy grew more quickly than any other capitalist economy except Japan during the 1950s and 1960s. Import controls and other protectionist measures led to a significant expansion of local manufacturing to supply the white consumer demand augmented by NP policies.[55] According to the Governor of the Reserve Bank, after 1948 monetary policy was changed with a view to achieving 'the highest growth rate with a stable and external environment'.[56] In effect, far from undermining economic growth, the NP's apartheid policies created the conditions for rapid accumulation by all capitalists. Most took advantage of government interventions in the labour market and its decimation of black trade unions to drive down their labour costs. Real African industrial wages which had risen by more than 50 percent between 1940 and 1948 now fell continuously for the next five years and did not reach 1948 levels until 1959. In the gold mining industry, as late as 1969, real African wages were still below the level of 1896.[57]

Apartheid thus proved to be good for every white's business. Whatever their moral and theoretical qualms with NP racial policy, I know of no anglophone liberal businessman who declined to profit from this NP 'interference' in the 'free market', and raise their workers' wages.* The NP government's overall assault on the employment practices, living standards and organisations of black workers clearly allowed a number of smaller and less competitive undertakings to survive and even flourish. The intensified exploitation, general level of profitability and rise in the gold price following the 1949 devaluation of Sterling, all contributed to a large and sustained inflow of foreign capital. Much of this new foreign investment went into an increasingly diversified manufacturing sector. When coupled with the growing diversification of the mining houses into manufacturing industry after the war, this accelerated the process of transition to corporate capitalism – or what marxists term monopoly capitalist relations of production.

The 'anti-monopoly' NP did little to hinder this process. The responsible minister admitted in parliament that its sole measure – the 1955 Regulation of Monopolistic Conditions Act – was 'not anti-monopolistic legislation'.† Indeed, the NP government actually *promoted* the transition to monopoly capitalism in a number of ways. The state-owned Industrial Finance Corporation and Industrial

---

* In April 1970, I heard NP Planning Minister Carel de Wet make the perfectly reasonable point to student hecklers at the University of the Witwatersrand, that his government did not oblige Mr Harry Oppenheimer to pay his black mineworkers lower wages than their great-grandparents had received in 1895. He added that all employers were free to increase their workers' wages should they feel that the latter were not earning enough.

† Cited Davies *et al.*, vol. 1, p. 23. The Bill was denounced in the NP caucus as a 'pathetic piece of legislation which does not give the state the necessary powers to act effectively against the dangers of monopoly'. Eight rural nationalist MPs took the unprecedented step of refusing to vote for this government measure, leading to a sharp caucus debate over whether they should be disciplined: Schoeman, *Van Malan tot Verwoerd*, 118-19.

Development Corporation both encouraged 'rationalisation' through amalgamation and mergers in various industries. Tariff protection and tax and fiscal policies all favoured efficient firms. The fostering of a merchant banking sector, a money market and the overall centralisation of credit and finance all encouraged the trend towards concentration and centralisation.

Thus while the NP government explicitly set out to nurture Afrikaner business, its overall policy climate created the conditions for the rapid accumulation of capital in all sectors. It likewise facilitated a significant modernisation of many of South Africa's archaic, British-derived, business practices. Between 1948 and 1957, real GDP increased at an annual average of over 5 percent. While this dropped to just over 3 percent between 1957 and 1961, in the period 1962 to 1974 real GDP grew at an annual average of 6 to 8 percent.[58] The overall economic prosperity began to blunt some of the edges of the NP's Afrikaner assertiveness in the 1960s.

This fed into other growing tensions in its ranks. While all sections of Afrikaner nationalism's variegated social base had benefited directly from NP rule, they did so unevenly. By far the major material beneficiaries were the major Afrikaner enterprises (see Chapter 7). But even here, the 'positive' impact of NP rule tended to exacerbate provincialist tensions in the entire nationalist movement, and led to sharp conflict in the NP caucus.

This nationalist infighting centred on the question of the definition of the Afrikaner nationalist project, whom should it serve, and which of these social forces was the most authentic representative of the Afrikaner *volk*. During the first decade of NP rule these conflicts took the predominant though not exclusive form of a struggle between the petty bourgeoisie of the Transvaal and Orange Free State on the one hand – also organised in the Afrikaner Broederbond – and the financial and farming interests represented by the Cape establishment on the other. The fact that the NP was also the governing party – representing not only the interests of its class base, but also concerned to secure the conditions of general capital accumulation – gave a particular character to the way in which these intra-nationalist conflicts were fought out in the various political terrains of Afrikaner nationalism. It also meant that these internal conflicts had an important impact on the working out of state policy. Both of these aspects are explored in the following chapter.

Chapter Four

ENEMIES ON THIS SIDE OF
THE HOUSE*

The struggle for nationalist hegemony, 1948–58

J. G. Strijdom
"The Lion of the North"...

The Lion of the North

---

* The title of the chapter is drawn from British parliamentary lore. The maiden speech of a new Tory
MP turned into a tirade against his and Britain's 'enemies' in the Labour Party across the aisle. A
veteran Tory frontbencher is then reputed to have risen to commend the 'enthusiasm' of his 'young
friend', chiding him that with time he would discover that 'your enemies are on this side of the
House. The people on the opposite benches are your opponents.'

The history of Afrikaner nationalism is one not just of ceaseless battle with its British, black and other perceived enemies; it is equally one of long internal struggles and conflicts. The worst of these was the profound *broedertwis* (division between brothers) during World War II. For five long years, Dr Malan's *Herenigde* NP waged a surprisingly intense and sometimes violent struggle for nationalist hegemony with the Nazi-inclined *Ossewa Brandwag* (OB), and other smaller groupings. Many commentators have stressed the ideological nature of these divisions, and particularly the overtly fascist orientation of the OB and groups such as Oswald Pirow's *Nuwe Orde* (New Order) and Louis Weichart's *Gryshemde* (Greyshirts). Still others see this struggle as a reflection of the strategic ambivalence at the core of nationalist political culture – the parliamentary tradition of the NP ranged against various putschist tendencies.

There is truth in both explanations. The liberal Cape nationalism of Dr Malan certainly had little in common with the strutting *führerprinzip* proclaimed by OB leader, Hans van Rensburg. Nor did Malan's dignified parliamentarism resemble the *bloed en volk* mass hysteria cultivated by the OB. Yet ideological differences were not at the core of the dispute. Indeed, the muscular nationalism of such ferocious NP partisans as Verwoerd or Strijdom stood closer to OB ideologues like Prof. L J du Plessis or Dr P J Meyer than to their courtly *Hoofleier*. As the 1942 dispute over the Broederbond's Draft Republican Constitution made clear, few Transvaal nationalists had much regard for parliamentary institutions per se, seeing these as a mere means towards the achievement of the *volkstaat* (Afrikaner people's state).

The real issues of this *broedertwis* were ones that had plagued Afrikaner nationalism from the NP's birth: who was the legitimate spokesman of the *volk*? who was to control Afrikaner nationalism and 'its' agenda – the party, some other, broader grouping, or an amalgam of Afrikaner institutions? Implicit in the NP's self-definition as a *volksfront* lay the claim to be the sole authentic representative of the *volk*. NP *Hoofleier* Dr D F Malan described his party as the 'mother' of Afrikaner nationalism and its struggle for Afrikaner rights at all levels.[1] Regardless of the deep tensions and ideological divisions in the NP, its entire leadership core was determined not to brook even the slightest meddling by other nationalist organisations in what the NP defined as its own terrain and policy agenda. NP politicians saw their party as much more than the political *representative* of the Afrikaner *volk:* it was rather, the political *embodiment* of the *volk*. What was good for the NP was, by definition, good for the *volk*.

This meant that so long as a minimum policy consensus existed within the NP, it would collectively resist attempts from other organisations in the nationalist network to prescribe policy or to define the nationalist agenda.[2] *Within* the NP, it also meant that the mundane struggles for position, for territory and for personal advancement normal to any political party took on the dramatic gloss of a fight for the soul of the *volk* – for the definition of the entire nationalist project. These already considerable stakes were raised even higher once the NP came to office in 1948. Obliged to live the schizophrenic role of a populist and highly partisan political party charged with the good governance of an economy it professed to detest, the smallest policy decision was now minutely examined for its implications for the *volk*. And as NP government policy had a differential impact on the various components of this *volk*, the question of who controlled the party assumed a significance unknown in the NP's days in opposition.

As indicated in the previous chapter, the elaboration of government policies in the 1950s unleashed a spate of internal clashes over both the specific content and the mode of application of these policies. Most publicly in Dr Verwoerd's confrontation with the SABRA leadership, and less evidently in Strijdom's persistent efforts to keep the Broederbond in check, much of this friction boiled down to the determination of NP politicians to keep the reins of policy in the party's (i.e. their own) hands. Space precludes a detailed investigation of the internal Afrikaner nationalist conflicts of the 1950s.[3] In this and the following chapter I focus on but two of its aspects: the 'regionalist' tensions within the NP and the ongoing issue of who finally defined and controlled the nationalist *volksbeweging*.

North vs South

The National Party took office in 1948 far from united. The year-long electoral pact negotiations with the 'Klass Havenga's Afrikaner Party had left deep scars. Transvaal NP leader J G ('Hans') Strijdom had strongly opposed the pact, threatening to resign over the allocation of seats to Havenga's party. When overruled in the NP Federal Council Strijdom had convened a special congress of the Transvaal NP where he used all of his considerable influence to have the deal rejected. Thwarted even here, Strijdom reluctantly accepted the deal, but wrote to *Hoofleier* Malan that he would not work actively for the pact, and threatened to withdraw from politics after the election. Following the NP victory, Strijdom declined 'to make peace with Malan'. For his part, the *Hoofleier* (and now Prime Minister) would show visitors the letter from the Transvaal leader, commenting: 'That's Hans Strijdom for you! He threatened to resign after the election because he could not get his way with the allocation of seats and then he pushed himself to the front of the queue and asked for a Cabinet post'.[4]

The animosity between the two persisted. Throughout the first six years of NP rule, the Prime Minister and Transvaal leader were 'frequently at loggerheads'.[5] In the words of a very well-informed right-wing nationalist journalist:

> One of the most unfortunate aspects of the first years of the National Party administration after its dramatic victory of 26 May 1948 was the clash and later struggle between Dr D F Malan and Mr J G Strijdom. For the uninformed it might sound astonishing that this struggle almost led to an open break in the party shortly after it took power, but those intimately involved in these events know how deep the divisions ran and that they led Mr Strijdom to consider resigning from the Cabinet. So delicate was this issue in 1951, that National Party caucus

meetings were suspended for a lengthy period in an effort to heal the break between Mr Strijdom and Dr Malan.*

This is partly explained by the long-standing animosity between two men born into very different times and circumstances, and 'never on the same wavelength'.[6] Malan had resigned from the pulpit to edit *Die Burger* and lead the newly formed Cape NP in 1915. The puritanical and old-worldly NP *Hoofleier* was never able to hide his distaste for the fact that the much younger Strijdom had first married an actress and then divorced her. As his autobiography makes clear, Malan was not above sometimes cheap means of signalling his clear scorn for Strijdom. Despite common knowledge in the NP that the Transvaal leader preferred the older Dutch spelling of his name (Stri**j**dom), Malan consistently wrote it as Strydom. And Malan's younger wife had 'never tried to conceal the fact that she did not like M. Strijdom'.[7]

Born and raised in the Cape, the 'Lion of the North' for his part, was a small-town lawyer turned politician.† He had come to prominence at the end of his first term in parliament, when he proved to be the only Transvaal nationalist MP who declined to follow General Hertzog into fusion. The now *gesuiwerde* Transvaal NP consisted of 'one back bencher, one Member of the Provincial Council, one former senator, and a group of women'. Now the lone *gesuiwerde* NP Transvaal representative in parliament, this 'unknown and untried backbencher' was elected onto the Transvaal party's triumvirate leadership in 1934.[8] His two other triumvirs were the immediate past chairman of the Broederbond and head of its 'Political Commission', Professor L J ('Wickus') du Plessis, and Mrs E Jansen (wife of the then *smelter* and former and future NP Minister of Native Affairs and Governor General). Two years later, Strijdom became sole leader of the Transvaal NP, with AB 'Political Commissar' du Plessis as its chairman.‡ Hans Strijdom's personal integrity and commitment to and pursuit of republicanism, the advancement of the Afrikaans language and white *baasskap* were single-minded and absolute. His admirers regarded the Transvaal leader as the most principled man in the NP, and one who built the Transvaal NP from scratch. His more numerous nationalist detractors viewed him as a petty-minded man of limited intellect and imagination, elevated by circumstance beyond his capabilities.

---

* Schoeman, *Van Malan tot Verwoerd*, 9. Based on the journal and papers of Dr Albert Hertzog, this book and its equally lively sequel, *Vorster se 1000 Dae*, set out to show that the nationalists who followed Hertzog out of the NP in 1969 were the real bearers of the 'authentic' tradition of Strijdom and Verwoerd. However, Schoeman's later book on the Afrikaner Broederbond (*Die Broederbond*) reveals Hertzog's contempt for Strijdom and his less than starry-eyed view of Hendrik Verwoerd.

† Strijdom was the second Transvaal NP leader to rejoice in this title. It had first been accorded to the founder and leader of the Transvaal NP, 1914–29, Tielman Roos – a man who also cordially loathed Dr Malan.

‡ Prof. du Plessis was briefly given the official title of AB Political Commissar during the early 1930s: Pelzer, *Die Afrikaner Broederbond*, 148, 174.

Strijdom clearly resented the ongoing Cape insinuation that he had become Transvaal NP leader by default. He also had to battle to establish his leadership against the overwhelming influence in Transvaal Afrikaner nationalism of the more accomplished and highly active intellectual leadership of the Broederbond. He was particularly wary of the man from whom he had wrested leadership of the Transvaal NP, its chairman and deputy-leader in the 1930s – as well as the leading force in most contemporary Broederbond initiatives – the AB 'Political Commissar', Professor Wickus du Plessis. Strijdom's unrelenting efforts to establish the primacy of the Transvaal party in nationalist politics could be interpreted as an attempt to protect his own rather limited political domain from both the Cape NP and the AB. The 'Lion of the North' only really emerged as a strong leader after Dr. Verwoerd was appointed editor of the new Transvaal NP organ (*Die Transvaler*) by its Cape Nasionale Pers owners in 1937. Once Verwoerd proved not to be the *Keeromstraat* stooge Strijdom had expected, he remained the Transvaal leader's key lieutenant, confidant and strategist – as well as the *real* power in the Transvaal NP – until Strijdom's death in 1958.*

However the conflict between Malan and Strijdom went beyond the purely personal, to embody firstly their different political styles, and secondly, the sometimes deep differences between Cape and Transvaal Afrikaner nationalism. Malan and Strijdom 'were temperamentally very different ... The much more impatient Strijdom was always striving for a republic ... He and Verwoerd wanted to sweep all opponents within Afrikaner ranks mercilessly out of their way ... Dr Malan, on the other hand, wanted to bring together those who belonged together.'[9]

The *gesuiwerde* and *herenigde* brands of Afrikaner nationalism had always been marked by sharp provincialist tensions. Much of this turned around so-called 'southern dominance' which went beyond the Cape NP's overweening role in the federal party after fusion in 1934. Its Nasionale Pers associate controlled most nationalist newspapers and tried very hard to whip *Die Transvaler* into line in the late 1930s, withdrawing its investment when Verwoerd and Strijdom declined to comply. 'Northern' Afrikaner businessmen frequently bemoaned the *oorheesing* (domination) of the economic movement by the Cape insurance giant Sanlam – itself founded and run by the very individuals who set up and led both the Cape NP and Nasionale Pers. Widespread resentment of the 'southern' (i.e. Cape) dominance of the NP led to many efforts to promote 'northern' interests. The Afrikaner nationalism of the Transvaal NP was more militantly republican than the 'liberal' Cape nationalist tradition. And reflecting its very different social composition, the Transvaal NP was more radically populist than a Cape party then still dominated by many of the same notables who had formed it and its official Nasionale Pers in 1915.

---

* Strijdom had initially opposed the appointment of the then Cape-based Verwoerd, whose private secretary later wrote of their relationship: 'rarely, if ever, did Mr Strijdom make an important speech without prior consultation' with Verwoerd – F Barnard, *13 jaar in die Skadu van Dr H F Verwoerd* (Voortrekkerpers, Johannesburg, 1967), 49.

Transvaal nationalists always doubted the republican credentials of their Cape colleagues, suspecting them – with some justice – of a residual attachment to the British Commonwealth and concern for the rights of English-speaking whites. Indeed, the first open breach between Malan and Strijdom after 1948 centred on this very issue. Malan had 'wholeheartedly' supported India's request that it remain in the Commonwealth despite its adoption of a republican form of government. *Die Doktor* saw this as a precedent for South Africa. But, outraged by the mere idea that a South African republic would retain any links with Britain, Strijdom used characteristicly racist rhetoric to attack his leader's action, bluntly telling Malan that the Transvaal 'would have nothing to do with a coolie republic'.[10]

Many Transvaal MPs likewise doubted Malan's commitment to apartheid, believing – again, not without reason – that much of the Cape NP leadership did not accept the need to destroy existing 'Coloured rights'. They were quick to blame the NP's difficulties in securing the enactment of its legislation to disenfranchise Coloured voters on Cape 'hesitation' and the 'incompetence' of the first responsible minister, Dr Eben Dönges – who succeeded Dr Malan as Cape NP leader in November 1953.*

The underlying causes of this rift between Malan and Strijdom were the very different social composition of the NP in the Cape and the north, and their diverging conceptions of the overall nationalist project. However, the more immediate issue grew out of the changing power-bases and relative weight in the NP's federal structures of the rival provincial NP barons. The intense jealousies and conflicts within caucus and Cabinet turned around a struggle for position, territory and patronage in a party transformed by its electoral triumph.

The 1948 election fundamentally altered the relative strengths of the provincial parties within the caucus. Whereas ever since 1934 the Cape NP had contributed by far the largest number of nationalist MPs (and still 23 out of 48 in 1943), the 32 seats won by the Transvaal party in 1948 gave it six more MPs than the Cape. Every nationalist knew that it was the electoral gains made by the Transvaal NP which put the Malan government in office. This Transvaal predominance in the caucus increased with each election.† Yet *Hoofleier* Malan and many of his Cape lieutenants seemed blind to this new reality. They were unwilling either to reward the Transvaal party for its breakthrough or to grant it adequate representation in the Cabinet. *Die Doktor's* first government contained seven Cape ministers and only three Transvalers – one of whom, Dr Jansen, was leader of the Natal NP though he held a Transvaal seat. Although Strijdom now led the biggest provincial NP, and was effectively the number-two man in party protocol, he was assigned the insultingly minor Lands and Irrigation portfolio.

---

* Schoeman, *Van Malan tot Verwoerd,* chap. 4, presents a partisan Transvaal account of this protracted episode. After handing over the Cape leadership to Dönges, Malan retained the NP *Hoofleier*ship for a further year.

† The Transvaal NP won 43 seats in 1953, to 30 for the Cape NP. In 1958, the respective figures were 48 and 33. Heard, General Elections in South Africa, table 25, 60 and table 38, 83.

His sidekick Verwoerd was so outraged by 'the shoddy treatment meted out to the Transvaal', that he and the entire *Die Transvaler* editorial committee 'seriously considered attacking Malan and the Cabinet in an editorial and then resigning *en bloc*'. Strijdom instructed him to desist.[11] Strijdom and the entire Transvaal caucus were further enraged by Malan's express refusal to include Verwoerd in his first Cabinet, despite the fact that a Transvaal MP was prepared in effect to hand over his seat to the editor of *Die Transvaler*.*

Throughout the 1950s, nationalist politics were marked by the ongoing efforts as the Transvaal NP fought to wrest control of the federal NP, the National Party government and its agenda from the Cape. The caucus study groups were deeply implicated in this offensive against 'liberal' Cape nationalism, and particularly against what many northern nationalists saw as the 'weakness' of Interior Minister Dönges on the issue of the Coloured franchise. This partly explains Dr Malan's broadside against the study groups as 'little governments' working with outside bodies (see p. 51 above). This provincialist struggle came to a head in two successive contests for the post of NP *Hoofleier*.

A perfectly ordinary person: J G Strijdom's leadership

The 84-year-old Dr Malan finally retired at the end of November 1954. In the seven weeks prior to his departure Malan violated all NP tradition and scandalised his own supporters with blatantly underhand efforts to block Strijdom's accession to the leadership. Instead, *Die Doktor* vigorously promoted the claim to the *Hoofleier*ship and Premiership of the 72-year-old former leader of the Afrikaner Party, Finance Minister N C ('Klaas) Havenga.

Malan first announced his resignation at an unscheduled Cabinet meeting he called suddenly on a public holiday on 11 October. This was the day before Strijdom was due to fly overseas for extended medical treatment, and after Strijdom's leading Cape partisan, Foreign Affairs Minister Eric Louw, had already left the country on a lengthy tour of foreign capitals. The aged Prime Minister openly urged his ministers to choose Havenga – provoking an angry rebuttal by Dr Verwoerd. Malan then convened a public meeting in Paarl to plead Havenga's case. In a special statement released only to the Cape NP organ *Die Burger*, the Premier hinted that he would ask Governor General Jansen (no friend of Strijdom) to exercise his constitutional prerogative to 'use his own discretion to ask someone else to form a new government'.

As the longtime right-hand man of General Hertzog, the Free Stater Havenga had always been anathema to Verwoerd and Strijdom. Not only had they both first opposed Malan's electoral pact with the *oud-smelter*, they were also aware that Havenga 'did not favour the republican objectives … [or] removing the Coloureds

---

* Strijdom tried to persuade Malan to make Verwoerd Transport Minister, and Transvaal MP J Wilkens agreed to resign his safe seat so that Verwoerd, who had narrowly lost his bid for election to Parliament in the Alberton constituency, could enter parliament as a Cabinet Minister.

from the common voters' roll in the Cape Province or of abandoning representation for Blacks in parliament'.[12] Havenga had only rejoined the NP when his AP merged with Malan's party in 1951. However, the Transvaal rejection of Havenga went way beyond offended *gesuiwerde* purism. Malan's attempt to block Strijdom's logical succession was perceived as yet another attack on the Transvaal NP – an outrageous attempt to keep the federal NP in Cape hands. Havenga was almost as old as Malan and could only be a caretaker Premier until the new Cape leader, Dr E Dönges, could make *his* move to claim the *Hoofleier*ship.

The depth of the divisions created by Malan's intrigues is clear in the very different versions of the affair later given by adherents of the various factions. Transvaal partisans describe a devious Cape conspiracy to force Havenga on the party, with Malan, Dönges and Cape NP head secretary P W Botha at its forefront. Later accounts by the most partisan Cape politicians speak of their embarrassment at Malan's scheming and claim that senior Cape NP figures privately, and successfully, begged a now deeply alienated Havenga to stand down.

In the end, the 61-year-old Strijdom was elected unopposed and Havenga joined Malan in an immediate and resentful political retirement. Malan's intervention served only to cast a shadow over his own long career. It permanently destroyed what was left of his relationship with Strijdom. A meeting between the two at Malan's retirement home in Stellenbosch was arranged with 'great difficulty'. It lasted but 10 minutes and the two men were 'barely able to engage in small talk'.[13] Strijdom then 'broke all contact' with his former leader, firmly rejected all suggestions that he visit *Die Doktor*, and never spoke to him again. The incident strengthened northern demonology of the machinations of *die suidelike belange* (southern interests) and severely weakened the Cape NP's standing with the other provincial parties. This succession struggle also had unprecedented fallout within the Cape NP leadership. At the September 1955 Cape NP congress Strijdom partisans around Foreign Minister Eric Louw alleged that the head secretary of the Cape party, P W Botha, had orchestrated these embarrassing attempt to short-cut the succession and launched an ultimately unsuccessful attempt to remove Botha from his post.*

Most nationalists regard Strijdom's short reign as *Hoofleier* and Prime Minister as a mere interregnum between the two colossi of NP history – Malan

---

* For a somewhat apologetic discussion, see the authorised biography of one of Malan's closest Cape lietutenants in D and J de Villiers, *Paul Sauer* (Tafelberg, Cape Town, 1977), 111-12 and the official Cape NP version in J J van Rooyen, *Die Nasionale Party: Sy Opkoms en Oorwinning – Kaapland se Handeel* (Cape Town, 1956) 9-11. The De Villiers' second official biography discusses P W Botha's own role and Strijdom's refusal to reconcile with Malan – *P W*, 37-9. See also the somewhat apologetic account of Malan's biographer, H B Thom, *D F Malan* (Tafelberg, Cape Town, 1980), chap. 16. In *Van Malan tot Verwoerd* (Beaumont) Schoeman gives a much more detailed – and credible – pro-Strijdom version of this affair (and a diametrically opposed acount of Botha's preferences and role to that described by the De Villiers), 76-100 and 114-17. For Malan's feeble attempt to justify himself five years later and to counter all the 'fibs' (*stories*) that grew up around the affair, see his autobiography, *Afrikaner – volkseenheid,* 238. On Louw's efforts to dump P W Botha, see Schoeman.

and Verwoerd. In a book dealing with South Africa's first six Prime Ministers, the man who ran the State Information Service under Malan, Strijdom and Verwoerd calls Hans Strijdom 'the single perfectly ordinary person among all the brilliant ones'.[14] Feared for his ruthlessness and long memory for political slights, the Lion of the North evoked neither the deep loyalty nor the status of uncontested *Volksleier* enjoyed by both his predecessor and – eventually – his successor. Never able to rise above his image as a petty provincial partisan, he acquired a reputation for nepotism when he reached outside of parliament to include his brother-in-law in his first Cabinet.* Even prominent Transvaal nationalists were outraged at this appointment.[15]

Nor did Strijdom ever overcome his resentment of the Transvaal intellectual Broederbond leaders whose brilliance and voracious appetite for flashy initiatives had threatened to eclipse his own leadership of Transvaal nationalism in the 1930s and early 1940s. Present in the NP caucus were senior *Broeders* such as Dr Albert Hertzog and (AB chairman between 1938 and 1942) Dr Nic Diederichs. Their respective efforts in the 1940s to organise the Afrikaner Mine Workers' Union and the *Reddingsdaadbond* had sowed the real seeds of the NP victory. Strijdom had personally pleaded with Hertzog to stand as an NP candidate in 1948. Yet he pointedly ignored this rich vein of younger political talent and declined to appoint any of them to his Cabinet – preferring far less competent men whose loyalty to the leader was absolute. Future State President Diederich's complaint to Albert Hertzog was that the 'Lion of the North' was a 'showman', who 'sought applause' rather than 'solving the cardinal problems'.[16]

Clearly in poor health and probably already dying at the moment of his accession, Strijdom did little to distinguish himself as Premier. His administration was marked by a sole political accomplishment – the expansion of the Senate to impose NP legislation to disenfranchise Coloured voters. Yet this cynical by-passing of the Constitution embarrassed even his most ardent partisans, and served to reinforce Strijdom's well-deserved reputation as an unimaginative and heartless racist elevated by circumstance way above his level of political competence.

Strijdom's death from heart disease in August 1958 unleashed another sharp 'north–south' struggle for control of the NP. For the first time in the NP's 44-year existence, the leadership actually came to a caucus vote, pitting the three major provincial NPs against each other. The senior NP parliamentarian, OFS leader, Acting Prime Minister and Minister of Justice, C R ('Blackie') Swart, believed the *Hoofleier*ship to be his by right of service. His claim was disputed by both Cape leader Dönges and Strijdom's political *alter ego*, Dr Verwoerd. A vote along predominantly provincial lines left Swart in last place as Verwoerd swept past an embittered Dönges on the second ballot.†

---

* Naming Jan de Klerk (father of F W de Klerk) to the Senate.
† The first ballot gave Verwoerd 80 votes to 52 for Dönges and 41 for Swart. On the second ballot Verwoerd beat Dönges by 98 to 75 votes. Schoeman gives a detailed account of the internal caucusing: *Van Malan tot Verwoerd*, 8.

The foreigner who was always right

Hendrik Frensch Verwoerd became South Africa's sixth Prime Minister in September 1958, just six days before his fifty-seventh birthday. Long notorious as the NP's most implacable extremist, his victory over the mild-mannered Dönges signalled the end to various lingering liberal fantasies that the NP could somehow be turned from its proclaimed path. With Verwoerd in the Premiership, the implementation of Grand Apartheid began in deadly earnest.

Hendrik Verwoerd's own personality seemed to embody a lethal mixture of the myriad rampart anxieties and insecurities transfiguring Afrikaner nationalism on the one hand, and its supremely arrogant, yet deeply fearful, racist convictions on the other.* The centrepiece of his evolving vision of apartheid was the preposterous notion that the Africans who comprised the majority of South Africa's population were not in fact 'South Africans', but belonged instead to one of (a changing) number of 'ethnic nationalities' – i.e. tribes. This translated into the NP's absurd claim that there was no majority in South Africa, but rather a patchwork of ethnic minorities. Yet this fiery prophet of an exclusively white and 'Afrikanerised' South Africa, this man who sternly instructed all blacks that they were not permitted to consider themselves South Africans, was himself not even a native of the country. Born of Dutch parents in Amsterdam, Verwoerd was brought to South Africa as a two-year-old when his parents left The Netherlands at the end of the South African War and took up life in the Cape.

His foreign birth, schooling largely in English-language schools in South African and Rhodesia, and the fact that many nationalists still privately referred to him as *Die Hollander* (the Dutchman), seemed to produce in Verwoerd a life-long need to prove 'his loyalty to Afrikaner institutions'.[17] Fired by the maximalist fanaticism of the convert whose proclaimed ethnic allegiances were always being questioned behind his back, Verwoerd was also possessed of a fierce ambition. He never seemed to suffer the slightest doubt about either his own destiny or abilities. As a young student he told a number of friends, including a future Judge-President of the Cape, that he would one day be Prime Minister. And during an interview on his 1921 application to be admitted to the Stellenbosch University theological school, he had replied to a query from a senior Cape cleric as to why he wanted to join the ministry, that this was none of his questioner's business, but was a

---

* Verwoerd has been the subject of a number posthumous biographies. Given the intense emotions his politics inspired, the grisly manner of his death in 1966, and the fact that his legacy then became the central bone of contention in the various splits in the National Party, these biographies unfortunately either fall into the category of nationalist hagiography (Scholtz's two volumes) or outright denunciation (Hepple – see Bibliography). The most superficial of them all is in English – Brian Kenney, *Architect of Apartheid* (Jonathan Ball, Johannesburg, 1980) – while the best is probably still the somewhat dispassionate entry in the *Dictionary of South African Biography,*: F J du Spies, E Theron and J J J Scholtz, 'Verwoerd, Hendrik Frensch', vol. 4, pp. 730-40. Yet none has yet adequately captured the extremely complex, driven personality and the extra-ordinarily machiavellian career of the man commonly seen as 'the architect of apartheid'.

matter between himself and God. He then withdrew his candidacy.[18]

Verwoerd earned a doctorate in psychology from Stellenbosch University in 1924. His dissertation bore the revealing title of 'The Blunting of the Emotions' (*Die afstomping van gemoedsaandoeninge*). In keeping with the national metaphor of his adopted people, Verwoerd too had to pass his years in the wilderness – 10 frustrating years at Stellenbosch University, first as Professor of Applied Psychology and then of Sociology and Social Work. His entry onto the national scene followed the publication in 1932 of the massive Carnegie Commission enquiry into the 'Poor White Problem'. The Stellenbosch Professor of Social Work was one of the organisers of the October 1934 *Volkskongres* on this issue, and delivered the main paper of the conference – a denunciation of the effects of the anglicisation of Afrikaners and a plea for 'discrimination in favour of the white worker'. Professor Verwoerd argued that blacks competing with whites for urban employment should be sent back to the Native Reserves, even if no work awaited them there.[19]

Verwoerd's constant need to prove his claim to ethnic purity may well have been tested at another, personally more difficult level. In 1927 he had married Elizabeth (Betsie) Schoombee. Common racist gossip among English-speaking opponents of Verwoerd made frequent reference to the fact that 'anyone' could tell that Betsie Verwoerd's appearance was not as pure white as her husband's ideology. Given white South Africa's hyper-active racial sensors, it is possible that *Die Hollander* heard and was wounded by such frequent allusions to his wife's presumed racial origins.

Verwoerd's first 36 years in his adopted country were lived largely in the Cape. Yet his real *entrée* into the stratosphere of nationalist politics came when he moved to the Transvaal in 1937, ostensibly as the intended instrument of a Cape takeover of the nationalist politics of South Africa's most populous and turbulent province. The ferment in the Transvaal after fusion, and the pathetic weakness of its *gesuiwerde* NP under Hans Strijdom had aroused much disquiet within the Cape *gesuiwerde* establishment. Led by the founder, chairman and real *éminence grise* of Sanlam and Nasionale Pers, Willie Hofmeyr, the inner core of this Cape establishment decided that the time had come to give the Transvaal *gesuiwerdes* their own newspaper.* Though intensely suspicious of Hofmeyr's motives, Strijdom eventually accepted the Nasionale Pers offer to establish a Transvaal subsidiary, Voortrekker Pers, to publish the official organ of the Transvaal *gesuiwerde* NP. Yet Hofmeyr was equally adamant that the new

---

* See Paul Sauer's account in Meiring, *Tien Politieke Leiers*, 131-2. Brother of the Secretary for National Education, first cousin of child prodigy and Smuts's deputy, J H Hofmeyr, and nephew of the revered leader of the Afrikaner Bond, 'Onze Jan' Hofmeyr, advocate Willie Hofmeyr had successively founded the Cape National Party and *Die Burger* (then published in Dutch as *De Burger*) in 1915. Declining the proferred leadership of the Cape NP, Hofmeyr had invited Dr Malan to leave his pulpit to edit *Die Burger* and lead the new party. Three years later Hofmeyr set up the trust company, Santam, which would eventually spawn Sanlam in 1921. See N J le Roux, *W A Hofmeyr: Sy Werk en Waarde* (Nasionale Boekhandel, Cape Town, 1953).

newspaper, *Die Transvaler*, was to be both a moderating influence on the exploding radicalism of Transvaal nationalism, and would remain firmly under Cape control.* Over Strijdom's objection, he insisted that its editor come from the Cape. At Paul Sauer's suggestion, Hofmeyr rescued the frustrated Professor Verwoerd from his 10-year purgatory at Stellenbosch University and named him *Die Transvaler*'s editor – despite the fact that this teacher of Social Work had not even one day's journalistic experience.†

Yet again, Verwoerd seemed driven by the need to prove his own credentials. From his very first editorial on 1 October 1937, the new editor confounded his patron's expectations that he would be a moderating voice in Transvaal nationalism. In one of the more revealing career moves of a man who never suffered fools gladly, Verwoerd hitched his star irrevocably to that of the single-minded yet far from brilliant Hans Strijdom. He gave Strijdom unstinting support, and some would say real backbone and direction, in the Transvaal leader's two-front battle to establish his own position with respect to both the pervasive influence of the Cape, and the young Broederbond professors engaged in redefining nationalist ideology in the Transvaal. Verwoerd soon became a member of the Transvaal NP's Head Committee, and then of the party's Federal Council, 'gaining a strong following in the party'.[20] He also soon moved into the Broederbond leadership, serving through the 1940s on its *Uitvoerende Raad* (Executive Council).

As editor of *Die Transvaler*, so sharply did Verwoerd delineate the line between the Cape and Transvaal variants of *gesuiwerde* nationalism that Willie Hofmeyr soon withdrew Nasionale Pers' investment in disgust.‡ Yet Verwoerd's almost symbiotic and even sycophantic, relationship with Strijdom meant that, unlike many of the other Transvaal Broederbond intellectuals, he always accorded absolute priority to the interests and role of the party in evolving Transvaal nationalism. Verwoerd's personal political opinions were closer to those of his co-authors of the Broederbond's authoritarian 1942 Draft

---

* Le Roux, *W A Hofmeyr.* Six of the nine members of the board of directors were Hofmeyr's Cape appointees. The Transvaal NP had but two members of the board of this, its official organ.

† Sauer not only proposed Verwoerd's name, he was the man who made the offer on behalf of Willie Hofmey to the man who would later become his leader. Given Verwoerd's total lack of journalistic experience, Sauer had originally proposed that the Professor be made assistant editor, but Verwoerd declined these terms. The irony of Sauer's choice lies in the fact that Verwoerd nurtured a lifelong disdain for the urbane and ironic Sauer's brand of nationalism. Using the gratuitously insulting English pronunciation of Sauer's first name ('Paul' rather than the Afrikaans 'Pole'), on more than one occasion he told Albert Hertzog that 'I have always wondered what Paul Sauer is doing in the National Party' – Schoeman, *Van Malan tot Verwoerd.*

‡ When their paper got into financial difficulties in the early 1940s, the Transvalers swallowed their pride and sounded out Hofmeyr on his conditions for renewed support. Yet according to the man who made the approach, Hofmeyr woud offer no more than to buy Voortrekker Pers shares at 38% of their normal value. He also insisted on additional conditions so severe that the Transvalers vowed to sink or swim on their own and cursed the Cape yet again. Meiring, *Ons Eerste Ses Premiers*, 122.

Republican Constitution than to NP *Hoofleier* D F Malan who vigorously denounced the document. However when the majority of the northern intellectuals rallied to the *Ossewa Brandwag* in its conflict with the NP, Verwoerd remained the most outspoken and effective partisan of the party. With Strijdom, he was the most remorseless pursuer of the OB's destruction. Not incidentally, when the NP emerged victorious from this conflict, Verwoerd had climbed to the top of the pecking order among this highly competitive group of political intellectuals. His vigorous interventions against the OB effectively ended the political careers of many of them (see below,). Henceforth they would be readmitted to the fold only on Verwoerd's terms – and as his underlings.

Die Hollander thus came to the Premiership in September 1958 carrying heavy political baggage. He also found himself in an uncomfortably delicate political position. The new Prime Minister was already far and away the most hated figure in South Africa – and not just among the black majority subjected to his racist social engineering. Much of the white population still supported the United Party, and regarded Verwoerd as the man 'whose misconceived policies would yet be the ruin of South Africa'. So intense were the opposition attacks on him and his policies that he had offered to resign at the end of 1957, telling Strijdom he feared he was becoming a liability to the NP.[21]

Verwoerd brought to the NP *Hoofleier*ship his well-earned reputation as a Transvaal extremist. To make matters worse, provincial sensitivities had been deeply bruised by the leadership election. The entire Cape nationalist establishment in particular had a long and unhappy history of dealing with Verwoerd's total conviction of the superiority of his own political reasoning and persistent refusal to compromise. The man who worked under him first for 12 years at *Die Transvaler* and then for a further four as the Director of State Information describes Verwoerd's forbidding political personality in the following terms:

> Did anybody in the course of their life ever have so many arguments as Dr Verwoerd, without [the latter] ever once being bested? It did not matter how well prepared you came to [argue with] him, he usually had the first and always the last word … His memory for opposition and opponents was long and his mercy very meagre.[22]

In effect, Verwoerd owed his elevation to the Premiership to Strijdom's expedient expansion of the Senate two years earlier. Verwoerd's parliamentary career before the April 1958 general election was spent as President of the Senate. Realising Strijdom was ailing, he had sought a base in the House of Assembly in the April 1958 election, becoming *Hoofleier* with just two months' experience in the Lower House. Verwoerd's own supporters estimated that at least 50 of the 73 NP senators voted for their former President in the caucus election.[23] This gave him at best only 48 votes from the 101 sitting Nationalist MPs, or five fewer than Dönges. Nor was Verwoerd more popular in the Cabinet. Many of his ministerial colleagues had been offended by his notorious intellectual arrogance and the growing power of his department. Ben Schoeman and other ministers had frequently clashed with the Minister of Native Affairs in Cabinet.[24] In the run-up to the April 1958 election Verwoerd had come under fire within the NP for turning the Ministry of Native Affairs into a 'state within the state'. Albert Hertzog had told a 1958 election meeting that Verwoerd wished to resign his portfolio as he 'could not stand the suspicion of his own people'.[25]

Yet once again, *Die Hollander* had been protected by Strijdom, who declined to accept his offer to resign. Verwoerd's intimate relationship with the Lion of the North also fostered great jealousy in the Transvaal NP leadership. Only two of Strijdom's eleven Cabinet ministers supported Verwoerd in the election and he was openly opposed by three of the four other Transvaal ministers – one of whom had nominated and another seconded Swart's candidacy.* In parliamentary debates immediately after his election, Verwoerd was apparently so upset by the reticence of his ministers to defend him from aggressive UP attacks that he delegated one of his younger supporters to ask the NP chief whip to speak to them officially. Ministerial support in the debate was still not forthcoming.[26]

However, nationalist reaction against Verwoerd went beyond caucus and Cabinet. Many SABRA intellectuals had been battered by his savage criticism of any who dared question his decisions on the pace and thrust of apartheid policy.† Verwoerd had pointedly resigned from SABRA at its May 1958 annual conference and led attacks on Afrikaner 'parlour intellectuals who venture to question the national [party's] policies'.[27] This was a clear reference to former Broederbond and Transvaal NP chairman, and once leading *Ossewa Brandwag* figure, Prof. L J du Plessis.‡ Other former OB nationalists now in the NP also carried powerful memories of their new *Hoofleier's* relentless pursuit of the downfall of the OB in the 1940s.

The new Premier thus needed to build bridges to many nationalists. He sought to mollify the Cape NP by offering its leader the Finance Ministry, which Dönges had long coveted. Resisting strong personal antipathies, he kept Paul Sauer in his Cabinet, and gave a deputy-ministership to Dönges' right-hand man, head

---

* Respectively, Transport Minister Ben Schoeman and Strijdom's brother-in-law, Labour Minister Jan de Klerk. The third Transvaal minister to oppose Verwoerd was Finance Minister Tom Naudé. The two ministers supporting Verwoerd were M D C de Wet Nel and P K le Roux. The latter declined to second Verwoerd's nomination, however. Schoeman, *Van Malan tot Verwoerd*, chap. 8.

† The virulence of Verwoerd's assault on the evidence given by SABRA's Profs L J du Plessis, Nic Olivier and Dr Gert Scholtz to the parliamentary commission on Separate University Education Act led the editor of the Cape NP organ to defend them as 'having a deeper and more lasting influence on public opinion than most MPs and even many Ministers'. *Die Burger*, 11 January 1958.

‡ Chairman of both the AB's wartime 'General Policy Committee' which produced the Draft Republican Constitution, and its 1939 and 1950 Economic *volkskongresse*, Wickus du Plessis had angered his former committee colleague Verwoerd with a speech criticising efforts to develop the reserves. However Verwoerd's deep antipathy towards Du Plessis went back to the 1940s. The two 'could not stand each other and had furious clashes in the [Broederbond] UR' – Serfontein, *Brotherhood*, 80.

secretary of the Cape NP, P W Botha. And killing two birds with one stone, he offered another deputy-ministership to Balthazar Johannes (John) Vorster – son-in-law of one of the founders of the Cape-based Nasionale Pers group, and former OB general.* To consolidate his own position, Verwoerd now turned to the body on whose executive council he had long served, the Afrikaner Broederbond. He went out of his way to cultivate former OB figures in the Broederbond. At the 1958 AB congress held just four weeks after the NP election, Verwoerd began his speech referring to his own role in the NP/OB conflict as a 'struggle between friends (*vriende*) who were trying to find the road to the Promised Land'. Declaring this friendly rivalry over he stressed his eagerness to 'move forward together'.†

This same AB Congress replaced the incumbent Bond chairman – Stellenbosch University Rector H B Thom – with former OB propaganda chief Dr P J Meyer. This was also widely interpreted as part of the Transvaal's settling of accounts with the Cape.[28] It may even have been inspired by Verwoerd – given his history of antagonism to Meyer, it certainly could not have occurred without his approval. Over Cabinet opposition Verwoerd then appointed Meyer to the key position as head of the South African Broadcasting Corporation (SABC), marking an astounding – and for Verwoerd, very rare – reconciliation with former OB partisans and one of his own major personal enemies.‡ However, true to his past, Verwoerd rehabilitated only those OBs loyal to his own vision. His treatment of his old nationalist enemy, L J du Plessis, bordered on persecution, culminating in Du Plessis' 1959 expulsion from the party he had once led in the Transvaal. One study hints that hounding by Verwoerd was an important factor leading to Du Plessis undergoing a frontal lobotomy in 1963.[29]

The Broederbond and the Transvaal party were Verwoerd's major base in his long struggle to whip the Cape NP into his line. However it was to take him fully three years to establish mastery over caucus and Cabinet. He was finally able to do so by orchestrating two themes whose counterpoint resonated through the early 1960s – the crisis unleashed by the Sharpeville massacre, and the revivalist orchestration of the Afrikaner civil religion during the campaign for the republic.

---

* Thereby consolidating the (then still friendly) rivalry between Vorster and P W Botha. Botha's official biographers find it 'interesting' that although both were promoted first to deputy ministers and then full members of the Cabinet on the same day, 'on both occasions Dr Verwoerd first summonsed Botha and then Vorster to offer them their posts' – D and J de Villiers, *P W*, 96. Ironically, Vorster was sitting in Botha's office when the latter received the call from Verwoerd – J D'Oliveira, *Vorster – The Man* (Ernest Stanton Publishers, Johannesburg, 1977), 125.

† Schoeman, *Van Malan tot Verwoerd*, 182. The word *vriende* translates literally as friends, but was also one of the Broederbond code words to refer to another Broeder in public.

‡ A self-proclaimed wartime Nazi, Meyer gave his son the unheard-of name 'Izan' (Nazi spelled backwards). In a June 1975 interview Meyer told me that he had withdrawn from active politics in 1946 because 'I had run against a wall', and indicated that Dr Verwoerd was the main builder of this wall. Albert Hertzog claimed that Verwoerd had decided in the early 1940s that Meyer's 'wings should be clipped'. Schoeman, *Die Broederbond*, 45.

Chapter Five

OLD BOOKS
AND NEW SADDLES

Sharpeville and the crisis and revival of Afrikaner faith

Striving for a Republic. Verwoerd and the Broederbond

Black South Africans had not passively received the National Party's unfolding vision of their place in the Afrikanerised new order. Throughout the 1950s, each new layer of apartheid was met with growing black opposition. Inspired by Gandhi's vision of passive resistance, and encouraged by the nationalist groundswell throughout Africa, the African National Congress (ANC) launched a series of mass campaigns designed to force reform out of the government. At the opening of the 1960s, a number of rural areas were simmering with incipient revolt and violent protests had begun to shake the cities. The new decade was but days old when nine white policemen were killed in the black township of Cato Manor in Durban. In this context Verwoerd announced that the white electorate would be consulted in a referendum on the desirability of South Africa becoming a republic. At the beginning of February, British Prime Minister Harold Macmillan told a shocked South African Parliament that it had better adjust itself to the 'Winds of Change' sweeping an anti-colonial revolution through Africa and Asia.

Now we are going to have big trouble: The Sharpeville crisis

South Africa entered its then gravest ever crisis in March 1960. The ANC had announced a campaign against the Pass laws to begin on 31 March, to complement its ongoing struggle for a £1 a day minimum wage. Refusing an invitation to join this initiative, the rival Pan Africanist Congress (PAC) precipitously called its own campaign for 21 March.* In the first afternoon of the PAC campaign, panicky white policemen opened fire on an unarmed crowd in the southern Transvaal township of Sharpeville. Sixty-nine people were killed and hundreds more wounded. Other African demonstrators were killed in Cape Town's Langa and Nyanga townships.

The Sharpeville, Langa and Nyanga killings kindled international outrage and massive domestic protests.† Thousands of Africans burned their passes and parts of the country moved into open revolt. A series of local confrontations with the police culminated with a march on Parliament by 50 000 Africans on 30 March – though they dispersed on the spurious promise of a later meeting with the Justice Minister. A State of Emergency was proclaimed on the same day. Marching Africans in Durban broke through police cordons to hold illegal rallies in the city centre. The ANC and PAC were outlawed on 8 April.[1] Opening an agricultural show the next day, Verwoerd was twice shot in the head at point

---

* The PAC had been formed in April 1959 by militant 'Africanists' who failed to take over the Transvaal ANC leadership at its November 1958 congress. See Davies *et al.*, *The Struggle for South Africa*, vol. 2, pp. 297-302.

† The United Nations later proclaimed 21 March to be the International Day Against Racism. Huge rallies against apartheid held in London after Sharpeville led to the founding of the British Anti-Apartheid Movement.

blank range by a white man later declared to be deranged. Somehow David Pratt missed all vital tissue and Verwoerd survived.*

These events provoked a flight of foreign capital. Share prices on the Johannesburg Stock Exchange plummeted. The Governor of the Reserve Bank blamed a £68 million 'reversal in the balance of payments' on 'the riots ... which forced the government to declare a state of emergency'. All business groups reacted strongly. The Stock Exchange President called for 'immediate and positive steps' to restore confidence. The nationalist chairman of the Wool Board urged business leaders to pressure the government 'to amend its policies ... or else'.[2] Echoing this invitation, the leading Afrikaner industrialist Anton Rupert privately pleaded with Verwoerd 'to grant land ownership to blacks in Soweto' or even 99-year or 30-year leasehold.[3] A mid-May joint statement of major employers' organisations (including the Afrikaanse Handelsinstituut) called for the settling of the grievances of urban Africans – such as pass laws, influx control, curfew regulations and the liquor laws.†

In a separate statement, Assocom had stressed the urgent need for policies which 'imparted to non-whites a sense of inclusion in shaping the Union's future'.[4] This led Verwoerd to retract his earlier acceptance of an invitation to open the 1960 Assocom Congress, angrily denouncing business leaders for behaving like 'an opposition party'. Anticipating a similar speech he was to deliver as Prime Minister sixteen years later (p. 195), Deputy Education Minister B J Vorster instructed an AHI meeting that businessmen should 'attend to their own affairs', and leave governing to the government. Later in the year the Prime Minister again denounced 'the campaign conducted against South Africa by certain businessmen' as part of the opposition attack on his proposal to convert South Africa into a republic.[5]

Yet the killings at Sharpeville, Langa and Nyanga troubled many Afrikaners, and led to wide repercussions in Afrikaner society. Alluding to the repeated cry 'My child is Dead!' of Afrikaner nationalism's unofficial Poet Laureate and theologian of apartheid 'Totius' (Prof. J D du Toit), the young Afrikaner poetess

---

* He was rushed to Johannesburg's General Hospital, and transferred the following day to Pretoria Hospital. Nationalists spoke darkly of the inadequate care he had received from 'the English' medical personnel in Johannesburg. The Prime Minister was first placed in a casualty ward with 60 other patients, and his bodyguard was 'visibly upset' with the attitiude of certain nurses – Schoeman, *Van Malan tot Verwoerd*, 202. A senior nurse on duty at the time confirmed that when the Johannesburg General received the first call that the Premier was being rushed in with bullet wounds in the head, 'we all thought it was a joke, nobody took it seriously'. Personal communication. Verwoerd's secretary cites an 'alleged' statement by the hospital superintendent that the Prime Minister "was accorded no VIP treatment. ... To the hospital staff and authorities he was simply a 'casualty', no more or no less" – Barnard, *13 Jaar*, 77.

† Though handed to the government on 12 May, publication was delayed for three weeks. See *Cape Argus*, 3 June 1960. These organisations included the AHI, Assocom, the Federated Chambers of Industry, the Steel and Engineering Federation of South Africa and the Chamber of Mines. For a useful summary of the reactions of various business groups and individual businessmen, see *A Survey of Race Relations in South Africa, 1959–1960* (South African Institute of Race Relations, Johannesburg, 1961), 90-4.

Ingrid Jonker captured the moral revulsion the massacre evoked in some Afrikaners, and eerily anticipated its later consequences:

Die kind is nie dood nie	The child is not dead
die kind lig sy vuiste teen sy moeder	the child lifts his fists against his mother
wat Afrika skreeu skreeu die geur	who screams Africa shouts the scent
van vryheid en heide	of freedom and the veld
in die lokasies van die omsingelde hart	in the locations of the cordoned heart
Die kind lig sy vuiste teen sy vader	The child lifts his fists against his father
in die optog van die generasies	in the march of the generations
wat Afrika skreeu skreeu die geur	who are shouting Africa shout the scent
van geregtigheid en bloed	of righteousness and blood
in die strate van sy gewapende trots	in the streets of his warrior pride
Die kind is nie dood nie	The child is not dead
nòg by Langa nòg by Nyanga	not at Langa not at Nyanga
nòg by Orlando nòg by Sharpeville	not at Orlando not at Sharpeville
nòg by die polisiestasie in Philippi	nor at the police station in Philippi
waar hy lê met 'n koeël deur sy kop	where he lies with a bullet through his brain
Die kind is die skaduwee van die soldate	The child is the shadow of the soldiers
op wag met gewere sarasene en knuppels	on guard with rifles, saracens and batons
die kind is teenwoodig by alle vergarderings en wetgewings	the child is present at all gatherings and law-giving
die kind loer deur die vensters van huise en in die harte van moeders	the child peers through house windows and into the hearts of mothers
die kind wat net wou speel in die son by Nyanga is orals	the child who wanted just to play in the sun at Nyanga is everywhere
die kind wat 'n man geword het trek deur die ganse Afrika	The child grown to a man treks all over Africa
die kind wat 'n reus geword het reis deur die hele wêreld	the child grown to a giant travels through the whole world
Sonder 'n pas	Without a pass*

* 'Die kind wat doodgeskiet is deur soldate by Nyanga' from *Ingrid Jonker: Versamelde Werke*, third, revised edition, © 1994 by the Ingrid Jonker Trust. Published in 1994 by Human & Rousseau, Cape Town. 'The child who was shot dead by soldiers at Nyanga' from *Selected Poems* by Ingrid Jonker, translated from the Afrikaans by Jack Cope and William Plomer, © 1988 by the Ingrid Jonker Trust. Published in 1988 by Human & Rousseau, Cape Town.

Ingrid Jonker was the daughter of nationalist MP and censorship advocate Dr Abraham Jonker. She struggled to publish the volume containing this poem. It was rejected twice by one publisher. Another, whose chairman was Dr Verwoerd, contracted to publish and then tried to force her to scrap this and two other poems. Only the threat of legal action got the volume published intact in 1963 – though Ingrid had to agree to shorten the title to 'Die Kind' (The Child). Dr Jonker later became publicly estranged from his rebel daughter over her attitude to censorship. She committed suicide by drowning at the age of 31 in 1965.

This extraordinary poem and its author are now inscribed in the pantheon of South African democracy. In his first state-of-the-nation address to South Africa's new non-racial parliament in May 1994, President Nelson Mandela said of Ingrid Jonker: 'She was both a poet and a South African. She was both an Afrikaner and an African. She was both an artist and a human being. In the midst of despair she celebrated hope. Confronted by death, she asserted the beauty of life. To her and others like her, we owe a debt of life itself.' He then read part of *The Child* to Parliament, as 'a few heads from the ranks of the predominantly white and Afrikaner (NP) opposition kept nodding'. *The Star*, 25 May 1994.

Other prominent Afrikaners gave even more damaging vent to their guilt and sense of a need for an end to the madness. Twelve influential ministers of the three Dutch Reformed Churches proclaimed their rejection of apartheid as an unethical policy without scriptural foundation, and denounced the racial hatred it caused.[6] A simmering interdenominational dispute over the responsibility of the Dutch Reformed Churches for the thrust and consequences of government policy culminated in the fateful agreement of the Synods of the Transvaal and the Cape NGK as well as the smaller *Nederduitsch Hervormde Kerk* (NHK) to take part in a consultation with the World Council of Churches. Held at the Cottesloe residence of the University of the Witwatersrand in December 1960, this meeting released a statement of consensus known as The Cottesloe Declaration. The statement condemned racial segregation of churches, declared there to be no scriptural grounds for prohibiting racially mixed marriages, denounced the migrant labour system, stressed the right of all to own land and condemned incarceration without a free and fair trial.[7]

The sheer scale and depth of the crisis seemed to have given momentary pause to even the most obdurate white supremacists. When first told of the Sharpeville massacre, Dr Verwoerd turned to his parliamentary benchmate, Ben Schoeman, and observed: 'Now we are going to have big problems'.[8] The then leader of the liberal Progressive Party, Jan Steytler, told a supporter that Verwoerd had been so unsettled by the reaction to Sharpeville that he had seriously considered resigning. He was reportedly dissuaded by the Leader of the Opposition, Sir de Villiers Graaff, who allegedly visited the Prime Minister promising full UP support for firm measures to restore order.[9] Graaff's own version of events claims that, persuaded of the gravity of the situation, he accepted an urgent personal appeal from Verwoerd to instruct the 'stunned' UP caucus to reverse its decision to oppose the Bill banning the ANC and PAC.[10] The then Progressive Party (and former United Party) MP for Houghton, Helen Suzman, says of the United Party during the Sharpeville crisis and State of Emergency:

> During all of this turmoil, there was a deathly hush from the Official Opposition. Under the cloak of the emergency regulations, Parliament was the only open forum from which the country could be kept informed of what was happening. However not one speech of condemnation, not one protest was issued from the United Party ranks.[11]

Whatever the United Party's complicity with Verwoerd, important nationalist voices seemed to hesitate longer than did the Loyal Official Opposition. *Die Burger*'s influential editor called in his 'Dawie' column for rapid action to ease the 'grievances of the urban Bantu', even if this meant 'the large scale changing or even scrapping' of cherished ideas.[12] At the last Cabinet meeting before the attempt on Verwoerd's life, senior Ministers Dönges, Ben Schoeman and Paul Sauer all pleaded that 'serious consideration should be given to scrapping' pass books for Africans. Verwoerd was visibly irritated by the suggestion, and the

Cabinet was divided on whether to agree to a request from the UN Security Council that Secretary General Dag Hammerskjöld visit South Africa to discuss the government's racial policies.[13]

While Verwoerd was recovering from the assassination attempt, many Transvaal nationalists were persuaded that the Acting Prime Minister and prominent exponent of the 'Cape line', Paul Sauer, was involved in a dark conspiracy with various business groups to form a coalition government.* Ten days after the attack on the Prime Minister, and without consulting Verwoerd, Sauer delivered a famous speech declaring 'the old book of South African history' to have been 'closed' at Sharpeville. He called for a 'rethinking' of Native policy, higher wages for black workers and various other reforms, particularly to the pass laws. He also argued that the government should seek the direct 'cooperation' of all employers' organisations. Sauer had shown the text of his speech to Cape leader Eben Dönges and to acting Transvaal NP leader, Ben Schoeman. Both claimed to agree with him, but declined to express such sentiments publicly. Schoeman warned Sauer: 'you are going get into big trouble [jy gaan bars] if you say that'.[14] Seeing this speech as either an attempt to bind the government to new policies, or part of more sinister manoeuvrings towards coalition, MPs and ministers attacked Sauer in caucus.

For a while things seemed finely poised. In April and again in May, Sauer, Dönges and Schoeman were now joined by the OFS' Jim Fouché in arguing to the Cabinet that the State of Emergency should be ended.[15] However possibly strengthened by Sir de Villiers Graaff, and certainly convinced that only Divine intervention had saved him from David Pratt's bullets, Verwoerd issued a statement from his hospital bed that he would not be bent from his course. In another statement read to Parliament on 20 May, Verwoerd responded to all the demands, petitions, submissions and proposals since Sharpeville. Praising the 'good intentions' of their authors, he dismissed them all as lacking 'sufficient facts at their disposal to test the effects of their proposals'. The Government 'saw no reason to depart' from its policies.[16] Just seven weeks after being shot, Verwoerd returned to work at a public gathering to celebrate the fiftieth anniversary of the founding of the South African state. He now clearly sought to rally the *volk* to his own conviction that his narrow escape confirmed his role as God's elected Afrikaner Moses destined to lead his people to the republican promised land.†

---

* Schoeman, *Van Malan tot Verwoerd*, 12. Given the events of the 1930s, most nationalists considered the mere idea of coalition as treason to the Afrikaner cause.

† So negligible seemed the after-effects of Pratt's bullets, that following Verwoerd's first speech to parliament two months after the assassination attempt, a friend of Progressive Party MP Helen Suzman asked in astonishment: 'Good God, didn't that bullet (sic) do anything to Verwoerd?' Suzman replied: 'Sure, it cleared his sinuses' – Suzman, *In No Uncertain Terms*, 68. Verwoerd's apparently genuine belief that he had been saved by God to fulfil some divine purpose led the *Cape Times* cartoonist henceforth to depict the Prime Minister as always connected by a direct line to the heavens.

Saddle up! The republican revival and the coming of 'The Rock'

Under the slogan 'Saddle Up! The Republic is coming', the NP's campaign for the Republic led to a great outpouring of faith in Afrikaner nationalism's civil religion. Yet even this revivalist enthusiasm did not end Verwoerd's internal political problems. Both the nature of the coming Republic and its relationship with Britain occasioned deep divisions within the NP. Broederbond chairman Piet Meyer and many Transvalers dreamed of an 'authentic' Christian-national and thoroughly 'Afrikaner' republic – one both radically different from the racially exclusive parliamentary system inherited from Britain, and determinedly outside of the British Commonwealth. While enthusiastic in its support for the idea of a republic, the Cape NP on the other hand was loath to abandon the parliamentary form of government. And the export-oriented wine, wheat and fruit farmers at the core of the Cape NP support base were desperate to retain access to the Commonwealth's system of trading preferences for member nations. The Cape NP was unbending on the issue of a South African Republic remaining within the Commonwealth.[17]

For once, Verwoerd was obliged to compromise. The NP went into the October 1960 referendum firmly committed to a parliamentary republic *inside* the Commonwealth. Though the ghost of Hans Strijdom may well have been mortified – this was after all the ostensible issue which divided the Transvaal leader from Dr Malan after 1948 – the white electorate was mollified. The NP won the referendum on the Republic with a close, but still comfortable majority of 74 580 votes (52 percent) in a 90,8 percent poll.* Unable to persuade the other Commonwealth Heads of Government to swallow republican apartheid, Verwoerd withdrew South Africa from the Commonwealth on the achievement of the purely parliamentary republic on 31 May 1961. A ceremonial State President replaced the Governor General, all reference to the monarchy was expunged from the South African Constitution, and little else changed in its constitutional arrangements.[18]

The long campaign had allowed Verwoerd to play to the hilt the role of *Volksleier* saved by Divine purpose. The failed assassination attempt had immeasurably increased his standing among Afrikaners. His apparently inflexible refusal to accede to any dilution of apartheid and the Afrikaner fervour during the referendum campaign further increased his stature. To the tens of thousands of ectatic nationalists who gave Verwoerd a hero's welcome at Johannesburg's Jan Smuts Airport on his return from London, *Die Hollander*'s withdrawal of South Africa from the Commonwealth simply solidified his reputation as the proud Afrikaner republican who had freed South Africa, as he put it:

---

* However the 'No' vote swept Natal Province, and all the major cities except Pretoria. While the 'Yes' forces prevailed in all three other provinces as well as in 'South West Africa', their majority in the Cape was only 0,3% (or less than 50% once the spoiled ballots were counted). Heard, *General Elections in South Africa*, table 50, 113.

[F]rom the pressure of the Afro-Asian nations who were busy invading the Commonwealth. We are not prepared to allow these countries to dictate what our future should be ... Therefore, we go now forward alone. We are standing on our own feet.[19]

With the achievement of the Republic, Verwoerd's once-shaky position as *Hoofleier* became secure. Yet rumblings of policy discontent within the party continued. In July 1960, *Die Burger* editor Piet Cillié had argued for 'dramatic' movement on NP policy towards the so-called Coloureds, insisting that Coloured voters 'must be permitted' to elect Coloured MPs, and calling for 'strong leadership' to realise this principle.[20] The Cape NP organ returned again and again to this theme, in direct confrontation with the Minister of what was now called 'Bantu Affairs'. It could only have done so with the approval of the Cape NP leadership. In his comment on the Cottesloe Declaration, Cillié warned against trying to hide what he called 'an acute crisis of confidence within nationalist Afrikanerdom on racial questions'. Declaring that the NGK delegates to Cottesloe were 'no liberals', he warned that the declaration would have to be taken seriously unless the NP planned an all-out attack on the Afrikaner churches.[21]

This was indeed exactly what Verwoerd had in mind. The acceptance of the December 1960 Cottesloe Declaration by delegates from the Cape and Transvaal Dutch Reformed Churches represented the gravest danger to Verwoerd's position and policies. The Prime Minister had reluctantly recast apartheid theory within the more contemporary idiom of decolonisation and self-determination. This allowed NP supporters troubled by the moral implications of Strijdom's simple notion of perpetual white *baasskap* (domination) again to believe in the moral defensibility of apartheid. In the context of rising African nationalism, this meant of course that Afrikaner nationalism did not have to follow Sauer's prescription and 'close the old book' of white racism. By directly challenging the moral (and scriptural) legitimacy of Grand Apartheid theory, the Cottesloe Declaration was a political time bomb thrown into the heart of the nationalist establishment. Should the broader church synods confirm their delegates acceptance of the declaration, church and party would be brought into direct conflict.

Cottesloe thus struck directly at the moral legitimacy of apartheid in Afrikaner eyes. It was a dagger held to the heart of the embattled NP *Hoofleier* and a direct assault on his interpretation of racial policy. Verwoerd threw all of his remarkable political energy into a desperate battle to undermine the credibility of the NGK's Cottesloe delegates and to get the churches to reject the declaration. His major ally in this battle was the new editor of the NGK mouthpiece *Die Kerkbode*, Dr A P Treurnicht. Despite his acquiesence to the early stages of the Cottesloe consultations, Treurnicht now used his paper to denounce Cottesloe as 'an unacceptable *coup d'état*', and mobilised its opponents inside the churches and other central organs of Afrikaner nationalism in a full-scale assault on the declaration.* A campaign of vilification was launched against the unfortunate clerics who had accepted the declaration on behalf of their churches, and the Broederbond lobbied remorselessly against Cottesloe at local level.† Each of the Afrikaner churches eventually repudiated the Cottesloe Declaration and withdrew from the World Council of Churches in protest at its 'interference' in South African politics. Not until the 1980s did the Afrikaner churches again dare question the morality of apartheid.

Though the Cottesloe crisis was finally settled in Verwoerd's favour, the question of Coloured voters proved less simple for him to resolve. This issue still touched deep divisions in the entire nationalist establishment. In the Cabinet, surprising voices echoed *Die Burger*'s call for Coloured representation by Coloureds in parliament. Foreign Minister Eric Louw (usually on the far right of the Cabinet), the man soon to take over the Free State NP, Jim Fouché, and the venerable Transvaler Tom Naudé all supported the idea, as did Cape leader Dönges.[22] The call was taken up by others within SABRA and the NGK. Press reports indicated that an Hermanus meeting of Afrikaner intellectuals decided to establish pressure groups to induce a change in government policy. Discussion groups 'composed of prominent Afrikaners and English-speaking business and professional men' drew up an eleven-point programme calling for adequate Coloured parliamentary representation by Coloureds and the restoration of the parliamentary representation of Africans by whites.‡

Not yet himself convinced of the inevitability of a 'Yes' majority in the upcoming republican referendum, and therefore cautious of any move which might further divide the NP, Verwoerd had to wait before moving to quell the dissidents. However once the referendum was safely out of the way, he took the offensive towards the end of November 1960. Telling his lily-white wife that he was not the man who would lead the Afrikaners to 'bastardisation', Verwoerd publicly rejected the plea for Coloured representation by Coloureds as 'a springboard for the integration of the races, leading to biological assimilation'. A week later he vowed to erect 'walls of granite' around all aspects of apartheid – which by now he had taken to calling the policy of 'separate freedoms'[23].

Verwoerd again mobilised the full range of Afrikaner conservatives in an all-

---

* As a member of the NGK study commission which prepared many of the Cottesloe decisions, Treurnicht had voiced no objections during the preparatory stages. When he later vociferously denounced the declaration to the Cape NGK Synod, senior churchman A J van der Merwe remarked acerbically: 'it's a pity he did not then give us the benefit of the wisdom he has bestowed on us today.' Quoted in A Ries and E Dommisse, *Broedertwis: die verhaal van die 1982-skeuring in die Nasionale Party* (Tafelberg, Cape Town, 1982), 59.

† See A H Luckhöff, *Cottesloe* (Tafelberg, Cape Town, 1978), especially 163-7. This issue broke the loyalty to Afrikaner nationalism of the son of a Broederbond founder and himself chairman of the Emmarentia AB division. Dr Beyers Naudé then became one of the most outspoken and courageous white opponents of apartheid.

‡ *Sunday Times*, 30 April 1961; *Rand Daily Mail*, 29 July 1961. Verwoerd's longtime SABRA opponent, Professor Nic Olivier, was a leading member of this group.

out attack to impose his own orthodoxy on the panoply of nationalist organisations and to isolate 'the liberal-inclined Cape line'. Intense pressure was brought to bear on the dissidents in all Afrikaner organisations. A SABRA congress on 'The Position of the Coloured People' planned for April 1961 was precipitously postponed indefinitely in February. At the regular SABRA congress of that year Dr Verwoerd 'was behind the action' in a purge which replaced its 'liberal' vice-chairman (and member of the 'Hermanus group'), Prof. Nic Olivier and five other Cape academics on the SABRA executive with conservative Verwoerd loyalists.[24]

However the conflict within the caucus on Coloured policy continued. So strong was the reluctance of the Cape NP leadership to force its official mouthpiece to toe the Prime Minister's line that not even the February 1961 intervention of the NP Federal Council could resolve the issue. In June 1961 the Cape NP was forced to call a special regional conference to bring the dissidents into line. However Verwoerd's masterstroke was to elevate the dominant politician in the Cape NP, its feared head secretary between 1948 and 1958, P W Botha, to full Cabinet rank in August 1961. Botha was given the Coloured Affairs portfolio – and thereby the political responsibility for bringing his Cape party to heel.*

This finally stilled the overt criticism in the party hierarchy. However, in calling an early general election for October 1961 Verwoerd provoked much speculation that he had been at least partly motivated by a desire 'to eliminate waverers' in NP ranks.[25] Such wavering was confined neither to the Cape nor even to 'liberal' nationalists. Right-wing white trade unionists formed a Conservative Workers' Party and put up four candidates to oppose the NP – which they accused of having 'betrayed the interests of White workers' and promoting white unemployment by concentrating on developing industry bordering the African reserves. This appeal to white workers fell on deaf ears. The new party won a total of just 6 220 votes and no seats.[26]

The 1961 election marked another sea change in white politics. Whereas the NP had only first won a majority of white votes in the Republican referendum, now, just a year later, it took a decisive majority – 63,7 percent of the votes in the constituencies it contested – to give it 105 of the now 156 seats in Parliament. Electoral support for the NP had now extended beyond the Afrikaner laager to encompass wider groups of white South Africans terrified at the spectre of African nationalism at home and to the north. The UP was reduced to just 44,4 percent of the vote in the constituencies it contested, and only 49 seats in parliament. Its 'National Union' ally won one other seat and joined the UP soon

---

* Verwoerd was well aware that Botha's iron control over the machinery of the Cape NP would ensure the compliance of its members. In the 1958 *Hooleier*ship election, the Cape Verwoerd partisan and senior Cape Cabinet Minister P K le Roux declined a request to second Verwoerd's nomination. Le Roux told *Die Hollander*'s organisers that he was 'rather afraid to do it becuase he would arouse P W Botha's ire' – Schoeman, *Van Malan tot Verwoerd*, 144-5.

afterwards. Although the liberal Progressive Party won 33,8 percent of the votes in the seats it contested, the 'Progs' saw their presence in parliament plummet from the 11 MPs who had left the UP in 1959 (to be joined by an independent at the end of 1960), to the lonely voice of Helen Suzman representing the richest constituency in the country.*

Walls of granite

The NP's 1961 triumph was also a personal vindication for Verwoerd. His leadership had been contested in the party, his politics and persona vilified in the 'English' and international press. Now the election made it clear that most white South Africans were more than ready for his promised walls of granite around their privileges.

Verwoerd was true to his word. State spending on the military increased by 63,6 percent between the budget years 1960/61 and 1961/62, and by just under 80 percent the following year. By the beginning of the 1970s, the military budget was 747 percent of what it had been at the start of the 1960s (increasing from R44 million to R329 million). Spending on the police force too was increased dramatically to deal with the threat to white power.[27] Under the supervision of the new Minister of Justice, B J Vorster, South Africa was rapidly turned into a grubby (and increasingly corrupt) little police state.[28] Vorster's own experience as a detainee during World War II shaped that way in which he conceived and applied his policies to root out the 'cancer' of subversion. As he later told his biographer:

> I realised that if the security forces had to play according to the rules it would be like fighting an implacable and vicious enemy with one hand tied behind your back. I was not going to send my men into battle with one hand tied behind their backs. I saw very clearly right from the outset because my own experiences during the war had given me clear insight into the whole thing ... I knew the whole thing from both sides, from the inside and from the outside.†

Detention without trial, house arrest and the banning of organisations and individuals were used to devastate the black opposition – itself forced to make the difficult transition to clandestinity. The torture of political prisoners became standard practice. Lengthy prison terms and a number of death sentences were handed out to organisers of political resistance. By 1964, the underground

---

* Heard, *General Elections in South Africa,* table 55, 144 (however, Heard gives the number of NP seats as 99). Comparisons of each party's share in the overall total vote are meaningless given the large number of uncontested seats in this election (47 for the NP and 20 for the UP). Using a highly complicated formula, Heard (145) comes to what he calls an 'inaccurate' estimate of 53,5% total support for the NP in contested and uncontested constituencies.

† D'Oliveira, *Vorster – the man,* 130. Vorster also claimed that some of the measures he introduced were biblically inspired – specifically by Solomon's house arrest of Shimei, Kings 1:2, 36-46.

networks of the ANC and the PAC had been wiped out, the various rural revolts brutally suppressed, and the member unions of the South African Congress of Trade Unions bled white.

A general climate of fear infected the entire society as the regime moved to impose strict censorship and close down any questioning of its ethnic balkanisation of South Africa. For over a decade, the only overt opposition to the evolving lunacies of grand apartheid was confined to the lone, uncowed voice of Helen Suzman in Parliament, a very few courageous journalists and to student groups. This was perhaps the bleakest period in South Africa's dismal history. The relentless, paranoid witch hunt for perceived enemies, the morally-blind and fanatical implementation of the smallest details of apartheid, the Mother Grundy censorship, and the imposition of fundamentalist Calvinist values on the broader society, all conspired to reinforce the most mean-spirited, petty-minded and ignorant parochial philistinism in public and intellectual life. These were years when *Black Beauty* was banned as subversive literature; when the Pretoria Museum was forced to close an exhibition on evolution; when 'swimming on Sundays' was condemned as a moral outrage; when prominent theologians could seriously claim that the devastating drought of 1966 was God's punishment for the fact that white women had adopted the miniskirt; when the whole society thrilled to salacious (and frequent) newspaper reports of the prosecution under the Immorality Act of pro-apartheid Dutch Reformed Church clerics, and thousands of other white males, who had slept with black women.

Hendrik Verwoerd's South Africa was a paradise for the satirist. But whites in general, and Afrikaner nationalists in particular, possessed not the slightest capacity to laugh at themselves – and even less for criticism. When the *Rand Daily Mail* ran an exposé of the appalling conditions under which white political prisoners were held, the government hauled the paper into court, hounded its editor and journalists, and denounced it as a fellow traveller of communism. The *Mail*'s circulation never really recovered, and the rest of the supposedly 'free' press was thoroughly cowed.*

And of course for most South Africans, the obscenities of 'moral' apartheid were no laughing matter. Denied all social and political rights, the black majority could only fantasise about the diminishing freedoms left to the white opponents of the regime. For blacks under the Verwoerd government, life was indeed nasty, brutish and short. As Steve Biko later noted:

> No average black man (sic) can ever at any moment be absolutely sure that he is not breaking a law. There are so many laws governing the lives and behavior of black people that sometimes one feels that the police only need to page at random

---

* BOSS agent Gordon Winter claims that the *Mail* was set up by the head of what was then called Republican Intelligence, General H J van den Berg, who planted the story on the newspaper in the first place – *Inside BOSS* (Penguin, Harmondsworth, 1981), chap. 8.

through their statute book to be able to get a law under which to charge a victim.*

Subjected to forced removals from the 'black spots', endless pass raids, the mind-numbing racist bureaucracy in the labour bureaux, Africans were constantly reminded who was *baas* in the land of their forefathers. And as Verwoerd pressed ahead with his planned 'self government' for the 'ethnic homelands', black South Africa was given the news that it was soon to be deprived of even this third-rate citizenship. The *baas* decreed that as 'temporary sojourners' in a whites-only country, blacks were no longer even considered to be South Africans. They would be given 'separate freedoms' in places many had never seen.†

At the head of this all stood Hendrik Frensch Verwoerd. During the last five years of his Premiership *Die Hollander* totally dominated his party, the Cabinet and the South African state. He increasingly came to be regarded as *Die Rots* (The Rock) on which not just nationalist rule but indeed the fate of 'White Civilisation in Africa' rested. Through a vigorous struggle in all the important organisations of Afrikaner nationalism Verwoerd had appropriated for the right wing the mantle of true Afrikaner nationalism, with himself as its infallible leader. A leading Cape nationalist journalist and editor later wrote of Verwoerd's Premiership:

> As if this was the most natural thing in the world, he regarded himself as the leader of all Afrikaners, and as the arbiter of what was good and bad for them. And he did not hesitate to intervene in areas over which he was totally incompetent to judge. Who does not now shudder at his attack on Van Wyk Louw's *Pluimsaad Waai Ver*? [see below p.128] Who would still applaud his instructions to the [Dutch Reformed] Churches? [the Cottesloe affair – DO'M] … (and here I remind myself of someone who said that South Africa has really only had two dangerous men – Alfred Lord Milner and Dr Hendrik Verwoerd).‡

---

* *I Write What I Like* (Harper & Row, San Francisco, 1978), 75. Rob Nixon comments that most blacks 'could enter, with no effort at all, a life of lawlessness: legality was, under the circumstances, the more taxing status to maintain'. 'Harlem, Hollywood and the Sophiatown Renaissance', paper to Canadian Research Consortium on Southern Africa, Research Seminar Series 2-93/94, 5 November 1993, 20-1.

† Even in these 'self-governing' bantustans, *baas* Verwoerd would impose his will. Faced with strong opposition from the Xhosa paramount chiefs in the Transkei region chosen for this apartheid experiment, the Prime Minister nonchalantly created new 'traditional' paramount and other chiefs, using them to overturn the Transkei voters' rejection of his chosen client black politicians in this bantustan's first election.

‡ Pienaar, *Getuie van Groot Tye*, 50. Since Lord Milner was Whitehall's hated pro-consul who had tried to extinguish the Afrikaans language after the South African War, it is difficult to imagine one Afrikaner nationalist paying a more deadly political insult to another than equating the once-revered *Volksleier* with the arch *volksvyand* (enemy of the *volk*), Milner.

While the Cape NP in general and *Die Burger* in particular continued to play the role of the loyal opposition, the forces of the Cape were politically isolated. Verwoerd maintained this alliance against Cape finance and the Cape NP by centralising power in both party and government into his dual role as national leader of the NP and Prime Minister.

This was unprecedented in NP history. Malan had run an 'undisciplined' Cabinet. Iron man Strijdom was too sick to exercise stringent control over his ministers. Verwoerd's centralisation of power led to a shift in the nature of political relations within the NP – between the party and 'its' government and between the NP government and the other organisations of Afrikaner nationalism, particularly the Broederbond. The Cape party was now isolated both within the party as a whole and in the state apparatus itself. These years saw a marked diminution in the powers of both individual ministers and the Cabinet. The Prime Minister took final responsibility for all crucial decisions and often announced these to the Cabinet without consultation. One conservative foreign observer remarked that the *Hoofleier* treated his Cabinet Ministers like 'schoolboys'.[29] Probably his least favourite minister, Paul Sauer, later noted that 'nothing in his Ministers' Departments escaped Dr Verwoerd's attention. At Cabinet meetings he frequently knew more of their own affairs than the Ministers themselves.'[30] His successor told the first Cabinet meeting after Verwoerd's death that 'Dr Verwoerd was an intellectual giant. He did the thinking for each one of us'.[31] His inflexibility often produced 'tense meetings, discussions and interviews which were totally dominated by him', leading more than one of his ministers to label him 'dictatorial' after his death.* The NP caucus likewise had its political independence severely curtailed and was simply not informed of a number of crucial policy decisions before these were laid before parliament.

There is some irony to this. Verwoerd finally secured his absolute domination of all levels of the party via the expedient of working through the Broederbond, the churches and other organs of Afrikaner nationalism to isolate the moderate Cape NP and its allies. So extensive was his use of the Broederbond that during his Premiership, the AB Executive Council under the arch conservative P J Meyer in many ways displaced the Cabinet as the Prime Ministerial policy sounding board. Yet what Meyer and his partisans forgot during their cosy relationship with the Premier was that, more than any other NP politician, Verwoerd jealously guarded NP control over government policy. As the personification of the party, *he* was the final arbiter. The Bond's increased influence depended on this personal link with the Prime Minister and *Hoofleier*. That it did not mark a change in the institutional relationship between the NP and the other organs of Afrikaner nationalism became very clear after Verwoerd's death.

---

* Though none had dared bell this cat during his Premiership. See Sauer in De Villiers, *Paul Sauer*, 124, and Diederichs and others cited in *Rapport*, 21 September 1975.

The striking centralisation of power in Verwoerd's hands was not just a product of his own domineering personality. As indicated in the following chapter, such was the balance of forces within Afrikaner nationalism during these years that the *verkrampte* (conservative/reactionary) elements connived in this shift in the dynamic within party and state in order to consolidate their own position against the Cape and the broader emerging *verligte* (enlightened) trends. However, Verwoerd's autocratic, centralised leadership in no sense ended the contradictions and conflicts within organised Afrikaner nationalism. It simply displaced them into other terrains. If an iron discipline of the majority was maintained in the NP to keep the Cape in line, these conflicts spilled over into sharp struggles in all other organisations of Afrikaner nationalism, from church and cultural groups to business groupings.

Chapter Six

BEHIND THE SEALED
FOREHEAD*

Internal divisions in the golden age of apartheid

Die Hollander

---

* 'The sealed forehead' is poetess Ingrid Jonker's image in 'Madeliefies in Namakwaland' to describe what she later called her *vrot* [rotten] *volk (Ek dryf in die wind)*. Jonker, *Versamelde Werke*, 84, 132.

The years between 1964 and 1972 are sometimes described as 'the golden age of apartheid'. As the South African economy grew faster than almost any other capitalist country, white living standards went through a veritable revolution. By the end of the 1960s, the vast majority of white families owned at least one motor car and employed at least one servant. Very many had their own private swimming pool. Luxury industries sprang up to cater to the exploding white demand. This collective white consumer orgy was uninterrupted by black resistance to apartheid. Once political stability had been reimposed by Justice Minister Vorster's iron hand, the most significant political battles of the decade were fought within the ruling NP.

When Verwoerd goes?

To the outside world, Afrikaner nationalism seemed resolutely united behind the firm and uncontested leadership of Dr Verwoerd. Verwoerd himself increasingly acquired the aura of the infallible *Volksleier* sure of his own direction, and in whose resolute hands the *volk* could entrust its glorious future. Yet inside the granite walls of this apparent nationalist monolith, Afrikaner society was rife with cultural, ideological and political ferment. While almost none yet dared question 'the Rock's' domination of party, government and state, after 1963 virtually every level and organisation of Afrikaner civil society came to be riven by surprisingly acute struggles between the emerging verligte and verkrampte wings of Afrikaner nationalism, squaring off for control of its entire project. The lines of division now began to transcend the largely provincial cleavages of the 1930s, 1940s and 1950s.

Four culminating events acted as the catalyst towards a whole new nationalist ball game. The first was the achievement of the Republic in May 1961. Ironically, the final realisation of this long-cherished nationalist dream removed one of the rallying points, one of the key symbolic props on which Afrikaner nationalism had been built. Now freed of all constitutional links with Britain and 'standing on our own feet' outside its Commonwealth, as Verwoerd put it,[1] Afrikaner nationalism could no longer avail itself of its old British bogeyman to mobilise the *volk*. The leading verligte journalist of the day later reflected that once South Africa became a republic, 'Afrikanerdom no longer had a political definition – the *volksbeweging* (people's movement) was gone.'[2]

Perhaps even more important than the achievement of the Republic was the manner of its achievement. Well aware that the NP had not yet won over a majority of the white electorate, throughout the 1960 referendum campaign the NP Cabinet and caucus had been haunted by the fear that the opponents of the republic might carry the vote.* Despite some resistance from caucus purists, it

---

* Verwoerd told Albert Hertzog that the NP was still 'some 70 000 votes behind the United Party', Schoeman, *Van Malan tot Verwoerd*, 186. On caucus fears that the referendum might be lost, see ibid, 188.

was decided that the NP would abandon its Afrikaner exclusivity and make a clear appeal to 'English' voters 'to create a republic on lines acceptable to all'.[3] Verwoerd went so far as to consider seriously the creation of the office of Vice-President, to be filled by an English speaker. However, faced with the insistence of Albert Hertzog and others that such a step would alienate many Afrikaners, he abandoned the scheme.

In the outpouring of ethnic sentiment during the campaign, few die-hard Afrikaner nationalists suspected that they harboured a viper in their breast. *Volksleier* Verwoerd saw the appeal to English voters as much more than a tactical step. Foreign-born, *Die Hollander* had long held the view that the establishment of a republic would eliminate the conflict between Afrikaans- and English-speaking whites. He believed that the republic would fashion a common (whites-only) *South African* nationalism in which political cleavage would occur along 'normal' conservative/liberal lines. As he put it in his statement on first being elected NP leader:

> *Above everything*, I look forward to the happy day when all of us will be so joined together by a common patriotism *into one people* with two languages that [the] political differences that might exist will no longer be based on [ethnic/linguistic] sentiment.[4]

For Verwoerd, the main cultural objectives of Afrikaner nationalism had been secured with the advent of the republic. Henceforth the NP should concentrate less on pursuing purely Afrikaner interests than on the resolution of the racial question via the Bantustan scheme. He told the 1961 Transvaal NP Congress: 'I see the National Party today ... as a party which stands for the preservation of the White man, of the White government in South Africa.'[5]

This came perilously close to the 'two stream' South Africanism which had led General Hertzog to destroy his own National Party in the 1930s, and as such was anathema to many nationalists. Yet most put this down to electoral rhetoric and gratefully entrusted the divine Afrikaner mission to Dr Verwoerd's capable hands. Even when Verwoerd took the unheard-of step and appointed two English-speaking former United Party members to his Cabinet in November 1961, very few Afrikaners expressed opposition.* The point was not lost on a few nationalists, however. The definition of 'the nation' on which the NP social project of 1948 had been built was now being reordered by Verwoerd. His new social project stressed *white* as opposed to purely Afrikaner unity – albeit exclusively through the NP – in order to achieve the new mission of implementing Grand Apartheid. This was an effective abandonment by the *Volksleier* of the sacred goal

---

* However, such was the Afrikaner/English tension that while both A E Trollip and Frank Waring were reportedly desperate to be appointed – Waring having proposed himself to Verwoerd a year earlier – both initially declined to join the NP. Only when Verwoerd insisted that party membership was a precondition of their appointment did they concede.

of 1948 – the Afrikanerisation of South Africa and the full realisation of the *volkseie*. A few of the more prescient of the NP's ethnic purists now began to have doubts about the long term implications of various facets of Verwoerd's policy.

The first of these was the evolving schema of Grand Apartheid. The granting of self-government to the Transkei bantustan in 1963 led to growing disquiet among 'loyal supporters of the party' that Verwoerd 'was busy dividing up the country into tiny Bantu statelets'. This unease extended to more than a few NP caucus members, and even its Chief Whip 'spent many sleepless nights' worrying over the implications of the 'Homelands' policy.* Hankering after the direct racism of the late Lion of the North, a small group of NP members formed a 'Back to Strijdom' group to promote a return to simple white *baasskap* and the abandonment of such silly notions that Africans had the 'right' to 'freedom' in parts of South Africa. Led by Pretoria University Professor C F van der Merwe, other disgruntled nationalists formed a 'Save South Africa' circle, which turned itself into the Republican Party in 1964 to oppose the NP and its concept of independent homelands.†

This remained a minuscule trend. Very few nationalists would yet dream of leaving the party or directly confronting Verwoerd. However within the highest reaches of NP and Broederbond a group of right-wingers led by Minister of Posts and Telegraphs Dr Albert Hertzog was quietly organising. During the turmoil in the NP at the end of the 1960s, then Prime Minister John Vorster told the caucus that before becoming a full minister in August 1961, he had been approached by Hertzog 'to form a right-wing group against Dr Verwoerd who was moving too far to the left'. Three other Cabinet Ministers and a number of MPs made similar allegations.‡

The core of what later became known as the 'Hertzog group' seemed to have formed around an obscure Pretoria-based secret organisation known as the *Afrikaner Orde* (Afrikaner Order – AO).§ Serfontein alleges that the AO set

---

* Schoeman, *Van Malan tot Verwoerd*, 227-30. In the quote on 'tiny Bantu statelets' cited from p. 228, the use of the Afrikaans diminutive form (*Bantoestaatjies*) indicates contempt for the idea.
† The new party fielded 22 candidates against the NP in the 1966 election, winning 3,3% of the vote in the five Pretoria seats it contested for a total of 8 212 votes. Heard, *General Elections in South Africa*, table 22, 167-8, and table 62, 172-3.
‡ Quoted in Serfontein, *Die Verkrampte Aanslag*, 201. Hertzog and his supporters vigorously denied these allegations. When forced out of the NP in 1969, their newly formed *Herstigte* (Reconstituted) NP laid claim to the 'authentic' nationalism of Strijdom and Verwoerd. Photographs of the martyred Verwoerd dominated the HNP Pretoria headquarters. Yet the party's programme was an implicit rebuke to Verwoerd, advocating that Afrikaans become South Africa's sole official language and making no mention of independence for the bantustans.
§ Formed by Albert Hertzog in 1942 to take the Pretoria City Council out of 'English' hands, the AO rested on the principle of absolute loyalty to its leader, and worked mainly to consolidate national-ist interests in Pretoria. Many of its members also belonged to the Broederbond. The group had a strong presence in most Pretoria state departments and among MPs elected from the Pretoria area – five out of 12 in 1966. Foreign Minister Hilgaard Muller remained an AO member until 1968 when the NP forced the organisation to disband. See ibid, 25-7. For a radically different account, see AO member and chief Hertzog publicist Beaumont Schoeman, *Vorster se 1000 Dae*, chap. 5.

itself the task of building a power-base in the NP in 1963, and that in 1965 Hertzog told an AO gathering which included at least one other MP that it was now doubtful whether they could any longer regard Verwoerd as a 'suitable' leader of the NP.[6] All of this remained very much a subterranean trend until the assassination of Dr Verwoerd in September 1966, after which an open fight developed for control of the NP.

Albert Hertzog had long had an ambivalent relationship with the NP, its leadership and particularly Hendrik Verwoerd. As a member of the Broederbond executive committee during the 1940s, Hertzog had overtly opposed the NP's claims of political hegemony, allying himself with the OB-inclined AB leadership – though not with the OB itself. In particular, Hertzog distrusted and disliked the two men who led and thought for the Transvaal NP, Strijdom and Verwoerd.* Though invited by Strijdom to stand for the NP in 1948, Hertzog formed his own 'secret "circle of friends"' (*Die Afrikaner Orde?*) to run his campaign in Ermelo, thereby provoking much conflict within his constituency party.[7] Once elected, he was shocked at both his own distance from power (he had hoped for a Cabinet post), and how under the 'dictatorial' parliamentary system imposed by 'the English', all the key decisions were made by 'this man they call the Prime Minister'.[8] This self-confessed 'socialist' then organised his own caucus 'study group' in the 1950s and 1960s to fight within the NP for the policies he favoured.[9]

Whatever his earlier reservations about Hendrik Verwoerd, by the 1960s Hertzog claimed to be among the *Hoofleier*'s most loyal followers. He also maintained a deep personal friendship with the Prime Minister. The two men regarded each other as what Afrikaners call *huisvriende* (close friends). And Hertzog was far too sensitive a politician to be seen to question Verwoerd's now virtual Papal infallibility in nationalist ranks. Rather, he and his cohorts seemed to be preparing a base from which to strike for control of the party once Verwoerd retired as expected around 1970.

The then political correspondent of the Johannesburg *Sunday Times* and recipient of leaks from all sides in the NP conflict, J P H Serfontein, has written at length on the Hertzog group's strategies.[10] These involved the secret organisation of supporters and the consolidation of common positions on the key issues of the day. However, their preparations for a post-Verwoerd era concentrated on staking out the parameters of a politically correct Afrikaner nationalist social project, and its corollary, attacking the credibility of what

---

* In a book on the Broederbond largely based on Hertzog's diaries, the Minister's longtime publicist and confidant stresses Hertzog's 'aloofness with respect to the [National] Party' during the war years. Schoeman declares that Hertzog's diary displays an 'inimical' attitude towards the Transvaal NP leader, who acted 'like an idiot'. Verwoerd was condemned as 'a great individualist' marked by 'weaknesses' and 'overweening ambition'. Schoeman, *Die Broederbond*, 21-4. The revelations of Hertzog's private opinions contrast sharply with the same author's earlier attempts to depict Hertzog as Verwoerd's closest confidant in the late 1950s and 1960s – *Van Malan tot Verwoerd* and *Vorster se 1000 Dae, passim.*

Hertzog called 'the dangerous liberal influence on the National Party exercised by *Die Burger* and certain NP politicians from the Cape'.[11]

The offensive began in 1963 with an organised letter-writing campaign in the Transvaal nationalist Sunday weekly, *Dagbreek* (Daybreak) directed against its editor, Dirk Richards and other verligtes.* In November the group proposed a '*Volkskongres* for the struggle against Communism' to be held in April 1964. This congress was clearly intended to lay the rightwing's claim to champion the hottest issue uniting nationalists. The Cape was not caught napping, however. Piet Cillié denounced the congress as doing 'more danger to anti-communism, which in South Africa is currently strong, resolute and purposeful, than to communism'.[12] The anti-communism congress provoked great controversy in NP ranks. The resident government expert on communism wrote to *Die Transvaler* that 'it is doubtful if there has ever been a congress in this country which has had as little to say on the congress theme as this one'. The storm around the anti-communism congress was seen by some as 'the big event which gave an indication of the real plans of the Hertzog group'.[13]

This controversy had barely abated when a second catalytic event served to prod an emerging verkrampte vision into strong defensive action to shore up 'traditional' nationalist values.

Taking the *volk* out of *volkskapitalisme*? The economic struggle

One of the major Johannesburg mining houses, the General Mining and Finance Corporation, got into difficulties in 1964. With his own giant Anglo American Corporation, (Anglo or AAC) poised to take over General Mining, mining magnate Harry Oppenheimer decided that the time had come to open the doors of the business establishment to Afrikaner undertakings still largely confined to working in an ethnic and linguistic ghetto. Oppenheimer also clearly hoped that this would help shore up a moderating tendency in Afrikaner nationalism.[14] In August 1964, Anglo struck a deal with Federale Mynbou which gave the Afrikaans company control of General Mining at a fraction of its value. Mynbou was the mining subsidiary of the Sanlam-controlled Federale Volksbeleggings (see below).

This deal unleashed a furious storm in Afrikaner ranks. Anglo American, and the Oppenheimer family, were the very personification of the mythical 'Hoggenheimer' beast, so long depicted as the major enemy of Afrikanerdom. Verwoerd, Hertzog, Blaar Coetzee and other Cabinet Ministers openly criticised the deal as 'an attempt to co-opt Afrikaners', and Verwoerd secretly appointed the Hoek Commission to enquire into Anglo's vast holdings and role in the South

---

* Richards referred to 'Hertzog's grape-shot commando' – Serfontein, *Die Verkrampte Aanslag*, 8, 51-2. There is a double irony to their choice of target. Hertzog sat on *Dagbreek*'s board of directors, and the newspaper would soon come under fire from the 'liberal' Cape Nasionale Pers (see below).

African economy.* A verkrampte journal later reported that Mynbou made a R10 000 donation to the NP in an attempt to still the criticism.[15] In another right-wing journal, itself later to become an issue of lively conflict in the NP, 'A Concerned Afrikaner' (Jaap Marais or Beaumont Schoeman?) predicted – correctly as it turned out – that:

> The next step will be to build up and portray the men of *Mynbou* as being the real leaders of the Afrikaners and as representing the force of 'moderation' and 'progress'. Other Afrikaner financial leaders will follow suit, and each time a new Oppenheimer–Afrikaans deal is closed, there will be less and less criticism, to the point of disappearing altogether.[16]

The brouhaha over this affair laid bare a long-simmering contradiction at the heart of the Afrikaner economic movement. During the birth and infancy of the economic movement in the 1930s and 1940s, nationalist discourse had been overtly anti-capitalist. The economic woes of all Afrikaners were laid at the door of 'capitalism'. Perhaps the then worst insult in the Afrikaner lexicon had been to accuse someone of being a 'capitalist' or 'capitalistically-oriented'.† Together with all other nationalist organisations, the NP had flirted with the rhetoric of socialism. Some went much further.‡ Yet this fierce rejection of the 'foreign capitalist system' extended neither to private property nor to the outrageous exploitation of black workers – both at the core of traditional Afrikaner values. On the contrary, the problem most nationalists had with capitalism was that it was controlled by 'foreigners' and by 'monopolies' – by 'the English' and 'the Jews', rather than by Afrikaners themselves. The chairman of the October 1939 Broederbond *Ekonomiese Volkskongres* (Economic Congress of the *Volk* – EVK) clearly spelled out the aim of the new economic movement to 'mobilise the *volk* to capture this foreign capitalist system and adapt it to the needs of our *volk*'.[17]

Yet right from the beginning there were differences over the meaning of this *volkskapitalisme* and whom it should serve. The Cape insurance company, Sanlam, had joined the Broederbond as a co-sponsor of the economic movement.

---

* Interview with Beaumont Schoeman, 30 June 1975. The Hoek Report was never officially published. However, Schoeman had access to a copy in the hands of Albert Hertzog. The report's findings form the basis of Schoeman's own denunciation of Anglo American and *Die Geldmag* ('Finance Power'), in his 1980 publication, *Die Geldmag: SA se onsigbare regering* (Aktuele Publikasies, Pretoria). See section on the report, 49-52. This book gives a very hostile version of the General Mining takeover and its impact on Afrikaner nationalism, 78-89.

† Rural cooperatives almost succeeded in stifling at birth the official offspring the Broederbond's *Ekonomiese Volkskongres* by accusing Federale Volksbeleggings of being more interested in profit than in service to the *volk*. See O'Meara, *Volkskapitalisme,* 191.

‡ On Albert Hertzog's self-proclaimed 'socialism', see Schoeman, *Die Afrikaner Broederbond, passim.*. P J Meyer, the Broederbond and SABC chairman after 1958, had published a remarkably sympathetic history of white trade unionism which ended in an eloquent plea for Afrikaner socialism – *Die Stryd van die Afrikaner Werker* (Pro-Ecclesia, Stellenbosch, 1944) The book was favourably reviewed in the Communist Party newspaper, *The Guardian.*

Indeed, the elaboration of the official AB strategy to be laid before 'the *volk*' at the first EVK had been entrusted to a three-man Cape committee appointed by Sanlam.* These gentlemen left no doubt that the aim of the economic movement was to mobilise the savings of all Afrikaners so as, in the words of future Cape NP leader and Finance Minister, Eben Dönges, 'to increase ten-fold the number of Afrikaner employers in commerce and industry'.† These Afrikaner 'employers' were to be paid 'in the jingling coin' of profit. The Broederbond and Sanlam had already decided that the principal official fruit of the EVK was to be a new investment company *Federale Volksbeleggings* (Federated *Volk's* Investments). Sanlam's actuary, M S Louw, confirmed that the new Sanlam-controlled investment company would be driven by profit rather than sentiment. He bluntly told the delegates that Afrikaners had to ape Hoggenheimer: 'If we wish to achieve success ... a finance company must be established which will function in commerce and industry like the so-called finance houses of Johannesburg.'‡

Such was the success of this Broederbond/Sanlam cooperation in the economic movement that when a second EVK was convened in October 1950, the FAK organ reported that the delegates 'are mainly from commerce and industry'.[18] But now the anti-capitalist rhetoric and populist pretensions were gone. Afrikaner capital had been consolidated. The *volk* was officially declared 'rescued' from poverty. The new goal was to consolidate the existing undertakings. Now promoted to Sanlam's managing director, M S Louw announced in his keynote address that this new Afrikaner business 'can only evolve under the protection of an old, strong company, or with the support of the most influential organisation'.[19] Only Sanlam fitted either description. Louw's three-point programme was a virtual injunction to the *volk* that its duty lay in consolidating Sanlam's now wide interests.

Yet within the economic movement, and particularly in the Transvaal, important voices had always contested this claim that what was good for Sanlam was good for the *volk*. The Broederbond had established an *Ekonomiese Instituut* (EI) of the FAK to implement the decisions of the first EVK. However, fears that this institute had fallen under the theoretical thrall of Sanlam's Louw and his collaborator Prof. C G W Schumann, were instrumental in the Broederbond's 1942 decision to set up an association of Afrikaner business groups.[20] The founder and longtime president of this *Afrikaanse Handelsinstituut* (AHI), J G ('*Kaalkop*' – 'baldy') van der Merwe, warned its 1944 Congress against the 'big undertakings' and the dangers of 'monopoly'. He repeated this warning in even stronger language in his farewell Presidential address nearly twenty years later.[21]

Afrikaner business grew rapidly under the benign eye of the NP government

---

* Its actuary M S Louw, Dr Dönges and Prof C G W Schumann, Dean of Stellenbosch University's Commerce Faculty. See O'Meara, *Volkskapitalisme*, 109-10.

† Quoted in E P du Plessis *'n Volk Staan Op*, 114. Interesting in light of their later differences, he was echoed on this point by Dr Verwoerd, ibid, 121.

‡ Quoted ibid, 115. Sanlam's corporate motto translated as 'Born out of the *volk*, to serve the *volk*'. See O'Meara, *Volkskapitalisme*, chap. 8.

in the 1950s (see pp. 139-42). As larger undertakings emerged in the Transvaal as well as the Cape, the earlier anti-capitalist rhetoric disappeared from the mouths of even its most ardent erstwhile proponents.* The longstanding tension over the different interpretations of the *volk*, and who best personified 'its' economic struggle, grew apace. Many small northern traders shared the view that the success of the economic movement was to be measured not in the growth of a few economic giants, but in the advancement of 'the small man'.[22] Fear of Sanlam's size and loosening ties with the *volk* were accentuated by its success in profiting from the flight of foreign capital after Sharpeville to invest heavily (and cheaply) in industrial shareholdings. However, the rising tensions in the AHI were not simply between larger and small undertakings. An overlay of provincialism was also present among larger northern undertakings jealous of Sanlam's size. This was echoed in Dr Verwoerd's oft-repeated claim that 'the Cape' was too close to 'the capitalists'.[23]

The announcement of Mynbou's acquisition of General Mining led to a vigorous battle over the soul of the economic movement. The editor of *Die Vaderland* (and former executive officer of the business-dominated South Africa Foundation) condemned the deal in highly partisan terms:

> So far as we can make sense of these 'breakthroughs', it looks to us more like a breakthrough for the Afrikaner financial institutions which stand behind *Federale Mynbou* – Sanlam, *Federale Volksbeleggings*, Bonuskor, or whoever else – into a larger and more profitable field for their investment capital. This sounds good, but it is also in effect the death blow for an ideal which goes as far back as the *Reddingsdaadbond*: ie. to win for the Afrikaner, no matter how heavy and difficult the going, an ownership position and share in South Africa's mining industry. This [dream] is over. *Federale Mynbou* is only a name: its original character and goal now disappears into General Mining – even with an Afrikaner Chairman – devoured by a greater entity. There will now certainly be greater opportunities, and in time, even senior positions, for Afrikaans-speakers in the mining industry. But the original idea is dead – buried in Hollard Street [the Stock Exchange] in a twenty-four carat coffin.[24]

Economic Affairs Minister and former key figure in the Economic Movement, Nico Diederichs denied all the naysayers, proclaiming that far from Federale Mynbou being swallowed up by Anglo American, through the deal the Afrikaner had 'captured and important share of a world hitherto beyond his grasp'.[25] The controversy precipitated a rancorous and public fight for control of the Afrikaanse Handelsinstituut. A week after the announcement of Mynbou's takeover of General Mining, fourteen prominent Afrikaner businessmen – some

---

* In a 1962 speech entitled 'The role and task of the entrepreneur in the capitalist economy', former *Reddingsdaadbond Hoofleier* and then Minister of Economic Affairs, Nico Diederichs, had no hesitation in insisting to the Johannesburg *sakekamer* (Chamber of – Afrikaner – business) that profit was more important than service. *Volkshandel,* January 1963. Diederichs could not have said such a thing twenty, or even ten, years earlier.

from very large concerns and almost all from the north – sent a circular to all AHI members alleging that 'one big organisation [read Sanlam] and its friends' were trying to take control of the institute. Warning of a consequent 'disaster for the medium and smaller independent Afrikaans enterprises which form the biggest part of the AHI', the circular explicitly inveighed against cooperation between Afrikaners and English business.[26] At the September 1964 AHI congress, the circular's organiser, Dr A J Visser, ran for the institute's Presidency against the new managing director of General Mining, Dr Tom Muller (brother of the soon-to-be Foreign Minister, Hilgard Muller). Verwoerd lent his personal support to Visser, whose organisers spread the word that 'the choice is really between HFO [H F Oppenheimer] and HFV [Verwoerd]'.

In the end, Muller thrashed Verwoerd's candidate and verligte businessmen won a clear majority on the AHI executive.[27] In sharp contrast with its usual effusive reporting, the AHI organ, *Volkshandel* barely discussed the congress in its October 1964 issue. Muller's victory did not end the conflict within Afrikaner business, however. This grew so acute in the following year that the AHI cancelled its scheduled 1965 annual congress, just as Dr Verwoerd warned that the growth of Afrikaner business must never be allowed to be used as a tool against Afrikaner interests.[28] By now the once private conflicts in the nationalist ranks were becoming increasingly public. This was particularly true of what was to become the third catalyst of a new kind of nationalist politics, the now hotly contested terrain of Afrikaner culture.

'Wind through a musty house': Afrikaner cultural politics

The overt battle for the soul of Afrikanerdom began in May 1964. Over the relentless opposition of four members of its Faculty Council, the authoritative *Akademie vir Wetenskap en Kuns* (Academy of Science and Art) finally bit the bullet. Fully two years after its publication, they awarded the prestigious Hertzog Prize for prose to Etienne Leroux's highly controversial novel, *Sewe Dae by die Silbersteins* (Seven Days at the Silbersteins).* Condemning the book as 'the best propaganda for communism', a group of verkrampte academics, churchmen and journalists launched an all-out, and eventually unsuccessful attempt to wrest control of the *Akademie* from the 'liberals'. The *Silbersteins* incident is widely regarded as the turning point which 'first exposed the juxtaposition between the inward-looking and the outward-looking Afrikaner'.[29] A leading Afrikaner critic and playwright later humorously summed up its impact:

> Do you really want to know where a man stands in South African [white] politics, or how much of a churchgoer he is, or if he is *verkramp* or *verlig*, or which

---

* *Silbersteins* tells of the surreal events befalling the promising son of an Afrikaner family during a madcap week spent on a fantastic Cape model farm. He ultimately fails in his quest to meet his future bride, the daughter of the farm, Salome Silberstein. The novel is a parody of the Creation, and can also be read as a parable of the failure and corruption of the nationalist project.

newspaper he reads, or what sections of which newspaper he reads carefully; or do you want to know if he is an honourable man, or has a screw loose, or can be easily enraged, or whatever else you might need to know? Use South Africa's best test question! Ask him: 'Sir, what do you think of the *Silbersteins*?' He *will* answer the question. He will do so, because he will feel he must. And then you will quickly be able to deduce whether he is a Vorster-man, a *verkrampte*, or a 'Sunday Times-er'; you will know whether he is a rumour mongerer or an editorial yes-man, or a follower of *Die Kerkbode* ... Because ever since we began our fight over the *Silbersteins* in 1964, everybody has an opinion on it – even those who have read the book.[30]

The *Silbersteins* controversy touched perhaps the most profound nationalist nerve of all – the one controlling the constant synapses between culture and politics. 'Cultural' issues had always stood at the very heart of Afrikaner nationalism. The protection and advancement of the Afrikaans language was perhaps *the* most important *raison d'être* for the NP's existence. The Broederbond too had come into being in the realm of what nationalists called *kultuurpolitiek* (the politics of culture – as opposed to *partypolitiek*, or party politics), and still vigilantly patrolled its borders.

Yet this again raised the issue of who defined 'acceptable' Afrikaner culture, and the related but different issue of the link between *kultuurpolitiek* and *partypolitiek*. Most were agreed this was the domain of civil society and *not* of the NP. *Here* at least, the Broederbond reigned supreme. Yet *partypolitiek* had a resonance even in this undisputed Broederbond terrain. Ironically, it was Verwoerd himself who inadvertently opened the Pandora's box. His assertion that the main cultural objectives of Afrikaner nationalism had been achieved with the founding of the Republic, and his consequent turn to the English, threw the whole question of the link between culture and politics – indeed the entire definition of the Afrikaner *volk* – into public debate.

Not only verkrampte nationalists were troubled by this development. Fresh from organising the resistance against the verkrampte takeover bid in the *Akademie*, its verligte Chairman, Prof. P J Nienaber, warned the 1965 *Akademie* annual general meeting of growing danger to Afrikaner culture now that the NP no longer gave priority to its defence. Verwoerd angrily replied that 'cultural leaders should know that they can no longer be political leaders'.[31]

However, the entire field of Afrikaner culture was in even deeper turmoil by the early 1960s. Here again, the traditional nationalist approach fell victim to longstanding contradictions now propelled centrestage by the very success of the NP social project. The rise of Afrikaans had long been associated with the struggle to transform it from a spoken to a literary language. Even before the publication in the first decade of the century of the first Afrikaans work of real literary merit, Eugene Marais' poem *Winternag* (Winter's Night), Afrikaner writers had occupied a special place in the hearts of all nationalists, revered as cultural heroes, frontline fighters in the battle for the Afrikaans language.

Of course, a few of them clearly chose political sides opposed to the nationalist mainstream. Marais himself had fought a lonely battle against the obscurantism of President Paul Kruger and his South African Republic in the 1890s. Poet Uys Krige had allied himself with the international struggle against fascism in the 1930s. Although essentially a lyrical poet, Krige's impassioned *Lied van die Fascistiese Bomwerpers* (Ballad of the Fascist Bombers) was a scathing denunciation of right-wing politics of the time – and by implication of the Broederbond, the pro-German NP and the many fascist sympathisers in their leadership and ranks. The poem's entire long third-to-last stanza could also stand as a description of Pretoria's destabilisation policy in southern Africa from 1980 to 1989, and some of these lines wonderfully sum up the underlying sentiment of NP security policy from 1960 onwards:

Sterf! demokrate, republikeine!	Die! democrats, republicans,
Sterf! anargiste, godloënaars!	Die! anarchists, atheists
Sterf! rooi gespuis!	Die! red scum![32]

Some Afrikaner poets, notably Olga Kirsch, had warned of the laager mentality enveloping Afrikanerdom at its moment of triumph.[33] Yet, as a Jew, Kirsch could be discounted as not being a real Afrikaner, and she soon emigrated to Israel. Others also expressed their dissent by going into voluntary exile.* However, the overwhelming majority of Afrikaner writers had always identified with the political struggle of their *volk* – whatever their sometimes acute personal struggles of conscience and retrospective horror at some of the policy turns of Afrikaner nationalist politics and ideology.† Much of the mainstream writing until the 1960s grappled with issues of the individual and collective identity, with the struggle of the new language to establish itself, with the perceived history of oppression by the British and with the devastating impact of urbanisation. With a few exceptions‡ – often encouraged and cultivated by Uys Krige – mainstream

---

* Elizabeth Eybers settled in The Netherlands, but continued to write sporadic poetry in Afrikaans. Barend Toerien became a US citizen, also occasionally producing Afrikaans poetry. Returning to his native Germany, Peter Blum for a time denied any association with South Africa. Breyten Breytenbach effectively exiled himself in Paris.

† N P van Wyk Louw, whom many consider the greatest Afrikaner poet, constantly wrestled with these issues in his poetry (see e.g. his 1930s *Raka* epic and the 1942 bestiary of the subconscious, *Gestaltes en diere*) and in his critical and other essays (with titles such as 'Loyal Opposition' – 1939 – and 'Liberal Nationalism' – 1958). For an interesting discussion of Louw's evolution from a Fichtean to a 'liberal nationalist', see G Olivier, 'N P van Wyk Louw and R F A Hoernlé: Notes on liberal and nationalist discourse in South Africa, 1933–1939', paper to Institute for Advanced Social Research, University of the Witwatersrand, 30 May 1994.

* Jan Rabie composed the first Afrikaans existential novel in the early 1950s (*Mens-alleen* – Man alone), although he wrote it in English and then translated it. But he found no publisher for ten years, and his later *Een-en-Twintig* (Twenty-one, the symbolic age of adulthood – 1956) and *Ons, die afgod* (We, the idol – 1958) were published first. Throughout much of this time, the most creative Afrikaans work was being produced outside of the official mainstream by the 'Coloured' poet, S V Petersen.

Afrikaans literature had become particularly sterile by the 1950s, provoking frequent calls for its renewal.

This was achieved with vengeance in the 1960s. A group of younger poets, novelists and playwrights – many of whom who had spent time in Paris – revolutionised both the traditional themes and now-sterile forms of mainstream Afrikaans literature. Formally coming together in the shortlived literary magazine *Sestiger* (Sixty-ite), these writers explicitly confronted what playwright Bartho Smit called the 'crisis in our concept of reality'.* They were a disparate literary circle. Some, like Smit and novelist Etienne Leroux were staunch nationalists, who remained loyal to the NP throughout the ructions caused by their work.† Others like Jan Rabie and Ingrid Jonker had already moved into open dissent, soon to be followed by André Brink and Breyten Breytenbach.

The *Sestigers* were initially more concerned with form than with what Smit called 'undermining themes'. Nevertheless their feverish literary experimentation swept like a gale through the musty house of Afrikaner culture, blowing down what *Sestiger* chief editor Brink labelled the 'ornamental burial urn' of official culture.[34] By European and American standards, their work would hardly have been considered *avant-garde*. And while surprisingly little of it was yet explicitly political, many *Sestigers* were revolted by the smug, provincial materialism of the newly emerging Afrikaner urban middle class.‡ Especially in their exploration of the *anomie* and alienation of mass society, and in the first timid treatment of sexuality, the *Sestigers* went where no other Afrikaner writers had dared go before:

> At heart, *Sestiger* was a tentative grouping towards independence. The younger and more radical followers of the group wished to rid themselves of authority, to speak in their own authentic voice. André Brink desired, among other things, to introduce full and frank sex into fiction, Rabie to carry his skirmishes against

---

* Quoted J Cope, *The Adversary Within*, 143. Here again strike the manifold ironies of Afrikaner nationalism. The group was originally given a moribund right-wing magazine, *Sestig* (Sixty) in an attempt to draw younger Afrikaner writers out of the clutches of the liberal literary journal *Contrast*. When the initial editorial committee included 'Coloured' poet Adam Small, the magazine's owners demanded his removal. The committee, including its nationalist members, refused and modified the name of their new journal. It lasted two stormy years before falling under the control of Afrikaanse Pers, whose chairman was Dr Verwoerd. See ibid, 100.

† Smit was the head of the literature department of the powerful Transvaal nationalist publishing house, Perskor. Even the virtual total ban on the professional staging of his work from 1962 to the mid-1980s could not propel him to abandon the nationalist cause. See Cope, *The Adversary Within*, 143-64. Etienne Leroux was the pen name of Stephen le Roux, the son of NP Cabinet Minister, S P le Roux.

‡ Particularly Rabie, Jonker, Brink and Breytenbach. Brink later built an entire novel around his disgust for the new Afrikaner bourgeoisie – *Gerugte van Reen* (Human & Rousseau, Cape Town, 1978 – published in English as 'Rumours of Rain'). For another poisonous portrait (by a non-Afrikaner) of the pseudo-sophistication of the new urban Afrikaner elite, see the character Brandt Vermeulen in Nadine Gordimer's novel, *Burger's Daughter* (Viking Press, New York, 1979).

racism and historic misconceptions into the hearts of his contemporaries, Ingrid Jonker 'to hide away in the violence of a simple recollection', Etienne Leroux to laugh with the devil at the fear surrounding him. Those [*Sestigers*] on the right, including even adherents of the Broederbond, might drag their feet in public, but in the silence of their creative work they could express a stubborn self-will, displaying what Brink detected as the schizophrenia running through the Afrikaans writers of all persuasions.[35]

The *Sestigers* polarised the staid Afrikaner cultural establishment. A few echoed N P van Wyk Louw's delight at this vigorous literary renewal, and themselves began to pursue other previously taboo subjects. A less adventurous majority hesitantly swallowed their doubts, and with the granting of the 1964 Hertzog Prize to Leroux's *Silbersteins*, nervously admitted the *Sestigers* into the official Pantheon. But a deeply offended minority regarded these writers as dangerous cosmopolitan degenerates and their coronation as proof of a dire internal threat to the integrity of Afrikaner culture and nationalism.

The verkramptes now went to cultural war. Led by the chairman of the Pretoria Division of the Broederbond, director of the Afrika-Instituut, and former SABRA and *Akademie* chairman, Professor P F D Weiss, they launched an offensive to protect what Weiss called 'authentic Afrikaner cultural values' against 'liberal and communistic infiltration'.[36] When they failed to take over the Akademie they formed themselves into the *Christelike Kultuuraksie* (Christian Cultural Action – CKA) and vigorously contested the 'right' of the *Akademie* to play a leadership role in Afrikaner culture. Yet they made another unsuccessful bid for control of the *Akademie* in 1967.

The remainder of the 1960s saw an all-out battle for the control of Afrikaner cultural institutions and the definition of 'acceptable' Afrikaner culture. The Broederbond, the churches, the Afrikaans press, politicians and eventually the NP itself were all drawn into this struggle. The verkramptes were successful in preventing the now verligte *Akademie* from awarding the 1966 Hertzog Prize to the 'leftist' Uys Krige. Then Justice Minister Vorster warned: 'Award him, and you'll get hurt.'[37] This remorseless hounding of whatever and whomever the verkramptes considered 'liberal' spared nobody. When Dr Verwoerd attacked the political deviationism of a play by Afrikanerdom's national poet, N P van Wyk Louw, the verkrampte literary warriors declared open season on Louw and his works.* Yet here too they bit off more than they could chew. Playing on the Afrikaans pronunciation of the name of the self-appointed verkrampte cultural commissar, Professor Weiss (and his equally shrill wife), Louw savaged the

---

* Verwoerd's attack took place at the same ceremony where Vorster had bullied the *Akademie* – the official celebration of the Republic's fifth anniversary held on the hallowed ground of the Voortrekker Monument. Louw had been commissioned to write a play for the occasion. Though deeply patriotic in tone, *Die Pluimsaad Waai* was a more rounded depiction of the strength and failings of the Boers in the Anglo-Boer War than the usual hagiography. Verwoerd expressed a wish for a generation of writers who would 'also praise the achievements of our *volk'*.

cultural pretensions of this 'Weiss-squad', declaring their accumulated talents insufficient to produce even 'one decent little short story'.*

Despite Verwoerd and Vorster's interventions, most NP politicians were reluctant to become embroiled in the desperate cultural skirmishes. However, this was not the case with the opening up of a fourth terrain of struggle, one which itself aggravated all of these conflicts and finally forced them into public attention.

The Empire strikes back: *Keeromstraat* and the great Afrikaner press war

The 'provincialist' strains in Afrikaner nationalism had always been closely linked to the fortunes of its press groups. One of the important reasons for this after 1948 was that the capture of the *Hoofleier*ship by north or south brought with it very lucrative government printing contracts for the house publisher of the victorious province.† During the conflicts of the early 1950, the Cape Nasionale Pers group had made a number of attempts to set up its own newspaper in the north. Defending his patch with his habitual tenacity, Transvaal leader and later *Hoofleier* Strijdom finally scuttled the *Keeromstraat* initiative 'by ensuring that the required import permit for the necessary newsprint was refused'.[38] Yet the north was at a disadvantage in the press wars. While *Keeromstraat* had an absolute monopoly in its Cape bailiwick, and also published the organ of the Free State NP (*Die Volksblad*), in the Transvaal three separate nationalist press groups each produced their own newspaper, and stood in differing relationships with the provincial NP.‡

Following its numerous political reversals in the early 1960s, and faced with the threat that *Dagbreek* would launch a national Sunday newspaper, in 1965 *Keeromstraat* tried again to do what it had failed to do with the selection of Verwoerd as *Die Transvaler* editor in 1937, and again in 1953 – to 'let the voice of the Cape be heard in the north'. To Verwoerd's rage, and over his express inter-

---

* *Die Burger,* 31 January 1967. Again, the use of the diminutive *(kortverhaaltjie)* reinforced Louw's contempt for his opponents. When, in April 1968, another verkrampte proposed the establishment of a Verwoerd Prize for 'patriotic literature', Louw castigated this as akin to a 'Stalin Prize' and led most of the literary establishment in a successful fight against the proposal.

† Thus, e.g. 98 % of the R3m spent by Department of Information on publications in 1977 was awarded by the responsible minister – the Transvaal NP leader and member of the Perskor board, Dr Connie Mulder – to the Transvaal nationalist press group, Perskor – *New York Times,* 10 May 1978. And this amount was peanuts in the overall state printing expenditure.

‡ Thus, with the Transvaal leader as chairman of its board, Voortrekker Pers published the Transvaal NP organ, *Die Transvaler.* Under its chairman Prof L J du Plessis, Dagbreektrust put out the former OB-inclined Sunday weekly, *Dagbreek.* The paper moved closer to the NP after 1951, and Strijdom organised a consortium to buy up a large shareholding in 1953 to become chairman of its board. First set up by General Hertzog and then controlled by Havenga, Afrikaanse Pers published the evening daily *Die Vaderland.* The latter two groups merged in 1962 to form Afrikaanse Pers (1962) Beperk, which merged with Voortrekker Pers in 1972 to form the giant Transvaal Perskor group.

diction, a Nasionale Pers Sunday newspaper, *Die Beeld* (The Image), started publication in Johannesburg at the end of October 1965. Verwoerd refused ever to read the paper, and the head secretary of the Transvaal NP, Jack Steyl, instructed his officials and organisers that a decision had been taken to boycott the paper.*

Like the *Sestigers* in the cultural field, *Die Beeld* brought a refreshingly new style and focus to the deadly dull world of official Afrikaner journalism. While entirely loyal to the NP, and clearly avoiding overt provincialism, it also began to report on what was previously never discussed in public – internal nationalist conflicts. In particular, it took up the *Sunday Times* campaign against the 'white-anting tactics' of the Hertzog group. In the pages of *Die Beeld*, nationalist politics now became news rather than a ritual incantation of faith.

Its coming provoked a furor in nationalist ranks. The verkramptes were enraged that the hated *Keeromstraat* had dared first to enter their protected Transvaal bailiwick, and then to publicise their activities. Using other Afrikaans newspapers – particular *Die Vaderland* and the new Pretoria daily, *Hoofstad* (Capital City), edited by arch conservative Dr Andries Treurnicht – they launched a four-year offensive to drive *Keeromstraat* out of the Transvaal, and the 'liberals' out of Afrikaner nationalism.

But the verkramptes were not the only nationalists offended by the blatant Cape incursion into Transvaal territory. Once again, the recurrent ironies of Afrikaner nationalism assert themselves. The principal loser in *Die Beeld*'s arrival was *Dagbreek*, whose verligte editor, Dirk Richards, had himself been among the earliest verkrampte targets. The circulation war between the two newspapers was a costly and sordid business. Richards estimated that together, *Dagbreek* and *Die Beeld* were losing the then enormous sum of R1,25 million annually. Richards's increasingly frantic attempts to save his newspaper led to openly provincialist attacks on *Keeromstraat*, both by himself and the verkramptes he despised.†

This great Afrikaner press war provoked great tension and unheard, of conflict in the NP. Old north–south rivalries resurfaced. Transvaal leader Ben Schoeman angrily denounced Cape leader P W Botha as 'a simple mouthpiece of Keeromstraat'.‡ But these tensions were soon overlaid by the new concern with the open verkrampte attempt to proscribe the limits of politically correct

---

* Verwoerd wore (and used) at least four of his hats – Prime Minister, *Hoofleier,* Transvaal leader and chairman of both northern press groups – in his attempt to prevent this incursion as 'politically undesirable' and one likely to provoke 'political consequences … repercussions and conflict'. The Nasionale Pers board bluntly told him that he was confusing his various roles. Pienaar, *Getuie van Groot Tye,* 46-9.

† See, e.g. Richards's columns entitled 'Where is this great press struggle leading us?', *Dagbreek,* 3 July 1966; 'Where is *Keeromstraat* leading us?', 17 September 1967; and 'special correspondent' (i.e. Beaumont Schoeman), '*Nasionale Pers* comes north in search of what has been lost by the South', 15 October 1967. In 1967 *Dagbreek* took over the sensationalist *Die Landstem* (the Voice of the Country) and renamed itself *Dagbreek and Landstem.*

‡ (Beaumont) Schoeman, *Vorster se 1000 Dae,* 246. Ben Schoeman became Transvaal NP leader in 1966, and P W Botha took over the Cape leadership in the same year.

nationalism, and to shape government policy after the assassination of Dr Verwoerd. The press war was an essential factor in forcing the Hertzog group into the open, and exposing its tactics, as the whole issue of 'group formation' in the party rapidly became a major political news story. The details of this conflict can be read elsewhere.[39] Suffice it here to say that the press war of the 1960s was the catalyst leading to the open 'verligte/verkrampte struggle' in the NP and its expulsion of Hertzog and his followers in 1969. And despite the provincialist overtones of the press war, the broader conflict between these two emerging visions of Afrikaner nationalism now cut right across provincial lines, leading to new alliances in nationalist politics.

The press war also marked another turning point in the development of Afrikaner nationalism. Whatever the original political motivations of *Keeromstraat*, as business undertakings, both Nasionale Pers and its various Transvaal competitors were ultimately driven by commercial considerations. The dynamic and imperatives of a nakedly capitalist battle for circulation between two nationalist press groups was eventually allowed to achieve the once inconceivable and rupture Afrikaner nationalism's most precious and hard-built political asset – Afrikaner *volkseenheid* (unity of the *volk*). Thanks to the commercial needs of the southern and northern press groups, Dr Malan's famous aphorism – *Bring bymekaar wie bymekaar hoort!* (bring together those who belong together) – seemed now to have been corrupted into *bring by die bank wat by die bank hoort* (bring to the bank what belongs in the bank).

The short- and medium-term political consequences of this sea change are explored in Part II.

PART II

NEW BOTTLE, SOURING WINE

'Jolly John' Vorster and the crisis of apartheid

Die vroegre boere paradijs
is nou één molshoop, groot en grijs.
TOTIUS: Trekkerswee

Our former rural paradise
is now one great, grey molehill.
TOTIUS: *Trekkerswee*

Uit tonnels van die nag tuur
ek oor rook en mis as ysterspore
my in kringe van die stad instuur.

Out through tunnels of the night I peer
and through smoke and mist as iron rails
steer me into the radius of the city.

Teen dakke en skoorstene blink
die son, soos in 'n leeggelopte dam
op bottleskerwe en geroeste sink ...

The sun glints againt roofs and chimneys
like an emptied dam
on bottle shards and rusted zink ...

Uitendelik valse sysfers neergekrap
kon ek uit vet van viskafees
na 'n paradyis ontsnap.

By scribbling down false figures
I finally escaped from the fat of fish & chips shops
to find a paradise.

Na tuine van die nag, waar neonligte blom,
het ek met haar gevlug; maar by my was
die vrees – die rekenmeester kom.

Then I fled with her to gardens of the night
where neon lights bloom; but with me always was
the fear – the auditor is coming ...

'n Pennieslotmasjien se kake
spoeg 'n kaartjie na my uit:
'Wees veral versigtig met geldsake'

The jaw of a slot machine
spits out its card to me:
'Be especially cautious in money matters.'

O die vrees! as die rekenmeester kom
hoe sal ek kan verantwoord
en verslag gee van sy eiendom?...

Oh the fear! when the auditor comes
how can I give account
and answer for his patrimony? ...

O week na week gebond
'n haas aan die ovale kring
en agter my ses honde ...

Oh week after week bound
like a hare to the oval track
and chased by six dogs ...

as die rekenmester kom! ...

when the auditor comes! ...

Excerpts from 'Ballade van die Grysland' (Ballad of the Grey Land) by D J Opperman,
which first appeared in *Versamelde Poësie,* Tafelberg and Human & Rousseau,1947.
Reproduced by permission of Tafelberg Publishers.

I

Chapter Seven

SOME ARE MORE EQUAL

The changing social composition of the Afrikaner *volk*

Afrikaner advancement?

The Afrikaner nationalist solidarity of the 1940s and 1950s was built on the myth of a classless *volk,* organically united through oppression by 'British imperialism'. This oppressed and exploited *volk* would have to be 'rescued' by a great collective *Reddingsdaad* (Act of rescue/redemption). As Dr Verwoerd had pointed out at the October 1939 *Ekonomiese Volkskongres,* the most effective instrument to 'rescue' Afrikaners, was 'that of state power'.[1] The NP government heeded this advice on taking power in 1948, expressly setting out to improve the economic position of all components of the disparate class alliance which comprised Afrikaner nationalism (see pp. 74-80 above). This policy of sustained Afrikaner favouritism succeeded beyond the government's wildest dreams. However, its consequences were not those wished for by the proponents of *volkseenheid.*

Reddingsdaad accomplished: The social impact of NP rule

According to the Population Census, whites made up just 19,3% of South Africa's 16 002 797 inhabitants in 1960. Afrikaners accounted for 58 percent of this white minority (compared with 38 percent for English-speakers, 1,4 percent for those who chose to classify themselves as bilingual, and 2,4 percent for other language groups).[2] Their place in the South African economy was literally transformed during the first twelve years of NP rule. Columns 2 to 5 of Table 1 indicate the changing position of Afrikaans-speaking white males in the occupational structure between 1940 and 1960. Column 6 indicates their changing position relative to that of English-speakers, and column 7 lists the median income per occupational category. Table 2 indicates the position of Afrikaner women among economically active white females in 1960.

A number of aspects of this changing place of Afrikaners in the occupational structure should be noted here. The first was their rapid movement into the higher income sectors of the economy. While this data indicates clearly that Afrikaans-speaking white males were still not as well off as their English-speaking counterparts in 1960, there had been a notable closing of the gap in all the better-paid occupational categories during the first twelve years of NP rule.

Equally significant here was the rapid decline of the proportion of Afrikaner males in the three lowest income occupational categories: agriculture, forestry and fishery; manual labour; and the unemployed. The fact that the number of Afrikaners in these categories declined more rapidly than did the number of English-speakers again points to a closing of the gap lamented by Sadie and Pauw (p. 74 above).

This decline of the absolute and proportional number of Afrikaner males in the lower income categories highlights another significant change in the occupational structure of the white Afrikaans-speaking population – its growing

Table 1

Position of economically active Afrikaans-speaking white males in the occupational structure, 1946–1960

Occupational category col. 1	No. per 1 000 Afrikaners 1946 col. 2	No. per 1 000 Afrikaners 1951 col.3	No. per 1 000 Afrikaners 1960 col.4	Increase per occupation group 1946–1960		Median income per category 1960 (Rand) col.7
				Afrikaners col.5	English col.6	
1 Professional and technical	43,2	49,6	68,1	93,4%	67,4%	2 675
2 Admin., managerial and executive	30,7	41,2	42,4	69,8%	39,3%	3 308
3 Clerical	72,2	101,7	138,4	136,2%	33,3%	1 786
4 Sales	19,3	25,9	26,1	67,0%	45,0%	2 168
5 Agriculture, forestry and fishery	349,6	276,8	198,5	–30,1%	–22,1%	1 477
6 Mining and quarrying	45,3	49,4	46,5	26,5%	–24,6%	2 311
7 Transport and communication	94,7	93,3	102,0	32,7%	–25,8%	1 540
8 Artisans and production workers	204,7	236,1	271,3	63,2%	6,7%	1 473
9 Manual labourer	54,9	43,8	23,7	–46,8%	–42,5%	931
10 Service, sports and recreation	60,3	58,3	60,9	24,3%	–41,4%	1 483
11 Unemployed, occup. unknown	24,8	23,5	21,9	–11,7%	0,5%	n/a
Total economically active	1 000,0[+]	1 000,0[+]	1 000,0[+]	23,1%	14,6%	1,836

Source: Columns 1-6 compiled from census data listed in Van Wyk, *Die Afrikaner,* Table 8.1, 190-3, & table 8.2, 201-2. Column 7 compiled from census data listed in *ibid*, Tables 3.3 & 3.4, 53-6.

+ = Slight discrepancy due to rounding

stratification. Between 1946 and 1960 Afrikaners had moved massively into three distinct social categories: professional, managerial and executive (i.e. the upper middle class); clerical, sales and administrative (the middle to lower levels of the middle class); and skilled and supervisory workers (and away from manual labour). Rigid occupational criteria, educational barriers and different lifestyles together rendered very difficult any mobility *between* these three strata. The apartheid policies of the NP government performed the crucial function of partially ameliorating the earnings gap between these strata normally found in free market economies, thus at least partially sustaining the old myth of a classless *volk*. It likewise consolidated the relatively privileged and protected position of Afrikaner skilled and supervisory workers. Nevertheless, the stratification was real, and as column 7 of Table 1 indicates, the income gap between these categories would grow wider in the 1960s.

In 1946, 30,3 percent of Afrikaners were involved in agricultural occupations. This declined to 16 percent in 1960 (and to just 8,1 percent by 1977). The percentage of Afrikaners categorised as 'blue collar and other manual labour' remained virtually static throughout the 1950s (40,7 percent in 1946, and 40,5 percent in 1960). It then dropped precipitously during the boom of the 1960s, to reach a mere 26,7 percent by 1977, most of whom had moved into skilled, better paid positions. This was accompanied by a dramatic increase of Afrikaners in the 'white collar' categories – 29 percent in 1946, 43,5 percent in 1960, rising to a whopping 65,2 percent in 1977.[3]

Table 2

Occupational position of economically active Afrikaans-speaking white females relative to other white females, 1960

(Percentage of each language group)

| Occupational category | Afrikaans | Language group | | | Total | |
		English	Bilingual	Other	%	Number
1 Professional and technical	18,7	16,3	14,6	21,7	17,5	48 556
2. Admin., managerial and executive	1,1	2,4	2,7	3,3	1,8	5 093
3 Clerical	46,8	54,0	47,0	34,8	50,1	139 515
4 Sales	11,6	12,7	13,7	12,6	12,3	34 094
5 Agriculture, forestry and fishery	0,4	0,2	0,1	0,5	0,3	761
6 Mining and quarrying	0,0	0,0	0,0	0,0	0,0	56
7 Transport and communication	4,1	1,5	2,4	0,4	2,6	7 296
8 Artisans and production workers	7,8	5,0	10,2	12,9	6,5	18 202
9 Service, sports and recreation	5,4	5,2	5,5	9,1	5,4	15 044
10 Unknown and unemployed	4,2	2,8	3,7	4,7	3,5	9 675
Totals: %	100,0	100,0	100,0	100,0	100,0	—
Number	119 992	143 846	6 135	8 319	–	278 292

Source: Unpublished Table 2.24, *1960 Census,* cited in Van Wyk, *Die Afrikaner,* table 7.1, 170.

Thus while the NP government fostered rapid social mobility by Afrikaners, their share of the economically active white population still did not reflect their numerically dominant position among whites. Afrikaners comprised 50,7 percent of the total of 699 163 white males and 43,1 percent of the 278 292 white females identified by the 1960 Census as economically active.* The position of economically active Afrikaner women (Table 2) underscores the real but still

---

* The respective shares of English-speakers and other language groups were 43% and 2,3% among the white males, and 51,7% and 5,2% among the females. Calculated from table 2.24 of the final census tabulation, quoted in Van Wyk, *Die Afrikaner,* table 4.1, 70, and table 7.1, 70.

limited economic advances made by Afrikaners after the NP came to power. The ratio of Afrikaners to English-speakers among economically active white women was close to the inverse of the linguistic breakdown of the broader white population (43:52 as opposed to 58:38). This is partially explained by the later urbanisation of the Afrikaner population relative to English-speakers. It also reflects the *slower* erosion among Afrikaners relative to other whites of the rigid tradition of the homebound *vroe en moeder* (wife and mother). While white women formed part of the dominant and highly privileged white racial group, gender roles (and the associated male psycho-sexual anxieties) tended to be even more rigid in white South Africa than in other 'western' populations.

Table 3
Afrikaner percentage ownership in the private sectors
of the South African economy, 1938–1975

Sector	1938–39	1948–49	1954–55	1963–64	1975
Agriculture, forestry, fishing	87	85,0	84	83	82
Mining	1	1,0	1	10	18
Manufacturing & construction	3	6,0	6	10	15
Trade and commerce	8	25,0	26	24	16
Transportation	n/a	9,0+	14	14	15
Liquor & catering	n/a	20,0+	30	30	35
Professions	n/a	16,0	20	27	28
Finance	5	6,0	10	21	25
Miscellaneous	n/a	27,0	35	36	45
Aggregate	n/a	24,8	25,4	26,9	27,5
Aggregate excluding agriculture	n/a	9,6	13,4	18,0	20,8

Source: Data for 1938–39, and 1948–49, prepared by the *Ekonomiese Instituut* of the FAK, published in *Volkshandel*, September 1950. Data for 1954–55 and 1963–64 from J L Sadie, 'The Afrikaner in the South African Economy' undated mimeo (1974?). Data for 1975 prepared by J L Sadie, published in H Adam & H Giliomee, *Ethnic Power Mobilised*, 170-1.
+ = estimates.

These tables show that while virtually every Afrikaner household had benefited materially from fifteen years of NP rule, some became much more equal the others. Far and away the major beneficiaries were the members a new class of urban Afrikaner financial, industrial and commercial capitalists. This group had blossomed from an embattled infancy to potent adulthood under the benevolent care of the NP government. A leading Afrikaner economist calculated that the Afrikaner share in the private sector of the economy (excluding agriculture) more than doubled in the first twenty years of NP rule (see Table 3). Yet the benefits of the NP government's policy of Afrikaner favouritism were spread unevenly even within this newly consolidated class of Afrikaner financial, industrial and commercial capitalists. Table 3 shows that while Afrikaner entrepreneurs increased their share of the private holdings in many branches of the South African urban economy between 1948–49 and

1963–64, the greatest leaps forward for Afrikaner capitalists occurred in finance, mining, liquor and catering, and manufacturing and construction.

Cape interests dominated in each of these three sectors. In the 1960s, 'Afrikaner finance' consisted basically of just three groups: Sanlam and its numerous subsidiaries,* the Cape-based Old Mutual Insurance company, and – lagging some way behind – the Transvaal-based, Broederbond-controlled Volkskas Bank. The apparent explosion of the Afrikaner share of the mining sector between 1954–55 and 1963–64, is explained by the virtual gift of the General Mining and Finance Company bestowed on Sanlam's Federale Mynbou subsidiary by the giant Anglo American Corporation in 1964 (see pp. 120-24 above). Mynbou slowly increased its mining holdings until 1975, when, in short-lived cooperation with Anton Rupert's Rembrandt group, it secured control of another of the great mining houses, Union Corporation, to emerge as South Africa's second biggest mining house (now known as Gencor).

The Cape-based Rembrandt Corporation itself grew very rapidly after 1948, turning itself into one of the world's major tobacco corporations. Its liquor holdings were also very substantial, and together with a blossoming of the predominantly Afrikaner-controlled Cape wine industry, Rembrandt largely accounts for the accelerating Afrikaner share of the liquor and catering sector.

This rapid growth of the share of Afrikaner entrepreneurs in private manufacturing after 1948 is explained by four major factors. The profusion of state corporations and parastatals under National Party rule placed Afrikaners in positions of control in key manufacturing sectors. Secondly, government contracts and subsidies benefited particularly the Sanlam industrial investment subsidiary, Federale Volksbeleggings. Thirdly, the three major Afrikaner financial groups, Sanlam, Old Mutual and Volkskas, began to diversify their holdings, moving into manufacturing in the 1950s. And finally, the drop in share prices and flight of foreign capital following Sharpeville in 1960 was seized upon by Sanlam and Old Mutual in particular as a golden opportunity to increase their shareholdings in a wide range of manufacturing and other companies.

A number of other aspects and consequences of this NP-fostered growth of Afrikaner capital should be noted here The first were its trickle-down effects. Good Afrikaner entrepreneurs employed Afrikaner workers, Afrikaner clerks and Afrikaner managers. The corollary of the seizure by Afrikaners of a greater (though still minority) share of the white-owned urban economy was the growth of an urban Afrikaner managerial and middle class (see Table 1). This was reflected in the dramatic increase of the proportion of Afrikaners classified as 'white collar workers' between 1946 and 1977 (Table 1, p. 137 above).

Still, it bears emphasising that as the Afrikaner share of the non-agricultural sectors of the economy virtually doubled in the first fifteen years of NP rule, by far the major beneficiaries of NP Afrikaner favouritism were the Cape-based groups, Sanlam, Rembrandt and Old Mutual. The first of these had been formed

---

* Including, *inter alia,* Santam, Trust Bank, Bonuskor and Saambou.

and run by the very men who established the Cape National Party and its official press, and who sat with key Cape politicians on the board of Nasionale Pers. The second had been set up by the Broederbond but moved into the political ambit of 'the Cape' once Rupert established its first factory in Paarl. By the mid-1950s Rupert had long ditched his once fiery Transvaal nationalism for the milder version of his Stellenbosch neighbour, friend and fellow wine farmer, Cape NP baron and Cabinet minister, Paul Sauer. Rupert's violent break with Dr Verwoerd in the late 1950s was deeply regretted by the entire Cape hierarchy, which made many unsuccessful attempts to heal the breach.[4]

Almost as significant by the mid-1960s was a change in the accumulation needs and strategies of the Cape and smaller and newer Transvaal financial and industrial capitals. Elsewhere I have shown that the overall strategy of the Afrikaner economic movement during the 1940 and early 1950s rested on an intense effort to mobilise both the savings of Afrikaner workers and clerks on the one hand, and the latent money capital lying around in Afrikaner agriculture on the other.[5] The Afrikaner financial institutions supported and established by the *Reddingsdaadbeweging* then gathered up all these dispersed monies, consolidating them into productive capital under its control. When coupled with the great support given to Afrikaner undertakings by the NP government after 1948, this strategy achieved its intended effect of creating what had not existed before – a class of Afrikaner financial, mining and industrial capitalists.*

However, the very success of this strategy undermined the once total dependence of these undertakings on their original source of capital – i.e. the savings of the Afrikaner *volk* at large. To take just one example, Sanlam's total premium and investment income rose from R5 million in 1946 to R38 million by 1961, while its assets increased over eightfold during this period. Yet an even more significant change occurred in the *base* of these Sanlam assets and income. The proportion of Sanlam's total income generated by investments (rather than premiums received) rose from under 20 percent in 1946 to almost one third in 1961, in which year investment income alone was more than double its 1946 premium income.†

As the larger Afrikaner companies loosened their economic dependence on Afrikaner farmers and workers, so too did their interests become less tied to the economic well being of these social forces. Increasingly part of the once exclusively 'English' club of big capital, many of the larger Afrikaner undertakings displayed a waning interest in the versions of Afrikaner nationalism which stressed the mythical unity of an increasing polarised *volk*. An outraged *verkrampte* later wrote of the growing presence of Afrikaner capitalists in the 1960s:

---

* Afrikaner penetration of the commercial sector was far less certain. Table 3 indicates that the Afrikaner share of trade and commerce actually shrank from 24% to 16% between 1963–4 and 1975.

† *Inspan*, X,1, Oct. 1950, and *Sanlam Review*, 1971. Premiums were nothing less than the mobilised savings of [predominantly Afrikaner] policy holders.

A new generation of Afrikaners made its appearance in the decade of the Sixties. These were Afrikaans-speakers who succumbed to the temptation of quick wealth and all that went with it. Always in the shadow of the representatives of the English-speaking financial world, these Afrikaners decided that allying themselves with foreign (sic) financiers brought quicker results and greater dividends than any bequest offered to them by the *Reddingsdaadbond* and the Economic Institute [of the FAK] – even though this meant that they would have to renounce the ideals and principles of those Afrikaner institutions.[6]

The widespread anger at Sanlam in the 1964 brouhaha over the presidency of the Afrikaanse Handelsinstituut (pp. 120-24 above) reflected both the frustration of smaller, mainly northern undertakings at the 'Southern' dominance of Afrikaner business, as well as their fears that *Suidelike geldmag* (Southern financial power) was beginning to display some independence from the overall nationalist line. It also coincided with Verwoerd's own fears that Afrikaner business was becoming too independent of the party and too close to Hoggenheimer.

In this new climate of the mid-1960s Afrikaner capitalists and politicians 'took each other's hand on the road which led to a break with the interests of Afrikanerdom'.[7] In sharp contrast with the resolute refusal of the late NP *Hoofleier*, J G Strijdom, even to use state postal and transport services for himself and his family, under the Vorster government, nationalist politicians began to receive important material benefits (mainly in the form of shares) for advancing the interests of this or that company. Thus, e.g. in the storm over the allocation of fishing concessions in Namibia to a Sanlam subsidiary, one-sixth of the 2 million share-issue by this Suid-Kunene (Suidwes-Afrika) company went to prominent government officials and parliamentarians.[8] Cabinet ministers and deputy ministers likewise acquired large holdings in companies the prices of whose products were fixed by the government. Prime Minister Vorster received 1 000 shares in the newly established South African petroleum company, Trek Investments Limited in 1969, seven other Cabinet ministers each received 700 shares and two deputy-ministers acquired 500 Trek shares. The government in which so many of Trek's shareholders sat then duly gave its approval to Trek involvement in the construction of a petrol refinery in Richards Bay.[9] It is difficult to imagine D F Malan or Hans Strijdom approving such actions.

Its impact on these new Afrikaner urban capitalists and politicians aside, the first fifteen years of NP rule also had a polarising effects on Afrikaner farmers. The NP government largely succeeded in its various efforts to improve the economic position of predominantly Afrikaner capitalist agriculture (see p. 77 above). Yet here too, the impact of its policies was uneven and led to political ferment. Firstly, though net farming income increased by 55 percent between 1951/52 and 1962/63, this was less rapid than increase in other sectors. As a result, agriculture's share of the national income actually *declined* by 13 percent during the first thirteen years of NP rule.[10] However the burden of this relative decline was unevenly spread. NP agricultural policy explicitly favoured the more efficient and larger farms. It also had some success in its expressed long-term goal in reducing the number of farming units.[11] The number of whites in agriculture, forestry and fishing fell by over 35 percent between 1936 and 1960 (from 181 409 to 117 599), and by a further 22,4 percent during the 1960s (from 117 599 to 96 000).[12] While the number of white farms likewise declined from 118 097 in 1951 to 91 153 by 1960 (and 75 562 in 1976), their average size *increased* during the same period from 736,5 to 978,8 hectares (reaching 1 134,4 hectares in 1976).*

The mechanisation of South African agriculture began to take off in the 1940s. An index of this lies in the tripling of the total number of tractors from 6 019 in 1937 to 20 292 in 1946. Once the NP came to office, this process accelerated. The number of tractors per unit of farm land increased fivefold between 1945 and 1960, as the total rose to 48 422 by 1950, 87 451 in 1955, 120 920 in 1960 and 133 600 by 1964.[13] This led to a doubling of the overall volume of agricultural production during the first fifteen years of NP rule.

The average annual *real* incomes of white farmers grew by a whopping 7,3 percent per annum between 1960 and 1975. Yet here too the larger agricultural undertakings were the major beneficiaries.[14] However most white farmers were virtually totally dependent on numerous forms of state support. A commission of inquiry into agriculture reported in 1972 that the various forms of state assistance provided 20 percent of an average white farmer's income.† Even more important in sustaining the position of white farmers were the numerous and very strict labour controls at the heart of apartheid policies. These meant that black agricultural wages barely increased from 1866 to 1966.[15]

This almost total dependence of Afrikaner farmers on an enormous variety of state interventions in labour and other markets rendered them, and particularly the maize producers, as much as ten times less efficient than their European and US counterparts.[16] It also fostered a peculiar economic culture in South African agricultural capitalism. Two aspects stand out here. The first was the rising indebtedness and hence long-term vulnerability of white farmers.[17] Secondly, white farmers looked to the state to solve their problems. In particular, they feared any relaxation of this array of state supports for agriculture.

Yet once again, there were important sectoral differences within agriculture,

---

* J Nattrass, *The South African Economy: Its growth and change* (Oxford University Press, Cape Town, 1981), table 6.6, 109. Moreover, the slight decline in the Afrikaner share of agricultural capital (from 87% in 1938-39 to 85% in 1948–49 and 82% fifteen years later), pointed to the slow entry of major English undertakings into agribusiness.

† Marais/Du Plessis Commission, cited in Nattrass, *The South African Economy*, 119. State support for agriculture ranged from the operations of a Land Bank and price stabilisation payments to rebates on fuel, fertiliser subsidies, soil conservation measures, the provision of water, etc. Total state subsidies for white farmers amounted to R66,8 million in 1967, or almost double state spending on black education. F Wilson, 'Farming, 1866–1966', in M Wilson & L Thompson (eds), *The Oxford History of South Africa: Volume II* (Oxford University Press, New York & Oxford, 1971), 165.

which translated into brewing political conflict between Afrikaner farmers. By the mid-1960s, the South African Agricultural Union had virtually ceased its previously endless calls for an 'effective labour control system'. Natal sugar farmers in particular had begun to view the elaborate apartheid labour controls as 'a drag on the agricultural economy'.[18] Yet the SAAU was controlled by larger, more progressive farmers. Maize farmers, on the other hand, became increasingly upset at what they perceived to be the failure of the Broederbond-dominated SAAU to fight for their particular interests within the Department of Agriculture. They also felt that their interests were being prejudiced by the government's anti-inflation measures which 'did everything possible to keep the consumer price of maize as low as possible'. In a move which had substantial ripples in NP politics, maize farmers seceded from SAAU in 1966, to form their own organisation – the *Suid-Afrikaanse Mielieprodusente Instituut* (South African Maize Producers' Institute – SAMPI).

In general then, while Afrikaner farmers benefited massively from NP rule, these *boere* were becoming an increasingly differentiated group. Yet even the larger and more prosperous farmers were subjected to growing economic pressure. Their position was certainly very different from, and much more precarious than, that of the new Afrikaner monopolies and managers brought into prominence by the NP's Afrikaner favouritism. After twenty years of NP rule, the economic woes of Afrikaner farmers and the other less privileged strata of Afrikaner society could no longer credibly be laid at the door of 'British imperialism' and/or the policies of a 'pro-Imperialist' government. In other words, then, the achievement of both the political and economic aims of Afrikaner nationalism meant the disappearance of a single symbolic target against which all classes of Afrikaners could be mobilised with the promise of the good life once these demons were replaced by an authentic Afrikaner government. Given the increasing economic and social stratification of Afrikaans-speaking whites, by the mid-1960s it was very difficult to identify the common, collective interest of this highly differentiated Afrikaner *volk*. The only feasible way of doing so was to claim that the interests of the *volk* were those of this or that social class – or, in a more radical verligte way, those of the broader white nation.

This was made even more complicated by significant changes in the nature and composition of the Afrikaner elite enrolled as members of the Broederbond.

Richer cream: The Broederbond's changing occupational structure

The Afrikaner Broederbond membership saw itself as the *crème de la crème* of Afrikanerdom – an attitude which generated much resentment among non-members. The changing occupational profile of the *Broeders* tells much about the project and control of Afrikaner nationalism. In 1933, the 1 023 members of the AB had been predominantly teachers, academics, lawyers, farmers and clergymen. Ten years later, and despite the Broederbond's feverish efforts to launch Afrikaner business undertakings after 1939, its members still appeared to be trapped in broadly the same occupations. The Bond had 2 672 members in 1944. Stung by the Smuts government's ban on Broederbond membership by civil servants, AB Executive Council member Hendrik Verwoerd published a series of repudiations by the Bond's secretary, Ivan Lombard, in *Die Transvaler.* Here Lombard stated that fully one-third of the *Broeders* were teachers, and only 8,4 percent were civil servants. He concluded (incorrectly) that 'the rest are mostly farmers'.* Interviews I conducted with a number of men prominent in the Broederbond in the 1940s (including Lombard's predecessor as AB secretary and its later chairman, Dr P J Meyer), confirm that teachers, academics, clergymen and civil servants accounted for substantially more than half of its membership in 1944. Other prominently represented occupations included farmers, lawyers, journalists and politicians. Despite the AB's launching of the economic movement, and the entry into business of many of its members, few listed their occupation as 'businessman' in 1944. This probably reflected the still prevalent broad Afrikaner prejudice against the 'English capitalistic system', and business in general.

This prejudice was still present eight years later, when the first reliable broad classification of the occupations of AB members exists. The now heavy involvement of the Afrikaner urban elite in numerous Afrikaner business undertakings, and the official seal of approval given to capitalism by the second *Ekonomiese Volkskongres* of 1950 notwithstanding,[19] still *none* of the now 3 520 *Broeders* wished to classify themselves as a 'businessman'. In 1952 nearly three out of every five AB members was an 'educator'. Farmers accounted for just over a quarter of all *Broers*, with Dutch Reformed clergymen making up another 10 percent, and politicians less than 2 percent (see Table 4).

This changed rapidly in the 1960s and 1970s. Thirty years after the NP took power 'educators' were still the largest single category of AB members. Yet their absolute numbers had not changed significantly in a quarter of a century, and their share of the total membership had shrunk from close to 60 percent to just over 20 percent. Most significantly, businessmen and bankers had come from nowhere to make up the third largest category. One in every eight *Broers* were now in business. Almost as notable was the aging of the once young leadership which had used the Bond to transform Afrikaner nationalism in the 1930s and 1940s. By 1968, old age pensioners were the fourth biggest group, or one in sixteen of all *Broeders*. Their numbers had more than doubled in the following decade, and by 1977 pensioners accounted for just over one out of every ten AB members. This changing occupational structure of the Bond membership was also affected by internal NP struggles. To shore up his own shaky position, former Justice Minister Vorster ensured that many security policemen were admitted into this Afrikaner elite group once he became NP *Hoofleier* in

---

* *Die Transvaler,* 14 December 1944. The remainder of Lombard's rebuttal was published in instalments in *Die Transvaler* on 21, 28 and 30 December 1944, and 4 January 1945. The Smuts government had been moved to act against the Bond by a series of increasingly dire warnings by Military Intelligence. See the *Hofmeyr Papers,* file Ce, Archive of the University of the Witwatersrand.

September 1966. Serfontein argues that whereas there were relatively few policemen in the Broederbond in the early 1960s, 'by the end of the decade an extraordinary number of senior police officers had been recruited'.[20] By 1977 there were almost as many policemen as politicians in the Bond.

Table 4
Occupational profile of the Broederbond membership, 1952–1977

Occupational category	1952		1968		1977	
	Number of members	%	Number of members	%	Number of members	%
Educators	2 039	57,9	1 691	20,6*	2 424	21,6
Farmers	905	25,7	1 806	22,1	2 240	20,0
Businessmen & bankers	–	–	1 161	14,1	1 405	12,5
Pensioners	–	–	511	6,2	1 124	10,1
Clergymen	357	10,2	670	8,2	848	7,6
Public servants	–**	–	415	5,1***	518	4,6
Doctors	–	–	391	4,8	n/a	–
Legal	159	4,5	252	3,1†	390	3,5
Municipal government	–	–	170	2,1	290	2,6
Agriculturalists	–	–	n/a	n/a	265	2,4
Policemen (incl. Security Police)	–	–	154	1,9	212	1,9
Railwaymen	–	–	197	2,4	201	1,8
Politicians	60	1,7	210	2,6‡	186	1,6
Parastatal employees	–	–	71	0,9	165	1,5
Media	–	–	64	0,8§	117	1,0
Miscellaneous other	–	–	428	5,1	805	7,2
Total	**3 520**	**100,0**	**8 191**	**100,0**	**11 190**	**100,0**

* These included 24 rectors of universities and training colleges (i.e. virtually every Afrikaner rector); 171 full professors; 171 other university faculty; 468 headmasters, 121 school inspectors and 647 teachers.

** Public servants had been forced to resign from the AB by the Smuts government in 1944. However, the ban was relaxed on the NP assumption of power in 1948 and there were certainly more than a few senior civil servants in the Broederbond by 1952.

*** These included: 59 [permanent] secretaries or assistant-secretaries or government departments. 'With few exceptions, the heads of all civil service departments were and are AB members.'

† Including 16 judges, 67 magistrates, 13 advocates (barristers) and 156 attorneys (solicitors).

‡ These 210 politicians included: Prime Minister Vorster; State President Fouché; 19 Cabinet ministers and deputy ministers; 79 nationalist MPs, 28 NP Senators, and 69 of its MPCs; 18 party organisers.

§ In the print media this included 22 editors but only three reporters. South Africa had no television in 1968 (it was only introduced in 1976). *Broeders* in the state-controlled radio included the head of the SABC and 14 of its other directors and managers, four organisers, two news editors and two announcers.

Sources: 1952 – Giliomee, 'The National Party and the Afrikaner Broederbond', 39; 1968 – Pelzer, *Die Afrikaner Broederbond,* 34-5; 1977 – Serfontein, *Brotherhood,* 135-6.

The success of the Nationalist project of 1948 had transformed not just the social structure of the Afrikaner population. It had also led to a thoroughgoing *embourgeoisement* of the urban and rural elites which presided over Afrikaner civil society and enjoyed such ready access to 'its' National Party government. In the early 1930s, the Broederbond had set for itself the task of overseeing the urbanisation of Afrikaners and capturing the new urban poor for their new vision of Afrikaner Christian-nationalism. At the same time, the Broederbond also worked to bring into being something entirely new – a class of Afrikaner industrial, financial and commercial entrepreneurs. Its startling success at both these levels transformed the Broederbond itself. The young academics, teachers, clergy and lawyers who managed the project of the 1930s had been economically tied to Afrikaner rural and small town communities themselves being transformed by the rapid urbanisation of the Afrikaner population. In the Gramscian sense, these were 'organic intellectuals'. They had given the disintegrating *platteland* an 'homogeneity and an awareness of its own function not only in the economic, but also in the social and political fields'.[21] The very success of their project had turned themselves and their vastly expanded membership into powerful, and rich urban sophisticates. Now the Afrikaner intelligentsia had been largely sundered from its rural roots and preoccupations. Its members had been transformed instead into the organic intellectuals of Afrikaner capital.

The new class of aggressive, Afrikaner urban capitalists now made the running in the Broederbond, often sidelining the academics, clergymen and other intellectuals who had led the organisation in the past. The impact of this change on the Bond, and particularly for its role as the gatekeeper of Afrikaner nationalism, was largely negative in two senses. Firstly, the Afrikaner elite represented in the Broederbond of the 1960s was a far less coherent socio/economic grouping that was the case in the 1930s, 1940s and even the 1950s. The interests of its second and third largest occupational categories (see Table 4) were increasingly in conflict. This social differentiation among their leadership led, secondly, to a real *fragmentation* of the old network of Afrikaner nationalist organisations. All of this profoundly affected the Broederbond itself. An Afrikaner analyst of the role of organised business in the functioning of the South African state writes as follows:

> Since the late 1960s, the influence of the Broederbond, either as policy-maker or policy conduit, has steadily declined. This decline was associated with the expansion of Afrikaner economic power and the attendant divergence of socio-economic class and sectoral interests within the ranks of *die volk* (the volk). These trends and the associated ideological conflict were themselves related to the gradual fragmentation of the network. With all of this came the expansion of the range of common interests between Afrikaner and English entrepreneurs and business associations, as well as a gradual increase in government's permeability to non-Afrikaner business interests.[22]

This, then, is the context in which the internal nationalist conflicts of the late 1960s need to be understood. During the 1940s, the NP had overseen and organised the transition of the stereotypical *Boer* (Afrikaner farmer) from countryside to town. By the late 1960s, Afrikaners were thoroughly urbanised, and very many had been elevated into the urban middle and managerial classes. The NP was now obliged to grapple with the very different task of giving political cohesion to a changing class alliance in a period of apparent prosperity for all its elements – when the early demands of its original constituents had been largely met. The conditions which had first given rise to the nationalist alliance no longer existed, and its burning sense of political and economic mission was dissipated precisely by the NP government's achievements. The result was prolonged and painful internal conflict.

Chapter Eight

THE ROCK ... IS GONE!

The first verligte/verkrampte war

The many faces of John Vorster

White South Africa again went to the polls at the end of March 1966. The result was yet another triumph for Verwoerd. His NP swept 126 of the now 166 seats, leaving the UP with 39, and the Progressive Party still limited to Helen Suzman's lone seat. Although all but two of the NP's 126 MPs were Afrikaners, Verwoerd's party won now substantial votes from English-speakers.* Rejoicing in what was then the greatest election victory since the establishment of the South African state in 1910, the Transvaal NP organ interpreted the result as 'an overwhelming mandate for the implementation of separate development in all spheres'. Verwoerd proclaimed his conviction that 'throughout the country the English-speaking [white] people had given more support than ever before to the Government and its policy, and that this process would be extended'.[1] Many English-speakers joined in the celebration of the fifth anniversary of the Republic in 1966, reinforcing Verwoerd's belief that his vision of a new white unity was being consolidated.

The growing legend of Verwoerd's political invincibility was further reinforced three months after this electoral triumph. A split decision of the World Court in The Hague finally ended its long hearing of Ethiopia and Liberia's complaint against South Africa's stewardship in Namibia. By the casting vote of its American President, the court determined that it could not rule on the merits of the case. This avoidance of the real issue through the escape hatch of a technicality was deemed a great triumph in South Africa.† White South Africa's awe at Verwoerd's alleged mastery of African and international politics was compounded at the beginning of September. *Die Hollander* became the first South African Premier to host an African head of government in Pretoria by meeting with the Prime Minister of the newly independent Lesotho, Chief Leabua Jonathan – though he declined to lunch with the chief.

But this was the Rock's last hurrah. At 2:15 pm on Tuesday 6 September 1966, Hendrik Verwoerd was attacked at his desk in Parliament as he waited to deliver a major speech in the Prime Minister's budget vote. His assailant was Dimitrio Tsafendas, a parliamentary messenger then on the list of prohibited immigrants and for whom the police were supposedly searching. *This* assassin made no mistake. Stabbed first in the heart and then thrice more, the Prime Minister was rushed to hospital mortally wounded. He was pronounced dead on arrival, just two days before his sixty-fifth birthday, and eight years and four days after his election as NP *Hoofleier*.

The National Party, Afrikanerdom, and much of white South Africa were shocked to their teeth. Seconds after Tsafendas' attack on Verwoerd Defence

---

* After South Africa became a republic in 1961 there had been threats of secession from the pre-dominantly English-speaking white electorate in Natal. Now however, the NP's share of the Natal vote rocketed from 16,7% in the 1961 election to 40,6% in 1966. Heard, *General Elections in South Africa*, table 50, 113 and table 62, 172.

† The morning host of the Afrikaans service of SABC announced: 'I know we are not supposed to crow, but ... Cockle Doodle Doo!'

Minister P W Botha screamed in Afrikaans at Progressive Party MP (and vociferous Verwoerd opponent), Helen Suzman: 'It's you who did this. It's all you liberals. You incite people. Now we will get you. We will get the lot of you.'* The government Department of Information put out a film lamenting 'The Rock is gone!'† Verkramptes claimed that this was a professional hit. Hinting darkly at a conspiracy, they wondered who benefited from the police failure to detect Tsafendas – a man already once expelled from South Africa, whom verkramptes claimed had once been a member of the South African Communist Party and whose various police files allegedly included the note that he 'has communistic leanings'.‡

A week after the assassination, the NP caucus met to choose the new *Hoof-leier* and Prime Minister. One of the more junior members of the Cabinet, Justice Minister Balthazar Johannes ('John') Vorster, was elected unopposed at the relatively tender political age of fifty-one. Since Vorster's personality and his position and history in the NP were to play such a key role in the working out of its politics over the new twelve years, it is as well to dwell here briefly on these issues.

Will the party not split? John Vorster's leadership style

Viewed by the normal political considerations of Afrikaner nationalism, John Vorster should never have been elected NP leader. Almost everything in his political past told against him. A senior figure in the bitterly anti-NP *Ossewa Brandwag* during the 1940s, Vorster's Nazi sympathies had seen him interned for much the war. In the 1948 election he had publicly criticised the NP as undemocratic when it attacked his selection as the Afrikaner Party candidate in Brakpan. Vorster then fought the election as an independent. In a *Die Transvaler* editorial, Dr Verwoerd instructed Nationalists not to vote for the OB General.§ Vorster lost by two votes thereby denying an otherwise probable secure seat to the nationalist coalition. He had only joined the NP in 1951 and was elected to parliament in 1953. Though he represented a Transvaal constituency, he was

---

* The Speaker eventually extracted a mealy-mouthed apology from Botha – Suzman, *In No Uncertain Terms*, 69-71.

† Others were less sorrowful. The London satirical magazine *Private Eye* marked the event with a black-bordered cover and heavy-type headline: 'Verwoerd – A Nation Mourns'. Its inside cover showed a traditionally dressed African dance troupe leaping for joy! It was declared an offence to possess this issue in South Africa.

‡ See Schoeman, *Vorster se 1000 Dae*, 8-10. See also his book devoted to the assassination and the question of who inspired 'the communist' Tsafendas – *Die Sluipmoord op dr Verwoerd* (Strydpers, Pretoria, 1975). This book lists the numbers of the numerous police and other files on the 'unde-sirable' Tsafendas.

§ D'Oliveira, *Vorster – The Man*, 111. Vorster told this biographer that Verwoerd later apologised to him for the editorial.

widely regarded as a man of the Cape and never developed a strong personal political base within the Transvaal NP.*

Vorster had been elevated to the Cabinet in 1961. As Justice Minister, the former Nazi introduced the then most repressive regime in South African history. Promiscuous in his definition of the 'commie/pinko-liberal subversives', and remorseless in their pursuit, Vorster soon earned the reputation of the real hard man in the government. His success in destroying the ANC and PAC underground within two years won accolades in the NP. Some judged that he had become the party's foremost MP.† But Vorster seemed still haunted by a sense of insecurity over his standing in the Cabinet and party. His ministerial colleagues regarded him as 'one of the quiet ones who did not speak much at Cabinet meetings'. Deeply conscious of his low standing in party protocol, the day following Verwoerd's death Vorster had demanded of the four MPs who came to ask him to contest the leadership: 'Will the party not split if a junior [Cabinet member] becomes leader?' [2]

In 1966 Vorster ranked a lowly thirteenth in Cabinet seniority. As Minister of Justice and Police, he was ultimately responsible for the Prime Minister's safety. Yet Verwoerd was assassinated in Parliament quite literally under Vorster's myopic nose by a listed 'communist sympathiser' for whom Vorster's vaunted police were supposed to be hunting.‡ Such were the subterranean tensions within the NP in 1966, however, that there was only one other credible *Hoofleier* candidate – the senior Cabinet minister, and Verwoerd's deputy as leader of the Transvaal NP, Ben Schoeman.§ Even Vorster's organisers acknowledged that Schoeman had the backing of most of the Cabinet, and all of its more senior members, including many Transvaal ministers. [3]

---

* Born and raised in the Cape, Vorster was frequently wooed by at least part of the province's NP leadership. On the eve of his own retirement in 1964, the doyen of the Cape party, Paul Sauer, tried to persuade Vorster to return to the Cape and take over Sauer's Humansdorp seat in parliament. Sauer told the Justice Minister: 'You're no Transvaler, you're a man of the Cape, and it's now time that you came home. You have a duty to the Cape!' – De Villiers, *Paul Sauer*, 149. This led to a rift between Sauer and the man who regarded *himself* as the Cape heir apparent, Vorster's old rival, P W Botha.

† See, e.g. the column by Scott Haig in the *Sunday Tribune*, 7 July 1963, which decribes Vorster as 'the dominant ministerial figure of the [parliamentary] session', overshadowing even Dr Verwoerd.

‡ Vorster sat directly behind Verwoerd in Parliament. I have sat in both these seats, and the distance between them is less than three feet. Ironically, the first question on the Order Paper that afternoon was for the Minister of Justice. Having mislaid his own spectacles, Vorster borrowed those of his parliamentary bench-mate, P W Botha, in an effort to review the typed answer he was to give once the day's business began. So just as his police failed to find Tsafendas, Vorster did not see Tsafendas attack Verwoerd, and only looked up once he heard the scuffle as the aged and portly Finance Minister Dönges and Tourism Minister Waring wrestled on the floor with the assassin, who had drawn another knife and was trying to stab Dönges – D'Oliveira, *Vorster – The Man*, 178-9.

§ The aging Cape NP leader and unsuccessful *Hoofleier* candidate in 1958, Eben Dönges was briefly in the running, but had such minimal support that he soon withdrew.

2 *The Rock and the volk:* An avuncular **Hendrik Verwoerd** greets a triumphant crowd at the 1964 celebrations in Bloemfontein of the 50th anniversary of the NP. **Mrs Verwoerd** is on his right.

3 *Making friends:* An unusually gaudy **P W Botha** and **Mrs Elize Botha** welcomed at a July 1979 dinner in his honour given by the 'Friends of South Africa'.

4 *40 lost years:* President **P W Botha** *(right, front row)*, the Provincial NP leaders, their wives and much of the Cabinet singing the National Anthem. The occasion was a Stellenbosch meeting on the evening of the 40th anniversary of the May 1948 election which brought the NP to power. Visible are: *Front row:* Cape leader, **Chris Heunis** *(3rd right);* Natal leader, **Stoffel Botha** *(3rd left);* Free State leader, **Kobie Coetsee** *(left); Second row:* Constitutional Development Minister, **Dr Gerritt Viljoen** *(2nd left);* Speaker and former Law and Order Minister, **Louis le Grange** *(4th left);* Foreign Minister, **Pik Botha** *(5th left).*

Yet the Transport Minister too had political skeletons in his closet. Schoeman was one of the dwindling band of so-called *oud-smelters* whose sins had never been forgotten nor forgiven in some nationalist circles.* Despite the claims of his campaign manager that *oom* (uncle) Ben would win by eleven caucus votes, Schoeman withdrew the day before the ballot, telling the political correspondent of *Die Vaderland* that the reason was 'slanderous gossip, slanderous gossip even about my wife'.† In his own account, Schoeman says he did not savour the prospect of a showdown in the caucus. Once persuaded by a delegation of Vorster's supporters that he would lose, he withdrew believing that the choice of a new leader should be unanimous.[4]

Verwoerd had no obvious successor. His total dominance of both NP and government precluded the emergence of a number two in both. Given the now acute tensions in Afrikaner ranks, Vorster's very political weakness stood in his favour. Unlike Schoeman, he was not openly identified with any of the squabbling NP factions. He enjoyed wide respect for his tough performance as Minister of Justice, especially among the fifty-odd new nationalist MPs elected in March 1966. Vorster's robust anti-communism, his OB past, and his recent intervention in the storm over the proposed Hertzog Prize to Uys Krige (p. 128 above) were all seen by the verkramptes as proof of his essentially far right-wing views.

Indeed, the Hertzog group took the initiative in securing Vorster's candidacy. Hertzog's deputy (and his later successor as leader of the verkrampte breakaway *Herstigte Nasionale Party),* the MP for Innesdaal, Jaap Marais, led the delegation which first asked Vorster to allow himself to be nominated. According to Vorster, Marais put the issue in ideological terms, telling the hesitant Justice Minister:

> *Oom* John: we want to plead with you to make yourself available for the post of Prime Minister because you are the only one who ideologically conforms to the ideas of the Afrikaner.[5]

Yet Vorster's image in the NP was more than just that of the *kragdadige* (strongman) minister who had wiped out the 'communist' threat. His Cape origins, link through marriage to one of the founding fathers of the Cape nationalist establishment and relative uninvolvement in the growing attacks on

---

* Beaumont Schoeman claims that a week before his death Verwoerd had warned the verkrampte Albert Hortzog that his senior minister should never become NP leader because Ben Schoeman 'was a *smelter* who had with the world view of a *smelter'* – Schoeman, *Vorster se 1000 Dae,* 254. General Hertzog himself was not forgiven. When a group of nationalists sought to raise money to erect a statue to the founder of the NP, Verwoerd refused his approval. He argued that many Afrikaners still resented General Hertzog's role in the 1934 'fusion' crisis and break-up of the old NP – Schoeman, *Van Malan tot Verwoerd,* 154.

† Ibid, 258. On the other hand, however, the caucus poll conducted by Vorster's organisers on the eve of Verwoerd's funeral showed a total of 91 MPs and Senators supporting Vorster, against 57 for Schoeman, with 16 undecided – D'Oliveira, *Vorster – The Man,* 188.

Keeromstraat and its allies, all made the Justice Minister acceptable to the Cape NP leadership.* Moreover, before Schoeman withdrew, Vorster seems to have made a deal with Cape leader Dönges. In return for Cape support in the caucus leadership election he would endorse Dönges in the upcoming presidential election.† Vorster finally emerged as the unchallenged candidate because he enjoyed the backing of these two apparently contradictory factions.

This detail is essential to an understanding of the nature and style of Vorster's radically different leadership in both party and government. As the duly chosen *Hoofleier*, Vorster would automatically have succeeded Verwoerd as leader of the Transvaal NP. Every *Hoofleier* since the NP's inception had simultaneously occupied the office of leader of the party in his home province. This was the final political base of the national leader. But Vorster had not risen to the *Hoofleier*ship through the established route of promotion in his provincial party. His campaign manager's sounding of MPs had revealed opposition to his candidacy from various influential senior Transvaal Cabinet ministers. While the provincial leadership was his to claim by right of succession, with no natural political base in the Transvaal party, he must have realised that he would enjoy at best the grudging support of its organisation. Like most former OB nationalists, Vorster had a horror of again being burned in intra-nationalist infighting. Given that the developing NP verligte/verkrampte factionalism was now at its most acute in the Transvaal, he could get sucked into these struggles in a way which could rapidly lose him support in other provinces. Vorster thus announced that he would not accept the Transvaal NP leadership, offering it instead to his astonished and gratified erstwhile opponent, Ben Schoeman – neatly placing Schoeman and his supporters deep in Vorster's debt.

In both caucus and Cabinet the new *Hoofleier* strove to stand above factional conflicts and to bring all sides together through the prestige – and patronage – of his office as national leader. Given his own relative weakness in the party, Vorster abandoned Verwoerd's highly centralised, hands-on leadership. He presided over the Cabinet much in the style of a 'chairman of the board'. Telling his very first Cabinet meeting that 'Dr Verwoerd did the thinking for each one of us', he announced that he had no intention of following suit. Ministers were instructed to get into the habit of thinking for themselves: 'From now on everyone must know his own field, immerse himself in it and be in command of it.'[6] Full policy-making responsibility within state departments was restored to ministers. In sharp contrast to the practice of his predecessor, the new Prime

---

* Vorster's father-in-law, P A Malan, had helped form and lead the Cape NP, Nasionale Pers and Sanlam.

† Schoeman, *Van Malan tot Verowerd*, 258-9. Dönges duly narrowly beat the Transvaal's Jan de Klerk (father of F W) in the electoral college vote a few months later. Given the relative weight of the Cape and Transvaal parties, he simply could not have done so without Vorster's support. However, Dönges fell into a long coma and died in January 1968 without ever assuming office. Free State NP leader Jim Fouché then ascended to the Presidency.

Minister almost never intervened in the way his ministers ran their own departments.

Both of these departures were to be of vital significance in the factional struggles which followed. In effect Vorster's new style of leadership produced a significant shift in the terrain of internal struggle, one which was ultimately to weaken the faction which then still probably enjoyed close to majority support within the NP. With the *Hoofleier* now effectively without a provincial institutional power base within the party, his interventions in its internal struggles were largely made from the terrain of the state apparatus. The machinery of government itself came to play an increasingly important role in these factional struggles. This latter terrain would ultimately predominate over the former – state apparatus over party – reducing the significance of the party itself as a level of political organisation, and weakening those elements whose principal power base remained within the NP rather than the state. This was to play an important role in the evolving power struggles within the NP.

With verligtes like these ...: Defining the terms of the division

The cohesion of Afrikaner nationalism was severely undermined first by the achievement of its historic goal – the creation of the republic in 1961. Mission duly accomplished, the NP and the Broederbond cast around for a new *volkstaak* (task for the *volk*). But unity of Afrikanerdom was further eroded by the civil war between cultural commissars. Presented for a while as a 'provincialist' struggle, the great Afrikaner press war soon came to be seen as a sordid example of cut-throat capitalist competition between Afrikaners. The 'anti-capitalist' *volks-kapitalisme* of the 1940s and early 1950s was publicly buried and the realities of class-based competition and conflict within Afrikaner nationalism exposed for all to see.

The now raging verligte/verkrampte conflicts within the party grew out of such processes. They essentially pitted those forces which sought to preserve the Afrikaner nationalist class alliance of 1948 – dominated by the interests of farmers and the petty bourgeoisie – against those who realised that in twenty years the social basis of Afrikaner nationalism had shifted profoundly. The verkramptes appealed to the great traditions of the past. The verligtes sought to transform Afrikaner nationalist ideology and politics to suit the changing social composition and material needs of the *volk*. This is clear in the early definition given by the man who first coined these terms:

> '*Verkramp*' is the word which designates the attitude and school of thought manifesting itself in hostility to all that is new; an attachment to the existing; a resistance to renewal and a passion to continue with and extend patterns belonging to the past; negation, condemnation and suppression of new demands which in the march of history continually lead to new situations calling for creativeness and adaption. In short, verkramp is a traditionalist attitude which elevates tradition as such to principle and norm.

Applied to the context of race relations in South Africa, 'verkramp' is the rigid and inflexible traditionalism which pushes to extremes the pattern of separation of the races on the basis of a master/servant, more/less relationship and which seeks the perpetuation of this relationship.

'*Verlig*' represents the opposite extreme ... This school of thought aspires to unprincipled openness; to compromise and pragmatism; to a reckless innovation of new patterns based on experimental thinking.*

The verligte phenomenon was a response to the emergence of a class of aggressive, self-confident Afrikaner capitalists, whose interests now went beyond those of the narrow class alliance out of which they had emerged. Their redefinition of the nationalist project sought to drag it out of the laager and into the modern world.† This verligte project provoked a visceral rejection in the hearts of verkramptes. It was nowhere better expressed than in a celebrated article by the editor of *Hoofstad*, the former *dominee* Dr Andries Treurnicht:

> When some people get hold of the idea of renewal or the new, they see visions and sprout wings. Then everything simply has to change. Then everything linked to the past is considered worn out – this even extends to principles and standards. [But] new standards and new principles can mean only one thing, and that is the rejection of the Christian ethic, and of the morals and traditions which, through the centuries, have been built on this ethic. Is this what we want? No thank you!⁷

The verkramptes detested the cosmopolitanism of the cities and the corrupting influence of money. Though himself far from a verkrampte, poet D J Opperman well captured this sense of materialist corruption in his 1947 poem, *Die Ballade van de Grysland* (excerpt, p. 133 above). In the title of one of P J Meyer's many books, the verkramptes implored the *volk* to *Trek Verder* (Travel Further) into the laager of *volkseie*.

By the late 1960s, the verligte element was no longer principally based in the Cape, but had emerged as an increasingly strong element in the Transvaal as well. Just as had occurred in the Cape a decade earlier, the economic dependence of Transvaal businessmen on an alliance of all classes of Afrikaans-speakers had

---

* Professor W J (Willem) de Klerk, 'The Concepts, "Verkrampt" and "'Verlig'", in N Rhoodie (ed.), *South African Dialogue: Contrasts in South African Thinking on Basic Race Issues* (McGraw Hill, Johannesburg, 1972), 520-1. Wimpie de Klerk originally used both terms in a pejorative sense. However, once he left his Chair of Pastoral Philosophy at Potchefstroom University for the more glamorous world of journalism, he soon became acknowledged as one of, if not *the*, leading verligte.

† This conflict over 'the choice between tomorrow and yesterday' is wonderfully lampooned in André Brink's very funny parody of the verligte/verkrampte brouhaha, *Oom Kookie Emmer* (Ad Jonker/Uitgewer, Johannesburg, 1973). Here the issue which divides 'town and country, turned father against son, brother against brother, and church against state' (p. 9), is whether the imaginary tiny northern Transvaal town of Witgatworteldraai (literally: White[arse] hole-turning root) should replace its night soil system with flush toilets.

now been broken, and they too began to pursue independent economic and political policies. Their rejection of, and embarrassment with, the symbols and vision through which Afrikaner business had been forged, lay at the heart of the verligte reaction against *Trek verder verkramptheid.*

Broedertwis: Round one

The removal of 'the Rock' Verwoerd brought into sharp relief the various creatures whose titanic battles had been hidden under his shadow. The simmering nationalist conflicts on the cultural terrain, in press wars and for control over the peripheral organisations of Afrikaner nationalism, now slowly boiled over into an overt battle for control of the NP itself. At issue were the questions so long suppressed by Verwoerd's dominance and rigidity: what was the nature of the Afrikaner nationalist project after the achievement of the republic and all of the other goals of 1948? Did Afrikaner nationalism still have a specifically *ethnic* content, or could it afford to become more inclusive? How, and by whom were the *volk* to be held together as the very success of the nationalist project transformed the social position of Afrikaners, leading to an increasingly rapid class differentiation among them?

The first salvo was fired by the highly verkrampte Broederbond chairman, Dr P J Meyer. At the AB annual conference held a month after Verwoerd's death, Meyer explicitly set out to answer the questions posed in the last paragraph. Pointing to the creeping anglicisation of urban Afrikaners, he made an impassioned plea for 'the Afrikanerisation of the English-speaker', primarily through the education system:

> ... the English-speaker has to make the Afrikaans world-view his own; that he will integrate his ideals and life style with those of the Afrikaner; that he will adopt Afrikaans history as his own; that he will accept Afrikaans as his national language, alongside English as the international community language.[8]

Moreover, Meyer now appeared to make a power grab on the Broederbond's behalf. He argued that the NP was a organisation confined to the purely political realm. The Bond on the other hand was responsible for securing each of the four corners of what Meyer called the *volks*-pyramid of Afrikaner nationalism – the cultural, political, economic and educational.[9] The inference was clear – in the difficult days ahead it was to the Broederbond rather than the party that nationalists should look for principled leadership.

Broeder John Vorster must have clearly understood that the gauntlet had been thrown down. Yet without a secure personal political base, the new *Hoofleier* was in an impossible position. He told his white compatriots in his first address to the 'nation' that he would faithfully cleave to 'the path of Hendrik Verwoerd'.[10] *Die Burger* commented that Vorster's approach was:

... in direct conflict with the 'laager mentality' so frequently ascribed to the Afrikaner in general and the Nationalist in particular. Here we have an appeal and a challenge to move out into the world, to look outwards, to become involved, to seek our national salvation in participation rather than separation.[11]

Within months, Vorster and some of his more verligte ministers began modifying hallowed Verwoerdian policies. This occurred firstly on the issue of the admission of multiracial touring foreign sports teams. In a celebrated speech at Loskop Dam almost exactly a year before his death, Dr Verwoerd had announced that no racially mixed touring teams would be admitted to South Africa. Early hints that hallowed policy might be relaxed provoked shock and rage among the very men who had pleaded with Vorster to run for the *Hoofleier*ship.[12] The new Prime Minister also soon displayed a willingness to go even further than Verwoerd in opening the NP to the 'English-speakers' whom AB chairman Meyer had wanted to 'Afrikanerise'.

It gradually became apparent that Vorster saw the NP evolving into the party of a broader white South African nationalism rather than a purely ethnic Afrikaner version. This scandalised the Hertzogites. They mobilised for a full-scale, behind-the-scenes campaign against this new vision. A growing battle for the soul of Afrikaner nationalism then also focused on the issues of South African support for the illegal settler regime in what was then Rhodesia (now Zimbabwe); on Vorster's feelers about establishing diplomatic relations with independent African states; whether their accredited (black) representatives could reside in 'white' areas and send their children to 'white' schools; on immigration policy as a threat to the numerical preponderance of Afrikaners in the white population; and on money being spent on 'black development'.[13]

The internal NP conflict over these issues during the first three years of Vorster's leadership produced the most serious divisions in Afrikaner nationalism since the 1940s.[14] Despite Vorster's attempts to elevate himself above the fray, he was ultimately unable to remain neutral as his leadership became one of the principal targets of the verkrampte onslaught. Once again, both Vorster's political history and his Bonapartist leadership style were crucial in the working out of this *broedertwis*. Still seemingly insecure in his own position, and acutely aware of his lack of a political base within the party, the new Prime Minister displayed a remarkable hesitancy to confront the virtually open Hertzogite offensive to seize control of the NP's ideological agenda. Still scarred by his own experience of the nationalist civil war during World War II, for two years Vorster almost naïvely accepted the verkrampte professions of loyalty. As he himself later acknowledged to his biographer:

> But genuinely, at that time, I accepted their declarations of loyalty because I wanted to accept them ... All I can say about this eagerness of mine to accept their declarations of loyalty is that I fought one civil war with my fellow Afrikaners – I did not want to become involved in another.[15]

In the first years of his premiership, Vorster was fiercely criticised from all sides as being a weak leader. Broederbond chairman Meyer told senior AB officials, in December 1967 that 'our most important task is to get rid of John Vorster'.[16] Watching his brother's brief speech on the steps of Parliament just after his September 1966 election as NP *Hoofleier*, Dr Koot Vorster had declared that 'John looks eager to get to work'.[17] Yet so acute and personal were the attacks on the new leader that barely eleven months later the Transvaal NP leader Ben Schoeman was informed by his Cape counterpart, P W Botha, that Vorster intended resigning. The Prime Minister confirmed the report, telling Schoeman: 'I can no longer bear it.'[18] Persuaded to stay in office, Vorster was finally obliged to rely on various factional groups in the party simply to protect his own position. As the extreme right attempted to drive the verligtes out of the ranks of Afrikaner nationalism, Vorster leaned heavily on the Cape NP and its new leader, P W Botha. But he also increasingly turned to another support base.

As Justice Minister between 1961 and 1966, Vorster had built the Security Police into a formidable political force. Through his office, the police were propelled to the forefront of South African politics, giving its members a dangerous taste for their own growing power. Now Vorster began to use the Security Police against his own nationalist opponents, provoking bitter complaints by the Hertzog group. One of the more significant features of Vorster's premiership was his consolidation of a openly political role for the Security Police. The head of the secret Republican Intelligence, Vorster's old OB crony, General Hendrik van den Bergh, became the Prime Minister's closest adviser and political lieutenant (see pp. 211-12 below).

As the struggle with the verkramptes reached its height in 1969, Vorster turned Republican Intelligence into a new, special security service which would coordinate the activities of the Special Branch, the Security Police and the intelligence departments of the Defence Force, and report directly and exclusively to the Prime Minister. This new Bureau for State Security (the notorious BOSS) was henceforth Vorster's principal and most effective political base, one which could not be called to account by any faction in party and government, and remained under his own exclusive control. Principally through BOSS, the Prime Minister began to intervene directly in the internal politics of almost all of the organisations of Afrikaner nationalism, but particularly the Broederbond.[19]

Volks pyramid vs *volksfront:* The struggle for the Broederbond

The Afrikaner economic movement had first been organised and consolidated through the Afrikaner Broederbond. While substantial Afrikaner business undertakings had sprung up in the Cape long before the first *Ekonomiese Volkskongres*, Afrikaner business in the Transvaal was in many senses the real creation (and greatest achievement) of the Bond. The businessmen who came of age in this economic movement clearly understood the importance of control of the AB – still led by its highly verkrampte chairman, Dr P J Meyer. In the words of one of the verligtes' deadliest Afrikaner foes:

> That the AB served as a crucial contact network for its member was self-evident. This led interest groups to begin to show their heads in the organisation, particularly the ever stronger 'Afrikaner' financial power centres (*geldmagte*). Officials of certain financial institutions [read the Sanlam group – D O'M] went all out to sign up their colleagues, and succeeded handsomely. And just as these institutions became ever less Afrikaner-oriented, so too did their officials naturally have to follow suit and justify the new line inside and outside of the AB. In more and more [Broederbond] divisions a sentiment began to take hold which was foreign to the nature of the organisation.[20]

The verkramptes also sought to use their traditional base in the Broederbond against what they labelled the 'finance power of the South'. Indeed, as the struggle for the Broederbond reached a crescendo in late 1968, a move was mounted to portray the factional conflict as a simple confrontation between the AB as the guardian and soul of traditional Afrikaner values on the one hand, and the *nouveau riche* 'money capitalists' (*geldmag*) of the South on the other.* Hardly a week passed without one faction of this 'secret' organisation leaking the stratagems and plans of their opponents in the Bond to the despised 'English press'.[21]

As the ideological battle began to devour nationalist organisations, Vorster remained reluctant to move against the verkramptes. As he explained to his biographer:

> You [read 'I' – D O'M] more or less had the message that Hertzog was involved in the subversive group, but you still gave him the benefit of the doubt.[22]

The Prime Minister took a first hesitant step in February 1968. Firing a warning shot across the verkrampte bow, he stripped their leader of his most important portfolio.† He only began to confront them openly six months later, moving first to seize control of the Cabinet and party and then to bring the Broederbond under NP direction. When Hertzog refused Vorster's request to resign, he was fired from the Cabinet in August 1968.‡ Declaring that the churches and the party were the only Afrikaner institutions with the 'right' to an

---

* See *Veg*, November 1968. The Hertzog group in parliament was however compelled to repudiate this ultra-verkrampte journal.

† Hertzog lost the Ministry of Post and Telegraphs, but remained the Minister of Health. Vorster explained that he took this action 'not because I wanted to act against him [Hertzog], but because I wanted to create a [Cabinet] position for Basie [van Rensburg]'. Van Rensburg became leader of the Orange Free State NP following the elevation to the State Presidency of Jim Fouché on the January 1968 death of President-elect Dönges.

‡ Hertzog evidently believed that he could follow the example of his father in 1912, and force Vorster to dissolve the entire Cabinet. See Vorster's account quoted in De Villiers, *P W*, 97-9.

autonomous existence, the *Hoofleier* now insisted that the other Afrikaner institutions were simply 'support organisations' of the party or churches. Ironically, this was exactly the Verwoerdian view that Vorster himself had fought against in the OB during World War II. Standing in sharp contrast to the hallowed Christian-national principle of *Sowereiniteit in eie kring* (the notion that each social sphere was autonomous from the others), it doubly outraged those who still believed in the ideology of the 1940s.

Vorster now demanded total loyalty from the Bond and particularly its arch-verkrampte chairman (Vorster's former OB comrade), Dr P J Meyer. Meyer did not give up without a fight. At the first meeting of the Broederbond membership after Verwoerd's death, he had tried to stake the AB's claim to be the overall policy-making body of the broader nationalist movement. Throughout the next three years he worked closely with the Hertzog group to ensure the primacy of the verkrampte line. At one stage this led Cape NP leader (and Broederbond member) P W Botha to break the old vow of never discussing the Bond in public. Referring to the Broederbond by name and Meyer by inference, Botha announced that the NP would never be dictated to by 'outside organisations'.[23]

This struggle for control of the Broederbond reached its height in mid/late 1968. Meyer told the verkrampte group which had seized control of the local Pretoria NP organisations that Vorster had sent former AB secretary Dr Piet Koornhof to ask for his own resignation as Broederbond chairman. Koornhof was instructed to return to the Prime Minister with the message that Vorster would have to vote Meyer out of the chairmanship. Urging the Pretoria group to stay the course, Meyer told his guests that he would move into 'open confrontation' with Vorster at the upcoming *Bondsraad* (AB annual congress).[24]

The October 1968 *Bondsraad* was the really decisive moment in this long first round of the verligte/verkrampte struggle. The Prime Minister arrived unexpectedly and demanded the floor. He challenged the AB that to attack him was to undermine the unity of the NP, warning that splitting the party risked 'destroying the white man [not the Afrikaner! – DO'M] in South Africa'. Vorster also explicitly defended Afrikaner businessmen against the charge of 'selling out to Oppenheimer'. Referring directly to Federale Mynbou's still-controversial takeover of General Mining (pp. 120-4 above), the *Hoofleier* also sought to capture from the verkramptes the definition of who was a 'real' Afrikaner. Probing the significance of the verkrampte denunciation of Afrikaner businessmen, he asked rhetorically:

Once you have destroyed them and made them suspect, what remains of your Afrikaner concerns? To whom is the field then left?[25]

The Prime Minister had taken the measure of Piet Meyer. His intervention in the *Bondsraad* effectively marked the end of Meyer's willingness to move into 'open confrontation' with the party leadership. Passing his allies a note saying that 'he had changed his strategy', the Broederbond chairman declined to take up the Premier's challenge.[26]

In the end, Meyer was as much a prisoner of his political past as was John Vorster. Once the fastest rising young nationalist intellectual in the Transvaal, following the split between the NP and *Ossewa Brandwag*, Meyer's sojourn in the political wilderness had been even longer than Vorster's. Meyer had once been as ambitious as Verwoerd, with whom he was in almost constant conflict in the 1940s. This personal career strategy of this self-proclaimed 'Afrikaner socialist' was patterned on his reading of revolutionary history. In the early 1940s Meyer frequently told his intimates that 'Stalin could only have outmanoeuvred Trotsky because of his key position as secretary of the [Bolshevik] party'.[27] In the period just before the NP/OB split Meyer had occupied the post of secretary of almost all the key nationalist organisations *except* the National Party itself.* His associate, Albert Hertzog, noted in his diary:

> Piet Meyer indicated to me that he nurtured aspirations, and stressed the significance of the fact that he controlled the secretaryships of various things. He frequently joked that he knew how to work with the [Broederbond] Executive Committee to get his own way.

Meyer's central role and 'aspirations' so alarmed the equally ambitious NP 'party men' on the Bond executive that 'Verwoerd and Dönges ... decided that Meyer's wings had to be clipped'.[28] Obliged to resign most of his prized positions, the high-flying Meyer was one of the principal victims of the NP triumph over the OB. He withdrew completely from politics in 1946, only re-entering the scene when rescued as part of Verwoerd's attempt to consolidate his own weak position (see p. 96 above).

Like the Prime Minister he now declined to confront openly, Piet Meyer had learned the hard lesson that the party was likely to win all internal struggles. Like Vorster, once obliged to choose between principle and party, he would never again make the idealistic mistakes of his youth. When the Prime Minister made it clear that Meyer would have to take sides openly, the chairman abandoned both his claim that the Broederbond was the central organisation of Afrikaner nationalism and his erstwhile verkrampte colleagues in the Hertzog group.†

---

* These included: the Broederbond; the FAK (and its executive body, the *Afrikaner Nasionale Kultuurraad* – National Cultural Council); the *Ekonomiese Volkskongres*; the *Reddingsdaadbond*; the *Ossewa Brandwag*; *Trekmaats* (an AB front); and the Afrikaanse Handelsinstituut. He was also the founding editor of *Volkshandel*, treasurer of the *Ekonomiese Instituut* of the FAK and the organiser of Albert Hertzog's group seeking to take over the white mining unions, *Die Nasionale Raad van Trustees* (until he resigned to lead to OB's own labour organisation, the *Arbeidsfront*).

† Thereby earning himself their undying contempt. His voice dripping with scorn, Beaumont Schoeman advised me not to give much credence to Meyer's version of Afrikaner nationalist history, dismissing the AB and SABC chairman as 'a former employee' of Dr Hertzog. Once the Hertzogites were finally expelled from the NP in August 1969, Meyer made a feeble attempt to persuade Vorster not to use the AB against them. See Bond UR circular of 7 October 1969, cited in Schoeman, *Die Broederbond*, 140-2. However, Meyer soon acquiesced on the expulsion of Hertzogites from the AB.

In this struggle for the Broederbond, Vorster ensured that large numbers of security policemen were admitted to the Bond, giving the Prime Minister a secure base within the organisation itself. The 'highly irregular' manner by which 'Van den Bergh and his spies' were 'infiltrated into the Broederbond' provoked bitter verkrampte complaints.[29] The effect was to restrict even further the Bond's political independence, reducing it for the first time in its history largely to a platform for the leader of the NP. This accomplished, Vorster then required of the verkrampte Meyer that he purge from the Broederbond all verkramptes who would not toe the party line. He used the right to contain the right.[30]

In hindsight, many analysts put Vorster on the verligte side of the great Afrikaner divide of the late 1960s. This is true only in the very limited sense which would have also included Verwoerd among the verligtes – i.e. that the *Hoofleier* actively propagated the position that the NP was no longer an exclusively Afrikaner party, but rather one now devoted primarily to defending the interests of 'the white man', Afrikaner or English-speaking. But until almost the very end of this internal conflict, Vorster's major preoccupation and virtual sole objective was to hold the party together. Whereas Verwoerd was driven largely by his misbegotten principles (and huge personal ambition), the former OB General who succeeded him was a pragmatist desperate to avoid being labelled the man who presided over the first split in the National Party since the NP/OB war of the 1940s.

A truce of sorts brokered by Vorster between the factions at the end of 1968 produced a short-lived peace in the party. Eventually, however, the Hertzog group proved unwilling to compromise. The final declaration of war was delivered by Albert Hertzog's notorious 'Calvinism' speech of April 1969. Hertzog now proclaimed that Afrikaners were still fundamentally Calvinists, rooted in their church and religion. English-speakers on the other hand were basically liberals and, as such, vulnerable in the face of attacks by communist and left-wing groups. He concluded that if the English-speakers stood on their own, the white race would have collapsed in South Africa.*

Though Hertzog claimed to have given an advance copy to the NP chief whip, his speech was a barely concealed repudiation of attempts by Verwoerd and Vorster to broaden the base of the NP. Vorster could no longer put off a fight to the finish. It was now just a matter of finding the means to get rid of Hertzog and his cohorts in a way which contained the collateral damage. This was achieved at the September 1969 Transvaal NP Congress. Telling the delegates that the moment of truth had arrived, Transvaal leader Ben Schoeman demanded

---

* See Serfontein, *Die Verkrampte Aanslag,* 187-207, and Schoeman, *Vorster se 1000 Dae,* 224-39. In the furore which followed this speech, Dr Treurnicht's *Hoofstad* (30 April 1969) rushed to the defence of the verkramptes with the following rhetorical question: 'The question is who deviates from the principles of the National Party and who rejects the Christian-national basis of our entire social, educational, political and national life *[volkslewe]*? Without being falsely pious *[vroom]:* Who stands by the Lord and His Word?'

Congress support for a resolution on immigration policy, Afrikaner–English relations, admitting black diplomats to South Africa, and a new sports policy which would admit visiting international teams which had 'non-white' members. Eleven of the 1 000 delegates, including Hertzog, Jaap Marais and one other MP, voted against the resolution on sport policy. They were soon expelled from the NP, to be joined by a single Cape MP.

Against the advice of some of the verkramptes who had managed to avoid expulsion, the four expelled MPs then formed the ultra-verkrampte *Herstigte Nasionale Party* (Reconstituted Nationalist Party – HNP), with Hertzog as its leader and Jaap Marais as its deputy.* Vorster called an early election in April 1970 explicitly to break the HNP before it had a chance to organise. Hertzog's party lost all four of its parliamentary seats, and many of its candidates lost their deposits. This did not end the factional conflicts in the NP, however, and it was not until 1972 that all HNP members were expelled from the Broederbond.†

The man for the job: John Vorster and Afrikaner unity (i)

The NP had come to power in 1948 as the political organisation of an unruly Afrikaner nationalist social alliance. Its component class forces were held together by the ideological glue of a classless *volk* united in *Die Afrikaner se Republikeinse strewe* (the Afrikaner's struggle for the Republic). Yet by the mid-1960s, the very success of the NP policy of Afrikaner favouritism and the rapid economic differentiation of the Afrikaner population this produced had completely undermined the myth of a classless *volk* each of whose members were oppressed and exploited by British imperialism. The very achievement of the republic in 1961 eroded the ethnic mission of a *volksbeweging* united by an historic duty to free the *volk* from the British yoke. The ethnic glue which held the social alliance together for fifteen years dried and chipped in the process, and the nationalist alliance slowly began to unravel into fractious class forces.

For a while the widening cracks had been bridged by the sheer force of Verwoerd's overpowering personality and *koersvastheid* – his almost messianic belief in the continued possibility and necessity of nationalist unity. But the fantasy (and the social project) was buried with Verwoerd. Open class conflict now spilled over into the NP itself. The verkrampte reaction represented those Afrikaner social forces which had drawn the least material benefit from NP

---

* The HNP advocated making Afrikaans the sole official language. Its programme called for the vigorous implementation of 'pure apartheid'. It demanded the restriction of urban residential rights for blacks, stricter separation of housing and social facilities, and reduced state expenditure on all services for the black community. Economic growth should be restricted to a rate governed by the availability of domestic white labour and local capital. See Davies *et al., The Struggle for South Africa*, vol. 1, p. 154.

† In this year Meyer retired as Broederbond chairman. As a result of a verligte tactical error, he was succeeded by another former Hertzog ally who likewise declined to follow his erstwhile friends into the political wilderness, Dr Andries Treurnicht.

Afrikaner favouritism. The Hertzogites were disgusted by the crass materialist excess of the new Afrikaner bourgeoisie, distraught at its easy renunciation of the populist civic culture of Afrikaner nationalism for capitalist wheeling and dealing and personal position, and outraged by the now overt contempt in which these powerful *nouveaux riches* held their less fortunate *volksgenote* (fellow members of the *volk*). The Hertzogite agitation was a last-ditch rearguard action to defend the social alliance, the nationalist project and the political culture of 1948 – a desperate attempt to delay ceding the nationalist field to Afrikaner *geldmagte*.

Himself a self-proclaimed lifelong 'socialist', Albert Hertzog always insisted that the *volk* was comprised largely of workers and that the NP was above all a party of Afrikaner workers. He told Parliament in 1953: 'We on this side are partly a party of farmers, but *largely a party of workers.*'[31] Since his election to parliament in 1948 he had organised study groups, recruitment drives and even secret organisations such as *Die Afrikaner Orde* to propagate his vision of *ware* (authentic) Afrikaner nationalism. Hertzog surrounded himself with Afrikaner labour leaders, petty clerkdom and less successful farmers. Yet for all his ideological consistency and curiously principled stance, he failed to recognise the inevitable – that the changing social composition of Afrikanerdom rendered the alliance of 1948 untenable. Hertzog and his little band of true believers were trapped by their own ideological fantasies and past success. Farmers and workers *had* comprised the voting fodder for the NP victory in 1948. Indeed, Hertzog's long battle to capture the Mine Workers' Union had forged Afrikaner support for the NP where none had existed before. His efforts gave the NP its first ever toehold in (white) working-class constituencies – winning eight such seats in 1948. In this sense, Beaumont Schoeman was right: without Hertzog the NP would simply not have come to power in 1948.[32] But by 1965 the world and the *volk* had changed. Now most Afrikaners were urban professionals, members of a middle class as much bent on conspicuous consumption as their 'materialistic' English-speaking white compatriots. A return to the purist vision of 1948 was simply inconceivable.

In his frustration with Vorster's pragmatism, Hertzog forgot the lesson he had learned so well to wean Afrikaner miners from the Labour Party in the 1940s: workers cared more about their wage packet and about their other material interests than ideology. The political timing of this once-outstanding organiser was also now terribly awry. Whatever Vorster's ideological deviations from 'authentic' Afrikaner nationalism, so long as the ongoing boom continually increased Afrikaner workers' living standards, they would simply not give a hoot for uncle Albert's dire warnings of NP betrayal and machinations by Afrikaner Hoggenheimers. So to its eternal bemusement, the HNP won minimal support from the Afrikaner workers and poorer farmers it so militantly claimed to champion.* Like his father before him, Albert Hertzog went into the political

---

* Hence the despair of the editor of the HNP newspaper, *Die Afrikaner,* when he replied to my question as to why Afrikaner workers, lower-level civil servants and less well-off farmers had not joined the HNP in droves: 'I fear, Mr O'Meara, that my people *(volk)* are not ideologically rooted.' Interview with Beaumont Schoeman, July 1975.

desert for the sake of impractical political principle. But whereas Hertzog *père* had tried to force Afrikaner chauvinism to evolve into something less exclusive before the social composition of the *volk* made this achievable, the son preferred the role of the Afrikaner Canute – hopelessly but proudly trying to hold back the tide of the inevitable consequences of social change and class formation.

His unavoidable failure did not mean of course that verkrampte politics per se were now impossible, but rather that Hertzog's purist interpretation of what this project should now involve confirmed his inability to judge the art of the possible. A return to the always mystical ideological notion of the mythical unity of a classless *volk* was pure nonsense. *That* glue had forever disappeared. Now the verkramptes would have to work to *accommodate* and so dominate the new Afrikaner bourgeoisie in the NP, rather that try, *à la* Hertzog, to *displace* it.

The short-lived political genius of John Vorster lay precisely in his recognition of this fact and his success in moulding the political adhesive which broadly held most Afrikaners of all classes in the NP for another 13 years after the angry departure of the Hertzogites. Vorster's Bonapartism was in one sense a masterful recognition of the new limits of the possible. He understood that to prevent a fundamental split along class lines, the NP would have to decentralise itself into a series of fiefdoms in which those who remained inside 'the family' would still have privileged access to a brokered consensus among competing Afrikaner power centres. Vorster transformed the NP from the political embodiment of a *volksbeweging* in the service of the *volk,* into a party of pluralist power centres held together by patronage and insider access. So long as verkramptes and verligtes were prepared to accept the existence of the other, so long as neither insisted that theirs was the only 'authentic' way, the National Party could remain broadly united, and each would have access to the goodies in the command of the state. Such was the power of this patronage and so sweet were the benefits of insider access that remarkably few of those who secretly agreed with Hertzog were prepared to follow him into the political desert. In this sense Hertzog's faithful were both the victims of their own idealism and correct in their accusations that the NP had betrayed its core principles. They likewise correctly foresaw that an NP now based on the pluralism of patronage must become increasingly corrupt – politically and materially.

Vorster's carefully cultivated Bonapartist position above the NP factions thus had significant consequences for political struggles in the Cabinet. His accommodating chairman of the board approach to government generated greater political independence within the state apparatus for individual members of the Cabinet. Powerful ministers were now able to use their ministries as a base from which to stake out territory within the party, to become the barons of the NP, rather than vice versa as had been the practice in the past. And given that Cabinet appointments were the exclusive prerogative of the Prime Minister, this also reinforced their loyalty to Vorster and his 'pragmatism'.

After the expulsion of the Hertzogites the factionalist struggle within the NP was increasingly waged within, but more particularly between various government ministries. Specific ministries became identified with certain 'lines' within the NP, and interdepartmental conflicts were openly discussed in the Afrikaans press – an unprecedented development which reflected the fragile unity of Afrikaner nationalism (see Chapters 10–11).

This shift in political terrains of the conflict within Afrikaner nationalism grew partly out of the leadership style imposed by Vorster. While the economy was booming and the country enjoyed relative political prosperity, Vorster was able to sustain his Bonapartist role within party and government. Once the Hertzog group was driven out of the NP, the Prime Minister basked in enormous personal prestige and enjoyed great influence. Following the across-the-board successes of the NP against the HNP in the 1970 general elections, Vorster was able to reduce his previous heavy political reliance on the Cape NP and assume in reality the role he had cast for himself as the force uniting in his person all factions within the NP.

His appeal now reached beyond the 'traditional' constituents of Afrikaner nationalism. Vorster's opening towards English-speaking whites considerably expanded the support base of the NP, bringing much of the anglophone establishment into its ambit. This eased what was left of the Afrikaner/English ethnic tensions so long characteristic of white politics and society. It also facilitated even further cooperation between Afrikaner and 'English' business, thereby smoothing the way for further penetration of various sectors by Afrikaner monopolies such as Sanlam, Rembrandt, Volkskas *et al.*

However, it was possible to sustain this Bonapartist reconstruction of Afrikaner unity only so long as the NP government retained the ability to deliver sufficient benefits to all the Afrikaner power centres/interests seated around the NP table. To put this another way: the moment that a major power centre confronted a pressing need to change policies in order to protect its own particular fundamental interests, the NP would become decreasingly capable of maintaining its 'I won't rock your boat if you won't rock mine' consensus. Such a situation began to develop with the multi-levelled crises that emerged in the early 1970s and reached their full force in 1976. As this crisis unfolded, Vorster's Bonapartism was less and less able to find the magic formula which would enable him to accommodate all the conflicting versions of the Afrikaner project.

Chapter Nine

A FUTURE TOO GHASTLY TO CONTEMPLATE

The crisis of the mid-1970s

US Secretary of State visits SA, but fails to persuade Vorster to abandon apartheid

White South Africa and its ruling National Party entered the 1970s at the crest of the golden age of apartheid. The economy sailed apparently unharmed through a minor collapse of the Johannesburg Stock Exchange in early 1969. Business was still booming and white living standards continued to rise steadily. The black population seemed cowed into submission. Not even the appearance of militant 'Black Consciousness' student organisations led by Steve Biko at the end of the 1960s disturbed the general white complacency. Always blissfully ignorant of the dynamics of black politics, and the gathering rage among black youth, the theorists of apartheid persuaded themselves that the 'Black Man You're on Your Own!' message of this emerging Black Consciousness Movement (BCM) simply confirmed their own belief in the impossibility of non-racial politics. The state actually briefly encouraged the growth of the premier BCM grouping, Biko's South African Student's Organisation (SASO).

White power looked equally secure in the rest of southern Africa. The United Nations' challenge to Pretoria's administration of Namibia seemed to have fizzled, while the armed struggle of the SWAPO liberation movement offered scant threat to the superpower of the region. In what was then still known as Rhodesia (Zimbabwe), the illegal Smith regime seemed to be comfortably weathering international sanctions with the help of Pretoria and Lisbon. The incursions of ZAPU guerrillas in 1967 and 1968 had been beaten back. The rival ZANU movement was not yet able to gain access to Rhodesian territory. And the Portuguese colonialists boasted of winning their wars against national liberation movements in Angola and Mozambique.

Things also seemed to be looking up for Pretoria internationally. The 1970 British elections saw Harold Wilson's Labour Party government swept from power. Edward Heath's new Tory administration resolved to resume supplying arms to South Africa – and to settle the Rhodesian issue on terms approved by Pretoria. And still years away from his own Watergate nemesis, the new occupant of the White House agreed with Henry Kissinger that white power would not be overthrown in southern Africa. The Nixon administration conducted business as usual with all the region's colonial regimes, while US intelligence services strove to help Lisbon, Pretoria and Salisbury in their battles against African liberation groups.

The only apparent blips on white South Africa's rosy horizon at the beginning of the 1970s were nagging inflation and the growing irritant of an international sports boycott. However, this cosy perspective was soon confounded. As the decade unfolded Pretoria suddenly confronted a seemingly unstoppable series of domestic, regional and international setbacks. Taken together, their impact seemed to implode an entire series of economic, political and social conditions underlying apartheid. By the mid-decade, the early glittering promise of the 1970s had proved to be mere white fool's gold. With the country mired in crisis, neither John Vorster nor his successor proved able to forge the philosopher's stone to turn the dross of apartheid into economic growth and social peace.

The crisis confronting the South African state and its ruling establishment in the latter half of the1970s was complex and multi-levelled – an ensemble of simultaneous and mutually determining economic, political, ideological and cultural crises. Their combined effect generated what Gramsci has termed an organic crisis.[1] Again, space prohibits a detailed investigation of the full complexity of these intersecting crises. Rather, in this and the following chapters, I examine three interlinked elements: the broad dimensions of the growing crisis of capital accumulation; the rapid intensification of social and political struggles during the 1970s; and, thirdly, the emerging political crisis for the broad white establishment. The aim is to attempt to understand how these elements simultaneously helped to shape, and articulated with, the internal dynamic of Afrikaner nationalist politics to produce a crisis of the state in the particular form of 'Muldergate'. This will provide a basis for an assessment of the 'incessant and persistent efforts' (see p. 487 below) to remould the existing order after 1978.

Gold, fruit and machines:
The limits to growth in the apartheid economy

The South African economy began a downswing in 1973. This developed into a full-blown recession in 1976. By 1978 the apartheid economy was mired in a deep structural crisis of accumulation from which it has not yet escaped.* To understand this rapid collapse, as well as the nature and dynamics of this structural crisis, it is necessary first to grasp something of the limits to accumulation in the apartheid economy, and secondly, the significant changes in the domestic structure of South African capitalism during the great boom of the 1960s.

South Africa appears to have a modern, diversified economy. The only industrialised country in Africa, it was classified by the World Bank as the world's 24th largest economy outside the Comecon block in 1985, accounting for 60,8 percent of the total GDP of the 17 African countries south of the equator (including Madagascar).[2] Manufacturing contributed 24,5 percent to the 1988 South African GDP of R178,5 billion. This was almost twice as much as the second most important productive sector, mining, and more than four times as much as agriculture. Manufacturing has also historically been the dynamic sector of the economy, growing faster than other productive sectors in cycles of expansion.

South Africa industrialised after 1925 on the basis of *import substitution of consumer goods* for its relatively small population. Three factors played a central role in this process: heavy state subsidies for and protection of local agriculture and manufacturing; the cheap migrant labour measures which lay at the heart of the racial policies of all South African governments until the 1980s; and the flow

---

* The short burst of very rapid growth of 1980–81 was entirely due to the spectacular increase in the price of gold as a result of the Iran hostage crisis. Once the gold price began its overall downward turn during the 1980s, the South African economy was plunged back into recession.

of foreign capital first into the mining and later the manufacturing sectors. Taken together, these three elements fashioned a significant industrial base, producing consumer goods for a *domestic* market. The size of this domestic market, and patterns of demand within it, were both largely set by the racial policies of successive governments. The racially determined nature of consumer demand itself then acted as an important factor shaping, and limiting, the pattern of industrialisation through import substitution. This is seen in a number of ways.

Firstly, with the domestic market predominantly geared around the demand of the small white minority, the pattern of import substitution was tied very closely to this white demand. This tended to eliminate the possibilities of economies of scale in anything but those most basic wage good industries catering to a black demand – which latter was itself structured by low incomes and high levels of relative poverty. Secondly, at least until the early 1980s, the education system was explicitly designed to confine blacks to the lowest rungs of the labour market, training them only in the most basic literacy and numeracy.

Skilled, technical and professional work was reserved by statute for whites. This led to permanent and severe shortages of skilled and technical labour in all sectors of the economy, but most particularly manufacturing. It also militated against significant research and development initiatives, and hence the emergence of a domestic technological capacity. Thirdly, the large state subsidies to industry, and the high wage structure of *white* labour within it, when taken together with the overall generally low levels of productivity, meant that South African manufactures were simply not competitive on world markets. Their only external market lay in the narrow circle of neighbouring states. International abhorrence of apartheid further restricted the possibility of access to significant export markets.

The South African economy had become almost entirely self-sufficient in consumer goods by the 1960s. Yet it produced neither the technologies nor the heavy machinery and equipment needed both to manufacture these consumer goods and to service the other sectors of the economy. The vast bulk of the capital and intermediate goods used in all sectors of the economy was, and still is, imported. The Governor of the South African Reserve Bank estimated in 1987 that as much as 80 percent of the country's imports were comprised of capital equipment and intermediate goods, without which the economy could not sustain itself.[3] *Growing industrial capacity thus always implied increased imports of these crucial inputs.* Known in South Africa as the 'propensity to import', this in turn could only be sustained if ways could be found to raise the foreign exchange needed to pay for such imports.

Here lies the major structural difference between the apartheid economy and that of the small group of Asian countries which managed to industrialise during the 1960s. Unlike these newly industrialised economies, South Africa has failed to emerge as a significant exporter of manufactured goods. For over seventy years, its role in international trade has essentially been that of an exporter of gold and other strategic minerals to the developed market economies, and an importer of capital and intermediate goods, of oil and of arms from them. South Africa's trade profile is not that of a 'newly industrialising country' such as South Korea, but rather of an exceptionally well-developed exporter of primary products. Mineral products alone have consistently generated between 70 percent and 85 percent of its export earnings, with manufacturing barely accounting for 10 percent. South Africa's manufacturing sector is thus a net consumer rather than a net producer of foreign exchange, importing four times as much as it exports.

Since the end of World War II, South Africa has acquired the foreign exchange needed to pay for these essential imported economic inputs from just two sources: earnings from the export of primary products – predominantly minerals, and principally gold; and various forms of foreign capital inflows – investment, non-equity arrangements and loans.

This last point is crucial. It points to the fact that the pace and scale of industrial production has *always been absolutely limited by the capacity of the economy to generate inflows of foreign exchange* – either through trade, through direct or indirect investment, or through loans. This 'foreign exchange constraint' became a growing worry through the boom of the 1960s and then generated an outright recession in the mid/late 1970s.

House of cards:
The great boom of the 1960s

As indicated in Chapter 5, the Draconian measures after Sharpeville imposed the requisite political stability and labour docility for rapid growth. Between 1964 and 1969 fewer than 2 000 African workers were involved in labour stoppages in any single year. Once the underground networks of the ANC, Communist Party and PAC had been wiped out by mid-1963, the rest of the decade had been marked by almost complete political passivity among the black population. Not until the emergence of the Black Consciousness Movement in 1969 did an overt black political voice again challenge apartheid

This 'golden age of apartheid' from 1964 to 1972 was a period of very rapid capital accumulation. As the economy grew by an average annual rate of six to eight percent per annum, two interrelated aspects of the boom began to lead to a shift in the *domestic* structure of South African capitalism. On the one hand, the rapid increase in GDP growth was based on increasingly capital-intensive industrial production. Real capital stock per worker in the manufacturing sector rose by annual average of 3,15 percent during the 1960s.[4] On the other hand, this growing capital intensification gave rise to, and took place through, an accelerating process of acquisitions and mergers – more technically known as the centralisation and interpenetration of capitals. The ownership structure of the urban economy was transformed in the process, and the South African capitalist class effectively reorganised economically.

The major mining finance houses had begun diversifying into manufacturing and other branches of the economy in the early 1950s. This process was accelerated by the flight of foreign capital after Sharpeville as large local corporations began buying up shares at fire sale prices. By the mid-1960s, the big mining finance houses, and particularly the giant Anglo American Corporation, had emerged as major industrial groups. Large manufacturing concerns – most notably the Barlow group – likewise began to invest in mining, commercial and financial undertakings. And the leading financial institutions, and particularly the two largest insurance companies, Old Mutual and Sanlam, gathered up growing assets in all sectors. These years also saw a considerable expansion of finance capital. Merchant banks and other new institutions arose to facilitate the growing number of mergers and takeovers. As the range and variety of available credit services expanded, the monetary and banking sector was transformed.[5]

The 1960s thus saw the consolidation of large conglomerates with extensive interests in most branches of the economy. The traditional sectoral differences between corporate capital became less and less relevant. Once investor fears had been stilled by the post-Sharpeville crackdown, foreign capital poured back into South Africa – some R3 559 million between 1965 and 1974. By 1970, total foreign investment was estimated at R5 818 million, rising to R6 694 million in 1974. The average rate of return on capital invested in apartheid South Africa after 1964 was among the highest, if not the highest, anywhere. As late as 1974, 'the average American corporation received an 18 percent return on its South African investment, as compared with a return of only 8 percent in Britain'.[6]

The emergence of these new cross-cutting conglomerates led to significant shifts in relations within South Africa's capitalist class. Prior to 1960, the economy had been characterised by a sharp economic distinction and political antagonism between local and foreign undertakings. These effectively dissolved in the 1960s. More importantly from the point of view of this study, the decade also saw the first large-scale collaboration between English and Afrikaner conglomerates, provoking furious debate within the ranks of Afrikaner nationalism (see above pp. 120-4).

This growing English–Afrikaner business cooperation was also facilitated by new corporate ideologies and business practices. The haphazard, British-derived techniques of South African management rapidly gave way to an American-styled managerialism. Most of the white universities now set up schools of business. US business practices were extensively studied and copied. 'Scientific management' – with its obsession with personnel management, with optimum productivity, with budget and cost control systems and industrial organisation – became the new watchword of South African capitalists, both English and Afrikaans-speaking.

The boom thus transformed the domestic structure of South African capitalism, reorganising the capitalist class and changing the structure of production and accumulation. The dominance of capital-intensive production significantly modified the organisation of industrial labour processes, with important consequences for the position and interests of black and white workers. The introduction of increasingly sophisticated technologies led to a relative reduction in the number of workers needed to operate them, or, in other words, a decrease in the number of workers employed per unit of capital. It also changed the industrial division of labour among the employed. The old unskilled/skilled division of labour gave way to a distinction between semi-skilled operatives on the one hand, and technical/supervisory labour on the other.

Thus while large numbers of semi-skilled (African) operatives were being drawn into production during the 1960s, even larger numbers of unskilled African migrant workers were rendered redundant. This process marked a shift away from the reliance on cheap, unskilled *migrant* labour so long characteristic of South African industry, towards the consolidation of a stable, semi-skilled workforce now organised around *contract* labour. This changing nature of the urban labour force in turn generated two acute problems, both of which would eventually call into question apartheid's ability to sustain expanded accumulation.

Firstly, the number of unemployed African workers rose from 582 000 in 1962 to 750 000 in 1966. It reached 1 million at the height of the boom in 1970.[7] Under apartheid's influx control system, these unemployed Africans were supposed to be removed from the cities and dumped in the festering rural slums of the Bantustans. Secondly, the rising capital intensity in manufacturing also rendered large numbers of skilled white workers relatively superfluous to production, as their specific skills were now superseded by a growing need for technical/supervisory labour. Yet the jobs of white workers were protected by apartheid laws. As all supervisory, technical and professional work was reserved exclusively for whites, few skilled white workers thus lost their jobs in this changing organisation of the labour process. Rather, they were either retrained and/or converted into supervisors of gangs of African operatives. However, neither retraining nor reclassifying white workers solved the growing demand for technical, professional and semi-professional labour – shortages estimated at some 47 000 such workers in 1969.[8]

These technical labour shortages – in the midst of growing black unemployment – generated regular demands from big business for the easing of apartheid restrictions on the mobility, the employment and the training of African workers. Employers' organisations lobbied in vain to be allowed to cultivate a stable supply of semi-skilled African operatives with the right to permanent residence in the black townships surrounding the 'white' cities. They were equally unsuccessful in their pleas to be allowed to retrain African workers for technical labour. The restrictions on the employment of black workers imposed by the 1968 Physical Planning Act, and the entire Job Reservation system, were particularly criticised by all elements of organised business.

However, while these shortages of technical labour certainly held back even faster growth, the overall white prosperity and high profitability tended to mitigate the worst effects of such labour shortages. While the boom persisted, the maintenance of a rigid racial division of labour in industry did not seriously threaten the interests of the capitalist class. Indeed in their attempts to secure trained African labour to make up the shortages of technical workers, even the most liberal capitalists at times *defended* this racial division of labour.[9] Despite their growing frustration, few businessmen moved into open confrontation with the government during the 1960s.

The boom also aggravated, but temporarily concealed, another growing structural economic problem. Given South Africa's static role in the rapidly transforming global economy, the boom intensified the process of import substitution for a domestic market – whose size was itself constrained by the low-wage policies of apartheid. The rapid growth of capital-intensive manufacturing during the boom actually *intensified* the dependence of the South African economy on external inputs – particularly foreign technologies and capital and intermediate equipment. These imports had to be paid for by mineral and agricultural exports, or by other inflows of foreign capital. The continuing large influx of foreign investment during the boom thus cushioned the economy from the worst consequences of expanded imports. But more than a few economists were aware that the rapid growth of the boom years had rendered the South African economy even more vulnerable to the vicissitudes of the world economy and to the confidence of foreign investors.

Winds of change:
The recession of the 1970s

The boom began to tail off under the impact of growing inflation in the early 1970s. By 1976 a complex interplay of internal and external factors had produced a full-scale recession.* The volume of manufacturing output fell by almost 6 percent in the year 1974–75. In 1976 all sectors of industry, bar leather products and footwear, reported sharp falls in production and a collapse of domestic demand. Total investment in manufacturing declined by 13 percent between 1975 and 1977. The real growth rate was negative in the first half of 1976, nil in 1977 and negative again in 1978.[10]

In the context of an international recession and growing industrial, economic and political instability within South Africa itself and the southern African region as a whole (see below), the inflows of foreign capital which had sustained the rapid growth of the 1960s began to dry up. South African Reserve Bank statistics show a decline in the inflow of long-term foreign investment from R1 561 million in 1975/76 to R452 million by 1976/77. If this is coupled with the actual net outflow of short-term capital from the private sector, a net capital

---

* These included: the international downswing following the 1973 Yom Kippur War; growing political instability in South and southern Africa; a falling gold price; and specific, inept fiscal and monetary policies of the South African state. On the latter point, see Davies *et al., Struggle for South Africa.* vol. 1, pp. 54 ff.

outflow of R121 million occurred in the financial year 1976/77.[11] The recession also dramatically increased the number of unemployed African workers. By 1976, an estimated 2,3 million African workers were out of work. One economist calculated that a growth rate of 6,7 percent was needed simply to prevent this number from increasing.[12] At the same time, however, the shortages of skilled workers accelerated. By 1977, government figures showed vacancies for 99 000 workers in the technical, professional and semi-professional grades.[13] The pages of economic journals were filled with reports of bankruptcies, and the state was forced to abandon or defer major infrastructural investment programmes in steel, petrochemicals, transport and other sectors.

The impact of the recession was uneven, however. Many smaller undertakings were wiped out. This reinforced two interlinked processes begun during the boom of the 1960s – the increasing capital-intensity of industrial (and to a lesser extent, agricultural) production, and the interpenetration and centralisation of capital. The annual average rate of increase of real capital stock per worker in manufacturing rose from 3,15 percent in 1961–70 to 4,95 percent in 1971–73.*

The recession likewise accelerated horizontal and vertical integration in the economy. By 1981, eight conglomerates controlled over 60 percent of the assets in the private sector. A mere four years later, four of these conglomerates had been swallowed by the 'big four'. Anglo American, Sanlam, SA Mutual and Rembrandt now together controlled over 80 percent of the listed shares on the Johannesburg Stock Exchange.[14] Sanlam and Rembrandt had spearheaded the 'Afrikaner economic movement' of the 1940s. Their position at the pinnacle of South African capitalism further reduced the linguistic and political tensions between Afrikaner and English capital.

The worst effects of the recession were felt in the agricultural sector, still characterised by large numbers of relatively inefficient, labour-intensive, individual undertakings.† Heavily dependent on state subsidies and the apartheid cheap labour system, and racked by acute and growing indebtedness, many smaller individual agricultural capitals could not survive a recession. The number of individual farms fell by a third between 1960 and 1980, and the major conglomerates had each developed substantial agribusiness interests.[15]

Yet the impact of the recession on the different branches (and regions) of agricultural production was also uneven. Cape wine, deciduous fruit and wool farmers, together with Natal sugar growers, were generally less debt-ridden and less dependent both on state subsidies and on stringently controlled labour than was the single largest group of farmers – Transvaal and Orange Free State maize

---

* Beaudet, *Afrique du Sud*. Another study claims that the capital/labour ration increased by an annual average of 5% between 1965 and 1975 – M Williams (pseud.), *South Africa: Crisis of World Capitalism and the Apartheid Economy* (Winstanley Publications, London, 1977), 16.

† Of the 104 000 registered white-owned farms in 1960, 75% were farmed by individual owners, 22% were rented or sharecropped, and only 3% were farmed by managers. *Report on Agricultural and Pastoral Production* (Department of Agriculture, Government Printer, Pretoria, UG 70/1960), 5.

producers. Since maize farmers were the real backbone of the ruling National Party in these two provinces, their economic vulnerability had important political consequences.

The mid-1970s recession thus went beyond a normal cyclical downswing to reflect a profound structural crisis for South African capitalism – one which called into question its specific path of development over the past fifty years. It revealed very clearly that, under the prevailing internal political and social conditions, the South African economy was reaching the limits of industrial expansion based on import substitution and cheap labour. As such, the recession significantly affected the politics of capital. Virtually all business groups agreed with the 1972 Reynders Commission that further industrial expansion required a shift in exports. Further industrial expansion would have to be based on the development of a strong capital goods sector, and a shift in the emphasis of exports towards industrial rather than primary products.[16] This in turn implied changing the nature and training of the labour force. The cheap labour policies of the past were no longer conducive to growth. What had once been the central engine of economic growth – the abundant supplies of cheap, unskilled labour – was now turning into a constraining factor. Apartheid was becoming less and less profitable.

For the larger conglomerates – Afrikaner as well as 'English' – the recession posed the urgent need to change the domestic *conditions of capital accumulation*. Restoring profitability appeared to demand a complex restructuring of capital in all sectors to render labour more productive. This implied the need for an even more capital-intensive basis to industry, now linked to the need to reap the benefits of economies of scale.[17]

Moreover, the existing system of cheap migrant labour severely limited the size of the domestic market. Most businessmen were agreed that renewed economic growth also required an expansion of this market via higher wages for a settled black urban workforce. They were not, however, arguing for an absolute increase in their own wage bill. Rather, they favoured the introduction of semi-skilled, better-paid African labour to replace – and to undercut – the high-wage and relatively unproductive corps of white workers protected by the Job Reservation legislation. The pressing need to restructure the entire set of conditions under which labour was utilised within the South African economy on the one hand, and the structure of the market on the other, were now posed as urgent *political* problems for the capitalist class as a whole (see below).

These issues all went to the heart of Grand Apartheid policy and the National Party's hegemonic project. Any change would be seen as a direct threat both to the precarious position of smaller agricultural capital, as well as the protected niche of racial privilege enjoyed by organised white labour. The growing political battles within the white establishment around such issues were exacerbated by developing industrial and political instability throughout southern Africa.

Whose backyard?
The challenge to domestic and regional hegemony

The 1970s began with a massive strike of contract workers in South African-ruled Namibia, one which forced significant concessions out of the mining companies. This new labour militancy soon spread to the white heartland. From the end of 1972 and throughout much of 1973, South African industry was shaken by wave upon wave of strikes by African workers demanding higher wages and the right to organise.[18] These strikes began at the tail end of the great boom of the 1960s and in many ways heralded the onset of the 1970s recession. The mining industry was also beset by violent stoppages and strikes between 1972 and 1976. These were largely suppressed by force – eleven striking miners were shot dead at Carletonville by police summonsed by the Anglo American Corporation in 1973.

These labour struggles spawned the first fledgling black trade unions in a decade. Though overt black political discourse in the early 1970s was overwhelmingly shaped by the rhetoric of Black Consciousness, most of these new unions fought for a non-racial, class perspective. While relatively weak until the end of the 1970s, they managed to survive both the banning of organisers and the cultivation of docile alternatives by the state and employers.

The jolt to white power delivered by these strikes was soon reinforced by startling changes in the neighbouring countries. On 25 April 1974, exhausted by three losing colonial wars, the Portuguese Armed Forces Movement overthrew the world's longest-surviving fascist dictatorship in Lisbon. The consequent dramatic collapse of Portuguese colonialism in 1974–75 was a profound defeat for Pretoria's regional strategies to sustain the white-ruled 'buffer states' encircling South Africa. This first real shift in the regional balance of power elicited a striking response from blacks living under apartheid. In September 1974, the South African Students Organisation organised an illegal rally of 30 000 in solidarity with Mozambique's FRELIMO-dominated transitional government. Mozambican independence in June 1975 was widely celebrated in South African black communities. It was followed barely two months later by South Africa's first incursion into Angola, eventually turned back on the outskirts of Luanda by Angolan and Cuban troops, forcing the South African army into a humiliating withdrawal in March 1976 (see Chapter 11).

Despite a propaganda offensive to persuade shaken whites that the invasion of Angola had been a military triumph, black South Africans gleefully – and correctly – saw this withdrawal as an another important setback for the apartheid regime.* Yet NP insiders recognised that what verligte journalist Schalk Pienaar

---

* The state television service broadcast a particularly crude 'recreation' of such 'heroics' entitled 'Bridge 14' in May 1976. Newspaper headlines were emblazoned with choice quotes from the heroes. One wounded officer said of his alleged slaying of many of the Cuban soldiers, 'I did it for Christ.' BOSS defector Gordon Winter describes elements of this propaganda offensive, *Inside BOSS, passim.*

ironically labelled the *ligte mistykie* ('slight mistake') of invading Angola had been a disaster for Pretoria. The then Secretary for Information later described the SADF incursion into Angola as 'one of the greatest blunders in South African history'.[19] It certainly helped precipitate widespread black defiance which led to the historic events of 16 June 1976.

The growing militancy of South African blacks in the early 1970s had not been confined to working-class struggles. The Black Consciousness movement gradually reawoke and crystallised the political militancy of much of the black intelligentsia and youth. This culminated in the widespread revolt of June 1976 known as the Soweto uprising. Thousands upon thousands of black school-children defied bullets, tear gas and armoured cars in a three-month struggle for control of the streets. Hundreds died.* The slaughter of unarmed schoolchildren at Soweto gave the lie to Prime Minister Vorster's earlier attempt to defend his crackdown as Justice Minister in the 1960s with the claim that he had warned the South African Police: 'Heaven help anyone who ill-treats a child.'[20]

Yet unlike Sharpeville sixteen years earlier, 'Soweto' entered South African political culture not as a massacre but as a proud and glorious rebellion. Those who died were not seen as victims of apartheid but as heroes in the struggle to overthrow it. Soweto showed that significant numbers of urban black South Africans no longer perceived themselves as the passive victims of white power, but rather as the active makers of their own history. Sixteen years after Sharpeville, the schoolchildren of Soweto confirmed martyred Ingrid Jonker's prophetic vision that the baby killed at Nyanga in 1960 would return to haunt the regime:

> The child is not dead
> the child lifts his fists against his mother
> who screams Africa shouts the scent
> of freedom and the veld
> in the locations of the cordoned heart[21]

Like 'Munich' or 'Suez', Soweto was one of those rare historical catalysts which irreversibly transform the political landscape, whose very name becomes a metaphor for lessons learned by an entire society.† Soweto forced Afrikaner

---

* Official figures list 192 deaths from the 16 000 rounds fired by the Soweto police, with 1 439 injured. 'Other causes' claimed another 122 lives in Soweto, and 1 006 injuries. A further 20 people died under police guns on the East Rand, with another 92 in the Western Cape. SAIRR, *A Survey, 1976,* 86-7. A number of journalists who reported on the disturbances told me that they estimated that between 700 and 800 people died during the Soweto uprising.

† In a very different context, Joseph Nye has written about how such events impose 'discontinuous' or 'lumpy' learning on an entire society: 'Large groups or generations may learn by crises or major events which serve as metaphors for organising diverse sets of experiences.' See his 'Nuclear learning and US–Soviet security regimes', *International Organisation,* 41, 3, 1987, 398.

nationalism to abandon the cherished fantasy of shaping South Africa in its idealised image. Here lay a dual lesson. By destroying Andries Treurnicht's attempt to educate them in Afrikaans, the schoolchildren of Soweto tolled the failure of the NP's efforts to Afrikanerise South Africa. With minimal soul-searching, the nationalist establishment abandoned the quest for the Holy Grail of *volkseie* in favour of a broader white solidarity. Afrikaners learned that, in the end, most of them favoured Mammon over Mission.

Moreover, Soweto finally forced the NP to concede the one political advantage to which Verwoerd had been so determined to cling – its own belief in the morality of Grand Apartheid. The self-righteous sense of a divine mission to fashion 'separate freedoms' likewise rapidly gave way to a grubby and cynical scrambling to shore up white privilege and power. From now on, the NP would be largely on the defensive, desperately seeking ways to regain the political initiative – and to restore economic growth. Soweto turned the deep concern about the recession into a full-blown political crisis over securing a stable political future for renewed growth.

Black South Africa also learned crucial lessons in June 1976. Coming but four months on the heels of the humiliation of the South African army in Angola, and in many ways as a direct consequence of what most blacks perceived to be a stinging defeat for Pretoria, Soweto crystallised a growing sense that white power was vulnerable, that the hour of black resistance was approaching. It made it very clear that the old ways of apartheid could not continue, that change would have to come to South Africa.[22] Soweto regenerated a deep sense of pride in much of the black population. It was a key catalyst of the psychological liberation which the Black Consciousness movement had worked so hard to produce.

But here too the lesson learned was two-sided. Soweto marked both the greatest achievement and the beginning of the decline of Black Consciousness. The rebellion clearly revealed the limits of the student vanguardism at its heart, and the movement's failure to capture broad working-class support. Soweto thus crystallised a rapid reorientation of black politics. Many black organisations now began to draw a link between the apartheid policies of the NP government on the one hand and capitalism on the other.[23] White business grew concerned that black demands for an end to racial discrimination were beginning to encompass a rejection of capitalism itself, that in the words of South Africa's leading business journal, 'there is a general tendency for young Africans to be anti-free enterprise'.[24]

The second lesson of Soweto was to leave even deeper scars. The vast courage of the young rebels defying the might of the apartheid state helped to generate a revolutionary *élan* which transfigured the politics of black liberation in the 1980s. Its major beneficiary was a rebuilt ANC, which emerged as the dominant force in South African politics during this decade. However, the new political culture fashioned by Soweto was voluntaristic, maximalist and profoundly militaristic. It gave rise to an ultimately apolitical cult of 'the Young Lions' which eventually became a real political millstone for the ANC, hamstringing the organisation in negotiations, and significantly contributing to the confrontationalist culture of violence after February 1990.

The lessons of Soweto extended beyond South Africa. Following hard on Pretoria's humiliation in Angola, the revolt of black schoolchildren generated an enormous racial pride all over Africa. Soweto occasioned 'lumpy learning' throughout the African continent.[25] It reshaped perceptions of the conflict and the strategic options open. Mere schoolchildren had challenged the mighty Boers, forcing them to back down. This seemed to confirm the contention of radical African governments that resisting the military power of Pretoria did not automatically lead to disaster, that 'the Boers' were vulnerable. Soweto was thus also a crucial moment which significantly shaped an emerging militarist political culture throughout the whole of southern Africa – a culture which was to play such a crucial role in the unfolding regional tragedy of the 1980s.

Still, events in the rest of southern Africa continued to run against Pretoria. Escalating anti-colonial struggle in Namibia provoked the diplomatic intervention of the five leading Western powers. The Smith regime in Rhodesia came to be sorely pressed once ZANU guerrillas gained access in 1972 to Rhodesian territory through a corridor in FRELIMO-controlled areas of Mozambique's Tete Province. By 1977 the two Zimbabwean nationalist movements had formed a Patriotic Front which won wide diplomatic support. The days of white Rhodesia were clearly numbered.

South Africa also grew increasingly isolated from its Western allies. Britain finally abandoned its naval base at Simonstown in 1974, and the evolving geo-strategies of the US military no longer gave priority to control of the sea route around the Cape.[26] The new US Carter administration took a markedly tougher line on southern African questions than its Nixon–Ford predecessor. Meeting the American Vice President in Vienna in early 1977, a shocked South African Prime Minister was told that there would have to be 'one man one vote' in South Africa. With American concurrence, the 1977 UN arms embargo imposed the first mandatory sanctions against South Africa.

In this context of domestic and regional crisis, two interlinked sets of political issues moved centre stage. The first concerned the types of formative action needed to resolve each of these separate moments of crisis as well as the overall 'organic' crisis. This then posed, secondly, the issue of the appropriate political organisations and forms to carry out such 'reforms'. If the capitalist class and specific factions of the National Party were broadly agreed on the first issue, they were deeply divided on the second – the capacity of the NP government to implement such a restructuring.

The reasonable people? The politics of reformed capitalism

The years 1975–78 saw an explosion of politicking around the developing crisis. All organisations of the capitalist class joined in sharp debate over the character and scope of the required 'reforms'. Organised agriculture excepted, the employers' organisations were all in broad agreement on the general principles, if not always the details, of the economic, social and constitutional policy reforms essential to renewed prosperity.*

Organised business now demanded four general changes in economic policy. First was a relaxation of the array of apartheid restrictions on the mobility of African labour to permit its more profitable utilisation. The areas targeted by capital included influx controls, the administration of the pass laws, the labour bureaux system and various provisions of the Physical Planning Act. This was accompanied, secondly, by a demand for the abolition of Job Reservation policies restricting the employment and training of Africans in positions 'reserved' for whites. Following the Soweto uprising businessmen also began to demand improvements in the Bantu Education system so as to produce people 'suitably qualified' for employment in increasingly high technology production systems.

Issues of mobility and training then raised, thirdly, the need for a *negotiated* reorganisation of production. This implied modifying the Industrial Conciliation Act, which effectively excluded Africans from membership of registered trade unions. Businessmen were agreed on the need for some form of recognition *and control* of collective bargaining for African workers. Though differing over the particular desirable *forms* of recognition and control, most business leaders now argued that only trade union rights for African workers might ensure industrial peace.† The employers' organisations came together to form the South African Employers' Consultative Committee in November 1974, to 'coordinate and crystallise employer thinking on labour affairs ... [and] ... deal with labour matters and from an employers' point of view'. At its first meeting in January 1975, the committee discussed black trade unions.[27]

Finally, capital now demanded a reduction in state ownership and control of key areas of the economy. The 1974 and 1975 congresses of the firmly pro-NP Afrikaanse Handelsinstituut were particularly disturbed over what was termed 'creeping socialism'. Taxation policy also aroused much excited comment.‡ In one of those phrases which capture the almost endearing shamelessness of

---

* Specifically here I include: Federated Chambers of Industry (FCI): Associated Chambers of Commerce (Assocom); Steel and Engineering Industries Federation of South Africa (Seifsa); Afrikaanse Handelsinstituut (AHI); and the Chamber of Mines (CoM). Neither the South African Agricultural Union nor the South African Maize Producers' Institute went along with these demands. Only the FCI issued a public manifesto. I have distilled what follows from the public statements of the period.

† General Mining's Wim de Villiers called for 'strong company unions' which would enjoy the right to strike – inaugural address on accepting an honorary professorship at the Rand Afrikaans University, 25 March 1975. The AHI was divided over most desirable forms of collective bargaining. Its journal *Volkshandel* simply listed the four 'alternatives', February 1975. The FCI and Assocom seemed prepared to see the recognition of African trade unions. *Financial Mail,* 23 May 1975 and *Rand Daily Mail,* 20 June 1975.

‡ *Volkshandel,* June 1974, June 1975. Again, this marks an ironic turning point in the position of Afrikaner business. In the 1940s and 1950s the AHI had argued vociferously for exactly those kinds of state control over which it was now so agitated.

Afrikaner racism, the AHI executive director blithely explained that enhanced mobility for black labour, the training of black workers and reduced state expenditure were all essential, 'if we are to keep all that we have'.[28]

These issues of the mobility, employment and training of labour, of industrial relations, state economic control and taxation were all at the core of the apartheid project. The demands of the employers' organisations now effectively posed the need for far-reaching modifications to forge new political conditions and alliances capable of sustaining such economic 'reforms'. In effect, they were calling for a new hegemonic project.* Here were raised questions of both domestic and foreign policy.

The flight of foreign capital, difficulties in raising foreign loans, the arms embargo, the hostility of the Carter administration, intensifying regional liberation wars, the growing need for export markets for industrial commodities, all underscored the link between international respectability, regional stability and renewed accumulation. Once again, employers' organisations pressured the government for reforms which would ease South Africa's international isolation, renew the flow of foreign investment, guarantee Western support in Namibia and Zimbabwe, and, if possible, open the African continental market to South African products.[29]

However, the overriding concern remained the need to restore domestic stability. After Soweto, individual businessmen and the employers' organisations realised that mere reform of economic policy would not of itself recreate conditions of growth. Economic reform needed to be accompanied by a restructuring of social and political relationships. As the influential *Financial Mail* editorialised: 'If South Africa is to move beyond its current impasse, a new vision is necessary.' Given the general 'anti-free enterprise' attitudes of black youth and the widespread link drawn between 'government policy and the aims of business', the most urgent task was to persuade black nationalists of the 'merits of capitalism'.[30]

New organisations were set up to accomplish this task. All major business groupings supported the formation in 1976 of a 'Free Market Foundation' to 'spread the message of free enterprise to young blacks'.[31] On the joint initiative of Harry Oppenheimer of the Anglo American Corporation and Anton Rupert of the Rembrandt group, most of South Africa's major companies combined forces in 1977 to form the Urban Foundation (UF). The establishment of the UF 'introduced the role of a "specialist change agency" into the relationship between organised business and government'.[32] Its major objective was to assist in the development of a black middle class with 'Western-type materialistic needs and ambitions'. This was deemed essential because

> only by having this most responsible section of the urban black population on our side can the whites of South Africa be assured of containing on a long term basis

---

* See footnote, p. 488 below, for my definition of hegemonic project.

the irresponsible economic and political ambitions of those blacks who are influenced against their own real interests from within and without our borders.*

So blatant was the UF obsession with a black middle-class bulwark against revolution that it became an early and easy target of radical organisations.† It later instructed its officials to negotiate out of the public eye. Yet UF programmes were a barometer of capital's collective thinking. They reflected the recognition that different strategies would have to be pursued towards the various classes of the black population, and more particularly towards *urban* blacks. In the evocative terminology of Mike Morris, the UF now argued that it was essential to move away from the 'class suppression' apartheid was intended to introducte in the black population, towards the 'class differentiation' normal to capitalism.‡ The South African Institute of Race Relations and most white liberals had been arguing this for decades. Since the end of the 1950s, Harry Oppenheimer had used his immense influence and wealth to advocate such policies. By 1976 however, so severe had the crisis become that the full collective energies and attention of business could now be mobilised around these issues, to elaborate what was in effect the common programme of the capitalist class.

The UF, the major employers' groups, the press and individual enterprises all recognised the need to improve the 'quality of life' of target groups in the black population, in order to demonstrate the 'superiority of capitalism' and deflect black opposition to what was called 'the system'. Their proposals assumed that the black population in the cities was permanently urbanised and could not be

---

* Urban Foundation, quoted in Davies *et al., Struggle for South Africa,* vol. 1, pp. 122-5. The UF was clearly an organ of big business, claiming that the involvement of smaller undertakings in its programmes was 'impractical at the current moment'. By May 1981 it had received just over R32 million from 233 donors, 58% of whom accounted for over 90% of these donations and 14 of whom appeared in the *Financial Mail's* 'Giants League' of the largest South African Corporations, and a further 13 in that journal's 'Top 100'. More than half of the UF's funds came from seven large donors. Anglo American alone contributed R11 million, or 34% of UF funds. All the then other major monopolies and banks – with the notable exception of Volkskas – each donated at least R750 000, and some considerably more. See T Karon, 'The Urban Foundation', in L Cooper & D Kaplan (eds), *Selected Research Papers on Aspects of Organisation in the Western Cape* (University of Cape Town, 1982). For a UF apology, see R Lee, 'The Role of the Private Sector as a Catalyst for Social Change in South Africa', *African Affairs,* vol. 82, no. 329, October 1983.

† Thus, before its banning at the end of 1977, the South African Students' Organisation attacked the UF for 'sabotaging' the interests and unity of blacks by fostering a black middle class. *Rand Daily Mail,* 7 August 1977.

‡ 'State, capital and growth: the political economy of the national question', in S Gelb (ed.), *South Africa's Economic Crisis* (David Philip/Zed Books, Cape Town/London, 1991). By 'class suppression' Morris means the apartheid attempt to suppress capitalism's 'natural' process of class differentiation within the black population, lumping it all into one social (though not ethnic) category.

shifted back to the bantustans – as was still the declared aim of state policy. This echoed the 1948 Fagan Report, whose findings had been rejected by the NP government on taking office. However, this position was now supported by the Afrikaans press, by the major Afrikaans monopolies and by the AHI.[33] The emerging UF proposals separated the urban black population into two categories – labour and the emerging 'black middle class' – and advocated distinct policies towards each.

With respect to African workers, it was clearly recognised that a reorganisation of production geared towards greater labour productivity would necessitate raising black wages. This last gasp of South African neo-Keynesianism argued that higher black wages would increase demand and contribute to stimulating growth. Giving black workers the right to organise in recognised *and regulated* trade unions was seen as the best way to provide an *institutionalised* form of collective bargaining which would hopefully contain industrial conflict. The 'business community' would itself address the problems of housing and education for workers through the UF. While elaborating a range of policy proposals directed at black workers, the major ideological preoccupation of business lay with the black middle class.

The Urban Foundation's obsession with cultivating 'Western-type materialistic needs and ambitions' in the black middle class was explicitly designed to reduce the social isolation and alienation from capitalism experienced by middle-class blacks under the class suppression induced by apartheid. In a country in which full-scale racial segregation had *never* been seriously challenged by capital, and was still defended by most Afrikaner undertakings, building a common business front on such issues was a delicate task. A step-by-step approach was needed to avoid divisions among the UF's own constituents.

Improving black middle-class housing was seen as the first priority. Apartheid land laws classified the black townships as 'white areas' where blacks could own neither land nor housing. This meant that until the late- 1970s, middle-class urban blacks were forced to live in the very basic housing provided by the state in these townships. They had no legal means of upgrading their accommodation, of passing on property to their descendants, nor of realising the 'Western-type materialistic needs and ambitions' which so obsessed the Urban Foundation. It was also clear that the National Party government would never agree to granting property rights to this black middle class in the white-zoned black townships such as Soweto. The UF thus proposed a 99-year leasehold system to enable middle-class blacks to 'choose to live near others of a similar socio-economic background'. It urged that all aspects of so-called 'petty apartheid' be scrapped and that restaurants, hotels and other facilities be opened to blacks who could afford them.

White capitalists now also advocated increased opportunities for black businessmen. In concert with the National African Federated Chambers of Commerce (Nafcoc), assistance was provided to fledgling black business undertakings.[34] White business also favoured a relaxation of the Group Areas Act to allow black businesses into the central business districts of the cities – and to permit 'white' undertakings to invest directly in black townships. Again on the initiative of Oppenheimer and Rupert, the Small Business Development Corporation was established to provide loans to black entrepreneurs and labour intensive undertakings'.*

It was recognised that greater socio-economic mobility for middle-class blacks also necessitated a limited political accommodation. While a few individual capitalists may have privately accepted a universal franchise, this was still fiercely opposed by the capitalist class as a whole. In the words of Anton Rupert: 'After many African countries became free they got dictatorships like [Idi] Amin's. *We have to find a solution that won't end up giving us one man one vote.'*[35] At best, business proposed limited concessions deemed acceptable to one faction of the ruling NP. This was well expressed by the leading practitioner and ideologue of liberal capitalism, South Africa's most powerful businessman, Harry Oppenheimer:

> Since we're not going to get the nationalists out of power so quickly – much as I'd like to and see the Progressive Federal Party come in – one has got to find a means of doing social justice in a way that *the reasonable people* in the National Party might go for. This does shut out going for one man one vote in a unitary state, although clearly one's got to go for one man one vote in some form. I used to be very keen on a qualified franchise [the policy of the Progressive Party until 1977], but it's no longer practical. I think therefore one should go for everybody voting in some sort of federal society. We have go to look for our salvation to that fascinating business of constitution making.†

The years 1973–78 saw intense politicking around such issues by the capitalist class. New organisations were formed to push for 'reform', and existing organisations hammered away at these themes. This reformist hyper-

---

* Drawing a direct analogy with the *Reddingsdaadbond* of the Afrikaner economic movement in the 1940s, Anton Rupert described the Small Business Development Corporation as 'the beautiful face of capitalism' – Davies *et al., Struggle for South Africa*, vol. 1, p. 84. He seems to have forgotten that the 'Small Business Finance Corporation' established by the RDB, as well as its various other measures to stimulate small Afrikaner business, were admitted to have failed completely. The RDB had to take 'firm and unpopular measures' to recover its loans. See O'Meara, *Volkskapitalisme*, 140.

† Business International, *Apartheid and Business: an analysis of the rapidly evolving challenge facing companies with investments in South Africa*, 1980, 230, my emphasis. This document was a virtual manifesto of liberal monopoly capital in South Africa. Its wish list of the impossible concludes: 'If political stability can be maintained, a political dispensation acceptable to South Africa's black people introduced, inflation curbed and the training and mobility of the black workforce rapidly improved, South Africa's business environment in the 1980s could be excellent'. p. viii.

activity began to transform the established political terrain. The formation of groups such as the Urban Foundation to coordinate, channel and direct the collective activities of the capitalist class for reform, clearly illustrated the changing nature of business politics. This, in turn, was a major factor reorganising the terrain of white party politics.

This first occurred within the ranks of the opposition parties. In the 1974 general election, the liberal Progressive Party finally broke out of its Houghton ghetto. The Progs now took six seats from the moribund and deeply divided United Party. The UP split soon thereafter. Four of its MPs joined with the 'Progs' to form the Progressive Reform Party (PRP), and the UP continued losing support in by-elections. The Soweto uprising precipitated renewed efforts to reorganise the parliamentary opposition. An 'informal meeting of businessmen and academics' met behind closed doors in October 1976 to forge a new opposition party. The chairman of this grouping was Dr F Cronje, for many years the UP spokesman on finance, and chairman of the South African Breweries and Nedbank monopolies. Following protracted negotiations, the UP split in three ways in 1977. Six of its MPs joined with the PRP in the again-renamed Progressive Federal Party (PFP). The bulk of the United Party MPs merged with the minuscule Democratic Party of ex-NP Interior Minister Theo Gerdner, to form the New Republic Party.[36] The 1977 general elections saw the NRP reduced from 23 to 10 seats, and the PFP now became the official opposition with 17 members of parliament – compared with 134 for the NP.

This organisational realignment in the party political and other fields reflected a crisis of representation for the forces of monopoly capital. But it was hardly solved by the formation of the PFP and a few new extra-parliamentary groups such as the UF. By 1977 it was strikingly clear that capital's demand for purposeful, effective reforms would never be met by the Vorster government. In a celebrated editorial, the influential *Financial Mail* called on businessmen to mobilise the full force of what it called 'BUSINESS POWER' to force change upon the regime. The journal spelled out a 'baseline' programme for 'action by *organised business*' in seven areas.* The paralysis of the NP government was now the central issue of all white politics. The intense business politicking for reform now shifted to the terrain of the NP itself. Capital's crisis of representation hinged around just a single question – the capacity of the NP government to implement such a programme.

In effect, many of the economic, political, ideological and international conditions which sustained the entire post-1948 'apartheid' period had been

---

* Editorial, 8 July 1977, original emphasis. These 'key areas' were: the provision of infrastructure in black townships; some form of 'security of tenure' for urban blacks; compulsory education; minimum wage standards for urban black workers (farm labourers were not mentioned although they were the lowest-paid workers in the country); recognition of black trade unions; abolition of job reservation; and 'the full liberalisation' of trading rights for blacks in the (white-zoned) urban areas.

fatally weakened. Four mutually reinforcing 'sectoral' disruptions or crises had developed:

(a) the recession was transformed into a *crisis of accumulation*;

(b) the Soweto uprising sharpened the perpetual crisis of legitimacy of the apartheid state into a *crisis of hegemony*;

(c) Pretoria's dramatic reverses in southern Africa gave rise to a growing *crisis of regional hegemony*;

(d) All of this precipitated a *crisis of international relations* for the apartheid regime.

These intersecting moments of crisis congealed to provoke a full-blown organic crisis. Key individuals and factions in government and all leading business spokesmen now realised that the old order had to change. A series of economic, political, ideological and social relations would have to be restructured so as to resecure conditions of expanded accumulation. White politics exploded with political and ideological debates and manoeuvres designed to 'disarticulate old formations and to rework their elements into new conditions'[37]. This in turn generated:

(e) a *crisis of representation* within the power bloc. Taken together these five separate but intersecting moments then congealed into

(f) a *crisis of political organisation and political culture* within the hitherto relatively cohesive Afrikaner nationalist movement.

This latter element is examined in the following chapters.

Chapter Ten

BIDING TIME

The paralysis of the Vorster government

After Soweto: Bantu Administration Minister M C Botha prohibits blacks from occupying executive positions

Too little, too late: The Vorster government and the unfolding crisis

The state response to the crisis of the 1970s was complex and contradictory. Vorster's government initially exhibited uncharacteristic flexibility. Although a number of trade unionists were banned in 1973, the 1972–73 strike wave did not elicit the anticipated police attacks and general repression. The collapse of the Portuguese colonial empire in 1974 and the threatened disappearance of at least two of the 'buffer states' around South Africa – the prop on which Pretoria's regional policy had rested since 1960 – provoked a hasty rethinking of regional strategy. Expectations that South Africa would intervene in Mozambique, particularly during the abortive 'settlers coup' of September 1974, eventually proved unfounded.* Instead, Vorster surprised most of his critics with his celebrated 'give us six months' speech addressed to the international community in October 1974, described by President Kaunda of Zambia as 'the voice of reason' for which Africa had been waiting.

Out of this emerged an innovative two-pronged strategy. A programme of minor internal reforms involved the removal of certain 'petty apartheid' irritants (such as segregated park benches). Far more importantly, the so-called 'détente' policy sought out African governments prepared to cooperate with Pretoria. This was hinged around an offer to push the illegal settler regime in Rhodesia into negotiation with the Zimbabwean national liberation movements.†

For nearly a year, the détente policy met with stunning success. Most notably it led to active collaboration between the South African and Zambian governments on a range of issues. This in turn significantly reduced South Africa's international isolation, to the delight of foreign and local capitalists. So successful was the détente initiative that a senior ANC functionary later told me that by mid-1975 his organisation had began to fear that it might be excluded from every African state south of the Sahara. The obvious successes of the détente exercise gave John Vorster greater domestic and international prestige than any other previous South African prime minister bar Smuts.

This soon evaporated, however, African supporters of détente were driven onto the defensive by the first South African military intervention in Angola between August 1975 and March 1976. Yet Cuban involvement in the Angolan

---

* However the then (Permanent) Secretary of the Department of Information later alleged that Defence Minister P W Botha instructed the SADF to assemble an intervention force on the Mozambique border. Its entry into Mozambique was said to have been prevented only when BOSS agents sabotaged the vehicles. E Rhoodie, quoted in Rees & Day, *Muldergate*, 202. He repeats the claim in his own book, *P W Botha: The Final Betrayal* (SA Politics, Melville, 1989), 72. Former BOSS agent Gordon Winter tells a similar story, *Inside BOSS, passim.*

† To show his good faith, Vorster ended the longstanding South African parapolice presence in Rhodesia, withdrawing the unit and exerting strong pressure on the Smith regime. Again, Eschel Rhoodie claims that P W Botha had assembled a secret unit of 500 South African paratroopers to assist Rhodesia, and that Vorster stood the unit down in the nick of time. Rees & Day, *Muldergate.*

conflict also provoked significant African disquiet, and the issue split the Organisation of African Unity virtually down the middle. The eventual humiliating withdrawal of South African troops in March 1976 weakened those African governments still prepared to work with Pretoria. The remaining fragile impetus to détente crumbled after the brutal suppression of the June 1976 student protest in Soweto. Not even the most conservative African regime could now afford to be seen to be collaborating with a white minority government which shot down hundreds of unarmed black schoolchildren.

Taken together, the Angola fiasco and the Soweto uprising seemed to knock the direction out of the Vorster government. It was reduced to a mixture of vacillation and severe and bitterly cynical repression, the latter personified by two notorious statements from Police Minister, Jimmy Kruger. He justified the police use of live ammunition rather than rubber bullets during the Soweto rebellion with the assessment that blacks needed to be made 'tame to the gun'.[1] When news broke of the death in detention from brain injuries of the Black Consciousness Movement's founder, Steve Biko, Kruger declared that Biko's death 'left him cold'. He informed the Natal NP congress that Biko had died as a result of a hunger strike. A congress delegate then congratulated the Minister on extending to Biko 'the democratic right' to starve himself to death. Nationalist MP Frank le Roux went even further, boasting that he 'would have killed Biko'.*

In the aftermath of Soweto, the government was capable of only the most timid reforms. Prodded by newly appointed Foreign Minister, R F (Pik) Botha, it speeded up the elimination of 'petty apartheid'.† The training facilities for African workers had been extended in 1975. Job Reservation was now eased slightly, and two commissions of enquiry were appointed in 1977 to investigate the wider labour reforms advocated by businessmen. Comprised of representatives of the Department of Labour, white trade unions and employers' organisations, the Wiehahn Commission would enquire into the legislative framework of industrial relations. The Riekert Commission on the other hand would examine all other aspects of 'manpower utilisation'. The administration of the Pass Laws was also marginally eased.‡ A scheme for African 99-year leasehold in black townships was announced and minor concessions were made to Asian businessmen. The Theron Commission of Enquiry recommended

---

* Kruger, quoted *Rand Daily Mail,* 15 September 1977. The Police Minister later denied he had ever stated that Biko had starved himself to death. His reaction to Biko's death was the catalyst leading the UN to impose a mandatory arms embargo against South Africa. Kruger privately apologised to Vorster, who refused his proffered resignation. Pottinger, *The Imperial Presidency,* 47-8. Le Roux, quoted in *Cape Times,* 9 November 1977.

† *A Survey … 1977,* 5-7. Pik Botha announced in 1977: 'I am prepared to go to war over our right to exist, but I am not prepared to die for discriminatory signs on a lift [elevator].' Ibid.

‡ The employer's signature on every *dompas* was now only required at the beginning and the end of a labour contract, instead of each month.

various significant changes in the conditions of the so-called Coloured ethnic group. However most were rejected by the government.

Feeble attempts were also made to find an 'acceptable political dispensation' for the black majority. Announcing an 'internal programme of action' in February 1975, Vorster delineated three decades of development in NP racial policy. During the 1950s 'we had to separate what had been allowed over the years to mingle'. In the 1960s the NP had emphasised separate development: 'we created governments [in the bantustans], gave people status'. The third decade 'of our policy' involved the Prime Minister meeting the various [bantustan] governments. Summarising the achievements of NP racial policy, Vorster proudly declared: 'I discuss matters with them ... as one man to another ... as equals.'[2]

A system of regular consultations with bantustan leaders was now instituted. Vorster announced plans to give 'Cabinet status' to the government-appointed South African Indian Council and the elected Coloureds' Representative Council (CRC). Together with the NP Cabinet they would form an 'inter-Cabinet Council'. This scheme was wrecked by the refusal of the majority Labour Party in the CRC to cooperate. In 1976, the Minister of Information and the Interior, Connie Mulder, suggested using a more 'positive' term – 'plural democracy' – to describe NP racial policy.* It was announced in early 1977 that elected 'Community Councils' would replace the hated Urban Bantu Councils, destroyed during Soweto.

Other long-term initiatives were launched. At the end of 1976, Defence Minister and Cape NP leader, P W Botha was appointed to chair a special Cabinet Committee of senior party leaders, investigating possible constitutional changes.† Already beginning to march to his own drum, Botha argued that the inherited Westminster model had never really worked in South Africa. His report the following year recommended the introduction of an elected executive Presidency and a system of separate parliaments for whites, so-called Coloureds and Asians, each with its own Cabinet.[3] Botha's proposals were incorporated in the NP platform for the 1977 general election.

Yet all of these initiatives remained mere ad hoc response to pressure. The government lacked an overall strategy of reform, and its timid measures did little to contain the crisis. Political observers were virtually unanimous in the view that the Vorster government appeared rudderless in the face of the immense problems it confronted. Vorster's one-time close adviser, the leading

---

* Ibid. 5. Mulder was appointed Minister of Bantu Administration in January 1978 and renamed his new fiefdom the 'Department of Plural Relations'. This new apartheid nomenclature elicited a series of racist jokes. Thus, for example, an African peasant was labelled a 'rural plural', Africans in adult education schemes were referred to as 'extra-mural plurals' and the old Bantu Investment Corporation (BIC) was christened PRIC – for Plural Relations Investment Corporation.

† Including the leaders of both the Transvaal and the OFS NP, Connie Mulder and Alwyn Schlebusch respectively.

Afrikaner industrialist Dr Etienne Rousseau, commented that Vorster seemed to have lost all drive, that he was no longer receptive to new ideas and did not want to listen to advice from Afrikaner industrialists.[4]

The once 'verligte' Prime Minister was now backpedalling on notions of reform. A November 1976 Broederbond circular described Vorster's announcement to the AB *Uitvoerende Raad* of his 'profound analysis' that

> the recent trying months and weeks had convinced him anew that there is no way to handle race relations but the way of separate development. He added that the greatest legacy of Dr Verwoerd was his vision of separate homelands which could be developed to full independence. Without the homeland policy, he said, we would now have been in the same situation as Rhodesia. He called on the AB to take stock and throw everything into the battle to maintain and promote this policy.[5]

Vorster began to lash out at those demanding coherent, effective reform. In October 1976 he denounced a detailed Assocom memo proposing a programme of reform as 'interference' in the realm of government, angrily lecturing the Assocom annual congress that 'policy making' was the sole prerogative of government. Businessmen were bluntly instructed to confine their recommendations to the 'proper' channels and to refrain demands for 'radical' change.[6] 'The following year, Vorster was also enraged by a book by the chairman of the Afrikaner insurance conglomerate Sanlam which dared criticise state interference in the economy. Now the Prime Minister warned Afrikaner businessmen to 'keep out of politics'.*

By the end of 1977 it was evident to all observers that the government was simply incapable of acting decisively to address, let alone resolve, the manifold issues confronting the country. This almost complete paralysis of the Vorster government after Soweto grew out of three distinct but interlinked factors. The revolt of black schoolchildren underscored the increasingly divergent interpretations of apartheid policy within the NP and across the broad spectrum of the Afrikaner nationalist movement. Soweto in effect demanded the construction of a new hegemonic project. But this the government proved unable even to begin. It was hamstrung, secondly, by the Bonapartist management style of NP *Hoofleier* and Prime Minister John Vorster. Literally terrified of exacerbating the growing divisions among the faithful, Vorster seemed incapable of decisive, effective leadership. His inaction further aggravated the internal divisions and tensions. The now open NP policy conflicts then turned, thirdly, into an increasingly overt struggle for succession between the two major

---

* A D Wassenaar, *Assault on Private Enterprise* (Tafelberg, Cape Town, 1977). Sanlam had been formed by the very men who had founded the Cape NP, and had always stood at the heart of the Cape nationalist establishment. The book by its chairman was a thinly veiled assault on Vorster's leadership, and created a sensation in white politics. Wassenaar later admitted that the book was intended to stir things up, *Financial Mail,* 17 August 1979.

coalitions of political and bureaucratic power in both party and state. The first two of these aspects are discussed here, while the desperate battle for position in the succession race is described in the following chapter.

Divided house: Afrikaner nationalism after Soweto

The Soweto uprising struck directly at the twin pillars of the Afrikaner nationalist project – the Afrikaans language and state policy towards urban blacks. The imposition of Afrikaans-language instruction on Soweto schools in January 1976 was the direct result of the Broederbond's insistence on 'Afrikaans as a Second Language for the Bantu'.[7] The NP politician in charge of this policy was former Broederbond chairman and Deputy Minister of Bantu Administration and Education, Dr Andries Treurnicht.* He announced the abandonment of the policy less than a month after 16 June. This NP/AB retreat from the Moscow of their cherished 'Afrikanerisation of South Africa' was borne by most nationalists with minimal grumbling. Few realised that they had begun the long march towards apartheid's protracted Waterloo.

The unprecedented labour unrest of the early 1970s highlighted the absolute failure of apartheid's low-wage, migrant labour policies. Three years later, 'Soweto' then showed up the fatal triple flaws at the heart of 'positive apartheid'. Generations of influx control and forced removals had signally failed to turn the tide of what the NP once called the black *oorstroming* of the cities (p. 34 above). The refusal to acknowledge galloping black urbanisation rendered the government incapable of developing an urban policy acceptable to the black majority. And in sharp contrast to their elders at Sharpeville, the enraged youth of Soweto finally acted out the very worst of white South Africa's guilty nightmares – the fact that the regime could no longer rely on blacks being 'tame to the gun'. What would it do when they one day started shooting back? Prime Minister Vorster himself declared this 'a future too ghastly to contemplate'.

Soweto thus unleashed furious Afrikaner nationalist soul-searching, though few of the faithful departed for more liberal political churches.† While still cast

---

* The verkrampte Treurnicht was elected AB chairman 'by mistake' in May 1972, when retiring chairman Meyer had 'not effectively planned the campaign' to insert John Vorster's candidate, the verligte Dr Gerrit Viljoen. Two years later, Vorster's organisers made no mistake. 'Influential business groups like Sanlam and Rembrandt, along with BOSS and the Special Branch, were actively engaged' in securing Viljoen's election. Treurnicht was not even nominated to the Bond executive. Serfontein, *Brotherhood,* 117-18, 124.

† However, one prominent defector was Judge J F 'Kowie' Marais who resigned from the NP proclaiming that June 1976 had convinced him that the party he had joined in 1924 was incapable of change. Marais chaired the steering committee set up to bring together the parliamentary opposition, ending up as a PFP Member of Parliament. The political columnist of the Transvaal NP organ, *Die Transvaler,* Natie Ferreira, also resigned in disillusionment. See his book, *The Story of an Afrikaner: Die Rewolusie van die Kinders* (Ravan Press, Johannesburg, 1980).

within the overall framework of grand apartheid theory, an increasingly sharp debate within the NP focused on three fundamental aspects: the relationship between so-called petty apartheid and the grander aspirations of 'separate development'; the status of the urban black population; and constitutional arrangements which would satisfy urban black aspirations. Conflict over these issues slowly fashioned the fault lines which would first polarise and then eventually split the NP.

Many Afrikaner intellectuals agreed that Soweto underscored deep black grievances which required remedying 'if we are to keep all that we have'.* The first panacea was to 'abolish discrimination'. The Prime Minister announced that 'hurtful' and 'discriminatory measures serving no purpose' would be scrapped.[8] In the nationalist lexicon, 'discriminatory' measures referred to so-called petty apartheid. The NP recognition that racial *discrimination* was now 'unacceptable' simply led it to *reaffirm* the necessity for what it called the *differentiation* of grand apartheid theory. In this semantic pedantry lay all the delusions and hypocrisy of apartheid. Even after Soweto, Afrikaner nationalism remained wilfully blind to the fact that the real black 'hurt' did not stem from Africans being confined to second-rate segregated park benches. Rather, the growing rage of the urban black youth was provoked by precisely the absurd 'differentiation' dogma which held that they were not South Africans but 'nationals' of one or other 'homeland' which few urban blacks had ever seen. The most 'hurtful' aspect of apartheid was the rigorous implementation of influx control. Still, not even the most 'enlightened' verligte yet dared propose abolishing the *dompas*.

Moreover, despite the proclaimed intention to remove petty apartheid, practice seemed to confirm Andries Treurnicht's oft repeated contention that apartheid was indivisible – once you removed petty apartheid you would soon have to dismantle grand apartheid. Thus the apparent NP consensus on the theoretical need to ease the 'hurtful' aspects of petty apartheid broke down over the practical definition of both a 'discriminatory' measure and a 'useful' purpose. Agriculture Minister Hendrik Schoeman provoked nationalist outrage with his July 1977 statement that the Immorality and Mixed Marriages Acts were unnecessary. The party hierarchy 'cracked the whip', obliging Schoeman to retract. According to the verligte editor of *Die Transvaler*, Willem de Klerk, this incident gave all verligtes 'the fright of their lives', they were 'running scared'.†

Even more controversial was the question of urban policy. The NP had first been elected in 1948 viscerally rejecting the Fagan Commission's finding that

---

* In the mid-1970s the official term 'Bantu' was replaced by 'Black' to refer to the African majority. In what follows it is important to be clear that in Afrikaner nationalist terminology the word 'black' refers only to the African majority. It does not include so-called Coloureds and Indians.

† Then editor Wimpie de Klerk is the elder brother of F W de Klerk, and son of the 'father of job reservation', former NP Cabinet Minister and failed Presidential candidate, Jan de Klerk.

black urbanisation was permanent and irreversible. Apartheid was constructed on the fervent belief that Africans were 'temporary sojourners' in the 'white' areas. There simply as 'labour units', they would all eventually to return to their 'homelands'. P W Botha had told parliament in 1964 that there could be 'no permanent home or permanency even for a section of the Bantu in the area of White South Africa'.[9] In the 1960s, Cabinet Minister Blaar Coetzee had built much of his political persona around the claim that 1978 was the magical year in which the flow of Africans to the cities would begin to be reversed.* Now, however, prominent verligtes in the press, academia and even parliament began to advocate what the NP had always regarded as apostasy – recognition of the permanence of black urbanisation. *Die Burger*'s 'Dawie' columnist put the matter most forcefully, arguing that despite Transkei 'independence',

> the masses of black labour in the large industrial centres are, for all practical purposes, not removable. ... In the meantime the enemy is at the gate and the country is riven by tensions.

Four days later, 'Dawie' expressed the even more heretical opinion that the policy of 'separate freedoms' had failed. Existing NP policy meant the prospect of 'permanent unfreedom for important sections of the population'. White South Africa should accept the 'inexorable alternative: freedom in one plural society'. The 'top priority' was now the 'granting of co-equal citizenship' to 'people of different colour' in a 'newly devised constitutional structure'.[10]

Not all verligtes went this far. While *Die Transvaler* editor De Klerk was prepared to accept the permanence of African urbanisation, he argued that urban blacks could exercise their political rights only in the bantustans. He did concede, however, that so-called Coloureds and Indians should be recognised as 'full South African citizens' and be given separate political structures in which they might exercise 'full authority over their own affairs'. Yet other prominent verligtes agreed with Dawie. The Nasionale Pers Transvaal daily, *Beeld*, accepted that urban blacks were there to stay. A 'proper forum' for their 'dialogue' with the government would have to be found. The president of the *Afrikaanse Calvinistiese Beweging* (Afrikaans Calvinist Movement – ACB) and later Rector of Potchefstroom University, Professor Tjaart van der Walt, told an ACB conference that the bantustans did not represent urban blacks. Unless the government introduced fundamental social changes 'more and more Afrikaners would not, as Christians, be able to support it much longer'.

Piet Koornhof was the only Cabinet member to propose granting some political rights to Africans outside the bantustans. The Minister of National

---

* Coetzee was once asked by the verligte journalist, Schalk Pienaar, why he continued to insist on 1978 as the year of reversal, even though 'you know as well as I that [this claim] is nonsense'. Coetzee replied: 'Well, when 1978 arrives, hopefully I will no longer have to do with such things, and perhaps I'll already be dead. So what will I have to worry aout it then?' Pienaar, *Getuie van Groot Tye*, 63-4.

Education and of Sport advocated 'a coalition of autonomous and mainly territorially-based units cooperating within a political system providing for consensual decision-making'. Echoing P W Botha's earlier praise for the Swiss cantonal system, Koornhof stated that South Africa was moving towards adopting a similar system of 'plural democracies' which would eventually enable each group 'to participate in the central decision-making process'.*

The gathering verligte emphasis on change incensed many nationalists. Water Affairs Minister Braam Raubenheimer accused Afrikaner newspapers of 'disloyalty', charging they would create 'chaos' similar to that in Mozambique and Angola. Attacks on this or that NP newspaper had always been the coded means to strike at the politicians supporting such positions. Raubenheimer's offensive elicited a flood of support for the traditional apartheid idea, and suggestions for speeding up the process of 'separate freedoms'. With characteristic bluntness and mangled syntax, the adopted Afrikaner and Police Minister, Jimmy Kruger, announced that 'the urban black man is export labour (sic), whether they (sic) were born here or not'.† SABRA chairman and Broederbond Executive Committee member, Professor Carel Boshoff, warned that the growing numbers of urban blacks would make it increasingly difficult to ward off their political demands. Ways had to be found to establish a white majority in 'white' territory. This son-in-law of Hendrik Verwoerd proposed consolidating the 10 bantustans into four large blocs. Bantustan leaders who refused the proffered 'independence' would simply have to accept continued white domination. Insisting that 'we need a strong government, not a weak one', Transvaal NP leader Connie Mulder attacked any idea of cantons, of a federation or confederation as imposing concealed black control over whites!‡ Mulder was echoed by Treurnicht who denounced such proposals as contrary to NP policy. Other ministers and MPs expressed similar views.

The recommendations of P W Botha's special Cabinet Committee on constitutional arrangements were presented to a special meeting of the NP caucus in August 1977. The editors of Afrikaans newspapers were invited to participate in these caucus deliberations on Botha's proposal to establish separate parliaments for so-called Coloureds and Indians, and to set up an executive Presidency.[11] The plan provoked a storm among nationalists. It was denounced behind closed caucus and Broederbond doors for starting a process which would ultimately lead to 'a multi-racial political dispensation whereby a

---

* *Cape Times,* 24 May, 1977. Koornhof's opponents dubbed him *Piet Pompies,* a synonym for a loudmouthed buffoon. This nickname implied an even more derogatory reference, illustrating the coarse nature of private Afrikaner political discourse. The Afrikaans word *pompie* literally means 'little pump'. The saying, *eerste geruik, eie pompie gebruik,* translates delicately as: 'he who first smells [a fart] has used his own "little pump" '. As verligte point man on many issues, Koornhof's policies certainly left a foul odour in the noses of most verkramptes.

† Kruger had been born to Welseh parents and was adopted as an infant by an Afrikaner mining couple.

‡ Mulder had been elected Transvaal leader on the retirement of Ben Schoeman in 1972.

"non-White" could be declared President and the White Parliament lose its powers'. The AB chairman, Dr Gerrit Viljoen, had to intervene 'to prevent a major crisis'. A special circular was sent to all AB branches asking them to rally support for the new proposals at the September 1977 NP provincial congresses.[12]

Once again, the verkramptes took an indirect approach. The constitution proposals were eventually approved by both Cabinet and caucus, so they could not be attacked directly without risking expulsion from the party.* So the verkramptes took aim at the new sports policy of *Piet Pompies* Koornhof. Yet again the AB had to intervene. Just before the opening of the 1977 Transvaal NP congress, Broederbond chairman Viljoen published an article arguing that infighting over sports policy was undermining the achievement of 'the largest possible unanimity (sic) for a constitutional framework'. He urged nationalists not 'to blow up differences of ... a lower priority, for example, the sports policy'.[13] All four NP provincial congresses duly endorsed the new constitutional proposals which stood at the heart of the NP platform for the November 1977 general elections.

These disputes between verligtes and verkramptes often struck non-nationalists as insignificant. The reformists were certainly *not* proposing to break with grand apartheid. Indeed, arch verligte Pik Botha clearly expressed their (then) resolve to 'fight to the last man' rather than abandon the bantustan model. Nevertheless, this reformist acceptance of the permanence of black urbanisation and the need to find some form of political accommodation for urban Africans did mark a significant shift from apartheid orthodoxy and Verwoerdian inflexibility. The willingness of the new Afrikaner urban middle class to contemplate the previously unthinkable in their determination to 'keep all that we have' was beginning to take precedence over what many critics still regarded as Afrikaner 'tribalism'.† The sheer vehemence of the orthodox denunciation of such mild proposals pointed to the growing fissures in the nationalist alliance.

By the end of 1976, both in parliament and the country as a whole, the Nationalist Party was decisively divided over the political questions posed by these multiple crises. Under the dual pressure of mass struggle and consequent reformist demands from business, two very broad ideological currents crystallised across the Afrikaner nationalist spectrum. The 'conservatives' saw the solution to the crisis in speeding up the vigorous implementation of

---

* As was the nationalist MP for Carletonville, Cas Greyling, for his refusal to accept the NP's 1977 programme.

† The longtime executive director of the South African Institute of Race Relations expressed the common liberal fallacy when he wrote of these internal NP conflects that 'the Nationalist Party is based as much on tribalism as it is on ideology'. As a result, 'as far as the fundamentals of policy towards urban Africans are concerned, there does not seem to be any *significant* difference of opinions'. Kane-Berman, *Soweto*, 177, 178.

'separate development'. This meant resisting moves to reform labour and industrial policy. While willing to eliminate 'petty apartheid' and 'discrimination', and even to make some concessions to the black middle class, most conservatives refused to acknowledge permanent black urbanisation. They strenuously opposed any idea of black political rights outside of the bantustans.

The conservatives were also outraged by the business clamour for far-reaching reform. Vorster's splenetic attack on Assocom (p. 195 above) gave vent to their view that government was a 'sovereign' sphere, in which businessmen had no right to meddle.* Moreover, the fact that good Afrikaner undertakings allied themselves with 'Hoggenheimer' in this reformist cacophony was further proof of the sad dilution of the nationalist movement and the need to shore up its traditional policies.

With the collapse of the détente initiative and the strong condemnation of South Africa following the Soweto massacre, Vorster himself was increasingly identified with this conservative stance. He announced he had 'finished talking about [black] political rights'. Blacks working in the (white-zoned) cities had 'abandoned the place where they had political rights'. Their jobs gave them the right to nothing but wages. The Prime Minister declared that no future government could change the basic NP principle that urban blacks must exercise their political rights in the bantustans. But Vorster was not only ailing, he was unwilling to lead the verkrampte crusade. Transvaal NP leader, Dr Connie Mulder, was generally regarded as the NP baron closest to the conservative faction. Any consolidation of Mulder's position as Vorster's heir apparent was actively supported by the NP's 'conservative' wing.

Mulder was seen by many as the main target of what came to be called – in the English-language press at least – the NP 'reformists'.† Recognising the permanence of black urbanisation, this current argued – in the words of the then chairman of the Broederbond – that 'apartheid's original formulation cannot cope with this situation'.[14] Though clearly still operating within the overall framework of separate development, the reformists were predominantly concerned with the need to make limited concessions to the black middle class. Urban policy would have to be reformed along three lines: to provide for the training of black workers and the recognition *and control* of black trade unions; to open the channels for social mobility for the urban black middle class; and, most problematically, to find a form of political accommodation for urban blacks.

---

* This harks back to the *sowereiniteit in eie kring* principle of Kuyperian Afrikaner nationalism – the notion that God divided society into separate and rightfully autonomous ('sovereign') spheres. For a useful discussion of the roots and development of this notion, see Moodie, *Rise of Afrikanerdom,* 55-7 *et passim.*

† For a while the terms 'conservative' and 'reformist' tended to be used in place of what had been called 'verkrampte' and 'verligte' nationalists. Distinguishing between 'ideological hardliners' and 'pragmatists', Adam & Giliomee provide a useful sketch of their ideological and policy differences, *Ethnic Power Mobilized,* 219-20.

Along with leading Afrikaner academics and intellectuals, Afrikaner business now generally rallied behind the NP reformists. Indeed, the growing political weight of this broad NP reformist current reflected the substantial development of Afrikaner business in the 1960s, particularly in the Transvaal. Cape financial interests and the Cape NP were no longer isolated from the dominant forces in the other provincial parties – as they had been in the early 1960s. The Transvaal NP was now itself decisively divided on fairly explicit class lines. Its leader, Connie Mulder, was the great hope of the conservative faction. His appointment to succeed the reactionary M C Botha as Minister of Bantu Administration in January 1978 was widely interpreted as reinforcing his role as Vorster's *Dauphin*. Once in possession of this, the key apartheid ministry, Mulder immediately consolidated his position as verkrampte champion by informing Parliament:

> If our policy is taken to its logical conclusion as far as black people are concerned, there will not be one black man (sic) with South African citizenship … Every black man in South Africa will eventually be accommodated in some independent new state in this honourable way and there will no longer be a moral obligation to accommodate those people politically.[15]

Yet many Transvaal businessmen despised and detested Mulder. One prominent Afrikaner industrialist described the Transvaal leader to me as ' *'n doef'* (a fart). There now existed a strong 'reformist' opposition within the highest levels of the Transvaal party, broadly clustered around three influential Cabinet ministers – Labour Minister S P (Fanie) Botha, the Minister of National Education and of Sport, Dr P Koornhof, and Foreign Affairs Minister, R F (Pik) Botha.* Any future leadership election would be fought less along the provincial battle lines of the past than around the emerging policy cleavages.

The fall-out from Soweto produced a virtual political impasse between these two broad currents. In this context Vorster called a general election for November 1977, eighteen months earlier than was constitutionally required. Campaigning as the only party capable of dealing with the multiple crises confronting South Africa, the NP emerged with the then largest majority in South African parliamentary history, winning a total of 134 seats compared with the combined total of 30 for the three opposition parties.† The NP also captured significant electoral support from two social forces which had hitherto backed the now-defunct United Party – large numbers of English-speaking petty

---

* Both Fanie Botha and Piet Koornhof had been linked with Albert Hertzog's verkramptes in the mid-1960s, the former having in fact been a member of the delegation of younger verkrampte MPs who persuaded John Vorster to run for the *Hoofleier*ship.

† *A Survey … 1977*, 21. The parliamentary opposition was split between the liberal PFP – now the Official Opposition with 17 seats – the centre-right New Republic Party (10 seats) and the right-wing South African Party (three seats). Most members of the latter two parties soon decamped to the NP.

bourgeois whites and significant sectors of 'English' business. Verwoerd's dream had been realised. The white electorate was now divided along ideological rather than linguistic lines.

Ironically, however, this expanded electoral base simply compounded the centripetal forces pulling the NP in different directions. The governing party found it much easier to modify its electoral base than to modify its social project. This massive election victory *aggravated* the political inertia of both Nationalist Party and government. By now a large part of the problem lay in the ways in which political power was exercised under John Vorster.

The cork in the bottle: John Vorster and Afrikaner unity (ii)

Reflecting the growing stratification of Afrikaners, the intense post-Soweto policy divisions within the NP and across Afrikaner nationalism do not, in and of themselves, explain the government's paralysis. Verwoerd had found himself in a possibly even more difficult position after Sharpeville. In 1960, however, *Die Hollander*'s unshakeable sense of where he wanted to take the NP, and his iron determination to impose this policy vision on his fractious party, effectively ended the internal debate. Now, however, a soporific brew of Vorster's personal political history and his mode of political leadership lulled the government into inaction.

John Vorster's political persona was a curious blend of brutal directness and vacillation born of insecurity. As Minister of Justice, the former Nazi had seemed to take an almost personal delight in the incarceration and humiliation of those who dared challenge the master race. He later claimed in all seriousness that he had run the vast crackdown 'in the most humane way possible'.[16] His victims tell a very different story. A number of former political detainees have independently told me of being woken up in their cells on weekend nights by a less than sober Minister of Justice leading visiting junkets of nationalists come to gloat at 'you bladdy Commies who think you are so – expletive deleted – clever'. Afrikaner poet Breyten Breytenbach's savage 'Letter from Abroad to Butcher', dedicated to 'Balthazar', sums up what many South Africans felt about their new Prime Minister:

and you butcher,
you who are entrusted with the security of the state
what do you think when night reveals her
framework
and the first bubbling shriek is squeezed out
of the prisoner
as in a birth
with the fluids of parturition? ...
does your heart also stiffen in your throat
when you touch the extinguished limbs

with the same hands that will fondle your wife's mysteries?*

Vorster's personal vindictiveness was not only reserved for the enemies of Afrikaner nationalism, but was also well known in the NP. The doyen of verligte nationalism, longtime *Die Burger* editor Piet Cillié, once compared Vorster to his predecessor, saying that should he have to be slaughtered politically, he would always prefer that Verwoerd rather than Vorster commit the deed. Whereas Verwoerd killed quickly, cleanly and impersonally, 'when John Vorster goes for you, he goes for *you* ... and that can be very scary!'†

Shortly after taking office in September 1966, Vorster had gone to great lengths to lighten up his image. He was so often photographed on the golf course that the *Cape Times* cartoonist took to portraying the former Justice Minister as a jovial sportsman, putter in hand, a golfer's cap on his head. Once the NP's most feared minister, Vorster rejoiced briefly in the sobriquet 'Jolly John'. Yet the leopard could not easily turn into a pussy cat. Progressive Party MP Helen Suzman was herself so often bruised by the Prime Minister that even *Die Burger* once came to her defence. She recounts a revealing anecdote about John Vorster:

> A story going the rounds told of a photographer pleading with the normally grim-faced Vorster: 'Won't you please smile, Mr Prime Minister?' And Vorster, his mouth turned firmly down, replied: 'I *am* smiling.' I would relate this story, suitably demonstrated, as an apocryphal story, until one day I received a call. 'Mrs Suzman, that story is not apocryphal – I was the photographer.'[17]

Profoundly scarred by the nationalist wars of the 1940s, John Vorster had been elected NP *Hoofleier* and Premier because he did not offend any major faction of the party (p. 000). He was acutely aware of his lack of seniority, of the towering legacy of his predecessor, and of the fact that unlike all his predecessors, he did not rise to the *Hoofleier*ship from an already consolidated personal and provincial political base. His entire period in office seemed

---

* Extract from "Letter from Abroad to Butcher" by Breyten Breytenbach, which first appeared in Afrikaans in *Skryt,* Meulenhoff Publishers, Amsterdam, 1972. English translation by Breyten Breytenbach. Reproduced by permission of Breyten Breytenbach. Enraged as much by the reference to his marital sexual relationship (sacrosanct territory to all nationalists) as by Breytenbach's characterisation of his brutality, Vorster became obsessed with revenge on the poet. When Police Minister Jimmy Kruger informed Vorster of Breytenbach's arrest on a madcap clandestine subversive 'mission' to South Africa (1975), a beaming Prime Minister instructed him: 'Don't tell anyone else, and definitely not the press, not for a while anyway. I want some time to savour this for myself' – Kruger, quoted in L Weschler, 'Profile: an Afrikaner Dante', *The New Yorker,* 8 November 1993, 89.

† Quoted by the De Villiers, *PW,* 97. However Cillié misrepresents the depths of Verwoerd's own vindictiveness, reducing many nationalists who crossed him to less than nothing, personally as well as politically. See pp. 95-7 above.

marked by a lingering sense of insecurity and hesitancy.

Vorster's mode of leadership in the party was designed above all to contain NP conflicts, to preserve the party's tenuous unity. Indeed, it was the perceived weakness of Vorster's leadership which had fatally emboldened the Hertzogites in the late 1960s, persuading them that the real direction of the party was theirs for the taking. Vorster had been extremely reluctant to act against Hertzog and his followers, doing so only when their blatant sectarian manoeuvres threatened to split the NP.

The dramatic internal battles from 1966 to 1970 had deeply scarred the Prime Minister. They reconfirmed the painful lesson he learned in the OB during the nationalist civil war of the 1940s -- policy conflicts would destroy Afrikaner nationalism if allowed to get out of hand. In the words of one of his closest collaborators in the 1970s:

> Vorster had become ... obsessed with keeping unity in the National Party at all costs. He wasn't going to bring about the necessary changes if it meant stepping on toes. He'd had a great fright when the HNP broke away shortly after he became Prime Minister and he did not intend to be the catalyst for something like that again.[18]

Vorster had deliberately adopted a leadership style in party and government which would minimise the destructive effects of policy disputes. He strove to stand above the squabbling factions, holding them together through patronage and the prestige of his office. Once the Hertzogite threat had been disposed of in the 1970 election, this Bonapartist style worked well for a while.* But Vorster lost sight of the essential ingredient of his much-vaunted popularity and prestige in the early 1970s -- these years did not require him to demonstrate decisive leadership in the face of crisis and internal conflict. Never known as a man of vision, the Prime Minister had seemed content to tread water and drift with the political tide in the period of relative political calm in the NP between 1970 and 1974. Under his leadership the NP government lost the enveloping sense of purpose and urgency it seemed to enjoy under Verwoerd.

John Vorster's name is indelibly associated with what was then seen as the bold opening to Africa in 1974, the so-called policy of détente. But his own role seems to have been less than decisive. According to Eschel Rhoodie, the détente policy was the culmination of a joint initiative begun in the early 1970s. Rhoodie and the head of BOSS, General Hendrik van den Bergh, agreed 'to carve up Africa between them'. Rhoodie was responsible for contacting the movers and shakers in West Africa, Van den Bergh for East and Central Africa. Their objective was twofold -- to gain an air corridor over Africa for South

---

* 'Bonapartism' here refers not to Napoleon Bonaparte, but rather to his nephew, Louis, who presided over the Second Empire. The term is drawn from Karl Marx's magisterial analysis in *The Eighteenth Brumaire of Louis Bonaparte.*

African Airways flights to Europe (SAA was forced to take the long and costly route 'around the bulge' of Africa), and to win support from 'moderate' African states in order to split the OAU over the issue of cooperation with South Africa.

Long subject to low blood pressure, Vorster had apparently wanted to retire on his sixtieth birthday in 1974. He was dissuaded by the framers of détente, who needed Vorster to carry out their African initiative – as well as another aspect of their long-term plans (see below). However, the Prime Minister's enthusiasm for the African initiative was questionable. Rhoodie says of the historic meeting in Abidjan he organised in May 1974 between Vorster and the presidents of Senegal and the Ivory Coast:

> [W]e had to drag John Vorster kicking into Africa. Right from the start he seemed unwilling, even when we had conclusive proof that moderate African heads of State like Senghor and Houphouët-Boigny were prepared to meet him immediately in Africa. It took a great deal of time and trouble to get him to agree to travel with us, and we had exactly the same problems getting him to go to Israel. ... I was astounded with Vorster's reaction. ... We very nearly lost this opportunity because Vorster was so cautious. We were also due to have a further meeting with President Senghor, but this finally fell through because Vorster took so long making up his mind.[19]

Vorster's tendency to vacillate grew more acute after Soweto. He spent his last years in office trying to deal with the crisis in piecemeal, *laissez-faire* fashion. Rather than clear policy and resolute leadership, his principal concern seemed simply to hold together his increasingly divided party. Faced with factions and ministries demanding apparently opposing policies, Vorster's reflex was to appoint commissions of enquiry in an attempt to defuse the conflict. His politics of prevarication contrasted sharply with Verwoerd's firm leadership after Sharpeville. The *Hoofleier*'s unwillingness to choose sides decisively simply exacerbated both the overall crisis and the deep tensions within the NP and government. This exasperated even his closest advisers. General Hendrik van den Bergh grew so frustrated with Vorster's inaction that he is reported to have begun referring to his old friend and patron as 'the cork in the bottle. He was stopping the flow of development.'* The chairman of the Broederbond later characterised Vorster's last years in office, saying that the Prime Minister 'gave the impression that he was just sitting around and waiting for his retirement'.[20]

The problem went beyond Vorster's notorious unwillingness to confront major factions within the party. Equally to blame was his overall mode of Cabinet and government management. Following the intensely personal and

---

* Eschel Rhoodie, quoted in Rees & Day, *Muldergate*, 182. According to many insiders, 'cork' Vorster was now unstopping more than a few bottles of another kind. A number of nationalists independently told me of the growing unease at the Prime Minister's fondness for brandy and Coke. His face took on the red-veined hue of a heavy drinker.

highly centralised rule of Dr Verwoerd, Vorster had deliberately reverted to the *primus inter pares* model of Prime Ministerial rule. He ran his Cabinet as 'a skilful chairman', who 'conformed more to the team concept of Cabinet government in which "while the Prime Minister is leader, he is heavily dependent on his colleagues".'[21]

However, Vorster's Cabinet was never a team as such, operating on the British model of collective responsibility. The Prime Minister allowed his ministers to formulate both the overall direction as well as the detailed policy of their own departments. This meant that strong-willed ministers, such as a Ben Schoeman, a P W Botha or a Connie Mulder, in effect dictated policy to the Cabinet so long as they could get Vorster's overall approval. Decision-making 'was not infrequently a rather haphazard process involving only a tiny number of participants – a far cry from a structured team concept of government allowing for inputs from a variety of interested parties'.[22] The more powerful ministers were effectively in a position to determine overall government policy by presenting the Prime Minister with a *fait accompli*, and the Cabinet was reduced to an almost peripheral role in the overall elaboration of policy. Thus far from the Cabinet model of government Vorster professed to be following, decision-making resembled that of a weak feudal monarchy. Powerful barons made policy in their domains. They were free to act so long as they were careful to consult with King Vorster, through whom everybody was supposed to work, and at whose erratic pleasure ministers retained their fiefdoms. The result was, in the words of an American observer, 'an organizational and administrative nightmare'.[23]

In the context of the mounting crises and Vorster's declining health throughout the 1970s, this meant that no overall strategic nor policy leadership was forthcoming from the Prime Minister's office. As his ministers sniped at one another in public, the battle over terrain and policy degenerated into open warfare between various ministries. The Departments of Information and of Foreign Affairs were constantly at each other's throats over who really ran South African foreign policy. The broad direction of domestic and regional security policy pitted BOSS in a protracted guerrilla war against the Department of Defence.

Vorster's habit of delegating effective power in both party and government created a real leadership vacuum, which two contending bureaucratic coalitions now rushed to fill. From 1976 onwards they engaged in an ever more rancorous and increasingly public fight over territory and strategy. At issue were more than just opposing attempts to dictate policy by *fait accompli*. Given the Prime Minister's declining health, both groups also clearly sought to take control of the policy agenda to place themselves in the best position to grasp the wobbling crown when the *Hoofleier* and Prime Minister departed.

Chapter Eleven

FEAR AND LOATHING
IN THE NATIONAL PARTY

The struggle for the succession

P W Botha: 'Ladies and Gentlemen, there has been a small mistake'

In the years following the 1976 Soweto rebellion, the Vorster government was paralysed as much by the profound ideological divisions within the caucus and Cabinet as by leadership style of its ailing Premier. This led to a ferocious struggle between the two main centres of bureaucratic power in the government – a struggle as much over personal position as over policy direction.

The Crown Prince, the General & James Bond vs the Pangaman

The front runner in the succession race was the candidate of a Transvaal cabal whose three principal figures were strategically placed to exert an enormous influence on the broad direction state policy. These were: the Minister of Information and the Interior, Dr Connie Mulder; the head of BOSS, General Hendrik van den Bergh; and the Director of Mulder's Department of Information, Dr Eschel Rhoodie.

Connie Mulder was the cabal's front man and pivotal political figure. Elected leader of the Transvaal NP at the comparatively tender age of 47 following the September 1972 retirement of Ben Schoeman, Mulder was also elevated to the influential Broederbond *Uitvoerende Raad* (UR – Executive Council) in the same year.* No sooner did he assume the Transvaal leadership than Mulder set his sights on eventually succeeding Vorster. The only other likely serious contender would be Cape NP leader and Defence Minister, P W Botha. Most observers regarded Mulder as a shoo-in, and he was known as the NP's Crown Prince. Yet to ensure his defeat of Botha in a future leadership election, Mulder needed to match the latter's twin peerless political resources – absolute mastery of the machinery of his provincial party and a bureaucratic fiefdom in a crucial ministry which could translate into decisive policy influence. Time and hard work would take care of the first issue. The Transvaal NP had overwhelming weight in the NP caucus. Its 61 MPs and 19 Senators far overshadowed the Cape party's 37 MPs and 18 Senators – let alone the 24 caucus members from the OFS (traditional Transvaal allies in a 'northern' coalition against the Cape), and 13 from Natal. Mulder simply required Vorster to remain Prime Minister long enough for the new Transvaal leader to consolidate his hold on his provincial party – hence Mulder's reluctance to see Vorster resign in 1974.

Yet Mulder also needed Vorster and the Prime Minister's *éminence grise*, General van den Bergh, in order to build a bureaucratic power and policy base

---

* Mulder defeated two older and much more senior Cabinet colleagues for the Transvaal leadership – the verkrampte Bantu Affairs Minister, M C Botha, and the mildly verligte Labour Minister, Marais Viljoen. Mulder was first 'proposed' for membership of the Broederbond UR in 1968 (Wilkins & Strydom, *The Super Afrikaners,* Appendix 76), and was elected in 1972. Serfontein, *Brotherhood,* 118. This was anomalous as ever since Strijdom's Premiership it had become accepted practice that AB Executive members appointed to the Cabinet would resign from the UR. However, as indicated in a note on p. 164 above, the 1972 UR election was supposed to have installed Vorster's candidate. Mulder's election to the Executive was probably part of these failed ploys.

to rival Botha's Defence Ministry. Vorster's former OB comrade-in-arms and fellow wartime internee, Hendrik van den Bergh had been appointed to head the Security Police at the end of 1962. Apparently reluctant to take the job, he did so only on certain conditions:

> [O]ne of those conditions was that the Security Police as it then existed should be disbanded and that I would be able to draw to the new Security Police force the men that I either knew personally or knew as top policemen. ... I remember saying to John Vorster that if he gave us the weapons, then we would guarantee that no shot would be fired, that there would not be a revolution in South Africa.*

Having then created his own private fiefdom, responsible only to Vorster, Van den Bergh led the then Justice Minister's assault on the ANC and Communist Party underground in the 1960s. Appointed head of the new Bureau of State Security (BOSS) in 1969, and now statutorily accountable only to the Prime Minister, the general presided over all domestic and international intelligence gathering and evaluation, as well as counter-intelligence.

Van den Bergh personified the most paranoid and most vicious tendencies in Afrikaner nationalism. His activities ranged over all continents, seeking the downfall of anti-apartheid activists everywhere. BOSS was behind a bizarre six-year effort which eventually destroyed the career of the then leader of the British Liberal Party, leading to Jeremy Thorpe's prosecution (and eventual acquittal) on a charge of murder. Van den Bergh's elaborate plots allegedly went so far as a plan to spring Nelson Mandela from his Robben Island prison, and then have the ANC leader shot at a remote rural airstrip while Mandela was boarding a private plane which would ferry him out of South Africa.†

Vorster created BOSS in the first instance as his own eyes and ears in both party and state, shamelessly using the security apparatus in his battle with the verkramptes. Van den Bergh was Vorster's closest confidant and his most important adviser. According to the Erasmus Commission of 1978-79, the general was the real power behind Vorster's throne. Boasting that 'nothing happened in South Africa without me knowing about it', he told this commission that 'I am able with my department to do the impossible. ... I have enough men to commit murder if I tell them: Kill! ... I don't care who the prey is'.[1] The commission concluded that not only did Van den Bergh exercise

---

* Van den Bergh, quoted in D'Oliveira, *Vorster – The Man*, 141-2. Van den Bergh describes his dismay when he was first transferred from the Criminal Investigation Department to the Security Police in 1960: 'I was the most unhappy man in South Africa. I did not want to join the Security Police.' When Vorster asked him to take over in 1962, Van den Bergh had already submitted his resignation from the Police Force and signed a contract for a 'fantastic job' with a 'top South African financier'. Ibid. 140-1.
† See Part Two of Winter, *Inside BOSS*, especially chapters 22, 27 and 28. This former BOSS agent gives some idea of both the paranoia and scope of BOSS activities.

considerable influence over the Prime Minister, he sometimes made decisions for him:

> For that he sometimes held certain facts from Vorster and sometimes gave him only selected facts. Then again, there were times when he ignored Vorster's instructions. Sometimes he traded on the Prime Minister's name to gain his own ends. He was in charge of a formidable network of agents whose qualities he described in sinister terms. ... He told the commission arrogantly that if he wanted to do something, nobody would stop him and he would stop at nothing. ... He actually used his friendship with the Prime Minister to try and himself influence the course of events in South Africa.[2]

Mulder cultivated a close relationship with Van den Bergh, winning his committed support in the internal struggle against P W Botha. Yet Mulder also needed a public image to match Botha's reputation as a superbly effective Cabinet minister. Before being elected Transvaal leader, he had spent four years in the Cabinet as Information Minister. He and his department had not exactly distinguished themselves in promoting South Africa's image during this period. The Transvaal leader finally made his decisive move in 1972. Impatient with the cautious approach of his Secretary for Information, Gerald Barrie, and impressed by the aggressive views of maverick Information official Dr Eschel Rhoodie, Mulder elevated this sometime journalist over the heads of many senior bureaucrats to the post of (Permanent) Secretary of the Department of Information. Opposed by the Public Service Commission, Rhoodie's appointment was referred to, and confirmed by, the Cabinet.[3]

The new Secretary for Information had only contempt for his 'fuddy duddy' predecessors who had run the department as 'a super post office' peddling 'soft sell ... crap that ... included films of the flowers of South Africa and the freedom of an eagle in the Drakensberg mountains'. Rhoodie's flamboyant lifestyle and conspiratorial approach to his job would earn him the sobriquet 'James Bond'. Installing his brother Deneys as his deputy, Rhoodie drew up a detailed covert action plan to 'go after the opinion makers and decision takers in the Western world – by any means possible ... a propaganda war in which no rules or regulations count'.* In February 1974 Prime Minister Vorster and Finance Minister Nico Diederichs agreed to set aside a secret R64 million fund to finance Rhoodie's clandestine propaganda war. An informal Cabinet subcommittee of Vorster, Mulder and Diederichs would vet projects and spending.† Likewise dissatisfied with paucity of results achieved by the highly

---

* Rhoodie, quoted in Rees & Day, *Muldergate*, 170, 172. Written by two of the reporters who broke the story of 'the Information Scandal', much of this book is based on interviews with Rhoodie in exile.

† Rhoodie later insisted that Vorster submitted the detailed Information Strategy to the Cabinet on 11 March 1974 and that Vorster later swore under oath that the Cabinet both approved the strategy and appointed the oversight committee. Rhoodie, quoted in Rees & Day, *Muldergate*, 31.

conventional diplomacy of the Department of Foreign Affairs, they explicitly agreed that Foreign Affairs 'should be left in the dark ... and bypassed in certain circumstances'.*

To preserve secrecy, the funds would be allocated to the covert, arms procurement account of the Defence Department, and then channelled to BOSS and the 'G' funds of the Information Department. General van den Bergh 'was invited to sit in' on meetings of the Cabinet subcommittee – known as 'the Committee of Three'.† One senior civil servant said of the close relationship between 'James Bond' Rhoodie and the General, 'they are like twins'.⁴ Rhoodie's elaborate schemes became deeply intertwined with various BOSS activities. General van den Bergh clearly saw the new covert 'Info action' as an integral part of his own empire, and became 'a key figure in Information's covert ventures'.⁵

Labelled 'Operation Senekal', the Information Strategy was the centrepiece of the cabal efforts to promote Mulder's claim to the Premiership. In effect, Rhoodie was given a free hand. The Cabinet committee supposed to oversee his operations at best met on a sporadic, ad hoc basis: 'It was with the Mulder–Rhoodie–Van den Bergh triumvirate ... that the real planning and execution of the Department's secret programmes rested, rather than with the so-called Committee of Three.'⁶ Senekal involved multifarious, covert initiatives to suborn key opinion makers at home and abroad, and to seek control over various mass media, so as to shape the way in which information about South Africa was presented for public consumption. Rhoodie used the secret funds to buy, to bribe, to corrupt and to enrich both his targets and his collaborators. Sexual favours, outright theft, lies to Parliament were all part of the overall scheme. Some even hint darkly that the 'junta' were implicated in the still unsolved 1977 grisly murder of the South African delegate to the IMF

---

* Geldenhuys, *Diplomacy of Isolation.* The Foreign Minister, Dr Hilgaard Muller, was a career diplomat who had been stunned by his appointment to the Cabinet by Verwoerd in 1965. With no base in the party, no apparent political aspirations and no strategy beyond that of traditional diplomatic *politesse,* Muller was no match for the cabal's deliberate raid on his political turf. However, this changed dramatically following Muller's retirement in 1977. The new Foreign Minister, and former South African ambassador to the United Nations, R F (Pik) Botha had a definite sense of how he wanted to change South African policy and a horror of interference in his own bailiwick. Once Botha took over the Foreign Ministry, his department's behind-the-scenes wrangling with Mulder's Departments of Information and Van den Bergh's BOSS turned into an open war over political territory – one which excited much comment in the opposition press.

† Geldenhuys, *Diplomacy of Isolation,* 32. When Diederichs became State President later the same year, his place on the Cabinet subcommittee on Information was taken by the new Finance Minister, Natal NP leader Owen Horwood. Rhoodie told the *Rand Daily Mail* that Diederichs informed him that Defence Minister P W Botha had been given 'a general outline' of the projects proposed under the new Information Strategy, and 'had agreed that this was a good idea' (Rees & Day, *Muldergate,* 173). This does not gibe with his claim that the full project was submitted to the entire Cabinet in March 1974. For Botha's version, see De Villiers, *PW,* 126-9.

and National Party candidate in the 1977 elections, Dr Robert Smit and his wife.*

The scale and scope of 'Operation Senekal' would have beggared the imagination of even the author of the fantasy espionage novels from whose hero Rhoodie acquired his nickname. By 'James Bond's' own account, his almost 180 'projects' included, *inter alia*: attempts to purchase leading South African, British, French and American newspapers; establishing and financing both an international news magazine – *To the Point* – and a pro-government English-language newspaper in South Africa – *The Citizen*; purchasing numerous newspapers and magazines all over the world; subsidising pro-South African programmes on international television networks; setting up a 'moderate' black newspaper in the Bophuthatswana bantustan; funding the production of pro-South African movies with big-name stars; arranging Vorster's clandestine visits to the presidents of Senegal, Zaire and Ivory Coast and wrangling a state visit by former Nazi, John Vorster, to Israel; providing money to the president of the Seychelles; trying to bribe Nigerian politicians to recognise the 1976 'independence' of the Transkei bantustan; financing a Norwegian parliamentary party; underwriting (successful) election campaigns against US Congressmen and Senators hostile to South Africa; paying former US President Gerald Ford to address a Houston seminar on trade with South Africa; retaining Labour and Conservative Party members of the British Parliament to work for South Africa behind the scenes; compensating members of the Japanese Diet for 'their cooperation ... in regard to labour unions'; retaining a US public relations firm and numerous lobbyists to promote SA interests; financing special supplements on SA in Western media; identifying and wooing future political leaders in various countries; setting up 'neutral' international front organisations to promote South Africa; subsidising several supposed academic research institutes; paying the expenses of, and providing luxury accommodation and other perks and services – including sexual – to prominent local and international figures who spoke out for South Africa; purchasing vast luxury property holdings throughout southern Africa, the US and Europe.[7]

To accomplish all of this, Rhoodie set up literally hundreds of front companies in many countries, and moved around massive amounts of money between banks on four continents. He claims to have spent R85 million on Operation Senekal after April 1974.† At one stage R13 million 'disappeared' en route to *The Citizen*. Government attempts 'to recover the R13 million over a

---

* On the Smit murders, see Rees & Day, *Muldergate,* chap. 2. In a 1987 interview, only published after his own death in 1993, Rhoodie denies such allegations, suggesting that Smit was murdered because he got wind of a Defence Department slush fund for an eventual NP government-in-exile. *Noseweek,* vol. 2, no. 3, July 1993.

† Rhoodie, quoted in Rees & Day, *Muldergate,* 186. This compares with the R500 the Information Department spent on 'secret services' in 1962. When Rhoodie took over, the department had only 'two or three secret projects – and no budget to speak of'. Ibid.

period of more than a year failed – as the money had been put into private enterprise in a bid to help an ailing company'.[8] According to Rhoodie's one-time deputy, 'they were stealing money left and right'.[9] The allegations of corruption went beyond the realm of the financial. Some of the hardened journalists who spent months probing into the private lives of some of South Africa's most prominent politicians and key personalities in Operation Senekal were shocked by the sexual shenanigans. Though clearly constrained by libel law, they paint a picture of

> moral hypocrisy in which absolute power acted as an aphrodisiac to men who used their influence to seduce women both in South Africa and abroad.[10]

Operation Senekal effectively permitted the cabal to seize control of South African foreign policy. All the key initiatives of the period came from them, rather than the Department of Foreign Affairs. The lacklustre Minister, Hilgard Muller, protested the encroachment on his terrain, but lacked the both the political clout and bureaucratic muscle to reclaim his domain. In the cabal's game plan, Operation Senekal was complemented by two parallel undertakings designed to reinforce their hold over state policy – the détente initiative and the removal of aspects of petty apartheid which 'did not impinge on the overall objectives of separate freedom'.[11]

All this centred on the politics of image rather than substance. With Mulder's department in control of the presentation of South Africa's image abroad, and the manipulation of political perception at home, the Transvaal leader was poised to seize control of the policy agenda. His ally, General van den Bergh, had his tentacles into the darkest recesses of the state, controlling all its secrets, supervising many of its foreign contacts, manipulating many of its players and constantly plotting to checkmate P W Botha. BOSS maintained an active file on the Defence Minister and tapped his phone.[12]

Following Crown Prince Mulder's anticipated elevation to the Premiership, the cabal planned to set up a thinktank or 'Supreme Council' comprising key civil servants, leaders of commerce and industry, scientists, technologists, political scientists, military strategists, representatives of the country's intelligence and law enforcement services. According to Eschel Rhoodie, this Supreme Council 'would be responsible for all the country's forward planning on major political, socio-economic and capital works programmes'. It would make recommendations to the Cabinet, which would 'not be allowed to make major decisions on its own, without the Supreme Council first discussing the issue'. The chairman of this Supreme Council was to be none other than General van den Bergh, with 'James Bond' Rhoodie as his 'co-ordinating director'. Rhoodie believed that 'the General would probably have got a Cabinet post, because it would have been essential that he follow the council's recommendations into the Cabinet room'.[13]

The Cape NP leader was all that stood between the cabal and the realisation of these plans. United by their ferocious individual ambition, Mulder, Van den Bergh and Rhoodie all cordially detested and feared the equally ambitious P W Botha. Though the Defence Minister was still indulgently known as *Piet Wapens* (Pete Weapons) Botha in the NP, the cabal referred to him in private as 'the Pangaman' (Axeman) because 'you'd never know when he was going to lash out at you'.* Mulder's antipathy towards Botha was an almost inevitable consequence of the feudal structure of NP federalist politics. The leaders of the Transvaal and Cape parties were the two great NP barons, respectively presiding over the party's major political fiefdoms. Internal party battles almost always pitted one province against the other, with their leaders as the great structural rivals of NP politics. Since the NP's formation in 1914, every Transvaal/Cape leadership couplet had always been characterised by mutual disdain, and often by outright contempt and loathing.†

P W Botha was also the principal bureaucratic enemy of both Rhoodie and Van den Bergh. The Defence Minister regarded Operation Senekal as an amateur scheme run by cowboys, and made his opinion widely known.[14] Never reconciled to the fact that massive funds from his own secret account were channelled to the department of his chief rival for Vorster's shaky crown, Connie Mulder, Botha fought Operation Senekal at virtually every turn. On five separate occasions he formally protested this arrangement to two different Ministers of Finance. More than once he took his complaints to the Prime Minister.‡

Even more to the point, however, were Botha and the Defence Ministry's intense, ongoing war with Van den Bergh over turf and policy. Botha exercised firm hands-on leadership of the Defence Ministry. Taking over a creaking Broederbond fiefdom in April 1966, he had thoroughly reorganised the South African Defence Force (SADF), cultivated and promoted an entire cadre of younger military technocrats, and steeped himself in military lore and theory, and particularly counter-insurgency strategy.§ Throughout the late 1960s, the

---

* Rhoodie, quoted in *Muldergate*, 174. The original (black) 'Pangaman' perpetrated a series of brutal rapes and murders of white courting couples in the Pretoria area in the late 1950s and early 1960s. He was later hanged.

† General Hertzog's first Cabinet was more than once driven to the verge of an rupture by the mutual antagonism between the first Transvaal leader, Tielman Roos, and Cape leader D F Malan. The troubled relationship between Strijdom and Malan was discussed above (pp. 85-9). Strijdom and his successor Verwoerd openly scorned Malan's replacement as Cape leader, Dr T E Dönges. Ben Schoeman had described P W Botha as 'little more than a simple mouthpiece for *Keeromstraat*' – quoted in (Beaumont) Schoeman, *Vorster se 1000 Dae*, 246.

‡ Pottinger, *The Imperial Presidency*, 9. The Erasmus Commission noted Botha's persistent complaints against Operation Senekal.

§ Botha's sycophantic biographers claim that when Verwoerd gave Botha the Defence portfolio in 1966 he told his minister that he needed someone he could trust to prepare the Defence Force for the looming 'difficult times' and 'military confrontation'. De Villiers, *PW*, 221. On Botha's intensely personal relationship with the High Command, see Grundy, 'Rise of the SA Security Establishment'.

SADF had squabbled openly and violently with first Republican Intelligence and then BOSS over the appropriate response to domestic and regional security issues.

For Botha and his generals, Van den Bergh was nothing more than an 'astute (*skerpsinninge*) police officer' who did not understand that 'the Police and the Defence Force had totally different interests and needs'.[15] This military contempt for the security operations of the Police Force pre-dated Botha's tenure in Defence. Senior Army officers had deeply resented the fact that the deaths at Langa and Nyanga in 1960 were blamed on the military rather than on the incompetent police who had lost control and called on the army to shoot.[16] The military's battle with Van den Bergh continued over Katanga and over the Nigerian Civil War. In the words of former BOSS agent, Gordon Winter,

> The top men in Military Intelligence regarded themselves as 'non-political purists' who were only interested in vital matters of defence. They despised Van den Bergh's men as little peeping toms who crept around looking for people who disagreed with apartheid or Whites who slept with Blacks. And to some extent they were right.[17]

The creation of the Bureau for State Security in 1969 simply aggravated the rivalry and the military's pique. Falling under the direct control of Van den Bergh, and responsible only to the Prime Minister, BOSS became the central clearing house and coordinating station for all intelligence gathering, evaluation and counter-intelligence activities.[18] BOSS even established its own military evaluation division.[19] The Military Intelligence Section of the SADF (MIS) was relegated to a subsidiary role, and its budget slashed.* Given the intensely personal relationship between Vorster and Van den Bergh, the Defence Minister and his General Staff were now taken out of the loop on crucial security issues. Botha's biographers give a sense of his resentment over this issue.

> What made matters worse was the fact that under Vorster, Van den Bergh had a free hand. Everywhere where something was contentious, Van den Bergh turned up: in Europe, in North African countries, in Angola, in the secret projects of the Information Department, in Vorster's inner office.[20]

Worse still, Botha knew policeman Van den Bergh to be 'constantly sticking his nose in military business'. Again, the Cape leader's biographers use strong language to describe his outrage: 'If there is anything over which Botha would flay (*afslag*) somebody, it is outside interference in areas of his own personal responsibility.' Never a man to nurse his injured *amour propre* and sense of vio-

---

* The 1969 estimates of expenditure saw the Defence Force Budget for Secret Services shrunk from R790 000 to R39 000, while BOSS was given a budget of just over R4 million in the new 'Secret Services' item under the Prime Minister's vote. To add insult to injury, the Police vote for the same service almost tripled (from R412 000 to R1 218 000) – D'Oliveira, *Vorster – The Man,* 241.

lated personal turf in silence, Botha fought back with all his considerable political skill and notorious vengefulness. Once aware that Van den Bergh 'kept a security file on him (Botha)', and was tapping his telephone, the Defence Minister stormed into Vorster's office, threatening resignation, and warning the Prime Minister that 'Van den Bergh would be the cause of his own [Vorster's] downfall'.

BOSS had been established in the middle of Vorster's battle with the Hertzogites, in which his need for Botha's support was absolute. The Defence Minister made sure that 'he got his way' on the issue of MIS independence from BOSS, telling Vorster 'to wake up and not to lend his own ears to Van den Bergh'. Under intense pressure from both the Defence Force and BOSS, Vorster took his customary sideways exit. Barely months setting up BOSS, the Prime Minister appointed Appeal Court Justice Potgieter as a one-man commission to enquire into all matters relating to state security. Potgieter's brief included the question of whether the relevant state departments functioned 'properly and in a coordinated manner'.[21] His 1971 report essentially recommended maintaining the existing division of labour between the security services, reinforcing both BOSS's overall coordination role and its exclusive right to engage in covert intelligence gathering and evaluation. In terms of the Security Intelligence and State Security Act (SISA Act) of the following year General Van den Bergh was appointed to the newly created post of Secretary for Security Intelligence.

The Potgieter Report seemed a decisive BOSS victory over MIS. However what the commission took away with one hand, it returned with interest with the other. It gave MIS the residual right to gather domestic intelligence on matters related to the functioning of the Defence Department. Such matters could be, and were, very broadly interpreted (see below). Even more significantly, the 1972 SISA Act now set up an interdepartmental State Security Council (SSC) 'to advise the Government on the formulation of national policy and strategy in relation to the security of the country and the manner in which this should be implemented'. Both the Defence Minister and the Chief of the SADF were statutory members of the SSC. The SADF High Command now had its first institutionalist *entré* into what had hitherto been the exclusive preserve of BOSS. While Vorster did not make great use of the SSC, its mere existence gave the military a forum from which to contest some of the more weird and wonderful plans of Van den Bergh and the cabal.

On numerous occasions Botha complained so vigorously to Vorster about Van den Bergh that the 'violent quarrel' between the *Hoofleier* and the Cape leader over Van den Bergh became 'even more tense'. The ongoing war between the Defence Department and BOSS over territory and the broad direction of security policy grew out of a very different sense of the appropriate strategies and tactics. General Van den Bergh

> favoured a cautious and primarily diplomatic mode exemplified by Vorster's détente exercise, backed by a massive and covert foreign information exercise. Botha, conversely, believed in the judicious deployment of military force, both

open and covert, where it could help South Africa's interests. In some cases it was not so judicious – leading to the observation by one Cabinet minister ... that Botha was a 'convinced militarist'.[22]

The collapse of Portuguese colonialism after the April 1974 Lisbon *coup d'état* elevated this BOSS/SADF rivalry to a completely new pitch. Botha's enemies claim that he had prepared an direct intervention in Rhodesia by South African paratroopers once Vorster withdrew the South African para-police unit in 1974. BOSS took the tale to an unwitting Prime Minister who directly ordered the unit stood down. It is also alleged that, contrary to Vorster's express orders, the SADF was on the verge of intervening in Mozambique in late 1974 – and was again thwarted by BOSS agents.[23] But persistent skirmishing between BOSS and the SADF gave way to open warfare over the fact and consequences of South Africa's first military intervention in Angola from August 1975 to March 1976.

A *'ligte mistykie':* The first incursion into Angola

Nothing better illustrates the haphazard, almost chaotic nature of the last years of Vorster's rule than the débacle of the first SADF incursion into Angola, August 1975 to March 1976. South Africa was effectively dragged into a major war without the Cabinet's knowledge. The 'startled Cabinet' seems only to have been finally informed of the real nature and scope of South African involvement in Angola in January 1976 – five months into the SADF's then biggest operation since World War II, and after more than a few South African soldiers had been killed. Decisions were taken by a very small group of players, and those technically responsible for foreign policy were completely excluded. The Department of Foreign Affairs first realised that the South African army had undertaken a major offensive into Angola at the end of August 1975 when it received a formal protest note from Portugal – then still technically the colonial power.[24]

Still shrouded in official secrecy, the *ligte mistykie* of Angola remains the object of intense mutual recrimination and mudslinging. Eschel Rhoodie blamed the disaster on a militaristic P W Botha. Rhoodie's account insists that the Defence Minister unilaterally sent SADF troops into Angola to guard the Calueque–Ruacana border hydro-electric complex serving northern Namibia, and then authorised a 'hot pursuit' operation when these troops were fired on (by UNITA forces!) 30km into Angolan territory:

> Vorster swore to Dr Mulder and General Van den Bergh that he did not know what was going on until it was too late ... not even the Cabinet was informed about the 'pursue-to-Luanda' instruction, as Dr Piet Koornhof told me ... The decision to send the troops northwards of Caleque (*sic*) on a 600km 'hot pursuit' was Mr Botha's own and he presented Mr Vorster with a *fait accompli.*[25]

Botha's official biography tells a vastly different story of a gradually escalating South African involvement, with Vorster and the Cabinet consulted every step of the way.[26] The most detailed and authoritative existing account paints a barely credible picture of a total policy vacuum and slovenly decision-making.[27] Again, the problem appears to have lain with Vorster. The Defence Department presented the Prime Minister with an analysis of the implications of various policy options in June 1975. However, it took Vorster 'some months' to react. Each stage of the intervention seems to have been dictated by ad hoc response to events, rather than by a well-worked-out strategic plan and clear political objectives. Decision-making was confined almost exclusively to Vorster and Botha, with the Defence Minister 'the driving force behind their joint decisions, a man whose strong views more often than not prevailed'. In the absence of a well-considered set of strategic policy options, the Prime Minister seems to have become the prisoner of a four-phase operational plan of an initially gung-ho Defence Force. The political objectives of the intervention seem never to have been spelled out. Commanders in the field were hampered by the fact that 'crucial political decisions were often slow to materialise'. Not for the last time in South African history, the military seemed to turn Von Clausewitz on his head, with policy becoming the pursuit of war (and the enemy) by other means.

Vorster approved arming the UNITA and FNLA factions in July 1975.[28] In August, the SADF occupied the border region of Angola – ostensibly to secure the Calueque–Ruacana hydro-electric complex as well as refugee camps for fleeing Portuguese settlers. Over the next two months it was sucked deeper into Angola in a series of escalating hot pursuit missions against MPLA units. In mid-October the go-ahead was given for the two armoured columns, 'Foxbat' and 'Zulu', to engage the MPLA and Cubans in central Angola.* What then became the SADF northward punch into the heart of Angola halted on the outskirts of its capital Luanda in early November 1975. P W Botha's authorised biography describes how South African heavy artillery and bombers were directly involved in the FNLA attempt to take the capital on Sunday 9 November. Planned by South African Brigadier B de V Roos, the attack was on Luanda was a complete fiasco. South African Canberra bombers missed their targets, Holden Roberto and his FNLA troops arrived late for the attack, and Roos and his men had to be rescued by the South African frigate, *President Steyn*, leaving their artillery behind them.[29] By this time, there were 3 000 South African troops in Angola, including 1 000 conscripts.† Botha's December

---

* The SADF claims that this only involved 'about 300 advisors/instructors' and various arms. Robin Hallet quotes reports that by mid-October between 1 200 and 1 500 SADF troops were engaged – 'The South African Intervention in Angola 1975-76', *African Affairs*, vol. 77, no. 303, July 1978, 361. Geldenhuys regards the official figures as 'too low' and Hallett's as 'probably greatly exaggerated' – *Diplomacy of Isolation*, 77.

† I have been told by a number of SADF conscripts who were involved in this adventure that their unit was 'asked' to volunteer. Those who did so were immediately stripped stark naked, all possible identifying items – including their dogtags – were removed and every single item of their kit was replaced with nondescript equipment impossible to trace. They were told that if they were captured, the SADF would deny having anything to do with them.

proposal for a full-scale assault on Luanda, with 1 500 South African troops, was turned down by Vorster. By late December, the Chief of the Defence Force, Admiral Bierman, was expressing concern that South Africa could run out of ammunition. Task Force Zulu finally withdrew from Angola on 27 March 1976.

One of the key questions of the Angola affairs turns around the role of BOSS. Geldenhuys has Van den Bergh joining with the Department of Foreign Affairs in a chorus of 'powerful domestic voices raised against South Africa's involvement in the Angolan war'.[30] However, the general's role seems to have been more complicated than that of Vorster's house dove. Van den Bergh had directly advised Vorster to supply arms to the anti-MPLA forces. He was also deeply involved in negotiations with the CIA and US Secretary of State Kissinger to acquire overt American assistance to the South African intervention, conveying the striking belief in SADF circles that such assistance would be forthcoming. According to his co-conspirator Eschel Rhoodie, in late October/early November 1975 Van den Bergh told the *Cabinet* of

> CIA promises of support for a massive pincer attack on Luanda: South Africa and Savimbi from the south and Holden Roberto from the north-east with American equipment. I know that this was true because I was in Mobutu's palace at the time when Holden Roberto was asking Mobutu's blessing to launch his attack from the sanctity of Zaire. So was General van den Bergh.*

The BOSS head only appears to have begun his opposition to further South African participation in the Angolan war after the CIA indicated that the US would end its involvement. Until then he 'actually tried to make his Bureau rather than Military Intelligence the main vehicle for South African involvement in Angolan affairs'.[31]

The 1975–76 war in Angola eventually marked a conclusive turning point in the internal battles over security policy. Its importance is only underlined by the desperate efforts of each side to shift the blame on to the other. Whoever was responsible for the *ligte mistykie* of involving South Africa in Angola in the first place, both BOSS and the military were equally intent on winning the war and the *après guerre* – not only against the MPLA/Cubans but also against each other. However, they drew very different returns from the exercise. Both during the war and its thirty-month aftermath, BOSS was decisively outmanoeuvred by the Defence Department.

Despite the decisive MPLA/Cuban victory, domestic white opinion seemed persuaded by the government's propaganda message that its army had performed nobly if not heroically. The military reversal was blamed firstly on its inadequate equipment. The SADF's major artillery piece was still the WWII vintage 25-pounder, and South African troops had been devastatingly

---

* Rhoodie, quoted in Rees & Day, *Muldergate*, 195. This also contradicts Geldenhuys' (and implicitly Rhoodie's own but different) claim that the Cabinet was kept in the dark until January 1976.

outgunned by the Angolan and Cuban 'Stalin Organ' – the Soviet-supplied BM-21 multiple rocket launcher. Some of the conscripts involved claim that the South African Air Force (SAAF) 'lost its air superiority'. This dubious story has SAAF pilots telling troops that they had come up against 'technology they had never seen before'. That this was believed by this battered invasion force is almost as important as whether or not it was true. White soldiers simply could not credit that they had been beaten by black troops – both Cuban and Angolan. Whatever the truth of this latter story, the SADF failure in Angola simply confirmed Defence Minister Botha's long insistence on the need for even greater resources for his ministry, and intensified efforts to acquire more modern arms.*

The failure of the *ligte mistykie* was also blamed on the Americans – and by inference, on the man primarily responsible for coordination with the CIA, General van den Bergh. In the end, Van den Bergh became the victim of his own overextended power. Intelligence gathering and evaluation was the supposed exclusive preserve of BOSS. Both the SADF's June 1975 assessment of South Africa's options, as well as its strategic and tactical decisions in the field, were ultimately based on intelligence provided by BOSS. The military High Command held Van den Bergh personally accountable 'for misleading them about the extent of American support for the covert SADF operation'.†

In the recriminations following the debacle, Angola was judged to have been essentially an intelligence failure. BOSS had completely miscalculated American intentions and misread the American mood, being over-reliant on Kissinger's alleged verbal promise of support. Equally significantly, it also severely underestimated the capacities of, and support for, the MPLA, and hugely overestimated those of the FNLA and UNITA.[32] Even the most superficial and biased reading of the published literature on the military struggle against Portuguese colonialism made it patently obvious that of the three Angolan 'national liberation movements' only the MPLA possessed any military capability, only the MPLA had done any real fighting against the Portuguese.

Less than three months after the last South African troops left Angola, BOSS was again caught fatally off guard by the Soweto uprising. It had ignored the strength of opposition to imposing Afrikaans tuition on black schoolchildren, and failed to gather reliable intelligence about their organisations. This left the

---

* One member of the parliamentary delegation which visited Angola in early 1976 told me that Botha (and Progressive Federal Party MP Harry Schwartz) wanted to 'begin an arms race with the Russians'.

† Pottinger, *The Imperial Presidency*, 46. The US administration, and especially Secretary of State Henry Kissinger, had expressed consistent support for the South African incursion. However, the overt American intention to intervene was hobbled by the December 1975 Congress vote to cut off all funding for operations in Angola. The CIA mission turned into farce, leaving Pretoria, and more specifically, the SADF, holding the baby. See the book by the man in charge of the CIA's Angola intervention, J Stockwell, *In Search of Enemies* (W W Norton, New York, 1978).

regime unprepared for what happened, and unable to formulate any response other than the machine-gun.[33] Soweto was the then worst public relations disaster in the history of apartheid. With Van den Bergh handed much of the blame for its occurrence, the other members of the cabal were dealt the impossible card of trying to explain the massacre of unarmed schoolchildren. Not even the most sophisticated massaging of the managers of world information flows could undo the impact of the traumatic images of black children made 'tame' to Pretoria's gun. The dramatic photograph of a horrified black teenager bearing the corpse of 12-year-old Hector Petersen while a traumatised girl ran screaming beside him undid at a stroke whatever goodwill Operation Senekal had achieved for the apartheid regime over the four previous years.

Both Angola and Soweto seemed to confirm the SADF's longstanding complaint, firstly, that BOSS was incapable of collecting reliable intelligence and, secondly, that the entire BOSS security strategy relied on flashy diplomacy and individual contacts rather than substantive strategic planning. Van den Bergh was reputed to see South Africa's problems largely in terms of conspiracies by agitators. His counter-insurgency tactics concentrated on infiltrating informers into the ranks of the domestic and international opponents of apartheid, and indulging in baroque counter-conspiracies. All of BOSS's protracted efforts to forge links with various OAU member states focused almost exclusively on *individual* leaders within these states, offering them various inducements to alter their own individual political position, presuming that this would affect the general policy thrust of these states.[34]

This conspiratorial mentality was equally evident in the adventurist grandstanding of the Department of Information. Like Van den Bergh, both Rhoodie and Mulder operated on the white man's delusion that only leaders mattered. All you had to do was suborn the movers and shakers, and the idiot masses would fall into line. Structural problems, indeed apartheid itself, were not at issue. White South Africa could be protected by cynical manipulation of information and of image. Substantial change was unnecessary. What is really striking about Rhoodie's discussion of the cabal's plans for a Mulder Premiership, of a 'Supreme Council' and control of the Cabinet, is the total absence of any sense of the need for either cultivating black support or for strategic thinking.[35]

By the end of 1976, Botha and his Defence Ministry had developed a very different view of South Africa's future. The Cape leader described himself as 'difficult' and 'dissatisfied' and 'almost rebellious' during the last years of Vorster's Premiership.[36] Well aware that Vorster would not remain in office forever, Botha did all that he could to distance himself from the policies and practices of the cabal. Their antipathy towards him was returned in full measure. Botha and Van den Bergh clashed fiercely in the State Security Council.[37] Winter claims that the Cape leader 'got some of his top Military Intelligence men to mount a careful probe' into 'the secret projects mounted by BOSS in collusion with the Department of Information'.[38] Even more importantly, however, the SADF set out to elaborate a clear and public policy alternative to the conspiratorial tinkering offered by Mulder *et al.* Botha and his generals had also prepared a wider set of political alliances than the one on which the cabal relied.

The military–industrial complex

By the end of 1977, virtually all commentators were agreed that on the burning issues of economic, social and political policy, behind the overt face of hardline control and repression, the government was virtually rudderless.* Afrikaner intellectual circles were rife with discussions of the possibility of a *coup d'état*. Indeed, the SADF General Staff reportedly sent a memorandum to their Minister Botha pressing for a change of government and hinting at the possibility of a coup unless the Vorster government urgently introduced social and political changes to expand black political loyalty to the regime.[39]

This protracted paralysis of the Vorster government finally catalysed decisive political realignments. Two broad forces are crucial here: the military and the most powerful of South Africa's capitalists. They shared an increasing identity of interests, and their growing cooperation spilled over into similar strategic perspectives.

As the regional situation deteriorated, the Defence budget was again increased, rising from R327 million in the budget year 1971/72 to R692 million in 1974/75. Growing regional instability after 1974 and particularly the circumstances in Angola led to a further doubling of allocations for the military to R1 408 million in the two years 1974/75 to 1976/77.† Angola and Soweto crystallised SADF discontent with overall security policy. The Defence Force recast its own training, organisation, logistics and strategic projections to take account of the new regional and international realities. It fought hard for a rearmament programme to enable it to correct the severe deficiencies in equipment revealed in Angola. More significantly, the generals and Botha clearly concluded that war was far too an important business to leave to NP politicians, and particularly the directionless, haphazard leadership of Vorster. In the aftermath of Soweto the SADF lobbied for a complete strategic reformulation of South Africa's regional objectives and policies, insisting on the need for long-term planning and a coherent decision making process.[40]

---

* The then immediate past president of the South Africa Foundation and chairman of the Anglovaal conglomerate, Basil Herzov, said of Vorster's government, 'for years everything was stagnant'. *Financial Mail,* 28 September 1979. The Sanlam chairman expressed similar views, *ibid.* 17 August 1979.

† Frankel, *Pretoria's Praetorians,* table 2, 72. The Police Force Budget rose by just over 70% in this two-year period, from R119 million to R168 million – G Cawthra, *Brutal Force: the apartheid war machine* (IDAF, London, 1986), table IV, 259. Both the real funding allocated to the Defence Force, as well as the actual amounts spent, were higher than the Defence Budget. See Frankel, *Pretoria's Praetorians,* 74-5.

Steeped in the counter-insurgency lessons of Malaya, Algeria, Vietnam and the wars in the Portuguese colonies, Botha's strategic planners grew increasingly concerned with creating the broad set of conditions making for social stability. They argued that any such counter-insurgency struggle was '80% political and only 20% military'. The 1977 *Defence White Paper* proclaimed the SADF programme for a 'Total National Strategy' to meet the complex crisis confronting the state. The fundamental aim, according to the SADF official organ, was 'a guarantee for the system of free enterprise'.[41] This could only be achieved on the basis of a 'comprehensive plan to utilise all the means available to the state according to an integrated pattern'. This Total Strategy held that

> the resolution of a conflict in the times in which we now live demands interdependent and coordinated action in all fields – military, psychological, economic, political, sociological, technological, diplomatic, ideological, cultural etc. ... We are today involved in a war ... the striving for specific aims ... must be coordinated with all the means available to the state.[42]

However, such 'coordinated action' was no mere defence of a static status quo – political and economic reforms were essential to ensure the defence of the state. In the words of the then Chief of Staff of the SADF:

> The lesson is clear. The South African Defence Force is ready to beat off any attack ... but we must take account of the aspirations of our different population groups. *We must gain and keep their trust.*[43]

In effect, the Total Strategy doctrine argued that blacks had to be given a stake in the capitalist system, so that they would begin receiving the 'benefits' of that system, their 'quality of life' would have to be improved, thus supposedly giving blacks a commitment to the defence of capitalism in South Africa against the 'Marxist threat'. However the doctrine recognised that this would only be possible through the closest cooperation between the state and 'the private sector' (see Chapter 14). This was a far cry from the cabal's envisaged 'Supreme Council'.

The Total Strategy doctrine elaborated the ideological basis for overt collaboration between senior military officers and business leaders. It took up the loud appeals made in the early 1970s by the Sanlam vice-chairman and chairman of its massive Gencor mining subsidiary, Dr W J de Villiers, for 'cooperation between the public and private sector in an overarching strategy to ward off Marxism'. P W Botha's biographers stress his high esteem for Wim de Villiers, and the impact on Botha's thinking of the analysis by this key member of the Cape nationalist establishment.*

---

* De Villiers, *PW,* 159. Dr Wim de Villiers made a number of highly public pleas for such cooperation. His most coherent statement is found in his inaugural address on accepting an honorary professorship at the Rand Afrikaans University, 25 March 1975.

Cooperation between the captains of industry and the SADF generals grew out of more than just their converging strategic conceptions of necessary 'reform'. It also had a direct economic base. The imposition of the first arms embargo against South Africa in 1964 led to the emergence of a locally based armaments industry, supervised by the state-owned Armaments Development and Production Corporation (Armscor), under the ultimate control of the Ministry of Defence. By the end of the 1970s Armscor stood at the core of a new, indigenous military-industrial complex. The corporation had become South Africa's third biggest industrial group, with total assets exceeding R1 200 million.[44] While itself directly manufacturing a wide range of arms and other military equipment, roughly 60 percent of Armscor's production was contracted out to the private sector, together with much of its research. In 1976 alone, 25 000 contracts were handed out to about 1 200 private arms contractors. Of these, 50 'main contractors' were 'directly involved' in the manufacture of arms, another 400 subcontractors supplied major components, and the remaining firms delivered the 'nuts and bolts' to keep the war machinery running'. Frankel estimates that some 5 600 'business operations [were] linked into the defence establishment' at the end of the 1970s. These included the subsidiaries of virtually all of South Africa's major non-state conglomerates, as well as a number of high-profile multinationals such as IBM, Shell, Daimler-Benz and many others.[45]

Almost 29 000 people were directly employed by Armscor at the end of the 1970s. When added to those employed to fill military contracts, at least 100 000 people worked in South Africa's armaments industry. Armscor itself had the reputation of a relatively benevolent employer of blacks, who made up 43 percent of its 1978 workforce. Given the technology-intensive nature of its work and mandate, Armscor was 'sensitive to internal shortages of skilled labour in a manner reflecting current structural problems in the South African economy as a whole'.[46] Reflecting the preoccupation of all major employers with apartheid's restrictions on the employment, training and mobility of black labour (see p. 183 above), Armscor's concern with skilled labour shortages would have been communicated to the responsible Minister (Botha), and may well have played a role in his own known willingness to eliminate job reservation – contrary to existing NP policy.

In 1975/76 some R184 million was paid out in the domestic production of arms. This figure rose dramatically in subsequent years. Almost all levels and branches of the private sector were locked into a direct, and highly profitable, relationship with the miliary via the burgeoning armaments industry. Indeed, so close was the link between the major conglomerates and Armscor that in 1979, at the Prime Minister's request, South Africa's then largest industrial private corporation, the 'liberal' Barlow Rand group, seconded one of its key executives, Johan Maree, to act as Armscor's executive vice-chairman – in which capacity he sat on the highly influential Defence Planning Committee. The *Financial Mail* listed as one of Maree's achievements 'the heavy private sector involvement, both at board and production levels, in armaments production'.[47] This close integration of the military and the private sector through Armscor led one observer to conclude that in the corporation were concentrated 'the interests of capital intensive, mainly monopoly capital, the military apparatus, and the political organs of the state'.[48] Yet the link between the SADF and private capital went beyond arms production. Military contracts made up a substantial part of the production of the textile, mechanical engineering, electronic and building industries, and 'many segments of the private sector are today either directly or indirectly dependent on Defence Force contracts'.[49]

The discussion of the development of a 'military-industrial complex' in South Africa can be overdone, and the political cooperation between the military and business can in no sense be reduced to an identity of economic interest through Armscor. Nevertheless, by the mid-1970s business leaders and senior commanders had grown accustomed to working together, and clear agreement was emerging between on the need for 'reform' of apartheid to make it militarily defensible. In late 1977 the National Management and Development Foundation convened a crucial meeting of business leaders, senior military officers and Department of Labour officials, to 'enable each group to understand the other's needs'. Chaired jointly by a senior general and the chairman of a leading bank, the meeting was held *in camera* and under the cloak of the Official Secrets Act.*

The major political beneficiary of this cooperation was the man who ultimately presided over Armscor – Defence Minister P W Botha. As leader of the Cape NP, Botha was one of the two great barons of the NP. He had led the fight in the late 1960s to replace the verkrampte vision of Afrikaner nationalism with a broader (white) South African nationalism, at one stage directly confronting the Broederbond. Botha was first and foremost a creature of the Cape NP. He had worked throughout his entire adult life in the greatest intimacy with the Cape Nationalist establishment (see p. 257 below). By 1978 the linchpin of this establishment, the Sanlam financial group, had emerged as South Africa's second biggest conglomerate. Its chairman had written a scathing denunciation of Vorster's economic policies, and publicly demanded 'reform' in language little different from that of the 'liberal' Anglo American Corporation. The Cape NP, its press, and particularly its leader, were not insensitive to these demands.

But Botha was more than just Cape NP leader. As Defence Minister since 1966, he impressed his own 'managerialism' on the SADF and nurtured its commanding cadre of young generals. Known as *Piet Wapens* (Pete Weapons), Botha enjoyed close personal ties with the General Staff, was well read in military theory, and followed the detailed studies of counter-insurgency warfare

---

* G Moss, 'Total Strategy', *Work in Progress,* 11, 1980. The same banker had chaired the committee which presided over the dissolution of the United Party.

instituted by the High Command. Minister Botha shared his generals' concern with managing counter-insurgency. He had been particularly incensed at the failure of the SADF's 1975–76 Angola intervention, blaming Vorster's refusal to commit the necessary forces, and bad intelligence from BOSS. During the visit to Angola by a parliamentary delegation in early 1976, Botha petulantly referred all questions to Vorster, saying that he knew nothing about the operation.[50] Botha was also known throughout the NP as a superb organiser whose managerial skills had won him wide respect among younger technocrats in all state departments.

Writing in the early 1980s, Philip Frankel's study of civil–military relations in South Africa argues that Botha

[D]rew heavily on private sector advice during his tenure as Defence Minister, and since a 1977 meeting at the Rand Afrikaans University, which many analysts regard as the 'take off point' of the local military-industrial complex, Botha has frequently expressed the desire to 'unite business leaders behind the South African Defence Force'.*

Botha's wish began to be realised in the Muldergate crisis.

---

* Frankel, *Pretoria's Praetorians*, 88. The meeting here referred to is the one discussed above, held under the Official Secrets Act.

Chapter Twelve

MIGHTY TONGUES
TELL MIGHTY LIES

Muldergate:
The consolidation and victory of the 'reformists'

Muldergate: Let the best man win! (left to right: P W, Connie, Pik)

Oh what have you done Christine?
You've wrecked the party machine
Its not very rude
to lie in the nude
but to lie in the House – that's obscene!*

Throughout 1978 and much of 1979, the National Party and government were rocked by the worst political scandal in South African political history. The highly public unravelling of the myriad covert projects of Connie Mulder's Department of Information provoked seemingly endless political and financial uproar, immediately dubbed 'Muldergate' by South Africa's English-language press. First the Auditor-General, then the press and finally two judicial commissions of inquiry revealed massive corruption, systematic deceit and other abuses by all members of the Transvaal cabal. The affair eventually disgraced Mulder, Van den Bergh and Rhoodie and led to their complete fall from power. Muldergate also destroyed the career of John Vorster, forcing his resignation from the Premiership in September 1978, and then the State Presidency less than a year later. In making P W Botha Prime Minister, Muldergate accelerated both the process of reform and the final sundering of the National Party.

People in glass houses

Great floods of ink have been spilled over Muldergate and its consequences.[1] While most commentators have rightly seen the affair as both the apogee and symbol of a crisis of power and direction in the South African state, almost without exception the brouhaha has been cast in narrow and misleading terms. Outrage predominates. Three intersecting themes characterise most commentaries. Muldergate is judged to reflect, firstly, the 'moral hypocrisy' of men in power, who used their public positions to advance their private interests, financial and otherwise. The opposition English language press, and particularly the liberal *Rand Daily Mail*, concentrated, secondly, on the 'abuse of power', violation of 'mechanisms of democratic control' and 'the creation of a Frankenstein monster'. And drawing these themes together was, thirdly, the parable of the collapse of the austere Calvinist public morality of Afrikaner nationalism into 'bribery, corruption, deceit, lies'. In the words of one journalist turned politician, 'moral rot and decay ... was destroying the entire Nationalist edifice' from within.[2]

This is all true in so far as it goes. However, at another level, the intense moral indignation over Muldergate in the mainstream white press – including, later, some pro-NP newspapers – both contains its own 'moral hypocrisy' and conveniently masks the real *political* significance of Muldergate. Since I am

---

* In 1963, British War Minister John Profumo lied to the House of Commons about his sexual relationship with Christine Keeler. The 'Profumo affair' ended the political careers of Profumo and Prime Minister Harold Macmillan.

here concerned with this latter aspect of the affair, it is as well to dispose of the issues of 'corruption', 'abuse of power', 'deceit' etc. at the outset.

Such things were hardly new in apartheid South Africa. Glaring examples of collective and ministerial corruption were revealed in the 1960s (such as the 'Agliotti affair') with negligible political consequences.* 'Abuse' of power and of 'democratic norms' by the ruling party had been its prime means of sustaining itself in office since 1948 – and were vigorously defended as being in 'the national interest' by some of the newspapers now howling 'corruption'.

More fundamentally, in apartheid South Africa, such notions were a luxury available only to those who still expected gentlemanly behaviour from the regime. However, for the vast majority of South Africans the entire social edifice was structured to enrich a powerful few at the expense of the majority. Rotten to its roots, the system of white power and privilege was sustained only through the constant 'abuse of power' by a white minority – English-speaking as well as Afrikaners. For four out of five South Africans, Muldergate was no aberration, but rather the norm in and further confirmation of a thoroughly corrupt society. The self-righteous indignation emanating from a political and economic establishment which had grown fat off apartheid smacked of the rankest 'moral hypocrisy'.† And it fudged the real political question of Muldergate: why did this brouhaha assume such monumental proportions?

Cats' nest exposed: The Information Department scandal

The Auditor-General began examining the secret Information projects in April 1977. His February 1978 report tabled in parliament gave the first public notice of something seriously amiss in Connie Mulder's ministry. This report noted the department had been using funds without Treasury approval for over three years and criticised unnamed senior Information officials for unnecessary and extravagant oversees trips.

For six months prior to this report, the *Rand Daily Mail* and other English

---

* At the end of the 1960s, a businessman named Agliotti bought land at the end of the runway of Jan Smuts International Airport for R5 million, selling it back to the state for R95 million shortly thereafter. The *Sunday Times* campaigned unsuccessfully for years for an inquiry into ministerial collusion. Agliotti was eventually obliged to return much of his profits to the state.

† Thus the English-language press which editorialised so indignantly over Muldergate had never condemned the systematic 'abuses of power' which, eg, kept real African mine wages lower than they had been in the mid-1890s. Liberal editors seemed blind to the 'moral hypocrisy' of the liberal businessmen who owned and read their newspapers – and whose eloquent denunciations of apartheid were matched by a rigorous refusal to increase the appalling wages of their black workers. During the 1970 general election campaign I heard Planning Minister Carel de Wet scold heckling liberal students at the University of the Witwatersrand that nothing in government policy prevented Mr Oppenheimer from raising the wages of his black mineworkers should he be serious about improving the conditions in which blacks lived in South Africa. This may have been disingenuous, but it was also true.

newspapers had been investigating alleged 'irregularities' and 'corruption in high places' in the Information Department. From the outset, the press also focused on sexual high jinks among 'some of South Africa's most prominent politicians'.[3] Information Secretary Eschel Rhoodie dismissed these investigations in an extremely aggressive, and revealing manner:

> Tell those bastards I know about them. Tell them I have tape recordings about them. Tell them I know what they are trying to do. Tell them to go to hell.*

In May 1978, in response to reports of a large-scale seepage of South African capital abroad, Prime Minister Vorster appointed a one-man commission of inquiry under Judge Anton Mostert to investigate exchange control contraventions. Mostert soon encountered the large-scale evasion of exchange control regulations by the Department of Information. The evidence given to his commission was the dynamite which finally blew the lid off Operation Senekal, and shattered the careers of the entire cabal.†

The Auditor-General's report led to a hearing by a parliamentary select committee which recommended an investigation by the Treasury as well as the Public Service Commission. Despite Information Minister Connie Mulder's denials of any wrongdoing, investigating journalists slowly revealed detail upon juicy detail of the vast, well-financed and secret operations of the Information Department. Just two months after the Auditor-General's report, Mulder was finally forced to admit to Parliament that 'there has been a serious offence'. Blaming his officials, the Information Minister promised to take the necessary action. Less than three weeks later, Mulder made the first of what proved to be two fatal tactical errors. Under persistent questioning by opposition MPs, he assured Parliament that neither his department nor any other organ of the government had given funds to the recently founded pro-NP English-language daily newspaper – *The Citizen*.‡

---

* Quoted Rees & Day, *Muldergate,* 7. Rhoodie's department had no capacity to bug conversations. He could only have obtained such 'tape recordings' from one of the intelligence services of the state, probably BOSS.

† Here again are found the recurring ironies of Afrikaner nationalism. A staunch nationalist, before his elevation to the bench at the tender age of 43, Judge Anton Mostert was legal adviser to the giant Afrikaans Transvaal press group, Perskor, the chairman of whose controlling body was Connie Mulder. Mostert was also a close personal friend of Justice Minister, Jimmy Kruger – himself to second Mulder's nomination as NP *Hoofleier* in September 1978. Mostert's legal colleagues attributed his early elevation to the Bench to his friendship with Kruger. Yet Mostert was a key figure in the process which eventually caused the downfall of Mulder, John Vorster and Kruger himself. Mostert was later peripherally involved in other significant political developments (see p. 386 note, below).

‡ *House of Assembly Debates,* 21 April 1978, col. 5350, and 10 May 1978, col. 6626. Free State NP Leader Alwyn Schlebusch was so unimpressed by Mulder's assurances that the same day he told Vorster that P W Botha and not Mulder would be the next prime minister – Pottinger, *The Imperial Presidency,* 12.

This was an outright lie. It would later be confirmed by the Mostert and Erasmus Commissions that the Department of Information had set up *The Citizen*, had written its operating charter and was funding its monthly losses of R400 000. The department would eventually give R32 million (or almost half the money channelled from the Defence Special Account) to the newspaper – some R13 million of which was used by frontman Louis Luyt to subsidise his own troubled fertiliser company, which funds 'went missing' for over a year (see above pp. 214-15).*

The revelations about the 'cats' nest' in the Department of Information unleashed an unprecedented outcry within white politics. For the first time since 1948, the parliamentary opposition parties managed to seize the initiative. Their hounding of the government centred on their suspicion that it had been involved in the establishment of *The Citizen*. Yet ever more detailed revelations seemed unable to pin down definite proof. For almost five months Mulder and Prime Minister Vorster denied any government implication with *The Citizen*. 'James Bond' Rhoodie was made the scapegoat for the 'serious offences' admitted to by Mulder. The Department of Information was disbanded in June 1978, and Eschel Rhoodie went on premature retirement.

Behind the scenes, however, a massive cover-up was taking place. The final report of the Erasmus Commission revealed that Vorster had been directly informed of the scope of and financial 'irregularities' in the Information Department projects.† The Prime Minister told an informant that he would clean up the department after the elections of 30 November 1977: 'He could face everything [in the department], but just not the newspaper [*The Citizen* disclosures].' At this stage, Auditor-General Gerald Barrie had already demanded that Deputy Information Secretary, Deneys Rhoodie, 'should go'. This led General Van den Bergh to 'negotiate with Barrie over a solution to the problem'. After the NP triumph in the 1977 elections, Vorster was advised to reveal the Information abuses, fire Eschel Rhoodie and leave Connie Mulder out of his Cabinet. He rejected this advice as politically too costly. Once the Auditor-General's report was tabled and the press revelations began, General Van den Bergh took charge. According to Retief van Rooyen's evidence to the Mostert Commission:

> General Van den Bergh ... informed me that he had been to see the Prime Minister and Connie Mulder and told them that he had wanted to resign

---

* Luyt had first allowed the department to use his name as the ostensible principal in the department's attempt to buy out South African Associated Newspapers, owners of the NP's real *bête noire*, the *Rand Daily Mail*. When this scheme eventually failed, Luyt again agreed to act as frontman for the department in its establishment of *The Citizen* as a pro-government morning daily in direct opposition to the *Daily Mail*. See Rees & Day, *Muldergate*, chap. 14, 'Luyt's Confession'.

† Erasmus 2, p. 11. In evidence to the Mostert Commission one of the frontmen for the Information Department – advocate Retief van Rooyen – claims he told Vorster of theft and other abuses in October 1977. Unattributed quotations and information in this paragraph are taken from the edited version of this evidence in Rees & Day, *Muldergate*, chap. 13.

previously, but that he would save them. The people were saying that the Prime Minister, by his silence, was misleading the nation, that Mulder was lying. Van den Bergh then told them that he would save them and take over the evaluations, and he would manage project for project for the next two years. ... Any matter dealt with by the Bureau for State Security was covered by the Official Secrets Act, and he would therefore inform newspaper editors that any further writings on this matter would be a contravention of the Official Secrets Act. ... In other words, he would stretch the thing out for them until the whole thing was dead.[4]

Prime Minister Vorster indeed appointed Van den Bergh to evaluate the Information Department's secret projects, and a BOSS auditor, Louw ('Loot') Reynders, was mandated to investigate the department's secret expenditures.[5] Mulder was able to continue protesting his innocence, telling the September 1978 Transvaal NP congress that he had a clear conscience. The tumult over the Department of Information was 'only a storm in a teacup'.[6] However, the spill-over from the affair would soon entirely swamp first the ambitions and then the career of the NP Crown Prince.

Dogs around a bone: The battle for the Premiership

South Africa's third State President, former Finance Minister Nico Diederichs, died on 26 August 1978, after three years in office. Many observers commented that Prime Minister John Vorster looked exhausted at Diederich's funeral. Hospitalised three days later, Vorster was declared to be suffering from physical exhaustion and mild bronchitis. This occasioned feverish NP speculation over both his future and his likely successor. On 11 September, five days after being released from hospital, the Premier told the political correspondent of *Die Burger* that although he was feeling better, 'I'm like champagne without its sparkle'.* Although Vorster waited another week before informing his Cabinet that he would resign as Prime Minister and seek the vacant (and largely ceremonial) State Presidency, the overt battle for the succession was already well under way. With Connie Mulder and P W Botha as its central protagonists, this would become the 'biggest and most exciting power struggle in the country's political history'.[7]

Vorster's term as Prime Minister ended when his successor was sworn in following the NP *Hoofleier*ship election on 28 September, 1978. General Van den Bergh resigned the same day. In retrospect, these resignations seem to have been prompted by two overriding concerns. Firstly, as was later revealed, both Vorster and his favourite general were deeply implicated in the Information Department's schemes, including the funding of *The Citizen*. Were this to come out while Vorster was still Prime Minister, the political damage would have been immense. Vorster must have realised that in such an event he could rely on neither the support nor the protection of his party. Once elevated to the

---

* Ries & Dommisse, *Broedertwis: die verhaal van die 1982-skeuring in die Nasionale Party* (Tafelberg, Cape Town, 1982), 9. Such alcoholic similes were dear to 'the cork in the bottle'.

ceremonial Presidency, however, even his NP opponents would be forced to protect the Head of State.

Yet Vorster was in an impossible position. P W Botha's biographers report that in June 1978 Vorster had told *Die Burger*'s political correspondent, Alf Ries, that he wanted to retire soon and his only possible successor was P W Botha. But he added that 'he knew PW's temper; he did not know whether PW would be able to hold the party together'.[8] Curiously, Ries's own lengthy account of the protracted saga of Vorster's resignation and the battle for the succession makes no mention of this, despite his acknowledgement that *Die Burger* was very close to the Defence Minister. Rhoodie asserts that Vorster 'made no bones about his support for Pik Botha', and did everything he could to help him.* Vorster later told the Erasmus Commission that 'I did not think that he [Mulder] had a chance, and what is more, I told him that it was my considered opinion that he should not make himself available as a candidate'.[9]

However, Vorster had certainly clashed sharply and frequently with the Cape leader over the previous few years, and his actions until two days before the leadership election appeared to favour Mulder. Certainly, were Mulder to reveal what he knew about Vorster's own role in the Information Scandal, he could do far more damage to the retiring Prime Minister than could P W Botha. Vorster's best protection would have been a Mulder Premiership. A few days after Vorster was released from hospital, he was approached by P W Botha. Stressing that he was acting in his capacity as senior minister, the Cape leader told the Premier: 'There are frightening rumours going around. Can I discuss this with you? I would like to tell you what I am hearing.' Vorster declined comment, observing that 'my people [ie General Van den Bergh and Reynders] are busy investigating'.[10]

The timing of Vorster's resignation clearly helped Mulder, coming as it did just days after the end of the Transvaal NP Congress where Mulder had appeared to consolidate his position with a powerful speech against concessions and negotiations to 'appease the outside world'.[11] However, five days before the leadership election, Mulder made his second fatal tactical mistake. He leaked to the official organ of the Transvaal NP part of the report of Vorster's special BOSS investigator into the Information Department. Reynders noted that 'no malspending came to light' in his investigation of Mulder's old department. *Die Transvaler* concluded: 'This news will be welcomed by those members of the NP caucus organising support for Dr Mulder in the present leadership race.'†

This ploy very nearly succeeded. Just six days before the leadership election the key source of leaks to the *Rand Daily Mail* told its investigating journalist:

---

* Rhoodie, *P W Botha*, 43. Vorster had the Foreign Minister sit next to him at the press conference when he announced his retirement. According to Rhoodie, Vorster later described his support for Pik Botha as 'one of the biggest mistakes I made in my life, if not my biggest'.

† 23 September 1978. The then editor-in-chief of *Die Transvaler*, Willem de Klerk, later told the Erasmus Commission that the leak came from Connie Mulder. He in turn could only have got this information from General Van den Bergh or Vorster.

Hell Mervyn, you can't believe what's going on here man. They're fighting like dogs around a bone ... Connie's home and dry. It's all over bar the shouting. The General and Eschel have already started rubbing their hands.[12]

The overwhelming weight of the Transvaal in the NP's parliamentary caucus (80 out of 172 members) virtually ensured its candidate's victory if two conditions were met. Firstly, the Transvaal leader had to be able to count on the support of the overwhelming majority of his own caucus. But, secondly, to achieve the magic number of an absolute majority (87 votes), he *also* had to win substantial support from the 24 members of the Free State NP caucus. The old northern alliance of the Transvaal/OFS versus the Cape was thus the second essential key to victory. Mulder ultimately threw away both.

By 1978 the conflicts within the Transvaal NP had reached such a pitch that Mulder was finally unable to control his own party. More than a few Transvaal MPs had been upset by their leader's belligerent speech at the recent Transvaal congress. The MP for Florida (and the man later to come within five votes of keeping F W de Klerk out of the Presidency), Barend du Plessis, commented that 'if this was the sort of politics which was going to be practised in the following years, a disaster awaited the country'.[13] Defying all party protocol, precedent and discipline, two other Transvaal ministers put themselves forward as candidates for the *Hoofleier*ship against the leader of their provincial party – S P (Fanie) Botha (Labour & Mines) and the very junior R F (Pik) Botha (Foreign Affairs, no relation to either S P or P W Botha).*

Fanie Botha soon withdrew on the ostensible grounds that he did not wish to divide the anti-Mulder vote, and most of his support now switched to P W Botha.† Yet the continued presence of Pik Botha split the Transvaal vote, drawing off younger verligtes, and ensuring the defeat of Mulder – as the Foreign Minister and his supporters later admitted to have been their intention.[14]

---

* Both Transvaal Bothas were anathema to the verkramptes. S P Botha was a one-time junior associate of Albert Hertzog. Since his defection to the verligte camp, he was known by his verkrampte critics as 'Fanie Water' (pronounced *Faanie Vaarter).* This derisory reference to his sojourn as Minister of Water Affairs had roughly the same pejorative meaning as Margaret Thatcher's contempt for the 'wets' in her Cabinet. R F Botha for his part had been known since adolescence as *Pik* – argot 'shorty' – an ironic reference to his height. During his sojourn as Pretoria's ambassador at the United Nations, his blunt defence of his government's unpopular cause won him the moniker 'Pig' Botha from fellow diplomats. In September 1978, the 46-year-old Pik Botha had only been in the Cabinet for eighteen months, had never held a leadership position in the NP and stood a lowly number 16 in the order of Cabinet seniority. He too was hated by verkramptes for his equally blunt statements of the need to reform apartheid – once declaring that he was prepared to die to defend the Afrikaner's right to exist, but not to defend racially segregated lifts (elevators)

† Though some (like Barend du Plessis) turned to Pik Botha. *Die Vaderland* reported that Fanie Botha was the victim of *skinder stories* (slanderous gossip) during the 'cat and dog fight' for the leadership, 22 September 1978. This most likely dealt with the dubious state of his personal finances – which would eventually force *him* to resign under a cloud in 1983.

At first Mulder had been incensed by sheer audacity of Pik Botha's candidacy. But as what P W Botha called 'the ghost of Rhoodie' began to stalk the former Information Minister on the eve of the election, Mulder offered Pik Botha the leadership of the Transvaal NP if the latter would withdraw in his favour. One Transvaal MP said of the 'enormous pressure' placed on the Foreign Minister's Transvaal supporters: 'It was a call to blood, but it was in vain. Our repugnance (*afkeer*) for Dr Mulder was too great.'[15]

However, convinced right to the last that he would win, Mulder rejected a number of separate ministerial appeals to withdraw in favour of P W Botha. In the end, his own desperate tactics assured his defeat. Mulder's unauthorised leak of the Reynders report sparked two lethal interventions. Three days after the leak, and just two days before the *Hoofleier*ship election, Prime Minister Vorster issued a statement that only part of the report had been leaked. The statement added that *Die Transvaler*'s story neglected to mention that Reynders clearly stated he had no mandate to enquire into the 'merits and evaluations of policy decisions' regarding the secret projects. Reynders had therefore concluded he could not 'offer comment on the eventual spending of the payments which were made'.[16] Vorster's statement was an implicit repudiation of *Die Transvaler* story, and severely damaged Mulder's credibility. More significantly, Vorster must have known what the Erasmus Commission later revealed – that General Van den Bergh had subjected his employee Reynders to intense pressure to whitewash Mulder before the caucus vote on the *Hoofleier*.* The thieves were beginning to fall out.

By this stage, Vorster was himself under extraordinary pressure from even more damaging devils let loose by *Die Transvaler*'s whitewash of Mulder. A series of sensational developments were now precipitated by former Rhoodie frontman and the informant who had urged Vorster to fire Mulder after the 1977 election, advocate Retief van Rooyen. On reading *Die Transvaler* report, Van Rooyen was appalled by the idea that Mulder seemed on the verge of getting away with everything. As he later told the *Rand Daily Mail* journalists who frantically and unsuccessfully tried to contact him that weekend: 'I had put my head through the door of a potential dictatorship and what I saw there horrified the hell out of me.'† Van Rooyen immediately contacted his former colleague on South Africa's World Court legal team, Pik Botha, showing the Foreign

---

* Judge 'Mixed Metaphor' Erasmus wrote that when 'the total irreconcilability' of Reynders' report 'and the actual facts that where known at the time' was pointed out to the BOSS auditor, Reynders burst into tears 'and like a lanced boil, made a clean breast of things' – Erasmus 1, p. 82.

† Quoted Rees & Day, *Muldergate*, 72. Van Rooyen might also have worried that if Mulder were Premier, he would seek retribution for Van Rooyen's tales to Vorster and efforts to get the minister fired. This lawyer's role in the Muldergate *dénouement* is yet another example of the 'moral hypocrisy' of the affair. Van Rooyen had earlier represented the police in the notorious inquest into the death in detention of the Black Consciousness movement founder, Steve Biko. Mulder's actions 'terrified the hell' out of him, yet Biko's brutal death did not. Van Rooyen told reporters in America that 'Biko had been treated kindly by his interrogators'. *Rand Daily Mail*, 2 February 1978.

Minister secret Information Department documents. These amply proved Mulder's lie to Parliament and revealed the extent of the secret Information projects.

This unleashed dramatic manoeuvring at the highest levels of the NP. Pik Botha was apparently so shocked that his wife and supporters feared he had taken ill. In a highly conspiratorial manner he arranged a hasty meeting in Cape Town the next day with Cape leader P W Botha and Orange Free State NP leader Alwyn Schlebusch (Natal NP leader, Owen Horwood, was at an IMF meeting in the United States at the time). Van Rooyen repeated his story to the two Bothas, Schlebusch and two other Cabinet members, telling them that the hated 'English press' were on the verge of blowing the story and bringing down the government. Schlebusch was appalled by the revelations:

I felt the heavens were falling in on me. ... Remember, I was a provincial leader [of the NP] and a relatively senior member of the Cabinet. Now, for the first time in my life, I found out about the Information saga.

There and then the five Cabinet ministers decided to beard Connie Mulder and Prime Minister Vorster. Schlebusch, who had earlier urged Mulder to withdraw – and who also believed he had been instrumental in Fanie Botha's own withdrawal from the leadership race – was deputed to see Connie Mulder in Pretoria the same night. His account of their meeting is worth quoting in full:

When I arrived in Pretoria, I immediately phoned Connie and went to his house. I told him that certain revelations had been made to me. I was not prepared to reveal either their nature [n]or the name of the person responsible. In the light of these allegations and of the manner in which they were brought to my attention, I believed that I must now tell him that I was convinced that it was neither in his own interest, nor those of the party and the country, that he should present himself as a candidate for Prime Minister the following Thursday [28 September].

He replied that he could not give me this assurance. I then told him that as Free State Leader of the National Party I wished to make something very clear to him: if he did not become Prime Minister, I would let the matter lie. However, should he indeed become Prime Minister I would then immediately call a meeting of the Head Committee of the Free State National Party and try to convince its members to withhold their support from him as Prime Minister up and until such time as he agreed to appoint a commission of enquiry into all the allegations which had been made to me. He had nothing to say to this, but looked reasonably shaken. With this we parted.[17]

The five Cabinet ministers confronted Vorster with Van Rooyen's story on Monday 25 September. A startled Prime Minister told them, 'I am afraid there is much truth' to the tale, and promised to inform the full Cabinet at his last Cabinet meeting the next day.[18] However, 'falling apart (*afgetakelde*) and exhausted', the outgoing Premier only raised the Information issue the end of the Cabinet meeting, simply informing his ministers that he was going to release all three paragraphs of the Reynders report without comment or qualifications. Pik Botha objected. Confronting Vorster, the Foreign Minister announced he 'would not leave the table until all the other colleagues had also heard' what Vorster had told the delegation of ministers the previous day. The full Cabinet was then briefed on the full ramifications of the affair, 'for the first time'. Despite now being urged by several ministers to withdraw, Mulder still refused. A journalist who saw the Cabinet members emerge from this meeting described them as 'pale' and 'heavily dejected'.

While they had been meeting, other significant developments had taken place. The pro-Mulder Transvaal daily, *Die Vaderland*, reported that with the exception of the two other candidates themselves and only three other named ministers, the entire Cabinet supported Mulder. Once again Alwyn Schlebusch intervened, obliging the newspaper to place a front-page correction the next day in which the Free State leader said he was not only supporting P W Botha, he was organising actively for him. To the pro-Botha *Die Burger* and *Beeld* newspapers Schlebusch declared that the Cape leader also had the support of 20 or 21 of the 24 Free State MPs.*

Even following the confrontation in Cabinet Mulder still believed he would win, telling Pik Botha this when the Foreign Minister called him the day before the election to propose yet again that they both stand down in favour of the Defence Minister. Indeed, right up until the morning of the caucus vote, Mulder was still trying to lure Pik Botha into withdrawing. However, he had been mortally wounded by Vorster's revelations, which were soon common knowledge in the caucus. The *coup de grâce* came the day before the election when a rumour was spread among MPs that Mulder was about to be subpoenaed by the Mostert Commission and questioned about a R2 million Swiss bank account.†

Mulder's Transvaal NP organisers expected to win with 104 votes in the final round (87 were needed), while P W Botha was told by his Cape machine that he would win with 97 votes on the second round. Pik Botha's organisers' expectations ranged from 32 votes up to 'the high 50s'. In the event, P W Botha's organisers were closest to the mark. The first round of the caucus election gave 78 votes to the Cape leader, to 72 to Mulder and 22 to Pik Botha.

* *Die Vaderland*, 26 & 27 September 1978, and *Die Burger* and *Die Beeld*, 28 September 1978. Schlebusch said of the Free State-born Botha: 'We came from the same political and philosophical milieu' – De Villiers, *PW*, 104.

† This rumour prodded Pik Botha into dictating, and eventually destroying, a resignation letter to Vorster, on the grounds that he 'did not agree with the way in which the Information affair was being handled'. See Ries & Dommisse, *Broedertwis*, 18-19, and Pottinger, *The Imperial Presidency*, 14. Eschel Rhoodie alleges that Judge Mostert telephoned P W Botha's factotum Chris Heunis, who spread the story. He recounts that three caucus members swore to him that the rumour ('the most scandalous in the history of South African politics') was the reason they voted against Mulder – *PW Botha*, 42-3, 45-6.

All but two of the Foreign Minister's supporters then switched to his namesake. In the final round P W Botha beat Mulder by 98 votes to 74.[19] Just before the new *Hoofleier* emerged to address the crowd waiting in front of Parliament, the public address system broadcast the Radetzky march – a clear sign of things to come. Speaking to the crowd, Botha promised orderly, honest and effective government.

Rotten apple, rotten house

The purpose of the [Information Department's] secret fund had all the attraction of a lovely fresh apple, but the germ which could cause complete rot to set in was already there in the flowering stage because of lack of clarity in the existing statutory control – Judge Erasmus

P W Botha was elected the fifth NP *Hoofleier* since its 'purification' in the 1930s by a margin eerily similar to that which Dr Verwoerd had beaten Botha's own predecessor as Cape leader twenty years earlier – 98:74 for Botha as opposed to 98:75 for Verwoerd. Like Verwoerd, Botha inherited a bitterly divided party, with the recalcitrant and enraged Transvaal conservatives now playing the spoiler's role the Cape NP had performed within the NP between 1958 and 1962.

Mulder's mistakes had weakened his powerful Transvaal NP machine just enough for the Cape party to dream of recapturing its lost *Hoofleier*ship. By alienating the upright Alwyn Schlebusch, the Transvaal leader's various manoeuvres ensured that the essential support from the Free State was lost to himself, thereby putting the leadership beyond his grasp. It was a close run thing, however. As the new Prime Minister acknowledged, his victory was possible only because of the split vote of the Transvaal caucus. Pik Botha's defiance of the rules of NP political apprenticeship, and then his (and Alwyn Schlebusch's) dogged insistence that the Cabinet be fully briefed, were the decisive factors bringing the Defence Minister to the Premiership.* Without first dividing the Transvaal NP, and then destroying its leader's political credibility, and finally weaning the Free State NP away from the traditional ant-Cape northern alliance, it is inconceivable that any Cape leader could have again have become NP *Hoofleier*.

Just how decisive were these interventions was clearly revealed in the election for a new Transvaal NP leader following Mulder's enforced resignation from that post in November 1978. Here the darling of NP verkramptes, Dr A P Treurnicht, trounced the verligte Fanie Botha – despite the fact that Treurnicht was not even a full member of the Cabinet. Pik Botha was never forgiven for

---

* Rees & Day argue that the presumptuous candidacy of the neophyte Pik Botha was originally intended as a stalking horse for his other namesake, Labour & Mines Minister S P Botha, and that when the latter withdrew Pik got carried away – *Muldergate*, 76.

'leaving the Transvaal in the lurch and handing over the government to the South [ie, the Cape NP]'. The new leadership of the Transvaal NP worked to 'strip him of all influence and responsibilities in the party', removing him from its executive while Botha was en route to a meeting with the UN Secretary-General over Namibia.[20]

However, P W Botha's victory over Mulder was far more than just the result of the verligtes finding a fortuitous means to shortcircuit the old north/south rivalry. To the general surprise of the caucus, the verkrampte Mulder had been nominated by one of the more verligte Transvaal Ministers, Dr Piet Koornhof – giving rise to speculation that Koornhof had been promised the Transvaal leadership should Mulder win.* Mulder's seconder was the Police Minister, Jimmy ('the Mouth') Kruger. The Cape leader on the other hand was generally known to favour 'reform'. Yet he was nominated by his chief organiser and next senior Cabinet minister, the far from verligte Louwrens Muller, and seconded by Alwyn Schlebusch. Moreover, this was still a highly verkrampte National Party. Christopher Hill has estimated that the 77 of the then 133 NP members of Parliament were either very verkramp or somewhat verkramp, as opposed to the 56 MPs who were either very, or somewhat verlig.† The verkrampte majority would certainly not have supported the Cape leader out of ideological conviction.

P W Botha came to power determined to introduce reform. Yet his hold over his party was tenuous. Both the fact and the manner of his election had profoundly aggravated the longstanding and deep divisions in the NP (see previous chapter). The party's wounds were daily further deepened under the relentless cascade of new revelations about the Information Department. Botha moved quickly both to limit the political damage his rivals could still do him and control the flow of information. John Vorster had been sidelined, but, just 30 days older than Botha and still popular in the caucus, the former Prime Minister could well return to active politics should Botha launch ambitious reforms. Less than two weeks after the *Hoofleier* election, Vorster was kicked upstairs into the State Presidency vacated by Diederichs' death six weeks earlier. The parliamentary correspondent of the *Sunday Times* aptly comments:

> The reasoning behind the appointment was clear: as the largely ceremonial Head of State he [Vorster] would by precedent be forced to remain aloof from the party political arena. His views on the succession struggle, on the administration's new

---

* Although Mulder had on occasion defended Koornhof when the latter was attacked for his 'advanced' views. The night before the election, Koornhof phoned Pik Botha with the message that while he could not vote for him the next day, he wanted the Foreign Minister to know that on leaving Pretoria that morning his children had given him a sealed envelope with instructions only to open it on the plane. Their note read: 'Dad, vote for uncle Pik' – Ries & Dommisse, *Broedertwis,* 20.

† Cited in Geldenhuys, *Diplomacy of Isolation,* 64. The study focuses on the 1980 NP caucus, which was elected in 1977, i.e. these were the MPs who voted in the *Hoofleier* election.

reform policies and on Botha himself would remain his own, which was just the way Botha wanted it. It was a simple yet ingenious way of rewarding Vorster while at the same time gagging him.[21]

Botha then turned his sights on the flood of revelations. When Judge Mostert refused the new Prime Minister's request not to publish the transcripts of evidence given to his commission, the Prime Minister first tried unsuccessfully to ban their publication and then fired Mostert at the beginning of November. He subsequently appointed Judge Rudolf Erasmus to a conduct a formal inquiry into the Information affair, and had the *Rand Daily Mail* charged under the Commissions Act for publishing information subject to the Erasmus Commission's mandate.

The Erasmus Commission proved to be an effective damage control mechanism. It enabled the new *Hoofleier* to present the entire Information Affair in a manner least harmful to himself and his new government. Though clearly an interested party in these proceedings, Eschel Rhoodie makes a credible and documented case that the three reports of the Erasmus Commission were filled with inconsistencies, that they ignored crucial evidence and that Judge Erasmus had coached key witnesses, including Minister Koornhof, to produce an acceptable version of the affair.[22] Finance Minister Horwood denied ever being on the Information oversight committee, and explained his signature authorising the expenditure of R14,8 million on secret projects with the lame story that he covered the schedule with a piece of paper and signed at the foot of the page.*

Whatever the truth of these allegations, the Erasmus report became the accepted version. Prime Minister Botha then introduced an 'anti-gossip-mongering' Advocate-General Bill to prevent the press from publishing details on any official corruption without first laying the matter before the Advocate-General. Publication would be solely at this newly created official's discretion. Though negative response to this 'Gag Bill' from the Afrikaans press eventually led to its withdrawal, it had achieved its intended result. When the Erasmus reports appeared, the anomalies were overlooked and the fractured prose of Judge Erasmus was the final word on Muldergate.

The first Erasmus report in December 1978 fingered three villains who had already vacated the corridors of power – Rhoodie, Van den Bergh and Mulder.

---

* Horwood had long been a controversial figure. As the conservative Vice-Chancellor of Natal University in the late 1960s he had clashed frequently with black and liberal white students. He was mocked in liberal student circles for his lacklustre academic achievements, and was always referred to as 'Professor O P F Horwood, B.Comm (Second Class)'. During the 1970 election campaign he had been dogged by student hecklers. He dealt with them by asking them how their careers stood up to his long experience in the educational field. A junior lecturer in the Natal University Psychology Department brought the house down at one NP rally when he replied to this query as follows: 'Professor Horwood, unlike you, I have *two* degrees, *both* of them in the First Class'.

Following Judge Mostert's publication of the evidence to his commission in early November 1978, Botha told Plural Relations Minister Connie Mulder that he must resign from the Cabinet. Mulder tried to get President Vorster to intercede, but here too was advised to step down. Just seven weeks after coming within six votes of Botha on the first ballot for the *Hoofleier*, Mulder quit the Cabinet. He relinquished the leadership of the Transvaal NP three days later. Following the damning first report of the Erasmus Commission in early December Botha then insisted that Mulder resign from parliament.* The erstwhile NP Crown Prince was expelled from the party four months later – ironically on the very day on which white South Africa celebrated the anniversary of the establishment of the first white settlement at the Cape of Good Hope.

New State President John Vorster emerged relatively unscathed from the first Erasmus report. The judge accepted that Vorster only first heard of the gross irregularities from BOSS investigator Reynders in the latter part of 1978, endorsed his bona fides and declared his integrity 'unblemished'.[23] Five months later, however, Judge Erasmus's supplementary report made what some have characterised as an 'unconvincing' turn-around.[24] Now Vorster was said to have known everything from the outset, concealed the details and the gravity of the irregularities from the Cabinet, and was jointly responsible for the fact that they continued.† In a stormy meeting four days after the publication of the report, P W Botha turned down Vorster's plea for a review of these findings by either a Parliamentary Select Committee or a panel of judges. This obliged Vorster to resign from the Presidency in disgrace the next day, less than eight months after assuming office.

Throughout remaining four years and seven months of his life, John Vorster conducted a private vendetta against his successor, threatening on more that one occasion to return to politics and to lead the fight against Botha's reforms.‡ Convinced that somebody had altered Judge Erasmus's report, Vorster told friends on the day of his resignation that he 'had been quoted out of context and would fight its conclusions to the bitter end'.[25] In his last book Eschel Rhoodie produced photocopies of the original typewritten draft of this report, showing significant handwritten changes which Rhoodie claims have been verified by British and South African handwriting experts as matching the handwriting of

---

* Judge Erasmus declared the former Information Minister to have been incompetent in the administration of his department, and had exercised improper pressure on others to secure favourable results for himself – Erasmus 1, paras 11.345 to 11.401.

† Erasmus 2, p. 11. Mulder and Van den Bergh had given evidence against Vorster, and a private secretary told the commission of seeing a note from the Prime Minister instructing Mulder to lie to parliament about the funding of *The Citizen*.

‡ Former Transvaal NP leader Ben Schoeman publicly warned that should Vorster return to politics, *he* would do so too, but on the other side, and reveal things Vorster would prefer to keep secret – De Villiers, *PW*, 143. See Willem de Klerk's column 'Pynlike vrae', *Rapport,* 16 March 1980.

'an Afrikaans-speaking politician'.* When the *Rand Daily Mail* reported in November 1980 that the second Erasmus report had been annotated before publication, 'Pangaman' Botha denounced both the paper and its informant in parliament, asking 'who is the man who walks with a dagger in his hand to stab me in the back?'[20]

The shock resignation of John Vorster was the last overt political act of Muldergate. However, its fallout continued well into the 1980s, and the very bitter divisions in the NP were infinitely aggravated by the affair. This is examined in later chapters. Here it is as well to clear up the real political mystery of Muldergate. The National Party had never played politics by the Queensbury rules. It had always accepted *raison d'état* as a compelling rationale for any kind of behaviour, and had, and would, time and time again, used it to justify far more egregious crimes than those of Connie Mulder and Eschel Rhoodie. So why did Muldergate assume such massive proportions? Why did the NP allow what, in terms of its own political morality, were perfectly justified excesses to divide it so deeply and to scar white politics forever?

The answer lies in the political impact of the many-levelled character of the crisis of the 1970s on the key centres of power within the South African state and ruling class. In the final analysis, the paralysis of the Vorster government stemmed from the balance of, and conflicts and rivalries within and between, the social forces and individual politicians within the NP, the nationalist government and the state apparatuses. When the Auditor-General revealed the first irregularities in the accounts of Mulder's department, those forces within the ruling class arguing for 'reform', together with Connie Mulder's enemies in the National Party, were presented with an ideal opportunity to attempt the political discreditation of the major public figure of the NP right – Dr Connie Mulder himself. The Muldergate scandal is significant not so much for the degree of political corruption it revealed, but far more importantly, for the way in which it was used to effect a realignment of political forces within the state and ruling party.

To the extent that Muldergate has been seen as a political crisis, it has been analysed exclusively as a crisis for Afrikaner nationalism and the Nationalist Party and government.[27] While the imbroglio indeed marked the culmination of a long-simmering crisis both in the Nationalist Party itself and the NP government, it was far more that a simple, self-contained, internal crisis for Afrikaner nationalism. It is the central assumption of this chapter that Muldergate was both a product of, and a moment in, a much wider *crisis of the capitalist state as a whole* in South Africa. Its 'resolution' in the allegedly 'clean' regime of P W Botha likewise represents the attempted resolution of the

---

* *P W Botha*, 74-5. Again, Rhoodie suggests a deliberate conspiracy to get rid of Vorster who was slowing down Botha's legislation and playing far too active a role as State President, and was feared for the influence he 'could still exercise on National Party members behind the scenes'. Ibid. 46.

wider crisis of the South African state through the 'Total Strategy' proclaimed by Botha. As such, Muldergate is a useful prism through which to view the intersection between the politics of Afrikaner nationalism and the crisis of the South African state. It also highlights a great deal concerning the development of this state since 1978.

Most revealing here is the manner in which the leaks about the Information Department practices were made – and the way in which these leaks were then turned into the raw material of a political witch hunt against the right wing of the NP in general, Mulder in particular, and Vorster by implication. Eschel Rhoodie has alleged that the whole affair was a elaborately orchestrated *coup d'état* by P W Botha. He depicts both the Defence Minister and his senior officers as having been deeply involved in all the major Information projects, and provides *prima facie* documentary backing for some of these claims.[28] Clearly the former Information Secretary has his own axe to grind and has to be considered a tainted source. Yet it is not necessary to accept his gothic conspiracy theories to see a number of glaring anomalies in the affair – anomalies which clearly suggest that *somebody* was deliberately and systematically leaking information damaging to Mulder, and doing so in a manner unprecedented in the history of the NP and its government.

Three sets of facts stand out here. The first is that Gerald Barrie, the Auditor-General who issued the first damning report, was none other than Rhoodie's 'fuddy duddy' predecessor as Secretary for Information, fired by Connie Mulder in 1972 – and whose efforts in the Information Department Rhoodie contemptuously dismissed as 'soft sell crap' (p. 212 above). Leaving aside any personal motivation on Barrie's part, the funding for the secret projects came from the secret weapons procurement account of the Defence Department. Rhoodie claims that the Auditor-General was specifically *excluded* by statute from reporting on or even examining the spending of these funds. He also cites a letter from the then Head of the SADF, Admiral Bierman, to the effect that 'the Auditor-General was not even informed about the existence of Operation Senekal'.* It is thus not too far-fetched to conclude that somebody drew this to Barrie's attention and provided him with the detail he needed. *Cui bono*? Moreover, a copy of one of Barrie's handwritten and confidential reports to the Prime Minister fell into the hands of Kitt Katzen of the *Sunday Express*.† How? And again, who benefits?

The second anomaly deals with the way in which the *Rand Daily Mail* reporters got hold of the story. Mervyn Rees describes receiving a call out of the blue in August 1977 from 'an old friend and contact'. This person introduced the reporter to 'a highly placed civil servant' who told Rees:

---

* Ibid. 32. Here he names 'Act 6 of 1974'. The letter from Bierman is reproduced in the evidence to the Erasmus Commission.

† This led Rhoodie to issue a press statement accusing the Auditor-General of sabotaging secret operations and of contravening the Official Secrets Act. *Rand Daily Mail*, 6 May 1978.

There was corruption in high places. ... A lot of money was involved. Top people in government were not what they seemed. A personality very much in the public eye would not stand much scrutiny ... most of the scandal was to be found in the Department of Information and he named a woman who had been the mistress of a leading National Party politician.[29]

This source, code-named 'Daan', and another 'Deep Throat' code-named 'Myrtle' – 'somebody so close to the centre of Muldergate that it was breathtaking'[30] – provided much of the information which broke the story open, and directly precipitated Retief van Rooyen's crucial phone call to Pik Botha. Now it had long been established practice during the endemic factional conflicts of Afrikaner nationalism for one side or the other (and often both) to use judicious leaks to the anti-NP English-language press to gain advantage over its adversaries. This was regularly done by both sides during the protracted verligte/verkrampte war of the mid/late 1960s, for example.[31] However, such leaks were usually passed on anonymously, and it was unheard of for reporters on an anti-government newspaper to be given information which would obviously damage the entire government or endanger its secret projects.

What makes these leaks even more unusual is firstly that the original 'senior civil servant' approached the *Rand Daily Mail*, and secondly that he contacted its crime reporter rather than its political correspondent. The newspaper of choice in which to leak the dirt on one's internal opponents was the centrist *Sunday Times*. The respected political correspondent of the *Times*, Hennie Serfontein, was himself a none-too-liberal Afrikaner with an unparalleled knowledge of Afrikaner politics. The liberal *Rand Daily Mail* and its editor Allister Sparks, on the other hand, were loathed by every loyal nationalist (and most members of the United Party) as virtual traitors to white South Africa. Indeed, the Vorster government first tried to buy the newspaper's parent company, and then destroy it through subsidised competition from *The Citizen*. To leak *the* most sensitive state secrets to the *Mail* was close to high treason to most nationalists. And to leak it to its prize-winning investigative journalist was to ensure that the story would be followed with a vengeance. Yet very little in the actions of the Department of Information would have disturbed any nationalist. Most would probably have enthusiastically agreed with Rhoodie's ruthless propagation of apartheid South Africa's image, and, from the NP standpoint, these projects did a great deal of good. So, once again, who benefited from their exposure? and why use the very worst enemy of the National Party to achieve this end?

The final set of facts to be considered are the fascinating hints contained in P W Botha's official biography. This tells first of Botha's admittedly 'difficult mood' during the last years of Vorster's reign, and their 'violent quarrel' and 'serious differences' over Van den Bergh. More specifically, the book makes tantalising reference to Botha 'learning from his own intelligence service about goings-on which were queering the pitch of Defence', and makes clear the source of such 'goings-on' was Van den Bergh.[32] Although it is impossible to find the proverbial smoking gun on this issue, it is taken as established fact by more than one Afrikaner intellectual with links to the Cabinet that the first leaks to the press were provided by Military Intelligence.

Longtime BOSS agent Gordon Winter confirms such claims. He asserts that Military Intelligence first leaked information on CIA involvement in South Africa in 1977 in order to discredit General Van den Bergh who worked very closely with the CIA, particularly over Angola. Winter then goes on to allege that Defence Minister Botha

> got some of his top Military Intelligence men to mount a careful probe into various aspects of these [Information Department] projects. Armed with this information he saw that the time had come for him to get his own back on Vorster and Van den Bergh and bring himself to power at the same time … his next move … was the slow but sure leaking of information to South Africa's liberal press about the Department of Information secret projects. The notorious 'Info Scandal' was born.[33]

Winter is clearly also an unreliable source, and there is no irrefutable evidence on this score. However, the fact remains that the ongoing and extremely damaging leaks which sustained Muldergate and destroyed the careers of three of the most powerful men in South Africa were of an unprecedented nature and scale. The people who provided the leaks must have known that they were harming their own Prime Minister and his closest advisers. Source 'Myrtle' told the *Rand Daily Mail* that power 'doesn't go any higher than the people I am talking about'.[34] 'Myrtle', 'Daan' and other sources were apparently all senior players in the Afrikaner nationalist power game. They undoubtedly knew that by damaging Vorster, Mulder and Van den Bergh at a time when Vorster was openly ruminating about his retirement, the *only* possible beneficiary was the man who since the early 1970s had been arguing that the government was not moving fast and far enough – P W Botha.[35]

Once the initial leaks had been made they were relentlessly pursued by the English-language newspapers of the South African Associated Newspapers and Argus groups. Jointly owned by the Anglo American Corporation and some of South Africa's largest banks, these press groups were clearly hounding Mulder as part of a wider campaign to undermine the right wing of the NP.[36] Perhaps even more significantly, after some initial hesitation, the anti-Mulder campaign was taken up in the Afrikaans press, and particularly in the newspapers of the official Cape NP press group, Nasionale Pers. Its Transvaal morning daily called for 'a purge of elements … .who have imperilled our precious national unity', ie Mulder and probably Vorster.[37] While the newspapers of the Transvaal nationalist Perskor group also reported on the scandal, they did everything to protect Mulder, implying that the Transvaal NP leader (and chairman of the company with a controlling interest in Perskor) was not personally involved in the abuses – blaming it all on Eschel Rhoodie.

This open involvement of sections of the official National Party press in an explicit campaign against a government minister and elected leader of one of the provincial NPs (and by implication, against the NP *Hoofleier* and Prime Minister) would have been absolutely inconceivable in the past. It was the clearest possible index of just how deep were the divisions and conflicts within the party and government, and of the lengths to which the 'reformers' were prepared to go to discredit the NP right wing. Further evidence for this lies in the belief of other Afrikaner intellectuals that once the affair began to unravel, crucial disclosures to the press were made by the wives of (unspecified) Cabinet ministers.

The long campaign of press revelations and judicial inquiry around the Department of Information had fatally undermined the political credibility of the most prominent representative of the NP right wing at a crucial moment in the factional struggle for dominance both within the NP and the government. It led directly to Mulder's humiliating defeat which then marked a significant shift in the balance of class forces organised by the Nationalist Party *qua* party under the banner of Afrikaner nationalism. Through the victory of P W Botha, Afrikaner business effectively consolidated and now institutionalised its position as the dominant force in the nationalist alliance. Through Botha it announced its intention to modify some of the hallowed policies of this alliance, policies which went to the heart of the support for the Afrikaner nationalist alliance from white labour and certain strata of the petty bourgeoisie. The election of Botha broke the log jam in the NP and enabled the cautious introduction of policies for which Afrikaner business, together with all sections of monopoly capital, had long been pressing.

However, it cannot be emphasised too strongly that this was no simple struggle *internal* to Afrikaner nationalism. Afrikaner capital was now able to consolidate its hegemony over the other class forces organised by the NP only because of broader support outside of the party from other bourgeois organisations and institutions, and from the army itself. This is a crucial point. On its own, the 'reformist' wing of the NP would not have been able to defeat the right wing in an election for a new NP leader. Nor would it have been able to discredit the right as in any way representative of majority opinion within the party. To do so, the NP 'reformists' were compelled to rely on, and indeed play a relatively minor role in, a broader campaign by a range of capitalist interests (but particularly the 'English' press) against the leading NP verkramptes. The Muldergate scandal was unique in South African parliamentary politics not so much for the 'corruption' or 'abuse of power' it revealed, but because for the first time a coalition of capitalist interests both inside and outside the NP had intervened decisively in internal NP politics to isolate those interests hostile to the modifications to apartheid advocated by capital.

In conclusion, it is worth noting the parallel with the Angola débâcle. In the end, Muldergate was not just about 'moral hypocrisy' or 'abuse of power' or even about Mulder lying to Parliament. It bears repeating that such things were not unknown in either apartheid South Africa or its governing party. The *real* political issue was the sheer incompetence of Vorster's mode of government, and hence his inability to deal with the crisis confronting the entire white establishment. This organic crisis turned first into a political crisis for the entire power bloc, and then, because of Vorster's paralysis, a crisis for the National Party and its government.

At this level the political problem was Vorster's practice of allowing individual powerful ministers to undertake crucial and far-reaching initiatives without even informing the Cabinet. It was not P W Botha who broke with the principle of collective Cabinet responsibility inherent in the Westminster model. Rather, this was first done by John Vorster. In both Angola and the Information affair, the fundamental *political* point at issue was not the outrageous actions per se. In both cases, had the Cabinet been informed, the good nationalists within it would more than likely have endorsed the actions in question. Rather the problem lay in the *manner* in which these things were done. Because Vorster's mode of governing meant that the crucial networks of political support were kept in the dark, when the Cabinet *was* finally informed of the enormity of the deliberate deception in both cases, it was so taken unawares, and had become so defensive on both issues, that it was unable to counter the tide of opposition. Vorster's management style vastly facilitated the intrigue in the NP, and fatally sapped its sense of collective purpose. The leadership of the 'cork in the bottle' not only 'stopped all development', it created such a build-up of pressure inside the bottle that when it finally shattered, the exploding shards forever shattered the precious unity of the National Party.

This is explored in Part III.

PART III

ADAPT OR DIE!

The Botha regime, reform and the collapse of Afrikaner nationalism

(Ter herdenking aan 'n wonderlike era uit ons geskeidenis)

Die ander dag toe voel ek lam
ek wou 'n klein bietjie ontspan
en 'n boer maak 'n plan
ek sit my TV-set toe aan
jy sal nie glo wat ek sien
Op my TV-screen
Dit was 'n nare gesig
dit het my heeltemal ontstig
dit was 'n moerse klug
dit was PW se gesig
en langs hom staan oom Pik
wel ek dog ek gaan verstik
Koor *Sit dit af! sit dit af!*
         Sit dit af! sit dit af!
         Sit dit af! sit dit af!
         want dis 'n helse straf
Ek stap kombuis toe kry 'n bier
En skakel oor na TV4
O my gots wat het ons hier?
wat my TV screen ontsier
is daar nêrens om te vlug
van daai man se mooi gesig
Met sy vinger in die lug
gaan hy my lewe net ontwrig
in die programe in die lug
sien jy net PW se gesig
ek vat jy nou 'n wed
al die bure het M-Net!
(herhaal koor)
o, ek not esk sê jou dis finaal
voor julle my kom haal
en ek met al my verstand
in die gestig beland
as daar iets is wat my kwel
is dit my TV stel
         (herhaal koor en rafel uit)

(To commemorate a wonderful era in our history)

The other day I was feeling weary
I wanted to relax a bit
and a boer can always make a plan
I turned my TV set on
You won't believe what I saw
On my TV screen
It was an horrible face
it shocked me rigid
it was a complete farce
it was PW's face
and beside him stood uncle Pik
Oh I thought I was going to throw up
Chorus Turn it off! turn it off!
           Turn it off! turn it off!
           Turn it off! turn it off!
           'cos its a helluva punishment
I went to the kitchen to get a beer
And changed channels to TV4
Oh my God! what have we here?
What is defacing my TV screen?
Is there nowhere to escape
from that man's pretty face
With his finger in the air
he's going to disrupt my life
in the programmes on the airwaves
you see only PW's face
I will now take a bet with you
all the neighbours have M-Net [subscriber TV]
Chorus
Oh, I'm telling you for the last time
before you come to take me away
and I with all my intelligence
land in an institution
if there is anything that gets to me
it is [what I see on] my TV set
           (Repeat chorus and fade out)

Sit dit af (words and music by Johannes Kerkorrel) from the album *Eet Kreef!*, Johannes Kerkorrel en die Gereformeerde Blues Band, Shifty Music, 1989. Reproduced by permission of Shifty Music.

Chapter Thirteen

TO KEEP ALL THAT WE HAVE

The Total Strategy project

Constructive engagement

P W Botha became South Africa's eighth Prime Minister in September 1978 at the age of 62, forty-two-and-a-half years after he first took up service in the National Party. The second-oldest man to have entered the Premiership since the formation of the South African state in 1910,* the new Prime Minister took office determined to reform the creaking apartheid state. Throughout his almost eleven years in power, P W Botha was to place a greater personal stamp on the machinery and functioning of the South African government than any of his predecessors. His policies would provoke a traumatic split in the National Party three-and-a-half years into his reign. Since his own personality and ideological proclivities became key issues of political struggle during this period, it is necessary at the outset to clear up some of the widespread myths surrounding Botha's personal position and politics.

Pangaman, organisation man, reformer: The politics of P W Botha

On Botha's elevation to the Premiership, he was almost universally depicted in the press as a 'hawk' and a Nationalist hardliner. His personal belligerence and opinions seemed to reinforce this perception.[1] Like the contemporary conventional wisdom about both his predecessor and his eventual successor (see pp. 151 above and 384 below), this oversimplifies Botha's complex political persona, and misconceived the likely trajectory of his government.

On one thing friend and foe were unanimous, however: in the words of the founder of the Broederbond and longtime Speaker of the House of Assembly, P W Botha had always been 'a difficult man'. Long before his elevation to the Cabinet, Botha's prodigious temper and bullying tactics had terrified MPs and Cabinet ministers alike. His biographers go to great lengths in a unconvincing attempt to show that this was all just tactical bluster.[2]

Yet this notorious short fuse had usefully concealed another essential part of the new *Hoofleier*'s evolving political make-up. During his long ascent through the machinery of the Cape NP, Botha developed impressive managerial skills. His organisational and managerial flair was given full flower in the Defence Ministry, revealing an hitherto hidden side to the Cape leader – a technocratic pragmatism and impatience with policies that did not work. In his twelve years in the Defence Ministry, Botha completely reorganised what his two predecessors had turned into an arthritic Broederbond fiefdom. His vigorous campaign to promote and cultivate a younger, technocratic leadership cadre revived the military's sagging morale and generated a strong *ésprit de corps* in a rejuvenated and more professional officer corps. The Defence Minister also cultivated close political and even intellectual relations with his senior officers. Deeply enamoured of the macho rituals of the military, and widely read in

---

* D F Malan was 78 when he became Premier in 1948. While Jan Smuts had been almost 70 when *he* assumed the Premiership in September 1939, Smuts had first entered this office as a relative spring chicken on the death of Prime Minister Louis Botha in 1919.

254

military theory, Botha was familiar with the strategic concerns of the SADF High Command. To this extent *Piet Wapens* Botha could be relied upon at the time of his accession to the Premiership to reflect the thinking of the military, and could indeed legitimately have been labelled a militarist.*

Botha's stewardship of the military certainly reinforced his belief in two cardinal tenets of nationalist rule – an obsession with power and strength on the one hand, and the absolute necessity for 'order' on the other. Both revolved around the central issue of control. They fed into the new Prime Minister's long-standing sensitivity to the fact that he lacked a university education. This made him at once susceptible to and contemptuous of 'experts' in any field. However, most of those commentators who seized on Botha's temper, his bullying and militaristic tendencies, missed the fact that he had long embodied another aspect of Afrikaner (and especially Cape) nationalism – if confident that he would remain in control, he could be both flexible and imaginative. As he himself put it in his celebrated 1979 injunction to his fellow Afrikaners to 'Adapt or Die':

> I sat here this morning on the pavilion, looking and thinking to myself: Years ago there were young girls in Voortrekker costumes, now we have drum majorettes in short dresses. But has this made us a different people? No it has not, *we are still the same people, but circumstances have changed.* Long ago we rode in ox-wagons; now, when we can get hold of oil, we drive cars.[3]

Botha's long sojourn in Defence had taught him that while *objectives* might be easily specified, their achievement was a matter of strategy and tactics. The latter were both pragmatic endeavours. If one method did not work, you changed it. Replying to verkrampte critics that he had deviated from 'the course of the past', Botha habitually cited his mentor, Dr D F Malan:

> I am not deviating from my course, but – this is something I learned from Dr Malan, and I stand by it tonight – if I have to divert the road in order to keep to my course and reach my destination, I shall do that. Only a fool would keep travelling on the same road, even when it has been washed away, if there is a better road to reach his objective.[4]

Here lay the nub of the verligte/verkrampte divide. To the verkramptes, means and ends were indivisible. The Verwoerdian vision of apartheid was an issue of unshakeable *principle* – not just of where to go, but also of how to get there. The verkramptes read Afrikaner nationalist history as a ceaseless battle between principled, authentic *volksleiers* and opportunistic pragmatists. From this perspective, ever since the first arrival of the British, unprincipled

---

* A story went the rounds that while reviewing an immaculate, stony-faced and goose-stepping honour guard on a state visit to Taiwan in the early 1980s, Botha had remarked to an aide: *'These are my kind of people.'*

pragmatists had led Afrikanerdom into disaster.* This reflected an even deeper fear that, as the HNP chief publicist told me in 1975, 'my people (*volk*) are not ideologically deeply rooted'.⁵ Only through rigid adherence to the sacred principles of their civil religion could Afrikaners ensure their survival on the hostile southern tip of Africa. The verkramptes ceaselessly patrolled the ideological boundaries of Afrikaner nationalism in order to save the *volk* from itself.

The verligtes were equally concerned with the survival of the Afrikaner *volk* and its language. Yet, after the death of Verwoerd, they parted company with their verkrampte colleagues on how best to ensure this. In Botha's vision, clinging to policies that did not work represented the greatest danger to Afrikaner survival simply because it handed to the enemies of Afrikanerdom ever greater opportunities to mobilise ever more powerful forces against the beleaguered *volk*. Botha argued that Moscow's 'total onslaught' gained great strength from the fact that the international community regarded the Afrikaners who held political power in South Africa as 'a pig-headed (*moedswillige*) bunch who denied the legitimate rights of others'.⁶

Time and time again, Botha returned to this theme. He told the Natal NP congress that South Africa (ie, Afrikaners) now stood at the crossroads. The choice lay between 'the path of confrontation, bloodshed, nameless suffering, and the downfall of [white] civilisation in the country – or that of consultation and joint decision making with due regard for [racial] self determination'.⁷ Afrikaners and Afrikaner nationalism were the primary target of the Moscow-inspired 'total onslaught' against South Africa. The very survival of 'civilisation' was at stake. In this dangerous context Botha was determined not to allow himself to be 'pushed around' – not by Jimmy Carter, nor by Andries Treurnicht. All of his legendary singlemindedness was concentrated in his warning to all of his enemies: 'I will do everything that I deem necessary for our survival.'⁸ Attacking his verkrampte critics, the new Prime Minister challenged delegates to the 1979 Transvaal NP congress to get their priorities right: the issue was (Afrikaner) survival, not ideological sacred cows.⁹ Botha's biographers summarise his thinking on this issue:

> South Africa was now struggling for its life, and the total onslaught against it necessitated one thing above all others, namely change – rapid, visible change: the replacing of outdated political principles, the restructuring of race relations, the rejection of racial domination (*baasskap*), the removal of humiliating discrimination and injustice, equal opportunity and rights, fewer restrictions – and a new disposition.¹⁰

The Defence Ministry had also considerably widened P W Botha's sharply partisan political horizons. Now he seemed to realise that there was a world

---

* Thus Paul Kruger had triumphed over President Burgers. Christian de Wet had lost out to Louis Botha and Smuts. General Hertzog first led the charge against the compromises of Botha and Smuts, until he too was seduced into opportunism by 'the golden chains of imperialism'. His purist standard was then picked up successively by Dr Malan, Hans Strijdom and Hendrik Verwoerd.

outside the National Party, that he was required to defend interests beyond than those of the Cape NP. While always 'an intellectual prisoner of the group covenant', Botha gave a new twist to this old nationalist principle that individual security was possible only in the shelter of one's ethnic group.[11] He had led the charge against the Hertzog verkramptes in the late 1960s. The searing events of the 1970s reinforced his belief that isolation would doom Afrikaners. The NP had to look for allies and restructure the basis of its rule. Botha's construction of a domestic armaments industry had taught him he could work 'as a team' with that old nationalist *bête noire*, 'Hoggenheimer':

> I learned the hard way that while South Africa was being isolated by its enemies and by weak friends the only way we could survive was for the private and the public sector to join hands – without harming each other's individuality and without harming each other's freedom to act.[12]

All of these notions were embodied in the 1977 Defence White Paper in which Botha and his generals elaborated a clear strategy to reform apartheid. But, his close links with the military aside, P W Botha was first and foremost a political creature of the Cape NP machine – its leading, its most typical and its most powerful *apparatchik*. Botha rose to political prominence through the bureaucratic machinery of the Cape NP. In May 1936, barely 20 years old, he had abandoned his university studies to become the Cape party's first full-time political organiser. In this post, he was known as the 'agent' of both the NP and the Nasionale Pers press group which had first spawned the Cape NP. For ten years after 1948 he was its head secretary – and the Cape NP's chief hatchet man in the trying years when it had been obliged to cede paramountcy to the Transvaal party of Strijdom and Verwoerd. Appointed the federal NP's chief information officer in 1946, Botha also joined the Nasionale Pers board of directors when he became Cape NP leader on the resignation of Eben Dönges in November 1966.

The new *Hoofleier* had thus spent his entire adult life working in the greatest intimacy with, and sustained politically by, the forces which comprised the Cape nationalist establishment – Nasionale Pers, the wine interests of the Western Cape, but most particularly, the financial interests around Sanlam which had founded the Cape NP and continued to control its press. At an NP meeting called to celebrate his fifty years of service to the party, Botha named as one of his enduring influences the man who had successively founded the Cape NP, Nasionale Pers and Sanlam between 1915 and 1921, and remained the chairman of each until the early 1950s – Willie Hofmeyr.[13] Botha's accession to the Nasionale Pers board of directors consolidated the belief of the new Transvaal NP leader that 'P W' was just 'the simple mouthpiece of *Keeromstraat*'.*

---

* Ben Schoeman, quoted in (Beaumont) Schoeman, *Vorster se 1000 Dae,* 246. Botha paid his director's salary into the funds of the Cape NP. Once Prime Minister, he quickly ended the practice allowing Cabinet ministers (and the provincial administrators) to serve on the boards of press groups.

A sworn verkrampte enemy wrote in 1974 that no NP politician matched P W Botha's 'knowledge and experience of the harsh inner workings of [National] party politics'.[14] At the time of his elevation to the Premiership, Botha concentrated in his own political persona, the interests of the Cape party organisation and the political outlook of Cape Afrikaner finance, as well as those of the military High Command. His defeat of Connie Mulder marked a clear victory in the NP and government for the large capitalist interests in the nationalist alliance. This was virtually acknowledged by Sanlam chairman Andries Wassenaar in a remarkably frank interview eleven months after Botha assumed the Premier's mantle.*

The 'Total Strategy' was the incarnation of the emerging cooperation between the generals and the captains of industry – the embodiment of P W Botha's vision of 'reformism'. Yet the new Prime Minister faced daunting challenges at almost every level. His party was still reeling from the bruising struggle for the succession, and ideologically more deeply divided than at any previous moment in its history. The real locus of these division lay in the Transvaal NP – itself barely able to credit its loss of the *Hoofleier*ship to the Cape, and now led by a man whose whole life had been dedicated to holding an ultra-conservative line in nationalist politics. The entire state had been paralysed for at least two years. Policy initiatives were stalled, corruption was rampant and virtually the entire capitalist class was howling for reform of the main policy 'achievement' of 30 years of NP rule – apartheid and its entrenched bureaucracy.

Beyond South Africa's borders, the prospects were even more gloomy. Marxist-Leninist states had been established in Angola and Mozambique. White rule was visibly crumbling in what was then still known as Rhodesia, and a flurry of Western diplomacy had produced an internationally supported proposal for settling the Namibian question – UN Security Council Resolution 435. Himself strongly opposed to this scheme, the new Prime Minister would now have to finesse a way out of the trap in ways which would not turn the five major Western powers even more strongly against his NP government.†

During the last years of the Vorster administration, Botha had 'plotted the steps he believed necessary to galvanise the party and bureaucracy into action

---

* *Financial Mail,* 17 August 1979. Stressing Sanlam's estrangement from Vorster in the last years of his administration, Wassenaar notes that he had despaired of any policy initiatives from the government. Admitting that his sensational book *(Assault on Private Enterprise,* Tafelberg, Cape Town, 1977 – see p. 195 above) was designed to stir things up, he now pronounced himself delighted with the direction taken by Botha. He did, however, express reservations about the commitment to reform of unnamed Cabinet ministers – a clear reference to Transvaal NP leader, Dr A P Treurnicht. See also Wassenaar, cited in *Rapport,* 25 November 1979.

† It is important to remember that the West was living through what proved to be the last moments of its post-war Keynesian liberalism – with a Carter administration in the US, Britain still under a Labour Party Government, West Germany ruled by the Social Democrats, and a Canada before Trudeau's brief loss of power. In 1978, only in France was an overtly conservative government in office.

while simultaneously diminishing their influence'.[15] Once in power, he set out to deal with all these challenges in a seemingly systematic and thought-out manner. Having sketched out his overall strategic conception of how to change South Africa, Botha's government began working out the real policy content of reform. This was a highly politicised process. It obliged the new Premier to act vigorously firstly to consolidate his own somewhat precarious position, and then to steer his way through the new kind of National Party politics unleashed by his policies. This in turn led Botha to seek to cobble together a new political base for his government. The remainder of this chapter examines the strategies underlying the Botha reforms as well as their overall thrust and content. The acute politicking they engendered is discussed in the following chapter.

The Botha reforms were explicitly cast within the framework of what the new administration insisted *ad nauseam* was now a 'total national strategy' to turn back the 'total onslaught against [white] South Africa'. Two central intellectual inputs shaped the conception, elaboration and political implementation of this Total Strategy.

French lessons: Strategic reasoning and the art of the possible

The first was the writings of French strategist, General André Beaufre, who first coined the term 'Total Strategy'. The *oeuvre* of this former commander of French forces in Algeria dominated the evolving strategic culture of the SADF High Command.[16] The best existing account of civil–military relations in apartheid South Africa argues that Beaufre's various works were 'at the base of virtually every lecture at the Joint Defence College', during the 1970s and that the Total Strategy of the Botha government was 'essentially Beaufre writ large in the particular counter-revolutionary context of South Africa'.[17]

Beaufre's writings on South Africa were limited to three-and-a-half pages of pure description of the 'troubles' of the early 1960s.[18] While expressing some reservation about what he called 'the weaknesses and the exaggerations of South African racial policy', nevertheless from a 'purely technical point of view' *le général* expressed admiration for the 'efficiency and the expedition' with which order had been maintained by Pretoria. From this brief overview of South African government action Beaufre drew a conclusion which must have warmed the hearts of Pretoria's generals:

> [N]othing is fated to happen in history, provided one knows how to intervene in time. One can struggle against the trend [of history], one can create a new trend. *It is simply a matter of will and of faith.*[19]

The SADF did not read this French strategist for his vague description of (John Vorster's) determination to deal with the ANC and PAC in the early 1960s. Rather, Botha and his generals drew four lessons from Beaufre's overall conception of war and strategy.

The first grew out of Beaufre's reflections on his experience in France's failed counter-insurgency efforts in Indo-China and Algeria. Beaufre's entire *oeuvre* rested on the supposition that in the 'modern' (ie, post-WWII) age, the nature of war had been transformed by nuclear weapons and nuclear dissuasion. In this new époque of now necessarily *limited* war:

> [M]ilitary war is no longer decisive in the proper sense of the word. The always essential decisive political outcome [*la décision politique*] can only be brought about by the proper combination of limited military action and appropriate activity in the psychological, economic and diplomatic fields. In the past, the strategy of war was governed by military strategy and gave pre-eminence to military leaders. Today, however, it demands a *total strategy* directed by heads of government and in which military strategy plays only a subordinate role.*

This transformed modern warfare had thus become a total form of social interaction, whose predominant feature was the constant and totalising revolutionary assault (both communist and Third World nationalist) on the existing centres of power. Such revolutionary warfare was all-embracing and ever present. This meant that it was no longer possible, and was indeed suicidal, to separate military concerns from the political, the economic and the ideological realms. The persistent nature of the revolutionary 'total onslaught' necessitated total counter-strategies – i.e., strategies to combine all aspects of state policy in a series of mutually reinforcing actions geared to produce the desired results.

Here Beaufre introduced an important distinction between what he saw as the 'direct mode' of total strategy, in which 'the use or threat of military force is the principal means of action', and its 'indirect mode', in which 'various limitations prevent recourse' to direct force.[20] Even in the direct mode of total strategy,

> the use of military forces represents only one component of the necessary action. Such action, which is necessarily total, must prepare, reinforce and exploit the results expected from military operations by the appropriate action in the psychological, political, economic and diplomatic fields.[21]

For Beaufre, however, the cold war had given predominance to the indirect mode: '[S]ince the threat of atomic weapons paralyses direct strategy', the indirect mode of total strategy 'is probably the only strategy that one could [now] use.'[22] Here was the key lesson for Pretoria, and Beaufre's definition is worth repeating in full.

> Action through the indirect mode of total strategy is that in which the intended outcome should be attained essentially by non-military means; thus where military means play only a complementary role.[23]

---

* *Stratégie pour demain: Les problèmes militaires de la guerre moderne* (Librarie Plon, Paris, 1972), 21. Original emphasis. In this and other cases, my translation of the original French differs slightly from the published English translation. See the 'Note on Translation', p. xxi above.

This then led to the second lesson Pretoria learned from Beaufre – the decisive role of strategy. Beaufre was a strategic idealist. He defined strategy as 'the art of using force to resolve the conflict between dialectically opposed wills'.[24] Designing the appropriate strategy was *the* essential moment of successful counter-insurgency. What Beaufre called 'strategic reasoning' (*le raisonnement stratégique*) was the key to success.[25] Adopting the 'correct' strategy would be the decisive factor allowing the existing power holders to run against 'the trend [of history]' in the age of 'revolutionary warfare'.

This stress on the decisive role of the relative intelligence of the adversaries neatly confirmed the prejudices of Pretoria's new generation of military technocrats. As well-educated, experienced men, they were far better placed than the politicians to make the essential 'rational calculations', to exercise what Beaufre frequently calls 'the grey matter' (i.e., intelligence, or brain power) which, he argued, now 'replaces force' as the decisive factor in the 'dialectic of opposing wills' which was modern war.[26]

The third lesson Pretoria drew from Beaufre related to what the general called 'the aim of strategy'. In the classic tradition of Von Clausewitz, this was defined as 'the attainment of politically defined objectives'. However, Beaufre explicitly rejected Von Clausewitz's emphasis on victory in battle as the decisive moment in obtaining this desired result. Rather, in trying to identify 'the essence of the desired decisive outcome (*la décision*)' he turned to Lenin:

> In this dialectic of wills, *the decisive outcome is an event of a psychological nature* which one wished to produce in the mind of the adversary: *to convince him that it is useless to engage or to continue the struggle.*[27]

The crucial terrain of battle against revolutionary movements was thus psychological rather than military. Counter-revolutionary strategy must needs contest primarily *this* terrain. Control of information was therefore essential. The 'total strategy of limited war' was aimed at mass media and domestic public opinion.

> This domestic involvement of the 'mass media' is crucial. It is they who can mould public opinion to the point of making it accept the necessity of going to war. It is the media who can inculcate demoralisation of the public and make possible the *compromises which are the only type of result possible in limited war.*[28]

In this indirect total strategy, political, consensus-building weapons were more effective than coercion. While the latter should be kept to a minimum, effective indirect strategy requires a mixture of the subtle and the brutal. In specifying the *tactics* of indirect strategy, Beaufre speaks, *inter alia*, of wars of attrition (the 'erosion manoeuvre'), and the piecemeal slicing away of the adversary's material and psychological resources – the 'salami manoeuvre'. Force remained an essential, though secondary, component of each of these tactics. To achieve the appropriate balance between consent-inducing mechanisms and coercion, beleaguered governments should fuse strategic military planning with political policy.

Here lay the final lesson learned from Beaufre – the primacy of what he called *the political line*. Several aspects of this were significant for the SADF. The first was the need to assert the prestige of the state, its 'civilisation' and international support. This required an ideological offensive to reinforce the moral fibre of the state, to amass domestic and international goodwill and to demoralise the enemy.[29] The second aspect of the political line was the absolute necessity for 'thoroughgoing reforms which would undercut the demands [of the revolutionaries]'.[30] This latter aspect reinforced his central proposition that, in the end, *compromise with the revolutionaries* was essential. In this sense, for Beaufre, indirect strategy amounted in practice to 'a strenuous (*dure*) form of negotiations', whose only attainable objective was not the capitulation of the enemy, but rather 'to suggest to him that he consider as a possible compromise a solution which corresponds with our own political objectives'.[31]

Here too politics had to be in command of the gun. Returning to his proposition that designing a successful strategy was essentially a question of adopting the appropriate mode of reasoning, Beaufre argued that such a 'Strategy of Action' must needs be considered in its political and social context:

> Action occurs in the midst of events and seeks to cause some other event to take place. Thus, nothing is possible without an understanding of both these events in which one plans to intervene and the forces which will act or react to advance or to hinder the envisaged action....*[T]he total strategy of action can only function effectively if it stems from a political analysis* which allows it to diagnose the character and significance of the events in which it intends to intervene ... to identify the major evolving trends, to take the best possible measure of the strength of the currents which it will need to exploit or combat.*

Based on this essential political analysis, the key step in 'the form of reasoning particular to strategy' thus lay choosing the appropriate means to achieve the desired result. This depended above all on an accurate assessment of 'the vulnerabilities of the adversary' relative to the 'possibilities' open to the state.[32]

However, given the complexity of the questions at issue, and the technical difficulties and subtleties involved, strategic reasoning and 'the elaboration of the strategic plan' were, above all, 'the domain of specialists'.[33] The necessary 'osmosis between policy and total strategy' blurred the old distinction between politician and soldier. While Beaufre does not quite go so far as to suggest that

---

* *Stratégie de l'Action*, 131-2, my emphasis. Beaufre's medical metaphors are central to his analysis of modern war as an 'insidious infection' (mostly originating in Moscow), against which the 'vaccination' of indirect total strategy is more effective than military 'surgery' – *Introduction à la stratégie*, 116.

the military take command of policy, he argues that this 'osmosis' is much easier to realise should it 'occur in a single statesman – at once politician and strategist'.[34] At the very least, under conditions of modern total warfare, the traditional differentiation of civil–military functions has become redundant.[35]

This also neatly confirmed the conclusions General Malan drew from the Angola débacle: policy was too important to leave in the hands of NP politicians.[36] It was essential that the SADF move into a policy-making role in the state. As first announced in the 1977 Defence White Paper, the SADF generals had evolved their own 'Total National Strategy' to meet the new demands of the time. With P W Botha as Prime Minister they were given the chance to implement it.

American pie: The political art of managing reform

If Beaufre provided the framework for linking public policy and security strategy, the conception of the *process* of reform was heavily influenced, secondly, by the conservative American political scientist and theoretician of 'modernisation', Samuel P Huntington.* Huntington's theories of managed change to preserve the interests of the existing power holders had impressed Foreign Minister Pik Botha while the latter was serving as Pretoria's UN Ambassador in the mid-1970s. Botha invited the professor to South Africa in 1979 and closeted him with an equally impressed Prime Minister. Huntington's basic ideas on managed reform were spelled out in a celebrated address to the South African Political Science Association – described by an influential South African editor as the *'script'* for P W Botha's reforms.[37]

In Huntington's ultra-Machiavellian framework, successful reform from above depended on several key principles. Firstly, expectations should be lowered and grand promises avoided. This would reduce the political pressure on the reformer and enable him to get on with the process. The real nub of Huntington's analysis lay, secondly, in the importance he attached to the actual *process* of implementing reform. He stressed *ad nauseam* the essential requirement that this reform process be *managed* so as to preserve political stability. *Stealth and concealment* were vital. The reformer should conceal his goals with ambiguity and deception. A *strategy of transition* was the key to successful reform. It was less important to specify final goals than to know how to get there. The implementation process was even more important to the ultimate success or failure of reform than their content. Success depended more on the skilful control of the prolonged journey to reform than on its final destination.

---

* Director of the Harvard University's Center for International Affairs, Huntington's advocacy in Vietnam of 'forced march urbanisation' to deny the Vietcong a rural base (i.e., bombing of rural areas) had made him a controversial figure. His book on *Political Order in Changing Societies* (Yale University Press, New Haven, 1968), was the major conservative statement on modernisation.

The reformist political leader should change his allies and enemies from one issue to the next and convey different messages to different audiences. The reform programme should be broken down into various elements and each component be presented separately with no apparent linkage with the others. Each individual reform should be drafted secretly and revealed only to the minimum of political leaders whose support was essential. The absolute centrality of process to the overall success of reform thus demanded a high degree of *concentration of political power*.

All of this implied, thirdly, that reform should only be introduced from a position of strength. It should *never* be conceded when the state was on the defensive, nor should it be done so in response to radical demands. This in turn meant, fourthly, that the maintenance of strict law and order was essential to contain the inevitable reactionary opposition and revolutionary violence. The state must move ruthlessly to contain and crush its opponents if their opposition moved beyond the prevailing constitutional order. Fifthly and finally, the wise reformer would turn revolutionary violence against its perpetrators, using the fear it generated to expand the reformers' support base, to generate a broad reform coalition of business groups, moderate blacks and sections of the state apparatus to carry the reform through.[38]

The work of both Huntington and Beaufre was crucial in the overall process of working out and implementing the Botha reforms. They likewise had a significant impact on the way in which these reforms were presented for public consumption.

Now we have drum majorettes: Total Strategy and reform ideology

As formulated by the SADF generals, the Total Strategy was conceived as a *strategy* in the military sense: 'the function of rationally organising and directing the totality of [one's own] forces' with the objective of 'negating' and then 'remodelling or restructuring an adversary'.[39] The detailed elaboration of the content of the Total Strategy became an exercise in Beaufrian 'strategic reasoning'. Once the strategy was rationally delineated, its successful pursuit was predicated on 'strategic management' – 'the harmonisation [*agencement*] of a series of decisions having as their object a total or partial restructuring [either] of the social order ... [or] of an external, non-consenting entity'.[40] This implied the optimal use of resources through organising and directing economic, political, ideological and military forces.

True to Beaufre's vision, Botha's generals saw public opinion as the decisive terrain of struggle. Total Strategy ideology explicitly set out to redefine three important elements in official discourse: the nature of 'the war'; its contending forces – the definition of self ('us') and of the other ('them'); and the broad lines of Beaufrian defence ('compromise' or solution).

The fundamental problem was defined as external. All 'social and labour unrest, civilian resistance, terrorists attacks against the infrastructure of the

RSA, the intimidation of Black leaders and members of the security forces' were deemed part of a Soviet-directed 'total onslaught'. In the words of the 1982 White Paper on Defence this 'total onslaught' against South Africa sought to install a 'Marxist-oriented form of government to further the objectives of the USSR' to control the wealth of southern Africa and the strategic Cape sea route.[41] The ANC and other 'revolutionary' opponents of apartheid were simply 'being used as a Trojan Horse' by the Soviet Union.[42] Prime Minister Botha told parliament in 1978:

> South Africa is experiencing unprecedented intervention of the part of the superpowers. ... The Republic of South Africa is experiencing the full onslaught of Marxism and it must not be doubted that the Republic enjoys a high priority in the onslaught by Moscow. However, South Africa is also experiencing double standards on the part of certain Western bodies in their behaviour towards her. They are doing this in an attempt to pay a ransom to the [Russian] Bear whose hunger must be satisfied.[43]

This apocalyptic total onslaught discourse struck a deep chord in the white South African and in particular the Afrikaner racial psyche. It evoked the nightmare images of black hordes swamping the vulnerable settlements of 'civilisation'. The theme of abandonment by opportunistic Western powers likewise echoed the belief of Afrikaner nationalist ideology that these embattled outposts of 'civilisation' could not count on external succour, but would have to rely on their own forces for survival. However the ideology of Total Strategy now held that this was no *racial* conflict. Rather, as Botha told parliament, the battle lines were drawn between 'the powers of chaos, Marxism and destruction on one hand, and the powers of order, Christian civilisation and the upliftment of people on the other'.[44] Those who did not rally to the forces of order etc., were defined as part of the enemy.

Such ranting cloaked the consecration of an important redefinition of self ('us'), begun under Vorster. The 1969 NP expulsion of the Hertzogite verkramptes had hinged around the question of whether the NP was to remain the vehicle of exclusively Afrikaner nationalism, or had it become the bearer of a broader, bilingual, white South African nationalism?[45] Vorster had moved towards the latter definition. Now, however, drawing on Beaufre's stricture that compromise was the only possible solution, the 'South Africa' to be defended against the Prince of Darkness and the powers of chaos was not only unambiguously proclaimed a nation of all whites, but even included some elements outside the white population who were prepared to rally to defend apartheid's 'Christian civilisation' against Moscow's 'total onslaught'.

The notion that the Soviet Union was planning an all-out attack on white South Africa may have seemed a trifle exaggerated in Jimmy Carter's Washington (though certainly not in Ronald Reagan's). The preposterous claim that the West was prepared to sacrifice South Africa in order, in Botha's words, 'to pay a ransom' to the ravenous Russian Bear, was deeply revealing of white

South African paranoia. Yet this paranoia was fed by the tumultuous events of the mid-1970s. It was further reinforced by the April 1980 assumption of power by the self-proclaimed Marxist-Leninist ZANU (PF) in Zimbabwe. It grew even more acute following the onset of ANC military actions with its spectacular June 1980 attack on three Sasol refineries, and then its crippling of the Koeberg nuclear reactor in December 1982. All such events were presented as symptoms of this supposed 'Marxist threat' or 'total onslaught', and used to generate a war psychosis and consolidate support for the regime. One senior official admitted in an interview with an American researcher:

> There is a threat as perceived by government, but the concept of this threat is used for other reasons than the real threat: to bring people together whom the government thinks should be together.[46]

The Total Strategy sought to negate this 'total onslaught' through a remodelling of domestic and regional politics. Summed up in Botha's celebrated instruction to his fellow Afrikaners to 'adapt or die', the regime's overall project was cast in the terms of survival.

Survival in the face of the total onslaught depended on resolute measures to preserve state security. Domestic security policy now moved away from its reliance on old-style apartheid repression as practised by the departed Hendrik van den Bergh. Rather, in the words of Police Commissioner Johann Coetzee, the police now sought to defuse 'explosive situations' and avoid conflict through 'an effective information organisation and spy network'.[47] Coetzee's counter-revolutionary tactics assumed that 'a dynamic policy of change' would eventually undermine the extra-parliamentary resistance. For the moment, this resistance could be more effectively controlled by allowing it some latitude to organise, and by exploiting political tensions between the various groups.

Domestic security strategy was complemented a highly interventionist regional policy. Pretoria set out to reimpose its shattered regional economic, military and political hegemony, and through a sustained and brutal destabilisation of neighbouring states, sought to break up what it saw as the bloc of hostile forces confronting it.[48] Carried out at horrendous costs to the peoples, governments and economies of southern Africa, destabilisation led in March 1984 to a 'Non-Aggression Pact' (known as the Nkomati Accord) with socialist Mozambique seeking to end the economic and military offensive against it.[49]

Survival also implied another significant shift in state ideology. Overt official racism gave way to a discourse of economic growth and the wonders of supply-side economics. Blacks would be given access to the system and its benefits. Botha's first years as Premier coincided with Margaret Thatcher's vigorous monetarism and what George Bush once called the 'voodoo economics' of Ronald Reagan's supply-side *wunderkinder*. Now the old Verwoerdian maxim of 'better poor and white than rich and mixed' was replaced by a vision of 'power-sharing' and rapid economic growth to be fostered by private initiative freed of the interventionist shackles of the past. Economic growth would guarantee white living standards and make it possible to raise those of blacks. A record high gold price ($850 an ounce) in January 1980 produced an 8 percent growth rate in 1980 and 4,5 percent in 1981, reinforcing the ideological presumption that aggressive entrepreneurship was the foundation of successful reform.[50]

The SADF's original Total Strategy blueprint called for a 'comprehensive plan to utilise all the means available to the state according to an integrated pattern in order to achieve the national aims within the framework of specific policies'.[51] According to the Defence Chief (and later Defence Minister) General Magnus Malan, this required 'the management of South Africa's four power bases (the political, economic, social/psychological and security bases) as an integrated whole'.*

These quotations highlight the central conceptions underlying the Total Strategy. As the key to a successful defence against the total onslaught, change had to be *planned*. Doing so required identifying areas where reform was essential, and then elaborating 'specific policies' in these areas. For reform policies to be effective, the process had to be *managed*. Such management was an exercise of *power* – managing the 'power bases' of the state according to an 'integrated pattern'. Translated from General Malan's military/managerial jargon, three essential steps were envisaged.

The first was to spell out broad 'issue-areas' where change was essential. This was done in Botha's 'Twelve Point Plan' of August 1979 – a statement of broad, and deliberately vague, principles underlying the Total Strategy.[52] The second step was the more complicated – and highly politicised – process of working out the necessary policy changes. Such policies had to be 'integrated', i.e., be designed as a package of mutually reinforcing interventions at every level of society – as well as on the regional and international environment. Following Huntington's strictures on reform by stealth, it was vital that this be done without specifying final goals over which the government could be pilloried and to which it could be tied.

This discourse of strategic management implied, thirdly, that politics within the state would have to be transformed. Government policy was now conceived as a *rational* process of organising and directing the totality of state resources to maximum effect. The *rational logic of the strategy* had to prevail. Policy formation could no longer be left to the cut and thrust of consensus-building within the Cabinet and between ministries – a process built on the very different rationale of compromise oiled by patronage and geared to maintaining NP unity.

---

* Magnus Malan, 'Die Aanslaag teen Suid-Afrika', 14. His boss, on the other hand, identified 'five power bases in which the total national strategy must operate'. These were: the military, coordinated state administration, state-private sector cooperation, 'good neighbourly' relations between South Africa's 'population groups' (ie, races), and the religious foundations of the state. P W Botha, quoted in J J Scholtz, *Fighter and Reformer*, 35-6.

Standing Clemenceau on his head, politics now became too important to leave to the politicians. Coherent, directed and coordinated policy was essential to 'negate' the 'total onslaught' threatening the nation. Opponents of such 'rational' policies were opponents of reason itself – and no longer members of the same political club with common rules of behaviour. Questioning the strategy, they threatened national survival. Political power had to be concentrated so as to by-pass conflicts within the state. Botha and his generals could simply not permit the NP tradition of participation, contestation and political wheeler-dealing to derail the Total Strategy.

The adoption of the Total Strategy thus considerably raised the already high political stakes in the NP and transformed the rules of political behaviour within the South African state. Already in 1976 Botha had declared the (whites only) Westminster parliamentary system inappropriate to the demands of the times (p. 194 above). General Malan's 'management of South Africa's four power bases' implied on the one hand that the apparatuses of the state had to be transformed into lean, efficient management structures. It also implied that political relations within the NP and government had to be restructured and 'managed' to prevent the conservative opposition from undermining the Total Strategy project. This echoed the proposals of reformist Afrikaner intellectuals for a 'verligte dictatorship' (the so-called 'Bismarck option'), on the grounds that 'entrenched white democracy' was at the root of 'retarded change' and NP opposition to Botha's reforms.[53]

This view was broadly shared by English and Afrikaner capital, whose joint critique of Vorster's last years centred on his failure to develop a planned, coordinated response to the crisis. The problem was seen to have been the dominance of 'political' over 'rational' criteria in decision-making – and particularly the use of patronage to preserve the facade of NP unity. Traditional NP populism now rapidly gave way to a stress on technical rationality and 'scientific' policy making:

> [I]n the Botha administration ... a strong tendency has developed ... to present the whites as a modernising elite and to portray economic growth, training, job creation, food production, and above all political stability, which is seen as making all these things possible, as sufficient justification for National Party rule.[54]

Formulated by military technocrats not immediately identified, nor even necessarily concerned, with the partisan issues of party or faction, the new militarist Total Strategy discourse offered businessmen a more dispassionate long view of the requirements for the survival of the fundamental structures of South African society. Its central emphasis on *managed* change and the managed containment of conflict through the planned allocation of resources, echoed corporate managerial ideology. Its critique of state economic intervention, and view that wealth creation through private initiative was the key to reform, likewise resonated with capital's view of itself. Although it would later became evident that most capitalists mistook their own wishes for reformist deeds, the early thrust of the Total Strategy seemed to indicate that state and capital were in tune.

The adoption of the discourse of the Total Strategy also encouraged the spread of a new technocratic managerialism throughout the wider white South African society. Government, business, educational institutions, the media – seemingly the entire establishment – became infected by this craze for technocratic rationality. This effected a slow but profound change not just in the nature of political debate, but in the culture of white society. It led to an attack on all 'ideology' as somehow at variance with the pragmatic bottom line. Remarkably blind to its own ideological content, it led to fierce conflicts within the National Party over both the content and the process of the Total Strategy reforms.

Chapter Fourteen

NEO-APARTHEID

The Botha reforms

Dr Koornhof: 'Apartheid is dying – we're moving you out'

The first six years of Botha's rule saw a veritable explosion of 'incessant and persistent' efforts to resolve the crisis confronting the South African state.[1] In keeping with Beaufre's insistence that total strategy 'involves an *external effort* on the global scene',[2] domestic reform was accompanied by a diplomatic and propaganda offensive directed at Western governments. This painted the Botha government as engaged in the historic task of dismantling 'white domination' and worthy of support as the principal target of 'Soviet expansionism' in Africa. The advent of Margaret Thatcher, Helmut Kohl and particularly Ronald Reagan, gave Pretoria much-needed breathing space and at least tacit support. According to the American Assistant Secretary of State for Africa, the Reagan administration's southern Africa policy was designed to end South Africa's 'pariah' status and to reincorporate the Botha government in the 'network of Western security interests'.[3] This 'constructive engagement' provided vital aid and comfort to Pretoria's destabilisation of southern Africa after 1981.

Explicitly cast within the much-trumpeted 'total national strategy', the Botha reforms were designed as an integrated package in which each element was supposed to reinforce the effectiveness of the others. No doubt entirely unconscious of how he was echoing the murdered Steve Biko (p. 110 above), Botha himself told an NP congress that existing policy had carried the regulation of society 'to the absurd length that the State itself is to blame for the ordinary [black] man becoming a transgressor of law'.* The objective was to depoliticise as many issues as possible, and so deny targets to the 'total onslaught'. Policy changes in five broad areas sought to rework elements of ideological, economic and political life into a new settlement.

The impossible art: Reforming apartheid

The entire reform initiative hinged, firstly, around the expected positive effects of transformed economic policy. Botha's government formally abandoned the statist policies and Afrikaner favouritism which had underpinned NP rule since 1948. Even before Margaret Thatcher, Ronald Reagan and Helmut Kohl unleashed the monetarist assault on post-war economic orthodoxy, the new administration renounced thirty years of the NP's racial Keynesianism, committing itself to a gradual reduction of state control of key productive sectors. Economic growth was now to be fostered by an aggressive entrepreneurship unleashed by dismantling the interventionist policies the NP had followed since 1948. This growth was, in turn, supposed to make possible the maintenance of white living standards while raising those of blacks. The most significant early gesture was the 1981 sale of a large bloc of shares in the giant state oil-from-coal undertaking, Sasol. Government criticism of the previously interventionist philosophy of the South African Reserve Bank

---

* Address to NP Congress, Port Elizabeth, 29 September 1980, in Scholtz, *Fighter and Reformer,* 65. Black women were evidently beneath Botha's consideration.

mirrored the now Friedmanite contours of fiscal and monetary policy.

The deep divisions in the NP during the 1970s had turned around the thorny issue of policy towards urban blacks. This became the major preoccupation of the Botha government. Its second set of reforms directly addressed the business demand for transformed labour policies. Following the 1979 report of the Wiehahn Commission on Labour Legislation,[4] a series of reforms sought to stimulate labour productivity by providing a structure for negotiated and *controlled* changes in production processes. Statutory job reservation in manufacturing industries was abolished and restrictions on the mobility and training of African labour eased. Culminating in the 1981 Labour Relations Act, a gradual extension of trade union rights attempted to institutionalise and regulate industrial conflict, and, through tight controls on the unions, to isolate and depoliticise work place struggles. The state took itself out of direct involvement in labour conflicts, leaving it to capital and labour to negotiate their differences – through resort to a new Industrial Court if necessary. While clearly a defensive response of the state to the burgeoning democratic trade union movement, these so-called 'Wiehahn reforms' opened up a space for legal struggles by black workers which significantly contributed to the growth of their trade unions.[5]

The labour reforms were complemented, thirdly, by important changes in the overall conception of Grand Apartheid. The 1979 Report of Piet Riekert's Manpower Commission spelled out the central strategy to divide the African population into urban 'insiders' and rural 'outsiders'.[6] The bantustans would be preserved – and their 'independence' remained the central final goal of state policy. Now, however, the government jettisoned the old NP fiction that urban Africans were 'temporary sojourners', ultimately destined to return to their 'national states'. Harking back to the 1948 Fagan Commission which the NP had rejected on first assuming office, Riekert insisted that urban blacks finally be recognised as permanent residents in the 'white' urban areas.

This implied significant changes in the influx control system underlying apartheid. Those fully proletarianised Africans already employed in the cities and possessing so-called Section 10 rights would now be given the right of 'permanent' urban residence – and theoretically at least, even the right to move between cities. On the other hand, however, the bantustans were to be virtually sealed off from the urban areas, influx control considerably tightened, and the penalties on both African workers and now also white employers for violating the pass laws drastically increased.* This ambiguous concept of 'reform' was embodied in the so-called 'Koornhof Bills' of the early 1980s.† This legislation

---

* See the detailed discussion in D Hindson, *Pass Controls and Urban African Proletariat in South Africa* (Ravan Press, Johannesburg, 1987), chap. 5. Riekert's proposal for a rigid division between the African urban and rural populations had first been advocated from all employers' organisations – including the AHI – proposing methods of defusing the Sharpeville crisis in 1960.

† Named for the responsible Minister, Piet Koornhof – now in charge of *the* central apartheid ministry, the once-again renamed Department of Cooperation and Development (previously known as: Plural Relations; Bantu Administration; Bantu Affairs; and, in the 1950s, Native Affairs).

combined new restrictions on influx control with various social and developmental concessions intended to defuse urban African grievances. They implied that African political representation in 'white' South Africa would be limited to the level of local government. All other political rights could only be exercised in the bantustans.

The Wiehahn and Riekert reforms clearly sought to entrench overall white control and the underlying principles of apartheid. Yet, taken together, they went a long way towards meeting business demands for a more flexible labour policy which would facilitate the reorganisation of production on a more capital-intensive basis. These reforms also clearly envisaged that the resulting higher black wages would stimulate 'insider' demand in an economy now rejuvenated by measures to encourage private initiative.[7]

This latter element was likewise present in the fourth area of the reforms – the fetish made of improving the 'quality of life' of the urban black middle class as a 'bulwark against revolution'. New housing, education and employment policies now offered limited but real social mobility to this diffuse stratum. A few of the many apartheid restrictions on the activities of small black businesses were also lifted.[8] One of the Botha government's first measures was to end the ban on direct investments by white businessmen in the urban African townships. This had contradictory effects, however. While some small black capitalists seized the opportunity to attach themselves to white investors through 'joint projects', the influential National African Chambers of Commerce (Nafcoc) complained that black entrepreneurs were being squeezed out by white 'monopolies'.[9] Shebeens – black-owned bars – were legalised, and at the beginning of 1984 the government announced it would accept the recommendation of the Snyman Commission to amend the Group Areas Act so as to allow black businessmen to operate in the central business districts of the 'white' cities.[10]

Attempts to cultivate 'a black middle class' went hand in hand, fifthly, with the most complex and problematic aspect of reform – the search for an acceptable 'new political dispensation'. Here lay a real political conundrum. Soweto had clearly shown that old-style apartheid was manifestly not working, and that its maintenance now directly threatened both overall political stability and white South Africa's economic welfare. Yet the National Party would still have to force the country down a long and bloody political road before it would accept the obvious and inevitable solution of dismantling apartheid. As Botha's trumpeted *Twelve Point Programme* emphasised, the political reforms of the Total Strategy were cast strictly within two central tenets of existing apartheid doctrine: that South Africa was a country of a 'plurality of peoples and of minority groups'; and that the 'Black peoples' were to exercise their political rights in 'independent' states.*

---

* See Appendix II, points 1 & 3, p. 491 below. Botha's use of the plural 'Black peoples' underlined his firm belief that there was no African majority in South Africa, but rather that all Africans belonged to one of apartheid's 'ethnic nationalities'.

The period from 1979 to 1984 produced a series of weird and wonderful schemes designed to win the political collaboration of a small black elite, and so defuse mass opposition to apartheid – while at the same time reinforcing and accelerating the basic thrust of Grand Apartheid. The particularly convoluted and complex policies involved can only be sketched here.[11]

The constitutional reforms rested on tried and true practice. The black population was divided into supposedly mutually antagonistic racial, ethnic, linguistic and tribal groups, playing the one off against the other, and using antipathies fostered by Pretoria to construct a network of allies for NP rule. The most detailed existing analysis of Botha's administration concludes that the new Prime Minister

> spent the first three years of his office tackling the implementation of Verwoerd's 'grand apartheid' – the establishment of independent black tribal areas – with the enthusiasm of a convert and certainly with more verve than any of his predecessors ... without once renouncing the principle of independent homelands, he worked hard to make it more practical in application.[12]

Intense efforts were launched to consolidate the fragmented territory of the 10 bantustans. A Consolidation Commission was appointed to investigate a new consolidation plan. Its chairman, Hennie van der Walt, was later made Deputy Minister of Lands, with responsibility for consolidation.* These consolidation efforts were complemented by shifting regional development policy away from failed efforts to promote economic growth in the bantustans. A new 'deconcentration' approach rested on the principle of 'economic interdependence and political independence'.[13] South Africa was divided into eight (and later nine) 'development regions', each to be managed by a complex 'multilateral' decision-making system – a possible mechanism for the later incorporation of the bantustans into emerging 'consociational' structures (see below).

The Botha government also made frantic efforts to persuade more bantustan leaders to accept Pretoria's professed 'independence'. Venda did so in September 1979. The Sebe brothers, who ran the Ciskei as a family fiefdom, did likewise in December 1981 – rejecting the findings of their own Quail Commission that 90 percent of 'Ciskeians' were 'totally opposed' to 'independence'. Enormous pressure on the KwaNdebele leadership to do follow to this trend led to a virtual civil war in this region, and its eventual refusal to join the 'SABCTV' club.†

---

* He sabotaged his own work almost at the outset, by using in Parliament the worst of all racial epithets for blacks – 'kaffertjies' (here, again, the diminutive form indicates even greater contempt). Van der Walt was later arrested for embezzling almost R1 million from a trust fund and sentenced to seven years' imprisonment.

† The name given by wags to the consultative council incorporating South Africa and the 'independent' bantustans of Bophuthatswana, Ciskei, Transkei and Venda – and also the acronym for the entirely pro-government South African Broadcasting Corporation. On the issues of 'independence' for these bantustans, see Davies et al., Struggle for South Africa, vol. 1, pp. 221-3, 225-6, 235-7.

However, these efforts to extend Grand Apartheid were partially tempered by Botha's pragmatism. Verwoerd had conceived the bantustan scheme as an inflexible *principle*.* Botha on the other hand now accepted firstly that not all 'homelands' could be bullied into independence, and secondly that some form of political accommodation would have to be found for urban African 'insiders'. His grandiose vision of a 'confederation of Southern African states' was supposed to take care of the first issue. Originally intended to embrace virtually *all* of southern Africa, this 'constellation' was eventually limited to South Africa and the 'independent' bantustans.[14] A permanent liaison secretariat and a multilateral development council of ministers were established in November 1982 to promote 'good neighbourliness'.

The problem of the political accommodation for urban Africans eventually led to the granting of 'full municipal status' to elected 'Community Councils' in the urban African townships. The new Black Local Authorities (or BLAs) were given powers equal to white municipalities – though they lacked any real tax base to fund their activities. This process was intended to foster a small urban African political elite owing its position and livelihood to the apartheid system. The 1981 NP election manifesto suggested that these BLAs could also eventually be tied to the bantustans, thereby providing the basis of a political settlement in terms of apartheid doctrine.

Here, once again, the NP showed itself still incapable of abandoning the central fallacy of apartheid – that urban blacks could eventually be reconciled with their own denationalisation. These councils were entirely lacking in legitimacy. After the massive boycott of the 1983 Community Council elections, Minister Koornhof declared himself pleased with the 16 percent recorded poll.[15] Intended to satisfy 'the aspirations' of urban blacks, the hated councils would eventually spark the urban uprising of 1984–86 (p. 325 below).

A different approach was elaborated with respect to the so-called Coloured and Indian population. After assuming power, Botha appointed Alwyn Schlebusch to head a constitutional commission to elaborate on the 1977 constitutional proposals developed by Botha's own Cabinet Committee. The Schlebusch Commission reported in May 1980. On its recommendation the Senate was abolished and replaced by an appointed 'President's Council' of whites, so-called Coloureds and Indians charged with advising the State President. This body then elaborated a scheme for a tricameral legislature of white, so-called Coloured and Indian parliaments presided over by an executive State President with extensive powers. With various modifications these proposals were accepted by the government and the NP as a whole – at the cost of finally provoking a split in the NP in early 1982 (see following chapter).

---

* In the mid-1960s I heard the former leader of the old Progressive Party, Dr Jan Steytler, tell a party meeting of a chance airport encounter with a Cabinet minister. Steytler had challenged the minister that the NP's bantustan scheme would never work. The minister replied: 'Dit *moet* werk' (It *must* work).

After much manoeuvring, the regime won the collaboration in this scheme of the (coloured) Labour Party and groups in the South African Indian Council. The proposals were approved by two-thirds of the white electorate in a November 1983 referendum.[16]

The new South African Constitution which emerged in 1984 preserved apartheid's exclusion of the roughly 30 million Africans from any political voice in the central state. To the 2,5 million so-called Coloureds and the 1 million Indians it offered a subordinate role in a racially segregated tricameral parliament (see below). The political aspirations of the urban Africans who so preoccupied the Total Strategists were to be satisfied with the granting of 'full municipal status' to elected Black Local Authorities in the segregated townships. Supposed to be financially self-sufficient – though excluded by the Group Areas Act from access to rateable commercial and industrial property – the BLAs would be directly responsible for delivering basic services to their 'insider' populations, thereby hopefully 'depoliticising' issues such as housing, transport, medical services etc. As in the broader bantustan system – with which they might later link up – the BLAs were also intended to place on the political stage a small black client elite with vested interests in the existing system.

This 1984 Constitution rested on a 'consociational' theory of 'power-sharing' which favoured the protection of 'group identities' while stressing the need to forge structures of 'co-determination' and 'joint decision making' between (racial) groups. NP reformists seemed genuinely to believe that by opening up very limited access by black elites to selected and (still racially restricted) organs of government, their 'power-sharing' reforms would legitimate the apartheid state – at least among urban 'insiders' – and so defuse mass opposition. By finally allowing 'the black middle class' to develop appropriately middle-class consumption patterns (in strictly segregated areas) and by allowing it very limited and tightly controlled political participation, the Total Strategy sought to incorporate this group as junior partners in a new 'historic bloc' organised around defence of 'the free enterprise system' against 'Marxist tyranny'.

Here was the most explosive area of 'reform'. In effect, Botha's verkrampte critics were right. This new scheme was a barefaced theft of the 'race federation' policies of the defunct United Party. As such, it provoked outrage among many Afrikaner nationalists. Even tinkering with the white monopoly of political power was seen as betrayal of sacred principles. Huntington's stress on reform by stealth thus played a key role in the laborious process of defining the consociational structures of 'power-sharing', and building the political support inside and outside the NP. Botha was to fight a constant battle in both state and party in order to push through his reform programme. Its actual implementation led to an extensive reorganisation of the entire apparatus of government – which then transformed the way in which NP and state politics operated.

More manageable machinery: Reorganising the South African state

The writings of Beaufre and Huntington both emphasised that the successful implementation reform was partially dependent on fashioning government machinery capable of fulfilling two essential functions. On the one hand, the state administration would have to be responsive to the managerialism of the total strategy, and implement its reforms swiftly and efficiently. On the other hand, this machinery needed to be of a kind which would limit damaging internal political struggles, and marginalise the opponents of reform within the state. These prescriptions confirmed the reformist analysis that the disorganised structures of decision-making inherited from Vorster made it 'difficult for the central executive machinery to act swiftly to solve problems and crises'. A 1980 White Paper on the public service pleaded for 'a more manageable machinery of government'.[17] Botha's first years in office thus also produced a significant reorganisation of the South African state, leading to a decisive centralisation of power and a striking militarisation of the decision-making and administrative structures of government.

A three-phase 'rationalisation programme' set out to reorganise first the decision-making, then the administrative and finally the legislative machinery of government.[18] Phase One began in March 1979. In keeping with Huntington's injunction that managment of the reform process required a concentration of power, this phase led to a progressive and profound reorganisation of the structures of decision-making, and a marked centralisation of power in P W Botha's hands. As a first step, a Cabinet Secretariat was set up in an enlarged Office of the Prime Minister. During the Botha administration this Office of the Prime Minister (and after 1984, the Office of the State President) would turn into the virtual government of South Africa. Its head (later designated the 'Secretary-General'), former Commissioner of Prisons, Jannie Roux, soon developed into one of Botha's closest confidants. At times the Prime Minister seemed to rely more on Roux for crucial advice than on his own ministers. Roux's role as P W Botha's gatekeeper resembled that played by Bob Halderman in the Nixon White House, and this former police psychologist quickly engendered the same hostility and jealousy from government insiders. Reflecting white South Africa's addiction to the American 'Dallas' soap opera on its recently inaugurated television service, Roux was known behind his back by the unflattering sobriquet of 'JR'.*

The Cabinet secretariat over which Roux presided was radically reorganised, as was the mode of operation of the Cabinet itself. The twenty ad hoc Cabinet committees inherited from Vorster gave way first to six, then five and finally four permanent Cabinet Committees – for National Security, and Constitutional,

---

* Pottinger quotes the allegation of Roux's one-time prisoner, the poet Breyten Breytenbach, that as chief Prison psychologist Roux had been responsible for 'making psychopaths stand up and cheer when the opposing team scored a point during a soccer match – a bit of a strain especially for psychopaths'. *The Imperial Presidency*, 39.

Economic, and Social Affairs. A fifth 'Special Cabinet Committee' was established in 1983 to investigate the constitutional position of Africans, particularly those living outside the bantustans. These revamped Cabinet Committees were comprised of those ministers whose individual portfolios bore on the overall concerns of each committee, together with an unspecified number of the Prime Minister's appointees. Cabinet Committees were now given the right to make decisions. Ministers could refer particular matters directly to a Cabinet Committee without first going through the Cabinet itself. Each of the committees was headed by a minister nominated by the Prime Minister, but whose identity was not public knowledge. The Cabinet Committee Chairmen reported directly to the Prime Minister and their activities were coordinated by the Cabinet secretariat in his office.

This effectively reorganised the functioning of the Cabinet. Premier Botha abandoned the remaining vestiges of the Westminster fiction that, as the *primus inter pares,* the Prime Minister presided over a Cabinet of equals collectively charged with, and jointly responsible for, determining government policy. Rather, he became the hub around which all Cabinet functions and decisions revolved. Cabinet ministers held their portfolios at the Prime Minister's pleasure. They reported directly to him, and his Secretariat supervised the day-to-day operation of all facets of government. The ability of ministers to make policy in their field of responsibility was absolutely dependent on the approval of, and support from, the Prime Minister. Cabinet members were no longer feudal barons, relatively secure in semi-autonomous domains so long as they paid the traditional political tribute to the monarch (as had been the case under John Vorster). Rather, as traditional NP feudalism slowly gave way to an ever more absolute monarchy, Cabinet ministers became courtiers at the court of Emperor Botha, dependent on his favour, and powerful only so long as they retained it.

Of course the odd Cardinal Richelieu made his appearance. Certain ministers enjoyed privileged access to the Prime Minister, and they and their departments played a focal role in the emerging reform programme. In the early years of the Botha government, the newly minted 'Vice-President' Alwyn Schlebusch, Labour Minister *Fanie Water* Botha, and Minister of Cooperation and Development Piet Koornhof respectively took charge of the details of reform in the central areas of the Constitution, labour policy, and the place of blacks in both the cities and regional political economies.* They did not last very long, however. Schlebusch retired relatively unscathed in 1982, having fathered the NP's emerging constitutional plan and then presiding over its first fruit, the President's Council set up in 1981. Fanie Botha for his part lived through a period of some triumph from 1979 to 1982, winning much praise for his wide-ranging reform of labour relations. However he had already lit the fuse of his

---

* 'Cooperation and Development' being the new euphemism for the key apartheid ministry, Verwoerd's old Department of 'Bantu Affairs'.

own political self-destruction and was finally forced to resign over financial improprieties in 1983. *Piet Pompies* Koornhof lingered a little longer in Botha's favour. A research officer for Verwoerd's Department of Bantu Affairs for much of the 1950s, and briefly the chief secretary of the Broederbond in the early 1960s, the mercurial and often lampooned Dr Koornhof always liked to boast that he was the real inspiration behind the NP's new reformism. But he too had to cede his place in the sun. By the mid-1980s, P W Botha's long-time acolyte, Chris Heunis, was emerging as the dominant Cabinet minister. Central elements were sliced off Koornhof's ministry in 1983, to be handed over to Heunis's new super-ministry of Constitutional Development and Planning. Not yet in his sixties, Koornhof lost his Cabinet post in September 1984, to be sent into political exile first as chairman of the President's Council and then as ambassador to Washington.*

For almost four years Heunis grew ever more powerful. By the mid-1980s he was widely regarded as the NP's new Crown Prince. The 'continuous transitions' introduced by his Department of Constitutional Development and Planning seemed to be the very soul of the Botha reforms after 1982. By the end of 1985 Heunis's reach extended into almost all the nooks and crannies of government policy, and the minister was known as the Czar of reform.[19] But he too failed to deliver, and fell into dramatic disfavour with his mentor in 1986. Though he retained his portfolio, he lost many of his powers and most of his political influence (below pp. 339 ff).

In P W Botha's new system of four (and then five) permanent Cabinet Committees, by far the most important was the Cabinet Committee for National Security, commonly known as the State Security Council (hereafter SSC). Set up in terms of the 1972 Security Intelligence and State Security Act (p. 218 above), the SSC was the only Cabinet Committee to have a permanent secretariat. Under Vorster, it had met infrequently and played a purely advisory role. The first, and still classified, 1975 Venter Report into state administration had found that the SSC 'lacked the administrative means to fulfil its

---

* Koornhof's reputation as a 'liberal' went back to his controversial 1953 Oxford PhD thesis, 'The Drift from the Reserves of the South African Bantu', in which he argued that 'South Africa is one composite, one complex society, but one society'. This, he later claimed, led to death threats from verkramptes – in whose circles he also briefly moved – once he became an MP in 1964. Koornhof now describes apartheid as 'barbarous' *(wreed)*, 'loathsome' *(vieslik)* and 'inhuman'. He also argues that it 'did more damage, psychological damage, to us white people than to the black people'[!] – interview with Max du Preez, *Vrye Weekblad*, 14 October 1993. Yet he defended it passionately throughout the 1960s, 1970s and 1980s. As the reformist head of the principal apartheid ministry for 1978–84, he implemented some of its most notorious forced removals, declaring this to be a humane policy carried out in everyone's interest. In 1993, the 68-year-old former chief apartheid politician shocked the 'new South Africa' when he abandoned his wife of 42 years to move in with a so-called Coloured woman in her twenties. His peccadillos – for which his own government would have prosecuted him until the late 1980s – earned him a profile in *Penthouse Magazine* in February 1994.

functions'.[20] Vorster had tried to make up for some of this and the other bureaucratic chaos of his government by transferring supervision of the public services from the Ministry of Internal Affairs to the Prime Minister's Office in 1976. However, given the institutionalised confusion which underlay state decision-making practices under Vorster, this barely addressed the problem. According to the head of the SADF, General Magnus Malan, it was the débacle of the 1975–76 invasion of Angola which 'focused attention on the urgent necessity for the State Security Council to play a much fuller role in the national security of the Republic than hitherto'. An interdepartmental committee with strong SADF representation met to devise the organisational structure for 'the formulation of strategy at a national level'. Out of this emerged the components of what was called the 'national security management system' (NSMS).[21]

Inaugurated in August 1979, and 'designed to coordinate the government's executive functions' more efficiently,[22] the structures of the NSMS quickly became the central conduit for Botha's centralisation of power and militarisation of the state. At its pinnacle stood the revamped State Security Council. Soon dubbed the 'SS Council', the SSC was to play a pivotal role in the unfolding South African drama over the next decade.* It is therefore worth delving into its structure.

The Prime Minister presided over the SSC. Other statutory members included the Ministers of Defence, Foreign Affairs, and Law and Order, together with the following senior officials: the Head of the National Intelligence Service; the Chief of the SADF; the Director-General of Foreign Affairs; the Director-General of Law and Order, and the Commissioner of Police. Other ministers and officials could be coopted at the Prime Minister's discretion. By 1983 eight Cabinet ministers sat on the SSC in an apparently permanent capacity, together with other senior officials.†

The SSC had the statutory responsibility to advise on the formulation and implementation of 'national policy and strategy in relation to the security of the Republic'. This broad definition allowed Prime Minister Botha to bring a wide array of concerns to the SSC's attention. Everything deemed to be connected with the security of the state now seemed to fall under its purview – from foreign policy to the price of bread. It was inside the SSC that 'the utilisation of all the means available to the state to achieve specific objectives' envisaged by the Total Strategy was planned and managed. Between 1979 and 1984 the SSC emerged as the primary overall planning and decision-making body within the state.

Access to it was controlled by the Prime Minister – either through appointment to the key statutory ministerial, military and bureaucratic

---

* The NP government had long demonstrated a wondrous capacity to conjure up the most revealing acronyms. Wags now said of the SSC: 'From those wonderful people who brought you first BOSS and then PISCOM (the Parliamentary Internal Security Commission), here is their newest creation – the SS Council'.

† These included the Ministers of Constitutional Development and Planning, Finance and Justice, the SADF service Chiefs and Director of Military Intelligence.

positions, or by his explicit invitation to attend SSC meetings. While all Cabinet ministers could participate in meetings of the other three Cabinet Committees, those of the SSC were open only to its statutory and coopted members plus the Prime Minister's invitees. The SSC was exempted from the rule that Cabinet Committee decisions be subject to Cabinet ratification. The Cabinet was only informed of SSC decisions after the fact, and at the discretion of the Prime Minister. Meeting the day before the fortnightly Cabinet meetings, the SSC prepared the Cabinet's agenda.[23] In theory, the Cabinet could still overrule SSC decisions. Yet since these bore the imprimatur of the Prime Minister – backed by the most powerful Cabinet ministers, the military, the police and the senior state bureaucrats – SSC decisions generated what Seegers has aptly termed 'a decision-making momentum that was hard for the Cabinet to stop'.[24] The Council's Secretary later confirmed that during the entire Botha administration, no SSC decision was ever overruled by Cabinet.*

Though put in place in 1979, the broader structures of the National Security Management System did not emerge at the centre stage of government until after the 1986 Emergency. However its central institution – the SSC – played such a pivotal role in the Botha government after 1979 that it gradually changed the way in which politics worked within the South African state. As the full weight of centralised information flows and decision-making became to be felt, the rules of the political game and the roster of principal players within the state were decisively changed. The real political horse trading of government politics now increasingly shifted from Cabinet to the SSC.

In keeping with Huntington's formula for stealth and secret planning away from the cut and thrust of NP factional politics, the details and implementation of the reform programme were planned and debated in the SSC rather than broader Cabinet. Over time, *this produced a profound change in nature and trajectory of internal government politics.* The sets of bureaucratic interests identified with key SSC players slowly came to predominate over the old cast of politicians and NP insiders around whom the government had previously hinged. Influence within the government was increasingly confined to those ministers whose portfolio gave them a bureaucratic power-base within the SSC. Cabinet ministers who did not sit with their chief bureaucrats in the SSC were frozen out of key debates and lacked the political wherewithal to influence government policy. This sharply curtailed the influence within the SSC of Cabinet ministers coopted by the Prime Minister (and later, the President). Though they sat at the table, they did so in their individual capacities – without

---

* Cited, *Weekly Mail,* 23 June 1989. However, J Selfe argues that while SCC decisions were routinely approved, 'recommendations which have overtly political implications for the white electorate have been known to be rejected by the Cabinet'. 'South Africa's National Security Management System' in J Cock & L Nathan, *War and Society: The Militarisation of South Africa* (David Philip, Cape Town, 1989), 151.

their departmental heads and strategists to engage in the bureaucratic bargaining that determined policy.*

P W Botha's power to contain policy disputes and freeze his conservative opponents out of the real centres of decision-making was immeasurably strengthened. The old Broederbond magic circle which had for so long given Afrikaner elites such easy access to, and influence over, the inner councils of state, was effectively slowly frozen out of the power game. Its place around the fire was gradually taken by the new 'securocrats' of the National Security Management System. With the discourse of the SSC now dominated by the Beaufrian strategic management theories of the SADF – whose Directorate of Military Intelligence largely controlled the flow of information into the SSC and, for a while, functioned as its secretariat – the military in general, and Military Intelligence in particular, came to play a principal role in shaping the overall thrust of state policy.

A significant shift in power between the various security services also occurred. While senior Police commanders apparently enthusiastically endorsed the trajectory of the reforms and new state structure,[25] the NSMS led to a sharp reduction of Police power and influence within the state. The previous administration had been hinged around Vorster's close relationship with, and heavy reliance on, the Head of BOSS, General Van den Bergh. With Van den Bergh politically eliminated by Muldergate, Botha moved quickly to downgrade the general's fiefdom. BOSS was substantially purged of its old Security Police cadre and renamed the Department of National Security. However, when South Africa's inveterate political wags claimed that the old BOSS had now been replaced by new DONS, the department was given the name (and innocuous acronym) of the National Intelligence Service. Its new head, the 31-year-old Professor Neil Barnard, was an academic close to Botha's key ally – Free State NP leader Alwyn Schlebusch. Vorster's police state gave way to P W Botha's Praetorian regime.

This was equally evident in the second thrust of Botha's programme to reorganise the state – revamping the administrative apparatus charged with implementing reform. Over thirty years of NP rule, successive administrations had assiduously cultivated and protected the civil service as a key nationalist constituency. This had turned the state bureaucracy into a 'vast, expensive and politically loaded welfare system'.[26] Under this benevolent regime (p. 76 above), the bureaucracy had developed a formidable inertia and capacity to hobble effective policy initiatives from the Cabinet. Minister Koornhof had publicly compared the public service to a tortoise: leave it alone and it would plod on remorselessly, but try to push it along, and it would withdraw into an indestructible shell.†

---

* Eg, F W de Klerk.

† Pottinger cites another minister's favourite after-dinner joke: 'How does a public servant wink? Answer: He opens an eye' – *The Imperial Presidency*, 36.

Beginning in November 1979, the first aspect of Botha's revamping of the state administration set out to streamline the civil service. Lecturing parliament that 'the Public Service plays a crucial role in every total national strategy', Botha explained that he wanted a 'well-organised and well-staffed' civil service, which would be 'better equipped to meet the demands of the time'. The 40 existing government departments were rationalised into 22, under 18 ministries. The Public Service Commission was now charged with producing 'a smaller, but more effective and better paid' state bureaucracy. 'Private sector leaders' were appointed to oversee this work. Botha explained this business involvement as representing but one step in a 'policy of cooperation between Government and the private sector, including selected academics'.* Breaking the Broederbond stranglehold on senior appointments, Botha vigorously recruited highly capable professionals to fill key public service positions and gave them wider powers. In a step pregnant with vast (and largely negative) consequences for the civic culture, senior public service salaries were also brought into line with the private sector. With the upper echelons of civil servants now paid as much as top business executives, their decades-old loyalty to the NP and NP-government was increasingly replaced by bureaucratic loyalty to the forces which drove and dominated the market.

Just as significant, however, was the other side of this reorganisation of the state administration – the slow extension of SSC supervision of the overall administration of government departments and local government. Parallel administrative structures were established to work out the detail of strategies designed in the SSC and to coordinate the policy implementation at every level. The day-to-day workhorse of this new management system was the SSC Secretariat. Responsible only to the Prime Minister and headed by a senior general, the secretariat's staff was seconded from various government departments.† Its four branches supervised the gathering of the necessary intelligence, worked out appropriate strategies to propose to the full SSC, oversaw the control of information and coordinated the implementation of SSC domestic and regional policies. This division of labour was then repeated at every level of the NSMS.‡

The SSC Secretariat presided over the parallel administrative structures of the now reorganised state. 'Security related' activities of all government

---

* SAIRR, *A Survey ... 1979*, 6, 252. The business appointees were the ranking executives of Barlow Rand, South African Breweries, South African Mutual (formerly known as Old Mutual) and the Sanlam subsidiary, General Mining.

† Of the 100 officials seconded to the Secretariat 1979–87, 56% were from the National Intelligence Service, 16% from the SADF, 16% from the SA Police and 11% from the Department of Foreign Affairs. *Weekly Mail*, 3 July 1987.

‡ Each of its structures acquired four committees known by their Afrikaans acronyms. These were responsible for security issues (the *Veikom*), developmental issues (the *Semkom*), public relations and information control (the *Komkom*), and coordination and links with the overall command chain (the *Uitvoerende Komitee*).

Figure 1
Organisational structure of the South African State
under the National Security Management System

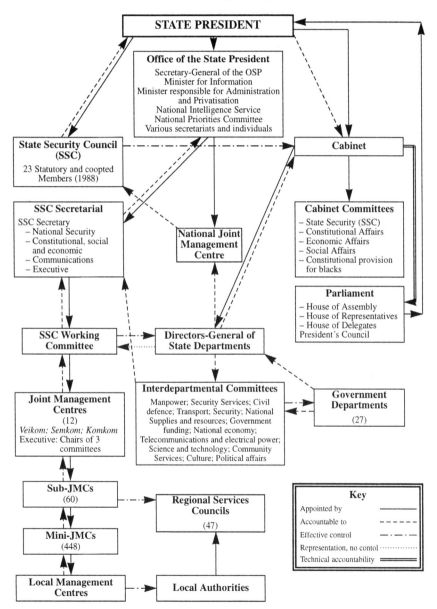

departments were coordinated by the SSC Working Committee, comprised of key members of the Secretariat plus the all department heads. These now integrated policies were implemented through 13 (and later 15) Interdepartmental Committees, each responsible for a particular area of security strategy affecting more than one department – eg, political affairs, manpower, the economy etc (see Figure 1, p. 285).[27]

Twelve Joint Management Centres (JMCs) were set up in 1979 to oversee the regional implementation of these policies. The geographical jurisdiction of 10 of these JMCs coincided with the Area Commands of the South African Defence Force, while two others were responsible for Namibia and other southern African states. In 1987, eleven of the twelve JMC chairmen were serving SADF brigadiers, while the twelfth was a police brigadier.[28] By 1988 a National Joint Management Centre presided over the 12 JMCs, 60 sub-JMCs, 448 mini-JMCs (covering local municipalities) and an unknown number of local management centres (LMCs covering the area of jurisdiction of a local police station):

> The NSMS was intended to shorten and simplify the bureaucratic chain of command. LMCs reported to mini-JMCs, who reported to sub-JMCs and so on up the line to the NJMC and SSC. ... Every government institution had to participate in one or the other committee of the NSMS on national, regional, sub-regional, mini-regional and municipal levels. The individual on the committees varied, but official representation by the most senior bureaucrats or her/his delegate was required.[29]

The third thrust of Botha's reorganisation of the South African state focused on recasting its legislative apparatus. Work here began with the July 1979 appointment of a Parliamentary Commission of Enquiry into the Constitution (Schlebusch Commission).* Following its May 1980 Report, the Senate was abolished in January 1981, and 12 nominated MPs were added to the elected parliamentarians. A 60-member 'President's Council' – including a few token so-called Coloured and Indian members – was appointed to work out new constitutional proposals. Its 1982 Report accepted 'the De Gaulle option' – the principle of an executive presidency – and argued further that the Cabinet should be drawn from *outside* parliament: 'Cabinet members must not feel constrained by immediate political and electoral considerations. *Their prime loyalty must be to the President to whom they owe their position.*' Departing

---

* This was the second Schlebusch Commission. In 1972 Alwyn Schlebusch was appointed to head a Select Committee of Parliament to enquire into the activities of four anti-apartheid bodies: the University Christian Movement; the National Union of South African Students; the Christian Institute of South Africa; and the South African Institute of Race Relations. Later known as the Le Grange Commission, the various reports of this first Schlebusch Commission led to the banning of members and officials of all but the last of these organisations. See, *A Survey ... 1972* and subsequent surveys for 1973, 1974 and 1975.

from the proposals of P W Botha's 1977 Constitution Committee for three ethnic parliaments, the report proposed a single legislature with 'segmental autonomy' for white, so-called Coloured and Indian members.[30]

However, even this relatively mild departure from the idea of ethnic parliaments was too much for the NP – and for its caucus members' hopes of an eventual Cabinet appointment. Following a well-publicised row between the Minister of Constitutional Development Chris Heunis, and the Chairman of the Constitutional Committee of the President's Council, Dr Dennis Worrall, the latter was packed off as South Africa's ambassador first to Australia, and then to Britain. The final package put forward by the government proposed an executive President and a tricameral parliament of three ethnic 'Houses'. These chambers would deal with 'own affairs'. The 'general affairs' of the whole population would be dealt with jointly between the three ethnic houses, with an absolute majority retained by the white House of Assembly. Demarcation disputes between the houses were to be settled by the President's Council, and ultimately, the President. Effectively elected by the majority party in the white house, the President would choose his Cabinet from the three ethnic chambers.[31] This arrangement came into force with August 1984 elections for the Coloured and Indian 'Houses'. The tricameral parliament was opened in September 1984 with P W Botha as the first executive State President.

Through his own secretariat, now known as the Office of the State President, Botha stood at the epicentre of the three spokes on the new wheel of power: the tricameral parliament through the Cabinet; the civil administration; and the State Security Council. Throughout his remaining five years in power, the new emperor was to continue this process of centralising – and personifying – political power. He moved to incorporate other areas, such as regional and local government, which had not been thoroughly recast during his first five years in office. After 1986, the National Security Management System was fully activated and the 'securocrats' seemed to replace the Cabinet as Botha's favoured, and most powerful, vassals. Before exploring these developments however, it is necessary to examine the political conflict fostered within the National Party and government by the first phase of reforms, from 1979 to 1982.

Chapter Fifteen

I'LL TAKE THE HIGH ROAD!

The end of *volkseenheid*

Power-sharing: The 1984 Constitution

On his accession to power in September 1978, P W Botha was painfully aware that despite his convincing majority over Connie Mulder, his own position was precarious. Neither was this master of NP politics blind to the fact that his determination to establish a new vision of Afrikaner survival would not go uncontested. At the very least it would unleash confrontation within the party and government over the preservation of hallowed NP policies. To implement reform Botha would have to consolidate his own power-base in party and state, while simultaneously negating his verkrampte critics. To do so, he launched a political offensive on a multitude of fronts.

Le parti, c'est moi: Riding the NP tiger

Botha's most immediate problem was his own party. Verkramptes still made up a majority of the NP caucus (p. 241 above). Their greatest power-base was the mighty Transvaal NP, itself still stunned by its loss of the *Hoofleier*ship to the Cape. The Transvaal party alone accounted for almost half of the nationalist MPs (61 out of 134, against 37 for the Cape), and close to two-thirds of the Cabinet Botha had inherited (11 out of 18 ministers, compared with five from the Cape and one each from Natal and the Orange Free State). Whatever their position on the verligte–verkrampte spectrum, many Transvaal nationalists tended to view the *Hoofleier*ship as theirs by right. Their new leader, Dr Andries Treurnicht, was not only supposed to restore the lost Transvaal ascendancy, he was also the new champion of the Verwoerdian hardliners. Embittered Transvaal verkramptes held secret meetings in the constituencies and launched a whispering 'campaign of slander' against the new Prime Minister, characterising Botha as

> an untried, quick tempered, bulldozing (*instormende*) alien who wanted to destroy everything along the white man's road. This was a campaign against the Cape liberal, the sell-out, the 'bald Father Christmas' who wanted to give everything away to the blacks.[1]

During his first year in office then, in his own blunt way Botha worked hard to win over the Transvaal party without either becoming its prisoner or giving advantage to Treurnicht and his verkrampte allies. The *Hoofleier's* first address to a Transvaal NP congress challenged the delegates to accept him or to get rid of him. Throughout his tenure, Botha preserved the Transvaal majority in his Cabinet, despite the Transvaal NP's declining weight in the caucus. Indeed, these efforts to smooth ruffled Transvaal provincialist feathers cost Botha the friendship of the man who had organised his leadership campaign – Transport Minister, and deputy-leader of the Cape NP, Louwrens Muller.

A full Cabinet member since 1968, by the mid-1970s Louwrens Muller was generally regarded as Dr Nico Diederichs' logical successor in the State Presidency. Unfortunately for Muller (and his equally ambitious opera singer wife, Hanlie Muller), Diederichs died just when John Vorster was again contemplating leaving active politics. When Vorster told the Cabinet of his intention to lay down the premiership in September 1978, Muller graciously offered to withdraw his own presidential candidacy should Vorster want the job. Muller was the chief organiser of P W Botha's own successful campaign for the *Hoofleier*ship. Once Botha was elected, Muller sat at the new Premier's right hand as the senior minister and Leader of the House of Assembly.

Vorster's shock resignation from the Presidency in June 1978 rekindled Muller's ambitions. He believed he had secured from Botha the promise that the *Hoofleier* would remain neutral in the battle for the NP nomination. However, Botha was in an impossible position. The leader of the House of Assembly (Muller), its Speaker and the NP Chief Whip were, like the Prime Minister, all Cape men. It was simply inconceivable that Botha could expect a still resentful Transvaal party meekly to accept that the Cape NP could now also lay claim the State Presidency. Despite first encouraging his old friend to seek the nomination, Botha tried to force Muller to withdraw. When Muller declined, Botha then instructed Cape MPs and *Die Burger* to oppose Muller's candidacy, and openly supported his opponent, the then President of the Senate, Marais Viljoen. Viljoen eventually beat out Muller by just seven votes in the caucus election for the NP nomination for the State Presidency. He could not have done so without Botha's interventions against Muller. The latter's resentment boiled over in Parliament the very next day. Without consulting his aggrieved colleague, the Prime Minister unilaterally announced the withdrawal of a section of Muller's controversial Advocate-General Bill. This was too much for Muller, and the erstwhile friends had a stormy confrontation. Accusing Botha of chasing him from his office, the by-now-enraged Muller resigned first from the Cabinet and then from Parliament and finally from the party for which he had worked for close to forty years.[2]

Botha's sacrifice of Muller on the altar of provincial equity at best avoided an open challenge on the grounds of provincialism. It did not remove the problem of the Transvaal party. Botha next set out to consolidate and reinforce the position of his Transvaal allies while neutralising his adversaries. This involved complex manoeuvring at five distinct levels.

Firstly, the Prime Minister sought both to marginalise the leading verkramptes in government and entrap them into complicity with his reform programme. The key Cabinet portfolios were reserved for Botha's own supporters. Louwrens Muller was replaced as senior minister and Leader of the House by the man who had run against Treurnicht for the Transvaal NP leadership, and who was, if anything, even more hated by the verkramptes than the Prime Minister, Labour Minister S P (Fanie) Botha.

Treurnicht himself was sharply reminded of his real standing in the power hierarchy. Elected to succeed Mulder as Transvaal NP leader with an over-whelming majority, in terms of NP protocol Treurnicht now ranked but second in the party after the *Hoofleier* himself. Yet he remained a deputy minister. For almost seven months Botha pointedly declined to promote this new 'Lion of the North' to full Cabinet membership. When finally obliged to take Treurnicht into the Cabinet, Botha gave him the insultingly minor portfolio of Public Works and Tourism. He soon changed Treurnicht's portfolio to that of Statistics and State Administration, thereby placing him directly on the reform firing line. Now responsible for more than 600 000 state employees, Treurnicht was required to implement the scrapping of Job Reservation and the dismantling of other safe-guards for white workers – reforms formulated by his arch-enemy, Labour Minister (and senior vice-chairman of the Transvaal NP) Fanie Botha. Just months after he was taken into the Cabinet, Treurnicht heard the Prime Minister tell a cheering Transvaal NP congress that his ministers 'would have to abide by the principles of the party and by policy as laid down by the Cabinet, or they would no longer find themselves in the Cabinet'.[3] Now bound by the principle of collective ministerial responsibility, or what Botha preferred to call *leierskap in rade* (leadership-in-council), and apparently unwilling to wage open war in the Cabinet, Treurnicht became, in Botha's words, 'a relatively passive (*swygsame*) member' of the Cabinet – and the frequent object of the Prime Minister's private scorn.* Other verkrampte Transvaal ministers were either simply excluded from the Cabinet (such as former Police Minister Jimmy Kruger) or kicked upstairs into the President's Council – a move which some denounced as 'provincialism'.†

Botha's second tactic in marginalising the Transvaal verkramptes was to expand Transvaal representation on the Cabinet, by bringing in reformists with impeccable nationalist credentials. An October 1980 Cabinet reshuffle saw the appointment of two other prominent new Transvaal ministers. Now finally surrendering the Defence portfolio, the Prime Minister selected the chief of the SADF and architect of the Total Strategy, General Magnus Malan, to succeed him. He likewise gave the Education Ministry to the Transvaler who presided over the Broederbond, the then Administrator of what Pretoria called South West Africa/Namibia, Dr Gerrit Viljoen.‡

* Botha, quoted Ries & Dommisse, *Broedertwis,* 59. Born and raised in the Cape, as a NGK minister Treurnicht had long been seen as an opportunist by the Cape nationalist hierarchy. Botha's biographers communicate something of Botha's delight in recounting the story of a chance street meeting in the mid-1960s with the venerated Cape church figure, Dr A J van der Merwe, in whose church Botha had once served as deacon, and who had fallen out with Treurnicht over the Cottesloe affair (note *, p 107 above). 'Brother P W', shouted Van der Merwe across the noise of the traffic, 'I see Brother Andries [Treurnicht] is turning his head towards politics.' 'Yes Doctor', replied Botha. Van der Merwe continued: 'Well Brother, all that I can say is that the church's gain is your loss.' Cited De Villiers, *PW,* 195. For a useful overview of Treurnicht's controversial career see Ries & Dommisse, *Broedertwis,* chap. 5.
† Former Water Affairs Minister Raubenheimer was thereby provoked into declaring at the 1980 Transvaal NP Congress that 'the Transvaal' would again oust 'the Cape' as the dominant force in the NP.
‡ Gerrit Viljoen had gained great kudos among the nationalist faithful as the moving spirit in the establishment of an Afrikaans university in 'the English' stronghold of Johannesburg. The first serving officer to be included in the Cabinet since the formation of the South African state in 1910, Magnus Malan, for his part, was the son of a prominent Transvaal nationalist family. His father,

However, Botha's Cabinet options were limited. The facade of NP unity demanded that major factions be reasonably represented in its Cabinet. Thus Botha's strategy to undercut the verkramptes focused, thirdly, on efforts to neutralise the Cabinet as an effective terrain of conflict between NP factions. This was the real import and reason for his new system of Cabinet Committees, of centralised Prime Ministerial rule 'in council' and the effective replacement of the Cabinet by the State Security Council as the primary decision-making institution of executive power. Botha's reorganisation of the entire apparatus of government transformed the institutional structures of the executive, while simultaneously altering the relationship between the executive and legislative branches of government. The reorganised form of state made it increasingly more difficult for the verkrampte opponents of the Total Strategy to mount an effective campaign against reform from within the state apparatus. In other words, the character of the terrains of political conflict in the state were deliberately and decisively altered in a way which undercut the NP right wing, forcing it back on to the terrain of the NP itself to combat what it saw as the betrayal of sacrosanct policies.

Yet here too Botha took the initiative, finding ways to undermine their ability to work against reform within the National Party. He did so, fourthly, by *fiat* – using the *Hoofleier*ship to redefine the relationship between the various levels of the NP, and in particular between the *Hoofleier* and the annual congresses of each of the provincial parties. At the first provincial NP congress after his election as *Hoofleier*, Botha simply decreed to the Natal NP delegates that in future no provincial NP congress could question government policy. They would have to restrict themselves to matters of 'principle'. This was a clear break with 65 years of NP tradition – and rested on a dubious interpretation of the party constitution which gave provincial congresses supreme decision-making powers.

Botha's choice of the Natal NP congress as the place to lay down the new line was deliberate and significant. Natal was the weakest of the provincial National Parties. Its English-speaking leader, the ineffectual Finance Minister Owen Horwood, had no personal political base independent of the *Hoofleier*, and, like his party, could be relied upon meekly to accept Botha's dictates.* Once the Natal NP had declined to oppose *Hoofleier* Botha's radical reordering

---

Dr A I Malan, had been a nationalist MP, Speaker of the House of Assembly and the longserving chairman of the Broederbond-run Volkskas bank. In the early 1960s, Magnus Malan's brother Avril had captained South Africa's then most successful postwar Rugby team – a huge political asset in white South Africa. General Malan had himself garnered a great domestic reputation, particularly during the propaganda campaign to depict the Angola débacle as a stirring success for the SADF.

* Horwood had been taken into Vorster's Cabinet in the early 1970s as the replacement for the retiring token English-speaking minister, Alf Trollip. So intense was the anti-Afrikaner feeling in certain sections of Natal's white population that this appointment gave rise to oft-repeated (and sexist) question–answer political pun: 'Q: Who would you choose to replace a Trollip in the Nat Cabinet?' 'A: Only a Horwood !' See also note, p. 242 above.

of NP politics, it became much more difficult for the Transvaal congress to do so without being seen to violate the sacred principle of *volkseenheid* (unity of the *volk*). With the *Hoofleier* effectively abrogating to himself the exclusive right to interpret NP policy, he also challenged the rank and file to risk provoking his well-known ire. While some congress resolutions dared speak of 'ambiguous and vague political statements', the once-lively NP congresses soon resembled 'nothing quite so much as Eastern European party jamborees – heavy on displays of loyalty, thin on substantive debate, ultimately rubber-stamp rallies'.[4]

The verkramptes certainly did not roll over and surrender to Botha's assault. Sharply reminiscent of the internal turmoil of the late 1960s, the growing NP factional conflict led to persistent caucus leaks and constant expectations of a decisive confrontation. However before discussing the internal NP conflicts during Botha's first three-and-a-half years in office, it is necessary to examine the fifth and final level of Botha's manoeuvring to entrench his reforms – the attempt to fashion a new social base for NP rule.

Open for business: The Total Strategy and South African capitalists

I argued in Chapter 12 that P W Botha had come to power partly as a consequence of the mid-1970s crisis of political representation of capital. He did not disappoint his new backers. The Total Strategy reforms of 1979 to 1984 largely met the business demands outlined in the *Financial Mail's* celebrated 'Business Power' issue.[5] Botha went out of his way to project his administration as the government of a broad alliance of all sections of capital. His reforms were warmly received by both English and Afrikaners businessmen. The head of the giant Barlow Rand industrial conglomerate spoke for all when, just six months after Botha entered the Premiership, he declared that relations between business and government 'had never been better', ascribing this cosy situation to the 'pragmatic approach' of the new Prime Minister.[6]

Much-publicised meetings in November 1979 and November 1981 brought together Cabinet, key officials and leading businessmen, and were hailed as symbols of a new cooperation between state and capital. Botha told the assembled capitalists at the 1979 'Carlton' Conference: 'We have our differences, but we are creating reciprocal channels to plan national strategy in South Africa as a team.' The doyen of liberal capital, Anglo American's Harry Oppenheimer, replied to the Prime Minister's address with the observation that he now saw 'greater reason for real hope in the future of the country than I have felt in many years'.[7]

Business enthusiasm for the new regime rested on more than just the latter's reformist stance. Now capital was given a wider *institutionalised* role within the reorganised state structures. Key executives of the major monopolies were brought in to supervise the reshaping of the civil service (p. 284 above). However, Botha was careful to include individual business leaders rather than the employers' organisations (such as Assocom, the AHI etc.). The roles and functions of existing advisory councils and commissions were expanded, and new ones brought into being. Perhaps the most important were the Prime Minister's Economic Advisory Council – dating back to the 1960s – and the Defence Advisory Board (disbanded in 1982 and partially replaced by the Defence Manpower Liaison Committee) and the National Manpower Commission. Representatives of South Africa's monopolies sat on all these bodies. An Afrikaner political scientist argued in 1982 that these 'corporatist consensus building' bodies functioned 'to resolve economic and political crises by the device of coopting interest organisations into policy process *where the government cannot, or will not, resolve the problems through party political and parliamentary modes of representation*'.[8]

This new cooperation with non-Afrikaner capital was highlighted by former Premier Vorster's complaint that: 'In my time I also talked to all the leading English businessmen, but I never involved them in planning and decision-making.'[9] Businessmen were certainly much happier with Botha's policies than those of Vorster. Backing off his long support for the Progressive Federal Party, Harry Oppenheimer suggested that capital's efforts for reform should now focus on what he called 'the reasonable people' in the NP (p. 187 above). Despite the PFP's opposition to the new political dispensation, all the major corporations supported the NP in the 1983 white referendum on the new constitution, contributing heavily to its campaign.

However, while eager to cooperate with Botha, business was not going to do so only on his terms. By 1981 there was evident frustration with the slow pace of change and Botha's apparent refusal to deal with opposition from the NP verkramptes. The Prime Minister came under increasing pressure from his new business allies to rid himself of Treurnicht, who was seen to be holding back reform. Between September 1978 and the dramatic events of early 1982, the NP government, the NP itself, and finally the broad gamut of organisations making up the Afrikaner nationalist movement were again key terrains of the battle for reform. This protracted conflict turned around the issue of the very nature of Afrikaner nationalism

Broedertwis: Round two

The most intense skirmishes of the battle between Botha's reformists and Treurnicht's verkramptes took place largely within the two crucial organisations of Afrikaner nationalism where Treurnicht *did* have strong support – the Transvaal NP and the Afrikaner Broederbond. In the process, the basic lines of cleavage within the National Party were effectively recast, leading ultimately to the dismantling of the post-1948 brand of organised Afrikaner nationalism.

Treurnicht's key base of caucus support lay among the organisers of Connie Mulder's failed campaign for the *Hoofleier*ship. The overwhelming majority of the MPs and MPCs close to Treurnicht were Transvalers representing rural constituencies (particularly in the Northern Transvaal), or those urban areas populated by state officials and/or Afrikaner workers.[10] Their complaints with the 'liberal' P W Botha reflected those of their constituents who generally made up those strata of the Afrikaner population which had not shared in the thoroughgoing *embourgeoisement* of their urban Afrikaner confreres. Leaving aside the personalities and political ambitions of the politicians involved, the profound Afrikaner *broedertwis* (division among brothers) of the late 1970s and early 1980s represented nothing so much as the agonised unravelling of the social alliance welded together in the 1940s by the Broederbond and National Party. They posed all the classic conflicts of Afrikaner nationalism: who best represented the *volk*? who was to interpret 'its' interests? The great difference with earlier internal struggles, however, was that in this second round of the battle for the Afrikaner soul, the principal lines of internal political cleavage were no longer drawn between the 'liberal' Cape and the conservative Transvaal. Now the real war was fought *inside* the Transvaal party.

The first shots were fired by the verkramptes, who desperately tried to rally their troops with the provincialist battle cries of the past. This worked well during the struggle between Fanie Botha and Andries Treurnicht over who was to succeed Connie Mulder as Transvaal NP leader. *Die Vaderland* quoted an unnamed member of the Transvaal NP head committee saying of Fanie Botha that 'people with Southern sympathies are not acceptable to us [in the Transvaal]'. Other Treurnicht supporters were quoted by his old newspaper *Hoofstad* as saying that 'the Transvaal leader must have a restraining influence in Cabinet to keep our verligte Cape friends in check'.* On his very first day in Cabinet, Treurnicht lived up to his billing by criticising fellow Transvaal minister Piet Koornhof's celebrated address to the Washington Press Club in which Koornhof had claimed that 'apartheid as you know it is dying'.†

Well aware that they could not yet risk going head to head with P W Botha, the Treurnichtites concentrated on trying to dislodge prominent reformists from key positions in the Transvaal party. Their four key targets were the two (unrelated) Transvaal Bothas (Ministers Fanie and Pik), Connie Mulder's replacement in the central apartheid Ministry of Plural Relations (now again renamed 'Cooperation and Development'), Dr Piet Koornhof, and the man who had himself displaced Treurnicht as chairman of the Broederbond in 1974, Education Minister Dr Gerrit Viljoen. Treurnicht had a number of public rows with the senior vice-chairman of the Transvaal NP (Fanie Botha). Numerous attempts were made to oust Botha from this position, and to replace other reformists in the head committee of the Transvaal NP with Treurnicht supporters.

Treurnicht's period as Transvaal leader was characterised by great tension

---

* Both newspapers quoted Ries & Dommisse, *Broedertwis,* 51. Fanie Botha had been a member of the Nasionale Pers board.

† Ibid. 82. However Treurnicht withdrew the comment when he saw the full text of Koornhof's speech.

and bad feeling within the Transvaal party. The open war between the Treurnichtites and Botha-ites helped consolidate a centrist group of 'peacemakers' around Agriculture Minister Hendrik Schoeman and the nephew of Hans Strijdom, Posts and Telegraphs Minister, F W de Klerk.* Ironically, the sheer intensity of the internal Transvaal conflict gradually eroded the provincialist tensions of the past. Now the battle was over two very distinct visions of Afrikaner nationalism – the 'adapt or die' realism as represented by *Hoofleier* P W Botha, versus the stress on sacred principles of the civil religion *à la* Treurnicht. The entire gamut of Afrikaner nationalism began to polarise around these two alternatives.

The Treurnichtites' heavy focus on the Transvaal was a major tactical blunder. In effect Treurnicht gave away his one great political asset – control over the dominant force in organised Afrikaner nationalism. But the Transvaal leader was essentially a political neophyte. Parachuted into the editorship of *Hoofstad* by Vorster in 1967, he had never been schooled in hands-on politics, in the real organisational nitty gritty of the Transvaal party. Always an ideas man rather than an effective political organiser, in the seven months preceding to his fatal confrontation with P W Botha, the Transvaal leader paid just one visit to his party headquarters – and that at the request of its head secretary.[11] As leader, he tended to take the Transvaal NP – and his place at its head – for granted, believing that one of his speeches was worth hours of grassroots organisation.

Outside their base in the Transvaal party, the Treurnichtites fought against reform in an indirect, guerrilla fashion. Rather than tackling the issues head-on in public, they indulged in apparently trivial quibbles which could not be interpreted as disrespect for the *Hoofleier*. Their complaints were persistently presented as matter of detail rather than principle. In private they waged full-out war in the closed meetings of local Afrikaner nationalist groupings, particularly in the Transvaal. Treurnicht was in great demand at *Rapportryer* meetings, where his opposition to reform was expressed clearly. Botha's biographers complain of a great campaign of slander against the new Prime Minister.[12] He was indeed the first *Hoofleier* to be attacked in public by his ostensibly retired predecessor. The verkramptes harboured great hopes of John Vorster. In March 1980 a leading Treurnichtite told *Die Burger* of the widespread feeling that 'John Vorster, Connie Mulder and Louwrens Muller should return to "save" the NP'. This informant added that 'Uncle John [Vorster] is keen for the thing'.[13]

In the months leading up to the final confrontation, the Treurnicht group also worked to place their own supporters in the influential positions of chairman of the NP's 22 caucus study groups. These study groups played a crucial role both in defining the terms of politically acceptable policy, and in mobilising caucus support for government legislation. As such, a study group chairman (never a

---

* Hendrik Schoeman had initially been a candidate to succeed Mulder as Transvaal leader, but had withdrawn 'in the interests of party unity' four days before the election.

woman in the NP) could exercise powerful political influence, or even constraint, on the responsible Cabinet minister. The study group chairmanships gave the Treurnichtites significant influence behind the scenes in the working out of the legislative programme of the government, and in defining the terms of the policy debate in caucus.*

However the overall strategic weakness of the Treurnichtites lay in the fact that, as a member of the Cabinet, their leader was obliged to concede that some modifications were necessary for apartheid to survive. P W Botha could, and did, often present Treurnicht with the choice of public confrontation and a split, or public reconciliation and humiliation. Nevertheless, on a number of occasions an open split very nearly occurred, particularly in the March 1980 brouhaha over the relatively minor issue of black participation in a traditionally 'white' school sporting event, the so-called 'Craven week'.† This row apparently convinced many Transvaal centrists that Treurnicht was bent on wrecking party unity.

Yet support for the far right in the NP in this period, particularly in the Transvaal, did appear to be substantial. By-elections in traditional NP farming and mining constituencies produced a swing of as much as 40 percent to the Hertzogite *Herstigte* NP, now led by Jaap Marais.‡ A large number of verkramptes were chosen by local NP branches as nominated Members of Parliament when the Senate was abolished in 1981 (above p. 286). Prime Minister Botha called an early general election in April 1981 in an attempt to secure the decisive dominance of his NP faction over the forces of the far right, and to stem the growing support for the HNP. In both the nomination contests for the Transvaal NP candidates, and in the election itself, the right emerged significantly stronger. P W Botha later told friends of his suspicion that the nomination contests were 'manipulated in order to undermine the NP'.[14]

The 1981 election saw the then biggest downturn in NP fortunes since it had come to power.[15] Its share of the vote fell from the 65 percent it won in 1977 to 53 percent. The beneficiaries were the three far right parties which contested the election: the HNP, Connie Mulder's hastily formed National Conservative Party; and a Broederbond-based faction calling itself *Aksie Eie Toekoms* (Action [for our] Own Future). Though they won no seats, the far right parties together

---

* Among the Treurnichtites who chaired caucus study groups were: Daan van der Merwe (Internal Affairs – to become the largest of such groups and responsible for 'Coloured' policy); Jan Hoon (Planning); Willie Snyman (Health); Tom Langley (Justice); Casper Uys (Agriculture) and Jan van Zyl (Posts and Telegraphs).

† See Ries & Dommisse, *Broedertwis,* 85-91. Highly revealing of Botha's own view of Treurnicht (and the Prime Minister's views on parenting) was his reply to the question of why he did not give even greater emphasis to his private statement to Treurnicht that he was repudiating the Transvaal leader's intepretation of the Craven week events: 'If one gives a child a thrashing in the bedroom, must you then announce it on the front porch?' – quoted *ibid.* 91.

‡ Marais had succeeded to the HNP *hoofleier*ship on the retirement from politics of the party's aged founder, Dr Albert Hertzog, in May 1977.

polled 192 000 votes, or 14 percent of the total – a fivefold increase over the 1977 vote for the far right. Their newly augmented electoral support was concentrated in the Transvaal, where almost a third of all rural votes went to the HNP. Marais' party also received 25 percent of all votes in the heavily rural Orange Free State. In some seventy constituencies the HNP had won more than 2 000 votes (enough to begin challenging the incumbent), more than sixty of them in the Transvaal. HNP leader Marais came close to defeating the Transvaal NP leader in Treurnicht's Waterberg constituency – a seat of great symbolism in Transvaal nationalism.*

A leading pro-P W Botha nationalist newspaper concluded that the extreme right had won 38 percent of the 'Afrikaner vote', that Afrikaner political unity was both a thing of the past, and that the NP should not seek its resurrection.[16] The HNP emerged from the 1981 elections with the bit firmly between its teeth, convinced that *its* moment would soon arrive. Charney comments appropriately:

> The most evident fact about the 1981 election is that it marked the point when it became respectable in the Afrikaans community to vote for the far right. The HNP lost its image as an oddball collection of ageing racist cranks. Indeed, one of the most striking things about the crowds who flocked to HNP election meetings was their very ordinariness. Some of the men had the long sideburns and slicked-down short hair favoured by Afrikaans Neanderthals, but there were also many well-dressed middle-aged men and youths.[17]

Support for the far right seemed to grow by leaps and bounds following the election.[18] Highly publicised defections by former MPs and NP local branches gave the impression of a groundswell towards the HNP, particularly in rural and poorer urban constituencies. Moreover a number of small far right organisations flourished, such as the openly-Nazi and semi-terrorist *Afrikaner Weerstand Beweging* (Afrikaner Resistance Movement – AWB), the *Wit Komando* (White Commando), and the more intellectual *Aksie Eie Toekoms*. All these far right groups, excepting the HNP, formed a united front known as 'Action Save White South Africa' in September 1981. Together with the HNP, the new alliance began to agitate openly against any South African withdrawal from Namibia, advocating armed resistance should the mooted UN peace-keeping force for Namibia ever set foot in the territory.

Far more serious for the NP, however, were the profound divisions in the Afrikaner Broederbond. Here, Prime Minister Botha inadvertently handed the verkramptes a significant weapon. In an effort to shore up support in the

---

* Having been the constituency of Transvaal NP leader and later Prime Minister J G Strijdom for nearly thirty years. Between 1934 and 1939, Waterberg was the only Transvaal seat consistently held by Dr Malan's *Gesuiwerde* NP. Treurnicht claimed the mantle of Strijdom and Verwoerd in P W Botha's NP – a claim sharply contested by Jaap Marais' HNP, which saw itself as the real heir of the 'authentic' Transvaal nationalist tradition. The was also strong personal antipathy between Marais and Treurnicht (below p. 306).

Transvaal NP and maintain a strong Transvaal verligte counterweight to Treurnicht in the Cabinet, Botha brought the then chairman of the Broederbond, Dr Gerrit Viljoen, into his Cabinet in late 1980. Since Viljoen was the verligte candidate who had defeated Treurnicht in the 1974 election for the Broederbond chairmanship in a campaign allegedly organised by Sanlam (see note * p. 196 above), this was an added insult to the right. In the event, however, it was a major blunder on Botha's part. Broederbond custom held that no man appointed to the Cabinet could remain on the AB executive. Viljoen was obliged to relinquish the Broederbond chairmanship, thereby handing this crucial post to the highly verkrampte and very active son-in-law of Hendrik Verwoerd, SABRA chairman Professor Carel Boshoff.*

Chairman Boshoff worked assiduously to distance the Bond from Botha's NP – quickly reasserting the independence the AB had lost under Vorster, Verwoerd and Strijdom. Under his frenetic chairmanship, the Broederbond soon became perhaps the most important verkrampte redoubt in the undeclared but now intense war for control of Afrikaner nationalism. Withdrawing its exclusive support for the NP in September 1981, Boshoff's *Uitvoerende Raad* reversed the policy adopted under Treurnicht's chairmanship to expel any *Broeder* supporting the HNP. The formation of the verkrampte political party *Aksie Eie Toekoms* from within the Broederbond in the same year also likely occurred with Boshoff's imprimatur.

Three little letters: The final break

By mid-1981, the divisions within the NP and all organisations of Afrikaner nationalism were deeper and more bitter that at any period since World War II. Battles within the party and government, together with intense opposition from within the state bureaucracy to Botha's policies were beginning to paralyse reform. Botha's biographers stress his own profound frustration at the lack of progress in the second half of 1981. Some of his closest NP supporters worried that NP conflicts were making the Prime Minister 'too accommodating towards everybody'.[19] His new capitalist allies were likewise deeply concerned, and began to make noises about reconsidering their relationship with the regime. The *Financial Mail* cited the now open questioning by 'concerned businessmen' over whether 'the very basis of what has been called 'the Carlton Contract' [between state and capital] was being shredded' as the Prime Minister 'did not deliver the material changes' he had promised at the 1979 Carlton conference. This always influential journal warned:

---

* I find it hard to believe that any of Botha's three predecessors would have blundered so badly. Indeed, each in their own way, Strijdom, Verwoerd and Vorster had worked very hard to keep the AB subservient to their own authority. Yet Botha was a man of the Cape – a province in which the Broederbond was far less active in the direction of nationalist politics. He may simply have failed to grasp the gravity of the situation in the Transvaal, or misunderstood the political culture and practices of its nationalism. He must certainly have regretted this step.

[I]f leaders and opinion makers in the commercial and industrial world are to continue to lend support to Botha they want the *quid pro quo* of a relaxation of the economic stranglehold of apartheid.[20]

The major conglomerates began to increase their pressure for reform. In mid-1980, the chairman of the giant Barlow Rand conglomerate convened 'an informal group of 10 major companies employing a total of 750 000 workers' for regular discussions over 'labour practices and problems'. An extremely high-powered delegation from this 'informal group' then met with the Prime Minister in October 1981, just before the highly public 'Good Hope conference' between the Cabinet, senior bureaucrats and 600 leading capitalists. Pressing for 'immediate implementation of reform measures', these businessmen presented Botha with a five-point 'programme of reform' based on 'months of detailed research'. They warned him that 'if his compact with business is to be meaningful', the Good Hope conference would have to come up with 'substantive proposals going well beyond regional development'.* Both Afrikaner and English-speaking business delegates to this Good Hope conference were notably cooler towards Botha's proposals than had been the case at their 'Carlton' conference two years earlier. Anton Rupert of Rembrandt reminded the Premier that 'if one has to leap over a yawning chasm, you can't do it in two jumps'.†

Clearly it was demanded of Botha that he abandon his concern to hold together the contradictory tendencies of the NP and press ahead with reform, regardless of the Treurnichtite opposition. Other channels in the monopoly/military alliance began to be used to push Botha into a final, formal break with the verkramptes. The *Sunday Express* reported that the 13 business leaders who sat on the Defence Advisory Committee had persuaded the Minister of Defence General Malan 'of the need to act' against Treurnicht and his supporters. This would suggest that Malan and other SSC members finally convinced an apparently hesitant P W Botha to precipitate a confrontation even at the risk of splitting the NP.‡

However, the Prime Minister was clearly waiting for some action by the verkramptes which would enable him to accuse Treurnicht of the 'deadly sin'

---

* 'Special Survey on Barlow Rand', *Financial Mail*, 13 February 1981, and *ibid.* 23 October 1981. This manifesto demanded rapid 'reform' in the areas of labour, education, housing, influx control and group areas. The content of these demands is analysed in 'South Africa: Strategy Conference of Government and Business Leaders', *Southern Africa Dossier* 4.60(E) (Centro de Estudos Africanos, Universidade Eduardo Mondlane, Maputo, 1981).

† Prompting Botha to reply: 'Yes, but before you jump, you have to be sure you will land on the other side.' De Villiers, *PW,* 164.

‡ See the article by the newspaper's chief reporter entitled 'Gen Malan persuaded P W to act', *Sunday Express,* 24 February 1982. The 13-member Defence Advisory Committee was composed of representatives of all of South Africa's major non-state monopolies and banks, together with the president of the Johannesburg Stock Exchange and chairman of the South African Agricultural Union.

of *volkskeurder* (schismatic).[21] The opportunity presented itself in February 1982. In keeping with his practice of sniping at what he saw as relatively minor issues raised by people lower in the nationalist hierarchy than himself, Treurnicht wrote to the editor of the official NP publication *Nat 80*, objecting to the latter's comment that under the proposed tricameral parliament, South Africa could obviously have 'only one government'. The Transvaal leader argued that there would soon be three separate governments for the three racial groups included in this scheme. Moreover, Treurnicht denied the publication's claim that the new constitution would institute 'healthy power-*sharing*', insisting instead that it would set up a *division* of power between whites, coloureds and Asians – thereby remaining faithful to the old Verwoerdian shibboleths. In Afrikaans, the difference between the two positions came down to just three letters: Botha's *magsdeling* (power-sharing) versus Treurnicht's *magsverdeling* (division of powers).

However Treurnicht had now made the mistake for which Botha had been waiting. In the usual slapdash fashion in which he conducted politics, Treurnicht seemed to have forgotten one crucial detail – that the Cabinet in which he sat had already approved the power-sharing formula. Botha now gleefully seized on Treurnicht's statement as an opportunity to force the issue. Assuming a self-righteous and injured tone, he described Treurnicht's intervention as an attempt to do an end run around a Cabinet decision and as a direct challenge to the policy and integrity of the *Hoofleier*. The trap was sprung in the regular Wednesday NP caucus meeting on 24 February 1982. Despite F W de Klerk's plea to delay a debate over power-sharing until the President's Council Report, Botha was now determined to use the opening Treurnicht's blunder had given him and press the issue.* Treurnicht's maladroit letter to the *Nat 80* editor was used to confront the wrong-footed Treurnichtites with an irrevocable choice – submit or leave. The Prime Minister's main Transvaal ally, Labour Minister Fanie Botha, proposed a caucus vote of confidence in P W Botha's leadership and his interpretation of party policy. Twenty-two nationalist MPs voted against the motion – including Treurnicht, and Education and Training Minister, Dr Ferdi Hartzenberg. Dissident MP Koos van der Merwe stormed out of the caucus, telling waiting journalists that he was 'finished with that Prog P W Botha'. This 'Prog' in turn ended the caucus proceedings by telling the Transvaal leader to 'go to the *Herstigtes* and Hertzog where you belong'.[22]

The long-anticipated NP split had finally arrived. Now the central question obsessing all observers was how would things turn out in the Transvaal NP? Would the provincial party support its own verkrampte leader against the reformist *Hoofleier* from the Cape? If this most important element in the NP

---

* *The Star,* 25 February 1982. Treurnicht's only Cabinet ally, Education and Training Minister Ferdie Hartzenberg, also asked caucus 'whether the matter could not be sorted out some other time' – presumably at the Treurnichtites' choosing.

turned against Botha, control of the machinery and funds of the Transvaal would give Treurnicht a formidable base from which to claim to represent the 'authentic' National Party.

Supremely confident of his dominance in the Transvaal NP, Treurnicht immediately called a meeting of its head committee for that Saturday – without bothering to inform his three vice-chairmen who found out about the meeting from newspaper reports. Fanie Botha and the two 'peacemakers', Hendrik Schoeman and F W de Klerk, then in turn called a meeting of the Transvaal NP executive the day before the head committee meeting set up by Treurnicht. Once again, the Treurnichtites were undone by their own lack of organisation. Convinced of their control over the Transvaal party, they did far less planning and organisation for the crucial meeting than did Botha's Transvaal allies – who soon selected as their main spokesman a man with impeccable Transvaal nationalist credentials, the centrist De Klerk.* After four days of great tension, Botha's Transvaal allies won a decisive vote of confidence in the head committee of the Transvaal NP, defeating the Treurnichtites by 172 votes to 36.

The Treurnicht forces had been completly out-manoeuvred and out-organised by the Transvaal reformists – whose masterstroke had been to bring the Prime Minister 'into the lions' den' to confront the dissidents in the Transvaal head committee. A stunned Treurnicht was suspended as Transvaal NP leader, and the dissidents were given four days to abide by the original caucus resolution.† While six of the original 22 dissidents duly ate the required humble pie, 16 MPs (15 from the Transvaal and one from the Cape) eventually refused to acquiesce and were expelled from the National Party. Two others soon joined them to bring the tally to 18. Treurnicht and Hartzenberg resigned from the Cabinet and Treurnicht was replaced as Transvaal NP leader by the forty-six-year-old scion on the Transvaal NP, F W de Klerk.

---

* Son of the longtime Transvaal NP head secretary, NP Cabinet minister and vanquished Transvaal NP presidential candidate against Eben Dönges on 1966 (note † p. 154 above), Jan de Klerk, F W de Klerk was also the nephew of J G Strijdom, and brother of the editor of the Transvaal NP organ *Die Transvaler.* No delegate going into the crucial meeting would have missed the symbolism of the nephew of the Lion of the North confronting one of Strijdom's successors both as Transvaal leader and MP for Waterberg, Treurnicht.

† Their humiliation is better conveyed in the Afrikaans original. The dissidents were instructed that they had to *neerlê* (lay themselves down before) to the resolution or face the consequences.

Chapter Sixteen

BACK TO THE FUTURE

The far right and the collapse of Afrikaner nationalism

The politics of the far right (left to right: Eugene Terre'blanche, Jaap Marais, Dr Treurnicht)

Your tortoise or mine? The social base and politics of the far right

The expulsion of the Treurnichtites from the NP led to much speculation about their possible alliance with the Hertzogite HNP. However, clear policy differences separated the two groups – as did the strong personal animosity between their leaders, dating back to the August 1969 expulsion of the then Hertzogites from the NP. Editor of the Pretoria newspaper *Hoofstad* at the time, Treurnicht had been a prominent spokesman and strategist of the Hertzog group. On the NP's expulsion of the Hertzogite MPs, editor Treurnicht had been coopted on to the 'Action Committee' set up to form Hertzog's Herstigte Nasionale Party. However, Treurnicht demurred, insisting that verkramptes should stay and fight *within* the NP – prompting Jaap Marais' exasperated reply: 'But Andries, we have been kicked out of the party now.'[1] Treurnicht was then deliberately used by Vorster to hound the *Herstigtes*. The HNP's bitterness against Treurnicht, and its conviction that he was a traitor to the verkrampte cause, was reinforced in 1972. As the newly elected chairman of the Broederbond, Treurnicht was obliged to accept Vorster's injunction to expel all *Herstigtes* from the AB – in clear violation of the much-abused clause 6 of its constitution forbidding 'party politics' in the Bond.

Now following their own expulsion from the NP, the Treurnichtites would have agreed to the formation of a new right-wing opposition party embracing both themselves and the HNP. They were adamant, however, that Treurnicht rather than Marais would have to be its leader. Yet in HNP eyes, the Treurnichtites were political Johnny-come-latelies. In the earthy metaphor of *Herstigte* luminary Cas Greyling, '*Andries wit handjies*' ('clean handies Andy') Treurnicht was little more than an emotional political *tweegatjakkals* (jackal with two [arse]holes), perpetually saying one thing and doing another.* The expulsion of Treurnicht and his followers from the NP simply proved the HNP's long-argued point. But now the opportunist Treurnichtites sought to reap for themselves the fruits of the HNP's twelve-and-a-half bitter years in the political wilderness. Treurnicht's holier-than-thou attitude and self-assumed mantle of the *gesuiwerdes* of the 1930s stuck in *Herstigte* throats, and Jaap Marais regarded him as little better than a General Hertzog.

Marais insisted his was the only legitimate party of the far right, inviting all disgruntled present and former members of the NP to join the HNP and fight for the 'authentic' nationalism embodied in Dr Verwoerd's 1966 NP manifesto. Treurnicht and his supporters on the other hand had publicly supported and indeed campaigned for the 1977 and 1981 NP manifestos – uttering many hard words about Marais and his party in the process. *Herstigte* stalwarts doubted the Treurnichtites' commitment to the 'real' cause, and felt they were not really to

---

* See his scathing letter to Treurnicht, cited Ries & Dommisse, *Broedertwis,* 159. A former nationalist MP, Greyling had himself been expelled from Vorster's NP for opposing its 1977 constitutional proposals.

be trusted – much like the *oud smelters* who had left the NP in 1934, returned in 1939, but most of whom again departed by 1942.

Thus after much speculation and some tentative soundings with other forces on the right, the Treurnichtites – joined by Mulder's NCP, the neo-Nazi AWB and *Aksie Eie Toekoms* – formed the *Konserwatieve Party* (Conservative Party – KP) on 20 March 1982. The KP founding congress, like that of the HNP over 12 years earlier, took place in Pretoria's *Skilpadsaal* (Tortoise Hall), occasioning many jokes about the nature of its politics. Andries Treurnicht was unanimously elected leader of the new party, and Connie Mulder resurfaced on its executive.

The Treurnichites also nurtured strong hopes that former Premier John Vorster would support the KP. While still in office Vorster had told his biographer:

> Once I retire I will retire for good. I would not like to hang like a proverbial millstone around my successor's neck ... I will avoid public statements.[2]

However, since his enforced and very reluctant retirement Vorster he had sniped continuously at Botha. Following the fateful NP caucus vote, the former Prime Minister had issued a statement supporting Treurnicht. Gleeful *verkramptes* confidently expected that their old *Hoofleier* would make an appearance at the KP founding congress, giving their new party real nationalist legitimacy and continuity. However, possibly detered by longstanding threats from his own former senior minister and former Transvaal NP leader, Ben Schoeman, to reveal things Vorster wished to keep secret, the ailing and resentful Jolly John stayed away, saying that his time in politics was over. In his absence, a number of other former NP Cabinet ministers announced their support for the KP, together with the widow of Dr Verwoerd.*

The KP proclaimed that it would again champion the Christian-national brand of Afrikaner nationalism, including 'our own [Afrikaner] people's particular identity, our right to a separate future and our right to self-determination'. However, unlike the HNP, the KP did not insist that Afrikaans be South Africa's sole official language. Nor did it follow the *Herstigtes* in seeking its legitimacy in Verwoerd's 1966 NP programme. Rather the KP declared itself faithful to Vorster's 1977 NP manifesto – allegedly violated by Botha's power-sharing schemes. It committed itself to rigid social segregation

---

* On Schoeman's threats of 'revelations', see note ‡ p. 243 above. The former Transvaal leader quickly denounced Vorster's support for Treurnicht as 'of no significance nor interest for me'. Schoeman added that, P W Botha is on the right road'. See Ries & Dommisse, *Broedertwis*, 136-7. Ex-ministers and other prominent nationalists now supporting the formation of the KP included: former Verwoerd associate and his successor as Minister of Bantu Affairs, Daan de Wet Nel; Louwrens Muller; former Police Minister Jimmy ('the Mouth') Kruger; former MP and Administrator of the Transvaal, Sybrand van Niekerk; ex-Natal NP leader Henry Torlage; and Broederbond founder and former Speaker of the House of Assembly, Henning Klopper.

and the abolition of all reforms introduced or discussed since Vorster's resignation from the Premiership.[3]

With the formation of the KP three political parties now claimed to be the genuine voice of organised Afrikaner nationalism. The NP retained a massive parliamentary majority and continued to govern South Africa. The KP had 18 MPs and a number of provincial councillors, while the HNP was represented neither in Parliament nor the provincial councils. Each party claimed to represent the Afrikaner *volk,* yet there were marked differences in their political bases of support. This is one of the major reasons why the far right opposition parties were never able to challenge the NP's predominance.

P W Botha's party now presented itself as the broad party of all 'patriotic' whites. This it saw as the real thrust of genuine Afrikaner nationalism. Moreover, under P W Botha the NP was clearly and proudly a party of big business. No longer speaking for 'the small man' against the monopolies, the Afrikaner 'Hoggenheimers' who now sat in the councils of Botha's government espoused stridently capitalist, indeed Friedmanite ideologies and spoke of building bridges across language and racial barriers. As a 'leading nationalist' told Craig Charney: 'Now the NP has become bourgeois itself, espousing middle class values and finding bridges across language and racial barriers.'[4]

Under Hendrik Verwoerd's leadership, the National Party had begun a slow turn towards 'the English' and ditched the *baasskap* formula of Strijdom. By 1982, a quarter of those who declared support from the NP in polls were English-speakers – compared to one out of every seven who voted for the NP in 1977. According to the pro-NP weekly, *Rapport,* declared support for the NP in polls had fallen from 82 percent in October 1976 to just 47 percent in April 1982 (though this crept back to 56 percent by October 1982).[5] This means that by October 1982 only 42 percent of Afrikaners declared themselves as NP supporters.

No longer representing the majority of Afrikaners, Botha's National Party was now also busy jettisoning Verwoerdian 'separate development' in favour of what the Prime Minister called 'healthy power-sharing and joint decision-making'. This had aggravated the class tensions in its own ranks. Indeed, some of the Afrikaner capitalists who earlier expressed delight with P W Botha's reforms went even further. The Sanlam chairman had 'chastise[d] the government for its racial policies and constitutional plans', urging the Schlebusch Constitutional Commission to accept 'the inevitability of total racial equality'.[6] This was indeed heresy to those who still cherished the formulae of Afrikaner nationalism's heroic age. It also directly threatened the perceived material interests of a range of Afrikaner social groups long included in the post-1948 nationalist alliance.

The ideological content of the reaction against Botha's reforms from within the ranks of this alliance was well expressed by Treurnicht when he argued in 1978 that 'if petty apartheid is completely eliminated, grand apartheid becomes stupid, superfluous and unnecessary'.[7] The form this reaction took was to focus on the alleged 'abandonment' of apartheid and Afrikaner favouritism by Botha's NP. Yet underlying this reaction was a concern with the shift in the class content of NP policies, and more particularly that the small farmer, the state bureaucrat and the Afrikaner worker were being pushed aside.[8]

The modifications to the influx control systems and the recognition of black trade unions were seen as threatening the structure of cheap agricultural labour on which smaller rural capitalists had so long depended. Maize farmers were particularly hard hit by what they saw as low official prices for their produce, rising labour costs and high costs of fertilisers and agricultural machinery induced by government policies. Despite the severe drought which ravaged South Africa between 1981 and 1983, the Botha government responded sluggishly to the demands of these farmers. NP agricultural policy had long favoured larger, more efficient farmers (above p. 77). By the 1980s, many maize farmers believed that the Botha government was far more responsvie to the needs of Cape and Natal export farmers than to those of Transvaal and Free State food producers. This issue had long simmered away behind many internal NP battles, and lay behind the formation of SAMPI in 1966.[9] SAMPI had represented the numerous smaller maize farmers and was widely regarded as 'an HNP-leaning body'.[10] In 1980, it merged with the body which represented the larger maize farmers, the South African Maize Specialists Organisation, to form the National Maize Producers' Organisation (NAMPO). In early 1983, Prime Minister Botha engaged in a slanging match in his office with NAMPO delegates, and the organisation 'has since stood out as a voice of the right'.[11] In sharp contrast to this perceived refusal to respond to the demands of maize producers, the Botha government seemed to fall over itself to extend favourable treatment to the large Western Cape wine farmers – themselves long a key support base of the Cape NP, and closely allied to the Sanlam and Rembrandt financial interests.* This produced strong support for the KP in maize-producing areas of the Transvaal and Orange Free State.

Negative fallout from the Botha reforms was also felt at many levels of the apartheid bureaucracy. The real earnings of whites in the public sector had declined sharply after 1974. One survey points to an average decline of 23 percent in real earnings in the public sector between 1979 and 1981.[12] When coupled with the programme to cut employment levels in the state bureaucracy, this no doubt precipitated fears among the lower ranks of this long-cosseted category that further reform would erode their carefully carved-out niche of privilege and power – one which traditionally rested on firm apartheid measures and large public sector employment. The far right parties clearly sought to

---

* Twelve of Botha's 37 Cape MPs were themselves wine farmers. Contrary to the recommendations of its own Monopoly Commission, the government approved the creation of the Cape Wine Distillers marketing monopoly in which Rembrandt soon emerged as a dominant force – although one of the stated objectives of the formation of Cape Wine Distillers had been to end the marketing war between the two liquor monopolies, Rembrandt and South African Breweries.

capitalise on discontent in the lower and middle ranks of the civil service. In a 1982 by-election the KP won a respectable 20 percent of the vote in the Waterkloof constituency, comprised heavily of bureaucrats and Defence Force officers.

Afrikaner labour had long been the most visibly restive group in the old nationalist alliance. Three months after Botha took office, white workers at the O'okiep mine went on strike to preseve job reservation. The government threw its support behind management against the (white) Mine Workers' Union (MWU), an historically unique rupture in the Afrikaner nationalist class alliance. The capture of the MWU by Afrikaner nationalists in 1947 had been a crucial moment in bringing the NP to power (p. 36 above). By the end of the 1970s, however, the union openly opposed the NP government, and now sought to coordinate all sections of white labour in a war against the Total Strategy reforms. The so-called Wiehahn reforms introduced by Labour Minister Fanie Botha effectively drove most strata of organised Afrikaner workers into strident opposition. Led by the MWU, the (largely Afrikaner) South African Confederation of Labour vigorously denounced the abolition of job reservation in the manufacturing sector (though not yet mining) and the recognition of black trade unions under the Industrial Conciliation Act. In the 1981 general election the MWU all but publicly aligned itself with the HNP. Its general secretary, Arrie Paulus, addressed a number of HNP rallies to 'put the workers' point of view'.

The HNP had been founded in 1969 on the conviction that the mainstream of the NP had sold out to 'Hoggenheimer' – now both Afrikaans- and English-speaking. From the outset, HNP strategy rested on the conviction that the inevitably declining material position of small farmers, lower-level civil servants and particularly Afrikaner workers would eventually bring these groups to support the HNP version of Afrikaner populism. The party clung to its mantra that this process would one day secure it a mass base among these three Afrikaner class forces, and so bring it to power.[13] Its faith seemed confirmed by the expulsion of the Treurnichtites from the NP. Yet the formation and political orientation of the KP again threatened to deny the HNP the mass support it sensed it had been on the verge of capturing after the 1981 elections.

This history and the policy differences between the KP and HNP led to much public bickering, and precluded anything but grudging and pragmatic cooperation. While both parties appealed essentially to the same social forces – Afrikaner farmers, workers and lower-level civil servants – the very different ways in which they cast their message made full-scale cooperation between them almost impossible.

Unashamedly and exclusively an *Afrikaner* party whose programme insisted that Afrikaans should be the sole official language, the HNP personified the anti-monopoly and anti-English strand of labour-oriented Afrikaner nationalism. To the extent that it sought to mould a nationalist class alliance, the HNP did so based primarily on Afrikaner labour, acting as a kind of 'poorer white' protest party. Pottinger well captures the embarrassed memories the party evoked even in many conservative middle-class Afrikaners:

> [T]he HNP people were so *gauche*. Apart from a few suspect academics, they counted among their followers figures from the sort of past most Afrikaners had spent two generations trying to flee – grease-stained semi-mechanics, *bywoner*-class farmers [rural squatters], grey lowest level public servants, those unable to make it even quarter-way in a world singularly crafted to white specifications.[14]

The HNP vigorously denounced Afrikaner monopolies such as Sanlam, lumping them together with Anglo American as part of the 'Hoggenheimer' enemies of the 'real' *volk*. The new Afrikaner urban managers and technocrats had sold their ascetic Calvinist cultural heritage for a mess of capitalist pottage, to become culturally indistinguishable from their 'English' golfing and yachting partners at exclusive clubs and casinos. As a protest party of the Afrikaner 'small man', the HNP was not overly concerned with the continued economic expansion and overall prosperity. Indeed, its 1969 programme advocated *limiting* economic growth to a rate governed primarily by the availability of skilled white labour, and never training black workers to take up the shortfall.

Some individuals in the CP might privately have supported such an austere Afrikaner populism.* Yet this was clearly not what was termed 'practical politics' in white South Africa. More fundamentally, its austere Calvinist vision of the future fundamentally misunderstood the lesson Albert Hertzog himself had been forced to learn in mobilising Afrikaner workers in the 1930s and 1940s: preaching at people was not the best way to win their support – catering to their material interests was far more effective. Small capitalist farmers usually aspired to be large capitalist farmers, not the culturally and ideologically pure but permanently poor *Boere* the HNP venerated. They were more concerned with freeing themselves from indebtedness than escaping the clutches of 'cosmopolitan' culture. Ditto for Afrikaner civil servants and workers, who were far more interested in their pay cheques than 'their' culture. They feared Botha's reforms not because they minded him cooperating with 'the English', but because this cooperation was likely to threaten their protected niche of privilege and power.

The KP on the other hand made no such mistakes. Its leadership was not drawn from the same rabid anti-monopoly Afrikaner labour traditions which sustained the HNP. Rather, the KP's emerging political culture owed more to the openly petty-bourgeois strand of Transvaal Afrikaner nationalism, now equally uneasy with the rabid anti-capitalist rhetoric of the HNP as with the new

---

* For example, Dr C J Jooste, editor of the KP newspaper, *Die Patriot*. As the longstanding director of the verkrampte South African Bureau of Racial Affairs (SABRA) – also headed by Broederbond chairman, Carel Boshoff – Jooste had authored a 'project Orange' for an exclusively 'white homeland' in a part of South Africa from which blacks (and their labour) would be permanently excluded. See Davies *et al.*, *Struggle for South Africa*, vol. 1, p. 277.

rampart free-marketeerism of P W Botha's NP. Unlike the increasingly marginalised potential Afrikaner lumpens cultivated by the HNP, the KP represented instead the more conservative middle groups of Afrikaner rural and urban communities. These people rejected the Verwoerdian 'better poor and pure' message of the HNP, aspiring instead to have their cake and eat it – to be both rich and pure. They were unable to recognise what P W Botha now saw so clearly – it was now one or the other.

Equally importantly, Treurnicht's party did not seek to mobilise an exclusively Afrikaner support base. Though staking proud claim to what it saw as 'real' tradition of Afrikaner nationalism – and indeed even invoking the Christian-nationalism of the 1940s and 1950s – Treurnicht's party sought to mobilise all right-wing forces in the white population, whether Afrikaners or not. The KP recognised that alienation with Botha's reforms was not confined to the petty bourgeois and labour strata among Afrikaners, but was also felt by many other lower-income whites. It assiduously cultivated those groups, particularly in immigrant communities. Former white Rhodesians, for example, provided a right-wing base in 'English' cities like Durban which the fervent Afrikaner exclusivism of the HNP could never hope to reach.

All of these factors made anything other than ad hoc and grudging cooperation between the two verkrampte parties very difficult, though negotiations between them continued intermittently. Nevertheless the far right made important electoral and other gains following the 1982 NP split. Almost a quarter of Transvaal NP district and branch committee members defected to the KP. By-election swings to the right in working-class and farming constituencies ranged from 10 to 27 percent.[15] The combined vote for the KP and HNP exceeded that of the NP in a number of by-elections – though their divided vote allowed NP candidates in through the back door. In others, the KP held on to seats it gained in the NP split and substantially increased the right-wing vote. Given its base in parliament, Treurnicht's party quickly emerged as by far the stronger of the two verkrampte parties. A month after the KP's formation, a poll put its support among the white electorate at 18,3 percent, while that for the HNP dwindled from 6 percent in January 1982 to 2,7 percent in April.[16] This simply accentuated *Herstigte* resentment, further compounded when Marais accused the KP of approaching senior *Herstigtes* to defect.

Yet despite its steady gains, extensive support for the far right appeared confined to poorer rural and urban constituencies. The NP's parliamentary majority was not remotely threatened until the very different political era of 1989 (see Chapter 20 below). In the November 1983 referendum over the 'new constitutional dispensation', the liberal and far right opposition to the NP's plan could muster only a third of all votes between them. As this was the fundamental issue over which the Treurnichtites split from the NP, it seemed to indicate something of the limits to KP electoral support.*

---

* Even in the 1992 whites-only referendum called to give F W de Klerk a mandate to negotiate a non-racial constitution, the verkramptes were not able to capture more than 32% of the vote.

Nobody for *volkspele*:
The end of the organised Afrikaner nationalism movement

The 1982 NP split forever destroyed Afrikaner political unity. It was the culminating moment of the process begun after shattering in the 1960s of the myth of the classless *volk* united by a common ethnic project. As suggested in Chapter 8, John Vorster had briefly succeeded in creating a new glue for the NP – that of pluralist patronage. But this too decomposed under the demands of the crises of the 1970s. In many respects Muldergate represented a virtual putsch, as the military, together with Afrikaner business, northern verligtes and the Cape NP seized control of the NP to force through a programme of reform. For three uneasy years, the verkramptes had tried to manoeuvre within the new regime. But the pluralist moment was over. The expanded NP centre could not hold. Such were the imperatives of the crisis that when Botha was finally obliged to choose between Afrikaner unity and the imperatives of capitalist stabilty, he opted for the latter – risking the dreaded charge of *volkskeurder* rather than maintain the now untenable system of Afrikaner pluralist patronage.

The effective expulsion of the Treurnichtites was the end of the road for *volkseenheid*. No longer would it be possible to follow Dr Malan's classic injunction to 'Bring together those who belong together by inner conviction!' Nobody could continue the pretence that verligtes and verkramptes still belonged together – their political convictions, policy prescriptions and interests of their respective social bases were all now mutually incompatible. The departure of the Treurnichtites from the NP decisively shattered what remained of the social, political and electoral alliance which had sustained Afrikaner nationalism since 1948.

It led to similar rifts in all the other nationalist organisations. Given the central role of the Afrikaner Broederbond in first moulding and always sustaining the Afrikaner nationalist alliance since the 1940s, the first fallout of the NP split was felt in the AB. Its Treurnichtite chairman, Professor Carel Boshoff, sought to use the Broederbond to rally opposition to the NP's proposed new Constitution for South Africa. However the Bond's executive committee approved the NP plans in 1983, and Boshoff resigned as chairman, to be succeeded by the verligte Professor J de Lange – himself author of a report on educational reform judged too far-reaching by the Botha government. Treurnicht also resigned from the Broederbond in early 1983, claiming that it was being used as an NP front and had betrayed its principles.

These two former AB chairmen, Treurnicht and Boshoff, then became the prime movers in the establishment of a new 'Afrikaner cultural front' in opposition to the Broederbond. Their *Afrikaner Volkswag* (Afrikaner national guard – AV) was launched in May 1984 amid great verkrampte fanfare – and derision in the mainstream Afrikaans press. All far right groups were prominently represented at the AV's founding congress, together with a number of former NP Cabinet ministers and other prominent Broederbond members.

Not a secret society like the AB, the AV sought instead to mobilise all Afrikaners for the verkrampte vision of Afrikaner nationalism. It clearly expected that substantial numbers of Broederbonders would eventually switch allegiance to the AV. Here again, the two intellectual founders of the AV allowed fantasy to cloud their understanding of the real mechanics which had made the Broederbond such a powerful machine – its formidable network of patronage. For fifty years, Broederbond membership conferred ready access to economic, political and social inner circles and virtually guaranteed a successful career. It had taken the AB nearly twenty years to construct the great influence it finally achieved from the 1940s onwards. Without similar networks of patronage the *Volkswag* stood not a chance of displacing it.

The split in the Broederbond was mirrored in other important organisations of Afrikaner nationalism. Not even the sacrosanct domain of the three Dutch Reformed churches escaped these divisive effects. Surveys by Afrikaans newspapers suggested that more members of the *Gereformeerde Kerk* supported the KP than the NP (45:37), while party support among the *Nederduitsch Hervormede Kerk* was evenly divided between the KP and NP (40:40). Among members of the largest of the mainstream Afrikaner churches – the *Nederduitse Gereformeerde Kerk* (NGK), sometimes referred to as the National Party at prayer – support for the KP stood at 31 percent in the Transvaal, but only 15 percent in the three other provinces. This compares with corresponding NGK support for the NP at 55 percent in the Transvaal, and 68 percent in the other provinces.[17]

The medium-term impact of the split fell hardest on the NGK, as the church slowly began to question its rigid segregationist dogma and politics under the impact of the Botha reforms. Conflict over this issue simmered on within the NGK over the next few years. In November 1986, verkrampte dissidents finally moved into open rebellion against the 'liberal onslaught' supposedly pushing the NGK in a direction through in which 'the uniqueness of the Afrikaner nation can be destroyed'. Most of the dissidents then left the NGK in June 1987, to form the *Afrikaanse Protestantse Kerk* (Afrikaner Protestant Church – APK). A smaller group of dissidents organised themselves into a *Nederduitsch Gereformeerde Bond* (Dutch Reformed League) within the NGK to oppose the 'liberal' direction taken by the church. Former AB chairman Carel Boshoff was elected vice-chairman of this group.[18]

The aftermath of the formation of the KP included early indications that the giant Transvaal-based press group, Perskor, might support Treurnicht's party. This speculation rested largely on the increasing animosity to P W Botha of Perskor managing director, Marius Jooste. While there clearly were verkramptes on the Perskor board, the hostility to the Botha line grew mainly out of an economically rooted territorial pique. On Botha's accession to power, the Perskor group had lost to the Cape-based Nasionale Pers group a number of exceedingly lucrative state printing contracts it had held since the 1960s. Moreover, replaying the great Afrikaner press war of the mid-to-late-1960s, an intense circulation battle between the Perskor and Nasionale Pers Transvaal morning dailies – *Die Transvaler* and *Beeld* respectively – was clearly being won by the latter. To shore up its position in this war of giants, Perskor had given false circulation figures to the Audit Circulation Bureau – thereby acquiring greater advertising revenue than its real circulation levels merited. When this practice came to light, Nasionale Pers instituted a multi-million Rand civil suit against the Transvaal group. As Cape leader, and former Nasionale Pers director, P W Botha was seen by many key Perskor figures to be allied with his Cape colleagues.*

In this renewed North/South press war, those hostile to Botha were not necessarily Treurnichtites. Yet Perskor managing director Jooste's September 1982 dismissal of the arch-verligte editor of *Die Transvaler*, Willem de Klerk, was widely interpreted as a precursor of a declaration of support for the KP. This would clearly have been opposed by the chairman of the Perskor controlling group, former Transvaal NP leader Ben Schoeman. Despite Schoeman's once-intense antipathy to P W Botha, the gruff *Oom Ben* had now thrown his full support behind the reforms, publicly warning ex-Prime Minister Vorster that should the latter continue his public criticism of Botha, Schoeman would start telling tales that Vorster would not like made public. In the event, however, Jooste conveniently died at the height of this speculation at the end of 1982, and Perskor was forced to withdraw *Die Transvaler* from the morning daily market in return for Nasionale Pers dropping its suit for damages.[19]

The protracted 'North/South' press war was an important mirror of the collapse of the ideological unity of Afrikaner nationalism. This ruthless struggle for dominance between the official presses of the Cape and Transvaal NPs likewise made a mockery of any notion of *volkseenheid*. Yet again sheer naked profit was the driving force pitting north against south. The same was true of the nasty public fight which erupted between Sanlam and Anton Rupert's Rembrandt Corporation in the second half of 1982. Rupert had been a crucial silent partner supporting the 1975 contested takeover of the ailing Union Corporation by Sanlam's mining subsidiary, General Mining. By the early 1980s, the tobacco merchant set his eyes on a move into mining – allying himself with the northern-based, Broederbond-controlled Volkskas bank in an unsuccessful bid to wrest control of General Mining from his former ally, Sanlam. His eventual failure led him into a intemperate public attack, in 'the English press' no less, on Sanlam's business practices.[20]

All of this reflected the more profound collapse of the class alliance on which Afrikaner nationalism had been built since 1948. The decisive split in its two most basic institutions – the National Party and the Broederbond – together with the now deep soul-searching in the Afrikaner churches – finally shattered the

---

* Recalling the observation by the Perskor chairman, former Transvaal NP leader Ben Schoeman, that Botha was nothing more than the 'simple mouthpiece' of Nasionale Pers – (Beaumont) Schoeman, *Vorster se 1000 Dae*, 246.

entire nationalist edifice so carefully erected in the 1940s. Neither the KP nor HNP was remotely capable of rebuilding it. Their failure was a measure of the success of the post-1948 NP project in transforming the social composition of the Afrikaans-speaking white population. This transformation in turn rendered impossible the remoulding of the political unity of all Afrikaans-speakers. The large, self-confident class of Afrikaner capitalists brought into being through NP policies was not likely to abandon either its economic power or its now affluent, materialistic lifestyle for mystic appeals to the unity of the *volk*. Like their English-speaking compatriots, Afrikaner businessmen and managers were now exclusively concerned with the economic bottom line – an element radically absent in both the KP and *Herstigte* appeals to the departed Afrikaner past.

Thus, while the KP was to crystallise substantial support for its verkrampte politics, and while it was able to win considerable ·backing in local-level political battles, sheer demographic and sociological realities doomed it at best to be medium-sized parliamentary opposition party. By the early 1980s a parliamentary majority for the far right was as probable as the HNP persuading the directors of Sanlam to return to the *trek verder* (trek further) politics of the 1930s. Treurnicht sounded the last hurrah. Even while he was fighting his rearguard action against Total Strategy reforms, his opponent, General Pieter Willem Botha, was himself obliged to wheel his forces to face a far more formidable foe on its left. And while Treurnicht departed to defend the abandoned ramparts of the nationalist past, the Total Strategy was being confronted with a deadly struggle over the future of white South Africa and its racist privileges.

This is explored in Part IV.

PART IV

STUMBLING TOWARDS THE RUBICON

The terminal crisis of apartheid

nuwe alfabet

new alphabet

As jy A sê moet jy B sê
A is altyd teen apartheid
B is blind vir kleur

If you say A you must say B
A is always against apartheid
B is colour-blind

ek wil jou skryf broer maar jy's verder
as die vorige eeu as 'n stamland
as gedig of dokument

I want to write you brother but you're further
than the last century than a motherland
than a poem or document

As jy A sê moet jy B sê
A is altyd teen apartheid
B is blind vir kleur

If you say A you must say B
A is always against apartheid
B is colour-blind

soveel gidse laat my in die steek
van soveel kante probeer ek by benadering
jou benader – hoe meer klede ek afgooi
hoe kouer rondom my hoe verder blyk jy te wees

so many guides leave me in the lurch
from so many sides I more or less try
to approach you – the more garments I cast off
how colder around me how further you seem to be

As jy A sê moet jy B sê
A is altyd teen apartheid
B is blind vir kleur

If you say A you must say B
A is always against apartheid
B is colour-blind

my oë kom nie uitgekyk aan doringbome dommelend
tussen rooigras en kiewiete my breidun bene
my tuin gevlek met vragte rose – net vir my kinders
lê ek my lewe neer

My eyes can't get enough of these drowsy thorn trees
between red-grass and plovers my thread-thin legs
my garden smudged with roses – only for my
     children lay I down my life

hier leer ek skryf – ek kan nie anders nie

here I learn to write – I cannot do otherwise

Antjie Krog, *Lady Anne*, Taurus, Johannesburg, 1989. Reproduced by permission of Antjie Krog.

Chapter Seventeen

NINETEEN EIGHTY-FOUR

The Total Strategy unravels

P W Botha declines to discuss the State of Emergency with Bishop Tutu

Reviewing economic prospects for 1983, the Johannesburg *Financial Mail* was not overly sanguine. The spectacular domestic boom of 1980–81 had been sliced off at the knees by the end of the US hostage drama in Iran. As international speculative fever abated, the domestic growth rate plummeted in tandem with the falling gold price. The economy was in a 'winter trough'. Yet, seemingly unaware of George Orwell, the *Financial Mail* reassured its readers that it was 'the broad consensus of most local economists' that 1984 would see a 'marked upswing in the SA economy'.[1]

Still, such unlettered optimism did seem justified in the last months of 1983 and first eight months of 1984. Now freed of the shackles of the Treurnichtites, the Botha government pressed ahead with its constitutional plans, racking up a string of ever more spectacular successes. The new constitutional dispensation won an enthusiastic reception from National Party Congresses. A propaganda blitz and series of high-powered speaking tours halted the drastic decline in NP popularity which had followed the February 1982 departure of 'Dr No' Treurnicht. By May 1983, polls revealed that the NP had regained its 56 percent popularity level of the April 1981 election (up from 47 percent in April 1982).[2] The November 1983 white referendum on the NP's constitutional proposals was a personal triumph for Prime Minister Botha. The plans won the enthusiastic endorsement of almost all sections of the white establishment bar a now isolated PFP. Despite the combined opposition of the parliamentary parties to the NP's right and to its left, two-thirds of the white electorate approved the new constitution and the tricameral parliament. P W Botha described this victory as his 'greatest moment'.[3]

It was soon eclipsed by even more remarkable victory. Premier Botha stunned most observers in March 1984 by concluding a Non-Aggression Pact with Samora Machel, President of Marxist-Leninist Mozambique. In his address at the signing ceremony Botha pointedly referred to his ongoing vision of 'a veritable constellation of states of Southern Africa'.[4] The 'miracle' of Nkomati received rapturous reviews from South Africa's business community. In the words of the Assocom chief executive:

> Most businessmen today – in the aftermath of the Nkomati Accord with Mozambique. new arrangements with Swaziland, conciliatory remarks by President Kaunda of Zambia, and peace moves in South West Africa (Namibia) – stand closer to the Prime Minister's goal than ever before. Businessmen have an enormous stake in the success or otherwise of recent developments in Southern Africa, especially Mozambique.[5]

Nkomati seemed to unlock the door to international acceptance so long barred to apartheid South Africa. Foreign Minister Pik Botha declared that 'the way to the world' lay 'through Africa'. Assocom gave 'top priority' to preparing a 'radical new master plan aimed at boosting two-way trade with black Africa', and to prove to African governments that 'free trade flows hold the key to economic growth'.[6] Such was the perceived scope of the triumph that various South African newspapers seriously discussed the possibility that one of the Bothas (P W or Pik) might win the 1984 Nobel Peace Prize.

There is some poetic justice to the fact that 1984 saw the culminating moments of the regional and domestic components of the Total Strategy – the Nkomati Accord in March, and inauguration of the tricameral parliament in September. The casual observer could be forgiven the conclusion that South Africa was indeed on the cusp of a new historic settlement – that P W Botha had truly succeeded in diverting the 'ghastly future' the furtive contemplation of which had so disturbed his predecessor.

Barely a year later, however, these triumphs had turned to ash. These two culminating events rapidly came to highlight the fatal flaws in, and absolute limits to, the Total Strategy. In doing so they precipitated its dramatic unravelling barely days after the inauguration of the tricameral parliament.

The fallacy of (total) strategy (i): Reform and the realm of the possible

P W Botha had come to the Premiership in 1978 as a result of a *putsch* by reformist elements in the NP. Inspired by General Beaufre, his Total Strategy project sought to both to sustain the position of the existing power bloc and regenerate conditions for renewed economic growth.

In terms of Beaufre's conception of politics, the key to success of such a strategy lay in *legitimising the new political arrangements*. This was possible, the general insisted *ad nauseam*, only through *compromise* with the revolutionaries – by taking on board the central aspects of their programme in such a way which both preserved the position of the stakeholders in the existing system and drew the teeth of the revolutionary demand for social transformation. Successful counter-revolutionary strategy thus demanded change, not for its own sake, but change predicated on a correct reading of the realm of the possible:

> T]he total strategy of action can only function effectively if it stems from a *political analysis* which allows it to diagnose the character and significance of the events in which it intends to intervene ... to identify the major evolving trends, to take the best possible measure of the strength of the currents which it will need to exploit or combat.[7]

Continuing Beaufre's medical metaphor, effective treatment was possible only if the ailment was correctly diagnosed. Here lay the central failure of Pretoria's version of Total Strategy. Botha and his generals had all read Beaufre, and quoted him endlessly. But they failed to understand him. Or perhaps their own deeply ingrained racism blinded them to the fact that it was not enough to *reform* apartheid: the minimal compromise which would have 'undercut the demands [of the revolutionaries]' required *scrapping* apartheid.[8]

For three-quarters of South Africa's population Botha's trumpeted reforms changed almost nothing. The regime had no plan to give the majority of South

Africa's population the vote, to scrap the racial classification of every inhabitant at birth, to end the racial division of the land. After six years of reform, all Africans were still subject to regular pass raids and 'endorsement out' of the so-called 'white' areas if they did not have the right stamp in their *dompas* – now renamed a 'passport' or 'citizenship document'. Literally hundreds of thousands of Africans were still convicted under the pass laws every year. *Piet Pompies* Koornhof's 'humane' policy of forced removals still dumped tens of thousands of them to 'adapt or die' in the arid bantustans. The neo-apartheid Total Strategy still denied Africans all political rights in the land of their forefathers. Blacks were still stripped of their South African citizenship by white administrative *fiat*. African workers went on queuing at the pass offices and labour bureaux. They still sweated in the mines by day, were cooped up in the compounds by night. The millions of jobless continued to rot in the bantustans. Black South Africans could be forgiven for wondering what, if anything, had changed under the Total Strategy. General Beaufre might have asked exactly the same question.

Indeed the fundamentals of this system had been reinforced by Botha's reforms. The Riekert recommendations made the influx control system far stricter, and sharply increased penalties for its infringement. While business leaders continued to agitate for the 'full' enforcement of the Riekert recommendations on labour mobility, little or nothing was said about the plight of the millions of 'outsiders' whom the report insisted should be firmly barricaded in the bantustans.

The Total Strategy reforms also led to an *intensification* of political repression. Strengthened security legislation sanctioned an even more ruthless and cynical level of violence against the regime's opponents. The profound militarisation of the state extended the SADF's control over virtually every facet of daily life. All that had changed here was that a better-organised and better-equipped repressive machinery emerged, based on a more powerful and coherent strategy and more efficient structures for apartheid's defence against the majority of the population.

This meant that the sudden concern with the 'quality of life' of a small section of the oppressed black population, the recognition of black trade unions, the petty concessions to the black middle class, the 'new constitutional dispensation', the 'Non-Aggression Pacts' extorted from neighbouring states, did *not* signify the collapse of apartheid. Rather, this first phase of reform sought to *modernise* apartheid rather than abolish it.

Yet while at one level the Total Strategy reforms indeed seemed to consolidate rather than change the apartheid status quo, they nevertheless *did* alter South African politics in a number of ways which worked against the existing stakeholders.[9]

Perhaps most significant in the long term was the fact that the apartheid regime was driven on to the moral defensive. The crises of the 1970s obliged the NP government to jettison its overt ideology of racism. The Total Strategy finally conceded that white supremacy was neither part of the natural order nor some Divine plan. While racism remained the base of state policy, the regime now conceded that this was in some sense both wrong and should be changed. This was a crucial retreat from the 'moral' foundations of Grand Apartheid which Verwoerd had worked so hard to lay. His 'walls of granite' were finally breached in the process.

In effect, then, the Botha regime admitted that there existed no moral nor ethical basis for its own rule. The SADF generals' recipe for 'victory' – 80 percent political, 20 percent military – was an implicit recognition that unless the regime could somehow legitimise the existing order, it was doomed to failure: that the highest and thickest 'wall of granite' could not defend it. Through the Total Strategy the apartheid regime effectively conceded the moral, ideological and cultural initiative. It sought to replace its abandoned ideology with a technocratic modernising discourse. This would work only should it be able to live up to its own ideological claims and deliver social stability and general prosperity while it slowly did away with the petty inequities of the past. By clinging to its modernised version of neo-apartheid, the Botha government held on to a policy which its own expressed ideology now clearly labelled as illegitimate. Here was the central contradiction of all its reformist pretensions – because it refused to abandon the central elements of Grand Apartheid theory, it could not legitimate its own reforms. Because its analysis failed to grasp that the central problem was the theory and practice of apartheid itself, its solutions were doomed to failure.

This was made even more certain by two of the central changes introduced by the reforms. Firstly, the attempt to incorporate black trade unions into an institutionalised and tightly controlled industrial bargaining system simply placed on the political stage a new and powerful actor. The Wiehahn reforms gave black trade unions the space they needed to grow and the legal protection to flex their muscles. Far from acting to consolidate the system, this radically strengthened the force of black resistance to neo-apartheid.

Secondly, the entire thrust of neo-apartheid rested on what Mike Morris aptly terms the move from 'class compression' to 'class differentiation' in black communities.[10] Verwoerdian apartheid had cast all blacks into the same ethnic boat and suppressed the mechanism of social differentiation and mobility 'normal' to capitalist society. Under pressure from the Urban Foundation and other business groups, the Botha government now relaxed *some* of the restrictions on the black middle class, allowing it a measure of social mobility. In Dr Verwoerd's terminology, the government had been obliged to lead the new black petty bourgeoisie to the 'green pastures' of white middle-class privilege. But it only permitted this new elite to look on rather than to graze there. By refusing to permit this social group to take its place with its (white) class confreres, the Total Strategy reforms in effect compounded its discontent and intensified its determination to remove the remaining barriers to full participation (particularly in political life).

Ungovernability: The black reaction to reform

Following the 1981 collapse of the gold price, the dogmatic monetarist policies of the Reserve Bank and Finance Ministry simply aggravated the impact on South Africa of the renewed international recession. The economic growth rate fell from 8 percent in 1980, to 4,5 percent in 1981 and then less than 1 percent in 1982.[11] The mild recovery of 1983 could not be sustained. In a terrible blunder of monetarist dogma the Reserve Bank had lifted some exchange controls in 1983, immediately prompting the four biggest British investors to withdraw their capital from South Africa.* An austerity budget in 1984 led to record interest rates, a sharp economic contraction and a growing exodus of foreign capital.

Just as the struggle in the NP seemed to have been resolved in the reformists' favour, the Botha government was confronted with a severe recession. This undermined its ability to cushion the impact of its reforms on disaffected whites. It also shattered some of the assumptions underlying Total Strategy. The recession provoked sharp wage struggles by a burgeoning trade union movement given wider legal and bargaining rights by the reforms. These in turn took on an increasingly open political hue.

The Riekert 'insider/outsider' strategy likewise provoked strong resistance from mushrooming squatter communities and an explosion of local struggles around housing, transport, education and other community issues after 1980. Often linked to trade union issues, the emerging local linkages and organisation provided the base for an attempt to generate a national political movement.

The striptease by which the regime elaborated its 'new political dispensation' also had the opposite to its intended effect. The blatant determination to retain effective power in white hands enraged rather than mollified middle-class blacks. The 99-year leasehold and other schemes to improve their 'quality of life' simply reinforced the point the regime would never allow blacks to enjoy a normal middle-class lifestyle. While the real thrust of the mounting opposition came from trade unions and the largely working-class community organisations, smouldering black middle-class anger fed into the renewed *political* groundswell which crystallised with the formation of the United Democratic Front (UDF) to oppose the 'insider/outsider' legislation of 1983.[12]

A growing sense that the political initiative lay with the resistance was reinforced by the ANC's escalating armed actions. Many ANC attacks were explicitly linked to community struggles – bolstering a sense of local power. Spectacular operations (such as the rocket attack on military headquarters in Voortrekkerhoogte and the disabling of the Koeberg nuclear plant) seemed designed to demonstrate the ANC's ability to strike anywhere. This armed

---

* And reimbursing them in foreign currency to the tune of over a half-a-billion Rand. See 'Background on Recent Disinvestments by Foreign Capital from South Africa', *Southern Africa Dossier,* 23.40 (E), Eduardo Mondlane University, Maputo, July 1983.

propaganda had a dramatic impact on black political morale, strengthening a belief that 'the Boers' were vulnerable, and could be shaken by organised political action.

The Nkomati Accord and the inauguration of the tricameral parliament first accentuated this politicisation and then ignited a full-scale uprising. Nkomati brought home the political truth that black South Africans would have to rely on themselves to end apartheid – that an externally based guerrilla army was not going to march into Pretoria to liberate them. In doing so, Nkomati gave some impetus to the resistance. It also soon obvious that Pretoria was simply not implementing its undertaking to end the destabilisation of Mozambique. When Foreign Minister Botha was forced to acknowledge that the SADF had violated the Accord (see below), this simply reinforced the widespread belief that 'you can't trust the Boers'.

But the real turning point came with the process leading to the inauguration of new constitution. The elections for the Black Local Authorities (BLAs) and then the Coloured and Indian Houses of Parliament galvanised an organised boycott. Less than 20 percent of registered voters appeared at the polling stations. The laborious attempts to legitimise reformed apartheid through 'consociational democracy' culminated with the new 'power sharing' dispensation regarded as even less legitimate, even more of an insult to politicised blacks, than the pure white parliament it had replaced. If the 1976 Soweto uprising had sharpened the perennial illegitimacy of the apartheid state into a crisis of hegemony, the very attempt to address this issue via the 'new dispensation' provoked a full-blown crisis of physical control over the black population.

Discontinuous transition: The state and the urban uprising

Barely weeks after the inauguration of the tricameral parliament, the new Lekoa BLA raised rents to generate revenue. This ignited a violent demonstration in the Sharpeville township which soon spread to other areas of the Witwatersrand. The army moved into black townships for the first time since the 1960s, provoking South Africa's then biggest political strike in mid-November 1984.[13] This strike transformed a local black school boycott into a national affair under the slogan 'Liberation now, education later'. The government detained the strike organisers together with the leadership of the two democratic trade union federations.

And so the uprising began. In January 1985 the ANC called on black South Africans to make the country 'ungovernable', and the resistance spread across the country. By the end of 1985, 155 townships were affected. A limited State of Emergency was declared in July, covering broad regions of the country. The main target of the uprising was the black local councillors, police and informers, all seen as agents of apartheid. Twelve councillors were killed, the homes of more than 300 were damaged and 240 resigned their posts. The BLA system set up the year before virtually ceased to exist. Black policemen had to be housed in white areas, and the state's administrative control of the black areas was destroyed.[14] The summary and horrible execution of suspected informers by firing a gasoline-doused tyre around their necks, soon shut down the police intelligence network into black politics. Emerging 'street committees' and 'people's courts' began to provide an embryonic form of alternative – often very harsh – local administration, hailed by the ANC as the first step in the establishment of 'dual power'.[15]

The uprising caught the Botha regime with its strategic pants down. The installation of 'elected' Black Local Authorities and inauguration of the tricameral parliament were supposed to have bought substantial time for Heunis's Department of Constitutional Development and Planning to work out the thorny issue of how to deal with the African majority. Nothing else was on offer, no long-term vision of how to proceed beyond the 'power-sharing' arrangements of 1984 had yet been elaborated. Yet instead of defusing black anger, the new constitutional dispensation provoked a seemingly uncontrollable black uprising, and forced the government immediately to respond to the clear political demand to end apartheid. As 1985 progressed, tension grew sharper within the NP between those who saw the tricameral parliament as positively the white man's last concession, and those who were beginning to see it as a stage on a long process of opening up the political system. Polled support for the NP which had been virtually steady at 56 percent between May 1983 and November 1984 declined again to 47 percent in April 1985.[16]

Ironically it was precisely the vociferous proponents of 'strategy' who themselves now lacked a strategy. Just like Botha's despised predecessor, they now responded with piecemeal measures – a mixture of extreme repression and ad hoc attempts to extend the reforms. More than 35 000 troops were used in black townships in 1985. Thousands of people were detained and nearly 2 000 blacks were killed in political violence. Still broadly based on Police Commissioner Coetzee's counter-insurgency strategy (see p. 266 above), domestic security policies combined large-scale detentions and restriction of known leaders and activists with intense efforts to exploit deep political tensions within the extra-parliamentary resistance. It was calculated that it would be easier to control a hobbled, but still legal, extra-parliamentary resistance than one forced underground, and that the outright banning of the democratic organisations would not only incur great international opprobium, but more importantly would destroy frail remaining hopes that the black middle class could still be won over to 'reform'.[17]

The overall policy thrust in 1985 seemed to confirm that legitimising the state through extending 'consociational democracy' down to provincial and local levels (or in apartheid jargon, 'tiers' of government) was still seen as the key to 'undercutting' the grievances of the 'revolutionaries'. In November 1984 Constitutional Affairs Minister Heunis reversed earlier policy and announced that BLAs would no longer be linked to the bantustan 'governments'. Now these councils would be included in the proposed Regional Service Councils – themselves designed to administer the provision of services to white and black communities. An early 1985 Cabinet reshuffle dissolved the remnants of the principal apartheid ministry – and until the 1980s, the greatest political fiefdom within the Cabinet – the Department of Cooperation and Development. To the already immense jurisdiction of Heunis's Department of Constitutional Development was now added control of virtually every aspect of the lives of black South Africans.

This confirmed Heunis as the *primus inter pares* in the Cabinet. It also signalled that the regime was being forced beyond the Grand Apartheid conception of territorial separation which still underlay the Riekert reforms of the Total Strategy. It now moved haltingly towards a new vision of white power secured through the racial control over white community interests (segregated social services, residential areas, etc.) and 'power-sharing' of major government functions (general affairs). In May 1985 an NP official pamphlet admitted that the bantustans had failed and that a different form of political incorporation of the black population would have to be found.[18] It was announced in December that South African citizenship would be restored to those blacks residing permanently in South Africa who had lost their citizenship with the 'independence' of four of the bantustans. The 1985 NP provincial congresses and the 1986 Federal Congress endorsed the principle that blacks were to be incorporated into 'all levels of decision-making up to the highest level'. This led to Botha's full-page newspaper advertisement proclaiming his government's commitment to 'the principle of a united South Africa, one citizenship, and a universal franchise'.[19] And tacitly admitting the failure of the new political dispensation, a 'National Council' would investigate a new constitutional framework. Following the President's Council Report on urbanisation, the state replaced yet another of the basic props of apartheid – the influx control system – with a policy of 'orderly urbanisation' in early 1986. The result was a veritable flood of black squatters to the cities, undoing all the minutely planned efforts to control urbanisation since 1948.

These tentative 1985 reforms ignored the fact that the destruction of most Black Local Authorities throughout the country had removed a central foundation on which the consociational mansion was supposed to be constructed. The hastily formulated plans for extending consociation simply emphasised the inherent design flaws and the fact that the architects no longer seemed to know what they intended to build.

Violating Huntington's prescriptions for successful reform from above, the regime fell into the trap of being seen to concede reform from a position of weakness. The NP reformists clearly hoped that their tentative 1985 forays out of the *laager* would be seen as the beginning of the end of apartheid by urban black professionals who would then turn on, and bring under their control, the steely-eyed children whose bricks, Molotov cocktails and necklaces threatened the state's control of the townships. Yet far from appeasing middle-class blacks, these reforms appeared to confirm yet again that the regime would never undo apartheid: that the best it could offer was crumbs from Botha's table. This made no sense when the uprising and the international reaction against the regime seemed to promise that the urban black elite might very well soon have the whole cake to itself. Far from calming black political tempers, these measures simply fuelled the deep rage through the black population.

The uprising and the growing international reaction against the regime pointed to the impossibility of reform by stealth. In the absence of the requisite political stability and 'order', Huntington's notion that the *process* of reform was more important than the final objective was simply untenable. South Africa's black majority had always insisted that it could not cooperate with Botha until it knew (and accepted) his real goals. But now Botha's business allies and conservative Western governments began to insist that the regime spell out its 'hidden agenda'.

Take the money and run: Domestic and international capital

The post-Nkomati business euphoria rapidly gave way to a sense that 'on the political front ... the wheels have begun to fall off', as one influential businessman put it.[20] With the November 1984 Vaal stayaway seen to mark 'a new phase in the history of opposition against apartheid', Assocom, the FCI and AHI sent a joint telegram to the Minister of Law and Order warning that his detention of union leaders endangered 'a very delicate labour situation'.[21] This was followed by a surprisingly strong joint declaration handed by most employers' organisations to the visiting Senator Edward Kennedy, and calling for 'meaningful political participation for blacks', the end to forced removals and negotiation with legitimate black political leaders.*

The worst fears of business were realised in 1985. The insurrection spread rapidly, and the revolt took on radically anti-capitalist rhetoric. The banner of the banned South African Communist Party was raised at huge rallies. And in November 1985 a new, overtly political trade union federation was formed – the Congress of South African Trade Unions (Cosatu). Uniting most black trade unions in an explicitly socialist discourse, Cosatu also proclaimed its adherence to the broad liberation struggle led by the ANC.[22]

P W Botha's erstwhile business allies now seemed to begin to realise that the Total Strategy could never win the acquiescence of important strata of the black population. The government appeared to be losing control domestically, and had no strategy beyond futile ad hoc measures and repression. Moreover in September 1985 Pretoria was obliged to admit to 'technical' violations of the Nkomati Accord amounting to a virtual declaration of war against

---

* *Financial Mail,* 18 January 1985. This memorandum was signed by the AHI, Assocom, the Chamber of Mines, the FCI, Seifsa and Nafcoc.

Mozambique.* The two jewels set in the Total Strategy crown in 1984 – the new political dispensation and the Nkomati Accord – had proved to be cheap fakes. Their false glitter had sparked a vast uprising and discredited and further isolated South Africa.

Growing business disenchantment with Botha's leadership was matched by foreign investors and Western governments. *Business Week* estimated that the average return on foreign investment in South Africa dropped from 20 percent in 1980 to 5 percent just five years later. South Africa attracted almost no real new foreign investment in the early 1980s.† The relaxation of exchange controls in the euphoria of 1983 immediately precipitated the departure of the three largest non-banking foreign companies listed on the Johannesburg Stock Exchange. This involved a net disinvestment of some R604 million – a sum greater than the GDP of Swaziland. Between September 1984 and September 1985, 18 American companies pulled out or reduced holdings in South Africa, repatriating assets and profits totalling $493 million.[23]

When coupled with substantial current account deficits, this produced a net decline of foreign reserves of over R4,7 billion between 1981 and 1984, even despite inflow of some R5 billion borrowed abroad. Total foreign debt soared from US$16,9 billion at the end of 1980 to US$24,3 billion four years later. The ratio of external debt to GDP increased from 20,3 percent to 45,7 percent, and debt servicing payments doubled.‡ The structure of this debt made South Africa extremely vulnerable to pressure from its international creditors. Short-term loans rose from 19 percent of total foreign liabilities in 1980 to 42 percent by 1984. In July 1985 the Chase Manhattan Bank announced that it would not roll over short-term loans to South Africa maturing in August.

Clearly something had to be done to restore foreign confidence. Carefully planted leaks by Foreign Minister Botha created the firm expectation in Western and African capitals that President Botha would reveal his final blueprint for

---

* These included: building an airstrip inside Mozambique for Renamo; supplying it with new communications equipment ; maintaining regular radio contact between its headquarters and the SADF headquarters; regular SADF air drops of 'humanitarian' aid to Renamo camps in Mozambique; ferrying its commanders into and out of Mozambique by submarine; and a series of visits to Renamo headquarters in Mozambique by a South African junior minister while SA paratroopers 'secured' the area. See the report of the press conference given by Foreign Minister Pik Botha and Defence Minster Magnus Malan, *Financial Mail,* 27 September 1985.

† *Business Week,* 23 September 1985. While the total stock of foreign capital invested in South Africa rose from R12,3 billion in 1980 to R27,9 billion in 1985, this increase was almost entirely accounted for by the rapid depreciation of the Rand – which almost halved in value during this period – and reinvested profits. Unless otherwise noted, all data in this and following paragraphs are drawn from various issues of the South African Reserve Bank *Quarterly Bulletin.*

‡ Commonwealth Foreign Ministers Committee, *South Africa's Relationship with the International Financial System: Report of the Intergovermental Group,* London, 1988, 4. Measured in the rapidly depreciating South African Rand, external debt almost quadrupled from R12,6 billion to R48,2 billion in the period 1980–84.

reform. Foreign journalists were told by the Foreign Minister that the President would announce the release of Nelson Mandela and possible talks with the ANC in his 15 August address to the Natal NP Congress in Durban.[24]

These expectations were not fulfilled, however. The then South African ambassador to London later alleged that Transvaal NP leader F W de Klerk 'persuaded' Botha to change his planned speech, as the intended reforms would unsettle the upcoming Transvaal Congress – itself much more important than the outside world. De Klerk vigorously denied such claims, insisting that 'P W Botha himself had amended the text'.[25] A common story going the rounds at the time held that Botha had fully intended to make a reformist announcement, but had somehow got into an altercation with a black taxi-driver, and in a characteristic state of rage changed his mind on his way to deliver the speech. That such a tale was believed by many whites was an eloquent statement on the condition of their government and its leader.

Whatever the reasons, the notoriously thin-skinned President launched into the diatribe of a tempestuous lifetime. Claiming that his government had already crossed 'the Rubicon' of reform and found its own 'course of reasonableness', Botha's theme was 'we shall not abdicate'. His hectoring tone and truculent style incensed businessmen and foreign governments almost as much as his refusal to go beyond his discredited 'reforms'. Bitterly reviewing past support businessmen had given Botha, the *Financial Mail* concluded: 'for their pains, Botha has dashed their hopes and eroded their wealth'. Headlined 'Leave Now!', this exceptionally strong editorial declared Botha to be 'hopelessly out of his depth and [he] should forthwith go into a well-earned retirement'. This influential journal called for 'a government of national reconciliation which draws into it members from *all* sectors of society and all shades of opinion'. Its editorial was accompanied by a biting, and amusing, analysis by a psychiatrist of the 'non-verbal leakage' of Botha's body language, described as 'a portrait of a man at the end of his tether – saying one thing in words, while his body betrays insecurity and weakness'.[26]

Pretoria's appalled foreign creditors were even more pointed. All banks now joined Chase Manhattan's refusal to renew the $10 billion in short-term loans maturing at the end of August. South Africa was forced to suspend debt repayments and reinstitute exchange controls. The Rand lost fully one-third of its already declining value in the week following 'Rubicon', and net capital outflow in 1985 reached R10,5 billion. The disinvestment movement moved from the cramped offices of anti-apartheid organisations to boardrooms worldwide. By 1987 over 250 foreign companies had withdrawn from South Africa.[27] Conservative foreign governments now seriously considered real sanctions against South Africa.

Rubicon killed off unified business backing for Botha. This support had been based above all on the central Total Strategy premise that the crisis could be *managed*. Botha's new directions, his reliance on young generals and technocrats, his implementation of reform even at the cost of splitting the NP, had all engendered a comfortable sense that a new, open-minded managerial elite had replaced the blinkered ideologues who had run the NP for so long. However, Botha's bumbling, nervous defiance in the Rubicon speech, and his failure to announce a major reform thrust to take the initiative from the stone-throwing children in the townships finally buried any business belief in either his managerial competence or that he had any idea of what to do next.

Later claiming they had been 'deluded' into believing that Botha really intended to reform apartheid,[28] major English undertakings began to explore new positions and seek new alignments. A joint statement by Assocom, the FCI, Urban Foundation and National African Federated Chambers of Commerce (Nafcoc), called for the end to the State of Emergency, the release of Nelson Mandela and negotiations with the ANC.[29] Their call was echoed by the editor of the nationalist daily, *Die Vaderland*.[30] The month after 'Rubicon', a group of South Africa's most important anglophone business leaders flew to Lusaka to hold 'cordial' discussions with the ANC hosted by Zambian President Kenneth Kaunda.*

In November 1985, all major business groups (except SAAU) formed the Private Sector Council on Urbanisation. This sought to work out a new urbanisation policy to replace the pass laws and to 'forge an alliance for change with the business sector as the first and central building block'.[31] The FCI drew up a 'Business Charter and Action Programme' calling for legal equality, a universal franchise, freedom of association and movement, the right of management to manage, privatisation and deregulation of the economy, and an expansion of the scope and incentive for private entrepreneurship.[32]

Most Afrikaner businessmen were equally dismayed by 'Rubicon'. The Sanlam chairman reportedly denounced Botha for squandering a 'once in a lifetime opportunity' by sprouting 'clichés better used at a *Boere saamtrek*' (rural Afrikaner rally).[33] Acknowledging that relations with the NP government had 'reached a low point', the AHI president obliquely chided that 'political developments have not kept up with ... expectations'.[34] One of Afrikaner capital's heroic figures went so far as to declare apartheid to have been a 'disaster and tragedy' equal only to the Anglo-Boer War. Jan Marais now called on business leaders to 'press upon the government a programme of action for 1986 which would include political reform, economic deregulation, privatisation and massive tax cuts'.[35] He was soon echoed by the Sanlam chairman's denunciation of the 'ad hoc and uncoordinated' measures to date. In a jibe which must have hurt the proponents of Total Strategy, this most influential of all Afrikaner businessmen called on the government to spell out 'clear goals' in a 'longterm national strategy'.[36]

However, Afrikaner business as a whole was more circumspect in its public expression of disappointment with the 'Rubicon' paralysis. Most Afrikaner

---

* See various interviews, *Leadership South Africa*, 4, 3, 1985. Premier Milling CEO Tony Bloom was 'surprised and overwhelmed by the cordiality of the meeting. I sometimes worry that we got on a bit too well.'

businessmen still enjoyed close personal and political ties with the regime. Many were heavily dependent on government contracts, and few had extensive links with foreign undertakings. Clearly not yet prepared to contemplate the release of Nelson Mandela, nor talks with the ANC, Afrikaner businessmen joined in neither the 'leave now' clamour of the *Financial Mail* nor the trek to Lusaka.[37] Indeed, the international outcry and bankers' sanctions following Rubicon sparked something of a nationalist revival among Afrikaner business. The AHI organ, *Volkshandel*, assumed a defensive, close-ranks-against-the-foreigners tone long thought laid to rest.[38] Referring to the August Assocom/FCI/UF/ Nafcoc joint statement, the AHI bitingly declined to join 'in any form of pressure on the government designed to achieve specific goals'. Instead, it advised its members to have 'faith in the government's ability to handle the situation'.[39] In May 1986 the outgoing AHI president stressed the AHI's 'unconditional support' for Botha's 'reform measures'. Opening the AHI congress, former AHI president and chairman of Federale Volksbeleggings, C J F ('Kerneels') Human anticipated the strategy to come with a denunciation of 'soft options' and 'defeatism'. He called for a 'plan for victory' based on the need to re-establish 'stability' and the 'upward movement' required to bring the 'third world' (blacks) nearer to 'our first world situation'.[40]

Rubicon shattered the shaky and new-found political unity of South Africa's capitalist class. All business leaders were still agreed on the need for further reform, including political reform. Yet Rubicon revealed basic divisions over the scope of the desired political reforms. It again brought to the fore exactly the same political question around which the whole Muldergate episode had turned – the capacity of the NP and its government to act as the vehicle of reform. But now the rules of the political game inside the government had changed dramatically and the National Party of 1985 was a very different political animal from that of 1978.

Who's the boss? Political struggles inside the state

Even before the urban black uprising really ignited, the failure of the SSC strategists to work out the next steps in their strategy had provoked sharp disagreements and growing rifts between the two great institutional clusters of state bureaucratic power. This first surfaced in open hostility between the SADF and the Foreign Ministry over regional policy, particularly towards Mozambique.

The Nkomati Accord and Foreign Minister Pik Botha's efforts to negotiate a broader settlement in Mozambique were wrecked by the SADF's continued support for Renamo. The so-called 'Vaz diary' and other documents captured by the Mozambican army in September 1985 contained highly embarrassing details of the SADF's deliberate violation of the Nkomati Accord. Then SADF Chief Constand Viljoen had advised Renamo 'not to be fooled by the schemes of Pik Botha because he is a traitor'. Viljoen variously described the Foreign Minister as a 'Soviet nark' and a stooge of US Assistant Secretary of State for Africa, Chester Crocker. These documents also showed that the SADF had bugged Pik Botha's negotiations with Frelimo and Renamo.[41] Indeed, when the Foreign Minister announced an agreement between the two in the October 1984 'Pretoria Declaration', the envisaged ceasefire was aborted by Renamo's abrupt walk-out.

Renamo was effectively under the operational control of the Special Forces Command of the SADF and totally reliant on it for training and supplies.[42] Had the SADF (and Commander-in-Chief P W Botha) really wanted Renamo to respect the Nkomati Accord and continue the Pretoria negotiations, this could have been achieved relatively easily. At the very least, President Botha and Defence Minister General Malan had it in their power to end SADF logistical, training and operational support for Renamo – as the South African government had solemnly undertaken to do in the Nkomati Accord. The very liberal South African interpretation of 'non-aggression' in effect involved sustained actions which would have been described as blatant acts of war in any language other than P W Botha's rendering of Afrikaans.[43] P W Botha had *never* brooked the slightest defiance of his own authority. Any state official caught deliberately flouting the President's declared will would have been instantly dismissed. The fact that the SADF continued its destabilisation of Mozambique and its support for Renamo could only mean that the generals knew that they did so with the implicit permission of their commander-in-chief.

Following the collapse of the Pretoria talks, the SADF sent Deputy Foreign Minister Louis Nel on a number of secret missions to Renamo bases in Mozambique, guarded by South African paratroopers. Nel's nominal boss, Pik Botha, was not informed.[44] This severely aggravated Pik Botha's relations with Defence Minister Magnus Malan. At the press briefing on the 'technical viola-tions' of the Nkomati Accord, 'the animosity between Malan and Botha ... was tangible'.[45] The affair also underlined the distance between President Botha and his 'reformist' Foreign Minister. That Pik Botha's deputy could have visited Mozam-bique only with the President's consent seemed confirmed when P W Botha promoted Nel soon thereafter. The sacrificial resignation of the Chief of the SADF, General Constand Viljoen, as the scapegoat for the Vaz diaries did little to ease Pik Botha's public humiliation and underlined growing divisions in the SSC.*

These were aggravated as the unfolding uprising undermined the assumption of Police Commissioner Coetzee's counter-insurgency strategy that a 'dynamic policy of change' would undercut the revolutionaries. The grisly township practice of 'necklacing' informers wiped out the cornerstone of Coetzee's approach.† Key Coetzee protégé and security strategist, the spy Craig

---

* Hence Rhoodie's later allegation that Pik Botha deliberately set up the Rubicon débacle as an act of revenge – *PW Botha,* 280 *et passim..*

† The 'necklace' involved placing a petrol-doused tyre around the accused's neck, and setting it alight. In an infamous speech, Winnie Mandela told supporters that black South Africa would lib-erate itself 'with our matchboxes'. ANC President Oliver Tambo eventually, though tardily, denounced the practice.

Williamson, resigned from the Security Police when his appeal for a more sophisticated approach to the ANC was rejected by President Botha. Other powerful Security Police voices attacked Coetzee's 'over-elaborate' tactics, advocating a total crackdown instead.[46] At a special meeting of the State Security Council in December 1985, Defence Minister Magnus Malan 'argued passionately for a tougher government posture'.[47] The regime had clearly lost the battle for domestic and international public opinion which lay at the heart of Beaufre's concept of Total Strategy. Yet given the international outrage provoked by daily television images of brutal police action, key reformists evidently believed the state could not risk being seen to take stronger measures to control the uprising.

This led to significant shift in security force tactics in late 1985, one seemingly based on the SADF experience with Renamo in Mozambique. Mass detentions, police raids and the military occupation of the townships continued. But now groups and individuals linked to the resistance were also subjected to attacks by black 'vigilantes' universally believed to be under police direction.* The extraordinary violence of these vigilantes 'paralyse[d] political opposition to an extent not achieved by the [regime's] Security Forces on their own'.[48]

By the beginning of 1986 the SSC was racked by sharp differences over the objectives and target groups of reform, as well as the relationship between security and reform. P W Botha and key securocrats were floating the possibility of black 'city states' and accelerated bantustan independence.[49] Minister Heunis now argued with his mentor that 'the city-state option' predetermined at best or contradicted at worst the new policy (announced by Botha at the end of January 1986) of including Africans into 'higher levels of decision-making via the negotiation process'.[50] Heunis's department on the other hand was informally negotiating with local UDF affiliates. Key voices in 'ruling circles' now began to argue that the real causes of the uprising and the appeal of 'revolutionary' politics was not the exclusion of 'the black middle class' from the political system (as the Heunis project assumed), but rather urban black economic deprivation. The proponents of this view advocated a move away from what the former director of Constitutional Planning and secretary of the Cabinet Committee on 'black constitutional development' described as Heunis's attempts to develop 'democratic participation' [sic], and move towards 'effective or cooptive participation'.† This view argued that both the ad hoc and reactive 1985 reforms and the weird and wonderful constitutional proposals being discussed in Heunis's department failed to address this fundamental cause of the 'unrest'. Made from a

---

* See N Haysom, *Mabangalala: The Rise of Right-wing Vigilantes in South Africa* (Centre for Applied Legal Studies, University of the Witwatersrand, Johannesburg, 1986). In May 1994 this lawyer declined President Mandela's offer of the post of Commissioner of the South African Police force – *Weekly Mail & Guardian*, 27 May 1994.

† Interview with Professor Willie Breytenbach, *Leadership South Africa*, 2, 6, 1987. According to Breytenbach, Heunis's critics argued that the 'revolutionary climate' was 'more a result of economic deterioration than political deprivations [of blacks]'.

position of weakness, such gestures encouraged 'the revolutionaries' to believe that they would win all their demands, or even bring down the government.* Contact between state officials and the UDF could only reinforce this perception and undermine the security forces' efforts to control the uprising.

These differences over the definition and practice of reform gelled into sharp conflict within the SSC and between the clusters of bureaucratic power. SADF generals were appalled by the bureaucratic inertia and sheer inefficiency of Heunis's great reformist empire. The minister's frequent and irritatingly incomprehensible exegeses on consociational theory threatened to destroy whatever credibility was left to political reform. Fearful that P W Botha's concession of the Cape NP leadership to Heunis in 1986 confirmed his status as heir apparent, virtually the entire security establishment fought to undermine the pivotal role of Heunis's department in determining and implementing 'reform'.

Sharp disputes also developed over how to balance the need to placate Western governments and bankers with the concern that the NP had already gone too far and was in real danger of a dramatic loss of support to the right. The two most important reformist ministers, Pik Botha and Chris Heunis, were increasingly concerned with the rumblings from the West. Transvaal NP leader F W de Klerk, on the other hand, bore the brunt of the assault from the right and led the faction insisting that the NP pay more attention to this front. President Botha slowly began to lend greater support to De Klerk's concerns than to those of his old reformist protégés – whose own sense of how far they could push their *Hoofleier* grew less sure. Addressing this international audience in early 1986, President Botha proclaimed his government's commitment to 'the principle of a united South Africa, one citizenship, and a universal franchise', promising to repeal the hated pass laws and establish a 'National Statutory Council' to negotiate with black leaders.[51] Euphoric at the generally positive international reaction to this speech, Foreign Minister Botha speculated to journalists on the inevitability that South Africa would one day have a black President. At the insistence of an outraged F W de Klerk, President Botha delivered a crushing public repudiation in Parliament of his loose cannon of a Foreign Minister, stating that Pik Botha was wrong, knew he was wrong and had no right to say such things.[52] On the same day, the highly respected leader of the Official Opposition, Frederik van Zyl Slabbert, dramatically resigned from parliament and the PFP, denouncing Botha's professed reformism a sham and parliamentary politics as 'grotesque ritual of irrelevancy'.†

---

* Best exemplified in Zwelake Sisulu's celebrated boast to the founding conference of the National Education Crisis Conference in early 1986 that the initiative had passed to 'the people'.

† *Weekly Mail,* 14 February 1986. Slabbert later revealed that four weeks earlier he told 'the top leadership' of his party that he would remain as leader only if the entire PFP caucus resigned their seats and contested the consequent by-election seeking a mandate to boycott Parliament until the Political Interference Act had been scrapped. Interview, *Leadership South Africa,* 5, 1, 1986. PFP *doyenne* – and its sole MP for 13 years – Helen Suzman was not among those consulted and was, and remains, outraged by Slabbert's action. See Suzman, *In No Uncertain Terms,* 246-7. Alex Borraine was the only other PFP parliamentarian to follow Slabbert's example.

With the inauguration of the executive presidency in 1984 P W Botha was shielded from the cut and thrust of parliament and party politics. Effectively eliminating the remnants of ministerial autonomy and collective Cabinet responsibility, the new political dispensation likewise terminated the old privileged access by Broederbond 'insiders' to the centres of power. In the new political order, the only real insiders who mattered were those who sat on the SSC. And there too, some were more equal than others. Now the only access which counted was to President P W Botha. As the sole arbiter of policy, the *Groot Krokodil* (Great Crocodile) took the imperial view of his presidency. Caught between his reformist technocrats and worried generals, his instincts were to support the latter. This widened the gulf between an ever more authoritarian and aloof President on the one hand and the Cabinet and caucus reformists on the other. Suggestions and criticisms from the old NP and Broederbond 'insiders' met with an increasingly hostile reception.[53] In at least one case, Botha's peremptory and angry dismissal of advice from a former longtime ally and key Cape Broederbond supporter led to the latter's total rupture with the 'prison' of the NP.*

Within the NP caucus a number of so-called 'New Nat' MPs began to challenge the leadership on issues such as the release of Mandela and talks with the ANC. Some openly discussed the possibility of major new political realignments under a new leader.[54] This gathering ferment in the NP accelerated the fragmentation of the old Afrikaner nationalist alliance, and had a significant impact on Afrikaner intellectuals. The ties of virtually exclusive loyalty to the *volk* and 'its' party had loosened in the 1970s. Now with the end of a Broederbond-moulded consensus, both the secular and clerical Afrikaner intelligentsia began to display more eclectic and often critical attitudes towards NP policies and its history. Many of the intellectuals and technocrats who had supported (and sometimes drafted) Botha's reforms moved into open dissidence.[55] The government had to intervene to prevent students at the most prestigious Afrikaner university, Stellenbosch, from travelling to Lusaka to meet the ANC. The 1985 discussions between key business leaders and the ANC were attended by the editor of a pro-NP Afrikaner newspaper,† despite the NP *Hoofleier*'s rant against such 'treason'.

Ferment within the Dutch Reformed Churches saw 16 theologians of the semi-state *Nederduitse Gereformeerde Kerk* (NGK) sign a 'confession of guilt' on the NGK's complicity with apartheid. The NGK's Western Cape Synod now reversed 40 years of NGK theology to proclaim the absence of a Biblical justification for apartheid.‡ The Synod 'completely abolished the theological

---

* See S J Terreblanche, 'My Stellenbosch se sprong na vryheid', in B Lategan & H Muller (eds), *Afrikaners Tussen die Tye*, Taurus, Bramley (SA), 1990. When this Stellenbosch economics professor resigned from the National Party, Botha dismissed him from the vice-chairmanship of the SABC Board of Governors.

† Harold Pakendorf of *Die Vaderland*.

‡ SAIRR, *A Survey ... 1985*, 629. Members of the church were urged 'to confess their participation in apartheid with humility and sorrow'.

and ethical justification the NGK had given to apartheid'. The NGK had long been considered 'the National Party at prayer'. Four out of five Cabinet ministers belonged to this church, together with the overwhelming majority of nationalist MPs. Announcing that 'the new Afrikaner is engaged in conquering his exclusivism' and 'recasting his political ideology', the new NGK moderator declared his church no longer to be

> the church of the Afrikaner volk or of the white man. These decisions say that the church is an open church, that it cannot be closed to people of other cultures. They tell the ordinary church member that there is no such thing as white superiority or black inferiority. They say that all people are equal before God. They say that there may not be under any circumstances a political policy based on oppression, discrimination and exploitation. We must move towards a community based on the principle of justice. ... The task of the church is to protest against unjust laws. And the protest must be based on the Scriptures.[56]

This dramatic reversal by the NGK led to an open split in the church and eventually triggered the formation of the *Afrikaanse Protestantse Kerk* (Afrikaner Protestant Church – APK) in June 1987 to defend NGK's traditional racist theology. Indeed, support for the far right continued to build during the 1984–86 uprising. A public sector pay freeze and reduction and elimination of other benefits reinforced the growing discontent of state functionaries. The dramatic collapse of farm income, soaring agricultural indebtedness and the April 1985 reversal of the decades-old practice of increasing the maize price, led to a series of unprecedented confrontations between Botha and the maize producers' association NAMPO.[57] The alienation of these core elements of the historic Afrikaner nationalist alliance saw thousands of former NP members joining Treurnicht's KP. The neo-Nazi *Afrikaner Weerstand Beweging* (Afrikaner Resistance Movement – AWB) began to break up NP meetings, proving itself capable of preventing even the NP big guns being heard in public meetings in the rural Transvaal. A sharp swing to the far right in series of by-elections provoked speculation that the NP could lose its parliamentary majority.[58]

By May 1986 South Africa was mired in an unstable and very violent impasse. The insurrection had destroyed local government structures, generating embryonic alternatives in some townships. Large-scale repression and military occupation of the black townships had failed to end the uprising. ANC military operations had risen dramatically and were increasingly being carried out by locally trained guerrillas.[59] Police spokesmen reported that 'new tactics' had made some townships virtual 'no-go' areas.[60] The regime had lost the political initiative and the support of its international allies. It faced the worst economic crisis in South African history and growing international momentum for sanctions. With its domestic base eroding, able to hold public meetings in its old Transvaal rural heartland only under massive police protection, its strategy in ruins and deeply divided over which course to follow at home and abroad, the Botha regime was seen to be floundering, and propped up only by its security forces. The perception began to take hold that the regime had lost but the resistance had not yet won.

By the beginning of 1986, at every level of social life, the South African state confronted a crisis whose severity went way beyond that which P W Botha had come to office determined to resolve. His Total Strategy had proved a total failure. The political initiative was firmly in the hands of the resistance in the streets, and the uneasy combination of reluctant, tentative ad hoc reforms and intense repression was clearly not going to return it to government hands. As the visit to South Africa of the Commonwealth Eminent Persons Group would soon make clear, basic choices would have to be made.

Chapter Eighteen

THE PURSUIT OF WAR
BY OTHER MEANS

The *Groot Krokodil*
and the time of the securocrats

P W-mobile (*Kragdadigheid* means determination to use forceful means)

By early 1986 the growing threat of international sanctions, calamitous Rand exchange rate and looming debt rescheduling negotiations all underscored the urgent need to improve Pretoria's international position. The State of Emergency was lifted in March, and the regime agreed to receive the Eminent Persons Group (EPG), charged by the Commonwealth Heads of Government with a last-ditch effort to try to find a solution to head off civil war in South Africa.

P W Botha had been warned by Pretoria's ambassador in Britain that receiving the EPG would effectively bind the government to giving very serious consideration to the group's eventual proposals. An intemperate rejection of such proposals would carry severe negative consequences, as would a refusal to allow the group to play the role designated by – among others – one of Pretoria's two remaining international protectors, Margaret Thatcher. Botha probably calculated that the EPG's presence would buy some desperately needed time to resolve the now raging policy divisions in the upper echelons of his government. Given the wide ideological differences between the group's seven members – two of whom had used their considerable influence to protect South Africa in the past, three others of whom had been among Pretoria's most strident and active international critics – he clearly also gambled that the EPG would be able neither to reach a consensus among itself nor broker an agreement acceptable to the ANC.* The group was given the 'categorical' assurance that Botha's government 'was prepared to contemplate negotiations with a completely open agenda where everything would be on the table'.[1]

This was a serious miscalculation. President Botha had always proclaimed his willingness to negotiate with the ANC providing it 'renounced violence'. He had written to the EPG that a 'suspension' of the armed struggle was 'a requirement for dialogue'.[2] A somewhat puzzled group was told by Pretoria's ambassador to London that Pik Botha's circumlocutious end-of-April letter responding to their 'possible negotiating concept' should be seen as 'positive'.[3] The EPG eventually proposed that the ANC suspend the armed struggle as a first step to its legalisation and to negotiations with the regime. The government initially neither rejected nor accepted this formula, which was then provisionally approved by Nelson Mandela in Pollsmoor Prison on 16 May and by ANC President Oliver Tambo in Lusaka the following day. The Commonwealth delegation was scheduled to meet the Cabinet Constitutional Committee on 19 May.

---

* The EPG members were essentially nominated by the more influential Commonwealth leaders. The group consisted of: Malcolm Fraser, the conservative Australian Prime Minister, 1975–83 (co-chair); General Olusegun Obasanjo, head of the Federal Military Government of Nigeria, 1976–79 (co-chair); Lord (Anthony) Barber of Wentridge, British Chancellor of the Exchequer during Edward Heath's Conservative Party government, 1970–74, and since 1974, chairman of the Standard Chartered Bank; former Indian Defence Minister, Sardar Swaran Singh; former Tanzanian Foreign Minister, John Malecela; Dame Nita Barrow, President of the World Council of Churches since 1983; Archbishop Edward Scott, Primate of the Anglican Church of Canada after 1971.

The regime now confronted a stark choice with just two days to respond. It could agree to negotiate while the ANC and the democratic resistance held the political initiative and the regime was perceived to be weak. It could prevaricate and press ahead with Heunis's complex plans for 'continuous transition'. Or risking further international action, it could renounce the EPG formula, move to crush the resistance and attempt to create new conditions which would favour 'power-sharing' on its own terms.

The public divergences over reform had already produced a Cabinet clash when President Botha refused to accept criticism from Heunis's department.[4] The need for a quick decision over the EPG formula finally ruptured whatever was left of the fragile SSC consensus. Heunis, Foreign Minister Pik Botha, and reportedly even Police Commissioner Coetzee, were not put off by the EPG formula and favoured accepting the logic of negotiations.[5] P W Botha and his generals on the other hand, however, were not prepared to negotiate from what they saw as position of weakness.

Barely hours before the scheduled EPG meeting with the Cabinet Constitutional Committee, the SADF attacked three neighbouring Commonwealth states. Pretoria informed the EPG that it was 'not interested in negotiations about a transfer of power'. The EPG concluded:

> while the government claims to be ready to negotiate, it is in truth not yet prepared to negotiate fundamental change, nor to countenance the creation of genuine democratic structures, nor to face the prospect of the end of white domination and white power in the foreseeable future. Its programme of reform does not end apartheid, but seeks to give it a less inhuman face. Its quest is powersharing, but without surrendering overall white control.[6]

With Pretoria's erstwhile friend, former Australian Premier Malcolm Fraser in the vanguard, the EPG recommended strong international sanctions against Pretoria as the only means to prevent a possible communist victory.

Regime consolidation: The 1986 State of Emergency

The decision to wreck the EPG initiative seems to have been taken in a narrow circle. As Botha's apparent preferred successor and Czar of the reformist bureaucracy, Chris Heunis reportedly claimed that he first heard of the SADF raids on a news broadcast shortly before he and other senior ministers were due to meet the EPG.[7] These attacks now catalysed a significant political realignment within and between the clusters of bureaucratic power in the state, leading to a dramatic shift in state strategy. With P W Botha now assuming an ever more imperious stance, his interventions were decisive in the unfolding pattern of white politics over the next two-and-a-half years. To grasp this pattern it is essential to understand something of the man's convoluted political psychology.

In his own terms, P W Botha had revolutionised South Africa since 1978 at great cost to the two institutions he had worked most of his adult life to build – apartheid and the National Party. He had taken what he clearly regarded as radical steps under intense pressure from the three great traditional enemies of Afrikaner nationalism – English-speaking businessmen (the Hoggenheimers of the nationalist demonology), foreign governments and capitalists (the *uitlanders* who had destroyed the Boer republics) and the restive black population (the 'Bantu' whom apartheid had sought to confine to their divinely ordained place as servants of the white race). For a short period between 1982 and 1984, he had worn the mantle of the great reformer and even that of statesman.

By mid-1986, however, Botha's carefully constructed and personally cherished image lay in shreds. Now instead of basking in the anticipated gratitude of Hoggenheimer, *uitlanders* and 'Bantu', he was universally derided as a buffoon, humiliated by psychiatrists and instructed to 'leave now' in the Hoggenheimer and foreign press. The most powerful Hoggenheimers had defied him to fly to Lusaka to talk 'treason' with the ANC. Previously loyal Afrikaners seemed to support this action. Interfering *uitlanders* tried to bend him to their will with threats of sanctions. Worst of all, he confronted an ever intensifying uprising by cheeky blacks who had forgotten their place, and, while killing white policeman, taunted *baas* Botha that his end was approaching. Moreover the President also clearly suspected some of his most powerful ministers and once-closest allies of intriguing with Hoggenheimer and *uitlanders* to replace him. Important policy differences had now opened up between him and the protégé whom he placed at the epicentre of the elaboration of reform, the Minister of Constitutional Development and Planning, Chris Heunis.

Botha blamed his long-time acolyte for the fact that the leader of the 'coloured' House of Representatives, the Rev. Alan Henrickse, 'was not going to play politics' the way Botha had intended intended him to. Instead of kowtowing in gratitude to the President who had made him Minister Without Portfolio, Hendrickse sought to build up his own fragile legitimacy with a serious of melodramatic confrontations with Botha. One 'inside source' told Swilling and Phillips:

> Heunis was the father of the tricameral parliament and during the early reform period he promised PW that if Hendrickse and [the leader of the majority National People's Party in the Indian House of Delegates, Amichand] Rajbansi came in they could be controlled. This proved to be a mistake. These guys came in and after an initial period of playing the game they started to become independent operators. This made it impossible for PW to have his way in cabinet or in the standing committees.[8]

Always hyper-sensitive and quick to bludgeon those he believed had slighted him, by June 1986 Botha had become deeply embittered and withdrawn. His warnings in the Rubicon speech that 'we are a proud and independent people', that he had shown 'great patience' and 'do not push me too far' were those of a man preparing to turn on his enemies.

A wide alliance of organisations of the democratic resistance had planned a three-day general strike on the tenth anniversary of the 1976 Soweto Rebellion on 16 June. Though attempts to enact legislation to outlaw such demonstrations were blocked by the 'coloured' House of Representatives, the regime simply could not allow such a show of strength by the black resistance. General Malan had argued for some time that the Heunis's 'dynamic policy of change' had achieved little and that existing security measures were inadequate to deal with the insurrection. He now apparently persuaded the President that a radical new counter-revolutionary strategy could recapture the political initiative. Ending two years of dithering, Botha now threw his weight behind an 'inner cabal' of SADF generals and other 'securocrats'. This transformed the balance of power in the SSC and led to a dramatic new crackdown. A nationwide State of Emergency was simply proclaimed by the President on 12 June. Parliament was not asked to give its formal approval. With Defence Minister Malan undertaking to restore order in the townships, the SADF assumed responsibility for domestic security from the police. Police Commissioner Coetzee went on premature retirement, and Chris Heunis lost his privileged access to the President. The Office of the State President gradually took over coordination of many of the 'welfare' functions of his department.[9]

The cluster of bureaucratic power around the security establishment was now clearly in ascendancy over the reformists grouped around Heunis and Pik Botha. However, the 'securocrats' were far from a monolithic force. Inter-service rivalries and territorial disputes continued to set Military Intelligence against the National Intelligence Service (formerly BOSS) and the Security Police, both jealous of the military pre-eminence. Within the SADF General Staff conventional counter-insurgency proponents did battle with the advocates of 'WHAM' (Winning Hearts and Minds) approach.[10] But their differences were less significant than the security establishment consensus that the principle of 'continuous transition' underlying Heunis's bumbling bureaucratic reformism was aggravating the unrest. The various levels of the security apparatus were broadly united around the need for a new, security-oriented strategy.

The generals were now able to reimpose their (revised) version of strategic management on Heunis's chaotic and ineffective 'reformist' empire. The maverick interventions of Pik Botha would again be reined in by a centralised, military-directed strategy, and the good cops (Pik Botha) bad cops (Malan *et al.*) routine of South African foreign policy would give way to a single vision of unwavering determination and power defying the international community to 'do your damnedest' – as the Foreign Minister challenged the international community once he had adjusted himself to the new reality.

The dominance of the 'securocrats' was felt at all levels of the state. While the battle for influence between the various sectors of the security establishment continued, the role of the National Security Management System (NSMS) expanded enormously (see pp. 281-6 above). For three years following the June 1986 emergency, the overall direction and implementation of state policy was effectively monopolised by the NSMS, with the SADF generals as its most cohesive force. They did not have a total monopoly, however. Adriaan Vlok's appointment as Law and Order Minister in 1987 saw Security Police interests assume a greater weight in the SSC.* Their influence increased with the establishment of a National Joint Management Centre (NJMC) to manage the State of Emergency under the supervision of the Office of the State President.[11]

Chaired by Vlok's deputy, Leon Wessels, the NJMC coordinated all aspects of the new strategy. It now activated the hitherto largely formal structure of Joint Management Centres (JMCs – see p. 286). The 11 JMCs each consisted of approximately 60 representatives of government institutions in that region under the chairmanship of the senior SADF (or occasionally, police) officer in the area. Their structure and function was replicated at a series of lower levels of local government (sub-JMCs, mini-JMCs etc. – see Figure 1, p. 285). The JMCs and subsidiary structures gathered intelligence and filtered it upwards to the SSC, formulated local strategies, coordinated the local implementation of broad policy directives and presided over the functioning of all local branches of government and the state bureaucracy. Through the JMC network, a structure of 600 or so key officials dominated the day-to-day workings of government, all tightly coordinated by the SSC.

The JMCs became the central institutions of day-to-day government on the ground. The entire apparatus of civilian politics was effectively marginalised, and the civil service largely reduced to implementing the directives of the SSC and JMCs. The NSMS soon came to preside over every facet of state policy, not just security-related issues. Its role was emphasised when the word 'Security' was dropped from its name and 'management by objectives' became official policy. The SSC secretary described the 'horizontal coordinating system' of the renamed National Management System as a 'useful tool' to coordinate all government departments and the private sector, and manage 'everything'.[12] This was the 'creeping *coup d'état*' which now became a staple topic of the opposition press.

Making tomorrow happen today: A new counter-revolutionary strategy

The 1986 Emergency was based on a redefined counter-revolutionary strategy. The generals argued that the problem had gone way beyond the 'total onslaught' to the creation of a 'revolutionary situation' in the townships.[13] Thanks to Heunis's ad hoc approach the state was bereft of a strategy to deal with the situation. Now rejecting (the misunderstood) General Beaufre as too vague,

---

* Although as a former Deputy Defence Minister, Vlok also enjoyed very good relations with General Malan.

E   RITUALS AND SYMBOLS

1 *The chosen leader of the chosen* **volk:** A bashful *Hoofleier,* **D F Malan,** greeted
by youths in the garb of the 'Second War of Liberation' (the Anglo-Boer War of
1899–1902) at Calvinia in 1947. They are singing the traditional hymn to the
leader, 'Lord, Let Your Blessing Shine Down on Him'.

2 *Volkskapitalisme?:* Finance Minister (and former leading light in the Economic Movement of the 1940s) **Dr Eben Dönges** and wife step out of their Cadillac to be welcomed to an 1964 NP rally by members of the Voortrekker youth group, bearing the then South African flag. Their black chauffeur is partially obscured by the flag at left.

3 *The politics of horse and buggy (i):* Transport Minister **Paul Sauer** escorted by the traditional *ruiterwag* (mounted guard) as he arrives to bid farewell to Dr Malan's old Piketberg constituency on his retirement in 1964. Note: (a) the NP *kruithoring* (powderhorn) symbol on the flag at left; (b) the unusual inclusion of a female *ruiter* at left.

3 *Who's for dinner?:* A hungry-looking Cape NP leader, the *Groot Krokodil* **P W Botha** *(2nd left)* sizes up a wary (and weary) Prime Minister **B J Vorster** as the Information crisis begins to unravel in 1978. **Mrs ('Tienie') Vorster** *(left)* and opera star **Hanlie Muller** (wife of Minister Louwrens Muller) seem oblivious of the gathering storm that would eventually drive their husbands from office.

4 *The BOSS:* **General Hendrik van den Bergh** *(left)* with Finance Minister and Natal NP leader, **Professor O P F Horwood** *(right)* just two months before Van den Bergh's September 1978 resignation as the head of BOSS.

5 *Dr No!:* **Andries Treurnicht** in full flow at a September 1982 Conservative Party meeting in Stellenbosch.

6 *There but for Cuito Cuanavale …?:* Defence Minister **General Magnus Malan** arriving at the September 1989 Presidential Inauguration of F W de Klerk.

SADF strategists turned to the evolving theories of Low-Intensity Conflict (LIC) being developed by the US armed forces, and their presumption that '[r]evolution and counter-revolution develop their own morality and ethics that justify any means to achieve success. Survival is the ultimate morality.'[14]

The SADF's own operation of Renamo against Mozambique's Frelimo government was a textbook classic of LIC 'pro-insurgency'. The LIC 'foreign internal defence' doctrine had been proven in the 'Crush, Conciliate, Negotiate' formula of the former SADF commander in Namibia, General Charles Lloyd.[15] This was now adapted to the 'area defence' strategy of the SADF, and Lloyd became the key SSC strategist, displacing General van der Westhuizen as chairman of the SSC secretariat in early 1987.*

The new strategy rested on the central LIC postulate that success demanded 'applying revolutionary strategy and principles in reverse'[16] – deciphering the logic and tactics of a revolutionary strategy and elaborating a counter strategy to pervert this logic, undo its cohesion, roll back popular gains and turn the revolution against itself. When combined with the work of US strategist John J McCuen, the LIC 'foreign internal defence' blueprint went beyond Huntington's Machiavellian reform-from-above to dream of an enforced remoulding and reorganisation of local communities from the base up. The chief SSC strategist told journalists that 'in the same way as the enemy', the new strategy was based on 'four main elements: constitutional, economic, social and security'.[17]

The latter was primary. P W Botha informed Parliament that 'security, order and stability in all of our communities are precondition for reform'.[18] His spokesman announced the further constitutional negotiations would occur only once the 'perception [that] a black government is obtainable in the near future has been thoroughly crushed'.[19] Absolute priority was now given to re-establishing law and order. The new strategy rested on the assumption that 20 percent of the black population were 'radicals', 30 percent were 'moderates' and 50 percent were uncommitted. The 'unrest' was the work of 2 000-3 000 agitators: '[P]ut them away and then you win the middle group' – the 50 percent uncommitted.[20] The SSC secretary declared that the first objective was to 'command, coerce and eliminate [!] the revolutionaries' in the townships.[21]

This led to a crackdown unparalleled even by South Africa's sorry standards. Rigorous censorship imposed in December 1986 ended the flood of damaging news and images to the outside world. Close to 26 000 people were detained between June 1986 and June 1987, compared with 6 000 in the preceding 12

---

* Lloyd had been the Commanding Officer in the three most important SADF commands – Namibia, Northern Transvaal and Natal. He was also the first chief of the SADF's special division of Internal Security. His immediate predecessor as SSC Secretary had been Head of the Military Intelligence, while Lt General van Westhuizen's own predecessor – Lt General André van Deventer – was the man who commanded the first South African invasion of Angola, 1975–76. Swilling and Phillips describe all three SSC Secretaries as 'military men with little sympathy for "dovish" … advice'. *Powers of the Thunderbird,* 64.

months. Almost half of them were less than 18 years old.[22] Prisoners, including children, were routinely tortured. Vigilante activity escalated drastically and death squads made their grisly appearance.[23] In keeping with the SADF's 'area defence' posture, particular attention was paid to eliminating local 'revolutionary' organisation within each 'area' of command.[24] The structure of street and area committees, civic associations and 'people's schools' which had mushroomed during the uprising was wiped out, their activists detained, in some cases charged with treason or 'eliminated' by death squads/vigilantes.

By the end of 1986 the SADF had re-established physical control over the townships, ended the uprising and driven democratic local and national organisations on to the defensive. The regime then moved to disorganise the remaining centres of resistance. New labour laws sought to emasculate the unions and outlaw strikes and boycotts. The February 1988 restrictions on 34 organisations effectively outlawed all forms of extra-parliamentary opposition.

The 'security' dimension of the new strategy went beyond South Africa's borders. Indeed, the abandonment of the reformist mask for military solutions was first felt in regional policy. In December 1985 the SSC publicly warned six neighbouring states to 'eliminate' the ANC from their territory or 'pay a heavy price'.[25] From the January 1986 South African-provoked *coup d'état* in Lesotho to the conclusion of the December 1988 agreement to end the war in Angola and implement the Namibian independence process, Pretoria dramatically escalated its destabilisation of neighbouring states, with Mozambique and Angola again its principal targets.[26]

With 'security' now seen as the absolute precondition of reform, this new strategy redefined the conception and content of reform, as well as its target groups. Magnus Malan argued that most blacks were less interested in democracy than in the 'satisfaction of their daily necessities'.[27] The 20:30:50 formula assumed that having 'eliminated' the radicals through 'hard war' measures, the state could win over the remaining 80 percent through 'soft war' measures designed to alleviate the appalling socio-economic conditions in the urban black townships. In the words of Major-General Wandrag:

> [D]rastic action must be taken to eliminate the underlying social and economic factors which have caused unhappiness in the population. The only way to render the enemy powerless is to nip his revolution in the bud by ensuring that there is no fertile soil in which the seeds of revolution can germinate.[28]

This second, economic, element of the new strategy stressed the *upgrading* of township infrastructure and basic social facilities. An SSC general said of blacks: 'if you want their support you can buy it'.[29]

Special attention was given to 34 townships where the uprising had gone the farthest in setting up alternative 'people's power'. These 'oil spots' were viewed as 'strategic bases' in which 'effective control over the population is regained', and R3,2 billion was earmarked for their upgrading – with a further R16 billion set aside to upgrade 200 additional townships.[30] Improving black access to urban housing was also given priority. Responding to a long-standing demand of organised business, the regime moved to create a black housing market by finally accepting the principle of freehold tenure in the black townships and privatising the state monopoly of township housing. Financed by private sector loans, its 'great housing sale' saw the private purchase of a third of state-owned township housing (or 105 000 units) by June 1989.[31]

The third and most ambitious aspect of the new strategy was its 'social element'. Through the provision of social facilities, extensive civic action programmes, 'civil education', 'co-optation of leaders' and the establishment of squads of 'special constables', the strategy sought to remake local communities in the state's image.[32] 'Counter-organisation' was the 'main weapon against the revolutionaries'. 'Sympathetic and helpful' state representatives would 'take the lead of all groups, classes, clubs and societies, with the organisation of social, career, sport, education, medical, religious and military activities' and win over the population.[33] The SSC secretary argued that such social programmes would prove to blacks that the SADF was 'concentrating not so much on making war, but on making love'.[34]

In order to be successful, this proposed restructuring of community life also required 'bringing the government down to the people'. The new strategy held that immediately following on the 'elimination of the revolutionaries', it was essential to set up effective local administration to deny the initiative to the revolutionaries. The Black Local Authorities were now resurrected under SADF protection, and the councillors who had fled during the uprising returned. The crucial step for the regime was the formal re-establishment of black civilian government over the townships. This was achieved in the October 1988 municipal elections which fully re-established the BLAs.

As the so-called 'third tier' of government, the BLAs were now assigned a central role in the 'redistribution' of resources from the white areas to black townships. This was to be achieved through establishment in 1987 of Regional Services Councils (RSCs), comprised of all municipal authorities, white and black, in a given area. Voting by size of tax base rather than population gave the white local authorities effective control of the RSCs.[35] Responsible for the provision of services such as transport, sewerage, lighting etc., the RSCs financed and supervised the upgrading of black townships through monies raised from new 0,1 percent turnover and 0,25 percent payroll levies on all business undertakings. They were also seen as a building block of 'power-sharing'.

This points to the final and most problematic element of the new strategy – constitutional reform. Despite his claim that blacks were not interested in democracy, Magnus Malan did recognise that 'a political solution is the hinge around which attempts to stabilise South Africa must turn'.[36] Yet policy in this area was confused and contradictory. On the one hand the NP seemed reluctantly to be confronting the error of its ways. President Botha finally acknowledged that apartheid had been 'a mistake'.[37] Transvaal NP leader F W de Klerk declared that the policy of his government was 'on the rocks'.[38]

Opening Parliament at the end of January 1986, the President in effect announced that the NP had jettisoned the Grand Apartheid concept of separate political systems for myriad 'national groups'. He abandoned almost 40 years of NP dogma with the statement that: 'We accept one citizenship for all South Africans. ... The peoples of South Africa form one nation.'[39]

Malan, Strijdom, Verwoerd and Vorster must have all turned in their graves. This was the very heresy the NP had been elected to destroy. Yet its *Hoofleier* now insisted that 'our nation [singular – D O'M] is a nation of minorities'. His regime was still determined to maintain white political control, under the guise that the 'rights' of 'minority groups' had to be protected. The [racial] 'group approach' was the only acceptable way to achieve 'the expansion of our democratic system'.[40] Minister Stoffel van der Merwe told the *Financial Mail* that while the government was committed to opening up political participation, the State of Emergency, the February 1988 banning of 17 organisations and 'external action in Angola' were all explicitly intended to 'send out signals that we are prepared to go to a certain point in the move towards power-sharing and no further'.[41] This provided no political solution to the moral dilemma long identified by Dr Verwoerd. Once the NP accepted a single South African citizenship and nationality, it could provide no moral justification for its determination to deny the vote to the majority of its citizens and exclude most of the South African 'nation' from participating in the political life of their country.

Botha's answer was that 'structures must be developed' through which black members of the South African nation 'can themselves decide on their own affairs up to the highest level'.[42] Two vague proposals tried to set these up, while simultaneously indicating the limits of power-sharing beyond which the regime would not budge. A 'National Council' under the President's chairmanship would give Africans an interim voice in government and prepare a new constitution to allow all South Africans to participate in government.* This step would be followed by the creation of 'own legislative assemblies for urban blacks and executive ministerial councils'. These 'separate power bases for each group' would then come together in a Council of State – a type of 'super-Cabinet' to share power over foreign affairs, law and order, defence and the economy.[43]

A National Council Bill was tabled in Parliament in 1986 and redrawn in 1987. Yet strong opposition to this 'toy telephone' from blacks already working within the regime's 'power-sharing' schemes meant it was never enacted. Most agreed with KwaZulu bantustan head, Chief Mangosuthu Buthelezi, that the release of Nelson Mandela was a precondition for participation. In April 1988, acknowledging that 'power-sharing' reforms had been too slow, Botha renamed

---

* *The Star,* 17 September 1987. It would consist of the bantustan leaders, nine elected representatives of blacks outside the bantustans, chairmen of Ministers' Councils of the three houses of Parliament and 10 presidential appointees.

the National Council 'the Great Indaba'. He announced proposals to allow the appointment of Africans to the Cabinet, the President's Council and the electoral college which elected the State President.[44] Though legislation providing for this negotiating forum was finally enacted in June 1988, the body never met. A Bill facilitating the appointment of Africans to the Cabinet was also tabled, but was blocked by the ('coloured') House of Representatives which insisted that the Group Areas Act first be repealed. By the time of P W Botha's stroke in early 1989, the national 'power-sharing' structures were no further advanced than at the declaration of the State of Emergency thirty-one months earlier.

Thus progress on the four elements envisaged in the new strategy was uneven. The regime succeeded in taking the political initiative away from the resistance and destroying the widespread notion that non-racial democracy was around the corner. It likewise succeeded in reimposing its local government structures on black communities. Upgrading schemes led to privatisation of black housing and some improvement in infrastructure. However, as the overwhelming black boycott of the October 1988 municipal elections showed, no headway was made in solving the basic political issues confronting the country. Meanwhile politics within the state had become even more fraught.

L'État c'est moi! P W Botha, the NSMS and NP politics

P W Botha and his generals appeared to wield absolute power after the 1986 Emergency. Nobody in the NP or government seemed prepared to risk Botha's ire by questioning this strategy, let alone fight for alternatives. Clearly aging, and probably ill, Botha became, if possible, even more imperious, but also ever more dependent on his generals.* Having thrown his weight behind the securocrats, he appeared to close his mind to alternative advice. His usually petty, often brutal and always demeaning treatment of those in his caucus and Cabinet who did not immediately bend to his wishes, and his open disdain for those outside his new magic circle made him a deeply loathed, but feared figure. A government mole reported that 'everybody [in government] is scared to death of the *Groot Krokodil*'.† Afrikanerdom's most respected journalist noted the prevailing belief among Afrikaner intellectuals that 'near absolute power had corrupted Botha politically'. In his late 1987 review of 'goings on' inside the NP, Willem de Klerk wrote that the President's

---

* Of the 23 permanent SSC members in 1988, at least 13 could be said to have been 'securocrats' – These included: the Minister of Defence; the Chief of the SADF and its four services (army, air force, navy and medical corps); the head of Military Intelligence; the Director of the National Intelligence Service; the Minister of Law and Order; the Commissioner of Police; the head of the Security Police; the Director of Security Legislation; and the Secretary-General of the Office of the State President.

† DMWW, 'Die Reisies is aan die Gang', 8. *Die Groot Krokodil* (The Great Crocodile) was the nickname given to P W Botha in the mid-1980s.

intolerance and bad-temperedness have reached new heights, and are serving to enforce conformity with an iron hand and a kind of reign of terror. He takes no nonsense from anyone, and everybody knows that they have to toe the line. This has brought a silence, for the sake of survival. Differences in emphasis have gone underground, for this is too dangerous a game in the vicinity of a powerfully intolerant man.[45]

Botha's generals seemed to enjoy his absolute protection – unless it suited him to use them as scapegoats for his own failures, as with the discarded SADF Chief, Constand Viljoen.* Defence Minister Malan and SSC secretary Lloyd appeared to many to be the real rulers of South Africa, answerable to none but the President. Despite frequent assertions that the SSC simply advised the Cabinet which retained full and final authority, the Cabinet was simply not consulted on a range of absolutely fundamental decisions over the direction and details of government policy. These included, *inter alia*: the May 1986 raids which scuttled the EPG; the declaration of the June 1986 State of Emergency; the February 1988 banning of the UDF and 17 other organisations.[46]

Civilian politicians were now almost completely marginalised. This extended even to NP barons like F W de Klerk who had no significant bureaucratic power-base (Botha had excluded De Klerk from the major Cabinet portfolios and hence from any significant role in the NSMS). It even included formerly trusted ministers like Pik Botha and Chris Heunis, who – unlike De Klerk – enjoyed some bureaucratic clout on the SSC. These key insiders were also effectively obliged to follow the *orders* of the soldiers who dictated the new strategy. Their bureaucrats were now supervised by the SSC and JMCs and reduced to implementing the directives of the NSMS. This generated huge resentment among those used to being at the centre of power. Many former insiders asked themselves the question posed by a government mole: 'what are we doing in this government if we do not even have a say over such matters?'[47]

In effect, under the State of Emergency conventional politics within the state – and particularly the NP – gave way to the commandism of Botha's 'Imperial Presidency'.[48] This was further reinforced by a far-reaching reform of regional government in 1986. The system of elected provincial councils set up in 1910 was scrapped. Now the provincial administrators and executive committees were nominated by the State President. Many of the powers formerly under the jurisdiction of the old Provincial governments (such as health, education and local government) were transferred to the three 'Ministers' Councils' of the tricameral parliament. This had a highly negative effect on the NP, as it removed yet another level of politics, politicking (and patronage) from the competence

---

* Viljoen had been chosen as the fall guy for the discovery of the Vaz diaries proving the SADF's sustained violation of the Nkomati Accord (p. 332 above). Resigning his commission, the general retired to his farm at the end of 1985. He re-entered public life as the 'saviour' of the far right in 1992 and was elected to South Africa's first democratic Parliament as leader of the (Afrikaner) Freedom Front in 1994.

of the respective provincial National Parties and their branches. The sole reason to work for the NP now lay in infrequent general elections (which could be delayed further by the State President). Ordinary nationalist MPs were now simple voting fodder for their President, and the only route to individual advancement lay in cultivating his erratic favours. The tricameral parliament and even the NP itself were reduced to a simple 'legitimising shells' for the national security state.

The festering demoralisation and cynicism among politicians and the civil service led to a startling increase in large-scale corruption at senior levels. A series of scandals in 1989 revealed a R650 million foreign exchange fraud and various other multi-million Rand scams. These implicated Cabinet ministers, the leader of the (Indian) House of Delegates, MPs, several government departments and multiple rungs of the state bureaucracy.

The 'experts' gathered at a national conference on corruption ascribed this phenomenon to the political evolution under P W Botha.[49] P W Botha had come to power in 1978 affirming his intention to reorganise the state bureaucracy and fashion a 'smaller, but more effective' civil service (p. 284 above). Yet Botha's Total Strategy reforms remained cast within the old Verwoerdian precept that black leaders could be bought off. Botha had continued Vorster's habit of placating white opponents with bureaucratic patronage. Thus far from reducing the public sector employment, ten years after Muldergate the situation was virtually unchanged. More than 10 percent of South Africa's labour force was still employed in central government, and fully one-third of all employees worked in the public sector.[50]

By 1989, the convoluted 'three-tier' system of government instituted by Botha had produced an extraordinarily bureaucratic state. The central government bureaucracy included the departments to manage 'general affairs' as well as three parallel bureaucracies for 'own affairs'. Each of the four 'independent' and six 'self-governing' bantustans were likewise endowed with 'national' bureaucracies and seconded white officials. Tens upon tens of thousands of additional functionaries served the networks of Regional Services Councils (47 planned in all) and Local Authorities. Coordinating all this were the still further parallel bureaucracies of the National [Security] Management System. These consisted of a Working Committee, 15 interdepartmental committees, a National Joint Management Centre, 12 Joint Management Committees, 60 sub-JMCs, over 400 mini-JMCs and an unknown number of Local Management Centres. To this chaotic morass of satrapies Botha now proposed adding nine black regional councils all working towards the creation of a 'National Council' or 'super-indaba'. By 1988, South Africa was governed by five 'presidents', nine chief ministers or chairmen of councils of ministers (soon to be joined by a Prime Minister), 14 Cabinets or ministerial councils, close to 300 Cabinet ministers, more than 1 500 Members of various Parliaments and/or legislative bodies, and literally tens of thousands of local councillors. All were paid by the state. All required massive infrastructures of telephones, copying machines, faxes, offices, secretaries, office furniture and supplies, transport etc., etc. All of this was paid for out of the shrinking coffers of the embattled state. By 1988, the wage bill for the state bureaucracy consumed close to 60 percent of the national budget of R53 billion, or roughly a quarter of South Africa's GNP.[51]

In effect, the Total Strategy had boiled down to 'Reform' through bureaucratic proliferation and patronage. This led to infinitely expanding government expenditure (see p. 354 below), giving rise to what one infuriated liberal journalist labelled 'reform by corruption':

> 'Reform' has turned out to be nothing more than and immense machine for spending money, for spreading the gravy to buy off the revolution. ... There is no coherence, no logic, no policy. There is just one vast, expanding bureaucratic pork barrel with thousands of greedy little snouts pushing and shoving to get into the ... trough. ... It is this theory of government as simple survival that President Botha has brought to the modern world. There is no need to hunt for a unifying theory in his constructions, there is no such theory. For the time being it seems expedient to make councils and anyway it pays well, so he makes councils by the dozen. Later he may abolish them. Meanwhile, the prosperity of the mandarins is teaching all South Africans of every race, what matters in this game: it is to get your snout into the trough, and to grab as much as you can get. For the manoeuvrable man with a flexible conscience, this is the time to get yourself elected to some council or other, or to get astride the floods of money that flow from the fiscus, or simply to pick up the contracts that flutter like confetti at a wedding in the name of 'privatisation'.[52]

In a keynote address to the Institute for Democratic Alternatives in Southern Africa, a longtime key Broederbond insider and former SABC vice-chairman blamed this now massive corruption on the NP's post-1948 policy of Afrikaner favouritism, which he characterised as sustained 'tribal patronage' and systematic and expedient perversion of democratic norms.[53] There had always been more than a hint of corruption under NP rule, even among the most convinced ideological purists. But this was intensely disapproved of in Afrikaner nationalism's puritanical Calvinist ethic. Muldergate had highlighted the dissonance between the overt moral code and the sordid reality of nationalist politics. Yet the successful pursuit of the Republican Holy Grail led to the withering both of Afrikaner nationalism's sense of purpose and of some of Afrikanerdom's central cultural norms after 1960. The final collapse of the organised Afrikaner nationalism following the Treurnichtite split in 1982 left a real moral vacuum at the core of the NP. Before probing its political consequences, it is necessary to explore the ways in which a now aggravated economic crisis was placing absolute limits on the regime's ability to maintain its new counter-revolutionary strategy.

Chapter Nineteen

ASINAMALI!*

The structural crisis of the apartheid economy

'We have no money!' Governor of the Reserve Bank to P W Botha

* *Asinamali!* (We have no money!) – the historical rallying cry in a series of bus boycotts by black township residents.

The fallacy of strategy (ii): The cost of counter-revolutionary warfare

P W Botha's various strategies were always expensive. Government spending increased by an annual average of 18,5 percent during his 10 years in office, rising from 25,1 percent to 27,3 percent of GDP.[1] The post-1986 strategy saw ever more state funds going to guns, taking the fat out of the 'butter' with which the generals planned to buy black support. A 'conservative' estimate of real 'security' spending put the figure at 25 to 30 percent of the 1987/88 budget or 8 to 9 percent of GDP.[2] Official estimates held that the economy needed to growth at an annual rate of 3 to 5 percent simply to keep pace with population growth. Implementing the welfare component of the new strategy would require a growth rate of 5 to 7 percent.[3] Yet real annual growth fell from an average of 5,8 percent in the 1960s to 3,3 percent in the 1970s and just 1,8 percent between 1980 and 1987.[4]

Significant changes in the way in which the GDP was generated made high growth rates even less likely. The proportion of GDP growth arising from private consumption expenditure rose from 42 percent to more than 80 percent between 1960 and 1987, while GDP growth from domestic fixed investment and exports declined proportionately.[5] The ratio of gross domestic fixed investment to GDP fell from 27,7 percent in 1982 to 18,7 percent in 1987, as real domestic fixed investment declined by 31 percent. By 1987 gross fixed investment had shrunk back to the level it had been in 1973.[6] This highlighted a crucial structural constraint on mounting state spending.

South Africa's role in international trade is essentially that of an exporter of gold and other strategic minerals and an importer of oil, arms, technology and intermediate and capital goods (see pp. 172-3 above). The Governor of the Reserve Bank estimated in 1987 that capital equipment and intermediate goods made up 80 percent of all imports.[7] Throughout South Africa's industrial history foreign exchange to pay for these essential imported inputs has come from two sources: earnings from primary products exports – primarily minerals and principally gold – and foreign capital inflows from investment, non-equity arrangements and short- and long-term loans. Access to all sources of foreign exchange became much more problematic after 1985.

The opening up of significant new gold streams in Canada, Australia and the US saw South Africa's share of world gold production fall from 51,9 percent to 32,5 percent between 1980 and 1986.[8] Government efforts to offset this decline boosted non-gold export volumes by around 23 percent and cut the volume of imports by 17 percent between 1984 and 1986.[9] However this could not compensate for declining world demand for base metals and minerals. By the beginning of 1989, real metal prices were approximately 45 percent lower than in 1962.[10] The failure of the gold price to rise significantly after the October 1987 stock market crash was widely read to confirm its long-term downward trend.[11] A $10 fall in the gold price equalled $200 million in lost export revenues to the state – only partially offset by production increases or working higher-grade stopes. This meant that gold and other mineral revenues were no longer a sufficient source of capital inflows to sustain the import spending necessary for the rapid growth of the South African economy.

The situation was made even worse by the drying up of other forms of capital inflow. South Africa's rapid economic growth during the 1960s had attracted high levels of direct foreign investment. This accounted for some 59 percent of foreign liabilities by 1970.[12] However, direct foreign investment declined sharply following the 1976 Soweto uprising, falling to just 34 percent of foreign liabilities by 1985. By the early 1980s, the predominant forms of capital inflow were short-term public and private loans. Together, these accounted for 42 percent of foreign liabilities in 1984, compared with 19 percent in 1980.[13] South Africa's external debt rose from US$16,9 billion in 1980 to $24,3 billion. Given the deteriorating value of the Rand, this meant that external debt as a proportion of GDP grew from 20,3 percent to 45,7 percent in just four years. Since foreign exchange inflows had slowed to a trickle, servicing this burgeoning debt had to be paid for out of whatever trade surpluses could be achieved in the face of international sanctions, and out of the country's declining foreign reserves. The 1985 debt moratorium following P W Botha's disastrous 'Rubicon' speech virtually closed South African access to international capital markets. But the haemorrhage of capital continued, reaching R19,3 billion in the years 1984 to 1987.[14]

Pretoria's 1986 and 1987 agreements with its international creditors froze $14 billion of this foreign debt until June 1990. Almost $8 billion of principal falling outside this 'net' was to be repaid between 1987 and 1990. A further $12,8 billion of the outstanding $21 billion would fall due in June 1990. Although the acceptance of Pretoria's proffered 'roll over options' by several creditors reduced the effective total due in 1990 to around $7 billion, it was calculated that any repayment of principal exceeding $1,65 billion in 1990 would place unacceptable strain on the economy.[15] Somehow Pretoria would have to lay its hands on the remainder of this enormous sum, while trying to stimulate the sluggish economy to facilitate the upgrading programmes essential to the 'soft war' component of the generals' counter-revolutionary strategy.

Trade sanctions further aggravated the negative effects of this debt crisis. A US General Accounting Office survey of South Africa's international export markets concluded that despite extensive sanctions-busting and the opening of new export markets, export earnings from items covered by US sanctions fell by $469 million in the first three quarters of 1987.[16] The impact of these trade sanctions seemed to decline in 1988 and 1989.[17] Yet when combined with the 'market sanctions' imposed by the international banks, existing official sanctions placed tight limits on economic growth and prescribed the regime's ability to finance its domestic and regional strategies. The vulnerable South African economy faced a real threat of even tougher sanctions. The far-reaching Dellums Bill had been presented to the US Congress in 1988, and the Commonwealth Foreign Ministers' Committee on South Africa was elaborating a programme of deeper financial sanctions against Pretoria.

However, even the fairly limited existing sanctions had a negative impact on the regime's ability to finance domestic and regional strategies. This became very clear in the short-lived economic upswing of 1988. 1988 was a relatively 'good' year for the South African economy. A 3,2 percent GDP growth rate was almost twice the 1981–87 average, and the first time in several years that real GDP growth had exceeded the rate of population growth.[18] A 13,1 percent increase in earnings from foreign mineral sales stimulated expansion in the manufacturing sector. The index of physical volume of production surpassed the October 1981 record high of 116,3 to reach 117,2 in November 1988. However this expanded activity also increased domestic spending on imports, thereby putting pressure on the balance of payments. A declining gold price threatened medium-term export revenues, and current account surplus fell from R6,1 billion in 1987 to R2,9 billion in 1988, as net capital outflow reached R6,7 billion. These factors then all put pressure on foreign reserves. In October 1988 South Africa's gold reserves were sufficient to cover just six weeks of imports. Total foreign reserves of R4,93 billion at the end of 1988 were less than 30 percent of the 1980 levels, and lower than those of Botswana. With looming debt repayment obligations estimated to require a R4 billion current account surplus in 1989 and R5 billion in 1990,[19] the 1988 upswing actually compounded the regime's financial difficulties.

The Finance Minister aborted the upswing in the third quarter with measures to curtail imports and reduce consumer spending. Blaming an 'internationally organised assault on the economy' for the fact that 'we are forced to label a modest growth of 3 percent in our economy [as] overheating', Barend du Plessis explained to a glossy business magazine:

> In the past we were able to live quite easily with annual [current account] deficits of several billion rands because we could finance them through fresh loans and equity investments. Now we have been precluded from the source of foreign funds. So we must put the brakes on the economy while the current account is still very much in surplus – exactly as we are doing now. That is time lost, growth lost forever. *Now the challenge will be to reduce our propensity to import during the growth phrase* through measures which make a higher growth rate possible without straining the current account of our balance of payments.[20]

Du Plessis' deflationary 1989/90 Budget sought to rebuild foreign reserves and strengthen the current account surplus while simultaneously *increasing* security spending. The total allocation for 'protection services' (Defence, Police, Justice and Prisons) increased by a whopping 22,6 percent to R16 billion, or 23 percent of budgeted state expenditure.* This now cut into funding

---

* Real spending on security was substantially higher as: (a) the secutity forces regularly exceeded their budgetary allocations; and (b) various forms of security expenditure were spread across the budgets of a range of other ministries such as public works, etc.

for other sectors crucial to state strategy. While his own allocation was increased by 19,2 percent, Education Minister F W de Klerk announced that the state of the economy had forced his department to revise its vaunted 10-year plan of 'equal education for all'.

South Africa's deteriorating position in world markets and long-term inability to maintain its developed infrastructure in the face of these structural constraints clearly bothered many business leaders. Yet the uneven impact of the crisis led to significant changes in the structure of capital and varying responses.

Once again, agricultural capital was the hardest hit. The collapsing value of the Rand sharply increased prices of essential imported inputs of mechanised agriculture, aggravating the indebtedness of farmers. By 1986 the total farming debt of R11,2 billion exceeded gross agricultural income (R9,9 billion) and was nearly ten times total agricultural profits, leading Assocom to warn that 'the banking system itself' was threatened.[21]

Yet the impact on white agriculture was, still yet again, uneven. Worst affected were Transvaal and Free State maize farmers. Neither half a billion Rand of subsidies nor reduced interest rates for agriculture seemed to improve their position. Some maize farmers replaced wage labour with labour tenancy. The number of white-owned farming units continued to decline rapidly.[22] By 1983 nearly three-quarters of gross farm income was generated by just 27,2 percent of white farmers. Yet even their position was growing less secure. The chairman of the Development Bank of Southern Africa argued that economies of scale produced by the trend towards ever larger farm units were 'exaggerated artificially through the subsidisation of large capital items'.[23] As the government moved to reduce agricultural subsidies, many larger farmers would be unable to meet their debt obligations. This was the context for P W Botha's showdown with the National Maize Producers' Organisation (p. 309 above).

Outside agriculture, this structural economic crisis had contradictory effects. Anywhere between 299 and 555 foreign multinationals disinvested from South Africa between January 1984 and April 1989.* This had a dramatic effect on business confidence. With most businessmen agreeing that 'we'll pay an enormous price [for disinvestment] in the medium and long term',[24] business confidence collapsed. Taking 1983 as a base line of 100, Assocom's Business Confidence Index fell to 78,6 in May 1986.[25]

Concentrated in those sectors hardest hit by the 1980s recession,

---

* The Investor Responsibility Research Center lists 277 withdrawals during this period, *Patterns of Multinational Corporations' Disinvestment from South Africa: A report for the UN Center on Transnational Corporations* (Boston, May 1989), 9. An additional 22 companies are listed in table 6 of a 1989 draft report on 'The Role of Transnational Banks in South Africa' prepared for the UN Commission on Transnational Corporations. The lists kept by the UN Economic and Social Council Commission on Transnational Corporations show 555 withdrawals. These, however, include both withdrawals from Namibia and, in a number of cases, count parent companies and their local subsidiaries as separate withdrawals.

disinvestment reinforced the already massive centralisation of ownership in the South African economy. The four major conglomerates rushed to buy the local operations of blue chip international companies like IBM (Barlow Rand), Barclays Bank and Ford (Anglo American). Their combined control of total market capitalisation on the Johannesburg Stock Exchange (JSE) rose from 70,3 percent to 83,1 percent between 1984 and 1987, with Anglo American alone controlling 60,1 percent.[26]

This extended the already vast operations of these conglomerates into new areas. Though huge Rand sums changed hands, these local conglomerates acquired the South African operations of major multinationals with capital which could otherwise have been invested in generating economic growth. This increasingly centralised ownership thus marked a form of forgone investment, contributing to stunted growth, particularly in industry. Manufacturing's contribution to total fixed investment fell to 14,2 percent by 1986 (from 21,6 percent in 1980), while that of mining rose to 60 percent.[27]

Yet disinvestment did *not* meant disengagement. Now freed of the negative implications of direct investment in the apartheid economy, at least half of the 'disinvesting' multinationals continued to earn large profits and exercise significant control over local operations, through the retention of non-equity links with their former subsidiaries.* In some cases disinvestment actually increased the share of the South African market held by the disinvesting multinationals. These non-equity links replaced direct investment as the key conduit of technology to the South African economy. Sanctions thus ironically *intensified* the dependence of local conglomerates on inputs from major multinationals.

The structural economic crisis also accelerated the trend towards the *export of indigenous capital*, begun in the 1960s and 1970s.[28] In 1981, the prestigious American business magazine *Fortune* reported that Harry Oppenheimer's Anglo American Corporation was the largest single foreign investor in the United States, controlling assets of $15 billion through its offshore holding company, Minorco.[29] Since it too moved a large part of its operations offshore in 1958, Anton Rupert's Rembrandt had mushroomed into the world's third largest tobacco multinational with interests in over 100 countries.[30] This export of local capital had increased dramatically when the Finance Minister succumbed to pressure from business and NP fantasies over the successs of the Total Strategy, and lifted exchange controls in 1983 – provoking the almost immediate disinvestment of the four largest British investors in South Africa.[31] Until these controls were reimposed following P W Botha's 1985 Rubicon speech, vast quantities of capital were legally exported from South Africa. Measured in the Rand currency, direct South African investment abroad more

---

* Including, *inter alia:* licensing, trade mark or franchise agreements; distribution contracts and/or management and technical assistance agreements. See Investor Research Responsibility Center, *Patterns,* Appendix E; and O'Meara, *Government Measures,* 89-93.

than doubled to R16,6 billion, while total foreign assets increased by 76 percent to reach over R30 billion.*

With the reimposition of exchange controls in 1985, outward transfer of capital was again strictly controlled. However Reserve Bank permission was relatively easily available to companies expanding South African export markets and engaged in 'sanctions-busting' activities.[32] Yet the major South African corporations accelerated their search for more secure investment opportunities outside South Africa, with the giant Anglo American Corporation (AAC) again in the forefront. Operating primarily through its Minorco holding company, Anglo seems to have been motivated by fear of nationalisations by a future ANC government and the relative decline of its massive gold mining operations.† One longtime AAC critic concluded that had Minorco's hostile takeover bid for the British mining conglomerate Consolidated Goldfields succeeded, R3 billion would have left South Africa, and the real locus of Anglo would have shifted overseas.[33]

This pattern of 'internal disinvestments' was a measure of the negative confidence of South Africa's major corporations in the country's economic future. In the context of the 1984–87 wave of disinvestment, and the constraints imposed by efforts to manage debt repayments, these internal disinvestments limited economic growth even further. The strategy of the state to defend its conception of white interest now erected further barriers to accumulation and exacerbated the longstanding structural crisis in the economy.

By the beginning of 1989, the various prongs of state strategy were thus sharply antagonistic. The absolute priority given to security undermined the government's capacity to fund the social and political 'reforms' judged essential to the counter-revolutionary strategy. An emphasis on growth to pay for this strategy itself threatened the priority given to the foreign debt repayment as a precondition of re-establishing access to capital markets. On the other hand, however, an absolute emphasis on building up the current account necessarily implied import restraint which threatened economic growth. Failure to achieve economic growth then put into question the capacity to finance the political

---

* South African Reserve Bank *Quarterly Bulletin,* March 1988. Adjusting these figures for the depreciation of the Rand (and hence higher Rand value of foreign assets) nevertheless shows a real increase in South African investment aborad of over 30%. *Ibid,* June 1988.

† While capitalisation of the gold mining industry increase sharply in the 1980s, its profitability relative to new major producing areas declined, and South Africa's share of global gold production fell (p. 354 above). By the mid-1980s most producing mines had been on steam for more than 30 years and the average gold yield per tonne of ore mined was less than 40% that of 1970 – *Financial Mail,* 18 March 1988. Annual average production cost increases of 18,3% far exceeded the 1980s inflation rate, while the overall tendency of the gold price was downwards, *Financial Mail,* 20 May 1988. The relative decline of the gold mining seriously affected the market value of gold holdings. The All Gold Index of the Johannesburg Stock Exchange fell from 1 774 in December 1987 to 1 266 in September 1988, reducing Anglo's control of total JSE market capitalisation from 60,1% to 49,5%. *Weekly Mail,* 10 February 1988.

strategy, and particularly the 'reform' element essential to restoring foreign confidence. And a lack of growth and consequent rise in the already huge levels of black unemployment implied a further risk of black political unrest. It also increased the political threat to the ruling National Party from disgruntled former supporters.

Once again, Pretoria's politically naïve and ideologically deluded strategists had been led astray by the perennial fantasy of the man on horseback – that the perfect strategy would yield the required results in the real world. Such 'strategic romanticism' tended to become obsessed with

> the rational elaboration of ... strategy and progressively distances itself from the practical realities and from the policy process. ... [It] reduces military planning to a science, in which strategy acts as the independent variable, while the structure of forces and purchase of arms plays the role of the dependent variables. Unfortunately, this is not how things work in the realm of politics.[34]

Nowhere was this failure to grasp the realm of the possible more clear than in General Malan's risible claim that 'for the masses in South Africa democracy is not a relevant factor'.[35] Nowhere was the strategic delusion more evident that in the SADF's belief that the recession-ridden apartheid economy had the resources to enable to regime to 'buy' black support. Once again the former disciples of Beaufre failed to learn his first lesson. Strategies could only work if the political analysis underlying them was sound. Once again, the generals failed to calculate both the real vulnerabilities of the regime and the core demands of their revolutionary opponents.

As this hopeless strategy worked to aggravate South Africa's grim economic situation, businessmen slowly began to organise themselves to deal with its real fallout.

Power of sanction? The Emergency and the politics of capital

The business response to the post-1986 counter-revolutionary strategy went through various phases. The imposition of the June 1986 State of Emergency had widened the divisions among capitalists already highlighted by the urban black uprising (p. 331 above). The AHI expressed regret that the state had been 'forced to take drastic measures' to fulfil its duty to 'maintain law and order' after 'all possibilities had been considered'.[36] The FCI on the other hand wrote to P W Botha that it 'strongly disapproves' of the Emergency, disassociating itself from 'the strategy of political repression and economic isolationism to which the SA government is apparently committed'. Botha's vitriolic reply lectured the FCI on its patriotic duty to help the government instead of its 'irresponsible criticism'.[37] Eight months after the imposition of the Emergency, a widely read financial daily observed that '[t]he once-cosy relationship between government and the business community ... has steadily deteriorated

... to the point where business leaders now exhibit excessive cynicism about virtually everything the government does'.[38]

However, confrontationalist tactics adopted by the FCI and individual businessmen wilted rapidly as President Botha unleashed the might of the state against his business critics. Most notorious was the hounding of Chris Ball, managing director of South Africa's largest bank, Barclays National (now First National Bank). Botha publicly accused Ball of financing January 1987 newspaper advertisements commemorating the ANC's 75th anniversary, and appointed the Munnik Commission to investigate. The commission criticised Ball's 'lack of candour' and questioned his judgement.[39] Several municipalities closed their accounts with the bank, obliging Barclays to deny claims that the affair had cost it 40 percent of its deposits.[40] Lest big brother's message went unheard, Botha opened the 1987 AHI congress with a stern warning that the private sector should confine itself to business matters and not to try to dictate to the government.[41] His sentiments and instructions almost identically matched those of John Vorster's diatribe against 'business interference in politics' at an Assocom congress a decade earlier (p. 195 above).

The big stick produced the desired results. Early in 1987 a lobby of 30-40 powerful members reportedly threatened to withdraw their special subscriptions to the FCI because of executive director Johan van Zyl's confrontationalist approach. Van Zyl was forced to resign, and the liberal FCI president – Shell (SA)'s John Wilson – was also replaced by the more conservative Hugo Snyckers.[42] The organisation came under pressure to merge with the stronger Assocom, which itself added the word 'Industry' to its name in 1988. A senior Anglo American executive opined that the FCI's financial and organisational woes grew directly out of its 1986 clash with Botha.[43] In 1990, the federation merged with Assocom to formed the South African Chamber of Business (Sacob), largely on Assocom's terms.

While most business leaders agreed with the Barlow Rand chairman that they 'had no option but to work for the removal of all bars to economic growth, even if some of those bars have a political flavour',[44] the style of such 'work' became both much less aggressive, and much less engaged with the state itself. Losing ground to the advocates of quiet consultation, liberal capital was badly disorganised. An article in a major business publication declared that its confrontationalist tactics of 1986 were now 'seen in most business circles as having been counterproductive'.[45] Two of the most outspoken liberal businessmen, Tony Bloom of Premier Milling and Gordon Waddell of the JCI mining house, emigrated in despair in 1987, blaming the state of 'politics in this country', and arguing that business had allowed itself to be trapped by P W Botha into a series of 'public relations seminars for the government'.[46] Cowed by the ferocity of the attack on Ball, most business leaders now appeared to agree with AAC chairman Gavin Relly that there was no 'quick fix, internal or external to South Africa's problems'.[47] Despite its fire-breathing rhetoric of 1985–86, this 'left wing' of capital had proved itself incapable of acting politically, of developing a strategy to mobilise the capitalist class and other social forces in favour of some kind of non-racial free enterprise option.

This failure reflected much more than the ongoing crisis of political representation of capital. It grew out of the fact that the crisis of 1984–86 went much further than that of Soweto a decade earlier. In the mid/late 1970s all elements of capital bar agriculture could rally round liberal capital's demands for restructuring the conditions of accumulation as expressed in the *Financial Mail*'s July 1977 'Business Power' issue (p. 188 above). While moving beyond the parameters of Grand Apartheid, these demands had called into question neither the form of the state nor the NP hold on political power. After the 1984–86 uprising, however, it was clear that attempts to win over even 'moderate' blacks must go way beyond the tricameral parliament and undo not just the NP political monopoly, but the existing form of the state. Botha's vision of 'reform' did not begin to include such options.

The only terms under which liberal capital could risk open confrontation with the Botha regime to secure a non-racial, but also non-socialist, alternative would be to find credible black allies capable of delivering powerful black support for such a project. The ANC was the only possible candidate. Here lay the rub. The ANC's programme called for a far-ranging redistribution of wealth and economic power. With socialist rhetoric the order of the day in black politics, the ANC seemed unlikely to abandon its economic demands for the egalitarian marvels of free enterprise. Many business leaders agreed with AAC executive director Zac de Beer that the ANC 'may wish to throw out the baby of free enterprise with the bathwater of apartheid', and that the primary political task of capital was 'to bring the benefits of the system more and more within the reach of our black citizens'.*

Developments in 1987 further reinforced business fears of a radical alternative. The locus of civil strife shifted from the streets to the factories. Nine million workdays were lost to strikes in 1987, a sevenfold increase over the record highs of 1986. Huge national strikes disrupted the retail and mining sectors, as well as the state-owned transport and postal services. A national metalworkers' strike was called off only after the state ruled it illegal. Emphasising a trend towards multi-plant strikes, many of these conflicts resulted in substantial gains by the unions.[48] As the first effective action by organised black workers in the public sector, the railway and postal strikes were a direct challenge to the state. The Congress of South African Trade Unions (Cosatu) was now the leading force in black resistance and the bearer of the mass anger that had fuelled the uprising. Cosatu was seen as even more radical than the ANC.

Liberal businessmen felt personally offended by both the strikes and the fact that the radical labour movement seemed to identify capital as part of the

---

* Quoted *The Citizen*, 17 September 1987. The Sanlam chairman expressed similar sentiments, *Business Day*, 16 July 1987. Neither proposed delivering such 'benefits' by raising black wages. Indeed, De Beer told a prominent trade unionist that black wages were already too high and should be reduced if South Africa was to compete on world markets. Personal communication.

problem rather than the solution. The chairman of various Anglo American subsidiaries argued in 1988 that business retreated from its 'extremely enthusiastic liberal initiative' of 1985–86 partly because 'the government has restored order'. However, even more important was what he called 'the politicisation of trade unions'. The massive upsurge of trade union militancy

> put management into a political frontline position where it doesn't belong and where it doesn't want to be ... businessmen get very angry with that sort of thing. They regard it as unfair ... business is more than irritated by the political tone of a great many of the unions.[49]

By 1987 most business leaders had come to agree with Kerneels Human that 'stability' had to be restored. Many were won over to the view that security was the precondition of reform, seeing in military-directed 'reformism' an efficient, decisive force capable of cutting through the bureaucracy of the Heunis empire to deal with the economic discontent underlying the unrest. Most agreed with the AHI chairman that the Emergency was 'conducive to improved business confidence' and 'essential to stabilise the labour market'.[50]

Business relief that 'the government has restored order' now began to translate into a general consensus on the need to curb the trade unions – or as Zac de Beer euphemistically put it, business now sought 'to filter that [political] tone out of the bargaining process through legislation'.[51] Business support for the anti-strike and other stringent provisions of the new Labour Relations Bill was almost universal. Employers generally now adopted a more abrasive approach to the unions. Many observers felt that Chamber of Mines deliberately provoked the massive August 1987 strike of black mineworkers, believing that an unprepared National Union of Mineworkers – the most powerful Cosatu union – could be weakened. The summary dismissal of 40 000 miners by the 'liberal' Anglo American Corporation forced NUM to call off the strike. And Cosatu met with scant success in attempts to persuade employers to condemn the Labour Relations Bill which would drastically curtail the right to strike and render unions liable for company losses during illegal strikes. In early 1988 'a select group of South Africa's most influential businessmen' issued a set of labour relations proposals which went even beyond those in the Bill.*

Like capitalists elsewhere, South African businessmen came to appreciate the economic benefits of military managerialism and a national security state.[52] Massive upgrading expenditure generated lucrative contracts and allowed white capital into the new black housing market. Thus, for example, while Zac de Beer regularly lashed out against apartheid – both as a key Anglo executive and

---

* These proposals favoured giving employers the right summarily to dismiss any alleged intimidators and 'where appropriate, shut them out of the workplace and place of residence'. Appeals on grounds of unlawful dismissal would have to prove that the employer acted in bad faith. For details, and an attack on these proposals by another (Afrikaner) businessman, see Christo Nel, 'Peer Pressure', *Leadership South Africa,* 7, 3, 1988.

as leader of the PFP after 1988 – he appeared to have few qualms about accepting huge contracts for the construction of apartheid facilities by his LTA company.* In February 1988 P W Botha announced an 'economic strategy' to finance the 'reform' programme. Soon dubbed 'Bothanomics', this envisaged saving R2,5 billion through a public sector wage freeze. The upgrading programmes would be financed through an estimated R70 billion raised by privatising state-owned corporations, and the tax base was broadened by replacing the General Sales Tax with a Value Added Tax.[53] This package adopted many of capital's longstanding demands – reducing public expenditure by attacking the earnings of (lower-level) public sector employees; shifting the burden of taxation away from companies onto individuals; and deregulation and privatisation. Business was enthusiastic in its support for this programme. The NP victory in the May 1987 white elections saw the JSE Industrial Index rise by 29 points to exceed 1 900 for the first time.[54] Taking 1983 as an index of 100, the Assocom 'Business Confidence Index' which had fallen to 79,1 in mid-1985 had climbed back up to 97,5 by the end of 1988.[55]

The business community as a whole seemed to withdraw from the political arena. The managing director of the South African Permanent Building Society seemed a lone voice when he taxed fellow businessmen for having been 'co-opted' by government and failing to address the war in Angola, mass poverty and forced removals. He warned that should business fail to exercise what he called its 'power of sanction' to ensure 'a brighter future for all', then

> numbers, apathy and disenchantment will break the ['capitalistic'] system, if revolution doesn't do so.

Bob Tucker further argued that what he called the 'disconcerting ... inconsistency' of 'the business community in South Africa' enabled the government to ignore the resolutions of organised business as not representing ' "the captains of industry", but merely ... the "hotheads" who participate in their formation'.[56]

Tucker's opinions created something of a stir. But most business leaders either agreed with the Seifsa director that Tucker had 'oversimplified' the issue, or with the Pick 'n Pay chairman that they were 'fighting for change in their own businesses'.[57] In contrast to capital's general condemnation of the State of Emergency and detention of trade union leaders in June 1986, the banning of 19 organisations and restrictions on Cosatu at the beginning of 1988 elicited only 'regret' from the FCI and Assocom. The former 'hotheads' now declared they

---

* 'Dr Zac de Beer: Dr Zackyll and Mr (Take you for a) Ride?' *Noseweek*, no. 2, July 1993. This issue produces photographs of the then chairman of the PFP (and later leader of the Democratic Party) smiling broadly as he hands over the keys to the new Pretoria headquarters built by LTA for the chief apartheid ministry (Cooperation and Development – formerly Bantu Administration). Minister Koornhof officially unveiled the cornerstone while a (black) police band provided the music. Apartheid was indeed profitable!

were 'not in a position to evaluate the security factor inherent in these measures'.*

Yet despite this new political quiescence, almost no capitalist believed that the crisis had been resolved or even that the government was on the right track. A national survey of business attitudes reported that 68 percent of businessmen considered 'present political policy' to be 'dampening' economic growth, while only 2 percent considered it to be 'stimulatory'.[58] Calculating that apartheid has cost the South African economy R78 billion by 1985, another study cited the estimate of 'leading business people' that without apartheid, the GNP per capita 'would be 50 percent higher'.† Two hundred business leaders held a quiet and unpublicised meeting with P W Botha and his Cabinet in early November 1986. The chairman of Old Mutual and longtime confidant of P W Botha declared he had no doubt that 'government got the message. The message from private enterprise was: "Hurry up [with reform]!" '[59]

As the immediate fear of a socialist revolution receded and sanctions aggravated the structural economic crisis, businessmen became centrally preoccupied with restructuring the conditions of accumulation over the medium and long term. Some of this focused on economic policy per se. A debate over neo-protectionist proposals for 'inward industrialisation' highlighted important divisions among the major conglomerates. Supported by the Sanlam chairman and leading Afrikaner economists, inward industrialisation envisaged import and foreign exchange controls and productive state investment to stimulate domestic demand for locally produced industrial products in a market expanded by the removal of restrictions on black urbanisation and business.[60] These proposals ran counter to the rabid free-marketeerism of mainstream anglophone business and financial press. An AAC executive's book on scenarios for the 1990s achieved cult status despite its banal conclusion that South Africa's options were negotiations and a booming economy or a stalemate with escalating violence, tighter sanctions and recession.[61]

By early 1988 the major obstacle to restructuring the conditions of accumulation was the government's refusal to acknowledge that it had no solution to the political impasse. In some business circles the concern over economic policy slowly shifted back onto directly political terrain. The chairman of a leading finance house and president of the influential South Africa Foundation lobby group argued in late 1987 that 'in the absence of strong parliamentary opposition on the left, business will increasingly find itself representing the opinions of those to the left of the government'.[62]

A remarkable series of *Financial Mail* editorials in early 1988 dissected the

---

* *Weekly Mail*, 15 April, 1986. The Chamber of Mines position was virtually identical, while the AHI did not react publicly.

† M Savage, University of Cape Town, cited 'Apartheid Barometer', *Weekly Mail* 27 November 1987. This R78 billion broke down into R8 billion in lost economic growth, R66 billion in lost growth opportunities, and R3,9 billion in implementing government race policies.

real political dilemma confronting capital. The government's constitutional initiative was 'dead'. In this 'policy vacuum' the regime was 'rudderless' and 'reactive', lacking vision and commitment to reform, and crippled by its obsession with protecting its right flank. Botha had proved to be the John the Baptist of post-apartheid South Africa rather than its Messiah. Yet the PFP too was in 'decline and disarray' – perhaps even 'dying' – and squabbling with the fractured Independent Movement (p. 373 below). While 'a charismatic leader could provide the catalyst for unity', the journal lamented that 'no such leader is in sight'. Ignoring its own Biblical parallels, it called on P W Botha to abandon his right wing and assume the real mantle of political Messiah, while pleading that the PFP save itself by appointing the leader of the so-called Coloured House of Parliament, Alan Hendrickse, to lead it out of the political wilderness.[63]

Other business debates took on a more directly political tone. At a March 1988 conference convened by the business focus group of the Five Freedoms Forum, important business leaders called for greater political involvement by business.[64] Two major obstacles stood in the way of such involvement, however. The *Financial Mail*'s pathetic attempts to convert P W Botha and revive the PFP simply underlined capital's political disorganisation. President Botha himself had become a major obstacle to restructuring the conditions of accumulation, and business could find no means of replacing him. The options of which had worked so well in 1977–78 were unavailable. The SADF was no longer a force for change – indeed its strategies were now a very large part of the problem. No influential and credible NP reformist politician lurked in the wings to play the role P W Botha had assumed for himself in the last paralysed year of the Vorster government – i.e., rally a new social alliance for reform and ruthless conquest of the NP. While Botha was now widely perceived to be ailing, his likely successor, F W de Klerk, was closely identified with the more conservative wing of the NP and was believed to have scuttled a number of reformist initiatives. Disorganised politically, capital had not yet found reliable political allies to displace Botha and launch another reform thrust.

This pointed to the second major obstacle to an effective business intervention to break up political impasse. With most businessmen still reeling under the twin blows of the radicalisation of black politics and the ferocity of Botha's attack on his business critics, it was essential that business develop a vision of a post-apartheid political and economic order capable of winning substantial black support. The *Financial Mail*'s plea that the despised and detested Hendrickse rally the opposition underscored capital's woeful ignorance of black politics. By mid-1988, however, major business efforts to overcome these two obstacles were under way. These would have a significant impact on politics within the state.

Chapter Twenty

ON THE ROCKS

The great crisis of
Afrikaner faith

Heunis to Botha: 'Stop this thing, I want to get off!'

Blowing in the wind: Questioning Afrikaner identity

The black uprising of 1984–86 and the abject failure of the Total Strategy together finally made it very clear to numerous nationalist intellectuals that white and Afrikaner privilege rested on outright racial discrimination and naked repression. Now abandoning the historic mission of Grand Apartheid, many were wracked by the guilty realisation that their 40-year collective project had always been doomed, at best wrong, and, as a growing number of Afrikaner theologians were coming to accept, was sinful to boot. Afrikaner intellectual circles echoed the bewilderment of a former architect of Bantu Education at how, as 'reasonable, intelligent people', they could have spent 'forty lost years' believing in the 'laughable conception' of apartheid.[1]

Afrikaner society as a whole was etched with a profound sense of malaise and self-doubt which few NP politicians dared yet voice. It found expression instead among a growing band of prominent dissidents in the heart of the old nationalist establishment. In the words of Afrikanerdom's most influential journalist:

> Significant Afrikaner circles are marked by a sense of collective guilt over injustice, moral protest against white domination and inequality, disillusionment with apartheid and its consequences, anger over warped ideology and a strong sympathy for the struggle for a post-apartheid democracy and representative government.[2]

The 'guilt' of middle-aged Afrikaners was turned into an angry rejection of apartheid by many of their children. This led to growing protest at Afrikaner universities previously slavishly loyal to the NP.[3] Younger Afrikaners rejoiced in a new anarchistic, angry and satirical Afrikaner punk rock music and poetry. This *Voelvry* (Feel free) music flayed the middle-aged Afrikaners who religiously followed the NP. One of its leading exponents, Ralph Rabie (aka Johannes Kerkorrel) explained the view of what he called the 'so-called alternative Afrikaners' who had 'now crawled out of the woodwork':

> We Afrikaners were always from the bottom of the barrel. We realise that many of the country's problems over the last 40 years must be laid at the door of the National Party and us Afrikaners. But we are angry about this. We are furious because our parents have fucked up everything.*

Their work was an often deeply moving denunciation of the obscenities of apartheid, and a longing for a South Africa freed from both the fact and fruit of NP rule.[4] Kerkorrel's song 'BMW' gives vent to the widespread disgust felt by

---

* Quoted in P de Vos, 'Nuwe lied van jong Suid-Afrika', *Die Suid-Afrikaan*, 21, June/July 1989. This article contains a very useful discussion on this new Afrikaner punk movement. No Afrikaans review would dare to print such words as *fok* (fuck) even a few years earlier.

many younger Afrikaners at the hypocrisy and inhumanity of the *nouveau riche* Afrikaner bourgeoisie and yuppies:[5]

Ons ry 'n BMW	We drive a BMW
Ons ry 'n BMW	We drive a BMW
Ons gaan elke jaar oorsee	Every year we go oversees
ons ry 'n BMW	we drive a BMW
ons sal nie jou 'n lift gee	we will not give you a lift
ons ry 'n BMW	we drive a BMW
vir rylopers sê ons nee	to hitch-hikers we say no
ons ry 'n BMW	We drive a BMW
moet ons alles dan verniet	so must we give away everything for
weggee?	nothing?
Nee!	No!
Ons ry 'n BMW	We drive a BMW
Polina gaan maak vir die miesies	Paulina! go & make some tea for the
tee!	madam!
ons drink net suurlemoen tee	we only drink lemon tea
ons ry 'n BMW	we drive a BMW
ons stem vir die PFP, die KP, die NP	we vote for the PFP, the KP, the NP
alles met 'n P, net nie die ANC, nee!	Everything with a P, just not the ANC, no!
ons ry 'n BMW	we drive a BMW
moenie politiek praat hier nie	don't discuss politics here
ons sal blou moord skree ...	we'll scream blue murder ...
ons ry 'n BMW	we drive a BMW
kan iemand asseblief my sonbril	Will somebody please pass me my
aangee?	sunglasses?
en het iemand nog 'n idee? *	And does anybody still have any ideas?

The names adopted by some of these self-described 'Children of Verwoerd' systematically mocked all of the holiest cows of the nationalist culture and sacred history.† Much of their work was a direct and deliberate desecration of the Afrikaner civil religion. André Letoit's ballad *'Swart September'* (Black September) viciously parodies the holiest of holies – the Afrikaans National Anthem of the white state – *Die Stem (van Suid-Afrika)* [The Voice/Call (of South Africa)] – written by former NP senator C J Langenhoven:

Uit die blou van ons gekneusdheid	Rising from our blue bruisedness
uit die diepte van ons heimwee	from the depths of our homesickness
oor ons ver verlate homelands	over our far forsaken homelands

---

* Ons ry 'n BMW', words and music by Johannes Kerkorrel from the album *Eet Kreef!*, Shifty Music, 1989.

† The most popular of these punk groups was known as *Johannes Kerkorrel en die Gereformeerde Blues Band* (Jonathan church organ and the Reformed Blues Band), an heretical play on the names of the 'official' Afrikaner churches. A co-author of the song 'BMW' cited above called himself *Daggadirk Uys* – 'dagga' being the South African name for marijuana, and Dirk Uys was one of the most revered Afrikaner heroes in the sacred history.

waar die tsotsi's antwoord gee	the cries of gangsters echo
Oor ons afgebrande skole	From our burned-out schools
met die kreun van honger kinders	with the groans of hungry children
ruis de stem van al die squatters	mumurs the voice of all the squatters
van ons land Azanië*	of our country, Azania.

These artists deliberately set out to change the outlook (and politics) of the Afrikaner youth. Again in the words of Kerkorrel:

> Each time one must always try to push your audience a little bit, to bring them to the point where they notice the absurdity of the paranoia over the ANC – this paranoia must be mocked, and this is what I want to do. I would like young people, young Afrikaners, to learn to be free. Most people would never think that the Afrikaner youth is not free, but ultimately they are absolutely unfree. They are expected to carry on the oppression here you know. They must shoot people and they hate it. [Young] People can't stand it any more. That's why they go so crazy when they hear our rock and roll.[6]

Other young Afrikaner artists and cultural activists even further to the left than the 'Feel Free' musicians criticised their lack of open political commitment. Still others derided the macho pretensions of their 'big cock rock', describing it as 'riding John Wayne-style to save South Africa'.[7]

Whatever its artistic or political shortcomings, this new music and poetry was an even more radical attack on the foundations of the very idea of 'the Afrikaner' than that of the *Sestigers* in the 1960s. The *Sestigers'* experiments with form and content had shattered the stultifying mould of 'official' Afrikaner culture. Yet for all their pathbreaking efforts, the *Sestigers* remained largely within the framework of the Afrikaans language. Indeed, a poet like Breyten Breytenbach raised Afrikaans to dizzying new lyrical and metaphorical heights. The work of the *Sestigers* dramatically confirmed *and developed* the power of the Afrikaans language. In doing so, these *enfants terribles* of the 1960s had strengthened the self-regard of most Afrikaners except the cultural flat earthers. As their eventual consecration in the Afrikaner cultural pantheon indicated, despite their often ferocious critique of Afrikaner nationalism, the work of the *Sestigers* had actually *reinforced* the desperate search for *eie*. This explains the huge audiences of the Afrikaner establishment which sat in Opera Houses in evening dress and rapture listening to Breyten Breytenbach flagellate them on his South African tours before and after his imprisonment. Outside of the relatively small

---

* 'Swart September', lyrics by André Letoit (Koos Kombuis) from the album *Niemandsland*, Shifty Music, 1989. Reproduced by permission of Shifty Music. 'Azania' was the name for South Africa used by the Black Consciousness movement and the PAC. For whites, this name had terribly radical connotations. This underscores their ignorance of black politics and particularly the fact that all ANC-aligned groups vociferously rejected 'Azania', preferring to use the word Africa in the name of their country. This poem also parodies the work of idealised nationalist poets such as C Louis Leipoldt, *Boerneef* ('farmer cousin', the pretentious pseudonym of I W van der Merwe), and N P van Wyk Louw.

fundamentalist circles, most urban Afrikaner nationalists were intensely proud of what the *Sestigers* wrought for Afrikaans literature and language. Even today, the more obdurate of the ethnic purists will tell you that despite his deplorable politics, nobody speaks or writes Afrikaans like Breytenbach.

This was hardly the case of the new writing and music. Not only did it represent a furious assault on the pretensions of Afrikaner nationalism and the ethnic mission, even more importantly much of the work was an frontal attack on the purity of the Afrikaans language itself. To the horror of the new cultural establishment, these writers and musicians mixed street Afrikaans with English and even words from African languages. The anarchic result was an always bracing, often lyrical, and occasionally extraordinarily powerful and moving linguistic synthesis. But it was never *suiwer* (pure) Afrikaans. These young Afrikaner cultural workers spat in the collective face of the nationalist cultural and political establishment. Their rapturous reception by alienated Afrikaner students seemed to signal that this central element of Afrikaner youth now openly and contemptuously dismissed any notion of *eie*. This compounded their lack of a clear sense of, and pride in, Afrikaner identity. These were precisely the children and the products of the forty lost years of Afrikaner rule and Afrikaner favouritism. Their contempt for not just the politics and ideology, but even the language and the *identity* of Afrikanerdom, was perhaps the most eloquent statement of the historical failure of the once-sacred ethnic mission. This is perhaps nowhere clearer than in André Letoit's agonised poem, 'Curriculum vitae':

(vir nog 'n nuwe werkgewer)	(for still another new employer)
My nooi is in 'n nartjie	My girl is in a tangerine
My ouma in die tronk	My grandma in the jail
My oupa is 'n try-for-white	My grandpa is a try-for-white
My pa is altyd dronk	My father's always drunk
My oom is in die Broederbond	My uncle's in the Broederbond
My boetie saag net meter maids	My brother only screws meter maids
My neef studeer nog vrugteloos	My nephew is still studying hopelessly
En my beste vriend het AIDS	And my best friend has AIDS
Die freaks dink ek is plastic	The freaks think I'm plastic
Die fuzz meen: skisofreen	The police reckon: schizophrenic
My predikant voel ek's 'n bietjie regs	My priest feels I'm a little right wing
Maar in my hart 'n goeie seun	But in my heart a good boy
My nooi is in 'n nartjie	My girl is in a tangerine
My ma vrees elke kommunis	My mother dreads every communist
My oom het 'n jacuzzi	My uncle has a jacuzzi
*En ek weet nie wie de fok ek is**	And I don't know who the fuck I am

---

* 'Curriculum Vitae' by André Letoit, from *Die Bar op de Aar: Ballades, Blues en Bevliegings* (Tafelberg, Cape Town, 1988), 70. Reproduced by permission of Tafelberg Publishers. In his poem *'Swart Transvaal'* (Black Transvaal) Letoit refers to 'Afrikaners, jaag-kakaners' (Afrikaners, hunt-shit-aners). It led to his cabaret with Kerkorrel, *Piekniek by Dingaan*, being banned from Nico Malan theatre.

In the context of what two leading Afrikaans writers labelled 'the destruction of the entire known world or way of life', this youthful disgust with official Afrikanerdom was echoed in other intellectual circles.[8] Veterans of Pretoria's border wars defied the SADF's ban on writing about their combat experiences. Their new and apocalyptic *grensliteratuur* (border literature) described the brutalised, amoral universe of these covert wars. One former member of the elite 'Reccie' unit (the Reconnaissance Commandos) depicted young Afrikaners as so brutalised by their military experience that language was reduced to a primal scream.[9] Hailed by some Afrikaner critics as an *avant garde* and liberatory expression, this exploration of the moral vacuum and chaos of South Africa's various southern African military adventures was denounced by at least one Stellenbosch-trained anthropologist as essentially legitimating white atrocities in Namibia and Angola.[10]

Still other Afrikaners also took up these issues, addressing a more mainstream audience. A lively Afrikaner intellectual review (*Die Suid-Afrikaan*) was started in 1985 to debate all the previously forbidden and unmentionable. It rapidly evolved into one of the most interesting publications in the country. It was soon followed by the spirited and highly original weekly newspaper, *Die Vrye Weekblad*. The paper both proudly asserted a deracialised and vibrant Afrikaner writing, and specialised in extremely courageous exposés of some of the darkest, most dangerous secrets of the state – issues virtually no other South African publication dared touch.*

The wind from Helderburg: The verligte challenge

The growing Afrikaner disillusionment with Botha's policies was also reflected in ferment inside the NP. Writing about this 'cauldron' a former key reformist insider described four distinct factions in the NP caucus. The 'PW Nats' remained strong on security and the Group Areas Act. They faced off against 'Fast Nats' (former verligtes) increasingly alienated from the leadership and its apparent lack of a reform strategy. Though likewise unhappy, the 'New Nats' still believed that the NP remained 'the best vehicle for reform'. However Botha's intransigence could soon turn many Fast and New Nats into 'Past Nats' who would leave the party.[11]

This came to pass in the May 1987 general election, which catalysed a slow reshaping of the topography of white politics. Campaigning under the slogan 'Reform yes, surrender no', Botha's NP depicted itself as the sole force capable of maintaining 'law and order', and vigorously attacked 'foreign interference' and particularly US sanctions. This appeared to work. The NP's parliamentary representation actually increased as its 52 percent of the vote gave it 123 of the 166 elected seats plus 10 of the 12 appointed MPs. Yet this was achieved largely at the

---

* Thus its exposé, *inter alia*, of Police and Army death squads in the so-called Civil Cooperation Bureau later obliged President de Klerk to appoint the Harms Commission of Enquiry in 1989.

expense of the PFP and NRP. The latter was virtually obliterated and disappeared soon after, while the PFP lost eight seats to the NP and its status as official opposition to the KP. The far right vote was double that of 1981. The KP's haul of 23 seats on 25 percent of the vote surprised even it own leadership. Yet the far right could have done even better. With its vote split between the KP and the HNP (which lost its only seat), the far right handed the NP nine seats in constituencies where the combined KP/HNP vote exceeded that for the nationalists.*

Yet the real significance of the 1987 election was not so much the KP advance as the dramatic events to the NP's left. During the election campaign Transvaal NP leader F W de Klerk acknowledged that 'our theory is on the rocks'.[12] Fast Nats now streamed through this breech to abandon the good ship NP. In January 1987 the nationalist MP for Randburg, Wynand Malan, left the Transvaal NP to fight his Randburg seat as an independent. He was soon joined Pretoria's Ambassador to Britain and former verligte MP, Dr Dennis Worrall who resigned his ambassadorship to stand as an independent candidate in the Helderburg constituency. This was the seat of Cape NP leader and Minister of Constitutional Development and Planning, Chris Heunis – the man who had summarily rejected the constitutional proposals of Worrall's 1982 President's Council Report and sent the ambitious Doctor Worrall packing to Canberra (p. 287 above). Worrall was clearly bent on revenge. The Independent roster was filled by Professor Ester Lategan who now opposed the NP candidate in the Stellenbosch seat of the leading Afrikaner university. The three former NP 'reformists' then formed a loose coalition known as the Independent Movement.

The Independents caught a real wave of discontent among Fast and New Nats, causing 'a great deal of concern within the NP'. The ruling party's own polls showed that 'up to 22 percent of NP supporters were prepared to take their coats and leave' Botha's party.[13] A large number of Stellenbosch academics expressed support for the Independent Movement.† Its credibility and prestige was immeasurably enhanced when one of the four most powerful figures in the Cape NP, Nasionale Pers managing director D P de Villiers announced his support for Lategan. De Villiers was immediately fired for 'betraying' his 'fellow combatants' by the man who had himself been the leading 'Fast Nat' of his day and perennial thorn in the side of Dr Verwoerd – former editor of *Die Burger*, now chairman of Nasionale Pers, Piet Cillié. Nasionale Pers was the bedrock of the political machine which P W Botha regarded as his personal political tool. It had been founded at the same time as, grown up with, and been both the voice and strongest defender of, the Cape NP. It is difficult to overestimate the jolt De Villiers' gesture must have given the party. It coincided

---

* *The Star*, 13 May 1987. An HNP representative had entered parliament for the first time in 15 years when one of the four former nationalist MPs expelled in 1969, Louis Stofberg, won a by-election in Sasolburg in 1985. Unable to hold the seat in 1987, Stofberg finally defected to the KP.

† Over 50% of Stellenbosch academics reportedly supported 329 of their colleagues who signed a manifesto and petition calling for speedier reform – *The Star*, 30 March 1987.

with the equally shocking resignation of the editor of the most influential NP newspaper and brother of Transvaal NP leader – Willem de Klerk of *Rapport* – in protest at pressure from his board, the Cabinet (and presumably his sibling), to adopt a more 'strongly propagandistic' editorial line.[14]

In the event, Malan was the only Independent Movement candidate to win a seat. However Lategan slashed the NP's Stellenbosch majority and Worrall came within just 39 votes of unseating Heunis – effectively erasing the latter's already fading hopes of ever succeeding P W Botha. The NP hierarchy reacted with something close to panic. Yet the three Independent Movement candidates were unable to sustain the momentum nor overcome their strategic differences and personal rivalries. The group soon split into Malan's National Democratic Movement (NDM) – which sought to build links with extra-parliamentary groups – and Worrall's more conservative Independent Party (IP). This reinforced the position of the 'New Nats' over the 'Fast Nats' in the NP caucus, as 'leftist nationalists … retreated into the laager and the old attitude that the NP must be edged towards more radical reform'.[15]

Nevertheless, the Independent Movement was a unique phenomenon in NP history. Leftward defections from the NP on this scale and stature were simply unprecedented. That a disaffected, *English-speaking* former nationalist MP could come within a whisker of unseating the man who had succeeded D F Malan, Eben Dönges and P W Botha as leader of the Cape party, and this in a predominantly Afrikaans constituency, beggared the imagination of most nationalists. It dramatically underscored the disaffection of former insiders from P W Botha's authoritarianism. It equally marked a dawning realisation that 'reformists' wishing to end the political impasse had also to break with what Willem de Klerk called President Botha's 'deadend street' politics.[16] And it underscored the fact that the once hard and fast rules of white politics were beginning to bend close to breaking point.

Despite their inability to sustain their own impetus, the Independents catalysed a slow, subterranean shift in attitudes in the NP establishment. It was carried considerably further by a series of meetings between the ANC and leading Afrikaners organised by former PFP leader Van Zyl Slabbert's Institute for Democratic Alternatives for South Africa (IDASA).* These meetings went a great way to building a groundswell for change within leading Afrikaner circles. In effectively demythologising the ANC in the collective mind of much of this Afrikaner establishment, the IDASA initiative slowly legitimised the once-unthinkable – that negotiations with the ANC were not just inevitable, but would happen sooner rather than later.

---

* The shockwaves of the first of these meetings – in Dakar, Senegal in July 1987 – rocked not just the NP. The PFP was divided by the unauthorised participation in the 'trek to Dakar' by a number of its MPs and other office bearers. They were all obliged to apologise to PFP leader Colin Eglin. The PFP witch hunt over the affair led to the resignation from the party of three of its MPs, and one of its representatives on the President's Council. Most of them then aligned themselves with Wynand Malan's National Democratic Movement. Some later ended up in the ANC.

This process was further facilitated by important changes the election wrought in the NP caucus and other party structures. The 1987 caucus was younger (70 percent under age 50) and better educated than ever. Fully one-third of its members were first elected in 1987. Its 12 English-speaking MPs were as many as sat in the PFP caucus. Moreover, a dozen of the 'New Nats' of the previous caucus had been promoted to deputy minsterships or the influential position of chairman of this or that standing committees.[17] Botha's high-handed leadership would sit even less well with his new caucus and Cabinet.

The 1987 election also accentuated the strains in the two major provincial NPs. For the first time since 1948, the Cape party now had one more MP than the Transvaal NP. Yet the election had left this newly dominant force in the caucus with major headaches. Unlike in the Transvaal, the Cape NP's problem was not the KP. The Treurnichtites had won less than 15 percent of the Cape vote and remained marginal in its politics. The well-knit Cape NP establishment had always been more cohesive than its permanently fractious Transvaal counterpart. Now, however, the Cape party faced a dramatic crisis of leadership and vision. The real force of the defections had struck at the very heart of the Cape nationalist establishment. Though P W Botha had relinquished the leadership of the Cape party to Chris Heunis the year before, he remained the immovable colossus of Cape NP politics. Deeply alienated by Botha's contempt for those outside the NSMS magic circle, much of the Cape establishment now probably secretly sympathised with the Independents' cause. Chris Heunis had never been much more than Botha's creature.* His verbose and often incomprehensible regular lectures on consociational and constitutional theory had made him something of a figure of fun in the Press. Now increasingly ignored by his truculent mentor, just 39 votes from losing his seat and clearly unable to deal with the KP in Parliament, Heunis lost much of his remaining political credibility and clout. The Cape NP could neither crawl out of Botha's political shadow nor openly oppose him without either being dumped in the political wilderness (*à la* De Villiers) or handing the NP caucus to the Transvalers and the generals.

Yet the Transvaal party too was in growing disarray. The brunt of the KP assault on the traditional NP bases of electoral support lay in the Transvaal. The Treurnichtites won three votes for every four cast for the Transvaal NP in 1987. This rendered marginal more than 20 of the Transvaal NP's 47 seats – including that of its leader, F W de Klerk in Vereniging. De Klerk's party had lost virtually all the rural constituencies and faced major problems in many urban areas. Now essentially an urban middle-class party competing with the PFP for the yuppie

---

* Heunis spent his entire political life in P W Botha's shadow. The chairman of the NP branch in Botha's George constituency in the 1950s, Heunis acted as his MP's understudy, representing George in the Cape Provincial Council from 1959 to 1970. Elected to Parliament at the age of 43 in the April 1970 general election, he had been taken into the Cabinet by a reluctant Vorster at P W Botha's insistence in 1974.

vote, it was able to preserve its fragile lead over the KP only by winning additional support from English speakers. While F W de Klerk had acknowledged that state policy was 'on the rocks', he was hobbled by Emperor Botha and frozen out of the NSMS magic circle. Seen as a conservative, and obsessed with the endless war against the KP, he was in no position to lead an anti-Botha groundswell.

The Transvaal NP's woes were further aggravated by the municipal elections of October 1988. It had defended itself from KP attacks during the 1987 white general election by campaigning on the issue of security. This had reduced the room available to the Treurnichtites to attack the National Party without being seen to question white power itself. But the KP was under no such constraints in the 1988 municipal elections. It now fastened on to the highly visible consequences of Botha's scrapping of the influx control system in 1986 – the mushrooming of black squatter communities in the 'white' urban areas. The NP had come to power in 1948 denouncing the black *oorstroming* of the cities (p. 34 above). D F Malan's party had steadfastly rejected that which the Fagan Commission had declared 'inevitable' in 1948 – the permanence and irreversibility of black urbanisation. Now, however, despite President Botha's insistence on 'orderly urbanisation', NP policy in effect conformed to the once-pilloried Fagan report. Playing on the fears of the poorer white electorate, the KP now cleverly evoked the NP's 1948 rejection of black *oorstroming* of the 'white' urban areas. This paid huge political dividends. Treurnicht's party captured control of most Transvaal municipalities except Pretoria and Johannesburg – in which latter city the NP displaced the PFP as the single biggest party.*

The NP had now irrevocably parted from its old rural and urban lower-class white base. But its appeal to the Afrikaans and English middle-class and yuppie vote was sharply undermined by both its lack of a viable constitutional policy as well as its now highly unpopular leader. Its political dilemma was accentuated by Botha's attempts to defer until 1992 the election for all three Houses of Parliament constitutionally due in 1989. To do so, he required the approval of the three Houses,. Still smarting from myriad humiliations at Botha's hands, the leader of the majority Labour Party in the 'Coloured' House of Representatives – the Rev. Alan Hendrickse – refused to comply unless Botha first agreed to scrap the Group Areas Act setting aside segregated residential and business areas. P W Botha was never a man to give in to what he regarded as political blackmail. He was less likely to do so when this came from a man whom he had fired from his own Cabinet for insubordination. And *Baas* Botha was certainly not going to bend to the will of a cheeky 'Coloured' who mocked Botha's frequent lectures to the House of Representatives that the

---

* Itself a major turnaround. In the heyday of Afrikaner nationalism in the late 1940s and early 1950s, the NP had been unable to hold meetings in Johannesburg without being physically attacked by outraged English-speakers and anti-fascists.

'coloureds' needed to display a little more gratitude to the leader of the party which 'had done so much for the Coloured people'. But behind Botha's always highly personalised view of politics lay another more serious consideration. The Group Areas Act was one of the few remaining legislative props of Grand Apartheid still in force. Should it be repealed before a general election, the NP risked provoking an even greater drainage of support to the KP, particularly in the Transvaal. The large number of marginal seats held by the NP made this an unacceptably risky step. And Transvaal leader F W de Klerk implacably opposed making such politically charged concessions.

By the end of 1988 the NP was dire straits. Frustration with Botha's leadership and cavalier marginalisation of all the structures of his party was rife. One MP warned of the 'disintegration' of the NP if Botha remained in office much longer.[18] Cowed by the generals' rhetoric, but deeply resentful at being ordered around by them, most politicians longed for the re-establishment of civilian control over the NSMS, for a return to 'normal' politics unhindered by either the men on horseback or their imperious President. While very few were prepared openly to challenge the transformation P W Botha had wrought in the NP and state, real committed political support for man who was once the great master of NP politics had virtually dissipated. With the government gripped by a growing sense of paralysis, a hidden but intense behind-the-scenes struggle for the succession led to much intrigue. As the year unfolded, a series of other developments began to shift the balance of forces against the regime.

Déjà vu all over again: The political crisis deepens

In October 1987, the SADF force occupying southern Angola turned back an Angolan offensive to capture the Jamba headquarters of Jonas Savimbi's UNITA group. The South Africans then won a decisive victory against FAPLA (the Angolan army) at the battle of Lomba River, massacring thousands of elite FAPLA troops. Emboldened by this triumph, the SADF then laid siege to the strategic town of Cuito Cuanavale. In doing so, however, Pretoria's generals fatally overreached themselves. Alarmed at the spectre of a South African breakthrough, the Angolan government desperately appealed for full-scale Cuban support. The Cuban government agreed, on condition that FAPLA dispense with what the Cuban high command regarded as the disastrous strategy and tactics imposed by Soviet advisers, and hand over strategic command of the battle to them.[19]

The battle for Cuito Cuanavale then soon turned into the largest conventional battle in Africa since World War II. The result was a disaster for Pretoria. While the SADF scored great success with pinpoint barrages from its G-5 and G-6 artillery guided by reconnaissance drone aircraft, in the end Cuban-piloted MIG-23s wrested air superiority from the South African Air Force (SAAF). The SAAF lost anywhere from five to 42 of its outdated but irreplaceable various versions of the Mirage combat aircraft.* The level of white conscript casualties grew politically unacceptable, and several battalions mutinied. Outflanking Cuban and Angolan forces eventually reached the Namibian border. The South African forces were virtually encircled and could not withdraw with their heavy equipment. The Angolan government urged the Cubans to annihilate the SADF forces in Angola, but Fidel Castro obliged Angola now to negotiate all issues with a suddenly much more amenable Pretoria. Four-party talks eventually produced the December 1988 Brazzaville Protocol. Signed by South Africa, Angola, Cuba and the United States, this provided for the withdrawal of South African and Cuban troops from Angola, and implementation within a year of the decade-old UN Resolution 435 on Namibian independence. Shifting away from his generals for the first time since 1986, P W Botha made the decision to settle the Namibian issue, 'on the basis of a carefully considered cost-benefit analysis by a senior intelligence officer'.[20]

Its military difficulties aside, by 1988 Pretoria was coming under growing international pressure, particularly from the US. The publication in early 1988 of a State Department report on Renamo atrocities in Mozambique severely embarrassed the Botha government. Using very strong language pregnant with huge symbolism in Reaganite America, the US Deputy Assistant Secretary of State for Africa described what had been done to Marxist-Leninist Mozambique as the most 'brutal holocaust against ordinary human beings' since the Nazis.† Pretoria's discomfort was aggravated by a *New York Times* editorial calling for a similarly authoritative report to 'expose South Africa's real hand in Mozambique'.[21] The Democratic Party platform for the 1988 US Presidential elections labelled South Africa a 'terrorist state', a position endorsed by its candidate Michael Dukakis. During the period when Dukakis was ahead of George Bush in the polls, his party's platform caused many sleepless nights in Pretoria.‡ The outgoing Reagan administration became manifestly less willing to shield Pretoria. Washington's growing cooperation with the Soviet Union had been vital in settling the Angolan conflict, and Pretoria feared lest its own regional interests be sacrificed by the US on the altar of superpower cooperation. Throughout the 1980s, Pretoria's various destabilising regional interventions had been central to re-establishing its definition of its own 'security'. By the end of the decade, however, they seemed to open a window

---

* The lower figure being losses acknowledged by the SADF, the higher representing Angolan claims.

† Quoted *Weekly Mail*, 5 May 1988. South Africa's Ambassador to Washington, Dr *Piet Pompies* Koornhof, attempted to persuade the State Department to delay publication of this Gersony Report. When rebuffed, he tried equally unsuccessfully to persuade Foggy Bottom that the report should be jointly published by South Africa and the US. Personal communication from a senior Mozambican diplomat.

‡ Under US law, the designation of a country as a 'terrorist state' carries very far-reaching and obligatory embargoes and sanctions, not just by the United States, but by all countries wishing to maintain good relations with Washington.

of vulnerability, which was then widened by other developments.

Sanctions began to loom very large in 1988. The mandatory UN arms embargo had proven decisive in Angola. While Israel, Taiwan and other states had no compunction in helping South Africa secure a wide variety of arms and equipment, modern fighter aircraft were another beast entirely. SADF Mirages had been shot down by MIG-23s, themselves long obsolete. No state was now willing to replace South Africa's Cheetah fighter aircraft – an update of the Israeli update of the long out-of-date French Mirage. And such aircraft had been crucial in the losing battle for Cuito Cuanavale.

Its options already severely circumscribed by the arms embargo, Pretoria faced the threat of heavy sanctions on other, even more worrying, fronts. The Dellums Bill before the US Congress sought to end virtually all US links with South Africa. The Commonwealth Foreign Ministers elaborated a strategy to undermine South Africa's international financial links. By mid-1988 employers and government were expressing fears that gathering sanctions moves would place added strain on gold and minerals. A senior Minister acknowledged that the February banning of 17 organisations was responsible for the growing sanctions pressure, and stressed the need to water down the Dellums Bill.[22] With Pretoria's foreign reserves lower than those of Botswana, and prohibitive debt repayments due in 1990, the Governor of the Reserve Bank warned in early 1989:

> If adequate progress is not made in the field of political and constitutional reform, South Africa's relationships with the rest of the world are unlikely to improve to any significant extent. In that event South Africa will probably remain a capital-exporting and debt-repaying country. The ideals of optimal growth, low inflation and a rising standard of living will not be achieved without adequate progress in the field of political reform.[23]

Still other international developments undermined the generals' strategy. Soviet *Perestroika* and US/USSR cooperation in Angola and other regional conflicts eroded the 'total onslaught' psychology. The Soviet Union was retreating from the Third World even before the fall of the Berlin Wall. By the end of 1988 it was placing strong pressure on the ANC to reach a negotiated settlement which guaranteed whites rights.[24] Not even Magnus Malan's most obdurate general could now credibly argue that every strike in South Africa was part of Moscow's grand design.

The single major achievement of the generals' strategy under the post June-1986 State of Emergency had been the re-establishment of 'stability'. The resistance had been driven on to the defensive, much of its fragile organisation shattered and its hopes of a quick victory over 'the regime' destroyed. Many employers began to turn on the trade unions in 1987, and even the powerful Congress of South African Trade Unions (Cosatu) began to retreat from its radical militancy after the failure of the August 1987 mineworkers' strike. The February 1988 banning of 17 organisations (including the UDF), and the interdiction of political activity by Cosatu was intended to give the regime the time to elaborate a strategy to legitimate the state. However, as indicated above (p. 377), this latter task now seemed beyond the capacities and imagination of the Botha administration.

Even more ominously, the enhanced 'security' established under the State of Emergency showed signs of beginning to unravel in 1988. At great risk to itself and its credibility, Cosatu called a three-day stay-at-home strike by all workers in June. Millions of workers turned this into the biggest ever stayaway in South African history. Emboldened by the clear support for Cosatu, and mobilised for a boycott campaign against the 1988 municipal elections, the dominant 'Congress' tendency in the extra-parliamentary opposition regrouped itself into the Mass Democratic Movement (MDM).* This led to a new explosion of mass resistance in the early 1989 Defiance Campaign – a campaign which also seemed to have learned from the voluntaristic and militaristic errors of the failed insurrection. The Congressites no longer sought to make the country ungovernable as in 1984–86, but rather to clog to death the functioning of segregated social services.

Law and Order Minister Adriaan Vlok boldly claimed that the government had developed a coherent 'master plan' to deal with the situation.[25] Yet unable to finance its grandiose upgrading schemes, nor create the climate for renewed economic growth, and again apparently unable to contain black anger at its own illegitimacy, the administration seemed reduced to simple crisis management. Himself clearly ailing, the imperious President retreated into further petulance. Lashing out at ministers involved in succession intrigues, threatening legislation against journalists who 'maligned or slandered' public figures, P W Botha opened the November 1988 Transvaal NP Congress pledging to 'fight this struggle to the bitter end'. He told the Natal NP congress that 'I am not even considering to discuss the possibility of black majority government in South Africa.'[26]

By the end of 1988 a powerful sense of *déjà vu* hung over white politics. P W Botha's administration was mired in an impasse remarkably similar to the one which had finished off John Vorster exactly a decade earlier. Just as in 1977, the National Party had won a major electoral victory in a 'law 'n order' campaign denouncing US interference. Just as in 1977, the previous Official Opposition was in disarray and had been replaced by a more vigorous force. Yet again the NP's massive election victory simply aggravated strains in the increasingly polarised party. Once again, its ailing and embittered *Hoofleier* had alienated his own political base, surrounded himself with a narrow magic circle of security advisers who were detested by the NP's civilian politicians. Like Vorster in early 1978, Botha had clearly run out of ideas, had lost the respect of much of his caucus and deeply resented the open battle for succession. The Botha govern-

---

* A debate in the (banned) UDF over whether to participate in the October 1988 municipal elections was won by the boycottists. See Seekings, 'What was the UDF?'

ment now seemed as paralysed as that of John Vorster, and for similar reasons.

P W Botha had clawed his way to the Premiership in 1978 at the head of a new political alignment, determined to resolve the myriad crises confronting the South African state. Twelve years of Botha's reforms left the South African economy in much worse shape than John Vorster's worst nightmares had ever feared possible. The failure of first the Total Strategy and then the strategy of low intensity domestic warfare left South Africa stuck in the future Vorster had once declared 'too ghastly to contemplate'. For all its pretensions of 'military science' and technocratic managerialism, the government of the *Groot Krokodil* lacked a creative political strategy even to manage let alone resolve the crisis. In an ironic parallel with the dilemma which had faced Jan Smuts's United Party government after World War II, Botha's tired and deeply divided NP government was completely unable to satisfy the conflicting demands emanating from its shrinking political base. Even less was it able to to respond to the calls for change from the increasingly restive major business interests – let alone develop an effective solution to the political problem posed by a volatile and restive black opposition.

After forty years in power, the National Party had come to recognise that its historic mission to impose apartheid on South Africa had failed. Key moral brokers of the Afrikaner establishment were even harsher in their judgement. While P W Botha could declare apartheid a 'mistake', and F W de Klerk acknowledged that the NP's policy was 'on the rocks', the entire society remained imprisoned in the crumbling but still standing ruins of apartheid. Yet the NP government seemed completely unable to demolish their foundations, and clung to power with petulance and viciousness.

The NP itself and its cantankerous *Hoofleier* had themselves become major political obstacles to the resolution of the crisis. South Africa had suffered its second major military reversal in Angola in thirteen years. It faced growing international pressure for real reform. All the elements of the crisis of the 1970s (p. 170 above) which Botha had set out so determinedly to address remained unresolved on the tenth anniversary of his coming to office. Now, however, each element of the crisis was immeasurably more acute than in 1978. Taken together, they threatened the very existence of the state. The leader of the NP government was just as paralysed as the man he had so ruthlessly run out of office. His party was but a shadow of what it had been in 1978. It now seemed extremely unlikely that South Africa's enormous problems could ever be solved while the NP remained in power. Indeed, its ongoing rule had became *the* central issue of a simmering civil war. At the very least, its leader would have to go. Even the NP press now recognised this fact. But no nationalist politician had the courage to bell *this* cat in the NP caucus.

Chapter Twenty-One

CROCODILE TEARS

The fall of P W Botha

Cry me a river!

Who's next? Line-up in the succession battle

The sharp and often underhand battle for the NP succession after the 1987 election simply underlined the absence of a powerful alternate vision to the 'deadend politics' of the *Groot Krokodil*. The main contender, Transvaal NP leader F W de Klerk, spent much time cultivating MPs ignored by Botha and building a base of support inside the now marginalised Afrikaner Broederbond. Ever since assuming the Transvaal leadership in 1982, De Klerk's main political concern had been to defend the NP's right flank against the challenge from the far right. This did not help his efforts to present himself as a man capable of finding the reformist solutions which had eluded P W Botha. Even De Klerk's adoring older brother writes apologetically that during this period, the Transvaal leader

> was still apt to make ultra-conservative noises in his attempt to halt the growth of the Conservatives; and if he was slowly edging towards a more enlightened [verligte] stand, he was also constantly qualifying his pronouncements with what were seen as more 'balanced' ones, confirming suspicions that he was hedging his bets and trying to accommodate divergent perspectives ... the mantle of conservatism still clung to him.[1]

Widely regarded as 'a man without real convictions, always looking over his shoulder [at the threat from the KP]', De Klerk saw his support slip in 1988.[2] Yet there were few other credible alternative candidates. De Klerk's main institutional rival, Cape NP leader Chris Heunis, had virtually no experience in dealing with the assault from the KP. He was himself in deep political trouble. Never seen as much more than as P W Botha's lapdog, any real hopes Heunis might have cherished were wiped out by his near defeat in the 1987 election. To make matters worse for Heunis, someone mounted 'an undercover campaign from within government ranks to demolish what remains of his prestige'. Two of his senior officials lost their security clearance in October 1988 in a effort to block the 'conception of [constitutional] reform ... evolving' in Heunis's department. This severely undermined what little was left of the Cape leader's clout in the SSC.[3]

The third figure in the race was Foreign Minister Pik Botha. To the intense ire of his presidential namesake, Pik Botha's supporters organised themselves into the 'Club of 22' and other front groups in 1988.* Yet the maverick Foreign Minister had many enemies in caucus and stood absolutely no chance of ever being elected *Hoofleier*. At best he could hope to repeat his 1978 role as king-maker. He seemed to realise this when he told his former leading organiser, Finance Minister Barend du Plessis, that he would not be a candidate, giving Du Plessis permission to launch his own leadership campaign.[4] Du Plessis sought

---

* *Financial Mail*, 10 February 1989. This club took its name from the number of caucus votes Pik Botha had won in the first round of the 1978 NP *Hoofleier* election.

to rally reformist opposition to De Klerk, winning praise as 'the man who can handle' the KP.[5] Yet the very fact that he was seen as a credible candidate under-scored the poverty of the choice. Du Plessis has been widely regarded as the front runner in a very crowded field for the title of South Africa's worst-ever Finance Minister.*

Other rumoured candidates for the *Hoofleier*ship included Defence Minister Malan and former Broederbond chairman Gerrit Viljoen. Yet, always uncom-fortable with the backslapping side of politics, General Malan had never been popular in the caucus. He preferred to tell people what to do than to try to win their support. He was so closely identified with the failure of P W Botha's various strategies that his chances of winning caucus support were slim indeed. His best hope lay in repeating what Margaret Thatcher had proved in the South Atlantic in 1982 – that military success could cancel all bets and swing the tide in the most unpopular leader's favour. Yet even though all the details of the war in southern Angola were again being denied to the public, most South Africans and all politicians were very well aware that things were not going the SADF's way in 1988.

Gerrit Viljoen for his part had never been able to overcome his remote professorial demeanour. Nor had he acquired the political art of cultivating support and building a personal base. By the end of 1988 he seemed to have lost whatever wish he may once have had to pursue the leadership quest.

Thus while P W Botha was clearly ailing throughout 1988, no strong leader had emerged, poised to take over the reins. The silent, but frantic manoeuvring for the succession simply compounded the regime's enormous political problems. However the vast logjam in white politics slowly began to evidence some cracks in the late 1980s. Just as in the impasse of the 1970s, the first signs of movement appeared in the ranks of the parliamentary opposition.

Get your act together!
The political reawakening of capital

The disastrous showing of the liberal PFP in the May 1987 election prompted the president of the South Africa Foundation and chairman of the Syfrets financial group to ask: 'has white business shifted to the right?' Responding negatively to his own question, Len Abrahamse expressed the view that 'in the absence of strong parliamentary opposition on the left, business will increasingly find itself representing the opinions of those to the left of the government'.[6] A group of influential Afrikaans- and English-speaking

---

* One businessman told me *à propos* Du Plessis' sojourn in the Finance Ministry: 'Any man who came make [Du Plessis' predecessor as Finance Minister, the far from brilliant] Owen Horwood look good, is indeed a genius, a veritable Prince of Mediocrity', Du Plessis was publicly criticised by the *doyen* of Afrikaner business, former Sanlam chairman, A D Wassenaar.

financiers, industrialists and retailers began discussions on how to mobilise this nascent business opposition, meeting quietly throughout 1987.*

In part these business leaders were motivated by the fear that Abrahamse was dead wrong in his assessment that business was not shifting to the right under the new security regime. Their later spokesman explained that they had been deeply worried by the 'alarming' proposals circulated by another 'select group of South Africa's most influential businessmen' in early 1988. This latter group of capitalists advocated an even tougher business attitude to organised labour than represented in the government's controversial Labour Relations Bill.† While their proposals reportedly met with 'outright ridicule' within the broader business community, they acted as a spur to a more proactive role by various business leaders.

Now deeply concerned that failure to achieve a minimum growth rate of 5 percent would 'prove to be disastrous', most businessmen agreed with Abrahamse's widely circulated April 1988 article arguing that renewed economic growth was impossible 'without the removal of statutory inhibitions' to full political involvement by all South Africans.[7] As the year unfolded, businessmen became increasingly angered by Botha's failure to deliver the privatisation and deregulation in his February 'Bothanomics' package.[8] Alarmed at Botha's blunt refusal even to consider lifting the 'insidious' '[State of] Emergency', major business leaders echoed Abrahamse's plea that 'we need to set this society free, not to strangle it'.[9]

The tone of the growing political debate among businessmen was also influenced by the publication in mid-1988 of the ANC's 'Constitutional Guidelines for a Democratic South Africa'. The ANC's proposed bill of rights, mixed economy and multi-party democracy were substantially less radical than many businessmen had feared. This seemed to confirm the reports from a series of IDASA-organised meetings between Afrikaner intellectuals and the ANC that accommodation with the ANC might just be possible on terms which did not 'throw out the baby of free enterprise with the bathwater of capitalism'.

Coordinated efforts were now made to address the two central political problems confronting capital – the lack of a programme of political reform acceptable to blacks, and absence of a credible political vehicle. Afrikaner

---

* This group included Chris Ball of Barclays Bank (he of the ANC advert fame), Chris van Wyk of Trust Bank, Neal Chapman and Zac de Beer of Southern Life (and, in De Beer's case, Anglo American), Mike Sander of AECI, Mervyn King of Tradegro. Former Judge Anton Mostert (who had played such a central role in the Information Department scandal) was also involved. See the article by the later head of the Consultative Business Movement, Christo Nel, 'Group Therapy', *Leadership South Africa*, 7, 4, 1988.

† Arguing, *inter alia*, that employers should be empowered summarily to dismiss anybody they regarded as an 'agitator', and 'where appropriate, shut them out of the workplace and place of residence'. Any worker appealing on the grounds of wrongful dismissal would have to prove that the employer acted in bad faith. See Christo Nel, 'Peer Pressures', *Leadership South Africa*, 7, 3, 1988.

business leaders now took the lead, building on the 1987 consultations launched by De Beer and others. As the perception took hold that 'we are in the last year or so of the Botha administration',[10] the Gencor mining house initiated a series of consultations with business and resistance leaders. These culminated the formation of a new business alliance, the Consultative Business Movement (CBM), in August 1988. The CBM recognised 'the inevitability of structural change in a socio-political and economic field' and 'the need for a transformation to a post-apartheid society in which the current polarisation can be overcome'.[11] As its chairman explained, the CBM was formed with the express purpose to challenge South African businessmen to 'define the real nature of their own power, and to identify how they can best use this not inconsequential power to advance the society towards non-racial democracy'.[12]

This followed a shake-up in the moribund liberal opposition Progressive Federal Party. The sustained *Financial Mail* attacks on the PFP (above p. 365) precipitated the resignation of its lacklustre leader, Colin Eglin. In the same month as the formation of the CBM, Eglin was replaced as PFP leader by one of the initiators of what turned into the CBM, the Anglo American executive director and former MP, Zac de Beer.* De Beer immediately announced his determination to seek unity with Dennis Worrall's IP and Wynand Malan's NDM.[13] His initiatives won aggressive support from key Afrikaner businessmen and intellectuals previously prominent in the NP.[14] The first meeting of the three opposition groups was held in the home of Louis Luyt – whose role as Information Department frontman in setting up *The Citizen* newspaper had been a key catalyst in Muldergate. Luyt told De Beer, Malan and Worrall that 'the business community wants you to get your act together'.[15] With financial backing from English and Afrikaner business, the three parties finally merged to form the Democratic Party (DP) in April 1989. The new party's programme called for non-racial democracy; the rule of law and an independent judiciary; freedom of speech, of voting, and of assembly; and private enterprise.[16]

The DP represented something new in white politics. Combining PFP organisation and experience, the NDM's extra-parliamentary credibility and Worrall's conservative appeal, it seemed to strike a chord in the heart of an Afrikaner establishment previously impervious to PFP blandishments. The negotiations to establish the new party had been chaired by the former editor of the Transvaal NP's official organ, and the brother of its leader, Willem de Klerk.

---

* Eglin had succeeded Jan Steytler as leader of the then Progressive Party in 1971. He was himself replaced as the PFP leader by Van Zyl Slabbert in 1979, and again picked up the reins following Slabbert's dramatic resignation in early 1986 (p. 335 above). De Beer for his part had first been elected to Parliament as South Africa's youngest-ever MP on the United Party ticket in 1953. He was one of the group of 11 MPs who left the UP to form the Progressive Party a year later, and lost his seat in the 1961 election. He joined Anglo American in 1968, rising rapidly in Oppenheimer's vast organisation. Re-elected to Parliament in the Prog breakthrough in the 1974 election, he had resigned his seat in 1980 to devote himself to Anglo American, serving as the chairman of many of its subsidiaries and sitting on the board of its parent company.

The elder De Klerk was widely tipped as the party's leader, only finally withdrawing his candidacy in order not to embarrass his brother once the latter was himself elected NP *Hoofleier* in February.[17] Former key Broederbond insider, vice-chairman of the SABC and one-time scourge of Afrikaner *oorbeligtes* (over-enlightened Afrikaners), Stellenbosch economics professor, Sampie Terreblanche, was a key financial adviser. Three former nationalist MPs, a former managing director of Nasionale Pers, and various prominent Afrikaner intellectuals and businessmen were present at the founding of the party.*

The formation of the DP was 'an unsettling development' for the National Party. Deeply concerned by what it regarded as the DP's 'considerable marketing value' among Afrikaner verligtes, the NP also feared that the rejuvenated and now much more *credible* liberal opposition would siphon off support among the English-speaking urban voters who were now all that stood between the NP and Treurnicht's KP.[18] These fears were soon confirmed. In a municipal by-election just two months after its formation, the DP took a seat away from the NP in an Afrikaner middle-class ward in Foreign Minister Pik Botha's constituency. This cost the NP its Johannesburg City Council majority. But by June 1989 other political developments had moved centre stage.

All the kings horses ... The demise of P W Botha

The more exhortatory Afrikaner histories like to refer to what one writer called 'the Hand that guides the fate of nations and men'.[19] This independent variable in South African history struck again barely two weeks into 1989. P W Botha was rushed to hospital on 18 January after what many regarded as his second mild stroke. With the *Groot Krokodil* now temporarily incapacitated, the senior minister, Chris Heunis, was sworn in as Acting-State President. Botha's illness put the simmering succession struggle onto the high boil.

The President made his first direct communication with the outside world two weeks after his stroke. Early on the morning of 18 February 1989 the chairman of the NP caucus, Boet Bothma, received a peremptory telephone instruction to present himself in the President's Tuynhuys office fifteen minutes before the 9 am opening of the weekly caucus meeting. On reading the letter from Botha handed to him by the President's private secretary, Bothma later recounted: 'I nearly dropped dead from fright and became completely weak in the knees.' The letter read as follows:[20]

---

* The latter included Gencor director Naas Steenkamp. The central role played by this group first taken over (as General Mining) by Federale Mynbou in 1964 confirmed both the analysis of Harry Oppenheimer that incorporating Afrikaner undertakings into the business mainstream would turn them into a long-term force for change, and the fears of verkramptes that 'Afrikaner capitalists' would destroy the historic mission of the *volk* (pp. 120-4 above).

Dear Friend

With reference to the deterioration of my health, I should appreciate it if you would lay this letter before the caucus. In my view the office of State President and the office of *Hoofleier*ship of the National Party should now be separated.

Therefore I should appreciate it if the Caucus of the National Party could now proceed to fill the post the *Hoofleier*ship so that I may be in a position to carry on with just the office of the State Presidency.

The State Presidency will then become a special force for cohesion in our country.

I thank all my friends for the trust and friendship in the past.

It is my sincere prayer that you may receive the special mercy of Almighty God.

With sincere greetings to you all

My blessing and wishes for success to you all

P W Botha.

The caucus was stunned. National Party chief whip Keppies Niemann could only reach for clichés, declaring 'you could have knocked us all over with a feather'. Neither Acting-President Heunis nor the other provincial NP leaders had been warned of Botha's intentions. There was even some doubt as to the constitutionality of his wish to separate the two posts, as it had been the clear intention of the framers of the new constitution that the leader of the majority party in the white House of Assembly (i.e., the NP) would always hold the post of State President.

The provincial leaders and their vice-chairmen retired to consider what to do. Transvaal NP vice-chairman Pik Botha explained that the President had earlier told him he wanted to avoid a repetition of the intrigue and infighting which had proceed his own election as *Hoofleier*. The man who had so masterfully disposed of NP 'Crown Prince' Connie Mulder in 1978 now reportedly feared that 'the guys (*die manne*) would turn on each other' once he was no longer on the scene. Hence his clear injunction to caucus that it should fill the *Hoofleier*ship 'now' – i.e., there and then. The Foreign Minister also tried to persuade the provincial leaders to return to caucus with the name of a consensus candidate.

When this proved impossible, it was decided to proceed directly to a caucus election. Blank ballots had to be borrowed from the chief secretary of the Cape NP – who promptly alerted *Die Burger*. The hunt for a ballot box ended in a storeroom in the old Senate Chamber. While a tense caucus waited to proceed, the whips ensured that nobody left the room or made a telephone call. Four candidates were duly nominated and agreed to stand: Acting-President, Cape NP leader and Minister of Constitutional Development, Chris Heunis; chairman of the Council of Ministers of the (white) House of Assembly, Transvaal NP leader and Minister of National Education, F W de Klerk; Foreign Minister Pik Botha; and Finance Minister Barend du Plessis.* Only Heunis was not a Transvaler, and only De Klerk was regarded as being on the conservative wing of the party.

Pik Botha was eliminated on the first ballot. The 16 votes he received were six fewer his disappointing tally in 1978. Just over half the Cape MPs supported Heunis, giving him 25 votes. Barend du Plessis came from nowhere to take second place with 30 votes to the 59 for De Klerk. In the second round 10 of Pik Botha's supporters switched to Du Plessis as the alternative verligte candidate. Five of them voted for De Klerk and Heunis garnered only one additional vote. The Transvaal leader retained his lead with 64 votes, to 40 for the Finance Minister and just 26 for Heunis. The hapless Cape leader was eliminated and the caucus prepared for the third and decisive round.

The vote tallies in the first and second round were not announced to the caucus, only the names of the candidates who went through to the next round. But there was great tension among the vote tellers as the stand-off now seemed between a verligte and a conservative candidate. The tellers realised that if all Heunis's second round supporters voted on ideological grounds, Finance Minister du Plessis would pip his provincial leader by just two votes. In the end, however, Du Plessis won only 21 additional votes to five for De Klerk. This was just sufficient for the Transvaal leader to edge out P W Botha's preferred candidate by 69 votes to 61.[21]

Following the obligatory caucus pleasantries after the vote, the new *Hoofleier* hurried back to his office to meet his wife who had been shopping that morning. Blissfully unaware of her changed status, Marike de Klerk had gone to the 18th floor of the Verwoerd building so that she could get a lift back to her official residence. There she had been given a garbled message from her husband to wait till he returned from the caucus meeting. When he finally arrived he answered her query about what was going on by telling her: 'I have just been elected by the caucus as the new *Hoofleier* of the National Party.' Herself no slouch in NP politics, a startled Marike de Klerk looked up from her parcels to ask: 'But what does that mean?' [22]

Most of the white political class shared her bewilderment. Once the events in the caucus were made public, absolute confusion reigned in political circles. The duly elected State President still lay basically incommunicado in hospital, but now no longer had a political base in the ruling party. Acting-State President Heunis had just been humiliated in the election for NP *Hoofleier*. Yet Heunis continued to exercise the vast constitutional powers of the Presidency and to scheme

---

* Pik Botha evidently decided to test the waters despite this earlier statement to his former organiser and now fellow candidate Du Plessis that the burden of the negotiations over Namibia meant that he could not see himself being available in a leadership election in 1988 or 1989. Three polls in July and August 1989 revealed that Pik Botha was still the most popular politician among the white electorate.

with his hospitalised mentor behind De Klerk's back. For his part, the newly elected NP leader seemed in political limbo. Though still chairman of the Council of Ministers in the white House of Assembly, as Minister of Education in the national Cabinet, De Klerk remained subject to the authority of a man he had just beaten in the leadership election and possessed no executive power to implement the policy of his party. Moreover, the new *Hoofleier* was entirely unsure as to the plans, and state of health, of the sick State President who made no effort either to congratulate him on his election nor to enlighten him on his future.

This uncertain situation was yet another example of how the country's politics were shaped by the volatile will of the *Groot Krokodil* rather than by any coherent and collectively agreed upon strategy. Botha had simply announced his preference for the French model of *cohabitation* between an executive President and the leader of the majority party who would now be made his Prime Minister. And because he wished it, this would happen. End of discussion. Yet these circumstances were absolutely unprecedented. None of the major actors had any clear idea of how to proceed. A period of great intrigue and manoeuvring began.

Some nationalist MPs regarded Botha's surprise resignation as NP leader as a 'masterstroke' to shortcircuit internal party conflicts. But most NP insiders were astounded that Botha had ceded his power-base as *Hoofleier*, taking this as proof that the *Groot Krokodil* had finally lost his celebrated political marbles, and that De Klerk could now move to pull his teeth.[23] Yet Botha might well have taken a calculated risk. His relations with De Klerk had deteriorated, and, openly favouring Du Plessis, Botha probably gambled that a precipitate election would enhance the Finance Minister's chances by preventing De Klerk mobilising Transvaal NP discipline in his favour. Had just five MPs voted the other way, the nephew of Hans Strijdom would have lost to the neophyte Du Plessis. But the old reptile could have been motivated by more an even Machiavellian calculation. Anticipating De Klerk's always predictable victory, by insisting on separating the powers of President and *Hoofleier*, Botha might have wanted to oblige the Transvaal leader to fight the upcoming general elections as the latter rather than the former. If as expected, De Klerk lost his marginal Vereeniging seat to the KP, the caucus was unlikely to elevate a loser to the Presidency. The way would then be open for Du Plessis.*

Deeply disappointed at his own dismal showing in the *Hoofleier* election, Acting-State President Heunis was widely believed to be conniving with P W Botha, and instrumental in his surprise return to work just one month after his resignation as *Hoofleier*.† Botha peremptorily denounced the 'indecent haste'

---

* One 'senior minister' said virtually as much to *Die Burger*'s political correspondent. Ries & Dommisse, *Leierstryd*, 98.

† *Cape Times*, 11 March 1989. Heunis denied these allegations, asserting that he had simply discussed the 'practical implications' of the division of powers with Botha, *Leierstyd*, 174. On his disappointment at the result, ibid, 112.

with which his successor as *Hoofleier* De Klerk sought to assume full power.[24] More irascible than ever, Botha made it clear he had no intention of relinquishing the Presidency, but following the French model, sought to elevate his office 'above partisan politics'. *Hoofleier* De Klerk would have to be content with his assigned role as the President's Prime Minister.[25]

But F W de Klerk was never anybody's fool. Acutely aware of his own vulnerability, the new *Hoofleier* simply had to force Botha out of the Presidency. On 13 March, over opposition from Du Plessis, Heunis and most Cape representatives, De Klerk won an 'ample majority' vote in the NP Federal Council for a resolution stating that it 'was in the best interests' of the country and the National Party that the NP *Hoofleier* 'occupy the office of State President'. The caucus then gave its unanimous approval to this resolution.[26]

And that was the effective end of the political career of P W Botha. The now toothless *Groot Krokodil* was obliged to agree to call a general election in September after which he would vacate the Presidency. Botha's drawn-out and petulant departure was marked by the most petty behaviour towards those whom he felt had turned on him. This signalled a man still totally unreconciled to being forced out of power. Botha never publicly congratulated De Klerk on the latter's election as *Hoofleier* – though he duly showed up to congratulate Dawie de Villiers when *he* replaced Heunis as Cape NP leader (see below). The *Groot Krokodil* summarily refused to attend a July farewell dinner organised in his honour by the NP Federal Council – although gilt-edged invitations had been sent out. His angry claim just three weeks before the September election that F W de Klerk had not informed him of his plans to visit Zambia with Foreign Minister Botha produced a unanimous and insulting statement from the Cabinet that the President's memory was faulty. In private, the Cabinet simply instructed Botha to resign forthwith. Fuming and friendless, the *Groot Krokodil* went on national television on 14 August to announce that since he was 'being ignored' by his Cabinet, he had 'no choice' but to resign.[27] F W de Klerk was sworn in as Acting-President the next day, and Botha retired to his cottage in the Wilderness, 53 years after he took up work as the Cape National Party's first paid organiser.

Botha's long political career ended in something close to disgrace because his arrogance blinded him to the basic political truism that even the most powerful politician must constantly stroke his supporters. He had begun his administration with a broken promise to the friend who had nominated him for the *Hoofleier*ship and managed his campaign in the caucus (p. 290 above). His elevation to the executive Presidency removed the last restraints on his always prodigious temper and arrogance. No longer constitutionally responsible to parliament, and freed of the political necessity of reporting to his own party caucus, Botha had snubbed his political allies and clients alike. He neglected and humiliated his caucus, and 'ignored' and insulted his Cabinet. The entire National Party was only too glad to return the compliment once he gave up his power of sanction and patronage with the *Hoofleier*ship. Not even Magnus

Malan went to his defence.* The man once acknowledged by his bitterest opponents as the consummate master of NP politics now personified his own contemptuous 1969 political epitaph for Albert Hertzog as 'an embittered political hasbeen'.[28] The wheel had turned the full circle. Just like the man *he* had manoeuvred out of politics, Botha considered himself betrayed by his once closest allies and his most senior ministers. Angry, isolated and forced out of office, just like John Vorster before him, the 73-year-old Pieter Willem Botha left in an almighty political huff.

---

* A 'veteran Cape nationalist' commented that in his long experience he had never know the caucus to rally so quickly and so unanimously behind a new leader as it did for De Klerk against Botha. Quoted Ries & Dommisse, *Leierstyd*, 187.

Chapter Twenty-Two

THE VIRTUE OF POLITICAL NECESSITY

F W de Klerk's National Party and
the art of the possible

"I don't care what the sangoma says. It's not going to go down well in the platteland."

F W de Klerk and the new National Party

Leader without fanfare: The position and politics of F W de Klerk

In February 1989 Frederick Willem de Klerk became the seventh man to lead the National Party at the age of 52. The contrast between the new and the old *Hoofleier* could not have been more marked.

P W Botha had spent much of his adult life apologising for the fact that he had no university degree. De Klerk received a *cum laude* law degree, and won various other academic awards. He had turned down the Chair of Administrative Law at Potchefstroom University on being asked to carry the NP standard in Blaar Coetzee's Vereniging seat when the latter was made ambassador to Rome in 1972. The highly volatile Botha had clawed his way up the NP hierarchy, his bullying tactics and furious temper sowing fear and cultivating enemies all around him. De Klerk was the scion of a famous political family. Known for his mild-mannered reasonableness, he had garnered the nickname (and role) of *vredemaker* (peacemaker or reconciliator) during the ferocious conflicts inside the Transvaal NP in the late 1970s and early 1980s. P W Botha rejoiced in all the flamboyant trappings and power of his presidential office. Seeming to derive personal pleasure from the low blows of factional conflict, the *Groot Krokodil* was liable to turn as quickly on his close political friends as on his enemies. His successor on the other hand appeared to live by the political credo he had announced on accepting the Transvaal NP leadership in 1982:

> I do not want to be a leader with fanfare, one who is carried on your shoulders and your applause. I want to be a leader who serves – not just from public platforms but also on a person to person basis. I do not want to be a factional leader and have fought against factionalism within the Transvaal National Party. I really want to be the leader of a team, always able to speak of *us*. I pledge you loyal leadership – loyal to the *Hoofleier*, loyal to the National Party in its broad federal context, but also loyal to the Transvaal.[1]

Perhaps the most ironic difference between these two men lay in their respective achievements over their time at the head of government. Botha had come to power trumpeting the need for strategy. Vastly enamoured of military theory, during his first six years in office he lost no opportunity to ram the idea of Total Strategy down the throats of his compatriots. Though himself much more of an intellectual than the always crude Botha, De Klerk on the other hand was a low-key politician, more attuned to one-on-one meetings than great strategic or theoretical constructs. Yet, in the end, *he* was the one who intuitively grasped the lessons of André Beaufre. Botha had talked endlessly of Total Strategy, but failed to understand what its French protagonist had really meant by political analysis and compromise. The *Groot Krokodil*'s disastrous relations with the press (including, in the end, the Afrikaner press) simply underscored his total failure to grasp Beaufre's insistence that 'modern' wars are won not on the battlefield, nor even in political struggle – they are won in the media. De Klerk was frozen out of most of the praetorian structures and practices of his predecessor's government, yet came to implement what Beaufre had deemed essential. His affable television manner and respectful treatment of the press won many more domestic and international political battles for the NP than all his predecessors combined. Botha was the reformist who, when push came to shove, could not break with the past. De Klerk was the conservative who would set South Africa on the road to real transformation.

This did not happen overnight, however. De Klerk came to the NP *Hoofleier*ship on the closest vote in NP history. Possessed of the most conservative track record of the four leadership candidates, he was deemed by domestic and international observers 'unlikely to move ahead of the National Party in its cautious agenda for gradual change'.[2] Yet he was also regarded as more 'pragmatic' than his cantankerous predecessor, closer to his caucus and likely to adopt a more 'open' leadership style.[3]

The political challenges facing the new *Hoofleier* were formidable. Still reeling from the confrontation with Botha, and feeling its way in the tense interregnum, the NP seemed to bounce from difficult problems to worse ones. Corruption scandals forced the resignation of three senior ministers within De Klerk's first year in office. The lack of a clear vision of viable reform deepened tensions in a troubled Cabinet.

The *Hoofleier* had to guard his back with great care. Having squeaked past Du Plessis and hamstrung by the uneasy division of power with P W Botha, De Klerk's authority was limited and his insecure leadership position threatened by powerful forces. With Botha poised to pounce on De Klerk's slightest mistake, Barend du Plessis was well placed to claim the leadership should the new *Hoofleier* falter. Stung by his failure even to match his low support in 1978, maverick Foreign Minister Pik Botha was always under suspicion of intrigue. Likewise humiliated by his own poor showing in the leadership election, and believed to have been instrumental in Botha's surprise return to office after his stroke, Cape leader Heunis's loyalty was at best half-hearted. In May 1989 he announced the government's 'new vision of the future'. His 'unique' and 'non-numerical democracy' envisaged freedom of association, a single Parliament for all voters and one national Cabinet to which Africans would be appointed. One former government insider described this version of power-sharing as coming 'as close to PFP policy as anyone could, short of resigning [from] the NP and crossing the floor of the House'. A furious President Botha summonsed his one-time acolyte to his office on 11 May. The fight between the two 'was said to have bounced off all four walls', and Botha apparently accused Heunis of betraying him. The next day, just three months and ten days after losing the *Hoofleier*ship election, Heunis suddenly quit caucus and Cabinet amidst speculation of a deep rift with De Klerk.[4]

This aggravated relations between the Cape and Transvaal parties. Although 'provincialism' seemed to have played little part in De Klerk's election, the Cape NP was not amused at the humiliation of its two immediate past leaders.

And De Klerk's own Transvaal party was the most vulnerable of the provincial NPs. It was certain to suffer heavy losses to the KP in September's looming election. But even worse, it now faced the prospect of a losing substantial urban support to the new Democratic Party which had the bit firmly between its teeth. The DP's confident forecast that it would hold the balance of power in a hung parliament after September did not seem inconceivable. At least one longtime NP observer reported widespread speculation that September's election could put the NP on the road to destruction.[5]

De Klerk's political difficulties were compounded by his uneasy relations with the security establishment, and particularly the SADF generals. Nursing their wounded military pride following a second major 'reverse' in Angola in fifteen years, the generals whispered that once again the army had been let down by politicians. If only P W Botha had not rejected Magnus Malan's proposed all-out frontal attack on Cuito Cuanavale, they would have showed those arrogant Cuban commies.* General Malan's own presidential ambitions were also buried at Cuito Cuanavale. Ill at ease with the pseudo-populist style, and obligatory 'hail-fellow-well-met' heartyism of NP politics, the general had done little to cultivate a personal political base within the Transvaal party. Although he had been made a vice-chairman of the Transvaal party, he was not popular among its membership and caucus.[6] Like his father before him, Malan had hitched his star a little too firmly to the Cape wing of the party. The Defence Minister must have realised that his fortunes would wane with the departure of his patron P W Botha. He may also have feared De Klerk's retribution for old political slights his family had given to De Klerk's uncle and father.†

Hoofleier De Klerk had never been a major player in the State Security Council. By early 1987 he had positioned himself to lead the groundswell in the caucus and the Broederbond which yearned to restore real civilian control over the government. Once elected *Hoofleier*, he took the first step. Just before President Botha returned to resume the Presidency in March 1989, the Cabinet rejected SSC advice and decided to release the hunger-striking detained leaders of the Mass Democratic Movement. This was the first time the Cabinet had

---

* Botha is said to have judged that the generals' estimate of 300 white casualties would be politically unacceptable.

† Magnus Malan's father, Dr Avril Malan, was a prominent Broederbonder, chairman of the Volkskas Bank for almost two decades and nationalist MP 1948–61. Siding with the anti-party faction in internal nationalist conflicts during the 1940s, he had clashed sharply with Hans Strijdom and Hendrik Verwoerd. Desperate for a Cabinet post, and well aware that Strijdom never forgot political slights, Avril Malan aligned himself with the Cape faction and worked feverishly to block the Transvaal leader in the 1954 succession brouhaha (p. 89 above). At one stage he went so far as to spread a rumour that Strijdom would not even find a nominator, thereby deeply insulting Strijdom's brother-in-law and chief organiser, Transvaal NP chief secretary Jan de Klerk. Returning from overseas just before the caucus election, Strijdom confronted Malan with his disloyalty to the Transvaal party, and the banker 'died a man disappointed in politics'. See Schoeman, *Van Malan tot Verwoerd*, chap. v.

overturned an SSC recommendation on a 'security' matter since the establishment of the National Security Management System in 1979. Seen in the resistance as a major victory, the release of the hunger strikers unleashed the MDM's impressive defiance campaign of civil disobedience, and the security services grew increasingly edgy.

The long interregnum between February and August 1989 thus saw De Klerk in an extremely delicate political situation within both party and government. Rallying the caucus against P W Botha shored up his position in the short term. But it offered no long-term security, particularly if the NP took the expected drubbing from the right and the left in the September election. A poll of increasingly restive business leaders revealed the judgement that the prospects for the new Democratic Party would largely depend on De Klerk's 'ability to undertake significant reform'.[7] Given his precarious position, *De Klerk simply had to make waves in order to stay afloat*, to swamp those who may have been dreaming of challenging him. His early signals that, once Botha had finally departed, his administration would move to a South African *glasnost* and maybe even *perestroika*, were clearly designed to appeal both to the DP's putative constituency and an international audience, making politically unthinkable any idea of an NP putsch against the new *Hoofleier*.

This certainly seemed to strike a chord internationally. Even the government of the Soviet Union declared its willingness to give De Klerk a chance.[8] But De Klerk's surprising new attitude was informed by more than crude political self-preservation. His isolation from the inner power circles under P W Botha left him sensitive to the desire for change in the Afrikaner establishment and an NP caucus whose 'class of 1987' had become very vocal.[9] By March 1989 the growing mass protests of the MDM's imaginative defiance campaign targeted the absurdities of De Klerk's 'group rights' version of neo-apartheid – empty white hospitals while black patients were forced to sleep on floors in 'their' facilities. This campaign captured massive international media attention. By now it was blindingly obvious even to the most intractable general that the post-1986 strategy had failed as miserably as the Total Strategy.

With negotiations looming on South Africa's scheduled repayment of unsupportable chunks of its huge international debt, a 1986-style crackdown was out of the question. Margaret Thatcher had personally told De Klerk that Western leaders wanted Mandela freed and a negotiated settlement to be reached in South Africa. The Iron Lady then wrote to De Klerk informing him that she 'would not be able to sustain her anti-sanctions stance forever'.[10] De Klerk's long obsession with consolidating the NP's right flank could clearly no longer form the basis of state policy. Something new had to be tried, and there were few alternatives left.

But before De Klerk could undertake new initiatives he had to win the general election on 6 September. For the first time since 1953 there was a real possibility of an NP defeat. Andries Treurnicht's Conservative Party argued that a return to Verwoerdian apartheid was the only way to take South Africa out of its crisis, and the KP expected to win as many as 60 seats.[11] The Democratic Party for its part announced that 'South Africa is ready for Western democracy'. The most vocal of its leadership *troika*, Dennis Worrall predicted the DP would pick up over 40 seats, and hold the balance of power in a hung parliament. The NP's new leader had acknowledged two years earlier that his party's constitutional policy was 'on the rocks'. Throughout 1988 and 1989 the NP caucus was sharply divided between those (like Heunis) who advocated open-ended constitutional negotiations through the 'negotiating forum' enacted in 1988 (p. 349 above), and those who favoured elaborating a constitutional blueprint before entering negotiations.[12] Neither faction had yet confronted the real political problem – that the NP would have to find some credible black political actors with whom to negotiate.

The 'new vision of the future' announced by Minister of Constitutional Development Heunis in May 1989 was little more than a stale rehash of his previous failed efforts to get even Chief Mangosuthu Buthelezi to enter his 'open-ended negotiations'. This 'grand constitutional aircraft' crashed and burned on take-off, incinerating its pilot's political career.[13] For his part, *Hoofleier* De Klerk favoured the approach of his principal political allies in the Broederbond. The 'Five Year Action Plan' adopted by the NP in June 1989 was based on one of four options spelled out in the AB's 'conceptual guidelines' for constitutional negotiations.[14] This NP 'blueprint for a new South Africa' enshrined the Broederbond's notion of 'freedom and equal rights', promising every South African the right to participate in decision-making at all levels of government, and spoke vaguely of universal suffrage and a bill of rights. The Broederbond's insistence on recognition of the 'interdependence of the different South African communities' was translated into the principle of self-determination in own affairs and joint decision-making on general affairs. The people who gave the world apartheid were now bent on ensuring that no [racial] group dominated the others, i.e., the whites.[15] It was hoped that this cracked record would play with the white electorate in the September election.

In the event, the election results were a disappointment for all the three parties running for the white House of Assembly. The NP made its worst showing in thirty years. For the first time since 1958 its overall share of the vote was lower than the combined vote for the opposition parties.[16] Losing 17 seats to the KP and 12 to the DP, De Klerk's party clung to power with 93 of the 166 elected seats. This was fewer than the NP of De Klerk's uncle Hans Strijdom had captured in the smaller parliament of 1958 (97 out of 150). The NP's slim 10-seat majority was even shakier than it looked, as fully 38 of its seats were reduced to marginal status. This traditional party of Afrikaner nationalism now enjoyed stronger support among English-speakers (50 percent) than Afrikaners (46 percent).

For its part, the KP of Andries Treurnicht finally broke out of its Transvaal ghetto to take six seats in the OFS and two in the Cape. Yet the KP's share of the vote rose by less than 5 percent over 1987 (from 26,4 percent to 31,2 percent), and its final tally of 39 seats fell far short of its hopes for 60 MPs.

Even despite the collapse of the HNP and a split NP/DP vote in some electoral districts, the KP captured only nine additional Transvaal seats, and saw the NP increase its majority in some constituencies the KP had expected to win.

The newly formed Democratic Party won 33 seats and 20,4 percent of the vote. This was an improvement over the combined totals of 21 seats on 17,1 percent of the vote won by the three opposition groups which had fought the 1987 election on the left of the NP . Yet DP support was still short of the 1981 combined PFP/NRP tally of 34 seats on 27 percent of the vote. The new party failed to capture a number of targeted seats, and won probably less than 10 percent of the Afrikaner vote. Its quest to seize the balance of power in a hung parliament proved illusory. Nevertheless this was a impressive showing for a party barely five months old, and the DP represented a real potential threat to NP attempts to turn itself into the natural party of the urban middle class.

Yet the most important pointer from the 1989 election simply underscored the truth that the real political weakness and glaring dilemma confronting the new De Klerk government lay *outside* both parliament and the realm of white politics. As whites went to the polls, over three million of their disenfranchised compatriots joined the two-day stayaway called by the extra-parliamentary MDM. Three times as many South Africans struck work as voted for the NP. The overall vote for De Klerk's party represented just 6 percent of the country's voting age population. But those who did not have the vote did not either passively accept the electoral renewal of the tricameral parliament. Twenty-three people were killed and hundreds injured in election night battles with the police. The level of force used by riot police against black protesters led one very angry, and courageous, 'coloured' police officer, Lieutenant Gregory Rockman, to denounce his colleagues as 'wild dogs'. Rockman told the world's press that when he looked at the police lining up to deal with young blacks, he 'could see the killer instinct in their eyes'. His comments were front-page news across the world.[17] The *Weekly Mail* opposition newspaper headlined the election results as: 'Nat: 93, Con: 39, Dem: 33, Hurt: 100, Dead: 23'.[18]

This election infinitely compounded the political pressure on the National Party. Frederick de Klerk was sworn in as State President on 20 September with his party haemorrhaging to its left and right and the MDM vowing to intensify the struggle. It was painfully clear that the halfway house between apartheid and democracy envisaged in the NP's 'Five Year Plan' was yet another nationalist trip into cloud-cuckoo land. And events outside South Africa were again moving against the regime. The ANC had been signalling its preparedness to negotiate for close to a year. The OAU's August 1989 Harare Declaration ratified the ANC's negotiation schedule, which then won wide international approval and was now due to be put to the United Nations. The international public relations disaster of the police riot during the elections, the groundswell of protest led by a confident MDM, and the now-wide willingness within the white establishment to deal with the ANC, all combined to threaten the De Klerk administration with a decisive loss of the initiative to the ANC. With the Commonwealth Conference and possibility of heightened sanctions just a month away, and debt renewal negotiations approaching a crucial phase, new initiatives were essential.

The road not yet taken: The reformist second coming

After forty-one years in power, by September 1989 the National Party had, in the words of Pik Botha, 'run out of alternatives'.[19] In a later interview with his brother, F W de Klerk echoed Willem's earlier turn of phrase (p. 374 above), telling him: 'By late 1989 it had become more and more clear to me that the government's emphases had landed us in a dead-end street.'[20] The fallout from the election finally convinced even Cabinet hardliners that something dramatically different would have to be tried. Warning of 'a maelstrom of increasing isolation, boycotts, sanctions and violence that can only lead to poverty and endless misery for the entire population', the hardline Minister of Law and Order, Adriaan Vlok declared: 'Everybody, including the Police, the government and the country, realises that the status quo cannot continue.'[21]

The Cabinet now determined to explore the means by which it could recapture the initiative. Starting from the recognition that, in De Klerk's words, 'we had to release Mandela', a series of Cabinet brainstorming sessions sought to find ways to 'normalise the political process'. But these Afrikaner Calvinists in De Klerk's inner circle also finally acknowledged that when P W Botha's government had jettisoned Verwoerd's version of 'moral' apartheid for the dubious expedient of 'power-sharing' in the early 1980s, it had cast off a priceless political resource – its belief in the morality of its own project. While the return to Verwoerdian apartheid advocated by the KP flat-earthers was no longer feasible, De Klerk stressed that the Cabinet was also determined to find a policy formula which would enable it to convince NP supporters that the party 'again' (sic) occupied 'the high moral ground'.[22]

Yet the regime's efforts to change the status quo confronted three political hurdles: it still lacked a clear set of credible policy proposals; it had found no significant black political group with which to negotiate; and De Klerk's room to manoeuvre was severely limited by the power of the securocrats under the National Security Management System. The new President moved to address all three.

As so often in the past, Namibia provided the laboratory. Legalising SWAPO had rapidly reduced it from mythical 'sole authentic representative' to a mundane political party hobbled by its own past brutalities, restricted ethnic appeal, disorganisation and limited electoral skills. Easily outmanoeuvred by Pretoria's manipulation of the enormous resources of state power, SWAPO was forced to agree to a constitution acceptable to all ethnic groups.

This might also be possible in South Africa. Legalising the ANC and freeing Mandela could eviscerate ANC international support and transform Mandela-the-myth into a fallible politician. Forcing the ANC into the organisational nightmare of transforming itself into a legal political party might undermine the romantic fetish of armed struggle and hold up ANC disorganisation to daily scrutiny by the hostile media. The ANC would have to translate the emotional appeal and literary elegance of the Freedom Charter into practical constitutional and economic proposals sufficiently radical to satisfy its constituency, yet flexible enough to weather the cut and thrust of negotiations with NP experts fighting for white survival. Learning the new rules of legal politics was likely to provoke ideological squabbles and personal rivalries in the ANC leadership, and unleash intense competition in black politics. All of this would reduce the pressure on the government. The NP could use the immense assets of state power to outmanoeuvre the ANC and dictate the terrain, the pace and the content of negotiations in ways Heunis had never been able to discover.

Yet powerful forces still opposed crossing *this* Rubicon. In January 1989 the Police Commissioner had declared the South African Police 'would not hesitate to take a stand against individuals' undermining the principle of no negotiations with the ANC. The Cabinet's rejection of Security Police advice on the March 1989 MDM hunger strike signalled its intention to reduce the securocrats' role. Even before the February 1990 unbanning of the ANC, the general who was the police 'specialist' on banned organisations complained that his men were 'frustrated' and 'confused' by De Klerk's new initiatives.[23] The new President confronted the dilemma of retaining the political loyalty of senior policemen while he clipped their wings.

The SADF presented similar problems. The government had long feared rank-and-file opposition to reform. During the 1982 NP/KP by-election confrontations, then SADF Chief Constand Viljoen had warned all ranks to stay out of politics.[24] But now opposition extended to the High Command and Military Intelligence had grown used to directing policy. Their blatant attempt to derail Namibian independence just days before the election for a Constituent Assembly showed the lengths some in the SADF High Command would go to disrupt negotiations in South Africa – and their open contempt for South Africa's own constitutional authorities.* This episode reinforced the need to bring the entire security establishment under civilian control. Afrikaans press handling of the mid-November Army and Police death squad revelations was reminiscent of a Mulder-gate in reverse – implying that it was time to rein in both police and SADF.[25]

Commander-in-chief De Klerk abolished the National Security Management System at the end of November 1989. The SSC secretariat was slashed, and the council reverted to an advisory role as a simple Cabinet committee divested of any decision-making authority. A week later mandatory white military service was halved, and the military budget and levels of manning cut. Overwhelming

---

* Acting on 'raw intelligence' provided by the SADF, Pik Botha had called a press conference just before the election, claiming that SWAPO guerrillas were 'invading' northern Namibia in contravention of the Brazzaville Protocol. He insisted that this would halt the election. The embarrassed Foreign Minister was later obliged to acknowledge that this information was based on 'forgeries', saying that he could not be held responsible for verifying information provided to him by Military Intelligence. *The Star,* 6 November 1989 and *Sunday Star,* 7 November 1989.

approval from the white political and business establishment then opened the way for what one nationalist newspaper termed the 'step we all knew would have to be taken, so long as it could only be taken later'.[26] A year to the day since becoming *Hoofleier*, De Klerk opened parliament on Friday 2 February 1990. Without notifying the National Party caucus, he announced the revocation of the thirty-year ban on the ANC and PAC, and the legalisation of the South African Communist Party forty years after it had been driven into clandestinity. The ban on all other proscribed organisations was also lifted. Nelson Mandela was released nine days later, and South Africa started down its long road towards a negotiated settlement.

Man of integrity? NP negotiating strategy

In contemporary South Africa, the very date of De Klerk's speech – 2 February 1990 – is widely used as a metaphor for the start of a new era. In his own address to the hundreds of thousands of South Africans who crowded into the Parade in Cape Town to hear him speak on the day of his release, Nelson Mandela declared the President to be 'a man of integrity' with whom he could work in good faith.[27] Conservative Party carping about 'treason' apart, the announcement of the unbanning of the ANC was greeted with unrestrained joy throughout the country. The Monday following the President's announcement, the liberal *Cape Times* ran a cartoon in which one white businessman said to another (parodying a well-known British army song of the South African War): 'We are marching to euphoria.'[28]

Yet De Klerk was no Saul converted by the sudden blinding light of non-racial democracy. As he later explained his decision to unban the ANC in an interview with his brother:

> Even now I have no doubts about the basic philosophy of the [National Party's] policy as formulated under P W Botha, but the way in which it was executed had become counter-productive. One must hold on to the initiative, and a policy must be capable of producing results and progress. We had to escape from a corner where everything had stagnated into confrontation.[29]

He and his Cabinet remained convinced 'that South Africa was shaped by ethnic powers and forces which cannot be denied'. 2 February 1990 was simply the result of a 'unanimous' decision 'to put this conviction to the test' of negotiation politics.*

Their constitutional strategy hinged around June 1989 Broederbond guidelines. Each 'component unit' of the population would control its 'own affairs', with 'general affairs' decided by consensus between the majority of

---

* De Klerk confidant, cited *Die Suid-Afrikaan*, 27, June/July 1990. De Klerk himself claimed that '[w]hat I said on February 2 was decided absolutely unanimously' by the Cabinet – W J de Klerk, *F W de Klerk*, 28.

each such unit in the national legislature.[30] While the Broederbond constitutional committee tried to flesh out these principles by studying the constitutions of countries marked by racial, ethnic or regional imbalances,* De Klerk quietly applied another lesson from Namibia – detailed constitutional blueprints were less important than irrevocably locking the ANC into negotiations. This ironically echoed discarded guru Samuel Huntington's stress on *process* over final goals. So long as the NP was clear on its *bottom line*, it could manage the process to control the results.

For at least two years following 2 February 1990, NP insiders saw the process of negotiations essentially as a simple extension and widening of the old 'consociational' approach.[31] Their buzz term was 'elite-pacting'. Through a process of bargaining, trade-offs and compromise, representative racial and ethnic elites would come to a 'pact' about South Africa's future. In 1990 this process was envisaged both as a series of stages to a settlement – talks (1990), negotiations (1991/2), abolition of statutory apartheid (1991/2), a referendum (1993) and implementation (1994) – as well as some kind of grudging 'joint rule' with the ANC. This view of things seemed to be concretised in joint Government/ANC declarations known as the Groote Schuur and Pretoria Minutes. Nine months after Mandela's release one former NP constitutional expert declared that so much progress was being made that 'an interim government is taking shape'.[32]

However, even for 'Afrikaner liberals' who had moved away from the NP, the bottom line remained 'group self-preservation'.[33] President de Klerk launched his February 1990 initiative talking of group rights and group or regional vetoes in an upper house. Throughout 1990, Broederbond constitutional strategists under the Minister of Constitutional Development, former AB chairman Dr Gerrit Viljoen, tried to refine this bottom-line model. Its apotheosis came with the October 1990 President's Council constitutional report.

Beyond its vision of process and bottom line, NP negotiation strategy initially rested on five assumptions: that the NP could stay united and hold off the far right during this process; that Western countries would accept some notion of group rights and lift sanctions; that sufficient numbers of conservative blacks would rally to an anti-ANC alliance to deny the ANC claim to majority representation; that state power could be used to sap the demands of the ANC negotiators, forcing them into compromise; and finally that the ANC was controlled by strong leaders who could command compliance from their radical constituents.

These assumptions proved only partially valid in 1990. The climate inside the NP caucus was indeed transformed. De Klerk's open leadership style and apparent greater concern for the caucus input into politics won some startling

---

* Fiji, Canada and Singapore attracted particular attention.

dividends. For forty years, the National Party had argued that a universal franchise would 'never' happen, that 'the Afrikaner' would fight to the death before giving 'his' country away to the blacks. In 1982, P W Botha had been forced to split his party and effectively destroy organised Afrikaner nationalism before either would accept a form of 'power-sharing' which patently and cynically kept all power firmly in white hands. Now in 1990 De Klerk had committed the NP to a process which could only ever result in exactly that which all nationalists had said they would never accept – one person, one vote. Despite his (false) claim to have 'restored' the caucus role as 'the decision-making body of the NP',* he undid this most sacred of NP dogmas *without even informing*, let alone consulting, his caucus or National Party congresses. Still, in stunning contrast to the haemorrhage to the right in February 1982, *not one single* NP official or Member of Parliament resigned nor even protested publicly. The only notable defection occurred after the April 1990 meeting at Groote Schuur between the Cabinet and an ANC delegation. When De Klerk sat down with 'communists', his former leader P W Botha now resigned his membership of the party he had served all his adult life But even the departure of the *Groot Krokodil* did not ripple the apparent calm of the new NP pond.

The explanation for this almost incomprehensible placidity lay more in the growing primacy of the survival instinct than in ideological and strategic consensus. De Klerk's leap into the dark of negotiation politics meant that the particular interests of the provincial NPs now paled into insignificance compared with the party's survival as the dominant force in South African politics (and its MPs' determination to hang on to their jobs and pensions). The individual political (and financial) fortunes of each MP were now directly bound to the success of their leader's negotiation strategy. Any embarrassment of him by caucus would play into ANC hands.

De Klerk's major internal problem remained the security forces. One canny NP-watcher judged that far from capitulating, the securocrats were planning 'to go on playing a central role according to their own vision'.[34] As De Klerk sidelined the generals and appointed the Harms Commission to enquire into illegal actions of the security forces, he had to move with great caution. According to sources in the Special Forces Command of the SADF, plots against De Klerk were 'commonplace' in this and other dirty tricks units after February 1990.[35] Support for the KP in SADF middle ranks also mushroomed. De Klerk thus reassured and protected senior officers whose support he needed to control the disaffection. Although the other services, and particularly the Air Force, were long overdue their turn at the summit, in naming a new SADF Chief in November 1990, De Klerk yet again gave the post to the Head of the Army, General A J ('Kat') Liebenberg. The new SADF chief had once presided over

---

* *Die Suid-Afrikaan,* June/July 1990. No NP *Hoofleier* had ever allowed the caucus to play a decision-making role. All were agreed that it was the parliamentary *vegorganisasie* of the government, and that it would be informed but not necessarily listened to.

the dirty tricks of the SADF's Special Forces Command.*

A modified version of the National Security Management System was quietly resurrected. Following the damning 1990 Harms Report on the army and police role in death squads the President rallied to support Defence Minister Magnus Malan, and hardline Law and Order Minister Vlok. Clearly reluctant to aggravate army and police discontent, De Klerk appeared to prefer to isolate the securocrats in government, slowly rein in their options and bind them to his vision of change. This meant turning a blind eye to much illegal activity. In return, an SADF political education programme won back much middle-rank support for the De Klerk line. The President only reluctantly shuffled Malan and Vlok into less controversial portfolios following the July 1991 scandal about covert security force financing and other support for the Inkatha Freedom Party.[36]

The validity of the other NP negotiation assumptions was sorely tested in the year following 2 February 1990. International acclaim for De Klerk's initiative promised an early end to sanctions. However sharp Western criticism led De Klerk to distance himself from the October 1990 President's Council Report on the constitution, and undermined NP conviction that group (i.e., racial) vetoes could be sold internationally. Likewise, government-commissioned surveys revealed lower support for its putative black allies than for the NP itself, while the ANC was leagues ahead of both.[37] By the end of 1990, it was clear that not even conservative blacks would support a 'group' system in which whites vetoed change. On the other hand, the government succeeded in forcing important concessions from ANC negotiators – most significantly on the armed struggle and indemnity issues. Yet this very success aroused strong ire among ANC supporters, accentuating ANC disquiet at the form and pace of negotiations.

The December 1990 ANC conference shattered facile delusions that the NP and ANC were in the same boat, and that the 'sharks to the left and the sharks to the right are not going distinguish between us when we fall over' – as Foreign Minister Pik Botha told his ANC dinner partner at the April 1990 Groote Schuur talks.[38] The ANC conference delegates voted to reject the leadership's proposals to moderate the ANC's sanctions policy – showing the liberation movement to be more than the passive vehicle of its own renowned and newly freed *Hoofleier*. The ANC plan for mass action to dictate the pace and form of negotiations now implied more than 'elite-pacting' with an aging Mandela and an affable Thabo Mbeki. The real problem remained the radical expectations of ANC supporters. The ANC conference underscored the fact that the National

---

* In which capacity, Liebenberg had organised SADF support for Renamo and Unita. As Army chief he had approved all operations of the hit squads which fell under the euphemistically named Civilian Cooperation Bureau ('when you've got them by the balls their hearts and minds – cooperation – will follow'). Liebenberg thus became the fourth army chief in succession to preside over the entire SADF.

Party's political survival would depend on moving beyond white politics to win the game of black politics as well. This required a political platform capable of winning support from more than just conservative blacks, as well as measures to reduce expectations in the ANC constituency.

The NP Cabinet met on Robben Island in mid-January to review its plans and tactics for 1991. A year following his historic speech of 2 February 1990, De Klerk opened the 1991 Parliament proclaiming the abolition of the Land Act, the Population Registration Act and other legislative pillars of apartheid. The NP finally committed itself to full democracy in a single state and measures to address black economic deprivation.[39] No longer bound to protect white privilege through 'own affairs' and group rights, its bottom line was now summed up in two words: 'standards' and 'order'. The NP's future lay in alliance with people who shared its values, not necessarily a white skin. This was clearly intended to demobilise the ANC's projected mass action campaign, and provide the basis for an anti-ANC political alliance in negotiations and in eventual elections.

A carrot and stick approach was now used with the ANC. De Klerk had broached the idea of a multiparty conference with Mandela in late 1990. A new initiative along these lines was launched in February 1991. The multiparty conference would work out 'common ground' and 'basic principles' before deciding the composition of the 'more formal body' to draw up the new constitution. This held out the prospect a semantic compromise on the ANC insistence on a Constituent Assembly. Parties to the conference would be offered a limited decision-making role in a form of a 'council of state' during the transition process.[40]

Yet the NP's overall line towards the ANC had clearly hardened. Open discussion of an anti-ANC Christian-Democratic alliance between the NP and right-wing black groups increased ANC suspicions that it was being sidelined. The frequent assassinations of ANC organisers and members by persons unknown (and never captured) led many of the organisation's militants to claim they now felt more exposed and more threatened than in the darkest days of P W Botha's State of Emergency. The Winnie Mandela trial increased tensions. By mid-1991 the ANC was overwhelmed by the feeling that it was the target of deliberate destabilisation. This led to its April ultimatum and subsequent withdrawal from negotiations.

The timing, targets and tactics of much of the violence of the first eighteen months after 2 February 1990 did indeed eerily echo the early stages of the destabilisation of Mozambique. Few commentators doubted that members or former members of the security forces were using their Mozambique and Angolan expertise to encourage destabilisation of the ANC. Revelations by former CCB members seemed to confirm these suspicions.[41] The widely-read *Africa Confidential* concluded that 'the hard men have served their Party and their tribe well ... [T]hey have rendered valuable service to the perpetuation of the National Party, by destroying the myth of ANC hegemony and establishing

[Chief Mangosuthu Buthelezi's] Inkatha [Freedom Party] as a national force despite its derisory level of support.'[42]

Not many observers believed that De Klerk was personally implicated in 'Third Force' violence. Yet the commander-in-chief did appear curiously reluctant to move to act against illegal action by members of his security forces. The Military Intelligence officer seconded to head the intelligence service of the military government in the Ciskei bantustan, Colonel Gert Hugo, stated on American television that such 'Third Force' violence stemmed from 'a strategy to prolong the negotiation process ... in the end to negotiate the best bargain for a small handful of individuals'.[43] De Klerk's prevarication throughout 1991 and much of 1992 on the issue of 'cultural weapons',* his evasive replies to questions about the security forces' role, and refusal to be seen to take decisive action to restore the damage to the climate of negotiation, all seriously undermined the spirit of good faith essential to successful negotiations. My own May 1991 interviews with NP insiders revealed that few grasped either the gravity of this damage or the need to repair it. When asked whether President de Klerk could have stopped the security forces' dirty tricks, SADF Colonel Hugo replied:

> He could have done more. The lack of, for example, putting a date after which no indemnity will be considered ... he is allowing the situation to continue which supports the [NP] politicians. He is prolonging the negotiation process. Not anywhere is a clearcut message being given: 'Stop your [destabilising] activities.'[44]

By mid-1991, the NP caucus had absorbed 30 MPs from the 'coloured' House of Representatives. Yet the demands of negotiation politics seemed to pull this new National Party in different directions. A 'peace conference' organised by F W de Klerk in May showed many of his new recruits and allies to be way to the right of the President.† Their presence strengthened a growing NP trend away from De Klerk's 'liberal' approach towards a position opposing reconciliation with the ANC and favouring strong security force involvement in firmly managed transition. This further complicated the President's position in his see-saw struggle to marginalise the securocrats. Just before he crossed the floor to the ANC, Democratic Party MP Jan van Eck's charged that a secret cabal of senior ministers and officials were plotting against the President.

However by the middle of 1991, the NP government had gone a long way to rebuilding the political *élan* it seemed to lose after 1973. The instant international acclaim De Klerk had garnered on 2 February 1990 won stunning

---

* So-called traditional weapons carried by Inkatha members and often used in violence against the ANC.

† 'Government members' expressed the opinion that at least some new Coloured Nat MPs would be more at home in the KP, and were shocked by Inkatha intransigence, *Vrye Weekblad,* 30 May 1991.

political rewards for the NP. South Africa was accepted back in the Olympics, and US sanctions were lifted. The ANC seemed weakened and struggling to define its own role. Many nationalists began to take seriously the prospect of a post-apartheid NP-led government.

The last half of 1991 and first quarter of 1992 saw the NP go from apparent strength to strength. The National Peace Accord of September 1991 laid the basis for multiparty talks, eventually opened in the forum known as the Convention for a Democratic South Africa (Codesa). A fabricated by-election defeat of the NP candidate by the KP in Potchefstroom in early 1992 gave De Klerk the perfect pretext to call a whites-only referendum in March 1992, seeking a mandate to negotiate a non-racial constitution with the ANC.* When he won the always predictable 68 percent approval from the white electorate, De Klerk interpreted this as a mandate to make a strong and vigorous stand on his 'bottom line' of group rights and an entrenched white constitutional veto.[45] Senior ANC negotiator Mac Maharaj commented that immediately following the referendum 'the government took the position: "ANC! I don't have to discuss with you." '[46]

De Klerk's hardline bravado after the March 1992 referendum squandered a marvellous opportunity to get the negotiations ball rolling. It played straight into the hands of the white (and black) far right. Afrikaners are a strongly legalistic people. After 2 February 1990, the KP had made some headway with the (technically legitimate) charge that De Klerk had no mandate from the white electorate to negotiate with yesterday's 'terrorists'. The referendum changed all that. With nearly seven out of ten whites endorsing the notion of a non-racial constitution, De Klerk had a real mandate. Even the most obdurate Treurnichtite would have to concede the legitimacy of negotiations. The President could have seized this opportunity to move ahead quickly. Instead he chose to interpret the vote as a mandate for a white veto in the new constitution. He stressed *as nauseam* the NP 'bottom line' that 'power-sharing' not majority rule was the only form of democracy acceptable to the NP. The ANC would have to accept this or no negotiations were possible.

This obstinacy quickly shattered the huge sentiment of goodwill the referendum victory for negotiations had elicited in the black population.† It reinforced black fears that *baas* De Klerk was up to old National Party tricks. A former Broederbond insider confirmed that following the referendum victory, the NP reverted to all of its 'old arrogance'.[47] But De Klerk's stance after the referendum had even more dangerous consequences. By stressing 'group rights' and ethnic fears, he played right back into the hands of the far right. Now they

---

* The NP fielded a no-name candidate in Potchefstroom, did almost no campaigning, and clearly knew long in advance that it would lose the seat to the KP. The 'shock' result was used to create a climate of panic to oblige even left-wing whites to vote for the NP in the referendum.

† The announcement of the result produced a number of joyful, mass demonstrations by black South Africans.

could claim that even De Klerk supported the view that each (ethnic/racial/whatever) group had the right to 'self-determination'. Instead of undermining the far right with his own new legitimacy, De Klerk unwittingly gave it new determination and new justification.*

The result was perhaps the most dangerous six months in South African history. At the end of December 1991 Nelson Mandela had taken the podium at Codesa to denounce De Klerk's manoeuvres and attempts to weaken the ANC. Mandela gave notice that if the NP wanted to play hardball, the ANC would do likewise. The April 1992 assassination of Communist Party secretary-general Chris Hani by a group including former Conservative Party MP Clive Derby-Lewis provoked an outpouring of grief and fury in black townships. It also removed one of the very few ANC leaders capable of holding back the bubbling rage among black youth and militants and contributed directly to the climate which led to a collapse of negotiations a month later.

The NP insisted on entrenching the constitutional requirement of a 75 percent vote in a future non-racial parliament to amend the new constitution. The ANC agreed to raise its own proposal from 66 percent to 70 percent, but balked outright at going any further. When the NP refused to budge, the ANC walked out. The collapse of Codesa on 15 May 1992 was followed by 'Mandela's referendum' – the 'Mass Action' campaign of massive strikes and demonstrations called by the ANC in mid-1992 to show to the government that real power lay with it in the streets.

In this fraught period, the grisly June 1992 massacre of 43 ANC supporters in the Boiphatong squatter camp generated vast black anger. When De Klerk visited the settlement the next day, his car was surrounded and pummelled by enraged residents. Television footage shows the President to have been understandably very nervous – he could easily have been killed. Once De Klerk's entourage had managed to escape, South African Police opened fire on the crowd without orders to do so. Television screens all over the world carried the eerily reminiscent image of white South African police again kneeling to fire on unarmed blacks. American television later broadcast footage of the officer in command screaming at his men in Afrikaans: 'Who told you to shoot? Nobody told you to shoot.' When Mandela visited Boiphatong, the crowd chanted at him: 'We want arms, we want arms.' Telling them that negotiations were 'in tatters', the ANC president announced in language eerily similar to that which he had used to signal the onset of the ANC's armed struggle in 1961:

> I can no longer explain to our people why we continue to talk to a government, to a regime, which is murdering our people. His [De Klerk's] method of bringing about a solution in this country is WAR. We are going to respond to that.[48]

---

* Hence the justice of Sampie Terreblanche's February 1994 evaluation of De Klerk's Presidency: 'He was more of a [partisan] politican than a statesman, and a better salesman than a politician.' *Vrye Weekblad*, February 1994.

Barely two months later a further 50 ANC supporters were shot to death near the Bisho capital of the Ciskei bantustan. The ANC general-secretary, Cyril Ramaphosa was among the thousands of demonstrators fired upon by Ciskei soldiers when the adventurist ANC leader Ronnie Kasrils led a charge on Ciskei territory. Had Ramaphosa been killed the consequences would have been horrendous.

Boiphatong, Bisho and the ANC's mass action campaign seemed to give both major actors pause. In the words of Stellenbosch political analyst Willie Esterhuyse:

> It was as if people looked into the abyss. This is where things will take us if we don't develop a strategy to compromise, to cooperate and establish a culture of cooperation. This looking into the abyss played a major role in bringing De Klerk and Mandela together ... Not just the government but all the white people got the following message from [the ANC's campaign of] mass action: 1) The ANC alliance has the ability to mobilise people and get them on the street; and 2) they have the ability to destroy the economy ... and everyone must accept that if we can't straighten out the economy, no democracy is possible.[49]

The ANC leadership was likewise sobered by the bloody consequences of Ronnie Kasrils's reckless behaviour at Bisho. Even before this massacre, the ANC had been brought up short by a presentation on the economy made by new Finance Minister Derek Keys to Mandela and De Klerk.* According to the ANC's Mac Maharaj, this presentation was 'truly devastating'. It convinced the ANC leadership that unless a political settlement was reached, 'this country is actually in danger of entering a downward spiral' with no hope of escape.[50]

Both parties now finally seemed to realise the full consequences of what De Klerk had done on 2 February 1990. In the context of the violent strategic stalemate between them, each would have to give a little. Since neither was able to defeat the other, the consequences for the country of the continuing hardball between them were, to coin a phrase, too ghastly to contemplate. The compromise General Beaufre had long ago insisted was the only realistic solution to a revolutionary war was now a strategic necessity for both the National Party and the ANC.

The result was the September 1992 'Minute of Understanding' between the ANC and National Party. The agreement caused howls of rage from Inkatha Freedom Party Leader Mangosuthu Buthelezi who had become used to his privileged relationship with the NP. It 'symbolised the end of all NP attempts to outmanoeuvre the ANC' and the beginning of real negotiations.[51]

---

* De Klerk's main rival for the *Hoofleier*ship in 1989, Finance Minister du Plessis, had suddenly resigned from the Cabinet pleading 'exhaustion' in 1991, just days after the outcry surrounding the collapse of a smallish bank. The CEO of the Gencor mining group, Derek Keys is widely regarded as one of the few competent Finance Ministers South Africa has ever had. Reappointed to the post by Nelson Mandela in May 1994, he resigned for personal reasons two months later.

412

Conclusion: The new National Party and the new South Africa

This is not the place to analyse the long negotiations which finally produced a draft constitution for South Africa at the end of 1993.[52] Suffice it to say that the constitutional agreement which came into force with the inauguration of a Transitional Executive Council in January 1994 led to elections in April 1994 and the establishment of a 'Government of National Unity' incorporating all parties which won 5 percent or more of the vote. This government will rule South Africa 'by consensus', but without the veto De Klerk fought so hard for, until 1999. The Parliament elected in 1994 is also charged with elaborating a new, permanent constitution for South Africa, one which has to be based on the constitutional principles already agreed upon by the NP and ANC.

Map 3: South Africa, provincial boundaries under the 1994 constitution

South Africa finally held its first democratic election on 27-29 April 1994. The run-up to the poll was marked by massive political violence and threats from the white and black far right to disrupt the elections. Less than two weeks before the vote, senior SADF officers made a formal presentation to the Independent Electoral Commission insisting that the security situation was such that the election would have to be postponed. After a virtual cross-examination of these officers by the IEC chairman, Judge Johann Kriegler, the commission declined to accept this advice. But with barely a week to go, the gods of politics seemed decide that South Africa deserved a break. Realising he had painted himself into a corner, Chief Mangosuthu Buthelezi reversed his longstanding refusal to participate in the elections and announced that his Inkatha Freedom Party would be on the ballot on 27 April. The white far right exploded a number of massive bombs which killed more than twenty people, but it too was emasculated on the eve of the election when police arrested 32 of its senior leaders, including the secretary-general of the neo-Nazi AWB.

And then, miraculously, the violence stopped. During the last five days in April South Africa basked in a remarkable respite of peace and reconciliation unique in the country's history. Despite massive disorganisation and long delays both at the polls and in counting the vote, almost all South Africans seemed to have experienced something of an epiphany during this, their first democratic election. Everywhere I went during this period, I was told by seemingly everybody I met that for the first time in their lives they felt proud to be a South African. And not a few blacks told me what the apocryphal Afrikaner was supposed to have said on the NP's surprise election victory 45 years and 11 months earlier: 'Now at last we have got our country back!'

Nelson Mandela was inaugurated as State President on 10 May 1994 in a profoundly moving ceremony. His inaugural address struck many of its listeners as a moment of absolution and unity the likes of which the country had not known since the first white settlement was started at the Cape 342 years, one month and four days earlier. According to one new ANC Member of Parliament, as SADF jets flew overhead trailing smoke in the colours of the new South African flag, even the leader of the (Afrikaner) Freedom Front, the former chief of the SADF, General Constand Viljoen, had tears on his cheeks. Once again, many South Africans, of all races and political persuasions, told me that they would remember this moment with joy all their lives. The foundations and symbols of their new 'rainbow nation' had been marvellously crafted.

F W de Klerk's new National Party won just over 20 percent of the vote (to 62 percent for the ANC) in this election. As South African television showed Pik Botha watching in some bemusement, and as Marike de Klerk sat on the presidential podium unconsciously but visibly wringing her hands, Frederick Willem de Klerk was sworn in as Mandela's Second Vice President. His National Party took four seats in a 27-member Cabinet. The NP also won control of one of the country's nine new provinces, in a controversial election in the Western Cape. A racist comic book prepared by the Cape NP seemed intended to stir up fears among the so-called Coloureds of *oorstroming* by Africans in the Western Cape, that black hordes were waiting to take over 'coloured' houses once the ANC took power. De Klerk was embarrassed by the affair and the Independent Electoral Commission obliged the NP to withdraw the offending booklet.

Nevertheless, the NP did win strong support among so-called Coloured voters in the Western Cape (though less so in the Northern Cape – see Map 3).

This, it believes, is an indication that the former victims of its apartheid policies now accept De Klerk's fervent message that 'We have changed'.* The *Hoofleier* of this new National Party seriously seems to believe his claim that the NP will be the majority party in South Africa's next election.

Here lies the rub. To fulfil its leader's hopes the National Party will have to strike way beyond its old and new electoral base and root itself in South Africa's huge African majority. Even leaving aside the fundamental question of whether large numbers of Africans will ever bring themselves to support those wonderful people who gave them forty-six years of apartheid, it is difficult to see what the NP can offer black voters that the ANC can't give them in buckets. The ANC has been forced to scale down drastically its once ambitious plans to restructure the South African society and economy. The Reconstruction and Development Programme of the Mandela government is a mild form of market-driven social democracy which focuses on bringing education, housing and health services within the reach of the majority of South Africans.

Yet the government's options are limited by the parlous state of the South African economy – not to mention the beady regard of the World Bank, the IMF and international financial markets. Miraculous changes will not take place in the next five years. Nevertheless, large numbers of black South Africans *will* have their lives literally transformed. The affirmative action campaign at the heart of ANC rule holds out the reality of jobs, position and rapid social mobility to the black middle class the NP tried so halfheartedly to woo throughout the 1980s. The NP was never able finally to replace its old policy of class compression for its proclaimed intention to allow class differentiation to flower in black communities. The ANC is under none of these constraints. The major beneficiaries of its rule will be the members of the burgeoning black middle class now flexing its political, social and economic muscles. It is simply inconceivable that this black middle class will rally against the ANC and to the National Party in the next five years.

Likewise for the urban African proletariat. The black trade union movement is now very well represented in senior government posts. Former Cosatu general secretary, Jay Naidoo, heads this team. As Minister without Portfolio Naidoo has been given the responsibility of overseeing all the economic reorganisation schemes of the new government. While black workers began to make increasingly strident demands of the ANC government in July 1994, there

---

* Although right up till his 'Man of the Year' interview with *Time Magazine* just before accepting the 1993 Nobel Peace Prize he shared with Nelson Mandela, F W de Klerk still insisted that 'seperate development was morally justifiable if you look at it as a constitutional option'. There had been nothing wrong with the concept of apartheid *per se*, nor with the fact that the black majority was never consulted over whether it agreed with this 'constitutional option'. For Nobel laureate De Klerk, the only problem with apartheid had been its unfortunate, and unintended – though unaddressed – consequences throughout the forty years of NP rule. *Time*, 3 January 1994 (Canadian edition), 43.

is still absolutely no hope that the centre-right National Party can win their support in the next five years.

So where does this leave the new National Party? It will clearly pick up some support between now and 1999. Most of this will come from the collapsing Democratic Party. It will win additional votes from marginalised rural blacks, and possibly even from some more conservative middle-class Africans. Yet electorally De Klerk's party has nowhere to go in the short term. It is now ironically doomed to play the role to which it so long consigned the parliamentary opposition to its left between 1948 and 1994 – that of the watchdog, and representative of big business, capable of slowing down parliament, but not changing it. De Klerk's dream of electoral victory in 1999 is about as realistic as Verwoerd's claim that apartheid was a 'moral'. However much the NP *has* changed, its capacity for political fantasy has not.

Here for the last time I will invoke the ironies which pepper the NP's history. In the end, Albert Hertzog was right. In jettisoning its Afrikaner exclusivism in the 1960s, the NP abandoned its soul. It current political dilemma turns around the issue always at the heart of its politics – *identity*. The NP has been forced to concede everything it stood against so violently throughout its life. Now it lives the classic crisis of identity of a political party which abandoned its original definition of itself almost 30 years ago, and which has never found a truly satisfactory replacement. The central question of Afrikaner nationalist politics still echoes through the NP's offices: *wie die donder is ons*? (who the hell are *we*?).

The NP was always a party of group identity. It always insisted on *volksgebondenheid* – that the individual drew his (never her for the NP) identify from the group. Its most pressing political problem today is that it no longer knows which group it represents: Afrikaners? white and brown Afrikaans-speakers? whites? the conservative centre right of all ethnic groups? big business? It knows (or knew) very well how to do the politics of exclusivist ethnic identity. It has not the foggiest notion of how to represent the full spectrum of 'the Rainbow nation' which is the new South Africa. Until it can resolve this question of identity, until it once again knows who are the *ons* (we/us) it represents, it stands no hope of ever winning an election in South Africa. De Klerk is simply whistling in the dark.

This does *not* mean, however, that the NP is either powerless or marginal. While its electoral prospects will remain distinctly limited in the short to medium term, De Klerk's new National Party does occupy two gatekeeping roles which ensure it substantial influence behind the scenes. The first is in the civil service. The settlement negotiated at the World Trade Centre basically leaves the existing civil service in place. Its ranks will be opened to blacks, and a large number of ANC members will be appointed to senior positions. Nevertheless, the NP will still command very strong support from within the state bureaucracy, and it has vast experience on how to use such support to derail policies it dislikes. It will use this power-base to define the limits of the possible, and to hamper the ANC-dominated government should the latter adopt policies which run counter to the NP's vision of the 'new South Africa'.

Its ability to do so will be reinforced by its second gatekeeping role. Under F W de Klerk, the once anti-capitalist National Party remorselessly presents itself as the real party of business in South Africa. The Second Vice President himself seems committed to a thoroughgoing monetarism. His party is regarded by both domestic big business and the international financial community as the watchdog on the excesses of the (not so) closet socialists in the ANC. This means that the NP remains well-placed to exercise strong restraint on Mandela's government. It will seek to use this power not so much in formal politics and in parliament, but in the corridors and boardrooms of real power. In the context of economic globalisation and structural adjustment, the National Party will demand for itself a crucial role in determining the limits of the elite consensus which shapes the policies of reconstruction and development.

Here, however, the NP might unexpectedly fall victim of its own history. During thirty years of NP ethnic favouritism after 1948, South Africa's (predominantly anglophone) white businessmen were obliged to find ways to work with, and gain access to, a government which did not directly represent their interests. After some initial hesitation, businessmen and state came to a mutually profitable *modus vivendi* – one which largely by-passed the formal structures of party politics. Now that political apartheid has been finally defeated, Nelson Mandela and his predominantly ANC government are likely to prove far more amenable, reasonable and less ideologically blinkered than NP leaders from Malan to Botha. At the time of writing (July 1994) there are already signs that capital will work out a comfortable relationship and easy lines of access to the post-apartheid state. It may very well be that despite considerable efforts to capture for itself the favours of the champion of big business, at this level at least, the NP's role might be less important than De Klerk imagines.

I should like to end this book with a vignette from the April 1994 election – one pregnant with unintended symbols. On Monday 2 May 1994, F W de Klerk conceded that the National Party had lost power. In a gracious, nationally televised speech to the NP faithful gathered at its Johannesburg headquarters, De Klerk called on his party to work together with the ANC to forge the new South Africa. Just as he announced that 'the National Party is no longer a white party', all the lights went out, and the hall was plunged into darkness. As millions of South Africans watched black television screens and heard De Klerk's voice struggling on valiantly, I'm sure that I was not the only one laughing at Fate's sense of timing and irony. Once the lights had come back on, De Klerk ended his speech by saying 'God Bless South Africa. *Nkosi Sikelel' i Afrika!*' (God Bless Africa – the ANC's longtime liberation anthem). The assembled *boere* (and other members of the new National Party) then burst into song. Some sang the old South African anthem *Die Stem*. Others valiantly tried to sing *Nkosi Sikelel' i Afrika* which had just taken its place with *Die Stem* as one of the new country's twin anthems. And still others burst into the one African song most whites have heard at some time in their lives, the work song *Tshotsholoza*. The resulting cacophony made marvellously funny television. It was also a wonderful metaphor for the political confusion facing De Klerk's new National Party as it struggles to find its role and its place in a country which now represents everything the NP fought against throughout its existence.

THEORETICAL APPENDIX

Understanding politics
in the apartheid state

[A]ll claims to knowledge are a quest for power (*jeu de pouvoir*) – they involve the manipulation of symbols with the objective of subjugating, silencing, or resisting other interpretations of reality. We believe that theory should be judged both in terms of its intrinsic merits (coherence, logic, etc.) and in terms of its consequences.[1]

Introduction

The South Africa state was born out of the merger in 1910 of Britain's four self-governing settler colonies in southern Africa. It became fully sovereign with the adoption by the British Parliament of the Statute of Westminster in 1933.* Explicitly built on a racially exclusive form of the Westminster model of British parliamentary democracy, and officially known as the Union of South Africa between 1910 and 1961, this state was transformed into a republic in 1961 – when it left the British Commonwealth. Beyond replacing the Governor General with a ceremonial State President, the first republic of 1961 altered almost nothing in South Africa's Westminster-derived constitutional arrangements. These provided for a strong central parliamentary government, with limited powers devolved to elected provincial councils in each of the four provinces.†

This form of state was transformed however with the establishment of the second South African republic – appropriately enough – in 1984. The Westminster model was replaced by a highly centralised and complex presidential regime, built around an executive Presidency, a racially defined tricameral legislature and a nebulous advisory body with limited powers, known as the

---

* The four British colonies which 'united' to form the Union of South Africa in 1910 were: the Cape, Natal, the Transvaal and the Orange Free State. In a 1923 referendum, the all-white electorate of a fifth settler colony, Southern Rhodesia (now Zimbabwe), rejected a proposal to join South Africa, opting instead for responsible government. Prior to the enactment of the Stature of Westminster, the South African government was constitutionally bound to enter into any war once the British Parliament had issued a declaration of war. This question of South Africa's involvement in Britain's wars was the catalyst for the formation of the National Party in 1914, and its 'reunification' in 1940.

† Thus the provinces administered, *inter alia:* education, health, roads. However, they were obliged to do so within the terms of national policy set by the Cabinet acting through Parliament, and administered by the various departments of the central government.

President's Council. The elected provincial councils were scrapped in 1986, and the Office of the President assumed responsibility for provincial government. This neo-apartheid state finally disappeared with South Africa's first truly democratic elections in April 1994. The new interim constitution provides for a neo-federalist presidential regime with a powerful (bicameral) central legislature elected on a mixture of proportional and regional representation. The five-year mandate of this new regime is also supposed to produce a new, permanent constitution for South Africa.

Between its formation in 1910 and transformation in 1994, the South African state enjoyed a long notoriety as the incarnation of constitutionally entrenched racism. Two aspects of this stood out.

Firstly and most importantly, in all the various forms it assumed during its first 84 years, this state always excluded the vast majority of its population from all aspects of political life, and denied them most other civil rights. Once white women were given the vote (though not yet full legal *persona*) in 1928, this exclusion of the majority was based solely on the grounds of race.* Actively propagated by virtually all white political parties, this policy of denying full citizenship to the black majority was elaborated and strengthened into *apartheid* (literally – 'separate-ness' or 'apart-ness') by the National Party after it regained power in 1948. As elaborated during the 1950s, apartheid theory came to hold that the tens of millions of Africans living in South Africa were not in fact South African nationals, but rather belonged to one of ten 'ethnic homelands' which would eventually become 'independent'. Thus black South Africans would exercise their rightful claim to citizenship outside of South Africa, and had no legitimate claim on citizenship in the white South African state.

This points to the second notorious feature of this racist state: for 56 of the 84 years of its existence, the white South African state was governed by a highly mobilised political party – the National Party – which self-consciously saw itself

---

* There were two partial exceptions. Firstly, the 1910 Constitution (the South Africa Act adopted by the British Parliament) saw a non-racial, property-based, male franchise in the Cape and (theoretically at least) Natal Provinces. In practice, although only white males could be elected to the Union parliament, this gave the vote to thousands of qualified 'non-whites', ie, male Cape Africans and so-called Coloureds. Their votes were judged to have been decisive in a number of constituencies. (In Natal a derisory number of 'non-whites' were able to exercise this theoretical right.) The white parliament voted to disenfranchise Cape Africans under the so-called 'Hertzog Bills' of 1936. Now placed on a separate electoral roll, Cape Africans elected four (white) representatives to the white parliament. Even this limited Cape African representation was abolished in 1960. Likewise, so-called Coloured voters in the Cape were removed from the common voters roll in 1956 and also given four separately elected (white) MPs; a representation abolished in 1968.

The second exception was the tricameral constitutional dispensation of 1984. This established racially separate Chambers of Parliament for the so-called Coloured and Indian populations, while preserving a monopoly of power in white hands. Africans remained entirely disenfranchised under this constitution. Only with the 1994 Interim Constitution did South Africa's African majority acquire the right to vote for the national parliament and other legislative bodies.

as the embodiment and instrument of Afrikaner nationalism, and which described its own apartheid programme as the realisation of the Afrikaner's divine mission in Africa. Even during the two 14-year periods when the NP was not in power, South Africa was governed by three Boer generals, each of whom had spent much of their respective careers fighting (quite literally) for Afrikaner rights. Two of these generals-turned-politicians went to their deaths defining themselves as Afrikaner nationalists, and one of them was himself the founder and longtime *Hoofleier* (leader-in-chief) of the National Party.*

More than any other society on earth, then, the South African state of 1910–1994 seemed to embody Clifford Geertz's celebrated claims for the primacy of what he termed *primordial attachments*:

> These congruities of blood, speech, custom and so on, are seen to have an ineffable, and at times overpowering, coerciveness *in and of themselves*.[2]

These supposedly self-evident ethnic characteristics of the South African state, together with the apparent primacy of ethnicity at most levels of its internal politics, led many analysts to explain these politics in largely, if not exclusively, in ethnic terms. The role of the ethnically exclusivist National Party (NP) in elaborating and implementing apartheid gave rise to the view that the NP was the simple instrument of, in the title of an influential book, Afrikaner 'ethnic power mobilised'.[3] In this type of analysis, the 'ethnic' character of the National Party (at least until the 1980s) is taken as sufficient both to explain itself and the ethnocentric policies which the party pursued until 1994.[4] How this helps us explain the (ethnic) NP's abandonment of its ethnically exclusive definition of both itself and the South African nation is less clear in this mode of explanation.

Such circular reasoning apart, this conventional wisdom about the apartheid state and its racial policies rests on another highly questionable premise. The racist policies of this supposed Afrikaner 'ruling ethnic group' have been widely depicted as directly suppressing and distorting the inherently colour-blind 'free market', and as such, deeply inimical to the interests of capital. This view is bolstered by the fact that South Africa was governed between 1948 and 1994 by a political party which, with the exception of most agricultural capitals and emerging Afrikaner finance, never really 'represented' the capitalist class. Indeed, throughout the 1950s, 1960s, and 1970s, the bulk of what marxists would call 'the capitalist ruling class' in fact regularly expressed opposition to apartheid policies – and in particular its rigid controls over the labour market.

---

* Respectively the first and third South African prime ministers, Generals Louis Botha (1910–1919) and the NP founder James Barry Munnik Hertzog (Prime Minister 1924–1939). The third such former Boer General was Jan Christian Smuts (Prime Minister 1919–1924 and 1939–1948). However by his second mandate Smuts had long abandoned even the veneer of Afrikaner nationalism to become an icon of the British Empire (see chapter 1 above).

Apartheid was thus widely seen to be in direct conflict with the logic of the free enterprise system.* This is all taken as self-evident, with the supposed primacy of primordial attachments now apparently confirmed by events in Central and Eastern Europe since the collapse of communism.[5]

The widespread notion that apartheid was inimical to South African capitalism was further reinforced during the black urban uprising of 1984–86 when P W Botha's government obstinately refused to accede to the demand of the major business groups to dismantle apartheid. The long 'crisis of apartheid' following the 1976 Soweto uprising was universally perceived internationally as a problem created by a recalcitrant, ethnic Afrikaner government. Up until the 1994 democratic elections, the conventional media take on South Africa still overwhelmingly echoed a prominent American journalist's musings on the 1976 Soweto uprising:

> The great problem for South Africa ... is essentially a problem for the Afrikaners since they hold the power in everything that matters.[6]

Understanding government policy then became, in the title of a recent book by South Africa's most respected and influential liberal journalist, one of grappling with 'the mind of South Africa' – read Afrikaners.[7]

This conventional view of the South African state rests on a series of mutually reinforcing logical and empirical errors which I have analysed elsewhere and will not repeat here.[8] Suffice it to say that it takes as given precisely that which requires to be proven, ie, the alleged primacy of ethnicity and the latter's virtually automatic translation into an exclusivist ethnic nationalism. Contrary to the journalistic conventional wisdom of the post-Cold War conflicts in Eastern and Central Europe, human beings do not always automatically respond in vast numbers to the beating of a nationalist/ethnic drum by this or that politician. History is replete with examples of peoples who have *refused* the invitation to ethnic mobilisation, opting instead for wider, more inclusive forms of identify and political mobilisation, or even changing their primary identities at this or that given moment.

Sometimes this even extends for those who have spent their lives propagating ethnic particularism. In the negotiations leading up to the 1993 adoption of South Africa's interim constitution, the National Party itself jettisoned almost every last element of its own, decades-old, ethnic programme and world view. Yet it fought

---

* This too is the source of the widespread perception of a basic contradiction between the apartheid state and the NP on one hand, and 'the economy' and business interests on the other. Merle Lipton's 1985 revision of this liberal conventional wisdom falsely reduced the marxist analysis of the capitalism/apartheid dialectic to the absurd proposition that 'capitalists want apartheid' – *Capitalism and Apartheid: South Africa, 1910–84* (Rowman & Allanheld, N J, 1985), 4, concluding that if capitalists neither 'wanted' apartheid labour policies nor supported the NP, then the marxist assertion that apartheid grew out of the structure of accumulation and class relations present in South African capitalism is false. Q E D. See esp. 372.

tooth and nail for the retention of a 'colour-blind' free market economy and the class privileges of its leadership. Which leads to a question: what was finally more important to this 'ethnic' party – its Afrikaner ethnic nationalism or the class interests of its leadership? One does not have to be a mechanistic marxist to conclude that, at the very least, the NP's own history and choices suggest that 'ethnicity' cannot simply be assumed to be either an instinctive human reflex, nor that it is *the* 'primordial' identity, nor indeed that where 'ethnic' sentiment exists that it translates directly and unproblematically into an exclusivist form of nationalism.

This would suggest, as I argue in the Introduction to this book, that social and political identities, and the translation of these identities into social and political action, are infinitely complex and dynamic aspects of human behaviour. As such, they cannot be taken either as given or as self-explanatory. I am persuaded that in order to explain such identities and their socio-political mobilisation, the analyst has to situate the particular group of people and socio-political phenomena to be analysed within the unique set of historical and conjunctural circumstances which define their understanding of both who they are and the options open to them.

I deal with this below. Here, however, I would note that the conventional view of the previously existing apartheid state also obscures one of the central issues of the current phase of South African politics. The dismantling of apartheid must address more than just the political consequences of apartheid (the exclusion of black people from the political system). It must simultaneously confront its social and economic legacy.

This challenge lies precisely in the realm of the 'art of the possible'. It is a question not only of the real balance of forces, and the limits and possibilities of the current moment, but also one of the skill and determination with which the new government acts within the realm of the possible. Politics, in all the various senses of the word, is at the core of the challenge confronting Mandela's government. In this book, I seek to make a modest contribution to the debate over what is possible in contemporary South Africa, by clarifying some of the political processes and struggles which led us to this current moment.

My discussion of the politics of the apartheid state is situated within a series of theoretical debates in South African social science which began in the early 1970s and continue to this day. A central preoccupation of these debates has been with the nature of and appropriate way to analyse the apartheid state. Most of the participants would have seen this debate as more than just the abstract musings of academics. Rather, exemplifying the underlying concern to find the best means to do away with the apartheid state, this debate implicitly echoed Jean Copans' observation: 'In order to combat state power, it is also essential to comprehend its sociological reality.'[9]

Competing paradigms of politics and change

During the 1970s a vigorous debate among South African social scientists focused on the relationship between capitalism and apartheid. The central protagonists in this debate were a disparate group of marxist scholars. Their work was an explicit and frontal attack on three key assumptions of the then prevailing (and now resurgent) liberal thesis on South Africa. Liberal analyses firstly saw apartheid as having been imposed from outside by a racist state on the inherently colour-blind logic of the 'free market', hence, secondly, absolving capitalism from any responsibility for apartheid. And, as most explicitly formulated in the so-called O'Dowd thesis, apartheid would eventually be brought down by the simple functional logic of the market – as the contradiction between the free market and racist limitations on this market grew acute, the former would displace the latter.[10]

The emerging marxist analysis of the apartheid state was by no means an unproblematic nor unified position.[11] Yet despite sometimes deep differences and antipathies, all these new marxist analyses of South Africa took as their starting point the conviction that the racist practices and policies which culminated in forty years of apartheid were integrally linked to the development of South African capitalism, and indeed, for much of the twentieth century, were an essential condition of capitalist accumulation in South Africa. If South African capitalism was inextricably linked with the development of apartheid, this implied, secondly, that any attempt to dismantle apartheid would have to address both the nature and consequences of this link. The democratisation of the apartheid state would necessarily involve going beyond the mere opening up the political system to the previously excluded (black) majority of South Africans – as difficult as this proved to achieve – to begin the democratisation of the apartheid economy. In this long struggle for democracy, marxist scholars likewise took sharp issue, thirdly, with the liberal notion that capital itself was the major agent of social change. Rather, they argued that the essential force which would do away with apartheid was the weight of mass struggle, in which the black working class would play the leading role.

This new writing in the 1970s rejuvenated the smug world of (anglophone) South African social science. Marxist analysis gained a currency within many South African universities, and seemed to be vindicated by the pattern of black politics in the 1980s. However, as its many critics, and indeed some of its own (and erstwhile) protagonists were quick to point out, this approach suffered from a number of theoretical deficiencies, which rendered its ability to explain the demise of apartheid more than somewhat problematic.*

---

* H Wolpe, 'Towards an Analysis of the South African State', *International Journal of the Sociology of Law*, 8, 4, November 1980. For a very different radical interpretation, see B Bozzoli & P Delius, 'Radical History and South Africa Society', *Radical History Review*, 46/7, 1990, 32-3. It should be noted, however, that this latter article is filled with important errors on the political and intellectual evolution of various trends of the 'radical' tradition. In particular, its treatment of 'structuralism' (24-5) is a tendentious caricature, often simply wrong – the authors attribute to the present writer theoretical influences I had not even read at the time – and highly sectarian. The structuralists are glibly accused of the not-so-slight crime of 'implicit Stalinism' (24), and, at various points, of 'idealism' without the slightest substantiation of these charges being offered.

The first lay in an almost functionalist conception of apartheid – as a set of policies which directly served the economic interests of capital and which were functional to rapid capital accumulation. While this was an important rebuttal of the claim that capitalism was 'innocent' of apartheid, it blinkered many marxist analysts to the impact of the changes in the structure of South African capitalism in the 1970s – changes which finally rendered apartheid 'dysfunctional' to capital accumulation. More than one marxist scholar argued that since capitalism in South Africa took the form of apartheid, the demise of the latter necessarily implied the demise of the former. This has left them peculiarly unable to explain the current state of affairs in South Africa, except through the lame notion that apartheid (rather than its legacy) is still alive and well under the Mandela government.

The second theoretical error grew out of the first – the almost universal instrumentalist conception of the state. In these terms, the apartheid state was treated as both monolithic and a simple instrument to be laid hold of by this or that 'hegemonic' fraction of capital, and wielded to serve its own particular interests. This ignored the vast contradictions within and between the various apparatuses of the state, evacuating exactly the theoretical territory to which purely gestural references were made – ie, the 'relative autonomy' of the state. It also eliminated any sense of the materiality of politics within the state, and indeed any notion of political process itself.

The third major problem with this analysis was its class reductionism – the tendency to reduce political parties and social actors to the simple agents of this or that class or class fraction. Their political practices were effectively read off from, and explained by, their economic interests. This form of analysis was simply unable to explain the process of real politics within the state except in terms of clashes between different classes or class fractions – and once again the relative autonomy of politics disappeared.

By the early 1980s, the shortcomings of these forms of marxism were being attacked from all sides. This coincided with the suicide of one of its leading sources of theoretical inspiration, Nicos Poulantzas, and the incarceration for the murder of his own wife of another theoretical guru, Louis Althusser. This was also the moment of the retreat into post-modernism and post-structuralism of much of the European left intelligentsia which had inspired South African theoretical marxism. In South Africa itself, many radical social scientists reacted against what some argued were 'top-down' explanations of apartheid and racism. Scholars were increasingly drawn to a more empirically oriented form of 'history from below', exploring in detail aspects of the contribution of popular forces and groups to the forging of apartheid society. This approach deeply enriched our understanding of the real history of South Africa.[12] However, perhaps in response to the new British cult of 'the Poverty of Theory', and its full-scale offensive against 'theoreticist' marxism, this turn to social history remained largely empirical in nature. Though much of this work was clearly underpinned by a rich theoretical tradition, very few of the social historians chose to make their theoretical concerns explicit. At same time, a particularly sharp and needlessly polarised polemic erupted between certain social historians and some of the defenders of the virtues of structuralism.[13]

The result was a prolonged retreat from theory. Despite a growing preoccupation with the South African state, little in this literature was explicitly theoretical. This appendix examines the various modes of analysis of the South African state which emerged in the 1980s and 1990s in response to perceived weakness in the marxist literature of the 1970s. It concludes with an exposition of what appear to me to by useful ways out of the theoretical impasse.

The debates of the 1980s and 1990s

The past fifteen years have seen a burgeoning literature on the apartheid state, much of it written from perspectives generally sympathetic to the democratisation of this state. Any attempt to group this literature into broad tendencies must necessarily gloss over differences between authors with similar approaches, and will miss most of the nuances in their work. Nevertheless, it still seems to me to be useful to attempt such a classification of the literature, on the condition that it is clearly understood what is at issue here. This is a debate over how best to analyse politics in the apartheid state, and, either explicitly or by implication, on what kinds of politics are most likely to lead to a thorough dismantling of both this state and its baleful legacy. Identifying theoretical trends and conceptual frameworks, and discussing their assumptions and weaknesses, is one fruitful way to advance this debate.

In the discussion which follows, I focus variously on three aspects in the literature – the ontological, the epistemological and the normative. In other words, I seek to classify the various analyses in terms of: a) the issues and/or the actors identified as central to their overall focus; b) the explicit and/or implicit modes of explanation at work in the overall conceptual framework; and c) the explicit and/or implicit political implications of the broad mode of analysis in question.

In these terms, I would argue that most the 'pro-democratic' literature on the apartheid state produced during the past decade falls into one or other of six very broad tendencies. The limited space at hand clearly does not permit me to do justice to all of this work, and I apologise in advance to any who feel that I over-simplify their own work. My aim is to highlight what seem to me to be various problems with the conceptual frameworks used by many (though clearly not all) of the authors whose work I place in each of these approaches. To the extent that I focus on particular authors, I do so because their work seems to me to be emblematic of a particular problem in the approach or trend in the literature.* Moreover, where appropriate I have also commented at length on what seem to me to be key theoretical influences on the approach in question. Again I do so because of what I see to be explanatory weakness in such influential work.

---

* For reasons discussed on pp. 451, this last comment does not apply to the fifth of these approaches, feminism and gender analysis.

(a) *The security state*

> In the political class struggle – as well as in its particular form of the military class struggle – it is never modes of production which confront each other, nor even classes, but always those *parties* and poly-class groups representing the capacity of one class to find allies for itself, or *military units*, which are likewise poly-class groupings.[14]

The first of these trends made its appearance at the beginning of the 1980s, and was particularly prevalent in the middle to latter years of that decade. This approach sought to 'open the box' of state politics in a new way – one which reflected crucial political developments inside that state after 1978. Attempting to comprehend the various reformist strategies of P W Botha's government, many authors paid particular attention to the role of the military in shaping the both the overall thrust and content of reform and the new decision-making and administrative apparatus which evolved under the Botha administration.[15] This literature was particularly concerned with questions of the military origins of strategy, and the attempt within a highly militarised state to realise this or that strategic initiative.

This work shed much light on the direction and limits of government policy. It further undermined the by then barely tenable liberal notion that the apartheid state was driven simply by Afrikaner nationalist ideology.[16] Yet it tended to oversimplify and exaggerate the military's role in internal state politics, occasionally coming close to explanation based on military conspiracies. This can largely be explained by the tendency of this literature to ignore the actual process of politics within the government, or at best to reduce it to competition between groups of 'securocrats'. The newly militarised state discourse was taken as sufficient proof that 'the military' was in control of the process of elaborating and implementing policy. At best, this rested on a vague notion of an alliance between generals and businessmen, though little attempt was made to explore the nature of this alliance.

This form of analysis also made the same mistake as many generals – to confuse the internal logic and precision of a strategy drawn up on paper with both the murky and contested processes of elaborating and implementing policy as well as with the subsequent struggles to adjust policy to deal with its own unintended consequences. The simple point seemed to have been lost that the definition of a strategy in the mind of a general, of the State Security Council or even the of State President guaranteed neither its adoption nor (a different process) its implementation in the desired fashion. More significantly, this analysis often also ignored the crucial fact that the adoption of a particular reform strategy as state policy did not mean that its opponents should accept that such policies would necessarily produce the effects and results desired by the state strategists. What was absent or drastically oversimplified in this mode of analysis was an understanding of the sharply contested internal politics through which 'the state' adopts, implements and modifies such strategies. This meant that those who still clung to this approach by the end of the 1980s were unable to anticipate the looming sea change in state politics, being both astounded by, and unable to explain, the dramatic policy shifts under F W de Klerk.

(b) The regulationists

[I]t is essential to acknowledge that socio-economic analysis does not directly explain the outcome (*la décision*), the moment which belongs above all to the realm of politics ... [W]ith the possible exception of Gramsci, none of Marx's successors have carried out a detailed and satisfactory investigation into the question of power.[17]

The second trend in the recent literature emerged in the mid-to-late 1980s. This was an attempt by a group of South African marxists to transcend the weaknesses of their 1970s view that apartheid was functional to capitalism. Some of this earlier literature had gone so far as the ahistorical suggestion that, in South Africa, apartheid and capitalism were to all intents and purposes the same thing. The struggle against apartheid was *necessarily* a struggle against capitalism in South Africa.[18] This was clearly a difficult position for a marxist to defend in the late 1980s. The theoretical reformulation was undertaken largely by a group of academics linked to the Economic Trends group of the Congress of South African Trade Unions (Cosatu). It sought to avoid the class reductionism and economic determinism for which much of the earlier South African marxist literature had been rightfully criticised. Rooted in the regulation theory of Michel Aglietta and Alain Lipietz, this approach rests on the assumption

that long waves in capital accumulation can be explained as a consequence of the successive creation and collapse of a supportive socio-institutional structure. ... Writers in the regulation/SSA [social structure of accumulation – D O'M] tradition argue that institutional structures (such as the welfare state) and state intervention (incomes policies and Keynesian full employment strategies) allowed for a balance between the growth in output (aided by techniques of mass production) and purchasing power.[19]

From this perspective, the particular regime of accumulation in South Africa until the early-to-mid-1970s was that of a form of 'sub Fordism' or 'peripheral Fordism' first characterised by Gelb as 'racial Fordism'.* Under this regime of

---

* S Gelb, 'The South African Crisis', *Transformation*, 6, 1987. 'Aside from its organisation of technology, Fordism consists of an economic and social policy, generally maintained by social contract, in the guise of corporatism or tripartism. This allows the state to manage the national economy in close cooperation with the large enterprises and major trade unions', R W Cox, 'Dialectique de l'économie-monde en fin de siècle', *Études internationales*, 21, 4, 1990, 696. This refers to the essentially Keynesian strategies of demand-led growth and the multiplier effects of relatively high wages and mass consumption as a spur to investment and productivity as the instrument through which to fashion social consensus and guarantee social peace.

accumulation, a form of industrialisation through import substitution was achieved via the 'Fordist integration of white workers and the white population in general, and the peripheral-Fordist integration of only a section of the black majority' and the 'exclusion' of the rest.[20]

By the early-to-mid 1970s, however, the growing political contestation by blacks of this 'racial Fordism', coupled with key changes in South Africa's integration into and role in the world economy, brought the growth model into crisis. The state was required to elaborate a new regime of accumulation and mode of regulation. In these terms, change is viewed as a consequence of 'crisis', which latter is itself conceived as 'a new terrain of contradictions in which the *regime of accumulation* of capital is no longer "guaranteed" by the *mode of regulation'*.[21] Morris argued that the key to a new mode of regulation is a new hegemonic project to resolve the national question and elaborate a new definition of the 'nation-people'.[22] By 1990, the central conjunctural question now became that of whether there would be a democratisation from below or from above.[23]

This approach provided a number of useful insights into the content of, and articulation between, South Africa's economic and political crises. I have myself borrowed from some of these writings, particularly from Mike Morris's various contributions. However, it seems to me that the regulationist literature is not without major problems.

The most acute grows out of its own closed theoretical structure. As Nicci Nattrass has pointed out, the key concepts of the regulationist model are posited as if they existed in the real world:

> The essential point is that before a regulation/SSA can be deemed to exist, it is necessary to conduct substantial historical analysis of key institutional and social relations as well as into central empirical trends, most notably the rate of profit and accumulation.[24]

Secondly, if everything in a crisis is *a priori* reduced to the regime of accumulation and mode of regulation, then analysis of the crisis becomes a fairly simple *a fortiori* form of empirical validation, if not simple illustration, of these core concepts. The analyst goes out and looks for 'the facts' which fit the model.[25]

This theoretically closed circle then leads to an economic determinism as blatant as that which its authors seek to avoid.[26] It rests on an implicit (and foreclosed) conception of causality and change: that crisis leads directly and automatically to policy changes – to the elaboration of new growth models and hegemonic projects. The mere existence of a crisis is taken as sufficient explanation of change. Nowhere does this literature grapple with the sharply contested *political processes* through which real living political and social actors struggle with each other to transform the abstract imperatives of 'crisis' and crisis resolution into concrete state policies, nor with the equally contested and complex politics around implementing such new 'accumulation strategies' and 'hegemonic projects'.

In the South African regulationist literature these real actions and policies of all class actors/political agents appear to be directly read off from the model and reduced to a simple search for new accumulation strategies and/or modes of regulation/hegemonic projects. At best, its analysis extrapolates from the perceived logic of 'the crisis' to explain policy choices and directions – as if 'the state' and 'capital' had read and were applying the precepts of Lipietz *et al.* – perhaps with the odd reference to a company report or government commission as 'proof' of some form of intentionality. Mike Morris does indeed acknowledge the need to avoid posing 'a deterministic relationship between economic crisis, political restructuring and redefinitions of the national question'.[27] Yet this reference to real political struggle inside the state seems largely gestural. When he and others of this school do try to grapple with such concrete conflicts, these are explained either in terms of the economic interests of 'fractions of capital' or as a direct function of the economic crisis and/or the political challenge of the oppressed majority.[28]

Politics is thus again reduced to conflict over the realisation of economic interests. The only real difference between the regulationist analysis and the forms of economic determinism of the old Poulantzian analysis is that since neither the market nor capital is able to regulate the functioning of any national economy, 'the intervention of an agency external to capital, like the state, *is necessary for this*'.[29] In these terms, the state is no longer the executive branch of the ruling class, but it exists to perform the necessary function of regulating the economy.

However, there are two problems with this insight. Firstly, while it may help explain the functional *necessity* of the state, it does not explain either its role or its 'relative autonomy' from the economy it supposedly exists to regulate. The second problem grows out of the first. If the regulationists are right that the state does indeed exist to perform the necessary function of regulation of the capitalist economy, it follows logically that their analysis of politics within the state can be reduced to the various functions the state is required to perform in order to fulfil this, its essential and necessary role. This is an unacceptably simplistic form of functionalism. The more astute regulationists attempt to avoid this functionalist trap through a return to Poulantzas and ascribing to the state a 'relative autonomy' in looking after social consensus and the national question. But since these are themselves necessary functions for accumulation to take place, and are thus intrinsically linked with the accumulation strategies which define the crisis, this relative autonomy is, in the notorious Althusserian last instance, part of its economic function.

Finally, this regulationist notion of the state also rests on a conceptual elision of 'government' and 'state' in which the state again becomes an rational actor, an historical subject rather than a site of struggle. 'It' elaborates new accumulation strategies and hegemonic projects, which usually don't work, and so the process begins anew. Conceived in this fashion, the state then becomes a kind of black box in which these things simply happen – or at best, the hidden hand of class struggle writes out new projects. The real living political struggles within and around the state, the haphazard nature of many of its policies, the highly contested ways in which they are implemented, the force of 'relatively autonomous' political cultures and bureaucratic routines, the role of the personalities of key political leaders – in a word, the *real* political world in which men and women are killed, tortured, imprisoned, or more mundanely, see their careers and ambitions realised or broken – all of this simply disappears into the grinding out of the theoretical logic of the regulationist model. Its most crudely reductionist variants sometimes read as if P W Botha, F W de Klerk and the rest were familiar with the works of Lipietz *et al*. The reader can almost hear De Klerk's richly accented Afrikaans as he tells his Cabinet: 'Listen, *okes*, our social structure of accumulation is beginning to crumble. I think we really need a new regime of accumulation and mode of regulation.'*

(c) State-centric analyses

> The historical process, in its most crystallised form, *simultaneously* has to do with social structure and human agency, social constraint and human volition, regularities and idiosyncracies.[30]

Other authors on the South African left have sought to go beyond the effective blindness to real politics characteristic of these first two approaches. What seems to me to be a third broad analytical trend in the recent literature has sought, explicitly or implicitly, to 'bring the state back in' and to 'open the box' or 'lift the lid' of state politics. These authors analyse state and politics in ways far more sophisticated (and helpful) than those which focus on the 'securocratic' state. Much of this literature echoes Hyslop's plea for a return to Weber's emphasis on 'the specific autonomous effects of political power' and that 'it is the accumulation of power in the state itself that needs to be analysed and understood'.[31]

In concrete terms, this translates into a recognition that the NP government's policies cannot simply be explained in terms of the interests of a dominant class or class fraction, nor in terms of the logic of capital accumulation.[32] Some of these authors also criticise the notion of a grand NP strategy either in 1948 or during the 1980s.[33] Still others argue that the conflicting political interests within the state and the ruling party were as material to the direction of state policy as was the need for new strategies of accumulation and hegemonic projects.[34] In

---

* My English rendition of this parodied imaginary conversation is no accident, since, like many analysts of South African politics, most of the regulationists failed to read what most of the protagonists of the apartheid state had to say to each other in their own language – Afrikaans. This led not only to much ignorance over the key transactions of state politics but also to a fundamental inability to grasp the content and significance of the dominant political culture within this state. Neither are in any sense reducible either to the logic of capital or the mode of regulation. It is roughly equivalent, in a Canadian context, to somebody writing about the Québec state and Québec nationalism by basing him/herself on the *Winnipeg Free Press*.

doing so, they stress the role and impact of the specific institutional structure of state politics at any given moment, and of the consequent institutional routines, and bureaucratic cultures 'that characterize the function of, not only the South African state, but all states', and thereby shape 'party and policy alignments'. This means that state action is both autonomous from, and articulates with, 'the economic'. Analysis of the state focuses on 'the logic of '"culture", [of] as well as personalities within bureaucracies in the formation of policy'. This 'New Research Agenda on South African Politics' needs also to explore how the thrust and dynamic of political conflict is affected by the changing institutional composition of the state.[35]

This focus has the great merit of taking politics seriously. These authors seek to grapple with the real politics of the apartheid state rather than imposing on these politics the abstract logic of the authors' own theoretical model. These writers often display a greater appreciation of the limits and possibilities of various political conjunctures than the (largely) structuralist texts they criticise. The best of this work has deeply enriched our understanding of both the development of apartheid and the operation of the apartheid state. Some of its also provides a rich theoretical synthesis.* However, much of the other literature on the internal workings of the state is uneven. It seems to me that in their haste to avoid the pitfalls of structuralism/class reductionism, some of these texts reproduce certain of the weakness of both traditional and contemporary liberal analysis of South Africa.[36] They tend either to overemphasise the political actors' stated views of both their own actions and the broader political process, and/or fail to grasp the real dynamic of state politics.†

---

* Eg, Posel, *The Making of Apartheid*, 'Lifting the lid...', and 'Sizing up the Population...'. Posel's work is marked by the strong influence of Weber and Foucault. Stanley Greenberg's work might also be considered to fall into this category – especially his *Legitimating the Illegitimate: State, markets and resistance in South Africa* (University of California Press, Berkeley/Los Angeles/London, 1987). Though explicitly Weberian, Greenberg's work – like that of Posel – defies neat categorisation. Though he has devoted much attention to 'opening the box' of internal state politics, I have somewhat arbitrarily classified Greenberg's work in the following section both because of his heavy attention to discourses of legitimation and because of his claim that the apartheid state was *not* autonomous. See note ‡ p. 442.

† Thus, eg, basing himself on a series of confidential interviews with nationalist politicians and functionaries, Steven Friedman in *Reform Revisited* asserts that in the last year of the Botha regime there were no real grand strategies, and that reform was the NP's way of muddling through in the hope that it would find a workable solution. In this text, Friedman was understandably concerned to correct the then prevailing conspiratorial notions of an iron grip on state policy by a cabal of 'securocrats'. While he was right to the extent that both the NP government and the broader party were no longer united around a single vision of how to proceed, he missed four essential points: (a) that such a grand strategy *had* been imposed by a hegemonic group within the NP and state between 1978 and 1984; (b) that the collapse of the reformist discourse shaped by this central strategic vision aggravated conflict among competing centres of bureaucratic power within both the National Party and 'its' government, and that this now raging conflict was itself a major obsta-cle to the elaboration of a new strategic consensus; (c) that in the period June 1986 till near

The real weaknesses of much of this type of analysis lie with its failure to confront what seem to me to be highly problematic issues in the dominant theoretical influences invoked by most (though not all) of these authors – the neo-institutionalist writings of Theda Skocpol and other proponents of a 'state-centric' approach.[37] Given the influence of the writings of Skocpol and other state-centric analysts, the remainder of this section is devoted to an examination of the theoretical validity of their approach. I will argue that while the intention 'to open the [black] box of [state] politics' points to a vital problem – the need to elaborate a coherent theory of the materiality of the political – both the metaphor of a hitherto closed box/lid and the way these theoretical models of state-centric analysis propose to open it seem to me to occlude central aspects of the process of change.

Metaphor is a endemic aspect of all theories – be it the architectural 'infrastructure/superstructure' of Marx, the 'closed box/lid' of various schools of political science, the 'state of nature' of realist theories of international politics or the 'texts' of post-modernism. Indeed, George Lakoff and Mark Johnson go so far as to argue that metaphor is fundamental to the entire process of human thought:

> The metaphor is not merely the words we use – it is in our very [psychological] concept of an argument ... We shall argue that human thought processes are largely metaphorical.[38]

The power of metaphor lies in its use of compressed imagery to convey, by association, an idea which might otherwise be inaccessible. I have myself had frequent recourse to metaphor throughout this book. Nevertheless, the pervasive use of metaphor in theory seems to me to be problematic for two reasons. Firstly, evocative imagery and association can be used to avoid the need to *think through* the relationship suggested by the image. This often leads to different and sloppy interpretations, and sometimes to controversy over the precise meaning of the metaphor. One of the best examples is the century-long debate over Marx's celebrated metaphor of base and superstructure, in the name of which people have died. The second problem with the use of associative imagery is the baggage that comes with the image in question, baggage which is often highly revealing of the *failure* of the particular metaphor to capture the relationship it is supposed to represent. Thus, the image of a closed box of politics necessarily carries with it the (Parsonian/Eastonian) notion of politics as a discreet, sealed, impermeable domain, accessible in thought only through an examination of its *internal*

---

the end of 1988, a loose coalition of 'securocrats' *did* again dominate the discourse of state policy, using their privileged access to P W Botha in a largely successful attempt to marginalise competing actors and perspectives; and d) that most key elements of both the government and the National Party still clung to a belief in the necessity of such a central strategic recipe to resolve the political problems confronting the state. This search for a new strategy was later to become a crucial element in the fall of P W Botha and then in the NP's turn to and comportment in the negotiation process.

contents, as seen only inside the box. What is inevitably lost in the metaphor of the box is the everyday truth that politics is shaped by, and in turn acts to shape, a much wider domain of social action of which it is an inseparable part.

Not surprisingly, this necessary consequence of the metaphor of the box is present in other aspects of the state-centric model. However, I would argue that as echoed in the work of Michael Mann and Anthony Giddens, Skocpol's state-centric model rests on a series of theoretical flaws which render its ability to understand state politics at least as problematic as that of the structuralism it criticises.* Space prohibits an extensive discussion here, but I will focus primarily of the work of Theda Skocpol as the trail blazer and most frequently cited of the state-centric theorists.[39]

Moving away from her early flirtation with the world-systems variant of neo-marxism, Skocpol's highly influential comparative study of state and revolution breaks with explanations that view the state as manifestation of social relations between collective (ie, class) actors.† Her conception of the state rests on three principles. The first stresses the need for what she calls 'a non-voluntarist structural perspective'.[40] The second emphasises the geopolitical framework of state action, and particularly the role of 'an international system of competing states' in shaping the interests, nature and institutional structure of the particular state to be examined.[41] Skocpol's third principle is that which she terms the 'potential autonomy of the state'. The state primarily exists to extract resources (for itself) from society, which resources it deploys in order 'to create and support coercive and administrative organizations', which are 'the basis of state power as such'. As a 'macro-structure', the state 'is no mere arena in which socio-economic struggles are fought out. It is, rather, a set of administrative, policing and military organisations headed, and more or less well coordinated by, an executive.' These 'fundamental state organizations' are 'at least potentially autonomous from direct dominant-class control'.[42]

Skocpol's notion of the 'potential autonomy' of the state is a curious one. On the one hand she insists on the need to move from the structuralism of the Poulantzian notion of 'relative autonomy' of the political (in which the economic

---

* Mann suggests that the power of the state is derived from: a) its functional necessity for the existence (maintenance) of complex civilised societies; b) the multiplicity of its functions; and c) its territorial centrality. Together these account for its autonomous power, rendering the state independent from civil society, and giving it the status of an actor (agent) with a will to power – 'Autonomous power of the State', *Archives européennes de sociologie*, 25, 1984. Giddens likewise stresses the independence of the globally ascendant nation-state from industrial capitalism – *The Nation-State and Violence* (University of California Press, Berkeley, 1987).

† Interestingly, Skocpol gives as one of the reasons for her break with marxism what she calls 'my early intellectual confrontation with the case of South Africa'. She amply illustrates the hold of ethnic analysis over a then marxist when she states: 'Working strictly in terms of class analysis, it was difficult to conceptualise, let alone adequately explain, the structure of the South African state and the political role of *the Afrikaners*'. *States and Social Revolutions: A comparative analysis of France, Russia and China* (Cambridge University Press, Cambridge, London & New York, 1979), xii (my emphasis).

instance is determinate 'in the last instance'). If the state is only 'potentially auto-nomous', this would suggest that under normal conditions it is *not* autonomous. So she seems here to propose a *weaker* notion of state autonomy than that held by the structuralists (who argue – metaphorically – that the 'lonely hour' of the last instance never comes). If the state is theoretically only 'potentially' autonomous, this implies that it only becomes autonomous in fact when 'its' own fundamental interests clash with those of the dominant social groups (class for Skocpol). Yet such a formulation is valid only to the extent that Skocpol's theorisation of the *conditions* under which this potential autonomy becomes real autonomy is deemed acceptable. This is the weakest part of her argument, leading her in fact to propose a much stronger, indeed absolute, notion of (supposedly potential) state autonomy than do many structuralists.

According to Skocpol, the state realises this potential autonomy under two conditions/situations. The first, and most fundamental, is in the realm of interna-tional politics. The state is potentially autonomous by its very place in the competitive system of states. In arguing for a focus on what political elites are 'actually doing', she replies that they are usually 'struggling to assert and make good their claim to state sovereignty'. They do so in order to 'enhance *national standing* in the international context'.[43] In her comparative analysis of the French, Chinese and Russian revolutions, she argued that the best way for the pre-revolutionary states to achieve enhanced national standing was through increased centralisation and deepened bureaucratisation – rendering these states both more powerful vis-a-vis their own societies and better able to participate in international rivalry. For Skocpol the basis of the state's potential autonomy is its involvement in the competitive international system:

> For international military pressures and opportunities can prompt state rulers to attempt policies that conflict with, and even in extreme cases contradict, the fundamental interests of a ruling class.[44]

I will return to the circular nature of this argument in moment. Here, however, it is important to note that Skocpol's conception of this international system, and the role of the state within it, rests explicitly on the vastly problematic and hugely contested 'realist' theory of an anarchic international system in which egotistical states are locked in deadly struggle for survival and power.

As literally hundreds of international relations theorists have pointed out, this realist approach rests on a series of extremely simplistic and reductionist assumptions. These include *inter alia*: An extreme form of empiricism which insists that realism has theorised the world 'as it really is', and that this 'objective' theory is the base for a 'science' of international politics;* a cyclical

---

* See H Morgenthau, *Politics Among Nations: The struggle for power and peace* (Knopf, New York, 1967), 4-5. While most realists cling to this insistence on their 'objectivity', the most sophisticat-ed realist text does acknowledge that the approach simply describes the world as state actors them-selves see it. See R Aron, *Paix et guerre entre les nations* (Calmann-Lévy, Paris, 1984), 97-102.

conception of history in which the actors change, but the patterns and logic of international politics remain constant;[45] an ahistorical insistence on the unchanging anarchic nature of the international system;* a metaphysical and essentialist conception of the state as a simple extension of an essentially Hobbesian human nature and thus necessarily egotistic entity;† an equally ahistorical, holistic and personified view of the state as a (monolithic) rational actor, rationally pursuing 'its' own national interest (or defending its own national security) defined in terms of power; and a Clausewitzian notion of war as both a key element in the rational pursuit of politics by this monolithic state, and an inevitable, and indeed necessary, part of the ongoing competition for power – one which establishes the very structure and distribution of power within the international system.‡ These universal realist principles themselves reside on a partial and ethnocentric reading of very limited slice of world history – that of the competing system of European states (mostly monarchies) between 1648 and 1914.[46] This is then turned into a particularly distorted ideal type, which the realists insist is the only legitimate way to analyse the world, since it

---

* Thus in the words of a prominent contemporary neo-realist theoretician, 'international politics has not changed fundamentally over the millennia' – R Gilpin, *War and Change in World Politics* (Cambridge University Press, New York, 1981), 211. Gilpin doubts whether contemporary analysts of international relations 'know anything that Thucydides and his fifth-century compatriots did not know about the behavior of states'. Ibid, 227. This has provoked Joseph Nye to reply that 'security dilemmas have existed since the time of Thucydides and they continue today, but... [a]fter all, Thucydides never worried about global debt, nuclear winter or the depletion of the world's ozone layer' – *Bound to Lead: The changing nature of American power* (Basic Books, New York, 1990), 178.

An illustration of the absurdities consequent upon the dogmatic, ahistorical nature of realism is to be found in John Mearsheimer's 'Back to the Future: Instability in Europe after the Cold War', *International Security*, 15, 4, 1990. Mearsheimer argues that the 'long peace' in Europe after 1945 was simply the result of the nuclear standoff of the bi-polar system. With the end of the Cold War, the necessarily anarchic nature of the international system will inevitably reassert itself, leading to a severe risk of military conflict within Europe (even between Western European states). Thus the only way to preserve peace in Europe is for the United States to preside over a controlled nuclear proliferation which would see Germany, Italy and other states becoming nuclear powers, thereby able to 'dissuade' potential aggression from their neighbours.

† The classic statement of which is the first principle of one of the great founding texts of modern realism: 'Political realism believes that politics, like society in general, is governed by objective laws *which have their roots in human nature.*' Morgenthau, *Politics Among Nations*, 4, my emphasis. Even those structural realists who do not rely on a theory of human nature necessarily end with an identical view of the state. See Aron, *Paix et guerre* and K Waltz, *Theory of International Politics* (Addison-Wesley, Reading [Mass.], 1979).

‡ See 'Introduction', P Kennedy, *The Rise and Fall of the Great Powers* (Random House, New York, 1987). Aron's magisterial realist statement begins with a long discussion of Clausewitz, *Paix et guerre*, 1, and his very definition of the specificity of international relations is of a realm characterised as 'the legitimacy and the legality of the recourse to armed force on the part of the actors' – 'Qu'est-ce qu'une théorie des relations internationales', *Revue française de science politique*, Vol. XVII, 1967, 310.

corresponds with the way the world 'really is'.

Skocpol's entirely uncritical assimilation of such 'realism' as one of the twin props of her state-centric perspective necessarily adopts the realists' insistence on the absolute autonomy of this system from societal actors. State sovereignty is the screen which separates domestic from international politics according to the realists. The two are entirely separate realms of politics, subject to entirely different laws and dynamics. But the external realm is primary because the very survival of the domestic realm of politics depends on the successful defence of sovereignty in international politics.[47] In the realists' Hobbesian world of an anarchic international system, the *raison d'être* of the state is to survive. State survival entails an endless and primordial obsession with national security. Here Skocpol falls into the same ahistorical reasoning as the realists, for whom nothing has changed in the nature of international politics since Thucydides first spelled out its rules. According to this mode of reasoning, the international imperatives confronting the contemporary South African state are the same as those of its apartheid predecessor (and little different from those of France of Louis XIV, England under Alfred the Great or the Athens of Pericles).

This ahistoricism is seen at another level. Despite her insistence on the need to place the state in the context of 'world historical events',[48] Skocpol conceives both the state and the (realist) geopolitical international system as *pre-existing* the emergence of capitalism, and thereby independent of it. Two theoretical confusions are to be found here. The first is to elide the forms of political systems which existed prior to 1648 (empires, monarchies, city-states etc.) with those which *slowly evolved* after the Treaty of Westphalia had entrenched the principle of sovereignty and the separation of the temporal from the spiritual realm of power – ie, the modern nation-state. To argue that contemporary Japan, seventeenth-century Britain, the Aztec empire and the Carolingian Empire can all be analysed as 'states' subject to similar international dynamics is a profoundly ahistorical form of political essentialism which renders problematic an analysis of the specificity of each of these political systems.*

The second confusion lies in Skocpol's notion of the relationship between the international system and global capitalism. While she is clearly right to insist that neither the state nor the international state system can be simply *reduced to* and read off from the dynamics of global capitalism (*à la* Immanuel Wallerstein), it is by no means axiomatic that the historical evolution of either can be conceived of *independently from* the evolution of international capitalism. What is required is a non-determinist theory capable of grasping their mutual interaction.

I return to this point below, in discussing my own view of the autonomy of the political. Here however it is also necessary briefly to examine the implications

---

* Nevertheless, this is exactly the universalist (and functionalist) claim made for 'the state' in much of the international relations literature which bears so heavily on the state-centric theorists. See, eg, J Huntzinger, 'L'universalisation de l'État-nation', *Introduction aux relations internationales* (Paris, Éditions du Seuil, 1987).

of the second condition of this notion of the potential autonomy of the state. According to Skocpol:

> State organizations necessarily compete to some extent with the dominant class(es) in appropriating resources from the economy and society. And the objectives to which the resources once appropriated are devoted may very well be at variance with dominant class interests. Resources may be used to strengthen the bulk and autonomy of the state itself – something necessarily threatening to the dominant class unless the greater state power is indispensably needed and actually used to support dominant-class interests.[49]

Here Skocpol does indeed acknowledge the need to explore not just the structure and interests of state organisations, but also to analyse the 'class forces and politically mobilized groups in society'.[50] Yet it seems to me that her argument is highly circular and *presupposes* exactly that which needs to be demonstrated – ie, state autonomy. State organisations are autonomous because they appropriate resources from the economy and society. But underlying this is the assumption that they can act in this manner precisely because they are – by their very nature – autonomous. This presumes that state organisations exist primarily to pursue their own need for resources, a need which is institutionally prior to, and independent of, the structure of power and the availability of resources in the economy and society.

I am not for a moment disputing that in the real world, this or that state apparatus (or more correctly, the power holders who are able to mobilise its particular institutional power resources) often do pursue objectives at variance with those expressed by key power holders in the economy (eg, the most powerful corporations). In apartheid South Africa, such autonomy was sustained over much of these 'forty lost years'. Rather, what is at issue here are two different questions, the first ontological, the second epistemological. The ontological issue is the question of under what conditions are such actions possible, and more importantly, under what conditions are they no longer possible. The moment that it is acknowledged that such resources are finite, and that the continued existence of the state depends on it not extracting so many resources as to threaten its own conditions of existence, then the *limits* to state autonomy become clear.

To illustrate with a concrete example. In the real world of politics it frequently occurs that, in pursuit of its own institutional resource requirements and interests, a state organisation, such as a municipal authority, may increase taxes on commercial property over the violent objection of major business interests. This action can indeed be explained in terms of the particular institutional logic and requirements of such a local authority. These policies can in no sense be reduced either to the imperatives of accumulation nor to the interests of the dominant fraction of capital. However, the ability of the municipality in question to sustain such policies – that is to say its ability to pursue its autonomous interests – is indeed *proscribed* both by the logic of accumulation and the social power of the dominant class. A severe recession would drastically curtail the revenue generated by such policies, as would the flight of capital from the city in question. Both would erode and eventually destroy the capacity of the municipality in question to pursue its autonomous institutional logic and objectives. Thus, again, while such policies are in no sense reducible to the logic of accumulation nor to the power and interest of the dominant class, nor are they completely autonomous from them. The autonomy is, precisely, relative rather than potential.*

Where does this lead the analysis of the apartheid state? It would suggest that despite its laudable insistence on the need to take account of the institutional logic of this state, and explore the materiality of its politics, the state-centric approach has not succeeded in its attempt to theorise the conditions of the autonomy of politics. Despite Sarakinsky's protest to the contrary, it does indeed implicitly conceive the state as a discreet entity pursuing its own autonomous logic outside broader social forces.[51] This approach provides a much-needed emphasis on state politics, but has failed to theorise them adequately.

This becomes even clearer in the epistemological issue at question in this mode of analysis. Despite Skocpol's pleas for the integration of the structural and autonomous moments, this has not been theorised. Her implicit mode of *explanation* of state action under the twin conditions of its autonomy is that of the rational actor. The state (conceived either as a monolith at the level of the international state system or as sets of state organisations) acts rationally in pursuit of defined objectives and interests. This is the essence of state autonomy – the ability to pursue its own (or its organisations' own) interests autonomous from those of the dominant class.†

These autonomous actions of state and state organisations are explained *ex post facto* by extrapolation from the occurrence we know to have taken place (or from the implementation of an autonomous policy), to impute an objective (the rational pursuit of an interest), a goal or an intention as the *cause* of this action, policy or occurrence. Ironically, this state-centric model shares this mode of explanation of politics with both the first two modes of analysis discussed above

---

* Thus, in Part IV of this book I argued that the exigencies of the crisis of accumulation in the late 1980s were such that the 'autonomous' state was ultimately unable to sustain its policy of 'buying' black support, its war in Angola or its desired constitutional options. While the accumulation crisis did not, as the regulations imply, lead directly to policy changes, it nevertheless had a number of crucial political effects both in state and civil society. Taken together these effects shaped the political process which led to De Klerk's turn of 2 February 1990.

† Mann likewise posits the state as a actor with a will to power, which fundamental interest 'it' pursues rationally. 'Autonomous power of the state'. Giddens argues that there 'are four institutional clusterings associated with modernity: heightened surveillance, capitalistic enterprise, industrial production and the consolidation of centralized control of the means of violence'. *The Constitution of Society*, 5. Because neither is wholly reducible to any of the others, he likewise develops a theory of state agency and autonomy explained primarily in terms of the international dimension of state action.

(the security state approach and the regulationists). Despite their wide differences, each of these three approaches to the South African state ultimately rely on what, in a very different context, Graham Allison long ago labelled the Rational Policy Model of explanation.[52]

According to this model, acting in the name of parsimony and theoretical elegance, academic political analysts tend to explain the twists and turns of state policy as the 'more or less purposive acts of unified national governments' (or, in Skocpol's terms, state organisations). For these analysts, the point of an explanation is to show how the actor or government could have chosen the action in question, given the strategic problem that it faced. This implies that policy or action is 'the realisation of some purpose or intention'.[53] Assuming that the actors in question make rational choices in pursuit of maximising values, the task of analysis is to identify, firstly, the key actors involved and, secondly, the *objectives* of the actors in question, in order to show how specific actions and policies are the result of rational choices in the pursuit of such objectives.

Thus the differences in the conception of politics between the three modes of analysis outlined so far are largely ontological – ie, to some extent reducible to: a) which groups and/or social forces they regard as the salient actors, and b) what they take to be the strategic objectives motivating their actions/behaviour. For the security-state analysts, the key actors are located within the state. These actors pursue the objectives specified by prescriptions of the securocratic vision of strategic management. The regulationists widen the cast of salient actors to include key business leaders and 'the state' itself. The objectives pursued by these agents are imposed on both state and capital by the requirements of the regime of accumulation. A situation of crisis eventually obliges key government decision-makers to make the rational decision to change policy (aspects of the mode of regulation) in an attempt to mitigate the negative effects on the regime of accumulation. The state-centric model posits either the entire (personified) state, or its various constituent organisations, as the central actors. This approach explains their actions as the realisation of an autonomous interest located either in international political competition or in extracting resources from society.

(d) Discourse analysis

It is proving beyond doubt that we find ourselves in *the age of the floating signifyer*, when word no longer attaches properly to thing, and no highbonding glues can help us. ... The undermining of the illusion of presence indeed goes back to the early days of the tendency and was famously developed by Roland Barthes in his great essay of 1968 on the Death of the Author ... What writes books is in fact nothing other than history, culture, or to be more precise, *language itself*. Indeed, so effective is language that it frequently has arrived early in the morning, sat down at the typewriter, and as good as completed half a day's work before the average so-called author has even showered, dressed and got through his breakfast croissant.[54]

A fourth, and probably the most influential (though also most diverse), trend in the recent literature on the apartheid state looks at state and politics in a very different way. While acknowledging the importance of actual institutional workings of and conflicts within the state, these analysts tend to focus more particularly on the elaboration of representations and subjectivity, on ideology and the role of ideological transformation in these conflicts within and between state departments. In sharp distinction to Skocpol's dismissal of legitimacy as a significant 'explanatory concept',[55] the issues of legitimacy, of modes of legitimation and of hegemony stand at the heart of this analysis. Many of these authors examine the particular modes and forms of representations through which 'the search for legitimacy' is elaborated. At the core of their work stands the question of language, and the ways in which, through discourse, language both shapes the terrain and the subjects and objects of politics and fashions the forms and ways in which power is expressed, exercised and reproduced.

Thus, Saul Dubow traces the working out of a segregationist ideology within the Native Affairs Department, documenting the ways in which the department consolidated and extended its powers.[56] Stanley Greenberg examines the practices of the various institutions of labour control and the significance of ideological shifts in attempting to legitimate an inherently illegitimate state. He argues that the elaboration of state structures is symptomatic of the *failure* of the state effectively to control the black population. His examination of 'the breakdown of state coercive institutions and the search for a legitimacy formula' is heavily preoccupied with 'the discourse on legitimacy'.[57] Both Dubow and Greenberg analyse the concrete institutional practices of state departments and the elaboration and changing content of the ideologies underlying them.

In a similar vein, Deborah Posel has focused on 'the new language' of legitimation/domination emerging under the Botha government.[58] Adam Ashforth's study of official discourse of race explores 'schemes of legitimation' which he reconstructs from the 'Grand Tradition' of commissions of enquiry into 'the Native Question'.* George Pavlich examines the South Africa company lore for capital's discourse on apartheid.[59] Martin Chanock explores how law works as a mechanism of power, and particularly how law constructs 'the categories of persons and their powers which are fundamental to the workings of any society'.[60] Kathryn Manzo sets out to demonstrate how 'South African politics are an effect of global power relations', asking questions such as: 'What is power? How does it operate? *How are relations of domination effected and reproduced?* How do changing power relations affect local struggles and modes of resistance?'[61] Linzi Manicom analyses the construction of gender in the South

---

* *The Politics of Official Discourse in Twentieth Century South Africa* (Clarendon Press, Oxford, 1990). Ashforth argues that the ongoing exclusion of Africans from citizenship in South Africa was largely an effect of a power/knowledge relation, in which the forms of categorising the population employed by these commissions was a key mode of legitimating forms of state and rule.

African 'state formation', exploring both state discourse and the routines and rituals of ruling.*

Of all the 'approaches' to the state which I have here somewhat schematically identified, this is by far the most disparate and difficult to categorise. This is largely explained by the wide diversity of the theoretical sources and influences on this literature. These range from Weberian hermeneutics and various forms of post-structuralism/post-modernism – from the 'post-marxist', neo-Gramscianism of Ernesto Laclau and Chantal Mouffe, through (most influentially) Michel Foucault's shifting analyses of the discourse of power, to post-modernism's *lider maximo*, Jacques Derrida and the cult of deconstruction† – to the Critical Theory of Jurgen Habermas and others.

These authors all reject the structuralist/instrumentalist conception of the state embodied in the 1970s marxist literature. Yet their theoretical diversity is reflected in widely differing conceptions of the state. At one end stands Greenberg's explicit adoption of Weber's definition of the state as 'the administrative and legal order that claims "to monopolise the use of force", to exercise "binding authority" "within a given territorial jurisdiction".' As such, the state 'is a complex terrain shaped by the interplay of political leaders, officials, class and allied actors and social divisions'.‡

---

* 'Ruling Relations: Rethinking state and gender in South African history', *Journal of African History*, 33, 3, 1992. This article is examined in some detail in the following section.

† However, a disciplinary and linguistic apartheid is in evidence here. Though increasingly present in historical and feminist studies, Western post-modernism remains less evident in South Africa social sciences than in the field of cultural studies – where its domination is barely challenged by the few remaining 'modernist' dinosaurs. Part of the reason for this, it seems to me, lies in the fact that many of the founding texts of post-modernism are written in a particular form of reflective and speculative French, which translates uneasily into the more empirically oriented English language. Very few of these texts have been read in the original. Nevertheless, some of the core ideas of post-modernism – particularly those of the end of the 'grand narratives' of 'modernity', of the impossibility of instrumental knowledge and of progress – have entered into the discourse of South African social science. For a useful brief discussion of the evolution of post-modernism, see Jean-Marc Piotte, 'Postmodernité et quête de sens', in *Working Papers* (Karl Polanyi Institute of Political Economy, Concordia University, Montreal, 1990). For a more fully realised discussion of both post-modernism and post-structuralism, see Pauline Rosenau's very useful *Post Modernism in the Social Sciences* (Princeton University Press, Princeton, 1992), together with her publisher's insert 'How to speak post-modern'.

‡ Greenberg, *Legitimating the Illegitimate*, 208, xvii. There is a real contradiction underlying Greenberg's concept of the South African state. On the one hand, he develops the somewhat unusual argument that the apartheid state was '[l]acking in autonomy'. This was so because the differentiation of state and market as 'theoretically distinct and autonomous spheres of activity' – a differentiation 'central to the legitimating discourse ' in capitalist societies – 'never arrived' in apartheid South Africa (9). This 'visible interpenetration of politics and economics' means that while the state regulates the market and the African working class, 'the development of the economic realm has been retarded. Markets and private entrepreneurs have not readily emerged as distinctive, self-regulating, productive, equitable [!] and public spirited [as they are under capitalism!? – D O'M]' (5). Because of its lack of autonomy, the state, on the other hand, 'has not

At the other extreme of this tendency are the more explicitly post-structuralist approaches. Manicom goes so far as to recount with approval Philip Abrams's view of the state as 'an ideological abstraction which in its appearance of unity and externality to society or social classes obscures the very relations and practices through which rule is effected'. In this perspective, the state is conceived as 'politically organised subjection'. Investigation of 'the state' thus not only involves

> an analysis of the institutional forms, practices and ideologies of its disaggregated parts, but also *the study of the way in which the relations and objects of rule are constituted* within and by what Poulantzas calls 'the institutional materiality' of the state.[62]

The key verb in this sentence (as in much of this approach) is 'constituted'. All the categories of 'the state' together with the 'relations and objects of rule' are 'historically constructed with discourse'. Together with the 'routines and rituals' of state rule, discourse fashions the '"moral regulation" inherent in state formation, the valorization of particular social and political relationships and identities and the marginalization of others'.[63]

The common thread in this literature is its attempt to deal seriously with language. However, its very theoretical diversity makes it virtually impossible to speak of a single analytical paradigm. Nevertheless, it seems to me that a large number (though again, not all) of analyses within this disparate literature *do* exhibit a fairly consistent and shared epistemological orientation. Thus I take as belonging to a common paradigm those authors – and only those authors – who assign explanatory privilege to discourse and (to a lesser extent) to symbolic rituals. These analysts are interested, above all, in the *construction* of the objects and relations of rule in discourse. Much of their work draws on Foucault's dual notion that micro-networks of power exist independently from the state, and that discourse reveals such relations of power and domination.[64] The analytical task thus lies in deconstructing all such social and political categories constructed by the prevailing modes of discourse, and in an exploration of the modes of construction of discourse.

There are a number of problems with this approach. The first is that many authors, and particularly those more explicitly working within a Foucaultian paradigm, completely eliminate agency, and hence the real world of politics, from their analysis of how social categories are constructed. Thus despite the title of his book, Ashforth barely considers politics in the conventional sense, reducing it instead to the conscious elaboration of 'schemes of legitimation' by

---

emerged as a universal institution mediating between conflicting parties and identified with the national interest, broadly conceived' [5]. This argument comes perilously close to a variant on the old liberal orthodoxy that a 'precapitalist' form of state is able to hold back the logic of the market. Greenberg's definition also implies that (this non-autonomous) state dominates, controls and runs the economy because it has the (autonomous) power to do so.

the 'experts' (as the bearers of the knowledge from which power is derived) sitting on the commissions.[65] This 'Grand Tradition' is the key to understanding the ongoing exclusion of Africans from citizenship in South Africa because in 'times of crisis for states' it often occurs that 'officially propounded accounts of social reality' are at such variance with 'that reality as it is lived' that these official accounts 'lose some of their usefulness in organising political subjection'. When these new realities

> adversely affect the interests of those sections of 'society' with the capacity to hamper the operations of state officials or threaten the stability of the state, difficulties in the reproduction of political power can be experienced. At this point *it becomes imperative* to develop new accounts; to develop new terms for referring to social reality. Commissions of enquiry are institutions ideally placed to engage in reckoning such schemes. In South Africa, our Grand Tradition reports do just that.[66]

Ashforth presents a functionalist notion of the conditions under which new schemes of legitimation come to be constructed. He sees such legitimation schemes as being consciously and intentionally elaborated as a direct result of the imperative to reproduce political power. This comes as close to the Parsonian functional imperative of 'pattern maintenance' as one can get without saying so. Commissions appear to act deliberately and consciously to preserve the existing order (or homeostatic equilibrium?).* Moreover his understanding of the 'politics' of these commissions of enquiry is unable to explain various crucial political issues.

The first is the link between commission recommendations and subsequent government policy. At least two of the commissions at the centre of this analysis had their core recommendations flatly rejected by the government of the day.† Neither of Ashforth's 'two key criteria' – 'the nature of the crises confronting the ruling orders at any particular time' and 'the official terms of reference and the general approach of the commission to its subject matter'[67] – provide the reader with the slightest means to understand why such 'schemes of legitimation' were rejected. He tells us that the phase of 'symbolic dialogue' between a commission's report and 'society as a whole' comes to an end 'as concrete decisions are made or not made, on the matters at hand or the report becomes no longer relevant to their consideration'.[68] Yet he simply ignores the how and why, the process, through which such 'concrete decisions are made or not made'.

---

* Ashforth imputes direct intentionality to the commissions which 'have sought to fashion workable schemes of policy by devising coherent schemes of legitimation', *The Politics of Official Discourse* – 3. Ironically, this functionalist mode of reasoning is strikingly similar to that of the regulationists.

† The report of the Fagan Commission was thrown out by the NP government when it assumed office in 1948. And the 17-volume report of the Tomlinson Commission ran counter to the interpretaion of apartheid favoured by Dr Verwoerd. Its central findings were never implemented (see pp. 33 and 71 above).

Ashforth insists that commission reports be seen as 'an authoritative statement relating to questions of political action with simultaneously limiting and empowering effects'.[69] The reader is completely unable to judge why such 'authoritative statements' lead to this rather than that 'political action', or might even become 'no longer relevant'. At best he argues that the 'knowledge of social realities they promote is integrally connected to the formations of state power'.[70] *How* they are connected is not explored. Again, the reader looks in vain for an explanation (eg) of the rejection of Dr Verwoerd of one of the central thrust of the 'truths' produced by the Tomlinson Commission.

Perhaps even more revealingly, nor does Ashforth's analysis begin to provide the means to account for another crucial realm essential to our understanding of political subjection – ie, how these 'schemes of legitimation' are 'received', wholly or partially assimilated, or rejected by the objects of state rule who are 'constructed' by such schemes – ie, 'the dominated'. In any but the most reductionist Parsonian notion, politics needs to be conceived as an ongoing set of struggles, not just *within* the state, but between the state and various levels of civil society. Yet this vital level of politics is likewise ignored. In practice, Ashforth's conception of 'politics' is limited to neatly elaborated sets of ideas and rules by experts.* Now, however loudly academics may proclaim that knowledge equals power, a reading of (say) the Tomlinson Commission by leaders and members of the ANC would not necessarily have convinced these black activists to accept the proposed new scheme of legitimation. Regardless of the 'truth' proclaimed by the Tomlinson Commission that Africans were not an homogeneous national group, key power brokers in black politics continued to act (and still do) as if they were such an homogeneous group – if you like to proclaim an opposite 'truth'. Thus, as knowledge-producing apparatuses intended to normalise various moments of domination, the Grand Tradition of Commissions of Enquiry may have brought some solace, some psychological comfort, to threatened white elites. However, this is a very narrow, and hardly original, explanation of 'politics' in South Africa and tells us precious little about power in that country. Gramsci long ago pointed to the distinction between the 'scholarly' or 'literary' forms of ideology on the one hand, and the 'practical' or 'popular' on the other.[71] The legitimation schemes proposed by experts belong squarely in the realm of the former and tell us precious little about the latter. Yet to understand South Africa requires just a little more than a reading, nor matter

---

* At best Ashforth discusses three stages exhibited by 'the discourse that is constituted through the institutional process of commissions of enquiry and embodied in their reports'. The second, 'persuasive stage of discourse' consists of 'symbolic dialogue with the society as a whole' in which 'truth criteria structure the terms of debate', *The Politics of Official Discourse*, 9-10. This seems to limit such 'debate' (and hence the 'truth' effect) of the commission to the white polity. This phase ends 'as concrete decisions are made or not made, on the matters at hand' – though, again, *how* and *why* such (policy) decisions are made seems not to interest Ashforth. The real world of process and politics is entirely absent. All that matters is the 'text' of 'discourse', and/or the 'symbolic rituals', of the state.

how methodologically sophisticated, of the Tomlinson Commission and the Freedom Charter.

Kathryn Manzo, on the other hand, clearly recognises that the 'dissemination and acceptance' of a particular 'truth' or 'norm' is bound to be uneven. It may not be accepted, or may only be partially accepted by 'the oppressed'. Indeed she argues that the latter case of partial acceptance by the oppressed of norms imposed by the dominant, is more typical of South Africa than the 'simple black/white dichotomy usually invoked'.[72] She explains such partial acceptance largely in terms of 'the differential effects of [the institutional discipline imposed by] mission schools and churches' and notions of a 'civilised/uncivilised dichotomy'.[73] This become a little more difficult to assert for the generation of Africans subjected to the 'universal' norms of Bantu education. The largescale (and violent) rejection of its 'truths' by millions of urban blacks over a period of almost 20 years is explained by the 'counter-discourse or hidden transcript of resistance to differentiation' embodied in Black Consciousness.[74]

But this is to explain social change in terms of a set of ideas embodied in discourse. Much post-structuralist analysis of South Africa evinces an intriguing intellectual irony. A very large part of the intellectual roots of this tradition lie in the radical social science of the 1970s. However, in its rejection of the structuralist and reductionist excesses of much of this literature, many post-structuralists veer perilously close to the epistemological idealism which was both the catalyst and the target of much of this radical, neo-marxist analysis.

The core problem lies in the theoretical weight assigned to discourse. That all language, all discourse, expresses relations of power and domination seems to me a fairly trite, if not self-evident, claim – and incidentally one advanced long ago by that arch-structuralist Louis Althusser in his notion of interpellation.[75] What remains to be explained in much of this literature are the necessary conditions of existence (rather than the discursive practice) which give rise to, and modify, various discourses, and/or ensure that one mode of discourse comes to dominate others.

To cite a pertinent example from South African history: Belinda Bozzoli has shown how a particularly 'South Africanist' subjectivity was laboriously and deliberately constructed over thirty years by intellectuals and publicists linked to manufacturing interests.[76] For much of this period, many of those whom we now consider 'Afrikaners' acted socially and politically in terms of this 'South Africanist' identity rather than the competing 'Afrikaner' identify likewise being constructed by Afrikaner nationalist ideologues. Why? Moreover, at a given point in time, and for a period of some 30 years or so, the 'Afrikaner' subjectivity seemed to win out over the 'South Africanist', despite the burgeoning discourse of South Africanism. Again, why? How? I hope that I have shown in other work that a large part of the answer lies: (a) in the failure of the forces propagating a 'South Africanist' identity to provide adequate economic and social resources to the various social forces simultaneously being targeted by the discourse of Afrikaner nationalism. This enabled (b) various organised Afrikaner nationalist groups to begin to address some of these neglected material interests; while (c) spinning an organisational web around the various target social groups. The result was a slow weaning away of many of these groups from 'South Africanism' for 'Afrikanerism'. This was achieved *not* by proclaiming the 'truth' of this subjectivity either in intellectual journals or from the rooftops – ie, not by discursive practice – but by rather by a conscious, planned, organised and politically directed attempt to provide for key economic, social and cultural interests neglected by those forces favouring the incorporation of the target groups within a broader South Africanism.

Discourse does not explain identity, even less those key episodes in South African history when large numbers of people began to act in terms of identities different from those apparently underlying their previous socio-political actions. It bears repeating that explaining such changes requires, minimally, an investigation of the *process*, and in particular, both the failure of the forces favouring the old subjectivities and the efforts of those proposing new ones, to win large-scale support. 'Texts' and 'symbolical rituals and routines' are grossly inadequate means to grapple with these key processes.

Like ideology, discourse is neither plucked from the air nor is it an independent variable. Like ideology, discourse both embodies and represents, in various mediated, distorted and mystified ways, underlying social relations. Thus, like ideology it can never be taken either as given nor as a social force in and of itself. I agree that it is essential to avoid the crude reductionism and/or economic determinism of some of the 1970s marxist writings on South Africa. I likewise agree that ideology and systems of legitimation have real, determinate effects in any society. However, the retreat into discourse analysis has in no sense answered the theoretical challenge posed by the earlier marxist literature: to elucidate at both the concrete and the theoretical levels the relationship between underlying relations and discourse. This can be put another way: what are the processes through which discourse is itself constructed? And the linked but different question of why do some discourses predominate and prevail over others? Under what conditions, and how, are discourses modified? Analysis which remains purely at the level of discourse itself answers the first of these questions in highly circular form (discourse is constructed through discursive practice). Yet it remains unable to *think* the latter questions, let alone answer them.

At issue here of course is Foucault's idiosyncratic notion of power, and particularly his notion of discipline as a form of power exercised both by continuous surveillance and more particularly by the workings of knowledge-producing apparatuses which present relations of domination as normal and natural:

> In a society such as ours, but basically in any society, there are manifold relations of power which permeate, characterize and constitute the social body, and these relations of power cannot themselves be established, consolidated nor

implemented without the production, accumulation, circulation and functioning of a discourse.[77]

It is difficult to give an authoritative version of Foucault's views on any issue, as his work, focus and definitions changed through his phenomenological, archaeological and genealogical periods. Nevertheless, Foucault seems to regard power as web of relationships throughout society, which, taken together, constitute subjects and endow them with capabilities.[78] Manzo restates the Foucaultian position underlying her own analysis as follows:

> Networks of power historically constitute subjects (or agents) whose struggles and conflicts frequently involve questions of identity and relations between the self and others. Power normalises relations of domination while disseminating ideas about what constitutes 'normality' in dealing with the various types of resistance that domination inevitably generates.[79]

The defining element of this Foucaultian conception of power lies in the 'power is knowledge/knowledge is power' couplet. For Foucault, particular forms of power directly imply specific fields of knowledge and vice versa. His disciples in South African studies have explored the construction of subjectivity (identity) in discourse in order to 'uncover the underlying relations of power'.[80] This work has examined 'the construction' through discourse of a range of identities – racial, ethnic, class and gender. It has also focused on the role of knowledge-producing apparatuses in the production of 'rules' and 'truth', themselves embodied in discourse, which both define inter-subjectivity and 'normalise' the mechanism of domination.

A number of points are relevant here.

Gramsci long ago authored the vital notion that the position of the dominant groups (class) in developed capitalist society rests less on coercion than on the engendered consent embodied in hegemony:

> The temporary universalisation in thought of a particular power structure, conceived not as domination but as the necessary order of nature.[81]

Foucault has taken this crucial insight way beyond the Gramscian notion of hegemony to argue that the production of 'truth' is more central to the exercise of power than are state institutions.[82] The notion that knowledge confers power and that power rests on certain forms of knowledge is as evident as it is trite. However, this in no sense means that power is *reducible to*, nor even knowable from, knowledge – nor vice versa. But this is precisely the assumption underlying much of this literature. By exploring the production of knowledge (of 'truth' concerning social reality) embodied in discourse, we are somehow presumed to be understanding power. At best, such analysis illuminates a *mechanism* of power, one among others.

Moreover, the virtual silence on political process evidenced by much of this discourse analysis leads to a highly mechanistic conception of the 'construction' of subjectivity in discourse. My own research on the elaboration by intellectuals of Afrikaner nationalist ideology in the period 1934–1948 taught me that these experts fought viciously among themselves. They struggled mightily in the realm of ideas – one former Broederbond chairman was even quite literally lobotomised as a result. The 'Afrikaner' subjectivity 'constructed' in the discourse of the 1940s was both highly variegated and the product of protracted and bitter struggle between such 'experts'. But the Foucaultian notion of discourse tends to reduce this highly political and politicised *process* to one of the statement of a recipe, of home truths, by intellectuals. Any acceptable analysis of the 'truths' which eventually emerged needs to be built on the notion of the political processes and struggles involved. I have yet to read an analysis of discourse in South Africa which does so.

I would argue that this mode of analysis rests on an inadequate and mechanistic notion of subjectivity. Here again, it seems to me that Gramsci's distinction between the 'literary' and 'popular' aspects of ideology (p. 345 above) is central to our understanding of the 'construction' of subjectivity. This discourse analysis likewise largely ignores the very different political process of the 'reception' of subjectivity once the experts have proclaimed their truths, once the knowledge-producing apparatuses have defined a particular form of domination as 'normal'. What is crucially left out of the equation here is *why, how, and under which changing conditions*, do particular groups of human beings come to accept a particular construction of their subjectivity rather than competing ones. Once again my research on Afrikaner nationalism indicates that the 'construction' of a particular Afrikaner subjectivity by Afrikaner experts went unheeded by key groups of 'Afrikaners' for much of the 1930s and 1940s. These individuals opted for other, competing identities (some as 'workers', others as 'South Africans'). Only fairly late in the game, and under very specific conditions and circumstances, did they come to assimilate the subjectivity embodied in the nationalist discourse. This means that in and of itself, the 'construction' of such identities through discourse is meaningless unless we have the means to explain the real historical (and highly political) process by which particular identities are discarded and others are received, adopted, assumed, *and transformed*. In the absence of such an analysis, which needs also to be *theorised*, explanation becomes another form of historicism: the outcome was inscribed in the process from the outset, therefore there is no need to explore the process.

I would take this further to question what seem to me to be a core epistemological premise underlying the various modes of post-structuralist analysis. Much of Foucault's work overtly repudiates both the possibility and the necessity of grasping 'the thing itself'. Language is conceived as primary and decisive:

> Expressing their thought in words of which they are not the masters, enclosing them in verbal forms whose historical dimensions they are unaware of, men

believe that their speech is their servant and do not realise that they are submitting themselves to its demands. The grammatical arrangements of a language are the *a priori* of what can be expressed in it.[83]

Or, even more clearly:

> In the descriptions for which I have attempted to provide a theory, there can be no question of interpreting discourse in order to use it to write a history of the referent ... What, in a word, we basically want to do is to dispense with 'things' ... [t]o substitute for the enigmatic treasure-trove of 'things' anterior to discourse, the regular formation of objects that are formed only in discourse. To define these *objects* without reference to the *substance of things* [*fond des choses*] but to relate them to the body of rules which enable them to form as objects of a discourse and thus constitute the condition of their historical appearance. To construct [*faire*] a history of discursive objects which does not sink them into the common depths of an original soil, but deploys the nexus of regularities which governs their dispersion ... I would like to show that discourse is not a slender skein of contact, nor of confrontation, between a reality and a language, the intricate mingling [*intrication*] of a lexicon and of an experience; I would like to show, with precise examples, that in analysing discourses themselves one sees the slackening of the apparently tight grip between words and things, and the emergence of a group of rules proper to discursive practice. These rules define not the dumb existence of a reality, nor the canonical use of a vocabulary, but the ordered system [*régime*] of objects ... practices that systematically form the objects of which they speak.[84]

Two points need to be made here. The first is that this formalism simply obliterates human agency.[85] Just as 'objects are formed only in discourse', so too are subjects 'constructed' by discourse. But in this mode of analysis they are seldom seen to be 'present' in real (and contested) process. At best, human agents are involved in the production of knowledge and discourse through which they 'construct' themselves and others. We have the 'text', who needs the author(s)?

The core of my disagreement with this mode of understanding the world lies in Foucault's view that the rules of discursive practice both 'constitute the condition of the historical appearance' of objects and 'systematically form the objects of which they speak'. That human beings live in and through language is self-evident. Language – 'broadly conceived as systems of signification that extend beyond mere words to include the symbols and structures of all ways of communicating (from the articulated to the subliminal)'[86] – is clearly central to 'the social construction of reality'. But this social reality is in no sense *reducible* either to language or to discourse. Yet again, one does not need to be a mechanistic marxist to argue that there is an irreducible difference between 'real' objects (Foucault's 'things') on the one hand, and the signs, symbols, words or concepts that we develop and use for such objects on the other. As Louis Althusser was wont to say, the concept of the dog does not, and never will, bark. Or to take another example. Any human being who walked the streets of

Montreal at midnight in mid-January would experience a physical sensation *regardless* of the symbols we might attach to this sensation. Naming this sensation 'warmth', or changing the sign given for the degree of such'warmth' from -30° to +30°, would not affect the subjective sensation experienced by this person . Nor would it prevent the death from exposure of anyone who lingered there without shelter or warm clothing. Some 'things' are not only prior to language, but do indeed exercise a tight grip over mere 'words'. 'Language is not life.'[87]

This would suggest that the analyst needs to explore not just the external reality and the symbol/signs/concepts which human beings assign to that reality, it likewise refutes a central precept of 'the descent into discourse' – that language is non-referential. I would argue that a coherent analysis of language (and of discourse) is possible only through an exploration of the mutual determination between the discursive practice and the aspect of social reality it seeks to (re)present.

I conclude this critique of discourse analysis with two brief points, the first methodological, the second entirely subjective. Too much of this work is 'constructed' around purely secondary, published sources. As the historian Bryan Palmer pertinently comments:

> If discourse is indeed the new interpretative key, all of that mucking around in original sources is hardly necessary. A few key 'texts' will suffice, and their creative 'reading' will offer up a history untainted by costly, often uncomfortable, research trips, years in front of the microfilm reader, or months breathing the dust of old archival documents.[88]

Of course, if the master Foucault's drift into genealogy entitled him to publish 'histories' which he explicitly acknowledged were 'fictioned',[89] his disciples could be permitted to feel a little less constrained by the real historical process (and its – clearly 'constructed' – record) than do those who believe in some real connection between words and things. Nevertheless, it seems to me that there is a direct correlation between such methodological reticence and the quality of the resulting analysis. With few exceptions, little of this discourse analysis resonates for me with a real sense, or feel, for what politics (or life) was like under apartheid. Confined to the tyranny of the text and of discourse, much gets reduced to a mechanistic 'construction' of a few dubious 'truths'.

(e) Feminism and gender analysis

Since the mid-1970s, a growing body of analysis has focused on the (different) issues of the role of women and gender in South African history. However, as Linzi Manicom notes in her authoritative overview of the paradigms of South African women's and gender history, this 'relatively small body' of literature has produced 'very little explicit theorizing of "the state" or state processes ... from a self-consciously gender or feminist perspective'.[90] In the only other published study of the place of gender relations and representations in the internal workings of the South African state, Deborah Posel likewise bemoans the paucity of such work.[91]

The gender analysis of the South African state represents a radical ontological departure from all pre-existing models. This work is consciously combative in the sense that it explicitly seeks to recast our understanding of, and approach to, state and politics. Despite its as yet relatively limited currency, gender analysis represents an important evolution in the analysis of the South African state, one whose claims for 'engendered' characterisation of the apartheid state need to be examined seriously. The different approaches used by Manicom and Posel provide a useful prism through which to evaluate a gender analysis of the state.

Both are explicitly concerned to criticise the instrumentalist perspectives of the South African state. In doing so, they also take issue with the

> tendency to treat power as a given, as if its mechanisms were either self-evident or uninteresting. Much more attention has been focussed on explaining why power has been exercised, by identifying those interests which state power has served.[92]

Both Manicom and Posel explicitly state that they are less concerned with 'questions of who rules and why, to one of how rule is achieved' or (the slightly different question) 'what forms power takes (at particular) moments and how it is exercised'.[93] Nevertheless, there are significant differences in focus, in methodology and in the explanatory models used by these two authors, differences which impact on their implicit and explicit conceptions of the place of gender in the mechanisms of power in South Africa. I will deal with these in turn.

Posel's article can be seen as a dialogue with certain historical data. Basing herself on intensive archival research, she sets out to analyse the long struggle over the state's attempts to institute a registry of African customary marriage in South Africa, and to draw explicit theoretical conclusions about the failure of this attempt. In answer to her own question concerning the forms of power and ways in which it is exercised, she insists on the need for two levels of analysis. These would involve:

> more detailed and systematic analyses of the internal institutional workings of the state ... [and] closer discussion of the prevailing discourses of power within state institutions, and the extent to which these representations are enacted in place. On both accounts *the politics of gender* ought to feature prominently.[94]

Posel's detailed analysis of the concrete politics surrounding such a register of customary marriage makes it very clear that she sees such 'politics of gender' at the core of power relationships in South Africa. Her explanation for the failure of state efforts to establish this register of customary marriage posits different sets of institutionally located (exclusively male) power holders, white and black, in struggle over different visions of 'patriarchy'. Despite her disclaimer about the need to focus on the 'how' rather than the 'who' and 'why' of power, her concrete analysis points explicitly to which interests (*who*) proposed and which opposed such a scheme, and *why* they did so. I will return to this in a moment.

Linzi Manicom's article on the other hand is concerned purely with paradigms and theory. Her central purpose is 'to discern the disruptions of prevailing understandings of state formation as these are urged by the inclusion of women and gender within the frame of historical analysis'. Going beyond recent critiques of 'inadequacies in current theorizing of South African state formation', she insists that the necessary rethinking of the South African state 'has fundamentally to integrate *the theoretical and epistemological implications of gender*'.[95]

Here lies the major difference between these two versions of gender analysis. Posel makes no broad claim for the specific theoretical and epistemological implications of gender. She explicitly argues that 'gender relations are relations of power', and concludes that 'the concept of "state power" should itself be disaggregated into an (unstable) amalgam of different styles of governance, each with particular mechanisms and imperatives of control'.[96] Her theorisation of this disaggregated amalgam of styles of governance rests on Barrington Moore's concept of authority:

> Authority – as a form of power accepted by both parties as having some legitimacy – can be conceptualised as an 'implicit social contract, and unverbalised set of mutual understandings' about the proper boundaries of obedience and disobedience, which is 'always being renegotiated' ... relationships of authority involve continuing processes of 'mutual surveillance and bargaining' during which the terms of the tacit contract are contested and renegotiated.[97]

Despite her frequent invocation of 'the discourses of power', the 'paradox of rule' which Posel analyses is in fact the process of politics. Gender is inscribed in the mechanism of political power, but does not in and of itself *explain* political power. Politics is ever present as a contested, and ongoing process.

Manicom on the other hand makes bolder claims for gender. Her insistence on its theoretical and epistemological implications means that the South African state

> should be understood not as unitary or coherent but as institutionally diverse with different objectives being taken up and produced as policy and practice. The project then becomes one of understanding South African state formation *as a gendered and gendering process*, of *exploring the different institutional sites and ruling discourses in which gender identities and categories are constructed*.[98]

Her starting point is the 'absence' of women in the South Africa state, or 'state formation' as she prefers to characterise it:

> Women are not present in 'the state' in more ways than one. Debate around the state in progressive South African history will show that women, historically and

today, have been negligible in state structures, that state policy has discriminated against women, oppressively so against black women, and that, indeed, the historical development of apartheid was predicated on state-enforced gender subordination.[99]

However Manicom argues that it is empirically and theoretically inadequate simply to 'bring women back in' as social agents hitherto ignored by South African historiography. Indeed, she criticises 'the socialist feminist tradition' for confining itself largely to 'inserting women into the historical picture and benignly incorporating their histories into the prevailing marxist theory'.[100] She argues that part of the reason for the failure adequately to rethink the state lies in the fact that much of the writing on women's history is located within the 'social history tradition'. The radical historians associated with this tradition rejected the 'theoreticist' neo-marxist explanations of the development of apartheid 'from above'. Instead, they stressed the necessity to focus on local social process, and particularly to pay attention to 'the perspective of the historical social actors'.[101] Their empirical work, and implicit voluntarism, involved a clear retreat from theory. Manicom emphasises the need to go beyond such empirical attempts to rediscover the agency of the poor, to reconceive the ways in which gender and state have been conceptualised in South African historiography. She argues that real explanation for the 'absence' of women from 'the state' lies in the fact that:

> [T]he very fundamental categories of state and politics – like citizen, worker, the modern state itself – are shot through with gender; that they were in fact historically constructed and reproduced as *masculine categories*, predicated on the subordination of women. *Gender is clearly a relation of power, of domination, of rule.* Yet gender does not feature in the race-class debate, even in its more recent incarnations, and it is certainly far from conventional to refer to *the masculinist state, the patriarchal state* – along with the colonial/segregationist/apartheid/capitalist/reformist state in South African history.[102]

This leads Manicom to criticise those writers engaged in 'rethinking the state' for their gender blindness, and particulary for their uncritical adoption of repro-duction of 'the *masculine* naming and ideological constructions of "labour", "the worker", "the blacks" that abound in the discourse of state and market in South Africa, historically and today'.[103]

Here lies a sharp difference between the two authors under review. Posel clearly regards gender as inscribed on the relationships of power. While she has argued that state power is always gendered, her concrete analysis nevertheless seems to regard gender as but one of many 'styles of governance'. Manicom on the other hand assigns a clear ontological primacy to gender. She first argues that the historical development of apartheid 'was predicated on gender subordination'. This leads her later to affirm that the 'premises of the long historical process of state formation are ones *predicated fundamentally* on gender'.[104] Understanding 'state formation as gendered' thus necessitates

[m]oving beyond the view of 'the state' or state policy as oppressing, neglecting, victimizing, protecting or denying 'women' as if the contents and the interests of this gender category are pre-given. It involves looking also at how gendered racial and class political subjectivity is *produced* and hierarchically organized *by state discourses and practices* as these vary across policy and institutions.[105]

If Posel and Manicom differ over the ontological primacy of gender, their implicit models of explanation are likewise at variance. Posel makes frequent recourse to the concept of gendered discourses of power. She likewise insists on the need to focus primarily on the mechanisms of power. However, when it comes to explaining the failure to set up a Registry of Customary Marriage, her underlying mode of explanation bears little resemblance to the post-structuralism suggested by her language. Instead, she identifies clearly located actors, defines their interests and points to the collusion between conservative African chiefs and various (white) apartheid officials in maintaining the marriage regime. Her explanation of why certain gender definitions/policies are adopted or not thus rests on a clear notion of political process and political struggle.

Manicom's analysis on the other hand is explicitly located within a post-structuralist framework. She argues that the element which distinguishes 'the gendered relations of ruling re/produced' in state practices and procedures, as well as in the social categorisation contained in official discourse, is 'the particular form of power and legitimation they bear'. This power derives not just from coercion, nor even from 'the rationalizing male and white supremacist ideology'. Rather, the power of 'gendered ruling relations and definitions' is located within 'their ongoing confirmation and materiality within state forms that organise political subjection'. This means that

'the state' in South African history should be understood not merely in terms of state policy that reflects patriarchal and racist ideology, but rather as *organized by gender* (and race) difference and subordination in its very formation.[106]

My comments in the previous section concerning the problems with the notion of a particular subjectivity 'constructed' through discourse apply equally here. What is absent in Manicom's analysis is a sense of politics, of struggle, of *process* in both the 'construction' and reception/assimilation of such engendered identities. This, I would also argue, is largely because her radically 'engendered' ontology creates as many analytical problems as its solves.

Much of the argument is circular, taking the primacy of gender as given, as self-evident, rather than as something to be established both theoretically and empirically. How do we 'know' that the state is and was 'organised by gender (and race)'?[107] Why not by class, or language, or ethnicity? This is affirmed but not demonstrated. While Manicom also criticises the notion of gender as being synonymous with women, here she makes no mention of the construction of psycho-sexual identities which go beyond the heterosexual. A consistent theory of gender would also need to explore the inherent homophobia of state discourse and routines of ruling.

More serious, however, is an essentialism differentially present in the core concepts of both authors. Throughout her article, Posel clearly points to competing conceptions of patriarchy held by various actors. However, patriarchy itself is nevertheless taken as an ahistorical given. This raises the question of whether the (differential) forms of subordination of women in (say) the Chinese empire of the Ming dynasty can be analysed with the same concept (patriarchy) used to analyse the highly differential forms of subordination of women according to race, class and linguistic group in apartheid South Africa. Manicom, for her part, criticises the analytical utility of the notion of 'the patriarchal state', insisting that 'the blunt concept of patriarchy occludes more than it illuminates'.[108] Nevertheless, her argument is shot through with, and hinges on, notions such as 'masculine categories', 'masculine naming', the 'masculinist state' and even 'the patriarchal state'. That which seems to render 'masculine' such categories as state, worker, citizen etc. is the fact that they are 'predicated on the subordination of women', or 'women's oppression by men'.[109]

This is far too bald a claim. I do not want to be misunderstood here. The (differential) subordination of (various racial, class, linguistic, and ethnic categories of) 'women' in South Africa (and everywhere else) is not in dispute for a second. Neither is the urgent need to develop analytical categories to explain such subordination, categories which can then inform the struggle to transform the various places different women occupy in social hierarchies. However, what *is* at issue are the terms and explanatory modes in and through which this differentiated subordination of various categories of 'women' (and 'men') have been analysed in the articles under review.

At least six sets of questions need to be posed here: (a) *which* 'women' are being subordinated? – all women, all in the same way? all women, but in different ways dependent on other elements in their 'constructed' identity, eg, race, linguistic group, class? only black women?; (b) these differential groups of 'women' are subordinated *by whom*? – by a 'masculinist' state? by all 'men'? by a white, middle-class English-speaking male power elite? by Afrikaner nationalist 'men'? all of the above?; (c) *why* does this differentiated subordination occur? – what do the dominant gain through such gender 'relations of ruling'? (d) *how* are each of these differentiated categories of women (and – in a consistent gender analysis – gays and lesbians) differentially subordinated by whomever is doing so? (e) *where* does this differential subordination of women fit in the overall structure of relations of domination/exploitation within the society? (f) *what* are the again varying power resources in the hands of such differentially subordinated women (and other subordinated groups) which allow them to struggle against, or accept, such subordination?*

---

* If this question is not posed, we are reduced to seeing 'the subordinated' (including women) as the simple victims of the power of 'the dominant'.

These questions need to be addressed theoretically and empirically. However Manicom directly tackles only the last of these questions, offering only a partial and, I would argue, inadequate answer.* This is quite deliberate on her part. Like Posel, she argues for a 'shift in theoretical preoccupation away from questions and *who* rules and *why*, to one of *how* rule is achieved'.[110] These relations of ruling are constructed through state discourse(s) through the 'routines and rituals' embodied in 'state practice'.

A number of points need to be raised here. Firstly, it seems to me inadequate to suggest a radical departure in the theorisation of the state based exclusively on the *mechanisms* of power. In such an approach, the central organising concepts of 'rule' and 'relations of ruling' rest on circular reasoning. Confining analysis to *how* the mechanisms of 'rule' reproduce entirely anonymous 'ruling relations' necessarily implies that 'rule' and 'relations of ruling' exist because they exist. It further implies that regardless of who was in power, who was ruling whom through what particular configuration of ruling relations, similar (anonymous) mechanisms (discourse and state routines and rituals) would reproduce such 'rule'. Now the issue of who is ruling whom in South Africa is hardly an innocent question, neither in day-to-day politics nor in the raging academic debates initiated by the 1970s marxist assault on the liberal consensus. It is, moreover, a question vital to a left feminist project.

I would argue that analysts can make sense of the particular modes and forms through which power is exercised in South Africa and elsewhere, only on condition that they simultaneously set out to answer the ontologically prior questions of who wields power the particular forms of power, under what (changing) conditions and why.[111] Of course this depends on one's definition of power. I would argue that power can most usefully be conceived as the differential ability of individuals, groups and institutions to mobilise a range of historically specific resources in such a way as to effect the options available to an array of other such actors. In these terms, empowerment involves obtaining *access* to such historically determined and situationally specific resources. Power is both *relational and relative*. It is held by X only in terms of his/her relationship with Y, in which one commands a combination of relatively greater resources than does the other. The nature and range of such power resources change over time. What was a crucial set of resources in one conjuncture or epoch – eg, the ability of certain institutional actors to define every individual's relationship to God and their prospects for salvation – becomes less so, or even irrelevant, in another. This means that we are obliged to ask: *who* acquires such

---

* Although throughout her text she also offers a partial and undifferentiated answer to the first, the second and the penultimate of these questions. She states that attempts within a functionalist South African marxism to accommodate 'women's oppression' obscured 'the specificity of women's oppression by men' (448). This clearly implies that in apartheid South Africa all women are oppressed by all men. It likewise clearly implies that gender domination (exploitation?) is the *primary* form of subordination in South African society.

differential access to these historically contingent sets of resources; *what* enables them to do so – or *why* do they gain access to such resource sets while others do not, or others gain access still other resources; *how* does the mobilisation of these sets of power resources operate, and what forms do power relations assume?

I would also argue what to a Foucaultian poststructuralist may seem pure heresy: that the forms and mechanisms of power differ, often radically, from society to society, and that regardless of similarities in the micro-networks through which power is reproduced, these differences matter. While relations of domination and rule persist in Nelson Mandela's South Africa, the mechanism and forms through which domination is secured are, happily, quite simply *not* what they were under P W Botha or H F Verwoerd. If this is not so, what was the whole anti-apartheid struggle about? Why waste one's time engaging in 'political' struggle?* Deconstructing the new discourse is an inadequate means to grasp the nature and contradictions inherent in such crucial change. Thus, to separate the 'how' from the 'who' and 'why' of power, and to privilege mechanism over conditions of existence, involves an arid formalism in which notions of 'rule' and 'relations of ruling' become residual categories devoid of explanatory power, and precisely unable to inform a credible transformative political practice.

I would take this critique even further to argue that Manicom's explicitly Foucaultian explanation of the mechanisms of power, or 'how [this anonymous] rule is achieved', is likewise inadequate. In common with most post-structuralists, Manicom argues that such rule is achieved through the 'construction' of 'political subjectivity'. This 'construction' is in turn '*produced and hierarchically organised by state discourses and practices* as these vary across policy and institutions'. She argues that the necessary new theoretical direction proposed by gender analysis must show how those fundamental categories of social and political analysis [state, citizen, worker etc.] '*came to be suffused with gender assumptions*'. The central achievement of 'the process of state formation' in South Africa lies in

> [t]he *representation* of such categories (and the broader social divisions of public and private, family and the economy, that underwrite them) as natural and neutral, and the obscuring of their normative gender, race, class and sexual attributes that denied political subjectivity in all who did not bear them.[112]

The explicit notion of the 'construction' of subjectivity here is devoid of sense

---

* This, it seems to me, is in fact *exactly* the necessary conclusion at which the logic of post-modernist epistemology obliges its believers to arrive. The grand narratives are all finished, universal historical subjects have failed and disappeared, 'reason' serves no liberatory purpose, all that is left are fluid networks of actors, each doing their own thing. Epistemological relativism leads to political relativism. We cannot in an epistomological sense, as opposed to an entirely subjective normative sense, 'know' that the form of state under Mandela is an improvement over that of P W Botha.

of process and politics through which such 'construction' comes about. The two central mechanisms Manicom identifies, discourse and state routines and rituals, do not simply appear on the historical stage fully-costumed and well-rehearsed – despite Foucault's insistence that it is the rules of discursive practice which constitute the condition of the historical appearance of the 'objects of discourse'.[113] State discourse (like policy) is a *constantly evolving outcome*, the result of political struggle at numerous levels *within and beyond* the institutional matrix which makes up the state. Treating discourse as text, as a result, fails to explain how and why such discourse is produced. Such an apolitical and ahistorical notion of discourse does not provide a sufficient explanation of *how* power is exercised in any given social formation.

A similar critique applies to the notion of state routines and rituals. The most fleeting investigation of, say, the long debate over the citizenship oath in South Africa, or the routines of issuing passports, reveals profound political struggles within and between the various power centres of the state. These struggles shaped the routines, rituals and symbols of state practice. Such state practices can neither be taken as given nor as immutable. Like the 'text' of discourse, they embody ongoing political struggle within and between the network of state institutions as well as between these state institutions and the myriad components of civil society. Thus any attempt to understand the (constantly evolving) construction of (multiple, fluid and constantly changing) identities in South African history (as elsewhere), needs go beyond mechanistic notions of discourse or state practice to analyse the real political processes by which this is achieved.*

There is a further ontological and conceptual problem here, one common – though in different ways – to both Posel and Manicom. Manicom makes repeated use of the notion of 'the relations of ruling'. She insists at various points throughout her article that such 'ruling relations' empower those whom state discourse 'constructs' as 'men'.† It would seem to me that a feminist analysis of the state, and particularly the apartheid state, would be forcibly impressed by the fact that not all 'men' are equally empowered by the discourse of this 'masculinist' apartheid state. To argue that P W Botha, Harry Oppenheimer and the poorest male squatter in Kayelitsha were all somehow beneficiaries of these relations of ruling of this masculinist state would be patently absurd. Yet this is exactly what is suggested by the notions such as 'the masculinist' (singular), or of [all] 'women's oppression by [all] men'. In apartheid South Africa, while

---

* That identity is both fluid and pluralistic is a key notion lost in the deconstruction of texts. I hope to have shown throughout this book, that while Afrikaner nationalist discourse clearly sought to construct all 'white', Afrikaans-speakers as 'Afrikaners' rather than as 'South Africans', for much of the National Party's history, the actual operation of the mechanism of power depended as much, if not more so, on whether one was 'constructed' as a 'Cape Afrikaner' or as a 'Transvaler'. These multiple (though evolving) identities were central to the question of who held power, and partially explain some of the key transformations of state politics.

† While Posel does not resort to such essentialist formulations, her use of the 'blunt instrument' of patriarchy is open to a similar critique – see p. 456 above.

white middle-class women clearly did not wield the same power resources as their male equivalents, they nevertheless enjoyed access to infinitely more formal and informal power resources than did even the most powerful black males. Throughout South Africa, the daily household psycho-drama of the white 'madam' instructing a truculent male servant (constructed as a 'boy'), was filled with myriad socio-sexual tensions. Yet however profoundly male black servants may have resented being ordered around by a mere 'woman', and whatever fears 'madam' may have harboured of potential sexual assault by her 'boy', both parties understood very clearly who was the more powerful, who could call on private and public resources to the detriment of whom. In such a case it is simply nonsense to talk of 'madam' being oppressed and subordinated by 'boy'. How undifferentiated notions such as 'the masculinist state', or 'women's oppression by men' helps us understand the specificity and complexity of such quotidian 'relations of ruling' is not clarified.

Thus, I would argue, while the normative implications of gender analysis pose the need for urgent political analysis and action, South African academic feminists have not yet come up with adequate theoretical categories necessary for such analysis and action. Despite Manicom's claim to underscore the 'theoretical and epistemological implications of gender', the latter remain unclear. While a radically different ontology has been proposed, the epistemology underlying her analysis is little different from some of the authors whom she takes to task for gender blindness. Posel's more modest claims on the other hand rest on a more credible – though still implicit – mode of explanation, yet one which still has to elaborate its own theory of the place of gender in politics. What remains to be accomplished in this work is exactly the task which Manicom announced – spelling out the specific theoretical and epistemological implications of inscribing a non-essentialist notion of gender on the broader analysis of the power relations underlying the South African state.

(f) Comparative theories of democratic transition

The final trend in the analysis the South African state which I wish to discuss lies more firmly within the mainstream of comparative Western political science than do the others. Unlike most of the analysts cited thus far, few of the authors in this paradigm ever regarded themselves as on the left. While all are preoccupied with the democratisation of the apartheid state, they tend, with one or two exceptions, to span the centre-right of the South African intelligentsia.

This approach focuses explicitly on the process (and prospects) of 'transition from authoritarian rule' in South Africa.[114] In particular, it examines, *inter alia*: the social and political preconditions for such a transition;[115] the forms of bargaining involved;[116] the notion of 'pact formation' between opposed elites;[117] the resources and objectives of the key elites and institutional actors;[118] and the various stages of such a transition.[119]

This work is highly uneven. Some of it is theoretically and empirically naive, using the analytical model discussed below as a set of verities through which to make predictions about the pace and forms of transition.[120] Reflecting its origins as the product of white, often Afrikaner, and mostly male social scientists, a large part of this literature is characterised by an ignorance of the political cultures, strategies and organisations of black politics, relying instead on the prescriptions of the theoretical model. On the other hand, however, the best of this work is often remarkably sensitive to the evolving positions and power-bases within black politics,[121] and provided often vital insights into the process of negotiations in South Africa, even before 1990.[122] Much of this analysis is also far more realistic about the prospects for transition, and the limits of change, than were many intellectuals on the left. These authors have 'opened the box' on South African politics in an often fascinating and useful way.

However, I would argue that they have done so *despite* rather than because of the theoretical model which underpins the vast bulk of this literature. This particular focus on South Africa politics is largely derived from the pioneering efforts of O'Donnell and Schmitter to provide a conceptual framework through which to analyse 'transitions from authoritarian rule'.[123] Part of its appeal to more conservative scholars lies in its emphasis in the key role of 'pacts' between a 'cartel of party elites' as the key to transition. This harks back – as is explicitly acknowledged by O'Donnell and Schmitter – to earlier theories of 'consociational democracy' in situations of 'deep-seated ethnic, cultural, linguistic, or religious conflicts'.*

Based on lengthy comparative studies of Latin America and Southern Europe, O'Donnell and Schmitter enquire into the 'uncertainty of the transition' in a context of

> '*underdetermined*' social change, of large-scale transformations which occur when there are insufficient structural or behavioral parameters to guide and predict the outcome.[124]

The concept of transition – 'the interval between one political regime and another' – is at the heart of this model. Such an interregnum is characterised predominantly by the fact that:

> the rules of the political game are not defined. Not only are they in constant flux, but they are also arduously contested; actors struggle not just to satisfy their immediate interests and/or the interests of those whom they purport to represent, but also to define rules and procedures whose configuration will determine likely winners and losers in the future. Indeed, those emergent rules will largely define which resources can legitimately be expended in the political arena and which actors will be permitted to enter it.[125]

---

* 'Tentative Conclusions about Uncertain Democracies', 41. For the full reference see endnote 123. O'Donnell and Schmitter do however extend their notion of 'pacting' to cover 'less communitarian cleavages, such as those of class, sector, region, institution or even generation'.

The transition has two central moments. The initial phase of *liberalisation* is 'the process of making effective certain rights that protect both individuals and social groups from arbitrary or illegal acts committed by the state or third parties'.[126] This controlled opening usually unleashes a range of unintended consequences which help shape the scope and extension of the process. The phase of *democratisation*

> refers to the processes whereby the rules and procedures of citizenship are either applied to political institutions previously governed by other principles (e.g., coercive control, social tradition, expert judgement, or administrative practice), or expanded to include persons not previously enjoying such rights and obligations (e.g., nontaxpayers, illiterates, women, youth, ethnic minorities, foreign residents), or extended to cover issues and institutions not previously subject to citizen participation (e.g., state agencies, military establishments, partisan organizations, interest associations, productive enterprises, educational institutions, etc.).[127]

On the basis of this distinction, O'Donnell and Schmitter proceed to a number of generalisations concerning the nature of the transition process and the eventual outcomes.[128] The addition of the concept of 'socialization' – the demand not just for 'formal equality of opportunity, but also substantive equality of benefits' – enables them to present a schema of the various likely 'regime configurations.'[129] The remainder of their long synthesis explores aspects of the various phases of transition. These include: the opening (and undermining of) authoritarian regimes; negotiating and renegotiating pacts; resurrecting civil society (and restructuring public space; convoking elections and provoking parties). They conclude by characterising the high degree of uncertainty and indeterminacy of transition as a 'multi-layered chess game' in which

> players not only form alliances to protect each other's positions; they may also elaborate rules which have the effect of isolating certain parts of the board and of neutralizing the players' behavior with respect to those positions in such a way that their moves may have little or no effect upon the eventual outcome.

This tumultuous and impulsive process is one of

> people challenging the rules on every move, pushing and shoving to get on the board, shouting out advice and threats from whenever they can – but nevertheless, becoming progressively mesmerised by the drama they are participating in or watching, and gradually becoming committed to play more decorously and loyally to the rules they themselves have elaborated.[130]

Politics is clearly at the heart of this approach. Its comparative analysis of the central role of competing power centres, institutions and various other 'mediating procedures' in legitimating the rules of political discourse and practice is both intriguing and insightful. The attraction of such a model for the analysis of South African politics after the late 1980s is evident. In many ways, the process of transition seemed to adhere to many of the generalisations presented by O'Donnell and Schmitter. Nevertheless, it seems to me, that its power lies more at the descriptive than explanatory level. The weakest part of the approach is its underlying explanatory model. A number of points should be noted here.

The first is the ancient conundrum of apples and oranges. Generalisations based on comparative analysis are useful only in so far as they remain just that – generalisations. What they obscure is the specificity, the uniqueness, of the case (polity, social formation etc.) in question, and particularly, the issue of whether the specific elements of that case are determinate, or whether the case follows the general trend. Thus, generalisations are not useful rules through which to approach a particular case. It is analytically legitimate to apply such generalisations to a specific case *only on condition that* the analyst demonstrate that the case does indeed 'fit'. While apples and oranges can indeed be usefully analysed as both belonging to the category of fruit, this latter category tells us little about the specific nature, composition, taste and nutritional value of either apples or oranges. And if I too can be allowed a metaphor, anyone who tried to bake an apple pie using oranges would end up with a gooey mess and a smoky oven.

There are a number of instances in which the 'fit' of the model to South Africa is questionable. In their chapter on 'opening (and undermining) of authoritarian regimes', O'Donnell and Schmitter insist on the primacy of domestic factors – and particularly 'divisions within the authoritarian regime itself' – in the transition.[131] I hope that my own concrete analysis of the collapse of the old apartheid state has underlined the critical significance of the internal politics around such internal divisions. Nevertheless, I hope that I have also made it crystal clear that external factors – sanctions, the looming inability to finance South Africa's external debt, military reverse in Angola, the collapse of the Soviet empire, the end of the Cold War etc. – were all likewise vital to an evolving (and overdetermined) configuration of power which made it virtually impossible for the apartheid regime to maintain its existing practices by late 1989. Likewise, I would very strongly dispute any attempt to apply to South Africa O'Donnell and Schmitter's claim that 'the timing of an opening towards liberalization' could not be 'correlated predictably with the performance of authoritarian rulers in meeting socio-economic goals'.* In the chapters dealing with the new counter-revolutionary strategy after 1986, I hope I have shown exactly the opposite – that the economic, social and political failure of General Malan's strategy to 'buy' black support on the basis of 'Bothanomics' rendered the strategy untenable and virtually obliged the regime to 'open' once P W Botha had been removed from the scene.

A related problem lies in the central notions of elite 'pacts' and elite 'pacting'

---

* I would further question the applicability of their analysis of 'The Cycle of Mobilisation', 26-8, as well as an overly militarised notion of an authoritarian regime, see 39.

which are at the core of this comparative analysis. O'Donnell and Schmitter define such pacts as

> an explicit, but not always publicly explicated or justified, agreement among a select set of actors which seeks to define (or better, to redefine) rules governing the exercise of power on the basis of mutual guarantees for the 'vital interests' of those entering into it.[132]

Explicitly elitist (or 'oligarchical') in form and content, such pacts 'move the polity towards democracy by undemocratic means'. Concluded by a limited number of participants representing the key political actors and institutions, such 'negotiated compromise' tends

> to reduce competitiveness as well as conflict; they seek to limit accountability to wider publics; they attempt to control the agenda of policy concerns; and they deliberately distort the principle of citizen equality.[133]

Once again, at first sight this seems a highly apposite characterisation of the process which produced first the interim constitution, and then Nelson Mandela's Government of National Unity in South Africa. However, it seems to me that the implicit notion of the bargain or 'deal' involved in such a 'pact' is at one and the same time overly static and overly deterministic in terms of its effects. While the authors do acknowledge the 'unintended consequences' of the political processes unleashed by such pacts, their notion implies an unacceptable, and in the South African case, incorrect, level of unanimity of intention between the competing 'elites' which conclude such pacts. In effect, the definition they present is one which mirrors the hopes of the conservative faction, not necessarily the 'revolutionaries' or challengers. One cannot reduce either the process of 'pacting' or its eventual effects to the wish list of the *ancien régime*.

Clearly the jury is still out on the eventual outcome of the 'pact' in South Africa, particularly in terms of its effect on the ANC's ability to deliver significant new resources to, and retain the support of, key elements in its political constituency. Nevertheless, it seems to me absurd to argue that Mandela, Slovo, Ramaphosa *et al.* set out ('seek') to do the things listed in the definition above. This was De Klerk's agenda, not the ANC's. There clearly *was* an elaborate compromise between a relatively small group of players. Moreover, as the ongoing Winnie Mandela saga illustrates, this compromise and the hard-line policy of 'national reconciliation' it entails, continue to elicit outrage from some of the ANC's complex support base. Nevertheless, key forces and actors within both the government and the ANC 'seek' to use this compromise to force change upon South Africa. Thus, Minister Without Portfolio Jay Naidoo who presides over the Reconstruction and Development Programme will not meekly accept F W de Klerk's version of the 'pact'. Nor will other key players in ANC's leading ranks. What is missing here is exactly that which O'Donnell and Schmitter set out to provide – a sense of process, of politics, of struggle.

A further problem with the approach lies in the concepts it uses to analyse what the authors stress to be *the* vital factor leading to such an opening – divisions within the authoritarian regime itself. Again while I am in absolute agreement that such divisions are of vital importance, O'Donnell and Schmitter do not develop adequate concepts either to describe or to think such divisions. Their notions of 'hard-liners' versus 'soft-liners' is both ahistorical and too rigid. Was F W de Klerk a hard-liner or a soft-liner? At which moment? And P W Botha in 1978 compared with P W Botha in 1988? By the end of 1989, even such 'hard-liners' as Law and Order Minister Adriaan Vlok had come to insist on the need for a radically new approach. On the other hand, however, a 'soft-liner' like Chris Heunis had gone down in political flames because he could not think himself beyond his rigid 'consociational' mindset. Thus, far more subtle, nuanced and *fluid*, notions of the internal divisions within the regime are essential if we are to be able to grasp their real weight in the unfolding political process. I will take up this question below, but it seems to me that these categories need to locate specific institutional actors both within (evolving) institutional cultures as well as within an (equally fluid) notion of their particular power-base and interests in particular conjunctures.

My final objection lies in the epistemological assumptions underlying the task O'Donnell and Schmitter set themselves. They explicitly set out to fashion the 'conceptual tools' to deal with

> choices and processes where assumptions about the relative stability and predictability of social, economic, and institutional parameters – and therefore of their descriptive and analytical power – seem patently inadequate.[134]

These concepts are 'distinctly political' and 'strategic'. They do acknowledge that 'macrostructural factors are still "there"', and that 'at some stage' these 'broad structures' do 'filter down to affect the behaviour of groups and individuals'.[135] However, they do not *theorise* how such a trickling down of structural effects occurs, and are content to stress that 'political calculations' cannot be deduced from, nor imputed to, such structures. This brings us back to the overpoliticised world of Skocpol, Mann and Giddens. While the political calculations of key actors during 'opening' and 'transition' clearly can neither be reduced to nor imputed from what O'Donnell and Schmitter term 'structural parameters', nor, would I argue yet again, are they comprehensible if *sundered from* such elements. What this amounts to is an affirmation of the real autonomy of the political, in a context where the authors acknowledge potential residual structural determination (which 'filters down'). Yet, and now unlike the state-centric analysts who *do* confront this problem, this is stated in ways which completely sidestep the consequent inevitable *theoretical* problem of how we are to understand either condition – the autonomy of 'the political' or the conditions under which 'structure' filters down – and what impact, forms and effects does such residual determinacy produce?

This inability to theorise the political, and hence power, leads on the one hand to such static notions as 'hard-liners' and 'soft-liners', and on the other hand to an overemphasis on the elaboration of new and constraining 'rules of the game'. As I've argued above, this produces an equally static – and implicitly pro-establishment – sense of politics and the possible. What gets lost in the process is that which the state-centric approach insists upon, a notion of agency and even of evolving strategies. Being unable to analyse the power-bases of key actors, except in highly circular political terms, this approach seems to me unable to grasp the nub of the politics it seeks to explore.

Rather than being 'underdetermined', as O'Donnell and Schmitter insist,[136] the political is exactly *overdetermined*. What is needed is a theory capable of thinking the parameters of such overdetermination. In the context of my critique of these six paradigms of politics and change in South Africa, this glib last statement presumes of course that my own analysis is free of such errors.

Towards a non-deterministic, materialist theory of politics

Socio-economic analysis needs to take account both of the importance as well as the limits of its object. Such analysis involves the study of nothing more nor nothing less than the economic and social *conditions* of political action and the development of ideologies. Such conditioning does not operate only in one direction. Political outcomes and ideological consciousness, in their turn, affect the evolution of the infrastructure. But how? To what extent? In this dialectic between the political and the economic, which instance is dominant, decisive 'in the final analysis'? There is no definitive answer to this type of enquiry. *The general idea* of historical materialism holds that the organisation of the production of the material necessities of life lies at the heart of all societies. While this notion conveys a profound reality, it says very little about the multiple ways in which such organisation is constituted and evolves through time and space. The relative weight of infrastructure and superstructure varies from epoque to epoque and society to society. Hence the necessity to pose the problem historically.[137]

By now I hope that it is clear that I take state and politics seriously. As embodied by my analysis of the politics of the apartheid state, as well as in the preceding discussion of existing paradigms, my aim has been to develop an approach which accounts for the real materiality of politics. I would suggest that such an approach needs to be both materialist and non-determinist. I remain persuaded that the twin underlying premises of historical materialism remain far and away the most illuminating and useful starting point. The first holds that before human beings can discuss how many angels can dance on a pinhead, before they can try to impose their answer to this question on others, or engage in politics, wage war, produce art, ideology, discourse etc. they have to feed, clothe and house themselves. In other words, they have to ensure the production and reproduction of all those goods necessary to satisfy their material needs as defined at any given historical moment. Their ability to engage in all other activities depends on their success in satisfying these (historically defined) material needs. This seems to me to be self-evident, whether, as Marx put it, such needs originate in their heads or in their stomachs. From this flows the second and most essential premise of materialist analysis: that the various, changing and stratified ways in which human beings organise themselves to ensure the production and the reproduction of these (historically defined) necessary goods shapes the conditions under which they live their lives, develop ideologies and engage in politics.

Marx formulated this much more dogmatically in his celebrated aphorism: 'It is not the consciousness of men (sic) which determines their being, but, on the contrary, their social being which determines their consciousness.'[138] This postulate has given rise to vast controversies both within marxism and between marxists and non-marxists. At issue have been questions of economic 'base' determining various aspects of 'superstructure', of forces versus relations of production, of economic determinism and causation. I do not intend to rehash these issue here, but will simply make two points.

Firstly, it seems to me that in trying to comprehend any political situation, social scientists require a non-deterministic notion of residual causality. It is the absence of such a notion – and indeed the effective epistemological denial of the very possibility of causality – which leads post-structuralism and post-modernism to endless relativism. If this be seen as my clinging to notions of a 'grand narrative', so be it.* Secondly, and most crucially, however, I would insist on a non-deterministic form of materialism. As indicated in the above quotation from Hentsch *et al.,* broad statements of the essential premises of materialist analysis simply identify the overall organised sets of (always historical) conditions which make human life possible. Interpreted in non-deterministic fashion they say *nothing* about these varying forms that such organisation takes, nor about their specific impact on political life. Detailed, concrete analysis of the various (and changing) class, ethnic, racial, gender and cultural forms such organisation took is essential in order to understand how people in twentieth-century South Africa set about to ensure the production and reproduction of their (differing) historically necessary goods. Such analysis needs also investigate the impact of such forms of social organisation in setting the parameters, the issues and the outcomes of political life.

The specific answers to such questions are not theoretically given. They can be arrived at only through detailed empirical analysis. However, a materialist epistemology also insists that 'the facts' of such empirical analysis are not neutral, they do not speak for themselves. In this view, no facts exist outside of theory. Each theory produces its own facts. So while theory cannot in and of

---

* However the post-modernist critique of 'modernist' grand narratives (such as marxism) rests not only on the forms of causality operating in such narratives but also on the privileging of a specific historical subject ('the proletariat', 'the nation', etc.) as the bearer of the liberatory project. The theory of politics presented here privileges no such subject.

itself answer the question of the materiality of the political in any specific case, it does and must tell us where to look in order to try to arrive at the answers. Empirical analysis in and of itself is impossible without a theoretical road map.* I would suggest that a non-determinist, materialist conception of politics needs to include the elements discussed under the following four broad categories.

Historical specificity

The theoretical attitude underlying this book and my approach to the problem of the state rests on an insistence on the historical specificity of both 'the state' in general, and all historically existing states. A number of points flow from this assertion. The first is that, contrary to the assumptions of various state-centric analysts, the particular form of political organisation known as 'the state' is not a universal and necessary form of organised power and rule. Rather, the modern state evolved under specific historical, geopolitical and cultural conditions following the Treaty of Westphalia in 1648. As Marcel Merle has stressed, the state form of organised political power was very different from, and should never be confused with, those of the various pre-existing and parallel forms out of which the modern state evolved.[139]

It is essential to be able to situate this distinction both historically and theoretically. Doing so requires, secondly, specifying what was historically unique about this new *and evolving* form of organised power and rule. Such elements would include, *inter alia*: the new configurations of power, social forces and social alliances underlying the state; its new institutional forms; the key role and functioning of the market in affecting these new power relations; the principle of sovereignty; the separation of temporal from spiritual power; the new historical subjects the state was deemed to represent (variously, commonwealth, nation, people, class, citizen, etc.) through the founding myth of a social contract; the underlying concept of public and private spheres; the notion of a monopoly of legitimate violence in the hands of this new political form. None of the above were present in the various forms of organised power and rule which preceded the state.

On the other hand, however, this theoretical notion of the historically specific nature of the state requires, thirdly, a clear sense of the (again constantly evolving) dynamics of the *conditions of existence* peculiar to the processes underlying this new emerging and evolving form of organised power. This is to insist that 'the state' did not emerge nor evolve in isolation. The core of my theoretical position holds that, as an historically specific form of organised

---

* This is of course disputed by those empiricists, like the prominent South African historian who told me in the seminar at Yale University: 'I don't have any pre-conceived theories or ideas. I just try to be hellish receptive to the evidence.' Is it still really necessary to point out that *all* analytical decisions about which issues to look at, how to go about selecting data, which 'evidence' to use and which to discard, *all* involve choices which are theoretically and epistemologically rooted – whether or not the analyst is conscious of his/her own assumptions? 'The evidence' never speaks for itself, it simply resonates (or not) with the analyst's own mental maps.

power and rule, 'the state' developed as an integral and essential aspect of a still ongoing wider process of global transformation whose original epicentre was located in seventeenth century Europe. To analyse the state thus requires situating it in this wider totality at the given moment of its historical evolution.

To spell this out: the modern state evolved in tandem with, and itself as a determinate element of, at least five other uneven but crucial historical changes. Taken together, these changes transformed human social existence on four levels – the international, the regional, the local and the domestic. Apart from state formation, these five other elements included: (a) evolving processes of class formation and class struggle which transformed the class structure of a wide range of social formations. The dominant dynamic of these uneven and situationally variant processes was to fashion two historically new social classes – the bourgeoisie and the proletariat – and to undermine the position of existing classes; (b) emerging and evolving local, regional and global forms of capital and capital accumulation, which – again, over time and unevenly – first produced, and then continuously transformed, industrial production. This in turn led to (c) to an unfolding domestic, local, regional and global division of labour – established by both economic and extra-economic factors (eg, war) – in which different regions and localities were placed in more or less favourable economic positions relative to other regions and localities. This in turn fed into and was itself shaped by (d) a hierarchy of extra-territorial power relationships, defining the various levels, configurations and structures of a competitive international political system; and (e) rapidly evolving forms, practices, techniques and technologies of warfare. Taken together, these six aspects of ongoing transformation fashioned what may be called the prevailing *global order* at given conjuncture, and shaped the cultures, practices and belief systems appropriate to this order.

While the state-centric theorists are clearly correct to insist that the state cannot be *reduced* to any one of the above factors, I would insist that neither can the state be sundered from, and analysed in isolation from, these the *historical conditions of existence* of the modern state. I will return to this central point in a moment. Before I can do so, however, a fourth point concerning the historical specificity of the state needs to be made.

The argument thus far assumes a very general notion of 'the state'. In order to be able to go beyond such broad generalities and to analyse this or that state in a given world historical and regional conjuncture, it is further essential to specify the *origins* of the particular state in question.

This is necessary for four reasons. Firstly, each state's origins establish its place in the prevailing global order at the moment of its birth. This historically determined 'place' in the global order, and ongoing domestic efforts to defend or modify this place, usually continue to influence the form, the nature and the issues of this state's domestic politics. Secondly, the origins of this or that state usually bequeath an institutional legacy (parliament, congress, army, presidency, form of bureaucracy etc.) which provides the key terrains, routines and rituals of state politics. These then act to shape the form of politics within that state.

Thirdly, the circumstances and struggles which give rise to the state in question also act to fashion its dominant social and political forces, shape its founding myths and establish the political cultures and ongoing political issues which project themselves into state politics long beyond the founding moment. And finally, these origins imprint themselves on the modes through which the state in question continues to interact with the overall conditions of existence of 'the state' in general. Taken together, these elements fashion what can be called the *hegemonic order* within each particular state at any given conjuncture.

To cite a concrete example. The contemporary French state evolved out of the complex socio-economic and political processes associated with the break-up of first feudalism and absolutism in Europe. Nevertheless, the form of the French state – be it in 1793, in 1850, in 1872, in 1946 or in 1959 – remained profoundly shaped by the domestic and international circumstances which together produced each of the five republics. The evolution of, and politics within, the Fifth Republic is incomprehensible without an understanding of the phenomenon of Gaullism, which is itself rooted in the domestic and international circumstances of the collapse of the Third Republic, the birth of the Fourth, and the latter's trauma with its Empire. In many ways the fundamental fault lines of French politics have little changed in two hundred years.* States are not born innocently, they carry their birthmarks with them throughout the lives, as do the domestic political forces in each state. On states too, 'the traditions of all the dead generations weigh like a nightmare on the brain of the living'.[140]

The apartheid state was a product of colonialism. The form of state established in 1910 was directly *imposed* by an external power under the specific historical fallout and prevailing correlation of domestic social and political forces at the end of the Anglo-Boer War. Its particular colonial origins placed the new state within an evolving international order in such a way as to shape its domestic politics for almost fifty years. The domestic hegemonic order remains fundamentally fashioned by the colonial experience to this day – an experience which engendered the twin national questions which dominated South Africa's political agenda from the moment of its birth.

Two fundamental characteristics shaped the evolving South African hegemonic order from the end of the nineteenth century. The social, political and military conflicts attendant upon Dutch and British colonialisms eventually forged a particular form of the wage relation and overall conditions of accumulation of capital in all branches of the economy which, until at least the 1970s, were predicated on the national oppression of the majority of the population. Given the form of state imposed by the colonial power, race became

---

* A colleague of mine conducted interviews in France in 1994 on the attitudes of various social groups with respect to the European Union. He recounts the following response of a descendant of the pre-revolutionary French aristocracy to his opening question of how the respondent saw conditions in France: 'Everything has gone to hell since '89.' It took the political scientist a few minutes to realise that his respondent meant 1789!

elevated to the primary criterion of inclusion/exclusion in the South African 'nation'. This reflected and reinforced a wage relation based on limiting access of the black population to land and urban areas outside of demarcated 'Native Reserves', permitting tight controls over the allocation and use of largely migrant, cheap black labour.[141] This in turn involved the establishment of a particular form of gender relations which bound African women to the reserves and to forms of 'traditional' domestic and chiefly authority – as well as that of the state – in ways which differed significantly from the relations of authority affecting African men.

The second fundamental feature of the emerging capitalist state in South Africa was that this 'racial capitalism' was then also overladen with, and itself partially shaped by, the unresolved residues of conflict between competing English and Afrikaner colonialisms. Following the Anglo-Boer War of 1899–1902, British colonial hegemony fashioned economic, social and cultural relations in such a way as effectively to exclude Afrikaans-speaking whites from ownership of capital in all sectors bar agriculture, and to leave most white Afrikaans-speakers with a deep sense of economic deprivation and cultural oppression. Once again, this was a gendered process in that it defined 'producers' as men and reinforced the ideology of *Vrou en Moeder* (Wife and Mother) which bound Afrikaner women to a particular form of subservience within Afrikaner families.

The construction and exercise of power in the state reflected these twin characteristics. In a period when universal adult suffrage was not yet achieved in Britain itself, the creation of a central South African state in 1910 rested on a tenuous compromise between competing colonial elites rather than on a broad consensus of the overwhelmingly white, and still exclusively male, electorate. Between 1910 and 1922 this absence of a consensual order pushed various elements of the white population into two serious armed rebellions and a number of violently contested strikes, all of which were suppressed militarily. These parallel and sometimes overlapping conflicts turned around three intersecting issues. The first was the place of this new state in the British Empire and particularly its relationship to Britain's international engagements and wars. The second was the position of white (male) workers in the racially exclusive state dominated by the interests of British capital; while the third turned around the unequal economic and political power of the two colonial populations enfranchised in the whites-only state. The working out of these conflicts between 1910 and 1922 together fashioned a system of party political representation in the white state in which language became a central – though far from the sole – criterion.

Only after the election of the so-called 'Pact' government of the National and Labour Parties in 1924 was a fragile 'South Africanist' consensual order forged around the notion of an interventionist state securing institutionalised minimum privileges for all whites regardless of their class position.[142] This order was reinforced by the extension of the political rights of citizenship to white women – though under the Roman-Dutch legal system they were denied full legal *persona.* However, this fragile consensual order was again called into question during the 1930s and then effectively destroyed during World War II by a burgeoning Afrikaner nationalist movement, all elements of which finally came to support a counter-hegemonic project aiming at a radical reconstruction of the state – one key element of which aimed to redefine the place of the South African state in the global order. Significant sectors within Afrikaner nationalism supported a campaign of armed sabotage against the elected United Party government.

The new Afrikaner nationalist leadership of the 1940s regarded an Afrikaner ethnic monopoly of political power and intensified exploitation of the politically excluded black population as the central means by which to overcome both its own deep sense of cultural marginalisation as well as its relative exclusion from access to capital. Their political project was cast in terms of ending the relative deprivation of white Afrikaans-speakers from all classes, but in ways which preserved the dominant position of the petty bourgeois leadership. On the other hand, however, significant changes in the structure of accumulation during this period generated a counter project for a limited restructuring of conditions of accumulation – and possibly even the political system itself – to admit elements of the black majority into roles from which they had previously been excluded. This further undermined the fragile consensual order, and helped produce the very narrow electoral victory through which the National Party assumed power on its apartheid programme in 1948.

Intense political struggles around the consensual vacuum during this period ensured that party political representation was again organised primarily along linguistic lines. The preponderance of Afrikaans-speakers in the white population, and constitutionally entrenched over-representation of (the mainly Afrikaner) rural interests in parliament meant that the political party supported by South Africa's then predominantly anglophone urban capitalist class lost office in the May 1948 general election. Hereafter, the other existing forms of the organised political representation of capital – and particularly the sectoral employers' organisations such as the Chamber of Mines, the Chambers of Industry etc. – became the most important forum for the political expression of capitalist interests and securing its access to the institutions and councils of the state.

Taken together, these points suggest that the analysis of politics in the apartheid state cannot be derived from a general theory of 'the state'.[143] It is essential to specify which state is being discussed, and *at which historical conjuncture.* Moreover, each of the three levels in the state at that particular conjuncture need to be specified: underlying principles; conjunctural dynamic of the various conditions of existence; origins and evolution of the specific state in question.

Structure and state autonomy

Here it is necessary to spell out my understanding of the question of the 'autonomy' of the state, or, as it is framed in a different paradigm, the 'boundary problem' of where politics and the state leave off and something else – economy, civil society, etc. – begins. It seems to me that neither the notion of 'relative autonomy' nor that of 'potential autonomy' are helpful formulations. While they do identify a real theoretical and analytical problem – that of the pertinent (and non-structural) effects of politics – they do so in a manner which does not lead to any but solutions based on circular reasoning.*

A more useful question might be to ask what are the *limits* of state power? This question has to be answered theoretically and empirically. The theoretical answer can only specify an ensemble of conditions which, singly or together, can be said to limit the autonomous action of the state.

The perspicacious reader may already have divined my answer to this question. It stems from my critique of Skocpol's ahistorical notion of the relation between state and international system. If, as I argued above, 'the state' in general needs to be conceived as an historically specific form of organised power and rule, then the limits of this power are set by the combined but uneven effect of the *particular conjunctural pattern and dynamic* of each of the essential conditions of existence of 'the state' – of the overall historical context within which the state in question emerged, evolved and exists. It seems to me evident that just as we cannot have anything but the most general (and hence analytically imprecise) theory of 'the state', neither can we have a theory of the state which does not rest upon the conditions outside of the state itself, conditions in and through which the state emerged, evolved and continues to operate.

To restate this argument more concretely: Most analysts would agree that it is impossible to understand the historical emergence and evolution of capitalism independently from the emerging and evolving forms of class formation and class structure in Europe in the fifteenth to seventeenth centuries. These transforming class relations were in turn partially fashioned by, and themselves fed back to help shape, the emerging and evolving forms of political power and modes of rule. The historical evolution of such evolving forms of organised power and rule is likewise simply unintelligible without an understanding of the changing nature, prevailing issue-areas, power configurations and forms of politics within a constantly evolving competitive international system. The latter is itself incomprehensible without a grasp of the changing nature, practices, techniques and technology of warfare – which itself had an at times decisive impact on the emerging forms of state, on patterns of class formation, on international, regional and local conditions of capital accumulation as well as on the various levels of an evolving international division of labour.[144]

I insist, therefore, not just on the historical specificity of both 'the state' in general or this or that particular state, I also argue that the attempt to theorise either or both of these levels of the state needs to locate the state within a complex, evolving, interdependent and interdeterminate totality. The particular 'fit', place, dynamic and weight of all of the various elements of this totality will vary

---

* Either 'the economic' is determinant 'in the last instance', or the international competitive system of states and/or organisational imperatives explain when the 'potential' becomes truly autonomous – although both conditions *presume* that states are autonomous. And so we go round the mulberry bush.

according to the particular historical moment, or conjuncture, under considera-tion. This means, once again, that we cannot develop a useful general theory of the limits of the autonomy of state and politics, one applicable to all historical conjunctures since the state began to emerge in seventeenth-century Europe. At such a general, ahistorical level, the most one can say is that the state will be auto-nomous only to the extent that the exercise of its power and policies do not have serious negative effects for any or all of its own external conditions of existence.

These conditions constitute the *structural limits* of state power and autonomy. But these too are at a fairly useless level of generality. These structural limits are present only in specific cases – ie, they vary from state to state, from historical conjuncture to historical conjuncture. One cannot determine the limits and impact of these structural effects in general. To do so requires what a once-renowned political analyst once called the concrete analysis of concrete conditions.* Of course a particularly skilful state strategy, or an adept – or demagogic – political leader might be able to push the envelope of the possible for a while. But, since the state has no existence outside of the larger totality, the forms of interaction and interdetermination between the various components of this totality will eventually act to limit state autonomy.

To illustrate such abstract notions in terms of their effects on the real concrete South African state, the forty lost years of South African political history discussed in this book spanned two distinct conjunctures in the evolving global order: the multilateralist Keynesianism of 1945–1971; and accelerating globalisation of 1971–1989. The National Party came to power in 1948 at a particular juncture in world history, the circumstances of which – until the mid-1970s – gave greater powers and latitude to states worldwide than at any moment since the foundation stone of the modern state was laid at Westphalia in 1648. However, following the unilateral August 1971 abandonment by the United States of the fundamental principle of the post-war Bretton Woods system, a very different dynamic took hold of the international order. Over time, this changing configuration began to limit state autonomy (not just in South Africa) in ways which would have been inconceivable in the period 1945–1971. It is important to spell some of this out.†

Taken together, the elements of the global order established by the post-war settlement – and in particular the compromise of the Bretton Woods system, the emerging Cold War, the social pact underlying generalised Keynsianism, and the new institutionalised diplomacy through the United Nations system – all had

---

* For a concrete idea of what is meant by such structural limits, see the example of municipal policies discussed on p. 438 above.

† Although this is beyond the scope of this book, it should likewise by noted that the Mandela government came to power in still another world historical conjuncture which can be said to have begun in 1990. This is characterised by two aspects: the international uncertainly following the end of the Cold War, and the rapid extension of all aspects – trade, monetary, financial, investment, etc. – of galloping globalisation. These then act to limit state autonomy in ways different from the two conjuctures mentioned above.

contradictory effects for states. On the one hand, they reinforced state autonomy, both with respect to the range of economic policies, and in terms of domestic social and welfare arrangements. The form of international economic cooperation established under the Bretton Woods system explicitly set out to reinforce state economic sovereignty.[145] This principle was further consolidated with the adoption by the United Nations of the right to self-determination. Economic sovereignty was further entrenched in reality by the long cycle of sustained economic growth until the early 1970s.

One of the consequences of this sustained growth cycle was to reduce pressures on all states to accommodate economic policies, interests and social philosophies which ran counter to those of the government of the day. However, this was true *only so long as the growth cycle was maintained.* The conditions of capital accumulation fostered by racial Keynsianism in South Africa produced sufficiently rapid economic growth to appease those capitalist interests unhappy at the 'market restraints' embodied in apartheid. At the same time it allowed the NP government to sustain racially exclusive employment and social welfare policies so as to maintain the broad alliance of support which had brought it to power – despite both the uneven transformation of the social forces represented in this alliance and the unequal returns its various constituent forces drew from NP rule.

On the other hand, however, the post-war settlement promoted a gradual but inexorable liberalisation of world trade and globalisation of the world economy and extended increasingly complex forms of interdependence between states. The long-term effect of these interlinked process was to curtail the autonomy of the South African state (along with almost every other state). Gradual trade liberalisation and economic globalisation underlay the long growth cycle of capitalism from the end of WWII till the early 1970s. This phase of burgeoning economic interdependence helped foster growth in the South African economy – widening its export markets and range of trading partners under the GATT; facilitating accelerated foreign investment drawn from countries outside of the relatively narrow network of pre-WWII investors (Japan, Taiwan, Israel, Germany, the US etc.); extending the process of import substitution behind protective tariffs; and fostering the horizontal (and later) vertical integration of ownership (leading to the emergence of domestic conglomerates).

This too all served in the short term to reinforce the autonomy of the South Africa state. Yet in the medium to long term, these processes actually rendered South Africa more vulnerable to external pressure. The combination of import substitution behind protectionist trade barriers and the unusually high rates of return on capital invested in the apartheid cheap-labour economy during the 1960s freed South African capitalists from the necessity to remain competitive on international export markets. This would eventually have highly negative long-term consequences. Unlike a number of other newly industrialising countries, during the long cycle of domestic economic growth, 1945–1972, South African policy-makers made little effort to modify the pattern of external trade and the country's role in the world economy. South Africa remained essentially an exporter of minerals and agricultural products, and an importer of capital equipment, technology, oil products and arms.

By the early 1970s, the evolving economic interdependence was confining South Africa's essentially resource-based external trade to an ever less favourable place in an increasingly globalised international division of labour. South Africa could sustain this profile only while its export markets were not threatened *and* so long as its access to international financial markets remained unchallenged. Both came under attack from the mid-1970s onwards. The growing crisis of accumulation then fed back directly into the political demands of various social forces. On the one hand, capital became more strident, and more active, in its demands for change. This was compounded by the changing composition of the NP's original support base. By the mid-1970s a powerful group of Afrikaner capitalists had emerged, now demanding essentially the same reforms as their anglophone compatriots. Their changing interests and political relationships were a crucial factor propelling changes in certain basic apartheid policies. These policy shifts then likewise fed back into internal conflicts within the National Party, and led, in the 1980s, to a radical reordering of its support base.

These contradictory effects were evident too in the growing political interdependence within the international system, and particularly its earliest manifestation, the effects of the Cold War. South Africa occupied an important strategic position in bipolar geopolitics. It is situated at the intersection of important global trading routes and commands access to both the Atlantic and Indian oceans.* South Africa was the largest single producer, outside the Soviet bloc, of a range of strategic minerals essential to the military apparatus of Western powers. It was the only industrialised state in Africa, in a region perceived by the West to be of growing strategic interest to Moscow. From the point of view of the NP-ruled state, the Cold War was a Godsend, in two senses. Firstly, the victim mentality of Afrikaner nationalism required a demonised external enemy. By the 1950s, and particularly after South Africa became a republic in 1961, the old British threat had been flogged to death and few nationalists still found it credible. But a world communist conspiracy to hand over the Cape sea-route, South Africa's minerals and all of its whites to Moscow (and its, black, domestic 'surrogates') – this was something to get really het up about. Secondly, and even more fortuitously, South Africa's particular position within the bipolar international political system meant that *while the Cold War persisted*, and despite the international opprobrium heaped upon it, Pretoria could count on its key strategic interests being defended by the United States. It could likewise take for granted that the major Western powers would

---

* Even after the major Western powers had abandoned the Simonstown naval base by the mid-1970s, the South African Navy's Silvermine facility offered unequalled surveillance of both the South Atlantic and the Indian Ocean. The intelligence it gathered became an integral part of US intelligence resources.

individually and collectively block effective international action against it.

However, here too, the contradictory effects of this growing interdependence were also to run against the South African state in the long haul, and to limit some of its areas of action. The practice, rules and most importantly, the *terrain* of diplomacy have been radically transformed since World War II. The emergence of a range of transnational actors (from the IMF to the World Council of Churches and multinational companies) and highly complex trans-governmental forms of diplomacy and international politics, has obliged all states to develop strategies and forms of diplomacy far more sophisticated than those of the pre-war and immediate post-war period. Despite its evident failures to preserve world peace, the United Nations system has vastly reduced the importance of bilateral diplomacy. A new – and highly unfavourable to apartheid South Africa – set of transgovernmental terrains of diplomacy has emerged, one which significantly reshaped the issue-areas of world politics. These new terrains, forms and practices of international politics empower those who acquire the ability to mediate and manipulate the various elements of complex interdependence. With the apartheid state barricaded behind its 'walls of granite', and frozen out of international political forums by a hostile bloc of Third World states, its ability to defend its own interests was increasingly eroded in this new era of the politics of interdependence.

Even more significantly, the nature of *power* in world politics has been transformed since the end of World War II. The traditional military–economic forms of power based on coercion have increasingly been displaced by what Joseph Nye has termed 'soft, cooptive power' based on the ability to define the terms of the international agenda.[146] As Eschel Rhoodie indeed realised, the key power resources in this regard are cultural, and in particular, the control over the flows of information.* From 1960 onwards, in order to defend its vital interests, the South African state built up its 'hard, command power' capabilities. These were used with great brutality and some success both domestically and in the South African region from 1975 onwards. However, once again, partially isolated from the world and despite Rhoodie's grandiose schemes, the South African government was completely unable to 'market' apartheid internationally, nor in this electronic age, to staunch the flow of highly damaging information and images to the outside world. By 1990, it had not only lost the (hard, command power) battle for Cuito Cuanavale, but it was being overwhelmed by soft, cooptive power far more skilfully manipulated by its domestic enemies. 'Soft power' is, by its nature, private, outside of the hands of the state – eg, CNN is not an instrument of the US state, and many may argue is a far more effective means of spreading an American world view than is a state agency such as the CIA. By contrast, the soft-power resources in the hands of the

---

* In his own perverted fashion Albert Hertzog also seized this truth. Hence his obstinate refusal as Minister of Posts and Telegraphs (1958–68) to countenance removing the state ban on the powerful medium he referred to as 'the little bioscope', ie, television.

apartheid state were few and far between, and simply not understood by its strategists – despite their reading of General Beaufre.

Finally, the processes of class formation inside and outside of South Africa worked to limit the options of the state. Apartheid was above all else an attempt to suppress class formation among the black population and, more particularly, to hold back the tide of black urbanisation. But this collapsed under the combined weight of a number of factors related to class formation. The NP's very success in fashioning an Afrikaner bourgeoisie in the first twenty years of its rule undermined the coherence of the social alliance which had brought it to power. This new Afrikaner bourgeoisie slowly developed a radically different concept of race relations from that fostered by Dr Verwoerd. Over time, this fashioned something of a common interest among the major capitalist groups to dismantle the – by now no longer profitable – labour, urbanisation and other policies associated with urban apartheid. Likewise, the process of class formation transformed the social composition of the *volk*, reducing the relative weight, and hence political clout, of the two class forces whose turn to the NP in 1948 had brought the party to power – white labour and white agriculture. This transformation of the social composition of the Afrikaner population was perhaps *the* key element underlying internal conflicts in both the NP and the wider Afrikaner nationalist movement from at least 1960 onwards.

Even more significant, however, was the simple failure of the NP's policies of class suppression within the black population. Despite the vast array of controls, despite hundreds of thousands of pass law arrests each year, the numbers and stratification of the urban black population steadily increased. This likewise had a number of effects which severely limited the autonomy of the apartheid state. The very rapid growth of the numbers of urban black youth crystallised a movement which, during the Soweto rebellion, destroyed attempts to 'Afrikanerise' the black population. I have argued that this political action from within civil society and directed at the state had spillover effects in the economy, in South African's international relations, and in its strategic policies. The combined effect of all of this was not only to oblige the government to seek ways of reorganising the modes of rule, but also to launch a protracted war between state and black civil society. The central place of black labour in the economy and the growing need for more skilled labour simply accelerated this process. By the mid-1980s, organised black labour had replaced 'the youth' as the single most powerful, and most militant force, in the burgeoning resistance to the state. Neither massive repression nor piecemeal reform was able to destroy this opposition.

Thus together and singly, each of these changing structural conditions acted to limit the range of state power, its sustainable policies and forms of rules in specific conjunctures. However, neither individually, nor even in their combined effects are these structural limits to state autonomy adequate to explain state politics and policies. What is required here are concepts which enable the analyst to grapple with the internal workings of the state in this context of (constantly varying, constantly evolving) structural limitation.

Agency, power and representation

My view of the state and politics rests on the assumption that it is essential to qualify this concept of the structural limits of state power by stressing the centrality of the pertinent effects of politics, in such a way as to include a notion of *agency*. As I argued in the Introduction to this book, I conceive the mutual interaction of such structural factors as impinging on the state and politics in such a way as the delineate the (evolving and fluid) boundaries, dimensions and topography of the field of state power. These structural factors set out the underlying rules within which the separate but linked game of politics develops its own rules. They spell out what kinds of overarching forces are at work, define the range of underlying issues of the moment, fix the players in their likewise changing relationships and roles, define the limits of their respective capacities and establish the parameters of possible outcomes.

In these terms, these structural dimensions can be viewed as the conditions of existence shaping the realm of politics and limiting its possible outcomes. On their own however, they do not *cause*, and nor are they sufficient to explain, either these processes or their particular outcomes. Such structural conditions do not directly determine the trajectory of a particular social or political process. While they do establish the *limits of what is possible* in a given conjuncture, they do not in and of themselves directly account for the collective and individual choices of the actors involved.

Ultimately, all social change, all outcomes, are the result of the mutual effect of an array of human choices. In order to account for such choices it is essential to introduce an understanding of politics, of political process and of agency. As we move analytically from the most general theoretical statements to attempts to grasp the operation of this or that concrete state in a particular conjecture, we need not only to investigate the determinate and limiting effects of structure, but equally to examine politics inside the state. This latter task has to be carried out in ways which enable the analyst to account both for these limiting effects as well as for the real materiality of politics.

My approach here embodies two intersecting but distinct levels of politics – those within the state, and those between state and the various elements of civil society. That which separates these realms of politics from each other, are the different power resources on which they rely.* State power ultimately turns around (and has as its key issue of contested control) the ability to command the instruments of legitimate, institutionalised and overwhelming violence. A complex matrix of rules and institutions play varying roles in this process, but the resources from which state power ultimately flows are, as Weber recognised, those of legitimate violence. Power in the various organisations and levels of civil society on the other hand, rests on an array of resources far too

---

* For my definition of power, see p. 457 above.

wide to specify here.* Most of these power centres of civil society regularly
wield their power resources in an attempt to influence the direction of state
policy. Their ability to do so depends, firstly on the nature and weight of their
power resources relative to both the other groups in civil society and to those of
the state itself, and secondly on the *access* such power resources give them to the
various decision-making institutions of the state.

This latter point is crucial, particularly in the analysis of South African politics under apartheid. Much has been made of the fact, for example, that for nearly
thirty years the major economic power holders in South Africa were not
'represented' in the ruling National Party. The marxist analysis of the 1970s
tackled this problem either by arguing that the 'hegemonic' class was not
necessarily the governing class, or by trying to demonstrate that the state
remained a capitalist state regardless of the professed attitude and policies of its
ruling party. However this analysis remained trapped within an essentially liberal
and instrumentalist notion of political representation – that political parties
should somehow directly 'represent' the interests of this or that social force, and
that these social forces control the state when 'their' party forms the government
and wields state power in 'their' interests. In both cases the analytical dilemma
is the same: to ask whom does this or that party represent, and whose interests
does the ensemble of state policies serve?

These questions are not unimportant, but they do not facilitate anything other
than an instrumentalist notion of power. I would argue the need for a different
notion of the relationship between state and social/class forces, one not constrained by a narrow idea of party political representation and instrumentality.

Simply because various actors in civil society are not directly 'represented' in
the ruling political party does not render them either powerless, or unrepresented
in the state. Thus, throughout the apartheid period neither black trade unions nor
big business were directly represented in the National Party. However both used
their range of power resources in such a way as to attempt to shape the direction
of state policy – and with varying degrees of success. Nevertheless, each commanded very different kinds of power resources, and each enjoyed vastly differential access to state institutions. This obliged black trade unions to employ more
confrontational modes of power mobilisation than those employed by big business. The new avenues of access to state machinery opened to black trade unions
after their legalisation in the early 1980s enabled them both to widen their range
of power resources and partially modify their mode of dealing with the state.

Not till P W Botha was anglophone capital in any sense directly 'represented'
in the National Party. Nevertheless, after a relatively short-lived panic when the
NP came to power in 1948, business interests found myriad routes of access to
and influence over decision-makers at all levels of the state apparatus. While

---

* These range from the coercive (the ability of, say, the Mafia to extract real loyalty through fear
induced by the threat of violence) through the ability to manipulate information to define the moral
and other terms of life (media, entertainment, religious institutions) to the ability to control the
ways and terms in which labour-power is used (in different ways, by enterprises and trade unions).

they were unable to budge the government on the fundamentals of its racial policies, the major employers' organisations, corporations and indeed individual businessmen all rapidly developed a *modus vivendi* with the NP government, with the various government departments, with regional and local governments. The relationships so established enabled these groups to achieve some success in having policies modified or adopted to suit their interests. Business interests were able to do so, where black trade unions were not until the late 1970s, because the vast range of power resources at the collective command of the capitalist class gave them unique access to all levels of the state – whether directly represented or not.

Thus, an analysis of state and state power needs to situate internal state politics within the context of the broader power issues involved in the politics between state and civil society. On this point however, I agree fundamentally with the state-centric critics of the cruder forms of neo-marxism. It is completely illegitimate to reduce state power to that of the dominant groups (classes) in civil society. It is equally illegitimate to reduce or equate the interests of various institutional actors in the state to this or that social group or class.*

The theoretical challenge is to develop an understanding of state power and state politics which, on the one hand accounts for its own autonomous rules, routines, roles and processes, while *simultaneously* building in the notion of the structural limits of such autonomy. My own approach draws on the notion of bureaucratic politics developed by Graham Allison.[147] Sharply critical of the prevailing 'rational actor' mode of explanation (see p. 440 above) and likewise sceptical of the explanatory power of organisation theory, Allison's path-breaking work on decision-making during the 1962 Cuban missile crisis gives a central place to politics inside and between state apparatus:

> Men share power. Men differ concerning what must be done. The differences matter. This milieu necessitates that policy be resolved by politics. What the nation does [in foreign policy] is sometimes the result of the triumph of one group over others, More often, however, *different groups pulling in different directions yield a result distinct from what anyone intended.* What moves the chess pieces is not simply the reasons which support a course of action, nor the routines of organisations which enact an alternative, but the power and skill of proponents and opponents of the action in question.†

Two central notions are introduced here. The first is that of agency – the power and skill of proponents and opponents. Allison's analysis of the Cuban

---

* Hence, despite its brilliance, Marx's own most powerful analysis of a real political situation, that of the process leading up to Louis Napoleon's ovethrow of the second French Republic, rests on a reductionist concept of politics – *la Montagne* equals the petit bourgeoisie, while the Legitimist/Orleanist coalition 'represents' the big bourgeosie – 'The Eighteenth Brumaire'.

† 'Conceptual Models', 707, my emphasis. The apparent gender-bias in this quote reflects the reality of power during the Cuban crisis. Men rather than women created the crisis, took decisions concerning it and eventually found a way to exit their own morass without destroying the planet.

missile crisis assigns a crucial role to the jockeying for position between institutional interests represented in the 13-member ad hoc executive committee formed to advise the President on the appropriate response to the Soviet installation of ballistic missiles in Cuba. He argues that it was Attorney General Bobby Kennedy's refusal to countenance an air strike or invasion of Cuba – asserted against the virtual consensus between all other ExCo members except Defence Secretary McNamara – which provided the essential bureaucratic clout and space for the slow consolidation of sufficient support for the eventual compromise choice of a partial blockade.

There is no doubt that such agency is central to the workings of politics. In the analysis in this book I have paid some attention to the impact on both the direction of state policy and the working out of internal National Party politics of the very different operating styles and political personalities of the various *Hoofleiers*. On more than one occasion, these were decisive in setting the trajectory of future developments. Thus, for example, Hendrik Verwoerd's almost paranoid conviction that he alone was right was vital in holding the line for the NP in 1960, when other powerful nationalists seemed to waver. The balance of forces between state and civil society and within the state itself were such that a different, and less resolute leader (a Dönges or even a Ben Schoeman, for example), might well have thrown his weight behind Paul Sauer and produced a very different solution to the Verwoerdian walls of granite.

Nevertheless, there are real structural limits to the efficacy of agency. Verwoerd got away with it in 1960 because of the particular configurations of the African and the international conjunctures created the political space in which he could manoeuvre.* However an entire Cabinet filled with determined Verwoerds could not have saved political apartheid in 1990. The boundaries of the possible had shifted to such an extent that no mere walls of granite could have held back the tide. P W Botha had been driven to a stroke by his attempt to straddle the middle ground. Whomever would or could have succeeded Botha in 1989 would have had to confront the same stark choices imposed by the shifting structural conditions – release Mandela and legalise the ANC (though not necessarily the Communist Party) or face the real possibility of dragging the country and the NP into permanent chaos.

Of course collective political suicide in defence of an ideological dogma is always an option, but one surprisingly rarely chosen by real politicians. Once Botha was forced out of power, the particular personality and apparently more

---

* The chaos attendant on the independence of the Congo and the fiasco of the UN Peacekeeping mission worked to aggravate domestic white fears of what a concession to African nationalism would entail. The U-2 incident shortly after Sharpeville, the Berlin crisis and the growing Cold War tensions until the end of the Cuban missile crisis all generated international tolerance for a crackdown on 'communists' anywhere. The restoration of political stability and of rapid economic growth in 1961 – sustained throughout the remaining five years of Verwoerd's life – significantly eased the strident pressure for change which major business groups had evinced during the Sharpeville crisis.

open style of F W de Klerk likewise helped shape some of the power relations, gaining considerable breathing space for his party and government in the months and years following 2 February 1990. De Klerk's skilful manipulation of the media and his intricate political bobbing and weaving following Nelson Mandela's release certainly helped hold back the inevitable for a time, gaining for himself and his allies far more favourable terms of settlement than would have been possible in 1990. But all of De Klerk's considerable Machiavellian skill could only defer but not avoid what was inevitably the only way forward after 2 February 1990 – a one person one vote election won by the ANC. The only other alternative, as President de Klerk belatedly seemed to recognise in late 1992, was an endless spiral of violence and the very real risk of the NP not just losing power, but that white South Africans could lose all of their vast privileges. This alternative truly was too ghastly to contemplate, and the decision was taken to adapt NP policy accordingly.

Two conclusions flow from this. This first is the absolute necessity to explore all the dimension of agency and to recognise its real, at times decisive, effects. This involves concrete analysis of the *political styles, personalities, belief systems and interests* of the particular actors in question. However, the second is to acknowledge the *real limits* of agency. This requires the analyst to spell out the terms and the conditions and processes in and through which these limits impose themselves, to demonstrate how such limits shape new directions in the actions of the agents in question. Yet again, both of these levels of analysis can only be stated theoretically in the most bald (and therefore analytically imprecise) terms. Explanation involves empirical analysis – the investigation of the real actions of real living agents under concrete and changing circumstances. This kind of inquiry cannot limit itself to mere 'text'.

A further crucial notion underlying Allison's view of bureaucratic politics is that of bargaining between institutionally located actors, commanding specific power resources and operating in terms of institutionally driven interests, routines and operating procedures. Once again, a number of points flow from this. This mode of analysis begins with an explicit rejection of the state as a monolith, an instrument or a rational actor – one whose actions can be comprehended retroactively by postulating objectives or intentionality on the part of the individual supposedly personifying the state at this or that given moment. Gavin Kitching's reflections on the debate over the Kenyan state are equally applicable to its South African counterpart:

> 1) [T]he state is *not* an agency of any single force in Kenya (i.e. it is *not* the agent of multinational capital or of indigenous capital, or of any 'fraction' of either form of capital), it is rather *a continual site of struggle* among all these forces, a struggle whose outcome is not foreclosed, and which continually results in contradictory policy outcomes; and (2) the state is not an 'it' – that is, it is not a unity, for the struggle outlined above, has, as one of its effects, the fracturing of the state and indeed of particular state institutions, into contending forces which themselves enter into conjunctural alliances and oppositions.[148]

In these terms it is necessary to investigate through empirical analysis which are the (changing) forces continually involved in struggle inside the state; what are their (changing) interests and political *modus operandi*; which (always changing) range of issue-areas are at the source of ongoing political conflict; and what kind of (always evolving) alliances and opposition are established, and on whose terms, in this or that conjuncture. Allison's contribution to such an analysis is the notion of 'where you stand depends on where you sit', ie, the idea that the particular interests which political actors defend, promote, struggle for (or, in Allison's terms, bargain), rest ultimately on their ability to command a range of power resources, the most important of which are bureaucratic/institutional.[149]

This conception of bureaucratic power-base contains a number of implications. Firstly, that in most circumstances, actors within the state almost instinctively defend the institutional and bureaucratic interests and routines of their immediate power-base rather than those contained in the state as a whole. Or more concretely, the powerful tend to conflate the particular interests of their particular power-base with those of the state in general. Hans Strijdom's dogged promotion of the Transvaal NP, even to the point of trying to scupper D F Malan's electoral alliance with the Afrikaner Party, is a useful case in point. More mundanely, conventional political lore has it that changing a minister's portfolio often leads the individual to advocate policies opposed to the ones s/he defended in his/her previous post. As NP *Hoofleier* and State President, F W de Klerk came to defend and promote radically different policies and interests from those he so tenaciously fought for while mere Transvaal NP leader from 1982 to 1989.

Secondly, while, in exceptional circumstance, a political actor will defend individual power resources outside those of his/her bureaucratic base (usually ideological or economic), his/her ability to do so effectively depends on the bureaucratic resources at his (and in the NP government's case, never her) command. While still a mere senator, Hendrik Verwoerd was able to do little to advance the particular view of the world he so passionately believed in. When promoted to the Cabinet in 1950 he was stunned to be made Minister of Native Affairs – he had wanted some more directly 'economic' portfolio. However, as a skilled political operator he not only began to transform the policies and politics of his new bailiwick, he gradually used this bureaucratic base to turn his department into the 'super-ministry' of the NP government. He was thereby able to 'out-bargain' a series of Cabinet ministers ostensibly more powerful than himself. This not only gave Verwoerd inordinate influence in shaping the wider contours of policy, it also enabled him to lay eventually irresistible claim to the succession to the *Hoofleier*ship. John Vorster and P W Botha used their powerful bureaucratic bases to similar effect. Botha was ultimately able to oust an apparently more powerful claimant (Connie Mulder) only by systematically undermining firstly Mulder's own bureaucratic power-base (the Department of Information), then his allies (particularly General van den Bergh and BOSS) and finally Mulder's hitherto unchallenged place as the most powerful baron and Crown Prince of the NP.

To summarise then: An analysis of state politics requires a complex and necessarily fluid understanding of the competing power-bases within the state, the various (and competing) political and bureaucratic cultures through which actors understand their place in the broader scheme of things, the institutional routines of key power centres, the issue-areas at the heart of state politics and the personalities of the individual actors concerned. This analysis has simultaneously to grasp the interaction between two levels of politics (within the state, and between state and civil society) as well as the (constantly evolving) limiting effects of structure under different conjunctures.

This is not a particularly elegant formulation. It reflects the fact, however, that politics in the real world rarely operate with the precision of Occam's Razor. Parsimony and theoretical elegance make for easily operationable theories of politics and power.[150] Examples would be the realism favoured by Skocpol, which understands state behaviour in international politics as a function of the national interest defined in terms of power, or the 'power is knowledge/ knowledge is power' couplet of Foucault and his followers. However, as Allison (among others) has cogently argued, such parsimony invariably distorts more than it illuminates.[151] Moreover, when such ideal types are elevated to the status of explaining the world as (allegedly) 'is', we move from simple empiricist distortions to something more pernicious.[152]

My own approach is radically opposed to any notion of ideal types. But while I reject Weber's epistemology at this (and other) levels, I agree with him by analogy on another. Weber argued that the construction of class needed to be investigated empirically, and not simply proclaimed theoretically. Likewise I would argue that we cannot develop a very useful theory of the limits of the state and politics at anything but the most (analytically useless) general level. My 'totalising' notion of state autonomy rests on the assumption that the real task of analysis is concrete and conjunctural. Particular states will experience different limits to their autonomy in different conjunctures – depending firstly upon how this conjuncture impacts on each of the conditions of existence of the state, as identified above; secondly on their mutual interdeterminacy; and thirdly (and often crucially) dependent upon the particular institutional forms of state power and the skill and determination with which political leaders develop effective responses to the political challenges of interdependence

My insistence on the necessity of in-depth empirical analyses of complex political process confronts a real methodological problem. Kitching's description of this problem in the Kenyan context applies equally to South African politics:

> That 'knowledge is power' is not merely a cliché. It is a true and powerful insight, well appreciated by all parties in the battle for access to and use of state power in Kenya. On all sides, that is hidden which it is in one's interests to hide, *and* that is revealed which it is in one's interests to reveal, or whose revelation may

damage an adversary. In this situation, social scientists sit around like starving sparrows, picking up crumbs of information where they fall, sometimes at first hand, more usually at second or third hand (from newspapers and other media).[153]

While this does not obviate the need for detailed research beyond mere 'texts', it does point to the fact that analysis often rests on inadequate, or even misleading information. There is no way round this dilemma in many cases. While the archives remain closed, no social science researcher will be able to say for certain what, for example, was the level of involvement of P W Botha in planning the systematic violations of the Nkomati Accord, or of deciding on the scale of brutality to be used in the destabilisation of the Frontline states. Mr Botha is probably not going to confess, and the relevant papers are likely either shredded or sealed. Nevertheless the analyst is obliged to come to conclusions on the understanding that these conclusions: a) are *provisional and probably flawed* – ie, likely to change as more reliable information slowly becomes available, hence the utility of good, well-researched history; and b) that they rest on theoretically coherent analysis, one conscious both of its own epistemological assumptions and of its normative consequences.

Crisis and change

The final conceptual building block in my theory of state politics in apartheid South Africa is that of crisis. This widespread use of the notion of crisis as an explanatory device has been cogently criticised by Deborah Posel.[154] She argues that much of the South African literature on the state and politics uses the concept of crisis in an illegitimate fashion. Analysis points to the existence of 'the crisis' of the 1980s, and then uses the mere existence of crisis to explain policy changes. Q.E.D. Posel is correct to underline the faulty reasoning embodied in such an argument. The mere existence of one state of affairs (a 'crisis') is insufficient, in and of itself, to explain the existence of another, and different state of affairs (new policies). To do so contains both the deterministic premise that crisis automatically generates change, and the historicist and teleological premise that the nature, trajectory and scope of this change (or crisis resolution) is already contained in the crisis as it develops. Not only is this empirically incorrect – in the real world crises can and do persist for long periods without producing change – but it also fails to understand *how* crisis can generate change and *why* some crises do so while others do not.

Nevertheless the concept of crisis still seems to me to be a useful concept to understand certain processes of change. This requires that its meaning is clearly spelled out, and that theoretical tools are developed to avoid such circular reasoning.

In analyses which seek to grasp the economic, social and political dynamics of a particular society, the term 'the crisis' usually refers to the mutual and combined action of a series of contradictions, pressures, conflicts and struggles to disrupt or even threaten the stability and overall structure of the established social, political and economic order. As such, the term encapsulates a range of different historical, social, economic, political, ideological and cultural processes. The concept of 'crisis' operates to condense and to compress into an apparent single whole what are in fact simultaneous and separate, though interlinked and mutually reinforcing, disruptions or crises. While these separate crises only exist in interaction with each other, each has its own distinct historical roots, rhythm and internal dynamic. Yet the unfolding of each discreet 'crisis' is also shaped and determined by its articulation with all the others in specific ways which, taken together, fashion the overall ensemble known as 'the crisis'.

Analysing 'the crisis' thus requires a complex task of both separation and condensation. On the one hand, the specific nature and dynamics of each separate crisis must be grasped. On the other, it is simultaneously necessary to explore the complex interaction of these separate crises, to show both their impact on each other, and how these different levels, moments, and rhythms fit together – how they are condensed into, and interact to shape, or overdetermine, the resulting ensemble known as 'the crisis'.

However, even such a nuanced understanding of the separate but interlinked moments of crisis does not avoid the problem identified by Posel. What is further required is a conceptual apparatus which adequately conceives of the ways in which crisis does, or does not, lead to change. For me, this apparatus lies in Gramsci's distinction between the *organic* and the *conjunctural* aspects of crisis – one underlying an influential work by John Saul and Stephen Gelb.[155] In these terms, a crisis is 'organic' when it involves 'incurable structural contradictions' – when the prevailing structure and strategies of accumulation on the one hand and the broad social and political order on the other, cease to reinforce each other to produce stability and economic growth, but rather undermine each other so as to call into question the overall structure of society, the state and the economy.

Such an organic crisis does not necessarily lead either to rupture of the social fabric or to revolution, but may persist for decades. Its outcome depends precisely on the second essential element of crisis identified by Gramsci. Gramsci understood the 'conjunctural' aspect of the crisis to incorporate what he called 'incessant and persistent efforts' to overcome these structural contradictions, and to conserve or defend, yet also subtly modify, the existing order. As Stuart Hall points out, such incessant and persistent efforts must go beyond mere adaptive and defensive measures to *formative* restructuring:

'If the crisis is deep – 'organic' – these factors cannot be merely defensive. They will be *formative*: a new balance of forces, the emergence of new elements, the attempt to put together a new 'historical bloc', new political configurations and philosophies, a profound restructuring of the state and ideological discourse which construct the crisis and represent it as it is 'lived', as a new practical reality; new programmes and policies, pointing to a new result, a new sort of 'settlement' – 'within certain limits'. These do not 'emerge': they have to be constructed. Political and ideological work is required to disarticulate old formations and to rework their elements into new configurations.[156]

These 'incessant and persistent efforts' identified by Gramsci are the terrain of struggle both to 'reform' the existing order and to transform it. In particular, they pose the question of the state as the essential site and focus of such work of disarticulation and formative action. The central political issue which emerges, is that of the capacity of the dominant forces in the state to overcome the effects of such structural contradictions – to cobble together a new settlement based on a new 'hegemonic project' incorporating a reordered *projet de société* (social project) and accumulation strategies.* 'Hegemony' in this sense then refers to a form of social consensus which legitimises and authorises a particular structure of economic, political, cultural and ideological power, winning for itself the approbation of 'common sense', as the only reasonable way of seeing things.

If these political struggles to construct such a new 'hegemonic order' succeed, a crisis may mark a potential turning point in social development. However, as Hall notes, this is a *turning point within limits* – one which may refashion but not transcend, re-*form* but not rupture, the basic pattern of economic, social, political and ideological relations.

A number of points are crucial here. Firstly, these 'incessant and persistent' efforts to fashion such an hegemonic project always involve real political struggle within and between the various forces, interests and institutions which comprise the existing nation and state. The real terrain of reform (of the conjunctural aspect of crisis) is therefore that of politics. The elaboration, content and prospects of any new hegemonic project cannot therefore simply be read off from the existence of an economic and/or political crisis. Rather, *reform needs to be analysed by a detailed focus on the concrete and complex process of political struggle within the state.* Anything else results in mechanistic and deterministic functionalism.

Secondly, the question of whether or not a crisis leads to a rupture of the social

---

* M Morris, 'State, Capital and Growth', 35. However Morris explicitly separates the elaboration of new accumulation strategies ('redefinition of the basic aspect comprising the existing growth model or the positing of radical alternatives to this model') from the development of new hegemonic projects ('the construction and maintenance of the social base of support for a particular form of state ... integrally concerned with unifying the nation around broad issues concerned ... [and] ... with who constitutes the nation, and who, in practice or theory, is excluded from the composition of the "nation-people"'). His definition of hegemonic projects thus specifically excludes economic objectives. I would argue, however, that a 'project' which attempts to reconstruct a new 'hegemonic consensus' in any given society (eg, Thatcherism) necessarily and crucially *includes* an explicit view of how wealth is created, by whom and how it is to be distributed. Thus what Morris terms the 'growth model' in any formative reform strategy is, for me, an integral part of the overall 'hegemonic project'. I therefore prefer to indicate any vision of who constitutes, and/or is excluded from, the nation or people, as well as the socio-political programme this entails, by a favourite term of Quebec nationalism – that of a *projet de société* (literally, a 'project of a society', poorly rendered as 'social project'). My use of the concept 'hegemonic project' refers to those programmes which envisage the construction of a new *hegemonic order* incorporating both an accumulation strategy and a social project.

fabric also depends on the counter-efforts by and strategies of the opposition bloc to render state action ineffective, and to undermine the politico-military bloc grouped around the state. A comprehensive understanding of the crisis, and of the ways in which it may unravel must thus grapple not only with these 'incurable structural contradictions' but must also be based on a clear analysis of the political struggles around attempts by the state to resolve the crisis and thwart the counter-strategies of the opposition bloc. Moreover, any but the most mechanistic understanding of the struggle between the rulers and the ruled needs to be predicated on a clear grasp of how this primary struggle is itself shaped by real political processes, political cultures and political conflicts *within* each of the two primary blocs.

Although hinted at in the opening pages, such a broad conjunctural analysis is unfortunately beyond the scope of this book. Rather, I have chosen to grapple with what seems to me the least understood aspect of both the organic and conjunctural crises in South Africa, ie, how the internal politics of the South African state form an integral part of the structural crisis, and how, on the level of the conjunctural crisis, the politics of the apartheid state interacted with, responded to, and sometimes derailed efforts of the democratic bloc to construct the political alliance needed to implement an alternative hegemonic project. Underlying the detailed analysis of the book is my concern with the central *political* question of the capacity of the newly reconstituted South African state to construct a new hegemonic project given both the domestic balance of forces and the highly unfavourable emerging global order in which a democratic South Africa now finds itself.

APPENDIX II

The Twelve Point Plan[1]

The only alternative for South Africa is to develop and apply a total strategy which must be based on the following:

1. The recognition of the existence of a plurality of peoples and of minority groups in the Republic of South Africa. They cannot be wished away.

2. The acceptance of vertical differentiation, with the built-in principle of self-determination on as many levels as possible.

3. The creation of constitutional structures for the Black peoples to make possible the largest possible degree of self-government in states consolidated as far as practically possible. Part of the right to self-determination of these states is that they should be allowed to develop towards independence as they themselves see fit. They should be helped to build the best possible economic future in cooperation with us.

4. The division of power between White South Africa, the South African Coloureds and the South African Indians in a system of consultation and co-responsibility where common interests are concerned.

5. The acceptance of the principle of own schools and communities wherever possible as fundamental for happy social conditions. This is not discrimination; this is a recognition of each other's rights.

6. The willingness to confer as equals on matters of common interest, with a healthy balance between the rights of the individual and those of the community. I am for the removal of hurtful and unnecessary discriminatory measures, but I am not in favour of forced integration or infringement of my own people's right to self-determination.

7. The recognition of economic interdependence and the properly planned utilisation of manpower.

8. The pursuit of a peaceful constellation of Southern African states with mutual respect for one another's cultural goods, traditions and ideals. To speak of a federation or confederation at this stage, is putting the cart before the horse. A covenant between states can only be established once there is a

will to do so. One first has to see to it that all those states become equal through interdependence and then leave it to them to determine to what they want to belong.

9. South Africa's firm will to defend herself in every practical way against outside interference.

10. To pursue as far as possible a policy of neutrality in the conflict between the superpowers and giving priority to South African interests.

11. The maintenance of effective decision-making by the State, which is based on a strong Defence Force and Police Force to guarantee orderly government, as well as its clean administration. Clean administration is essential on all levels.

12. The maintenance of free enterprise as the basis of economic and financial policies. This also presupposes the effective training and utilisation of manpower.

NOTES

Notes to Introduction

1   'Negotiations: What Room for Compromise?', paper prepared for the SACP organ, *African Communist*, leaked to the press in advance. See *The Star*, 1 October 1992.

2   Karl Marx, 'The Eighteenth Brumaire of Louis Bonaparte', in *K Marx and F Engels: Selected Works* (Progress Publishers, Moscow, 1968), 96.

3   D O'Meara, *Volkskapitalisme: Class, Capital and Ideology in the Development of Afrikaner Nationalism, 1934-1948* (Cambridge University Press, Cambridge, 1983), 4-11.

4   H Kenney, *Power, Pride and Prejudice: The years of Afrikaner nationalist rule in South Africa* (Jonathan Ball, Johannesburg, 1991).

5   See, eg, *inter alia*, H Dickie-Clark, 'Ideology and Recent Writings on South Africa', *Journal of Asian and African Studies,* XVIII, 1-2, 1983; H Giliomee, 'Constructing Afrikaner Nationalism' in ibid, and D Posel, 'The Meaning of Apartheid before 1948: Conflicting interests and forces within the Afrikaner Nationalist alliance', *Journal of Southern African Studies*, 14, 1, October 1987.

6   C Geertz (ed.), *Old Societies and New States: The quest for modernity in Asia and Africa* (Free Press of Glencoe, New York, 1962), 105. My emphasis.

Notes to Chapter 1

1   On the sectoral contribution to national income and the growing capital-to-labour ratio, see *Union Statistics for 50 Years* (Government Printer, Pretoria, 1960), S-3 and G-8 respectively. On share prices, see T R H Davenport, *South Africa: A Modern History,* 3rd edn (University of Toronto Press, Toronto & Buffalo, 1989), table 2, 537.

2   *Union Statistics.* For a succinct analysis of the wartime growth of the economies of the major belligerents, see J Keegan, 'War Production', *The Second World War* (Hutchinson, London, 1989), 209-19.

3   *Natal Daily News*, 13 April 1948.

4   NP Labour Minister Ben Schoeman, quoted in *The Star*, 28 May 1948.

5   See, eg, *Third (Interim) Report of the Agricultural and Industrial Requirements Commission*, UG 40/1941 (Government Printer, Pretoria), paras 160-91, and *Board of Trade and Industries: Investigation into Manufacturing Industries in the Union of South Africa,* First Interim Report No 282 (Government Printer, Pretoria), 42-6.

6   *Report of the Native Laws Commission of Enquiry, 1946-8*, UG 28/1948 (Government Printer, Pretoria – hereafter, the Fagan Report), paras 18-28.

7   *Report of the Witwatersrand Mine Native Wages Commission*, UG 21/1944

(Government Printer, Pretoria – hereafter, the Lansdown Commission), paras 201-3.

8 Major Piet van der Byl, quoted in M Morris, 'Apartheid, Agriculture and the State', *SALDRU Working Paper No 8* (University of Cape Town, 1977).

9 See M Morris, 'The Development of Capitalism in South African Agriculture', *Economy & Society*, 5, 3, 1976. See also B Hirson, 'Rural Revolt in South Africa, 1937-1951', mimeo, Institute of Commonwealth Studies, University of London, 1976.

10 See D Posel, 'Sizing up the Population: Statistics, statecraft and social transformation in South Africa', Keynote address to the 23rd Annual Conference of the Canadian Association of African Studies, Trent University, Peterbrorough, Ontario, 13 May 1995. This and the preceding paragraph draw on ideas in this address.

11 D O'Meara, 'The 1946 African Mineworkers' Strike and the Political Economy of South Africa', *Journal of Commonwealth & Comparative Politics*, 13, 2, 1975, 153.

12 *Union Statistics*, G-18.

13 *Race Relations News*, January 1945.

14 *Report of the Department of Labour for the Year Ended 31st December 1945*, UG 9/1947 (Government Printer, Pretoria), 19.

15 *Report of the Department of Native Affairs for the Years 1945-7*, UG 14/1948 (Government Printer, Pretoria), 19.

16 O'Meara, 'The 1946 African Mineworkers' Strike'.

17 See A Stadler, 'Birds in the Cornfield: Squatter movements in Johannesburg', in B Bozzoli (ed.), *Labour, Township and Protest* (Ravan Press, Johannesburg, 1979).

18 See Theoretical Appendix.

19 See O'Meara, *Volkskapitalisme*, chaps 1-2.

20 Quoted in D Lewis, 'The South African State and African Trade Unions, 1947-1953', mimeo, 1976.

21 Lansdown Commission, para. 65.

22 *Tribal Natives and Trade Unionism: The policy of the Rand goldmining industry* (Johannesburg, 1946).

23 *House of Assembly Debates*, vol. 48, col. 3098.

24 All figures on African farm labour in this paragraph are drawn from *Handbook of Agricultural Statistics*, table 6, 11.

25 Morris, 'Apartheid, Agriculture and the State', 14.

26 Agricultural and Industrial Requirements Commission, paras 90-8.

27 Morris, 'Apartheid, Agriculture and the State', 12.

28 W Finlay, 'South Africa: Capitalist agriculture and the state', B SocSci dissertation, University of Cape Town, 1976, 58.

29 Johannesburg Chamber of Commerce, *The Present Economic Position of the Union: A diagnosis, some comments and suggestions* (Johannesburg, 1949).

30   Finlay, 'South Africa', 75-6.
31   O'Meara, *Volkskapitalisme*, 190.
32   For a detailed analysis, see R H Davies, *Capital, State and White Labour in South Africa, 1900-1960* (Harvester Press, Brighton, 1979), esp. chap. 7. See also O'Meara, *Volkskapitalisme*, 238-42.
33   Quoted Davenport, *South Africa*, 343.
34   Heard, *General Elections in South Africa,* 31.
35   Fagan Report, paras 17-18.
36   Ibid.
37   Ibid, p. 33.
38   NP election manifesto, *Die Transvaler,* 21 April 1948.
39   NP economic programme, *Die Kruithoring,* 1 March 1944. These promises were repeated in the NP election manifesto.
40   Heard, *General Elections in South Africa,* 34.
41   *Verslag van die Kleurvraagstug-Kommissie van die Herenigde Nasionale Party.* An abbreviated version was published in *Die Burger* on 29 and 30 March 1948. A poor and often misleading translation is to be found in D W Kruger (ed.), *South African Parties and Parties and Policies, 1910-1960* (Human en Rousseau, Cape Town, 1960).
42   Sauer Report, reproduced in *Die Burger*, 29 March 1948. My italics.
43   *Natal Daily News,* 18 May 1948.
44   See D O'Meara, 'Analysing Afrikaner Nationalism: The "Christian-National" assault on white trade unionism in South Africa, 1934-1948', *African Affairs,* 77, 1978, 306.
45   Heard, *General Elections in South Africa*, 25.
46   Ibid, 45-6, and table 21, 45.
47   Ibid, table 17, 40, and table 20, 44.
48   Ibid, 38.

Notes to Chapter 2

1   For a magisterial account of these events, see M Roberts and A Trollip, *The South African Opposition 1939-1945* (Longmans, Cape Town, 1947).
2   D & J de Villiers, *P W* (Tafelberg, Cape Town, 1984), 23.
3   Cited O'Meara, *Volkskapitalisme*, 85.
4   On its efforts to keep these political tensions outside its own ranks and activities, see the official Broederbond history, A N Pelzer, *Die Afrikaner Broderbond: Eerste 50 jaar* (Tafelberg, Cape Town, 1979), 176-80. For a sharply differing viewpoint, see the opinions of the wartime AB Executive Committee member Albert Hertzog in B M Schoeman, *Die Broederbond in die Afrikaner-politiek* (Aktuele Publikasies, Pretoria, 1982), 17-54.
5   J D Shingler, 'Education and Political Order in South Africa, 1902-1960' (unpublished PhD dissertation, Yale University, 1973), chaps 9-11.
6   *Volkskapitalisme*, chaps. 4-15.
7   See the book by the one-time editor of the *Natal Witness,* G H Calpin, *At*

Last We Have Got Our Country Back (Buren Publishers, Cape Town, n.d.), 16.

8 See *Volkskapitalisme*, chap. 4.
9 Pelzer, *Die Afrikaner Broederbond*, 95-6.
10 'The Afrikaner Broederbond', Report by Military Intelligence, 23 March 1944, Hofmeyer Papers, file Ce, Archives of the University of the Witwatersrand.
11 Pelzer, *Die Afrikaner Broederbond*, 119-20.
12 Quoted in Military Intelligence Report.
13 Membership figures for 1925, 1933, 1952 and 1968, Pelzer, *Die Afrikaner Broederbond*, 32. Figure for 1977 from J P H Serfontein, *Brotherhood of Power* (Rex Collings, London, 1979), 136.
14 Schoeman, *Van Malan tot Verwoerd*, 120-1.
15 Pelzer, *Die Afrikaner Broederbond*, 177.
16 See Albert Hertzog's diary, cited in Schoeman, *Die Broederbond*, 17-54.
17 H Giliomee, 'The Leader and the Citizenry', in R Schrire (ed.), *Leadership and the Apartheid State: From Malan to De Klerk* (Oxford University Press, Cape Town, 1994), 106.
18 Serfontein, *Brotherhood of Power*, 84-8.
19 H Adam & H Giliomee, *Ethnic Power Mobilized* (Yale University Press, New Haven, 1979), chap. 8.
20 Quoted in H Giliomee, 'The National Party and the Afrikaner Broederbond', in R M Price & C G Rotberg (eds), *The Apartheid Regime: Political power and racial domination* (Insitute of International Studies, Research Series no 43, University of California, Berkeley, 1980), 21.
21 D F Malan, quoted in Schoeman, *Van Malan tot Verwoerd*, 30.
22 Quoted in Schoeman, *Die Broederbond*, 23-4.
23 P Meiring, *Tien Politieke Leiers* (Tafelberg, Cape Town, 1973), 136.
24 'The Head of Government and the Executive', in Schrire (ed.), *Leadership and the Apartheid State*, 70. All quotations in this and the next paragraph come from this source. See also A Seegers, 'Institutionalising a Cultural Style of Management? Afrikaners, the National Security Management System and state power', paper to the Conference of the Association of Sociologists of South Africa, University of the Witwatersrand, 2-5 July 1989.
25 T D Moodie, *The Rise of Afrikanerdom: Power, apartheid and the Afrikaner civil religion* (University of California Press, Berkeley, 1975).
26 K van Loggerenberg, 'Strukture van Oorlewing veg lustig voort', *Democracy in Action*, 6, 2, 30 April 1992, 17.
27 For a more detailed analysis of the points in this section, see O'Meara *Volkskapitalisme, passim*.
28 See Malan's autobiography, *Afrikaner-volkseenheid en my ervarings op die pad daarheen* (Nasionale Boekhandel, Cape Town, 1959), 233-4.

Notes to Chapter 3

1 On the AB's controversial Draft Republican consitution, see O'Meara, *Volkskapitalisme*, 129-30. Malan's NP was known as the *Malanzis* in Communist Party and trade union circles. One prominent CP author developed an elaborate (and false) conspiracy theory of the Nazi manipulation of this 'fascist' party via German agents in the Broederbond – B Bunting, *The Rise of the South African Reich* (Penguin, Harmondsworth, 1969). The most sophisticated attempt to theorise NP 'fascism' is Howard Simpson's *The Social Origins of Afrikaner Facism and its Apartheid Policy* (Almqvist & Wikselt International, Stockholm, 1980). See also P J Furlong, *Between Crown and Swastika: The impact of the radical right on the Afrikaner nationalist movement in the Fascist era* (University of the Witwatersrand Press, 1991). For a critique of the analyses of the NP as fascist, see O'Meara, *Volkskapitalisme*, 9-11.

2 See, eg, the report by the Head of Military Intelligence, 'The Afrikaner Broederbond' (n.d. – but from internal evidence, August 1944) in the Hofmeyr Papers, University of the Witwatersrand.

3 S Pauw, *Die Beroepsarbeid van die Afrikaner in die Stad* (Stellenbosch, Pro-Ecclesia, 1946).

4 S van Wyk, *Die Afrikaner in die Beroepslewe van die Stad* (Academica, Pretoria, 1968), table 8.2, 201-2.

5 Seegers, 'The Head of Government and the Executive', 54.

6 S van Wyk, *Die Afrikaner*, table 8.2, 201-2.

7 *Report of the Industrial Legislation Commission of Enquiry,* UG 62/1951 (Government Printer, Pretoria).

8 E Tyriakian, 'Apartheid and Politics in South Africa', *Journal of Politics,* 22, 4, 1960, 691.

9 See F A Van Jaarsveld, *Wie en wat is die Afrikaner?* (Tafelberg, Cape Town, 1981), 21-3. For varying interpretations of the history of the apartheid idea, see, *inter alia:* S Dubow, 'Afrikaner Nationalism, Apartheid and the Conceptualisation of "Race"', mimeo, 1990; H Giliomee, 'The Ideology of Apartheid', in Pierre Hugo (ed.), *South African Persectives: Essays in honour of Nic Olivier* (Die Suid-Afrikaan, Cape Town, 1989); D Posel, *The Making of Apartheid: Conflict and compromise* (Clarendon Press, Oxford, 1991); and N J Rhoodie & H J Venter, *A Socio-Historical Exposition of the Apartheid Idea* (Human & Rousseau, Cape Town, 1960).

10 See n. 41, chap. 1.

11 NP manifesto, reproduced in *Die Transvaler,* 21 April 1948. For the pseudo-academic reasoning behind the rejection of the Fagan Commission, and an overall flavour of the thinking behind apartheid, see the series of articles by Olivier and Van Eeden in *Inspan,* April to May 1947 and October 1948 to January 1949. These articles received the explicit editorial approval of this, the official FAK (ie, Broederbond) organ.

12 Abbreviated version of Sauer Report, *Die Burger,* 29 March 1948.

13 *Volkshandel,* June 1948.
14 *Inspan,* September 1948.
15 G Schüller, 'Stellenbosch en Sabra Jare', in Hugo (ed.), *South African Perspectives,* 7.
16 On the role of SABRA, see Lazar, *Conformity and Conflict,* 164-216.
17 H B Thom, *D F Malan* (Tafelberg, Cape Town, 1980), 279.
18 Schoeman, *Van Malan tot Verwoerd,* 40-8.
19 See (Ben) Schoeman, *My Lewe in die Politiek* (Perskor, Johannesburg, 1978), 224, 228 and 237.
20 See, eg, the extraordinary map of forced removals 1948-77 produced by the Black Sash – B Waite, *A Land Divided Against Itself: A map of South Africa showing the African Homelands and some of the mass removals of people which have taken place, also conditions in some of the resettlement areas* (Black Sash, Johannesburg, 1977). A detailed analysis of these removals is to be found in *Forced Removals in South Africa,* vols 1-5 (Surplus People Project, Cape Town, 1983).
21 See the annual *Race Relations Survey* published by the South African Institute of Race Relations. By far the best study of the pass system is D Hindson, *Pass Controls and the Urban African Proletariat* (Ravan Press, Johannesburg, 1987).
22 See D Posel, 'State, Power and Gender: Conflict over the registration of African customary marriage in South Africa c. 1910-1970', *Journal of Historical Sociology* (forthcoming).
23 Cited Davies *et al., The Struggle for South Africa,* vol. 1, p. 203. For a very different discussion of the Tomlinson Report and Verwoerd's reaction to it, see A Ashforth, *The Politics of Official Discourse in Twentieth Century South Africa* (Clarendon Press, Oxford, 1990), chap 5. This analysis is discussed in the Theoretical Appendix, p. 443 below.
24 The quotations in this paragraph are drawn from Schüler, 'Stellenbosch en Sabra Jare', 9-10.
25 On this incident see also: Hugo, *South African Perspectives,* 14-33, and Hollerman, 'The Great Purge', in ibid.
26 Quoted in F Troup, *Forbidden Pastures: Education under apartheid* (IDAF, London, 1976), 20.
27 W M Eiselen, 'Harmonious Multi-Community Development', *Optima,* 9, 1, 1959.
28 Cited Davies *et al., The Struggle for South Africa,* vol. 1, pp. 204-5. My emphasis.
29 Quoted Welsh, 'The Executive and the African Population', 157-8.
30 J Sadie, 'Die Ekonomies Faktor in die Afrikaner-gemeenskap', in H van der Merwe (ed.), *Identiteite en Verandering* (Tafelberg, Cape Town, 1975), 88.
31 Pauw, *Die Beroepsarbeid,* 243. For a detailed analysis, see O'Meara, *Volkskapitalisme,* 52-6, 81-3, 181-221.
32 J H Coetzee, *Verarming en Oorheesing* (Nasionale Pers, Bloemfontein, 1942).

33 Professor L J du Plessis, cited in E P du Plessis, *'n Volk Staan Op*, 104.

34 His address to the Congress entitled 'Consumer Associations', quoted ibid, 121.

35 NP economic programme in *Die Kruithoring*, 1 March 1944. These demands were repeated in the 1948 NP election manifesto, *Die Transvaler*, 21 April 1948.

36 The data in this paragraph are drawn from Seegers, 'The Head of Government and the Executive', tables 2.1 & 2.2, 40-1.

37 See ibid where Seegers discusses the six forms of fragmention of the state apparatus under NP rule.

38 K Pottinger, *The Imperial Presidency: PW Botha – the first 10 years* (Southern Books, Johannesburg, 1988), 36.

39 *Union Statistics for 50 years* (Bureau of Census and Statistics, Pretoria, 1960), H-29.

40 S S Brand & F R Tomlinson, 'Die Plek van Landbou in die Suid-Afrikaanse Volkshuishouding', *South African Journal of Economics*, 34, 1, 1966, 46.

41 C van der Merwe, 'Die Landbou Politiek', in J A Lombard, *Die Ekonomiese Politiek van Suid Afrika* (HAUM, Pretoria, 1967), 13-18.

42 *Reddingsdaadbond* chairman, cited in *Die Transvaler*, 3 October 1952. See O'Meara, *Volkskapitalisme*, 78-95.

43 Calculated from Steenkamp, 'Bantu Wages', 96.

44 O'Meara, *Volkskapitalisme*, 52-6.

45 A Stadler, 'The Party System in South Africa, 1910-1948' (unpublished DPhil dissertation, University of the Witwatersrand, 1970), 232-58.

46 S J Terreblanche, 'Corruption and the National Party', IDASA lecture at the University of Cape Town, 12 April 1989.

47 Seegers, 'The Head of Government and the Executive', 52.

48 South African Reserve Bank, *Quarterly Bulletin*, December 1974.

49 A D Wassenaar, *Assault on Private Enterprise: The freeway to Communisim* (Tafelberg, Cape Town, 1977), 123.

50 L Pretorius, 'The Head of Government and Organised Business', in Schrire (ed.), *Leadership and the Apartheid State*, 213.

51 J Sadie, 'The Afrikaner in the South African Economy', mimeo, n.d., 42.

52 O'Meara, *Volkskapitalisme*, chaps 13 and 14.

53 Johannesburg Chamber of Commerce, *The South African Economy and Future Policy* (1949) and *The Present Economic Position of the Union* (1949).

54 See Lazar, *Conformity and Conflict*.

55 See the interesting analysis of industrial policy by the then chairman of the Board of Trade and Industry, J J Kitshoff, 'Die Nywerheidspolitiek', in J A Lombard (ed.), *Die Ekonomiese Politiek van Suid Afrika* (HAUM, Pretoria, 1967), esp. 32-4.

56 G Rissik, 'Die Monetére Politiek', ibid, 89.

57 On African industrial wages, see Steenkamp, *Bantu Wages*, 96; for mining,

see Francis Wilson, *Labour in the South African Gold Mines* (Cambridge University Press, Cambridge, 1972), 45 and table 5, 46.

58　A Dickman, 'Investment – the implication for economic growth and living standards', *Optima*, 27, 1, 1977.

Notes on Chapter 4

1　Quoted in H Giliomee, 'The Leader and the Citizenry' in Schrire (ed.), *Leadership and the Apartheid State*, 104.

2　See, eg, the very sharp critique of the party on this issue by Broederbond Executive Committee member Albert Hertzog, cited at length in Schoeman, *Die Broederbond*, 17-34.

3　See Lazar, *Conformity and Conflict*.

4　Cited in Meiring, *Ons Eerste Ses Premiers*, 84, 107.

5　D and J de Villiers, *P W*, 37.

6　Ibid.

7　Meiring, *Ons Eerste Ses Premiers*, 107. On Malan's spelling of Strydom's name, see his autobiography, *Afrikaner-volkseenheid, passim.*

8　Meiring, *Ons Eerste Ses Premiers*, 101-2.

9　Ibid, 81.

10　Ibid, 85.

11　Schoeman, *Die Broederbond*, 34.

12　See J P Brits, 'Havenga, Nicolaas, Christiaan', in C J Beyers (ed.) *Dictionary of South African Biography* (DSAB), vol. 4 (Butterworth, Durban, 1981), 215-22. Quote from 219.

13　Meiring, *Ons Eerste Ses Premiers*, 82.

14　Ibid, 96.

15　See Schoeman, *Van Malan tot Verwoerd*, 113-14.

16　Diederichs is quoted, ibid, 151. See also Schoeman, *Die Broederbond*, chap. 1. On the central role of both Diederichs and Albert Hertzog in the evolution of organised Afrikaner nationalism in the 1930s and 1940s, see O'Meara, *Volkskapitalisme, passim.*

17　Meiring, *Ons Eerste Ses Premiers,* 125.

18　Ibid. Meiring's father was the chairman of the Admissions Committee who asked Verwoerd this question. On Verwoerd's early announcement of his intention to become Prime Minister, see ibid, and Kenney, *Architect of Apartheid*, 143.

19　E Theron, *HF Verwoerd as Welsynbeplanner* (Stellenbosch, Pro-Ecclesia, 1970), 83-5. For an interesting, if debatable, interpretation of Verwoerd's early career, including his role in the conference and its aftermath, see R B Miller, 'Science and Society in the Early Career of H F Verwoerd', *Journal of Southern African Studies*, 19, 4, December 1993.

20　Du Spies *et al., Dictionary of South African Biography*, vol. 4, p. 732.

21　Barnard, *13 Jaar in die Skadu van Dr H F Verwoerd*, 9.

22　Meiring, *Ons Eerste Ses Premiers*, 123, 125.

23 Schoeman, *Van Malan tot Verwoerd*, 136.
24 See Ben Schoeman, *My Lewe in die Politiek*, 224, 228, 237 *et passim*.
25 *Die Transvaler,* 24 March 1958, and Hertzog, quoted in Botha, *Die Parlementêre Verkiesing van 1948,* 28.
26 Schoeman, *Van Malan tot Verwoerd*, 149-51.
27 Verwoerd, quoted in *A Survey of Race Relations in South Africa, 1957-1958* (South African Institute of Race Relations, Johannesburg, n.d. [1958]), 17.
28 Personal communication from a former AB official.
29 Potgieter, 'Op die Voorpunt van die Tye: Hooftrekke van die Staatkundige Denke van L J du Plessis' (unpublished MA thesis, Potchefstoom University, 1972), 15-18.

Notes to Chapter 5

1 For a useful and fairly complete survey of these events, see *A Survey of Race Relations in South Africa, 1959-1960* (South African Institute of Race Relations, Johannesburg, 1961), 39-68. Hereafter, the various annual editions of this incomparable source will be cited as in the following example for 1965: SAIRR, *A Survey ... 1965.* The date of publication is usually the year after the one reviewed. See Bibliography.
2 Reserve Bank Governor, *Rand Daily Mail,* 11 August 1960; JSE President, *The Star,* 14 May 1960; Wool Board Chairman, SAIRR, *A Survey ... 1959-1960,* 90. 'Political pressure' forced Dr Moolman from this post in October.
3 See Rupert reminiscence in an interview, *Leadership South Africa,* 5, 4, 1986. For his public statement at the time, see *The Star,* 4 April 1960.
4 *Commercial Opinion,* June 1960.
5 Verwoerd attack on Assocom quoted in *Business Day,* 21 October 1986, and his musings on business and the anti-Republic campaign, *Die Burger,* 4 July 1960. Vorster to the AHI, *Die Burger,* 18 June 1960.
6 *Sunday Times,* 27 March 1960.
7 SAIRR, *A Survey ... 1961,* 64-8.
8 Quoted in (Ben) Schoeman, *My Lewe in die Politiek,* 260.
9 Personal communication from the son of the man to whom Jan Steytler recounted this incident.
10 Sir D V Graaff, *Div Looks Back: The memoirs of Sir De Villiers Graaff* (Human & Rousseau, Cape Town, 1993), 166-7.
11 H Suzman, *In No Uncertain Terms: A South African memoir* (Alfred A Knopf, New York, 1993), 52.
12 Piet Cillié, *Die Burger,* 26 March 1960.
13 Schoeman, *Van Malan tot Verwoerd,* 199-201.
14 See D and J de Villiers, *Paul Sauer,* 136-9.
15 Schoeman, *Van Malan tot Verwoerd,* 194-5.
16 See the summary in SAIRR, *A Survey ... 1959-1960,* 103-6.
17 Schoeman, *Van Malan tot Verwoerd,* chap. 11.
18 E Kahn, *The New Constitution* (Stevens & Sons, London, 1962), 3.

19   Quoted in A N Pelzer, *Verwoerd Speaks: Speeches 1948-1966* (Afrikaanse Persboekhandel, Johannesburg, 1966), 516.
20   *Die Burger,* 23 July 1960.
21   See his 'Dawie' column of 17 December 1960, as well as columns on 26 November, 3 December, 10 December, 31 December.
22   Schoeman, *Van Malan tot Verwoerd,* 194.
23   Scholtz, *Dr Hendrik Frensch Verwoerd,* II, 171, 162; SAIRR, *A Survey ... 1959-1960,* 133.
24   Theron, *H F Verwoerd,* 13, 14.
25   SAIRR, *A Survey ... 1961,* 3 September 1961.
26   *Sunday Times,* 3 September 1961. For NP reaction see *Die Vaderland,* 8 September 1961, and *Die Transvaler,* 9 September 1961.
27   See Frankel, *Pretoria's Praetorians,* table 2, 72. See also K Grundy, *The Militarisation of South African Politics* (Indiana University Press, Bloomington, 1986), 18; and G Cawthra, *Brutal Force: The apartheid war machine* (IDAF, London, 1986), table IV, 259.
28   The story of a defector from the key state intelligence service gives a very strong sense of the paranoid pettiness of the regime. G Winter, *Inside BOSS* (Penguin, Harmondsworth, 1981).
29   E Munger, *Afrikaner and African Nationalism* (Oxford University Press, Oxford, 1967), 59.
30   Cited by the De Villiers, *Paul Sauer,* 124.
31   B Schoeman, *Vorster se 1000 Dae,* 14.

Notes to Chapter 6

1   Pelzer, *Verwoerd Speaks,* 516.
2   Schalk Pienaar, quoted in *Rapport,* 12 January 1975.
3   Quoted in Pelzer, *Verwoerd Speaks,* 404.
4   Ibid, 162, my emphasis. See also Schoeman, *Van Malan tot Verwoerd,* 192.
5   *Rand Daily Mail,* 17 August 1961.
6   Serfontein, *Die Verkrampte Aanslag,* 27.
7   Schoeman, *Die Broederbond,* 25-6.
8   Ibid, 23-4.
9   Serfontein, *Die Verkrampte Aanslag,* 7-8. On Hertzog's 'socialism' ('which he did not announce from the rooftops'), see Schoeman, *Die Broederbond,* 20-1, 24-5.
10   Serfontein, *Die Verkrampte Aanslag.* Most of his claims and analyses were later confirmed by NP politicians.
11   Quoted ibid, 10.
12   *Die Burger,* 14 December 1963.
13   Serfontein, *Die Verkrampte Aanslag,* 52. Prof. Murray's letter to *Die Transvaler* cited on 53.
14   See interview with Ronald Segal, 'Portrait of a Millionare', *Africa/South,* 4, 3, 1960.

15 *Veg,* January 1969.
16 *South African Observer*, March 1965.
17 Prof L J du Plessis, quoted in E P du Plessis, *'n Volk Staan Op,* 104.
18 *Inspan,* November 1950.
19 Ibid.
20 Interview with first EI treasurer, Dr P J Meyer, June 1975.
21 *Volkshandel,* September 1944 and October 1962.
22 Ibid, October 1964.
23 See Schoeman, *Van Malan tot Verwoerd*, chaps 5, 6, 8.
24 'Editorial', *Die Vaderland,* 1 September 1964.
25 Quoted in Schoeman, *Die Geldmag,* 88.
26 Translated in full, *Sunday Times,* 30 August 1964.
27 Serftontein, *Die Verkrampte Aanslag,* 54-5.
28 Cited ibid, 55. See also Schoeman, *Die Broederbond,* 23-45, 78-82.
29 Justice Victor Hiemstra, quoted in Serfontein, *Die Verkrampte Aanslag,* 85.
     Hiemstra was himself one of the principal verkrampte targets.
30 Dr P G du Plessis, *Die Huisgenoot (Boekebylaag),* 14 November 1969.
31 Schoeman, *Vorster se 1000 Dae,* 50.
32 In Opperman, *Groot Verseboek,* 187. No Afrikaans publisher would touch
     the poem at the time, although it now takes its rightful place in Opperman's
     authoritative anthology of Afrikaans poetry.
33 See p. 17 above.
34 Quoted Cope, *The Adversary Within*, 126-7.
35 Ibid, 100.
36 Quoted Serfontein, *Die Verkrampte Aanslag*, 27.
37 Quoted ibid, 86.
38 Pienaar, *Getuie van Groot Tye,* 45. For Strijdom's version of this planned
     Cape 'invasion', see Schoeman, *Van Malan tot Verwoerd,* 102-8.
39 See, eg, Pienaar, *Getuie van Groot Tye*, chaps 9, 14, 16, 17, 22 *et passim;*
     Serfontein, *Die Verkrampte Aanslag,* chap. 9 *et passim*; and Schoeman,
     Vorster se 1000 Dae, chap. 9 *et passim.*

Notes to Chapter 7

1   Quoted in E P du Plessis, *'n Volk Staan Op*, 121.
2   Quoted in Van Wyk, *Die Afrikaner*, table 1.1, 1, & table 1.2, 2.
3   Data from J L Sadie, cited in H Giliomee, 'The Leader and the Citizenry',
     table 4.1, 109.
4   See Sauer's authorised biography, De Villers, *Paul Sauer, passim.*
5   O'Meara, *Volkskapitalisme*, chaps 13 and 14.
6   Schoeman, *Die Geldmag*, 55.
7   Ibid, 81.
8   See ibid, 90-5.
9   *Sunday Tribune*, 6 June 1971.
10 *State of South Africa, 1965: Economic, Financial and Statistical Yearbook for*

the Republic of South Africa (Da Gama Publications, Johannesburg, 1966).

11 On these policy objectives, see the article by Secretary for Agriculture – Van der Merwe, 'Die Landbou Politiek', 13-18.

12 Figures for 1936-60 from S S Brand & F R Tomlinson, 'Die Plek van Landbou in die Suid Afrikaanse Volkshuishouding', *South African Journal of Economics*, 34, 1, 1966. Figures for decline in the 1960s from Adam & Giliomee, *Ethnic Power Mobilized*, 162.

13 See S B Greenberg, *Race and State in Capitalist Development: South Africa in comparative perspective* (Yale University Press, New Haven, 1980), 94 and his statistical appendix, table C.2, 424.

14 Nattrass, *The South African Economy*, table 6.9, 125.

15 Wilson, 'Farming 1866-1966', 158-63.

16 Greenberg, *Race and State in Capitalist Development*, 94, citing the Marais/Du Plessis Commission of Enquiry into Agriculture.

17 Houghton, *The South African Economy*, 66.

18 See the important discussion of this issue, ibid, 97-100.

19 See O'Meara, *Volkskapitalisme,* 248-9.

20 Serfontein, *Brotherhood*, 136.

21 A Gramsci, *Selections from the Prison Notebooks* (Lawrence & Wishart, London, 1971), 5. On this point, see O'Meara, *Volkskapitalisme*, 53-6.

22 L Pretorius, 'The Head of Government and Organised Business', in Schrire (ed.), *Leadership and the Apartheid State,* 215.

Notes to Chapter 8

1 *Die Transvaler*, 1 April 1966; Verwoerd quoted in *Die Volksblad*, 5 April 1996. For a detailed analysis of the vote, see Heard, *General Elections in South Africa*, chap 8.

2 Ben Schoeman quoted in (Beaumont) Schoeman, *Vorster se 1000 Dae,* 12. Vorster quoted ibid, 14.

3 See the results of their sounding of each MP, D'Oliveira, *Vorster – The Man*, 189-92.

4 Ben Schoeman, *My Lewe*, 320.

5 Quoted D'Oliveira, *Vorster – The Man*, 184. Beaumont Schoeman confirms much of Vorster's account in his own version of these events in *Vorster se 1000 Dae*, chap. 1.

6 Ibid, 14.

7 'New standards mean rejecting Christian ethics', *Hoofstad*, 3 January 1969.

8 Quoted Serfontein, *Brotherhood,* 238.

9 Serfontein, *Die Verkrampte Aanslag,* 47.

10 Quoted *The Star*, 15 September 1966.

11 See the 'Dawie' column, *Die Burger*, 25 February 1967.

12 For Verwoerd's Loskop speech, see *Sunday Express*, 5 September 1965. On outrage at Vorster's moves away from this policy, see Schoeman, *Vorster se 1000 Dae,* chap. 2.

13 See J A du Pisani, *John Vorster en die Verlig/Verkramp Stryd: 'n Studie van die Politieke Verdeeldheid in Afrikanergeledere* (Instituut vir Eietydse Geskiedenis, Universiteit van die Oranje-Vrystaat, Bloemfontein, 1988), *passim.*

14 For very different, but fairly full accounts, see ibid; Serfontein, *Die Verkrampte Aanslag*; and Schoeman, *Vorster.*

15 Quoted D'Oliveira, *Vorster – The Man*, 220-1.

16 Quoted in Serfontein, *Brotherhood*, 101.

17 Quoted in Schoeman, *Vorster,* 13.

18 John Vorster quoted in (Ben) Schoeman, *My Lewe*, 334-5.

19 See Serfontein, *Brotherhood*, 98-125.

20 Schoeman, *Die Broederbond*, 131.

21 See Introduction to the book by the journalist who received most of these leaks, Serfontein, *Brotherhood.*

22 D'Oliveira, *Vorster – The Man*, 235.

23 Cited in Serfontein, *Die Verkrampte Aanslag*, 155.

24 Schoeman, *Die Broederbond*, 47-8.

25 Quoted in I Wilkins & H Strydom, *The Super-Afrikaners: Inside the Afrikaner Broederbond* (Jonathan Ball, Johannesburg, 1978), 182.

26 Schoeman, *Die Broederbond*, 48.

27 Quoted Serfontein, *Brotherhood*, 80.

28 Hertzog and Verwoerd and Dönges quoted in Schoeman, *Die Broederbond*, 45.

29 Schoeman, *Die Broederbond*, 67. See also Serfontein, *Die Verkrampte Aanslag*, chap. 10.

30 See Serfontein, *Brotherhood*, 111-25.

31 Quoted in Adam & Giliomee, *Ethnic Power Mobilized*, 161, my emphasis. On Hertzog's 'socialism' (which was *not* national socialism), see book by one of his closest followers and intermittent chronicler – Beaumont Schoeman, *Die Broederbond*, 24-34.

32 Schoeman argues that this point in his account of the struggle for control of the Mineworkers' Union, written under the pseudonym of Louis Naudé: *Dr Albert Hertzog, Die Nasionale Party en die Mynwerkers* (Nasionale Raad van Trustees, Pretoria, 1969). See my review of this fascinating book: 'White Trade Unionism, Political Power and Afrikaner Nationalism', *South African Labour Bulletin*, 1, 10, 1975.

Notes to Chapter 9

1 See 'Crisis and Change', pp. 486-9 of the Theoretical Appendix.

2 *South Africa's Relationship with the International Finance System: Report of the Intergovernmental Group* (Commonwealth Foreign Ministers Committee, London, 1988 – hereafter, CFMC), table 12, 87.

3 Quoted in *SA Barometer*, 1, 2, 27 March 1987, 20.

4 *Report of the Study Group on Industrial Development*, cited in P Beaudet,

'Afrique du Sud, crises et transitions' (PhD dissertation presented to Université du Québec à Montréal, 1990), table 12, 133.

5   For a detailed analysis of this process of centralisation and consolidation in the 1960s, as well as the history of the major companies involved, see Davies *et al.*, *The Struggle for South Africa*, vol. 1, chap. 2.

6   S Clarke, *Financial Aspects of Economic Sanctions on South Africa* (IUEF, Geneva, 1980); H Houghton, *The South African Economy* (Oxford University Press, Oxford, 1976), 76, 180-3; K Luckhardt & B Wall, *Working for Freedom* (World Council of Churches, Geneva, 1981), 38.

7   SAIRR, *A Survey ... 1977*, 215.

8   *The Economic Development Programme, 1965-70*, 86.

9   See, eg, the citation from Harry Oppenheimer in Luckhardt & Wall, *Working for Freedom*, 39.

10 SAIRR, *A Survey ... 1978*, 138.

11 R Davies, 'Capital Restructuring and the Modification of the Racial Division of Labour in South Africa', *Journal of Southern African Studies*, 5, 2, 1979.

12 C Simkins, 'Employment, Unemployment and Growth in South Africa, 1961-1979', SALDRU *Working Paper No 4* (University of Cape Town, 1979).

13 Davies *et al.*, *The Struggle for South Africa*.

14 For 1981, see ibid, vol. 1, pp. 61-4. For 1985, see R McGregor, *Investors' Handbook* (Purdey Publishing, Johannesburg, 1985).

15 *Abstract of Agricultural Statistics, 1987* (Department of Agricultural Economics and Marketing, 1987), 6.

16 *Report of the Commission of Enquiry into the Export Trade of the Republic of South Africa*, RP 69/72 (Government Printer, Pretoria). On business views, see, eg, the survey of the prospects of South African industry in *Financial Mail* Special Survey, 14 January 1977.

17 Ibid. The case for this is clearly spelled out in Harry Oppenheimer's 1981 annual statement as chairman of the Anglo American Corporation, *Rand Daily Mail*, 16 July 1981. For a later statement of a similar position, see the chairman's address to the 1983 Sanlam AGM, *Financial Mail*, 30 March 1984.

18 For a useful review, see Luckhardt & Wall, *Working for Freedom*.

19 Eschel Rhoodie, quoted in M Rees & C Day, *Muldergate: The story of the info scandal* (Macmillan, Johannesburg, 1980), 173.

20 Vorster quoted in D'Oliveira, *Vorster – The Man*, 160.

21 Jonker, *Versamelde Werke*, 74.

22 See, *inter alia*, J Brickhill, *Sowing the Whirlwind* (IDAF, London, 1977); A Callinicos & J Rogers, *Southern Africa after Soweto* (Pluto Press, London, 1977); B Hirson, *Year of Fire, Year of Ash* (Zed Press, London, 1979); J Kane-Berman, *Soweto: Black Revolt, White Reaction* (Ravan Press, Johannesburg, 1978); and R W Johnson, *How Long Will South Africa Survive?* (Macmillan, London, 1977).

23 See, eg, the position of SASO cited in Davies *et al., The Struggle for South Africa*, vol. 2, p. 307.

24 *Financial Mail*, 11 February 1977.

25 Nye, 'Nuclear learning and US-Soviet security regions', *International Organization*, 41, 3, 1987, 398.

26 A Santos, *Afrique du Sud: une stratégie dans l'impasse* (École des hautes études en sciences sociales, Cahiers d'études stratégiques, Paris, n.d. [1988?]), 22-3.

27 *Financial Mail*, 29 November 1974.

28 Cited *Sunday Times*, 25 April 1971. On AHI see also: *Rand Daily Mail*, 23 March 1973; *Financial Mail*, 23 May 1975; special issue on 'the black worker' of AHI organ, *Volkshandel*, February 1975; and report of 1975 AHI congress, ibid, June 1975. See also the editorial reaction to the Soweto uprising, ibid, July 1976. For Assocom's position see, *inter alia, Financial Mail*, 23 May 1975; for FCI see *The Star*, 29 May 1975, *Rand Daily Mail*, 20 June 1975, *Sunday Times*, 6 April 1975 and *Financial Mail*, 20 August 1976. *The Star*, 29 June 1976 reports on the position of the Chamber of Mines.

29 See *Financial Mail*, 11 November 1977.

30 Ibid, 8 July 1977.

31 Davies *et al., The Struggle for South Africa*, vol. 1, p. 125.

32 Pretorius, 'The Head of Government and Organised Business', 229.

33 *Rapport*, 8 June 1975.

34 See R Southall, 'African Capitalism in Contemporary South Africa', *Journal of Southern African Studies*, 7, 1, 1980.

35 Cited *Fortune*, 10 August 1981, emphasis added.

36 See SAIRR, *A Survey ... 1977*, 12-20.

37 See Stuart Hill, cited in the Theoretical Appendix, p. 487.

Notes to Chapter 10

1 *Sunday Times*, 19 February 1977.

2 *A Survey ... 1975*, 2.

3 Details in *A Survey ... 1977*, 7-9.

4 Quoted in Schoeman, *Die Geldmag*, 48.

5 Quoted in Wilkins & Strijdom, *The Super-Afrikaners*, 214.

6 B J Vorster, 'Address to the 74th Annual Conference of Assocom', October 1976, mimeo.

7 The title of an AB circular to its branches in September 1968. This was followed up by further circulars in 1971 and 1972. Wilkins and Strijdom, *The Super-Afrikaners*, 230-5.

8 Kane-Berman, *Soweto*, 179. Unless otherwise noted, the quotations in the remainder of this section are drawn from chap. 12 of this book.

9 *House of Assembly Debates*, 16 April 1964, col. 4337.

10 *Die Burger*, 6 & 10 November 1976.

11 See, *A Survey ... 1977*, 7-10.
12 Serfontein, *Brotherhood,* 125.
13 *Die Transvaler,* 13 September 1977.
14 Dr Gerrit Viljoen, quoted in *Rand Daily Mail,* 1 August 1978.
15 *House of Assembly Debates,* 7 February 1978, col. 579.
16 Vorster quoted in De Villiers, *P W,* 96.
17 Suzman, *In No Uncertain Terms,* 82. Here Suzman also cites an article by *Die Burger*'s political correspondent, entitled 'Why so hard on Mrs Suzman?'
18 Eschel Rhoodie, quoted in Rees & Day, *Muldergate,* 181.
19 Quoted in ibid, 181-3. See also D Geldenhuys, *The Diplomacy of Isolation: South African foreign policy making* (Macmillan, Johannesburg, 1984), 75.
20 Gerrit Viljoen, cited in Schoeman, *Die Broederbond,* 72.
21 Geldenhuys, *Diplomacy of Isolation,* 74. Here, Geldenhuys cites J Barber, *The Making of British Foreign Policy* (Open University Press, Milton Keynes, 1976), 13.
22 Geldenhuys, *Diplomacy of Isolation.* 74.
23 Grundy, *The Militarization of South African Politics,* 35.

Notes to Chapter 11

1 *Supplementary Report of the Commission of Inquiry into Alleged Irregularities in the Former Department of Information,* RP 63/1979 (Government Printer, Pretoria, 1979 [hereafter, Erasmus 2]), para. 12, V.11.386.
2 *Report of the Commission of Inquiry into Alleged Irregularities in the Former Department of Information,* RP 113/1978 (Government Printer, Pretoria, 1978 [hereafter, Erasmus 1]), paras 12.432-12.449.
3 Geldenhuys, *Diplomacy of Isolation,* 85-6.
4 Quoted Rees & Day, *Muldergate,* 8.
5 Geldenhuys, *Diplomacy of Isolation,* 75. See also Winter, *Inside BOSS,* chap. 38, 558 *et passim.*
6 Geldenhuys, *Diplomacy of Isolation.*
7 See Rees & Day, *Muldergate,* chap. 25, 'Tearing the paper curtain'.
8 *Rand Daily Mail,* 30 October 1978.
9 Former Deputy Secretary for Information, Les de Villiers, quoted in Rees & Day, *Muldergate,* 110.
10 Ibid, 5-6.
11 Rhoodie, quoted in ibid, 171.
12 Pottinger, *The Imperial Presidency,* 46. See also De Villiers, *P W,* 128.
13 Rhoodie, quoted in Rees & Day, *Muldergate,* 183-4.
14 See De Villiers, *P W,* 126-7.
15 Ibid, 128.
16 Personal communication.
17 *Inside BOSS,* 558.
18 SAIRR, *A Survey ... 1972,* 34-7.

19 Grundy, *The Militarization of South African Politics*, 43.
20 De Villiers, *P W*, 128. All unattributed quotations in the following four paragraphs are drawn from pp. 128-9 of this official biography.
21 SAIRR, *A Survey ... 1972*, 36-7. All information on the Potgieter Commission contained in this and the following paragraphs is drawn from pp. 34-7 and 69-70 of this publication.
22 Pottinger, *The Imperial Presidency*, 45.
23 See, *inter alia*: ibid, 45-6; Frankel, *Pretoria's Praetorians*, 106-7; Winter, *Inside BOSS, passim*; and Rhoodie, *P W Botha*, chap. 8.
24 Geldenhuys, *Diplomacy of Isolation*, 81, 79.
25 Rhoodie, *P W Botha*, 194-6.
26 See De Villiers, *P W*, 241-77.
27 Geldenhuys, *Diplomacy of Isolation*, 75-84. Unattributed quotations in this and the following paragraphs are drawn from this source.
28 All unattributed details in this paragraph are drawn from P W Botha's version of events as told to the De Villiers, *P W*, 256-75.
29 Ibid.
30 Geldenhuys, *Diplomacy of Isolation*, 80.
31 Ibid.
32 See Grundy, *The Militarization of South African Politics*, 90.
33 See the revelations by BOSS defector Arthur McGiven, *The Observer* (London), January 1980.
34 This is well conveyed by Winter, *Inside BOSS*. See also Rees & Day, *Muldergate*.
35 See Rees & Day, *Muldergate*, 183-4.
36 De Villiers, *P W*, 124.
37 Grundy, *The Militarization of South African Politics*, 43.
38 Winter, *Inside BOSS*, 558.
39 The source for discussions on the possibility of a *coup* is a personal communication, while *The Star* reports on the SADF General Staff memo to Botha (7 May 1980). This memo was also discussed in a US Congress Committee. See n. 1 in J Seiler, 'The South African Security Establishment: Rationalisation to what ends?', mimeo, Yale University, 1983.
40 See General Magnus Malan, 'Die Aanslag teen Suid-Afrika', *ISSUP Strategic Review*, November 1980.
41 *Paratus*, July 1979, 36.
42 Republic of South Africa, Department of Defence, *White Paper on Defence and Armaments Supply*, 1977, 5.
43 General Malan, quoted in *Rand Daily Mail*, 13 June 1979. My emphasis.
44 Unattributed information in this and the following paragraphs is drawn from the following sources: *Financial Mail*, 11 September 1981; Frankel, *Pretoria's Praetorians*, 73-89; M G Paul, 'Muldergate: A comment', *Work in Progress*, 23, 1983; and Davies *et al., Struggle for South Africa*, vol. 1, pp. 104-5.

45 Frankel, *Pretoria's Praetorians*, 87-8.
46 Ibid, 84.
47 11 September 1981.
48 Paul, 'Muldergate'.
49 Frankel, *Pretoria's Praetorians*, 88.
50 Private communication from an MP.

Notes to Chapter 12

1   Most English-language newspapers wrote of little else for more than a year. See also, *inter alia*, Pottinger, *The Imperial Presidency*, chaps 2-3; Rees & Day, *Muldergate;* E Rhoodie, *The REAL Information Scandal* (Orbis Publishers, Pretoria, 1983), and *P W Botha: The Final Betrayal;* De Villiers, *P W*, 95-138; Ries & Dommisse, *Broedertwis*, chaps 1-2; the three reports of the Erasmus Commission.
2   See, *inter alia*, Rees & Day, *Muldergate*, 5-6 and various *Rand Daily Mail* editorials, cited ibid, 137. The last quotation is by former *Sunday Times* editor, Joel Mervis, then a 'Prog' MPC – *Rand Daily Mail*, 3 May 1981.
3   Quoted in Rees & Day, *Muldergate*, 5. See also 2, 4-6.
4   Quoted ibid, 112.
5   SAIRR, *A Survey ... 1977*, 4.
6   *Die Transvaler,* 15 September 1978.
7   Ries & Dommisse, *Broedertwis,* 10.
8   De Villiers, *P W*, 111.
9   Quoted ibid.
10 Quoted ibid, 104.
11 *Die Transvaler,* 15 September 1978.
12 Source 'Myrtle', quoted in Rees & Day, *Muldergate*, 69.
13 Quoted in Ries & Dommisse, *Broedertwis*, 11. All unattributed quotations and information in this and the following paragraphs are drawn from chap. 2 of this book. For P W Botha's version of the 1978 NP leadership election, see De Villiers, *P W*, 102-13. Detailed accounts are also to be found in Rees & Day, *Muldergate*, chap. 9, and Pottinger, *The Imperial Presidency,* 7-15.
14 Pik Botha, quoted in Ries & Dommisse, *Broedertwis,* 10, and various of his supporters quoted in De Villiers, *P W*, 107-8.
15 Cited Ries & Dommisse, *Broedertwis,* 18.
16 Erasmus 1, paras 11.345-11.401.
17 Alwyn Schlebusch, quoted in De Villiers, *P W*, 105.
18 All quotations in this paragraph are drawn from P W Botha's authorised biography, ibid, 109.
19 Ibid, 104, 108. Ries & Dommisse, *Broedertwis*, 23.
20 De Villiers, *P W*, 110.
21 Pottinger, *The Imperial Presidency,* 21.
22 Rhoodie, *P W Botha*, chap. 3.
23 Erasmus 1, para 10.337.

24 Pottinger, *The Imperial Presidency*, 24.
25 Quoted in ibid, 25.
26 Quoted in De Villiers, *P W*, 143.
27 See Adam & Giliomee, *Ethnic Power Mobilized*.
28 *P W Botha*, 21-2, 24-5, *et passim.*
29 Rees & Day, *Muldergate*, 2.
30 Ibid, 26.
31 See introduction to both of Hennie Serfontein's books listed in the Bibliography.
32 De Villiers, *P W*, 124, 128.
33 Winter, *Inside BOSS*, 557-8.
34 Rees & Day, *Muldergate*, 26.
35 See De Villiers, *P W*, 124-5.
36 On the ownership structure of the South African Press in the late 1970s, see Davies *et al., Struggle for South Africa*, vol. 2, pp. 407-14.
37 *Beeld*, 1 November 1978.

Notes to Chapter 13

1 See, eg, the major article by Fleur de Villiers, *Sunday Times,* 1 October 1978, depicting Botha as an unimaginative hardman unlikely to introduce change. See also the interview he gave just before assuming the Premiership in which he trotted out some of the most rigid aspects of apartheid dogma – Anna Starcke, *Survival: Taped interviews with South Africa's power elite* (Tafelberg, Cape Town, 1978), 59.
2 On Botha as a 'difficult man', see Henning Klopper, cited Suzman, *In No Uncertain Terms*, 70. The NP chief whip expressed similar sentiments. Seegers describes Botha's temper as 'gothic', 'The Head of Government and the Executive', 60. On the fear Botha inspired as head secretary of the Cape NP, see footnote p. 108. For his biographers' attempts to reframe his personal nastiness, see De Villers, *P W*, 47-55.
3 Address to NP meeeting in Upington, 28 July 1979. See J J Scholtz, *Fighter and Reformer: Extracts from the speeches of PW Botha* (Bureau for Information, Pretoria, 1989), 17. My emphasis.
4 Quoted ibid, 6-7.
5 Interview with Beaumont Schoeman, July 1975.
6 Quoted De Villiers, *P W*, 151.
7 Ibid.
8 Quoted ibid, 177.
9 *Beeld*, 19 September 1979.
10 De Villiers, *P W*, 151.
11 K van Wyk & D Geldenhuys, *Die Groepsgebod in PW Botha's se Politieke Oortuigings* (Rand Afrikaanse Universiteit, Johannesburg, 1987), 48.
12 Botha, quoted in *Leadership South Africa,* 2, 3, Spring 1983.
13 Quoted Scholtz, *Fighter and Reformer*, 7.

14 Schoeman, *Vorster*, 246.
15 Pottinger, *The Imperial Presidency*, 35.
16 For Beaufre's extensive writings, see Bibliography.
17 Frankel, *Pretoria's Praetorians*, 46.
18 *La guerre révolutionnaire: Les formes nouvelles de la guerre* (Fayard, Paris, 1972), 279-82.
19 Ibid, 282. My emphasis.
20 *Stratégie de l'Action* (Armand Colin, Paris, 1966), 103, 112.
21 Ibid, 103.
22 *Introduction à la stratégie* (Armand Colin, Paris, 1963), 16-17. Beaufre slightly qualifies this point in *Stratégie de l'Action,* 112-13.
23 *Stratégie de l'Action,* 111.
24 *Introduction à la stratégie,* 16.
25 Ibid, 23.
26 Ibid, 117.
27 Ibid, 17. Original emphasis.
28 *La guerre révolutionnaire*, 24. My emphasis.
29 *Stratégie de l'Action*, 108-9.
30 *Introduction à la stratégie*, 113-14.
31 *Stratégie de l'Action*, 115. See also the section entitled 'Action as a compromise' in Beaufre's *Batir l'avenir* (Calmann-Lévy, Paris, 1967), 139-40.
32 *Introduction à la stratégie*, 18.
33 *Stratégie de l'Action*, 130.
34 Ibid, 132-3.
35 Ibid, 21.
36 See Malan, 'Die Aanslag teen Suid-Afrika'.
37 *Sunday Times* editor Tertius Myburgh, quoted in Rhoodie, *PW Botha*, 131. See Huntington, 'Reform and Stability in a Modernising Multi-ethnic Society', *Politikon*, 8, 2, 1981.
38 Huntington, 'Reform and Stability', *passim*.
39 J-P Charnay, *Essai général de la stratégie* (Editions Libre, Paris, 1973), 9.
40 Ibid.
41 *White Paper on Defence and Armaments Supply* (Department of Defence, Pretoria, 1982), 2.
42 W J de Klerk, *F W de Klerk: The man in his time* (Jonathan Ball Publishers, Johannesburg, 1991), 27.
43 Quoted Grundy, 'The Rise of the South African Security Establishment', 11-12.
44 Quoted ibid, 13.
45 *Rapport*, 23 May 1971.
46 Quoted in C Charney, 'Class Conflict and the Nationalist Split', *Journal of Southern African Studies*, 10, 2, April 1994, 272.
47 J Coetzee, 'Rewolusionere Oorlog en Teeninsurgensie', in M Hough (ed.),

Nasionale Veiligheid en Strategie met Spesifieke Verwysing na die RSA (ISSUP, Pretoria, 1981).

48 See R Davies & D O'Meara, 'Total Strategy in Southern Africa: An analysis of South African regional policy', *Journal of Southern African Studies*, 11, 2, April 1985.

49 See D O'Meara, 'Les couts de la déstabilisation en Afrique australe', *Afrique*, 4, 1, 1987.

50 SAIRR, *A Survey ... 1981*, 102.

51 *White Paper on Defence and Armaments Supply* (Department of Defence, Pretoria, 1977), 5.

52 *Rand Daily Mail*, 16 August 1979. The version Botha presented to the Natal NP Congress is reproduced in Appendix II.

53 See SAIRR, *A Survey ... 1980*, 2-3.

54 H Giliomee, *The Parting of the Ways* (David Philip, Cape Town, 1983), 150.

Notes to Chapter 14

1 See Theoretical Appendix.

2 Beaufre, *Stratégie pour demain: Les problèmes militaires de la guerre moderne* (Librarie Plon, Paris, 1972), 27. Emphasis added. See also Beaufre, *Stratégie de l'Action*, 76-80.

3 C Crocker, '"Scope Paper", Chester Crocker to Secretary of State Alexander Haig' (TransAfrica Forum, Washington, 1981).

4 *Report of the Commission of Inquiry into Labour Legislation*, RP 47/1979.

5 The gradual introduction of such measures, together with the debates and divisions they provoked within the democratic trade union movement, are discussed in Davies *et al., Struggle for South Africa*, vol. 2, pp. 325-9.

6 *Report of the Commission of Inquiry into Legislation Affecting the Utilisation of Manpower*, RP 32/197.

7 On the ways in which the Wiehahn and Riekert recommendations actually entrenched the basic provisions of apartheid, see 'Focus on Wiehahn', *South African Labour Bulletin*, 5, 2, 1979, and South African Congress of Trade Unions, *The Political and Economic Context of Recent so-called 'Reforms' in South Africa: Memorandum to the ILO,* June 1980. For a discussion from a very different perspective, see Ashforth, *The Politics of Official Discourse*, chap. 6.

8 See, eg, 'Special Survey on Soweto', *Financial Mail,* 25 March 1983.

9 Ibid, 47.

10 *Financial Mail,* 2 March 1984.

11 See the annual *Survey of Race Relations* published by the South African Institute of Race Relations for a useful year-by-year review of the twists and turns of these evolving policies.

12 Pottinger, *The Imperial Presidency*, 112, 114.

13 M Swilling & M Philips, 'The Emergency State: Its structure, power &

limits', in G Moss & I Obery (eds), *South African Review 5* (Ravan Press, Johannesburg, 1989), 71.

14 On the scope, and defeat of, the original 'constellation' proposals, see Davies & O'Meara, 'Total Strategy'.

15 *Financial Mail*, 16 December 1983.

16 For precise details, see SAIRR, *A Survey ... 1983*, and the interesting discussion in F Cachalia, 'The State, Crisis and Restructuring', *Africa Perspective*, 23, 1983, esp. 30-40.

17 Republic of South Africa, 'White Paper on the Rationalisation of the Public Service and Related Institutions', *Journal of Public Administration*, 15, 2, 1980, 49, 63.

18 D Geldenhuys & H Kotze, 'Aspects of Decision-making in South Africa', *South African Journal of Political Science*, 10, 1, 1983. The discussion which follows draws on this source.

19 For an excellent analysis of Heunis's rise and decline in the Botha government, see M Swilling & M Philips, 'The Powers of the Thunderbird: Decision-making structures and political strategies in the South African state', in Centre for Policy Studies, *Policy Perspectives 1989: South Africa at the end of the Eighties* (Johannesburg, 1989), 54-61.

20 Seegers, 'The Head of Government and the Executive', 59.

21 Malan, 'Die Aanslag teen Suid-Afrika', 14-15.

22 Seegers, 'The Head of Government and the Executive', 62.

23 *Sunday Times,* 11 July 1982.

24 Seegers, 'The Head of Government and the Executive', 62.

25 See article by Police Commissioner Johan Coetzee, 'Rewolusionere Oorlog en Teeninsurgensie'.

26 Pottinger, *The Imperial Presidency*, 35-6.

27 Malan, 'Die Aanslag teen Suid-Afrika', 15.

28 *Weekly Mail*, 3 July 1987.

29 Seegers, 'The Head of Government and the Executive', 63. Seegers's studiously gender-neutral description hides the fact that in the apartheid state *all* senior positions were filled by men.

30 For details, see SAIRR, *A Survey ... 1982*, 1-6.

31 See the detailed discussion of these proposals in SAIRR, *A Survey ... 1983*, 1 ff.

Notes to Chapter 15

1 De Villiers, *P W*, 176.

2 For various versions of the affair, see: ibid, 139-41; Ries & Dommisse, *Broedertwis*, 39-40; Pottinger, *The Imperial Presidency*, 52-3; and Rhoodie *P W Botha*, 82-9. Rhoodie's account includes photocopies of various of Muller's letters to Botha.

3 Quoted Ries & Dommisse, *P W*, 83.

4 Pottinger, *The Imperial Presidency,* 58.

5 8 July 1977. See p. 188 above.
6 Punch Barlow, cited in De Villiers, *P W*, 160.
7 P W Botha, quoted in Giliomee, *The Parting of the Ways*, 37. Harry Oppenheimer, quoted in De Villiers, *P W*, 160. For an evaluation of this Carlton conference, see 'South Africa: Strategy conference of government and business leaders', *Southern Africa Dossier* 4.60(E) (Centro de Estudos Africanos, Universidade Eduardo Mondlane, Maputo, 1981).
8 L Pretorius, 'Interaction between Interest Organisations and Government in South Africa', *Politeia,* 1, 1, 1982, 32. My emphasis.
9 Quoted in Giliomee, *The Parting of the Ways*, 37.
10 See Ries & Dommisse, *Broedertwis,* 120-1 *et passim.*
11 Ibid, 185.
12 De Villiers, *P W*, 176-9.
13 Quoted Ries & Dommisse, *Broedertwis,* 88.
14 De Villiers, *P W*, 180.
15 See C Charney, 'Towards Rupture or Stasis? An analysis of the 1981 South African General Election', *African Affairs*, 81, 1982.
16 *Rapport*, 3 May 1981.
17 Charney, 'Towards Rupture or Stasis?', 530.
18 This and the following paragraphs draw on 'The Far Right Challenge in South Africa', *Southern Africa Dossier* 6.30(E) (Centro de Estudos Africanos, Universidade Eduardo Mondlane, Maputo, 1982).
19 De Villiers, *P W*, 154-5.
20 *Financial Mail*, 14 August 1981. See also the strong Assocom statement cited in ibid, 16 October 1981.
21 On the great nationalist fear of *skeuring* (schism), see Ries & Dommisse, *Broedertwis,* chap. 1: 'Schism: Fear of a deadly sin'.
22 Van der Merwe, quoted in Ries & Dommisse, *Broedertwis,* 118; P W Botha quoted in *The Star*, 25 February 1982. The most complete account of this dramatic week is to be found in the book by leading Nasionale Pers journalists, Ries & Dommisse, *Broedertwis,* esp. chaps 8-12.

Notes to Chapter 16
1 Quoted in Schoeman, *Vorster se 1000 Dae*, 279.
2 D'Oliveira, *Vorster – The Man*, 249.
3 See the summary of KP founding congress and policy programme in SAIRR, *A Survey ... 1982,* 10-12.
4 Quoted in Charney, 'Class Conflict and the Nationalist Split', 270.
5 Cited in *A Survey ... 1982*, table 2, 274, and table 3, 275. There is a discrepancy in the NP's polled support in October 1982, given in these tables. Charney lists this as 51% in table 2 and 56% in table 3. I presume the former is a typographical error as the text speaks of 56% support for the NP in the October 1982 polls.
6 See the evidence of Sanlam chairman cited in the main editorial, *The Argus,*

16 November 1980.
7   *Rapport*, 24 November 1978.
8   See Giliomee, *Parting of the Ways, passim.*
9   On its key role in the 'fusion' crisis and the formation of the *gesuiwerde* NP in 1934, see O'Meara, *Volkskapitalisme,* Part I. Marais, *Die Stryd*, deals at length with the grievances of the maize famers and the formation of SAMPI.
10   Charney, 'Class Conflict', 278.
11   Ibid. On Botha's row with NAMPO, see *Financial Mail*, 4 February 1983.
12   J Lombard and J Stadler, 'Focus on Economic Issues', *Mercabank*, 31, 1982, 4.
13   Interview with chief HNP publicist, Beaumont Schoeman, July 1975.
14   *The Imperial Presidency,* 134-5.
15   Charney, 'Class Conflict', 273-4.
16   *Rapport,* 2 May 1982.
17   Charney, 'Class Conflict', table 4, 277.
18   *Race Relations Survey, 1987/8* (South African Institute of Race Relations, Johannesburg, 1988), 226-7. This was the modified title of the annual *Survey of Race Relations* from its 1986 edition onwards. The surveys after 1986 will henceforth be cited as in the following example: SAIRR, *Survey 1987/8*. For full detail, see Bibliography.
19   For Vorster's attack on Botha, see editorial in *Rapport*, 30 October 1980. For a brief history of positions taken, see 'The great Afrikaner press war ends in a Southern victory', *The Star*, 10 February 1983.
20   See interview with Rupert, *Financial Mail*, 3 September 1982.

Notes to Chapter 17

1   *Financial Mail*, 25 March 1983. In an editorial on 15 April 1983 the journal told businessmen: 'Don't Worry Lads, we're winning [the fight against the recession].'
2   Charney, 'Class Conflict', table 2, 274.
3   Quoted in De Villiers, *P W*, 366.
4   'Remarks by the Honourable PW Botha, DMS MP, Prime Minister of South Africa, on the Occasion of the Signing of the Accord of Nkomati: Friday 16 March 1984', mimeo, 4.
5   Raymond Parsons, quoted in *The Star*, 23 April 1984. The description of Nkomati as a 'miracle' comes from De Villiers, *P W*, 4.
6   Pik Botha, quoted in *The Citizen*, 22 February 1984. Assocom, quoted in *The Star*, 23 April 1984. On the international and regional perception of the Nkomati Accord, see R Davies & D O'Meara, 'Total Strategy in Southern Africa: An analysis of South African regional policy', *Journal of South African Studies,* 11, 2, April 1985.
7   Beaufre, *Stratégie de l'Action*, 131-2, my emphasis.
8   *Introduction à la stratégie*, 113-14.

9   The idea that the Botha reforms had *reinforced* apartheid, and hence validated the liberation movement's own response, was at the heart of Joe Slovo's strong verbal critique of the evaluation of the Total Strategy Rob Davies and I presented to the August 1982 UNESCO Conference on Social Sciences in Southern Africa, Universidade Eduardo Mondlane. See our 'The State of Analysis of the Southern African Region: Issues raised by South African strategy', *Review of African Political Economy*, 29, 1984.

10 'State, Capital and Growth: The political economy of the national question', in S Gelb (ed.), *South Africa's Economic Crisis* (David Philip/Zed Books, Cape Town/London, 1991).

11 SAIRR, *A Survey ... 1982*, 49.

12 See J Seekings, 'What was the United Democratic Front?', in D O'Meara (ed.), *The Politics of Change in Southern Africa*, Collected Seminar Papers, vol. 1 (Canadian Research Consortium on Southern Africa, Montreal, 1995).

13 *Financial Mail*, 16 November 1984.

14 For a monthly breakdown in 1984-85, see 'Unrest Chronology', *Indicator South Africa*, 4, 4, Autumn/Winter 1987, 22-6. See also *Political Conflict in South Africa; Data trends 1984-8* (Indicator Project, University of Natal, December 1988).

15 See its organ, *Sechaba*, April 1986.

16 Again reaching the low point it had achieved immediately following the February 1982 expulsion of the Treurnichtites, *Rapport*, 2 May 1985.

17 *Sunday Times*, 31 May 1987.

18 *... and what about the Blacks?*

19 *The Star*, 1 February 1986.

20 Tony Bloom, citing 'the views of many of my colleagues in business', *Financial Mail*, 16 November 1984.

21 *The Star*, 26 November 1984.

22 See the March 1986 Cosatu/Sactu/ANC communiqué reproduced in *South Africa Update* (CIDMAA, Montreal, 1986), 62.

23 On disinvestment following relaxation of exchange controls, see Centro de Estudos Africanos, 'Background on Recent Disinvestments by Foreign Capital from South Africa', *Southern Africa Dossier*, 23.40(E) (Eduardo Mondlane University, Maputo, July 1983). On the departure of American companies, see *Business Week*, 23 September 1985.

24 A senior editor of *Time Magazine* told me he was present in the Foreign Minister's office when Botha made this claim. Rhoodie asserts that Pik Botha deliberately spread this 'misinformation' in an attempt to force P W Botha's hand, *PW Botha*, 280.

25 See W J de Klerk, *F W de Klerk: The man in his time* (Jonathan Ball Publishers, Johannesburg, 1991), 20.

26 *Financial Mail*, 6 September 1985, original emphasis.

27 *Patterns of Multinational Corporations' Disinvestment from South Africa:*

A report for the UN Center on Transnational Corporations (Investor Responsibility Research Center, Boston, May 1989).

28   *Financial Mail*, 8 January 1988.
29   *The Star*, 29 August 1985.
30   See article by Harald Pakendorf, *Leadership South Africa*, 4, 3, 1985.
31   A Bernstein & B Godsell, 'The Incrementalists' in Berger & Godsell, *A Future South Africa*, 172.
32   *The Star*, 23 June 1986.
33   Quoted Rhoodie, *PW Botha*, 280.
34   *Volkshandel*, December 1985.
35   Quoted in ibid, March 1986.
36   Ibid, April 1986.
37   See, eg, Anton Rupert's statement in *Financial Mail*, 6 September 1985.
38   See, eg, its September 1985 editorial entitled 'The Message to the Outside [world]'.
39   Ibid, December 1985.
40   Ibid, June 1986.
41   *Gorongoza Documents* (extracts), Maputo, 30 September 1985.
42   See the very useful and extensive review of the debate over the nature of Renamo in Otto Roesch, 'A Paradigm Shift? Rethinking RENAMO's war', in D O'Meara (ed.) *The Politics of Change in Southern Africa* (Canadian Research Consortium on Southern Africa, Montreal, 1995)
43   See n. *, p. 329 above.
44   *Financial Mail*, 27 September 1985.
45   Ibid.
46   *Sunday Times*, 31 May 1987.
47   Pottinger, *The Imperial Presidency*, 330.
48   *Weekly Mail*, 4 April 1986.
49   SAIRR, *Quarterly Countdown*, Third Quarter, 8.
50   Swilling & Phillips, 'The Powers of the Thunderbird', 58.
51   *The Citizen*, 1 February 1986.
52   *The Star*, 8 February 1986.
53   A du Toit, 'White Politics: a post-election assessment', *Reality*, July 1987.
54   *Finansies & Tegniek*, 7 March 1986.
55   *Financial Mail*, 1 November 1985.
56   Interview with Johan Heyns, *Leadership South Africa*, 5, 5, 1986.
57   *Rapport*, 5 May 1985.
58   *The Star*, 29 April 1985.
59   *The Citizen*, 18 March 1986.
60   Police spokesman, Lt Attie Laubscher, quoted in *Weekly Mail*, 4 May 1986.

Notes to Chapter 18

1   Commonwealth Group of Eminent Persons (EPG), *Mission to South Africa: The Commonwealth Report* (Penguin for the Commonwealth Secretariat,

Harmondsworth, 1986), 132-3.

2   24 December 1985. This letter is reproduced as Annex 2, ibid, 148-9.

3   Ibid, 106.

4   M Swilling, 'The Politics of Negotiation', *Work in Progress*, Oct/Nov 1987, 18.

5   See the intriguing report by a government 'insider', *Die Man Wat Weet* (pseud.), 'Die Reisies is aan die Gang', *Die Suid-Afrikaan,* 14, April/May 1988 (hereafter DMWW).

6   EPG, *Mission to South Africa*, 125, 132.

7   M Swilling & M Phillips, 'Reform, Security and White Power: Rethinking state strategies in the 1980s', paper to the Annual Conference of the Association of Sociology of South Africa, University of Durban-Westville, July 1988, 23.

8   Quoted in 'Powers of the Thunderbird', 58.

9   DMWW, 8. Swilling & Phillips, 'Powers of the Thunderbird', 59 *et passim.*

10 Ibid. See also the interview with Willie Breytenbach, *Leadership South Africa*, 6, 2, 1987.

11 DMWW.

12 General Lloyd, cited in *Weekly Mail,* 23 June 1989.

13 Ibid.

14 S C Sarkesian, 'Low-Intensity Conflict: Concepts, principles and policy guidelines', *Air University Review*, 26, 2, 1985, 11.

15 See R Gordon, 'Anthropology and Counter-Revolutionary Praxis: The SADF case', paper to the Annual Conference of the Canadian African Studies Association, Queen's University, Kingston, 11-14 May 1988. On the 'pro-insurgency' and 'foreign internal defence' variations of LIC theory, see M T Klare, 'The Interventionist Impulse: US military doctrine for low-intensity warfare', in M Klare & P Kornbluh (eds.), *Low-Intensity Warfare: Counterinsurgency, proinsurgency and antiterrorism in the eighties* (Pantheon, New York, 1988).

16 'The Art of Counter-Revolutionary Warfare', a booklet distributed to leading politicians and bureaucrats by the SSC – *Weekly Mail,* 20 May 1988.

17 J J McCuen, *The Art of Counter-Revolutionary War* (Faber & Faber, London, 1966). General Lloyd, quoted in *Weekly Mail,* 3 October 1986.

18 Quoted in L Schlemmer, 'South Africa's National Party Government', in Berger & Godsell, *A Future South Africa,* 13.

19 Stoffel van der Merwe, *Financial Mail,* 18 March 1988.

20 DMWW.

21 General Lloyd, quoted in *Southscan,* 13 January 1988.

22 *Work in Progress,* 56/7, 1988.

23 For details, see *Now Everyone is Afraid: The changing face of policing in South Africa* (Catholic Institute for International Relations, London, 1988).

24 C Cooper, 'The Militarisation of the Bantustans: Control and

contradictions', in L Nathan & J Cock, *War and Society: The militarisation of South Africa* (David Philip, Cape Town, 1989), 178-9.
25   *Cape Times,* 12 December 1985.
26   See D O'Meara, 'South Africa's Destabilisation of the Frontline States, 1980-1987', Canadian Institute for International Peace & Security, *Background Paper No 20,* June 1988.
27   DMWW. See also the interview with Willie Breytenbach cited in n. 10 above.
28   *Weekly Mail,* 20 May 1988.
29   Quoted in *Newsweek,* 20 June 1988.
30   *Weekly Mail,* 20 May 1988.
31   *Race Relations Survey, 1988/9* (South African Insitute of Race Relations, Johannesburg, 1989), 193-223.
32   Swilling & Philips, 'Reform, Security and White Power', 28.
33   *Weekly Mail,* 20 May 1988.
34   Ibid, 23 June 1988.
35   SAIRR, *A Survey ... 1987/8,* 125.
36   Quoted in DMWW.
37   Quoted Schlemmer, 'South Africa's National Party Government', 38.
38   *Beeld,* 9 March 1987.
39   P W Botha, quoted in J J Scholtz, *Fighter and Reformer,* 53.
40   Cited in Schlemmer, 'South Africa's National Party Government', 13-14.
41   18 March 1988.
42   Opening of Parliament, 1985, quoted Scholtz, *Fighter and Reformer,* 28.
43   *Business Day,* 16 April 1987.
44   South African Institute of Race Relations, *Quarterly Countdown,* 10, 1988.
45   'Behind Closed Doors', *Leadership South Africa,* 6, 6, 1987.
46   DMWW.
47   Ibid.
48   The title of Pottinger's detailed analysis of the first ten years of the Botha government.
49   *Weekly Argus,* 30 September 1989.
50   Central Statistical Service, cited Rhoodie, *PW Botha,* 236. On the size of public sector employment in 1980, see Seegers, 'The Head of Government and the Executive', tables 2.1-2.11, 40-4.
51   Swilling & Phillips, 'Reform, Security and White Power', 34.
52   K Owen, 'You can't beat a system that's not supposed to work', *Cape Times,* 2 April 1988.
53   S J Terreblanche, 'Corruption and the National Party', IDASA lecture at the University of Cape Town, 12 April 1989. See also Terreblanche, 'The Dream Fades', *Leadership South Africa,* 7, 3, 1988.

Notes to Chapter 19
1   *South Africa Barometer,* 24 March 1989.

2   *Weekly Mail*, 11 March 1988.
3   Deputy Reserve Bank Governor, Jan Lombard, cited in Cock & Nathan, *War & Society*, 148.
4   Commonwealth Foreign Ministers Committee, *South Africa's Relationship with the International Financial System: Report of the Intergovernmental Group* (London, 1988), 12. Hereafter CFMC.
5   Ibid.
6   South African Reserve Bank, *Quarterly Bulletin*, June 1988.
7   Quoted in *South African Barometer*, 27 March 1987.
8   CFMC, 108.
9   Ibid, 18.
10 *Activities of Transnational Corporations Operating in South Africa and Collaboration of such Corporations with the Racist Minority Regime – Report of the Secretary General*, E/C.10/1989/8 (United Nations Economic & Social Council, Commission on Transnational Corporations, fifteenth session, New York, 5-14 April, 1989), para. 16.
11 *Business Day*, 26 September 1988.
12 *Statistical Presentation of South Africa's Foreign Liabilities and Assets, 1956-1981* (South African Reserve Bank, 1982).
13 South African Reserve Bank, *Quarterly Bulletin*, March 1988.
14 CFMC, 61.
15 United Nations Commission on Transnational Corporations, 'The Role of Transnational Banks in South Africa', Draft Report, 53.
16 *South Africa: Summary Report on Trade, Lending Investment and Strategic Minerals* (United States General Accounting Office, GAO/NSAID-88-228, 1988), 19-20.
17 D O'Meara, *Government Measures Against Apartheid South Africa on Areas Critical to its Economy* (Report to UN Centre Against Apartheid, July 1989), 126-30.
18 Centro de Estudos Africanos, 'The 1989/90 South African Budget and the Continuing Crisis of the Apartheid Economy', *Southern African Dossier*, 47.200 (Universidade Eduardo Mondlane, Maputo, 1989). Unless otherwise noted, all figures in this and the following two paragraphs are drawn from this source.
19 United Nations Commission on Transnational Corporations, 'The Role of Transnational Banks in South Africa', Draft Report, 53.
20 Interview, *Leadership South Africa*, 7, 4, 1988.
21 J Krikler, 'Problems of a Transition to Socialist Agriculture in South Africa', *South African Labour Bulletin*, 12, 5, July 1987, 95.
22 D Cooper, 'Ownership and Control of Agriculture in South Africa', in J Suckling & L White (eds), *After Apartheid: Renewal of the South African Economy* (James Currey, London, 1988), 2.
23 'Focus: The Great Economic Debate', Special Supplement, *Weekly Mail*, 30 March 1990, 5.

24 *Finance Week*, 5 May 1989.
25 *An Overview of Political Conflict in South Africa: Data Trends 1984-1988* (Indicator South Africa Focus, University of Natal, Durban, 1989).
26 *Weekly Mail*, 10 February 1988.
27 *The Star*, 20 March 1988.
28 On the early phase, see D Kaplan, 'The Internationalisation of South African Capital', *African Affairs*, October 1983.
29 *Fortune*, 10 August 1981.
30 Davies *et al.*, *Struggle for South Africa*, vol. 1, pp. 82-6.
31 See Centro de Estudos Africanos, 'Background on Recent Disinvestment by Foreign Capital from South Africa', *Southern Africa Dossier*, 23.40(E) (Eduardo Mondlane University, Maputo), July 1983.
32 CFMC, 39.
33 D Innes, 'Minorco: The biggest ever disinvestment', *Weekly Mail*, 31 March 1989.
34 H Kreplak & W George, 'La stratégie conventionnelle', in C-P David, *Les études stratégiques* (Éditions du Méridien, Montréal, 1989), 195-6. These authors borrow the term 'strategic romanticism' from Richard Betts, 'Conventional Strategy: New critics, old choices', *International Security*, 7, 4, Spring 1983, 146.
35 *Die Suid-Afrikaan*, 9, Winter 1986.
36 *Volkshandel*, July 1986.
37 *Financial Mail*, 8 July 1986.
38 *Business Day*, 6 February 1987.
39 Ibid, 4 May 1987.
40 *The Citizen*, 28 May 1987.
41 Ibid, 20 May 1987.
42 M Morris & V Padayachee, 'State Reform Policy in South Africa', paper to Conference of the Canadian Association of African Studies, Queen's University, 11-14 May 1988, 19.
43 Bernstein & Godsell, 'The Incrementalists', 307.
44 *The Star*, 10 November 1987.
45 G Lewis, 'Moving a Rock: Business and change in South Africa', *South Africa International*, XX, 2, October 1989, 86.
46 See interview with Waddell, *Leadership South Africa*, 6, 1, 1987.
47 Quoted in *The Star*, 14 September 1987.
48 See the analysis in G Ruitgers & D Nidrie, 'Curbing Union Power', *Work in Progress*, 57, December 1988.
49 Zac de Beer, interview in *Leadership South Africa*, 7, 3, 1988.
50 SAIRR, *Race Relations Survey, 1987/8* (Johannesburg, 1988), 386.
51 *Leadership South Africa*, 7, 3, 1988.
52 See Robert Reich's analysis of how American corporations moulded themselves on military practices after WWII: *The Work of Nations* (Alfred Knopf, New York, 1991), 51.

53 *Weekly Mail*, 12 February 1988.
54 SAIRR, *Race Relations Survey, 1987/88*, 385-6.
55 *Indicator South Africa*, March 1989.
56 'Another Man's Shoes', *Leadership South Africa*, 5, 6, 1986.
57 *Weekly Mail*, 15 April 1986.
58 *The Star*, 15 September 1987.
59 Interview with J G van der Horst, *Leadership South Africa*, 5, 6, 1986.
60 See J A Lombard, 'South Africa Looks Inward for Economic Growth', *Business Day*, 9 July 1986.
61 C Sunter, *South Africa and the World in the 1990s* (Human & Rosseau/Tafelberg, Cape Town, 1987).
62 Len Abrahamse, *Leadership South Africa*, 6, 6, 1987.
63 See editorials in the following 1988 issues: 1, 8, 22 January; 26 February; 4, 11 March; 8, 15 April.
64 G Borkman, 'Whiter Big Business?', *African Communist*, 117, 2nd quarter, 1989, 57.

Notes to Chapter 20

1 Professor J Boshoff, 'Veertig Verlore Jare', *Die Suid-Afrikaan*, 18, December-January 1988/89, quoted at length above.
2 W J de Klerk, 'Word die Afrikaners nou Liberaliste', ibid, 19, February 1989, 30.
3 See P de Vos, 'Protes op Afrikaanse Kampusse', ibid, 22, August/September 1989.
4 See, *inter alia*, the songs 'Hillbrow' and 'Donker Donker Land' on the *Eet Kreef!* album by Johannes Kerkorrel en die Gereformeerde Blues Band (Shifty Music, 1989), or André Letoit's lyrical (if homophobic) 'Sweet Paradise-blues', in *Die Bar op de Aar: Ballades, Blues en Bevliegings* (Tafelberg, Cape Town, 1988).
5 From the albumn *Eet Kreef!* (words: Daggadirk-Uys, Johannes K, André Letoit; music: Johannes K).
6 Quoted in De Vos, 'Nuwe lied van jong Suid Afrika'.
7 Singer Jennifer Ferguson, quoted ibid.
8 A Brink & A Coetzee, *A Land Apart: A contemporary South African reader* (Penguin, Harmondsworth, 1987), 13.
9 Alexander Strachan, *'n Wêreld sonder grense.*
10 See, respectively, H Koornhof, 'Works of friction: Current South African war literature', in Cock & Nathan *War and Society*, and R Gordon, 'Marginalia on *Grensliteratuur*: Or how/why is terror culturally constructed in Northern Namibia', *Critical Arts*, 5, 3, 1991.
11 W Breytenbach, *Leadership South Africa*, 6, 2, 1987.
12 *Beeld*, 9 March 1987.
13 W J de Klerk, 'Behind Closed Doors', *Leadership South Africa*, 6, 6, 1987.
14 SAIRR, *Race Relations Survey 1987/8*, 814.

15   De Klerk, 'Behind Closed Doors'.
16   'Word die Afrikaners nou Liberaliste', 30.
17   *Sunday Times*, 7 June 1987.
18   H Giliomee, 'Afrikaner Politics 1977-87: From Afrikaner nationalist rule to central state hegemony', in J Brewer (ed.), *Can South Africa Survive? Five minutes to midnight* (Macmillan, London, 1989), 8.
19   See the account based on Cuban military archives in E Dosman, 'Understanding the Cuban Role in Angola, 1975-1990', paper to the *Workshop on Angola*, Canadian Research Consortium on Southern Africa, Queen's University, 2 October 1993. This and the following paragraph are based on this unique source.
20   Swilling & Phillips, 'The Powers of the Thunderbird', 65.
21   23 April 1988.
22   *Weekly Mail*, 12 August 1988.
23   Quoted in *Die Demokraat/The Democrat*, June 1989.
24   See the address to the Annual Conference of the Canadian Association of African Studies by the director of the African Studies Institute of the USSR Academy of Sciences, Carleton University, May 1989.
25   *The Star*, 19 September 1988.
26   Botha, quoted in *BBC Morning Report*, 16 November 1988, and Swilling & Phillips, 'The Powers of the Thunderbird', 61.

Notes to Chapter 21

1   W J de Klerk, *F W de Klerk: The man in his time* (Jonathan Ball Publishers, Johannesburg, 1991), 18.
2   H Giliomee, 'Oktober Verkiesing: Nuwe Gesig van die Nasionale Party', *Die Suid-Afrikaan*, 17, October/November 1988, 25.
3   *Sunday Star*, 13 November 1988, and Swilling & Phillips, 'Powers of the Thunderbird', 60.
4   A Ries & E Dommisse, *Leierstryd: Die dramas rondom die uittrede van Pres. PW Botha* (Tafelberg, Cape Town, 1990), 9.
5   H Giliomee, 'Afrikaner Politics 1977-87', 9.
6   Interview, *Leadership South Africa*, 6, 6, 1987.
7   L Abrahamse, 'Presidential Address to 28th Congress of the South Africa Foundation', *South Africa International*, XVIII, 4, April 1988.
8   *Financial Mail*, 10 February 1989.
9   Abrahamse, 'Presidential Address to 29th Convention of Members of the South Africa Foundation', *South Africa International*, XIX, 4, April 1989.
10   DMWW, 'Die Reisies is aan die gang', 8.
11   *Weekly Mail*, 12 August 1988.
12   Nel, 'Group Therapy'.
13   *The Star*, 7 August 1988.
14   Ibid, 26 November 1988.
15   Quoted in *Sunday Tribune*, 20 November 1988.

16 *Weekly Mail*, 14 April 1989.
17 De Klerk, *FW de Klerk*, 104.
18 Ibid, 102-4.
19 L Naudé (pseud.), *Dr A Hertzog, Die Nasionale Party en die Mynwerkers* (Nasionale Raad van Trustees, Pretoria, 1969).
20 Bothma and Botha, quoted in Ries & Dommisse, *Leierstryd*, 91-2. Unless otherwise noted, all quotations in the following paragraphs are taken from chap. 5 of this book.
21 *Financial Mail*, 10 February 1989.
22 Ries & Dommisse, *Leierstryd*, 97.
23 See Die Man Wat Weet (pseud.), 'Die Groot Krokodil vergeet sy lesse', *Die Suid-Afrikaan*, 20, April 1989.
24 *Weekly Mail*, 10 March 1989.
25 *The Citizen*, 6 March 1989.
26 *Die Burger*, 14 March 1989.
27 Statement, *Cape Times*, 15 August 1989.
28 Schoeman, *Vorster se 1000 Dae*, 244.

Notes to Chapter 22

1   *Rapport*, 7 March 1982.
2   *New York Times*, 3 February 1989.
3   *Weekly Mail*, 3 March 1989.
4   Rhoodie, *PW Botha*, 283-4, and *Weekly Mail*, 12 May 1989.
5   H Giliomee, *Cape Times*, 22 June 1989.
6   *Weekly Mail*, 2 March 1990.
7   *Leadership South Africa*, 8, 3, May 1989.
8   See statement of the director of the Foreign Ministry's Department of African Countries, *New York Times*, 16 March 1989.
9   See chaps 2-3 of the book by his brother Willem, *FW de Klerk*.
10 S J Terreblanche, 'FW de Klerk verspeel sy kans om ware staatsman te word', *Vrye Weekblad*, February 1994.
11 R Taylor, 'Between Apartheid and Democracy: The South African election of 1989', in G Moss & I Obery (eds), *South African Review 5* (Ravan Press, Johannesburg, 1989), 58.
12 Giliomee, 'Afrikaner Politics', 9.
13 *Weekly Mail*, 12 May 1989.
14 See Afrikaner Broederbond, 'Basic Constitutional Conditions for the Survival of the Afrikaner', mimeo (transl.), n.d. (June 1989).
15 SAIRR, *Race Relations Survey, 1988/9*, xxv.
16 The following paragraphs draw on Taylor, 'Between Apartheid and Democracy', 61-4.
17 *New York Times*, 7 September 1989.
18 8 September 1989.

19   Interview, SATV, 31 December 1990.
20   De Klerk, *FW de Klerk*, 25.
21   Quoted in C Louw, 'Die SAP en die Pyn van Oorgang', *Die Suid-Afrikaan*, 24, December 1989, 19.
22   F W de Klerk, cited in W J de Klerk, *FW de Klerk*.
23   Louw, 'Die SAP en die Pyn van Oorgang'.
24   *Paratus*, November 1982.
25   See, eg, *Rapport*, 3 December 1989.
26   Ibid.
27   *Cape Times,* 12 February 1990.
28   5 February 1992.
29   De Klerk, *FW de Klerk*.
30   Broederbond, 'Basic Constitutional Conditions'.
31   Interview with the then National Party spokesman on Defence, Dr Boy Geldenhuys MP, April 1991.
32   Willie Breytenbach, 'South Africa: Towards 1994', mimeo, October 1994.
33   See, eg, Willem de Klerk, 'Word die Afrikaners nou liberaliste'.
34   André du Toit, Editorial, *Die Suid-Afrikaan*, August/September 1990.
35   Cited in *Africa Confidential*, 32, 9, 3 May 1991.
36   See G Maré, 'Inkathagate Revisited', *Southern African Report*, 7, 2, November 1991.
37   See D Nidrie, 'Apartheid's not dead, it just smells funny', *Work in Progress*, 72, February 1991.
38   Quoted in *Die Suid-Afrikaan*, June/July 1990.
39   *Cape Times*, 2 February 1991.
40   Minister of Constitutional Development, Gerrit Viljoen, quoted in the *New York Times*, 7 February 1991.
41   See *Vrye Weekblad*, 17 May 1991.
42   *Africa Confidential*, 9, 3 May 1991.
43   'Frontline', broadcast on station WGBH, Boston, 3 March 1993. Hereafter 'Frontline'.
44   Ibid.
45   See Terreblanche, 'F W de Klerk Verspeel sy kans ...'.
46   'Frontline'.
47   Sampie Terreblanche, interviewed ibid.
48   'Frontline'.
49   Ibid.
50   Ibid.
51   Terreblanche, 'F W de Klerk Verspeel sy kans ...'.
52   See, *inter alia*, S Terreblanche and S Friedman (eds), *The Long Journey: South Africa's quest for a negotiated settlement* (Ravan Press, Johannesburg, 1993).
53   Personal communication from a senior member of the IEC.

Notes to Theoretical Appendix

1   J-F Roux, E Keenes & G Légaré, 'Le néo-réalisme ou la reformulation du paradigme hégémonique', *Études internationales*, XIX, 1, mars 1988, 60.

2   'The Integrative Revolution: Primordial politics and civil politics in the new state', in C Geertz (ed.), *Old Societies and New States: The quest for modernity in Asia and Africa* (Free Press of Glencoe, New York, 1963), 105. My emphasis.

3   H Adam & H Giliomee, *Ethnic Power Mobilized: Can South Africa change?* (Yale University Press, New Haven, 1979).

4   See H Giliomee, 'A Question of Survival: The Afrikaner case', paper to the Fall Workshop of the Southern Africa Research Programme, Yale University, New Haven, 23 October 1992.

5   See ibid and Giliomee's '*Broedertwis*: Intra-Afrikaner conflicts in the transition from apartheid', *African Affairs*, 91, July 1992.

6   J de St Jorre, *A House Divided: South Africa's uncertain future* (Carnegie Endowment for International Peace, New York, 1977), 4.

7   A Sparks, *The Mind of South Africa* (Alfred Knopf, New York, 1990).

8   D O'Meara, 'Introduction', *Volkskapitalisme*.

9   'Pourquoi pas l'Afrique du Sud', *Les Temps Modernes*, 479-81, June-August 1986, 29.

10 The so-called O'Dowd thesis, elaborated in 1964 and based on Walt Rostow's much-ridiculed *Stages of Economic Growth*. Its author still clung to this notion in the mid-1970s. See M C O'Dowd, 'South Africa in the Light of the Stages of Economic Growth', in A Leftwich (ed.), *Economic Growth and Political Change* (St Martin's Press, New York, 1974).

11 For a critical overview by one of South Africa's leading marxist scholars, see H Wolpe, 'Towards an Analysis of the South African State', *International Journal of the Sociology of Law*, 8, 4, November 1980. These ideas are elaborated in his *Class, Race and the Apartheid State* (UNESCO, Paris, 1987).

12 For an overview, see Bozzoli & Delius, 'Radical History', 25-34.

13 See, eg, M Morris, 'Social Historians and the Transition to Capitalism in the South African Countryside', *Africa Perspective*, 5-6, 1978, and T Keegan, 'Mike Morris and the Social Historians', ibid, 7-8, 1989.

14 A Joxe, *Le rempart social* (Éditions Galilée, Paris, 1979), 42. Original emphasis.

15 This first came to the fore in G Moss, 'Total Strategy', *Work in Progress*, 11, 1980; D O'Meara, 'Muldergate and the Politics of Afrikaner Nationalism', *Work in Progress*, 22, 1982; D Geldenhuys & H Kotze, 'Aspects of Decision-Making in South Africa', *South African Journal of Political Science*, 10, 1, 1983; and K Grundy, 'The Rise of the South African Security Establishment', South African Institute of International Affairs, Johannesburg, 1983. It was later taken up in, *inter alia*, J Cock & L Nathan (eds), *War and Society: The militarisation of South Africa* (David

Philip, Cape Town, 1989); R Davies & D O'Meara, 'The State of Analysis of the Southern African Region: Issues raised by South African strategy', *Review of African Political Economy*, 29, 1983 and their 'Total Strategy in Southern Africa: An analysis of Southern African regional policy', *Journal of Southern African Studies*, 11, 2, 1985; R Davies, D O'Meara & S Dlamini, *The Struggle for South Africa: A guide to movements, organisations & institutions* (Zed Books, London, 1984); P H Frankel, *Pretoria's Praetorians* (Cambridge University Press, Cambridge, 1984); A Santos, *Afrique du Sud: une stratégie dans l'impasse* (École des hautes études en sciences sociales, Cahiers d'études stratégiques, Paris, n.d. [1988?]); M Mitchell & D Russell, 'Militarisation and the South African State', in C Creighton & M Shaw (eds), *The Sociology of War and Peace* (Macmillan, London, 1987); I Sarakinsky, 'State, Strategy and Transition in South Africa', mimeo, August 1988; A Seegers, 'The Government's perception and handling of South Africa's security needs', in D J van Vuuren *et al.* (eds.), *South Africa: The challenge of reform* (Owen Burgess Publishers, Pinetown (SA), 1988); 'Institutionalising a Cultural Style of Management? Afrikaners, the National Security Management System and state power', paper to the Conference of the Association of Sociologists of South Africa, University of the Witwatersrand, 2-5 July 1989; 'The South African Security Establishment: Theoretical and comparative impressions', in M Swilling (ed.), *Views of the South African State* (HSRC Publishers, Pretoria, 1990) and 'South Africa's National Security Management System', *Journal of Modern African Studies*, 29, 2, 1991; J Selfe, 'South Africa's National Security Management System', in Cock & Nathan, *War and Society*; M Swilling, 'The Politics of Negotiation', *Work in Progress*, October/November 1987, and 'Introduction to the Politics of Stalemate', in P Frankel, N Pines & M Swilling (eds), *State, Resistance and Change in South Africa* (Southern Books, Johannesburg, 1988); and M Swilling & M Phillips, 'The Politics of State Power in the 1980s', mimeo, Centre for Policy Studies, University of the Witwatersrand, 1988; 'Reform, Security and White Power: Rethinking state strategies in the 1980s', paper to the Annual Conference of the Association of Sociology of South Africa, University of Durban-Westville, July 1988; 'The Emergency State: Its structure, power and limits', in G Moss & I Obery (eds), *South African Review 5* (Ravan Press, Johannesburg, 1989); 'The Powers of the Thunderbird: Decision-making structures and policy strategies in the South African state', in Centre for Policy Studies, *Policy Perspectives 1989: South Africa at the end of the Eighties* (Johannesburg, 1989).

16   For an aggressive restatement of this liberal notion, and the idea that policy differences within the ruling National Party did not really 'matter', see the book by the director of the South African Institute of Race Relations, J Kane-Berman, *Soweto: Black revolt, white reaction* (Ravan Press, Johannesburg, 1978), chap. 12.

17 T Hentsch, D Holly & P-Y Soucy, 'Introduction: Les fondements marxistes d'une analyse de la société mondiale', in T Hentsch, D Holly & P-Y Soucy (eds), *Le système mondial: Rapports internationaux et relations internationales* (Nouvelle Optique, Montréal, 1983), 38, 40, emphasis in original.

18 See, eg, M Williams (pseud.), *South Africa: Crisis of world capitalism and the apartheid economy* (Winstanley Publications, London, 1977).

19 N Nattrass, 'Profitability: The soft underbelly of South African regulation/SSA analysis', *Review of Radical Political Economy*, 24, 1, 1992, 33-4. For the founding regulationist texts, see: M Aglietta, *Regulation et crise du capitalisme* (Calmann-Lévy, Paris, 1979), and various works of A Lipietz, *inter alia, L'accumulation intensive* (Maspero, Paris, 1979); 'Towards Global Fordism', *New Left Review*, 132, 1982; *Mirages et miracles: Problèmes de l'industrialisation dans le tiers monde* (La Découverte Paris, 1985); and 'New Tendencies in the International Division of Labour: Regimes of accumulation and modes of regulation', in A Scott & M Stoper (eds), *Production, Work, Territory* (Allen & Unwin, London, 1986).

20 P Beaudet, 'Afrique du Sud, crises et transitions' (PhD dissertation, Université du Québec à Montréal, 1990), 92-3.

21 Ibid, 106. My emphasis. For a useful discussion of these key regulationist concepts, see Gelb, 'The South African Crisis?' See also, *inter alia*: 'Introduction' to S Gelb (ed.), *South Africa's Economic Crisis* (David Phillip/Zed Books, Cape Town/London, 1992); M Morris, 'State, Capital and Growth: The political economy of the national question', ibid; and M Morris & V Padayachee, 'State Reform Policy in South Africa', *Transformation*, 7, 1988.

22 Morris, 'State, Capital and Growth'.

23 See the 'Conclusion' to Beaudet, 'Afrique du Sud'.

24 Nattross, 'Profitability', 33.

25 Cf. Beaudet, 'Afrique du Sud'.

26 For the regulationists, 'The processes of accumulation determines the dynamic of the wider whole,' Y Boyer, *La théorie de la régulation: Une analyse critique* (Éditions La Découverte, Paris, 1986), 111. For varying critiques of the theoretical and analytical shortcomings of regulation theory, see, *inter alia*, A Amdsden, 'Third World Industrialisataion: "Global Fordism" or a new model', *New Left Review*, 182, July/August 1990; S Clarke, 'Overaccumulation, Class Struggle and the Regulation Approach', *Capital & Class*, 36, Winter 1988; and J Holloway, 'The Great Bear, post-Fordism and Class Struggle: A comment on Bonefield and Jessop', *Capital & Class*, 36, Winter 1988. Nattrass, 'Profitability', questions the applicability of regulation theory to South Africa.

27 Morris, 'State, Capital and Growth'.

28 Again, see Beaudet, 'Afrique du Sud'.

29 Morris, 'State, Capital and Growth', 34. My emphasis.

30 W James, 'Materialist History, Materialist Theory: A response to Charles van Onselen', *Social Dynamics*, 9, 1, 1983 (my emphasis).

31 J Hyslop, 'Polar Night: Social theory and the crisis of apartheid', in G Moss & I Obery (eds), *South African Review 6: From 'Red Friday' to Codesa* (Ravan Press, Johannesburg, 1992), 177.

32 Ivor Sarakinsky argues forcefully against 'the belief that class interests, class struggle and accumulation are the main factors that have pressured the State to act in the way that it has/does' – 'The Impulse to Reform: The South African state from Vorster to Botha' (unpublished paper presented to the Department of Political Studies, Rand Afrikaans University, 4 September 1990), 1.

33 Taking issue with the idea of an apartheid blueprint, Deborah Posel explores the evolution of apartheid policy as 'having been forged through a series of struggles within and beyond the state, which forced the architects of state policy to adapt and revise many of their original strategies' – *The Making of Apartheid: Conflict and compromise* (Clarendon Press, Oxford, 1991), 5. Posel's later work directly poses the problem of how to open the box of state politics, 'Lifting the Lid on the South African State: Some historiographical reflections', paper to the Canadian Research Consortium on Southern Africa, McGill University, 25 November 1994. Steven Friedman disputes the notion, widely prevalent in the late 1980s, that government policy was animated by a coherent strategy – *Reform Revisited* (South African Institute of Race Relations, Johannesburg, 1988).

34 Eg, M Mitchell & D Russell, 'Political Impasse in South Africa: State capacities and crisis management', in J Brewer (ed.), *Can South Africa Survive? Five minutes to midnight* (Macmillan, London, 1989). John Lazar has examined the internal politicking within and between the various components of the Afrikaner nationalist alliance in the 1950s – 'Conformity and Conflict: Afrikaner nationalist politics in South Africa 1948-1961' (DPhil dissertation, Oxford University, 1987). Hyslop has not only sought to grapple with the nature and possibilities of the politics of negotiation, but has gone some way in trying to theorise his approach, 'Polar Night' and 'Introduction: Section 1 – The state and politics', in G Moss & I Obery (eds), *South African Review 5* (Ravan Press, Johannesburg, 1989).

35 Sarakinsky, 'The Impulse', 1, 2, and C Charney, 'From Resistance to Reconstruction: Towards a new research agenda on South African politics', *Journal of South African Studies*, 16, 4, December 1990, esp. 764.

36 Most clearly exemplified, *inter alia*, in Lipton, *Capitalism and Apartheid,* and L Schlemmer, 'South Africa's National Party Government', in P Berger & R Godsell (eds), *A Future South Africa: Visions, strategies and realities* (Westview, Boulder, 1988).

37 See, *inter alia*, T Skocpol, *States and Social Revolutions: A comparative analysis of France, Russia and China* (Cambridge University Press,

Cambridge, London & New York, 1979); 'Political Responses to Capitalist Crisis: Neo-marxist theories of the New Deal', *Politics and Society*, 10, 2, 1980; and 'Bringing the State Back In: Strategies of analysis in current research', in P B Evans, D Rueschemeyer & T Skocpol (eds), *Bringing the State Back In* (Cambridge University Press, New York, 1987). Other theoretically influential writings include: M Mann, 'Autonomous Power of the State', *Archives européenes de sociologie*, 25, 1984 and *The Sources of Social Power* (Cambridge University Press, Cambridge, 1986); and A Giddens, *The Nation-State and Violence* (University of California Press, Berkeley, 1987).

38   *Metaphors We Live By* (University of Chicago Press, Chicago, 1980), xxx.

39   Skocpol's work is uncritically invoked by Charney, 'From Resistance to Reconstruction' and by Sarakinsky, 'The impulse'. Mitchell & Russell, 'Militarisation', explicitly call for a state-centric analysis, adopting many of Skocpol's categories (and particularly her understanding of state autonomy). While they do add other 'restraints' on state autonomy, their theoretical position strikes me as highly contradictory and these authors end up 'opening the box' of the state by returning to a fairly simplistic notion of its dominance by its repressive apparatuses. In 'Lifting the Lid', Posel makes passing, and positive, reference to Skocpol's notion of autonomy, but her work cannot be considered to fall within Skocpol's paradigm. For an illuminating discussion of the applicability of various state-centric models to international relations theory, see F Keyman, 'Problematising the State in International Relations Theory', in W S Cox and C T Sjolander, *Beyond Positivism: Critical reflections on international relations* (Lynne Rienner, Boulder, 1994).

40   *States and Social Revolutions*, 14.

41   Ibid, 19-24.

42   Ibid, 29.

43   Ibdi, 164, 168.

44   Ibid, 31.

45   See, eg, P Kennedy, *The Rise and Fall of the Great Powers* (Random House, New York, 1987).

46   For an interesting critique of the highly partial nature of the realist reading of European history, see K Kaiser, 'Transnational Politics: Towards a theory of multinational politics', *International Organisation*, XXV, 1971. For a similar critique of the realists' Clausewitzian notion of war, see chap. 1 of John Keegan's, *A History of Warfare* (Hutchinson, London, 1993).

47   See Aron, 'Qu'est-ce qu'une théorie?'

48   Skocpol, *States and Social Revolutions*.

49   Ibid, 30.

50   Ibid.

51   'The Impulse to Reform', 5.

52   'Conceptual Models and the Cuban Missile Crisis', *American Political*

Science Review, LXII, 3, September 1969.

53 Ibid, 690 and also 691-7.

54 Malcolm Bradbury, *Mensonge: Structuralism's hidden hero* (André Deutsch, London, 1987), 1, 5, 21-2.

55 *States and Social Revolutions*, 31.

56 *Racial Segregation and the Origins of Apartheid* (Macmillan, Basingstoke, 1989).

57 *Legitimating the Illegitimate: State, markets and resistance in South Africa* (University of California Press, Berkeley/Los Angeles/London, 1987).

58 'The Language of Domination 1978-1983', in S Marks & S Trapido (eds), *The Politics of Race, Class & Nationalism in Twentieth Century South Africa* (Longman, London, 1987).

59 'Company Lore: South African business and its discourse on apartheid', unpublished MA thesis, Simon Fraser University, 1988.

60 'Writing South African legal history: A prospectus', *Journal of African History*, 30, 2, 1989, 273-4.

61 *Domination, Resistance and Social Change in South Africa: The local effects of global power* (Praeger, Westport [Conn.] & London, 1992), viii.

62 Manicom, 'Ruling Relations', 455, my emphasis. Philip Abrams, 'Notes on the Difficulty of Studying the State', *Journal of Historical Sociology*, 1, 1988.

63 Manicom, 'Ruling Relations', 452, 454, 456 *et passim*. The notion of 'moral regulation' is drawn from P Corrigan & D Sayer, *The Great Arch: English state formation as cultural revolution* (Oxford, 1985).

64 See, eg, Ashforth, *The Politics of Official Disclosure*, 5-6.

65 Ibid.

66 Ibid, 8-9 (my emphasis).

67 Ibid, 3.

68 Ibid, 10.

69 Ibid.

70 Ibid.

71 *Selections from the Prison Notebooks* (Lawrence & Wishart, London, 1971), 197.

72 *Domination, Resistance and Social Change in South Africa* (Praeger, Westport and London, 1992), 16.

73 Ibid, 16-17.

74 Ibid, 21.

75 *Lenin and 'Philosophy' and Other Essays* (New Left Books, London, 1971), 162. This point was noted in one of the key 'transitional' texts of early post-structuralism, E Laclau, *Politics and Ideology in Marxist Theory* (New Left Books, London, 1977).

76 *The Political Nature of a Ruling Class: Capital and ideology in South Africa 1890-1933* (Routledge & Kegal Paul, London, 1981).

77 M Foucault, *Power/Knowledge: Selected Interviews and other writings*,

1972-1977 (edited by C Gordon, Harvester Press, Brighton, 1980).

78 See ibid, 98.

79 Manzo, *Domination, Resistance and Social Change*, 2.

80 Pavlich, 'Company Lore', 2.

81 In the words of Gramscian scholar and theoretician of hegemony in international relations, R W Cox, 'Production and Hegemony: Towards a political economy of world order', in H K Jacobsen and D Sidjanski (eds), *The Emerging International Economic Order: Dynamic processes, constraints and opportunities* (Sage Publications, Beverly Hills, 1982), 38.

82 See P Rabinow (ed.), *The Foucault Reader* (Pantheon Books, New York, 1984), 51-75.

83 Quoted in R Harland, *Superstructuralism: The philosophy of structuralism and post-structuralism* (Methuen, London, 1987), 112.

84 M Foucault, *L'archéologie du savoir* (Éditions Gallimard, Paris, 1969), 64-7. Italics in the original, underlining is my emphasis.

85 On this point, B D Palmer, *The Descent into Discourse: The reification of language and the writing of social history* (Temple University Press, Philadelphia, 1990), 27.

86 Ibid, 3.

87 Ibid, xiv.

88 Ibid, 205.

89 *Power/Knowledge*, 193. Here Foucault is referring to his *Surveiller et punir: Naissance de la prison* (Gallimard, Paris, 1975).

90 'Ruling Relations', 445.

91 'State, Power and Gender: Conflict over the registration of African customary marriage in South Africa c. 1910-1970', *Journal of Historical Sociology* (forthcoming). I would like to thank the author for permission to cite from the pre-publication manuscript. Posel cites two unpublished gender analyses which focus on the state: K Eales, 'Gender Politics in the Administration of African Women in Johannesburg, 1903-1939' (MA dissertation, University of the Witwatersrand, 1991); and A Mager, 'Changing Constructions of Power and Gender in Ciskei, 1945-1968', paper to History Workshop Conference, *Democracy: Popular Precedents, Practice and Culture*, University of the Witwatersrand, July 1994.

92 Posel, 'State, Power and Gender', 1.

93 Manicom, 'Ruling Relations', 463. Posel, 'State, Power and Gender', 1.

94 Ibid, my emphasis.

95 Manicom, 'Ruling Relations', 445. My emphasis.

96 'State, Power and Gender', 1, 20.

97 Ibid, 19. Here Posel cites from Barrington Moore's *Injustice: The social basis of obedience and revolt* (London, 1978), 18.

98 'Ruling Relations', 465. My emphasis.

99 Ibid, 444.

100 Ibid, note 63, 464.

101 Ibid, 444. For a review (by two social historians) of the often antagonistic debates between the 'structuralists' and the social historians, see Bozzoli and Delius, 'Radical History'. For a concise restatement of apartheid made as much by struggles from below as from above, see Bonner *et al.*, 'The Shaping of Apartheid: Contradiction, continuity and the popular struggle', in P Bonner, P Delius and D Posel, *Apartheid's Genesis, 1935-1962* (Ravan Press/Wits University Press, Johannesburg, 1993).

102 Ruling Relations', 444. My emphasis.

103 Ibid, 460.

104 Ibid, 444, 456. My emphasis.

105 Ibid, 464. My emphasis.

106 Ibid, 457. My emphasis.

107 Ibid.

108 Ibid, 463.

109 Ibid, 444, 448.

110 Ibid, 463.

111 For a fascinating, if flawed, analysis of how the changing nature of power resources affects power relations in international politics at the end of the Cold War, see Nye, *Bound to Lead.*

112 'Ruling Relations', 464. My emphasis.

113 *L'archéologie du savoir*, 65.

114 Eg, F van Zyl Slabbert, 'The Basis and Challenges of Transition in South Africa: A review and a preview', in R Lee & L Schlemmer (eds), *Transition to Democracy: Policy perspectives 1991* (Oxford University Press, Cape Town, 1991), and Slabbert, *Quest for Democracy: South Africa in transition* (Penguin, Johannesburg, 1992). See also W van Vuuren, 'Transition Theory – Guidelines for a new politics in South Africa', paper to Research Colloquium organised by the Political Science Association of South Africa, Broederstroom, October 1990.

115 F van Zyl Slabbert, 'The Causes of Transition in South Africa', IDASA *Occasional Papers*, 32, 1990.

116 P du Toit, 'Bargaining in South Africa: Towards a balance of power, or a balance of terror?', *South Africa International*, 17, 1, 1986. See also his *Power Plays: Bargaining tactics for transforming South Africa* (Southern Publishers, Halfway House, 1991).

117 H W van der Merwe & L Liebenberg, 'Transition Politics in South Africa: Pact forming for negotiation and the role of new political leadership styles', paper to the Congress of the Political Science Association of South Africa, Rustenberg, October 1991.

118 S Booysens, 'Transition: The state and relations of political power in South Africa', *Politikon*, 17, 2, 1990, as well as her 'South Africa's Transition by Transaction: Changing power strategies and power resources', paper to the African Studies Association, Seattle, 1992.

119 W Breytenbach, 'South Africa: Towards 1994', mimeo, paper presented to

a seminar in the Political Science Department, McGill University, October 1990.

120 Eg, ibid.

121 See, eg, the work of Susan Booysens cited above and in the Bibliography.

122 See ibid; P du Toit, 'Bargaining in South Africa', and Slabbert, *Quest for Democracy.*

123 'Tentative Conclusions about Uncertain Democracies', in Section IV of G O'Donnell, P Schmitter & L Whitehead (eds), *Transitions from Authoritarian Rule: Prospects for democracy* (Johns Hopkins University Press, Baltimore & London, 1986). Other influential sources include S B Bachrach & E J Lawler, *Bargaining: Power, tactics and outcomes* (Jossey Bass, San Francisco, 1981).

124 'Tentative Conclusions About Uncertain Democracies', 3. My emphasis.

125 Ibid, 6.

126 Ibid, 7.

127 Ibid, 8.

128 Ibid, 9-11.

129 Ibid, 11-14.

130 Ibid, 66.

131 Ibid, 19.

132 Ibid, 37.

133 Ibid, 38.

134 Ibid, 4.

135 Ibid, 5.

136 Ibid, 3.

137 Hentsch *et al.*, 'Perspectives', 38. Original emphasis.

138 'Preface to a Contribution of the Critique of Political Economy', in *Marx & Engels: Selected works* (Lawrence & Wishart, London, 1968), 181.

139 'Les tribulations de l'Ètat', in M Merle, *Les acteurs dans les relations internationales* (Économica, Paris, 1988), 29-31.

140 Marx, *The Eighteenth Brumaire*, 96.

141 For a brief overview, see D Kaplan, 'The South African State: The origins of a racially exclusive democracy', *Insurgent Sociologist*, X, 2, 1979.

142 Bozzoli, *The Political Nature of a Ruling Class,* analyses the elaboration of a South Africanist ideology.

143 For a similar conclusion based on a different argument, see Bob Jessop, *The Capitalist State: Marxist theories and methods* (Martin Robinson, London, 1982), 211-13.

144 For an excellent demonstration of the historical interconnection and interdetermination between social structure, economic performance, the international division of labour, international politics and war, see J Keegan, 'Every Man a Soldier', *The Second World War.*

145 See, eg, C Deblock & B Hamel, 'Bretton Woods et l'ordre économique international d'après-guerre', *Interventions économiques*, 26, Automne

1994/Hiver 1995 (special issue: *De l'ordre des nations à l'ordre des marchés: Bretton Woods, cinquante ans plus tard*), esp. 21-5; and K Vergopoulus, 'Ajustment, instabilité, déséquilibre: Le retour de l'économie nation?', dans *Interventions économiques*, 22/23, Automne 1989/Hiver 1990.

146 *Bound to Lead*, chaps 2-6 *et passim*.

147 'Conceptual Models and the Cuban Missile Crisis'. See also his longer study, *The Essence of Decision: Explaining the Cuban missile crisis* (Little, Brown, Boston, 1971).

148 'Politics and Method in the Kenya Debate', in H Bernstein & B Campbell (eds), *Contradictions of Accumulation in Africa* (Sage Publications, Beverly Hills, 1985), 132. Original emphasis.

149 'Conceptual Models and the Cuban Missile Crisis', 711.

150 Morgenthau, 'Politics Among Nations', chap. 1.

151 'Conceptual Models', esp. 689-91 *et passim*.

152 For a useful discussion, see Kaiser, 'Transnational Politics'.

153 'Politics and Method', 131-2.

154 'Lifting the Lid'.

155 *The Crisis in South Africa* (Monthly Review Press, New York, 1981), 3.

156 Cited in ibid.

Note to Appendix II

1   P W Botha to NP Congress, 15 October 1979. Reproduced in J J Scholtz (comp.), *Fighter and Reformer: Extracts from the speeches of P W Botha* (Bureau for Information, Pretoria, 1989), 37-8.

BIBLIOGRAPHY

1 Official publications and papers

Aanvullende Verslag van die Kommiessie van Ondersoek na Beweerde Onreëlmatighede in die Voormalige Departement van Inligting, published as a special supplement to *Die Transvaler,* 5 June 1979.

Abstract of Agricultural Statistics, 1987, Department of Agricultural Economics and Marketing.

Activities of Transnational Corporations Operating in South Africa and Collaboration of such Corporations with the Racist Minority Regime – Report of the Secretary General, E/C.10/1989/8. United Nations Economic & Social Council, Commission on Transnational Corporations, fifteenth session, New York, 5-14 April 1989.

Board of Trade and Industries: Investigation into Manufacturing Industries in the Union of South Africa, First Interim Report No. 282, Government Printer, Pretoria, 1945.

Commonwealth Group of Eminent Persons, *Mission to South Africa: The Commonwealth Report,* Penguin for the Commonwealth Secretariat, Harmondsworth, 1986.

Handbook of Agricultural Statistics 1904-1950, Department of Agiculture, Pretoria, 1961.

Hofmeyr Papers, File Ce on the Afrikaner Broederbond, Archives of the University of the Witwatersrand.

House of Assembly Debates [Hansard], Government Printer.

Progress Made in the Implementation of the Declaration on Apartheid and its Destructive Consequences in Southern Africa: Second Report of the Secretary General, 4/45/1052, 4 September 1991.

Report of the Commission of Enquiry into Secret Organisations, RP 20/1965, Government Printer, Pretoria.

Report of the Commission of Enquiry into the Export Trade of the Republic of South Africa, RP 69/72, Government Printer, Pretoria

Report of the Commission of Inquiry into Alleged Irregularities in the Former Department of Information, RP 113/1978, Government Printer, Pretoria.

Report of the Commission of Inquiry into Labour Legislation, RP 47/1979, Government Printer, Pretoria.

Report of the Commission of Inquiry into Legislation affecting the Utilisation of Manpower, RP 32/1979, Government Printer, Pretoria.

Report of the Commission on Technical and Vocational Training, UG 65/1948, Government Printer, Pretoria.

Report of the Department of Labour for the Year Ended 31st December 1947, UG 38/1949, Government Printer, Pretoria.

Report of the Department of Labour for the Year Ended 31st December 1948, UG 50/1950, Government Printer, Pretoria.

Report of the Department of Labour for the Year Ended 31st December 1949, UG 50/1951, Government Printer, Pretoria.

Report of the Department of Labour for the Year Ended 31st December 1950, UG 71/1951, Government Printer, Pretoria.

Report of the Department of Labour for the Year Ended 31st December 1951, UG 45/1953, Government Printer, Pretoria.

Report of the Department of Labour for the Year Ended 31st December 1957, UG 29/1958, Government Printer, Pretoria.

Report of the Department of Native Affairs for the Years 1945-7, UG 14/1948, Government Printer, Pretoria.

Report of the Industrial Legislation Commission of Enquiry, UG 62/1951, Government Printer, Pretoria.

Report of the Native Laws Commission of Enquiry, 1946-8, UG 28/1948, Government Printer, Pretoria.

Report on Agricultural and Pastoral Production, UG 70/1960, Department of Agriculture, Government Printer, Pretoria.

Republic of South Africa, 'White Paper on the Rationalisation of the Public Service and Related Institutions', *Journal of Public Administration*, vol. 15, no. 2, 1980.

South Africa: Summary Report on Trade, Lending, Investment and Strategic Minerals, United States General Accounting Office, GAO/NSAID-88-228, 1988.

South African Reserve Bank 1921-1971: A Short Historical Review, Government Printer, Pretoria, 1971.

State of South Africa, 1965: Economic, Financial and Statistical Yearbook for the Republic of South Africa, Da Gama Publications, Johannesburg, 1966.

Statistical Presentation of South Africa's Foreign Liabilities and Assets, 1956-1981, South African Reserve Bank, 1982.

Summary of the Report of the Commission for the Socio-Economic Development of the Bantu Areas within the Union of South Africa, UG 61/1955, Government Printer, Pretoria.

Supplementary Report of the Commission of Inquiry into Alleged Irregularities in the Former Department of Information, RP 63/1979, Government Printer, Pretoria.

'The Role of Transnational Banks in South Africa', Draft Report to the United Nations Economic & Social Council, Commission on Transnational Corporations, 1989.

Third (Interim) Report of the Agricultural and Industrial Requirements Commission, UG 40/1941, Government Printer, Pretoria.

United Nations Declaration on South Africa. Adopted by consensus by the General Assembly at its Sixteenth Special Session on *Apartheid* and its Destructive Consequences in Southern Africa (New York, 12-14 December 1989), United Nations Centre Against Apartheid, Notes and Documents, 1/90, January 1990.

Union Statistics for 50 Years: Jubilee Issue, Bureau of Census & Statistics, Pretoria, 1960.

White Paper on Defence and Armaments Supply, Department of Defence, 1977.

White Paper on Defence and Armaments Supply, Department of Defence, 1982.

2 Newspapers and journals

Argus (The) (Cape Town)
Business Day (Johannesburg)
Cape Times (Cape Town)
Citizen (The) (Johannesburg)
Dagbreek en Sondagnuus (Johannesburg)
Democracy in Action (Cape Town – journal of the Institute for a Democratic Alternative in South Africa)
Die Burger (Cape Town – organ of the Cape NP)
Die Demokraat/The Democrat (organ of the Democratic Party)
Die Kruithoring (Johannesburg) (organ of the Federal Council of the National Party)
Die Oosterlig (Port Elizabeth)
Die Suid-Afrikaan (Cape Town)
Die Transvaler (Johannesburg – organ of the Transvaal NP)
Die Volksblad (Bloemfontein)
Financial Mail (Johannesburg)
Finansies & Tegniek (Johannesburg)
Finance Week (Johannesburg)
Globe & Mail (Toronto)
Indicator South Africa, University of Natal, Durban
Innes Labour Brief (The) (Johannesburg)
Inspan (Organ of the FAK & RDB)
Koers (Potchefstroom)
Leadership South Africa (Johannesburg)
New York Times
Quarterly Bulletin (South African Reserve Bank)
Rand Daily Mail (Johannesburg)
Rapport (Johannesburg)
SA Barometer: fortnightly journal of current affairs statistics (Johannesburg)
South African Observer (Pretoria)
Southern Africa Report (Toronto)
SouthScan (London)
Star (The) (Johannesburg)
Sunday Star (Johannesburg)
Sunday Times (Johannesburg)
Sunday Tribune (Durban)
Veg (Pretoria)
Volkshandel (organ of the Afrikaanse Handelsinstituut – merged with *Finansies & Tegniek* in 1986)
Vrye Weekblad (Newton)
Weekend Argus (Cape Town)
Weekly Mail (Johannesburg – after 1993, *Weekly Mail & Guardian*)
Work in Progress (Johannesburg)

3 Publications and papers of organisations, institutions and groups

Afrikaanse Handelsinstituut, *30 Jaar Gedenkuitgawe*, Pretoria, 1972.

— *30 Jaar Afrikaanse Handelsinstituut: Van Arbeider tot Uitvoerende Beampte binne 3 dekades* (ed. D J Greyling), Koöperatiewe Pers, Pretoria, 1972.

— *Republiek: Gedenkuitgawe Mei 1972*, Pretoria.

— Afrikaner Broederbond, 'Basic Constitutional Conditions for the Survival of the Afrikaner', mimeo (transl.), n.d. (June 1989).

Business International, *Apartheid and Business: an analysis of the rapidly evolving challenge facing companies with investments in South Africa*, 1980.

Catholic Institute for International Relations, *Now everyone is afraid: the changing face of policing in South Africa*, London, 1988.

Centro de Estudos Africanos, 'South Africa: Strategy Conference of Government and Business Leaders', *Southern Africa Dossier*, 4.60(E), Universidade Eduardo Mondlane, Maputo, 1981.

— 'The Far Right Challenge in South Africa', *Southern Africa Dossier*, 6.30(E), Universidade Eduardo Mondlane, Maputo, 1982.

— 'Novas Divisoes politicas no exercito sul africano?' *Dossier Africa Austral*, 16.40(P), Universidade Eduardo Mondlane, Maputo, 1982.

— 'Background on Recent Disinvestments by Foreign Capital from South Africa', *Southern Africa Dossier*, 23.40 (E), Eduardo Mondlane University, Maputo, July 1983.

— 'The 1989/90 South African Budget and the Continuing Crisis of the Apartheid Economy', *Southern Africa Dossier*, 47.200, Universidade Eduardo Mondlane, Maputo, 1989.

Centre d'information et de documentation sur le Mozambique et l'Afrique australe, *Southern Africa Update: an overview of political and social developments*, Montréal, May 1986.

Commonwealth Foreign Ministers' Committee, *South Africa's Relationship with the International Financial System: Report of the Intergovernmental Group*, London, 1988.

Indicator SA Focus, *An Overview of Political Conflict in South Africa: Data Trends 1984-1988*, University of Natal, Durban, March 1989.

Investor Responsibility Research Center, *Patterns of Multinational Corporations' Disinvestment From South Africa: a report for the UN Center on Transnational Corporations*. Boston, May, 1989

Johannesburg Chamber of Commerce, *The South African Economy and Future Policy*, 1949.

— *The Present Economic Position of the Union*, 1949.

Mining Unions Joint Committee, *Minutes*, Institute of Commonwealth Studies, London.

South African Institute of Race Relations, *A Survey of Race Relations in South Africa, 1957-1958*, Johannesburg, n.d. (1958).

— *A Survey of Race Relations in South Africa, 1959-1960*, Johannesburg, 1961.

— *A Survey of Race Relations in South Africa, 1961*, Johannesburg, 1962.

— *A Survey of Race Relations in South Africa, 1969*, Johannesburg, 1970.

— *A Survey of Race Relations in South Africa, 1972*, Johannesburg, 1973.
— *A Survey of Race Relations in South Africa, 1975*, Johannesburg, 1976.
— *A Survey of Race Relations in South Africa, 1976*, Johannesburg, 1977.
— *A Survey of Race Relations in South Africa, 1977*, Johannesburg, 1978.
— *A Survey of Race Relations in South Africa, 1978*, Johannesburg, 1979.
— *A Survey of Race Relations in South Africa, 1979*, Johannesburg, 1980.
— *A Survey of Race Relations in South Africa, 1980*, Johannesburg, 1981.
— *A Survey of Race Relations in South Africa, 1982*, Johannesburg, 1983.
— *A Survey of Race Relations in South Africa, 1985*, Johannesburg, 1986.
— *Race Relations Survey, 1987/8*, Johannesburg, 1988.
— *Race Relations Survey 1988/9*, Johannesburg, 1989.
— *Race Relations Survey 1989/90*, Johannesburg, 1990.
— *Quarterly Countdown*

4 Books, monographs, articles, dissertations and papers

Abrahamse, L, 'Presidential Address to 28th Convention of Members of the South Africa Foundation', *South Africa International*, XVIII, 4, April 1988.
— 'Presidential Address to 29th Convention of Members of the South Africa Foundation', Ibid, XIX, 4, April, 1989.
Adam, H, *Modernising Racial Domination: South Africa's Political Dynamics*, University of California Press, Berkeley, 1971
Adam, H & Giliomee, H, *Ethnic Power Mobilized: Can South Africa Change?*, Yale University Press, New Haven, 1979.
Adam, H & Moodley, K, 'The White Mind, Business and Apartheid', in E J Keller & L A Picard (eds.), *South Africa in Southern Africa: Domestic Change and International Conflict*, Lynne Rienner Publishers, Boulder & London, 1989.
Aglietta, M, *Regulation et crise du capitalisme: L'experience des États-unis*, Calmann-Lévy, Paris, 1976 (English version, New Left Books, London, 1979).
Allison, G, 'Conceptual Models and the Cuban Missile Crisis', *American Political Science Review*, vol. LXIII, no. 3, September 1969.
— *Essence of Decision: Explaining the Cuban Missile Crisis*, Little, Brown & Co, Boston, 1971.
Althusser, L, *Lenin and Philosophy and other Essays*, Pantheon, New York, 1971.
Amsden, A, 'Third World Industrialization: "Global Fordism" or a New Model', *New Left Review*, 182, July/August 1990.
Ashforth, A, *The Politics of Official Discourse in Twentieth-Century South Africa*, Clarendon Press, Oxford, 1990.
Barnard, F, *13 Jaar in die Skadu van Dr H F Verwoerd*, Voortrekkerpers, Johannesburg, 1967.
Bartels, D, 'Post-Structuralism and Empiricism/Posivitism: Siblings?', *Socialist Studies Bulletin*, no 28, April-June 1992.
Basson, J L, *J.G. Strijdom: Sy politieke loopbaan van 1929 tot 1940*, Wonderboom Uitgewers, Pretoria, 1980.

Bibliography

Bayart, J F, *L'État en Afrique: La politique du ventre*, Fayard, Paris, 1989.

Beaud, M, *Histoire du capitalisme, 1500-1980*, Éditions Seuil, Paris, 1981.

Beaudet, P, 'L'or de l'Afrique du Sud: Nuages à l'horizon', CIDMAA, Montréal, November 1988.

— 'Afrique du Sud, crises et transitions', Ph D dissertation, Université du Québec à Montréal, 1990 (a severely shortened version has been published as *Les grandes mutations de l'apartheid*, L'Harmattan, Paris, 1991).

Beaufre, A, *Introduction à la stratégie*, Armand Colin, Paris, 1963 (English edition, Faber & Faber, London, 1963).

— *Stratégie de l'Action*, Armand Colin, Paris, 1966 (English edition, Faber & Faber, 1967).

— *Bâtir l'avenir*, Calmann-Levy, Paris, 1967.

— *Stratégie pour demain: Les problèmes militaires de la guerre moderne*, Librarie Plon, Paris, 1972 (English edition, Crane, Russak & Co, New York, 1974).

— *La guerre révolutionnaire: Les formes nouvelles de la guerre*, Fayard, Paris, 1972.

Berger, P & Godsell B (eds.), *A Future South Africa: Visions, Strategies and Realities*, Westview, Boulder, 1988.

Bergman, L F, 'Technological Change in South African Manufacturing Industry, 1955-1964', *South African Journal of Economics*, vol. 36, no. 1, March 1963.

Berman, B, *Crisis and Control in Colonial Kenya: The Dialectics of Domination*, James Currey, Heinemann Kenya & Ohio University Press, London, Nairobi & Athens (Ohio), 1990.

Bernstein, A & Godsell, B, 'The incrementalists' in Berger & Godsell, *A Future South Africa,* 1988.

Beyers, C F (ed.), *Dictionary of South African Biography*, vol. 4, Human Sciences Research Council/Butterworth, Durban & Pretoria, 1981.

Biko, S, *I Write What I Like*, Harper & Row, San Francisco, 1978.

Block, F, 'The Ruling Class Does Not Rule', *Socialist Revolution*, no. 33, May-June 1977.

— 'Marxist Theories of the State in World Systems Analysis', in B H Kaplan (ed.), *Social Change in the Capitalist World Economy*, Sage, Beverly Hills, 1978.

Bloomberg, C (S Dubow, ed.), *Christian-Nationalism and the Rise of the Afrikaner Broderbond in South Africa*, Macmillan, London, 1990.

Bond, P, *Commanding Heights & Community Control: New Economics for a New South Africa*, Ravan Press, Johannesburg, 1991.

Bonmoni, G, 'La théorie gramscienne de L'État', *Les temps modernes*, no. 343, février 1975.

Bonner, P, Delius, P & Posel, D, 'The Shaping of Apartheid: Contradiction, Continuity and the Popular Struggle', in P Bonner, P Delius & D Posel (eds.), *Apartheid's Genesis, 1935-1962*, Ravan Press/Wits University Press, Johannesburg, 1993.

Booysen, S, 'Transition: The state and relations of political power in South Africa', *Politikon*, vol. 17, no. 2, 1990.

— 'Political power and the struggle for control over the state and transition in South Africa', Paper to the Congress of the Political Science Association of South Africa, October 1991.

Bibliography

— 'Facing electoral and transition challenges: Policies and strategies of the National Party', *CASE perspectives on transition politics in South Africa: Party, power and prospects*, CASE, Johannesburg, 1991.

— 'South Africa's Transitions: Changing Power Strategies and Power Positions', paper to the 35th Annual Meeting of the [U S] African Studies Association, Seattle, 1992.

Borkman, G, 'Whither Big Business', *African Communist*, no. 117, 2nd Quarter 1989.

Boshoff, J, 'Veertig Verlore Jare', *Die Suid-Afrikaan*, no. 18, Dec.-Jan. 1988/9.

Botha, J, *Verwoerd is Dead*, Books of Africa, Cape Town, 1967.

Botha, W A, 'Die Parlemetêre Verkeising van 1948: 'n ontleding van die faktore wat die verkeising beinvloed het', unpublished M A thesis, University of Pretoria, 1967.

Boyer, Y, *La théorie de la régulation: Une analyse critique*, Éditions La Découverte, Paris, 1986.

Bozzoli, B, 'English-speaking Ideology and Advanced Capitalism in post-Sharpeville South Africa', paper to the Oxford Workshop on Southern Africa, Institute of Commonwealth Studies, Oxford University, 27-29 September 1974.

— *The Political Nature of a Ruling Class: Capital and Ideology in South Africa 1890-1933*, Routledge & Kegan Paul, London, 1981.

— 'Marxism, Feminism and South African Studies', *Journal of Southern African Studies*, vol 9, no. 2, April 1983.

Bozzoli, B & Delius, P, 'Radical History and South African Society', *Radical History Review*, no. 46/7, 1990.

Brand, S S & Tomlinson, F R, 'Die Plek van Landbou in die Suid-Afrikaanse Volkshuishouding', *South African Journal of Economics*, vol. 34, no. 1, 1966.

Brewer, J (ed.), *Can South Africa Survive? Five Minutes to Midnight*, Macmillan, London, 1989.

Breytenbach, B, *The True Confessions of an Albino Terrorist*, Farrar Straus Giroux, New York, 1983.

Breytenbach, W, 'The Cauldron', *Leadership South Africa*, vol. 6, no. 2, 1987.

— 'South Africa: Towards 1994', mimeo, 1990.

Brickhill, J, *Sowing the Whirlwind*, International Defence & Aid Fund, London, 1977.

Brink, A, *Oom Kootjie Emmer*, Ad Donker, Johannesburg, 1973.

Brink, A & Coetzee, A, *A Land Apart: A Contemporary South African Reader*, Penguin, Harmondsworth, 1987.

Brits, J P, 'Havenga, Nicolaas, Christiaan', in C J Beyers (ed.), *Dictionary of South African Biography*, vol. 4, Butterworth & Co, Durban, 1981.

Browne, G W G, 'Die Fisikale Politiek', in J A Lombard (ed.), *Die Ekonomiese Politiek van Suid Afrika*, HAUM, Cape Town, 1967.

Bunting, B, *The Rise of the South African Reich*, Penguin, Harmondsworth, 1969.

Cachalia, F, 'The State, Crisis and Restructuring', *Africa Perspective*, no. 23, 1983.

Callinicos, A & Rogers, J, *Southern Africa after Soweto*, Pluto Press, London, 1977.

Carter, G M, *The Politics of Inequality: South Africa Since 1948*, Thames & Hudson, London, 1958.

Cawthra, G, *Brutal Force: The apartheid war machine*, International Defence & Aid Fund for Southern Africa, London, 1986.

Chanock, M, 'Writing South African legal history: A prospectus', *Journal of African History*, vol. 30, no. 2, 1989.

Charnay, J-P, *Essai général de stratégie*, Éditions Champ libre, Paris, 1973.

Charney, C, 'Towards Rapture or Stasis? An Analysis of the 1981 South African General Election', *African Affairs*, no. 81, 1982.

— 'The wooing of big business', *Management*, October 1982.

— 'Class Conflict and the National Party Split', *Journal of Southern African Studies*, vol. 10, no. 2, April 1984.

— From Resistance to Reconstruction: Towards a New Research Agenda on South African Politics', *Journal of Southern African Studies*, vol. 16, no. 4, December 1990.

Cillié, P J, *Tydgenote*, Tafelberg, Cape Town, 1980.

— *Baanbrekers vir Vryheid: Gedagtes oor Afrikaners se Rol in Suid-Afrika* (Selected and edited by P A Joubert), Tafelberg, Cape Town, 1990.

Clarke, S, *Financial Aspects of Economic Sanctions on South Africa*, IUEF, Geneva, 1980.

— 'Overaccumulation, class struggle and the regulation approach', *Capital & Class*, no. 36, Winter 1988.

Cloete, S, 'Characterising policy change in South Africa, 1980-1990: The games elites play', in F Cloete, L Schlemmer & D van Vuuren (eds.), *Policy Options for a New South Africa*, Human Sciences Research Council, Pretoria, 1991.

Cobbet, W, Glaser, D, Hindson, D & Swilling, M, 'A Critical Analysis of the South African State's Reform Strategies in the 1980s', in P Frankel, N Pines & M Swilling (eds.), *State, Resistance and Change in South Africa*, Southern Books, Johannesburg, 1988.

Cock, J & Nathan, L (eds.), *War and Society: The Militarisation of South Africa*, David Philip, Cape Town, 1989.

Coetzee, J, 'Revolusionere Oorlog en Teeninsurgensie', in M Hough, *Nasionale Veiligheid en Strategie met Spesifieke Verwysing na die RSA*, ISSUP, Pretoria, 1981.

Coetzee, J H, *Verarming en Oorheesing*, Nasionale Pers, Bloemfontein, 1942.

Cooper, C, 'The militarisation of the bantustans: Control and contradictions' in Cock & Nathan, *War and Society,* 1989.

Cooper, D, 'Ownership and Control of Agriculture in South Africa', in J Suckling & L White (eds.), *After Apartheid: Renewal of the South African Economy*, James Currey, London, 1988.

Copans, J, 'Pourquoi pas l'Afrique du Sud?', *Les Temps Modernes*, nos. 479-81, June-August 1986.

Cope, J, *The Adversary Within: Dissident writers in Afrikaans*, Humanities Press, New Jersey, 1982.

Cox, R W, 'Production and Hegemony: Towards a Political Economy of World Order', in H K Jacobsen & D Sidjanski (eds.), *The Emerging International Economic Order: Dynamic Processes, Constraints and Opportunities*, Sage Publications, Beverly Hills, 1982.

— 'Gramsci, Hegemony and International Relations: An Essay in Method', *Millenium*, vol. 12, no. 2, 1983.

— *Production, Power and World Order: Social Forces in the Making of History,*

Columbia University Press, New York, 1986.
— 'Dialectique de l'économie-monde en fin de siècle', *Études internationales*, vol. 21, no. 4, décembre 1990.
Crocker, C, 'Scope Paper', Chester Crocker to Secretary of State Alexander Haig, TransAfrica Forum, Washington, 1981.
da Silva, E, 'Mozambican Socialism and the Nkomati Accord', *Work in Progress*, no. 32, 1984.
Davenport, T R H, *South Africa: A Modern History*, University of Toronto Press, Toronto & Buffalo, 1989 (3rd edition).
Davies, R H, 'Capital Restructuring and the Modification of the Racial Division of Labour in South Africa', *Journal of Southern African Studies*, vol. 5, no. 2, 1979.
Davies, R H & O'Meara, D, 'The State of Analysis of the Southern African Region: Issues Raised by South African Strategy', *Review of African Political Economy*, no. 29, 1983.
— 'Total Strategy in Southern Africa: An Analysis of South African Regional Policy', *Journal of Southern African Studies*, vol. 11, no. 2, 1985.
Davies, R H, O'Meara, D & Dlamini, S, *The Struggle for South Africa: A guide to movements, organisations & institutions*, 2 vols., Zed Books, London, 1984.
Deame, S, 'Introduction' in T Eagleton, F Jameson & E Said, *Nationalism, Colonialism and Literature*, University of Minnesota Press, Minneapolis, 1990.
Deblock, C et Hamel, B, 'Bretton Woods et l'ordre économique international d'après-guerre', *Interventions économiques*, no. 26, automne 1994/hiver 1995 (special issue: *De l'ordre des nations à l'ordre des marchés: Bretton Woods, cinquante ans plus tard*).
Degenaar, J,*Voortbestaan in geregtigheid: opstelle oor die politieke rol van die Afrikaner*, Tafelfberg, Cape Town, 1980.
de Klerk, W A, *The Puritans in Africa: The Story of Afrikanerdom*, Rex Collings, London, 1975.
de Klerk, W A, Versfeld, M & Degenaar, J J, *Beweging Uitwaarts*, John Malherbe, Cape Town, 1969.
de Klerk, W J, 'The Concepts "Verkrampt" and "Verlig" ', in N Rhoodie (ed.), *South African Dialogue: Contrasts in South African Thinking on Basic Race Issues*, McGraw Hill, Johannesburg, 1972.
— 'Behind Closed Doors', *Leadership South Africa*, vol. 6, no. 6, 1987.
— 'Word die Afrikaners nou Liberaliste', *Die Suid-Afrikaan*, no. 19, February 1989.
— *F W de Klerk: The man in his time* (transl. H Snijders), Jonathan Ball Publishers, Johannesburg, 1991.
de St Jorre, J A, *House Divided: South Africa's uncertain future*, Carnegie Endowment for International Peace, New York, 1977.
de Villiers, D & J, *Paul Sauer*, Tafelberg, Cape Town, 1977.
— *P W*, Tafelberg, Cape Town, 1984.
de Villiers, R, 'Afrikaner Nationalism', in M Wilson & L M Thompsons (eds), *The Oxford History of South Africa,* Volume II, Clarendon Press, Oxford, 1971.
de Vos, P, 'Nuwe Lied van Jong Suid-Afrika', *Die Suid-Afrikaan*, no. 21, June/July 1989.
— 'Protes op Afrikaanse Kampusse', *Die Suid-Afrikaan*, no. 22, August/September 1989.

Dickie-Clark, H, 'Ideology and Recent Writings on South Africa', *Journal of Asian and African Studies*, vol. XVIII, nos. 1-2, 1983.

Dickman, A, 'Investment – the implications for economic growth and living standards', *Optima*, vol. 27, no. 1, 1977.

Die Man Wat Weet (pseud.), 'Die Resies is aan die Gang', *Die Suid-Afrikaan*, no. 14, April/May, 1988.

— 'Krokodil Vergeet sy Lesse', *Die Suid-Afrikaan*, no. 20, April, 1989.

D'Oliveira, J, *Vorster – the man*, Ernest Stanton Publishers, Johannesburg, 1977.

Dosman, E, 'Understanding the Cuban Role in Angola, 1975-1990', paper to the *Workshop on Angola*, Canadian Research Consortium on Southern Africa, Queens University, 2 October 1993.

du Pisani, J A, *John Vorster en die Verlig/Verkramp Stryd: 'n Studie van die Politieke Verdeeldheid in Afrikanergeledere*, Instituut vir Eietydse Geskiedenis, Universiteit van die Oranje-Vrystaat, Bloemfontein, 1988.

du Plessis, E P, *'n Volk Staan Op: Die Ekonomiese Volkskongres en Daarna*, Human en Rousseau, Cape Town, 1964.

du Plessis, L J, *Letters of a Farmer*, Johannesburg, 1951.

du Toit, A, 'Emerging Strategies for Political Control', in R M Price & C G Rotberg (eds.), *The Apartheid Regime: Political Power and Racial Domination*, Institute of International Studies, Research Series No. 43, University of California, Berkeley, 1980.

— *Die Sondes van die Vaders: 'n poging tot die verkenning van die Afrikaner-intellektueel in die komende legitimeits-krisis van die Afrikaner-nasionalisme en die apartheidsorde*, Rubicon Pers, Cape Town, 1983.

— 'White Politics: a post-election assessment', *Reality*, July 1987.

du Toit, A & Slabbert, F v/Z, 'South Africa as Another Case of Transition from Authoritarian Rule', in IDASA *Occasional Papers,* no 32, 1990.

du Toit, B M, 'Afrikaners, Nationalists and Apartheid', *Journal of Modern African Studies*, vol. VIII, no. 4, December 1970.

du Toit, P 'Bargaining in South Africa: Towards a balance of power, or a balance of terror?', *South Africa International*, vol. 17, no. 1, 1986.

— *Power Plays: Bargaining Tactics for Transforming South Africa* (Southern Publishers, Halfway House, 1991).

du Spies, F J, Theron, E, & Scholtz, J J J, 'Verwoerd, Hendrik Frensch', in C J Beyers (ed.), *Dictionary of South African Biography,* vol. 4, Butterworth & Co. for the HSRC, Durban & Pretoria, 1981.

Dubow, S, *Racial Segregation and the Origins of Apartheid*, Macmillan, Basingstoke, 1989.

— 'Afrikaner Nationalism, apartheid and the conceptualisation of "race" ', mimeo, 1990.

Dvorin, E P, *Racial Separation in South Africa: An Analysis of Apartheid Theory*, University of Chicago Press, 1952.

Eagleton, T, 'Nationalism, Irony and Commitment' in T Eagleton, F Jameson & E Said, *Nationalism, Colonialism and Literature*, University of Minnesota Press, Minneapolis, 1990.

Eiselen, W W M, 'Harmonious Multi-Community Development', *Optima*, vol. 9, no. 1, 1959.

— 'Die Ontwikkeling ven die Bantoe-volkseenhede na Selfstandigheid', in J A Lombard (ed.), *Die Ekonomiese Politiek van Suid-Afrika*, Cape Town, HAUM, 1967.

Esterhuyse, W P, *Afskeid van Apartheid: opstelle oor rassediskriminasie*, Tafelberg, Cape Town, 1979.

— *Die Pad van Hervorming: beskouinge oor die noodsaaklikheid van strukturele hervorming in Suid-Afrika*, Tafelberg, Cape Town, 1982.

— *Anton Rupert: Advocate of Hope*, Tafelberg, Cape Town, 1986.

Evans, I T, 'The Political Economy of a State Apparatus: The Department of Native Affairs in the Transition from Segregation to Apartheid in South Africa', unpublished Ph D dissertation, University of Wisconsin-Madison, 1986.

Evans, P B, Rueschmeyer, D & Skocpol, T, *Bringing the State Back In*, Cambridge University Press, Cambridge, 1987.

Ferreira, N, *The Story of an Afrikaner: Die Rewolusie van die Kinders*, Ravan Press, Johannesburg, 1980.

Finlay, W, 'South Africa: Capitalist Agriculture and the State', unpublished B Soc Sci (Hons) dissertation, University of Cape Town, 1976.

First, R, Steele, J & Gurney, C, *The South African Connection*, Harmondsworth, Penguin, 1973.

Fisher, J, *The Afrikaners*, Cassell, London, 1969.

Foucault, M, *L'archéologie du savoir*, Éditions Gallimard, Paris, 1969.

— *Power/Knowledge: Selected Interviews and other Writings, 1972-1977* (edited by C Gordon), Harvester Press, Brighton, 1980.

Fox-Genovese, E & Genovese, E D, 'The Political Crisis of Social History: Class Struggle as Subject and Object', in idem, *Merchant Capital: Slavery and Property in the Rise and Expansion of Capitalism*, Oxford University Press, Oxford, 1983.

Frankel, B, 'On the Theory of the State: Marxist Theories of the State After Leninism', in A Giddens & D Held (eds.), *Classes, Power and Conflict: Classic and Contemporary Debates*, University of California Press, Berkeley & Los Angeles, 1982.

Frankel, P H, *Pretoria's Praetorians*, Cambridge University Press, Cambridge, 1984.

Frankel P, Pines, N & Swilling, M (eds.), *State, Resistance and Change in South Africa*, Southern Books, Johannesburg, 1988.

Franks, P & Morris, P, 'Urban Black Government and Policy,' *SAIRR Topical Briefing*, South African Institution of Race Relations, Johannesburg, 30 May 1986.

Fransman, M *The South African Manufacturing Sector and Economic Sanctions*, IUEF, Geneva, 1980.

Franzen, D G, 'Die Beheer van Staatskuld', in J A Lombard (ed.), *Die Ekonomiese Politiek van Suid-Afrika*, Cape Town, HAUM, 1967.

Friedman, S, *Reform Revisited*, South African Institute of Race Relations, Johannesburg, 1988.

— 'The Shapers of Things to Come? National Party choices in the South African Transition', *Research Report No. 22*, Centre for Policy Studies, Graduate School of Business Administration, University of the Witwatersrand, February 1992.

— (ed.), *The long journey: South Africa's quest for a negotiated settlement*, Ravan Press, Johannesburg, 1993.

Furlong, P J, *Between Crown and Swastika: The impact of the radical right on the Afrikaner nationalist movement in the Fascist era*, University of the Witwatersrand Press, Johannesburg, 1991.

Gastrow, P, 'Towards a Convergence of Democrats', *Die Suid-Afrikaan*, no. 26, April 1990.

Gastrow, S, *Who's Who in South African Politics*, Ravan Press, Johannesburg, 1985.

Geertz, C, 'The Integrative Revolution: Primordial Politics and Civil Politics in the New States', in C Geertz (ed.), *Old Societies and New States: The Quest for Modernity in Asia and Africa*, Free Press of Glencoe, New York, 1963.

Gelb, S, 'The South African Crisis', *Transformation*, no. 6 1987.

— (ed), *South Africa's Economic Crisis*, David Philip/Zed Books, Cape Town/London, 1992.

Geldenhuys, D, *The Diplomacy of Isolation: South African Foreign Policy Making*, Macmillan, Johannesburg, 1984.

Geldenhuys, D & Kotze H, 'Aspects of Decision-making in South Africa', *The South African Journal of Political Science*, vol. 10, no. 1, 1983.

George, J, *Discourses of Global Politics: A Critical (Re)Introduction to International Relations*, Lynne Rienner, Boulder, 1994.

Geyser, D J, 'Die Arbeidspolitiek', in J A Lombard (ed.), *Die Ekonomiese Politiek van Suid-Afrika*, Cape Town, HAUM, 1967.

Giddens, A, *The Constitution of Society: Outline of the Theory of Structuration*, University of California Press, Berkeley & Los Angeles, 1984.

— *The Nation-State and Violence*, University of California Press, Berkeley, 1987.

Giliomee, H, 'Die Ontwikkeling van Selfkonsepsies by die Afrikaner', in H van der Merwe (ed.), *Identiteit en Verandering: Sewe Opstelle oor die Afrikaner Vandag*, Tafelberg, Cape Town, 1975.

— 'The National Party and the Afrikaner Broederbond', in R M Price & C G Rotberg (eds.), *The Apartheid Regime: Political Power and Racial Domination*, Institute of International Studies, Research Series No. 43, University of California, Berkeley, 1980.

— *The Parting of the Ways*, David Philip, Cape Town, 1983.

— 'Constructing Afrikaner Nationalism', *Journal of Asian and African Studies*, vol. XVIII, nos.1-2, 1983.

— 'Afrikaners and Apartheid', in A du Toit (ed.), *In Gesprek: Opstelle vir Johan Degenaar*, Die Suid-Afrikaan, Stellenbosch, 1986.

— 'Oktober Verkiesing: Nuwe Gesig van die Nasionale Party', *Die Suid-Afrikaan*, no. 17, Oct./Nov. 1988.

— 'The Ideology of Apartheid', in P Hugo (ed.), *South African Perspectives: Essays in Honour of Nic Olivier*, Die Suid-Afrikaan, Cape Town, 1989.

— 'Afrikaner Politics 1977–87: From Afrikaner Nationalist Rule to Central State Hegemony' in J Brewer, *Can South Africa Survive?*, 1989.

— 'Die Afrikaanse Politieke Geskiedskrywing', unpublished paper to conference on

Afrikaanse Geskiedskrywing en Letterkunde, University of the Western Cape, 16-18 October 1991.

— 'Broedertwis: Intra-Afrikaner Conflicts in the Transition from Apartheid', *African Affairs*, no. 91, July 1992.

— 'A Question of Survival: The Afrikaner Case', paper to the Fall Workshop of the Southern Africa Research Program, Yale University, New Haven, October 23, 1992.

— 'The Leader and the Citizenry', in R. Schrire (ed.), *Leadership and the Apartheid State: From Malan to De Klerk*, Oxford University Press, Cape Town, 1994.

Giliomee, H & Schlemmer, L, *From Apartheid to Nation-building*, Oxford University Press, Cape Town, 1989.

Gordon, R, 'Anthropology and Counter-Revolutionary Praxis: The SADF Case', paper to the Annual Conference of the Canadian African Studies Association, Queens University, Kingston, 11-14 May, 1988.

— 'Marginalia on *Grensliteratuur*. Or how/why is terror culturally constructed in Northern Namibia?', *Critical Art*, vol. 5, no. 3, 1991.

Graaff, Sir D V, *Div Looks Back: The memoirs of Sir De Villiers Graaff*, Human & Rousseau, Cape Town, 1993.

Gramsci, A, *Selections from the Prison Notebooks*, Lawrence & Wishart, London, 1971.

Greenberg, S B, *Race and State in Capitalist Development: South Africa in comparative perspective*, Yale University Press, New Haven, 1980.

— 'Ideological Struggles within the South African State', in S Marks & S Trapido (eds.), *The Politics of Race, Class & Nationalism in Twentieth Century South Africa*, Longman, London, 1987.

— *Legitimating the Illegitimate: State, Markets and Resistance in South Africa*, University of California Press, Berkeley/Los Angeles/London, 1987.

Grest, J, 'The Crisis of Local Government in South Africa', in Frankel *et al.*, *State, Resistance and Change,* 1988.

Grobbelaar, J, Bekker S & Evans R, *Vir Volk en Vaderland: A Guide to the White Right*, Indicator SA, August 1989.

Grundlingh, A, 'Sosiale Geskiedenis en Afrikaanse Geskiedskrywing in 'n Veranderende Suid-Afrika: Problematiek en Potensiaal', unpublished paper to conference on *Afrikaanse Geskiedskrywing en Letterkunde*, University of the Western Cape, 16-18 October 1991.

Grundy, K W, 'The Rise of the South African Security Establishment', South African Institute of International Affairs, Johannesburg, 1983.

— *The Militarization of South African Politics*, Indiana University Press, Bloomington, 1986.

Hall, S, 'Moving Right', *Socialist Review*, no. 55, 1981.

Hallet, R, 'The South African Intervention in Angola 1975-76', *African Affairs*, vol. 77, no. 303, July 1978.

Halliday, F, 'State and Society in International Relations: A Second Agenda', *Millenium*, vol. 16, no. 2, 1987.

Hamilton, N, *The Limits of State Autonomy: Post-Revolutionary Mexico*, Princeton University Press, Princeton, 1982.

Hanf, T, Weiland, H & Vierdag, G, *South Africa: The Prospects of Peaceful Change*, Rex Collings, London, 1981.

Haysom, N, *Mabangalala: The Rise of Right-wing Vigilantes in South Africa*, Centre for Applied Legal Studies, University of the Witwatersrand, Johannesburg, 1986.

Heard, K, *General Elections in South Africa. 1943-1970*, Oxford University Press, London, 1974.

Hentsch, T, Holly, D & Soucy, P-Y, 'Perspectives sur le système mondial', *Le système mondial: Rapports internationaux et relations internationales*, Nouvelle Optique, Montréal, 1983.

Hepple, A, *South Africa: A Political and Economic History*, Pall Mall Press, London, 1966.

— *Verwoerd*, Penguin, Harmondsworth, 1976.

Hindson, D, *Pass Controls and the Urban African Proletariat*, Ravan Press, Johannesburg, 1987.

Hindson, D & Morris, M, 'Political Violence and Urban Reconstruction in South Africa', Economic Trends Group Discussion Paper, Development Policy Research Unit, Economic History Department, University of Cape Town, September 1991.

Hirson, B, *Year of Fire, Year of Ash. The Soweto Revolt: Roots of a Revolution?*, Zed Press, London, 1979.

Hollerman, J, 'The Great Purge', in P. Hugo, *South African Perspectives: Essays in Honour of Nic Olivier*, Die Suid-Afrikaan, Cape Town, 1989.

Hollis, M & Smith, S, *Understanding and Explaining International Relations*, Clarendon Press, Oxford, 1991,

Holloway, J, 'The Great Bear, post-Fordism and class struggle: A comment on Bonefeld and Jessop', *Capital and Class*, no. 36, Winter 1988.

Horrel, M, *South Africa's Workers: Their Organisations and Patterns of Employment*, South African Institute of Race Relations, Johannesburg, 1969.

Horwitiz, R, *The Political Economy of South Africa*, Weidenfeld & Nicolson, London 1967.

Houghton, D H, 'Economic Development, 1865-1965', in M Wilson & L M Thompson (eds.), *The Oxford History of South Africa,* Volume II, Clarendon Press, Oxford, 1971.

— *The South African Economy*, OUP, Cape Town, 1976.

Houghton, D H & Dagut, J (eds.), *Source Materials on the South African Economy, Volume 2, 1920-1970*, Oxford University Press, Cape Town, 1973.

Hugo, P, *South African Perspectives: Essays in Honour of Nic Olivier*, Die Suid-Afrikaan, Cape Town, 1989.

— 'A Journey Away from Apartheid', ibid.

Huntington, S P, *Political Order in Changing Societies*, Yale University Press, New Haven, 1968.

— 'Reform and Stability in a Modernising Multi-ethnic Society', *Politikon*, vol. 8, no. 2, 1981.

Hyslop, J, 'Introduction: Section 1 – The State and Politics', in G Moss & I Obery (eds.), *South African Review 5*, Ravan Press, Johannesburg, 1989.

— 'Polar Night: Social Theory and the Crisis of Apartheid', in G Moss & I Obery (eds.),

South African Review 6: From 'Red Friday' to Codesa, Ravan Press, Johannesburg, 1992.

Innes, D, 'Minorco: The biggest ever disinvestment', *Weekly Mail,* 31 March 1989.

— 'Labour Relations in the De Klerk Era', in G Moss & I Obery (eds.), *South African Review 6: From 'Red Friday' to Codesa,* Ravan Press, Johannesburg, 1992.

Innes, D & Plaut, M, 'Class Struggle and the State', *Review of African Political Economy,* no. 11, Jan.-April 1978

James, W, 'Materialist History, Materialist Theory: A response to Charles van Onselen', *Social Dynamics,* vol. 9, no. 1, 1983.

— (ed.), *The State of Apartheid,* Lynne Rienner, Boulder, 1987.

Jessop, B, 'The Capitalist State and Political Practice', *Economy and Society,* vol. 9, no. 1, February 1980.

— *The Capitalist State,* Martin Robertson, London, 1982.

— 'Regulation Theory, Post-Fordism and the State: More than a Reply to Werner Bonefeld', *Capital and Class,* no. 34, 1988.

Johnson, R W, *How Long Will South Africa Survive?,* Macmillan, London, 1977.

Jones, S & Müller, A, *The South African Economy, 1910-90,* Macmillan, London, 1992.

Jonker, I,*Versamelde Werke,* Perskor-Uitgewery, Johannesburg, 1975.

Juta, C J, 'Aspects of Afrikaner Nationalism, 1900-1964', unpublished PhD thesis, University of Natal (Pietermaritzburg), 1966.

Kane-Berman, J, *Soweto: Black Revolt,White Reaction,* Ravan Press, Johannesburg, 1978.

Kaplan, D, 'The South Africa State: The Origins of a Racially Exclusive Democracy', *Insurgent Sociologist,* vol. X, no. 2, 1979.

— 'The Current Upswing in the South African Economy and the International Capitalist Crisis', *Work in Progress,* no. 16, 1981.

— 'The Internationalisation of South African Capital', *African Affairs,* vol. 82, no. 329, October 1983.

Karon, T, 'The Urban Foundation', in L Cooper & D Kaplan (eds.), *Selected Research Papers on Aspects of Organisation in the Western Cape,* University of Cape Town, 1982.

Keller, E J & Picard, L A (eds.), *South Africa in Southern Africa: Domestic Change and International Conflict,* Lynne Rienner Publishers, Boulder & London, 1989.

Kenney, H, *Architect of Apartheid: H F Verwoerd – an Appraisal,* Jonathan Ball, Johannesburg, 1980.

— *Power, Pride and Prejudice: The years of Afrikaner nationalist rule in South Africa,* Jonathan Ball, Johannesburg, 1991.

Keyman, E F, 'Problematising the State in International Relations Theory', in W S Cox & C T Sjolander, *Beyond Positivism: Critical Reflections on International Relations,* Lynne Rienner, Boulder, 1994.

Kitching, G, 'Politics and Method in the Kenya Debate', in H Bernstein and B Campbell (eds.), *Contradictions of Accumulation in Africa,* Sage Publications, Beverly Hills, 1985.

Kitshoff, J J, 'Die Nywerheidspolitiek', in J A Lombard (ed.), *Die Ekonomiese Politiek van Suid Afrika,* HAUM, Pretoria, 1967.

Bibliography

Klare, M T, 'The Interventionist Impulse: U.S. Military Doctrine for Low-Intensity Warfare', in M Klare & P Kornbluh (eds.), *Low-Intensity Warfare: Counterinsurgency, proinsurgency and antiterrosism in the eighties*, Pantheon, New York, 1988.

Koornhof, H E, 'Works of friction: current South African war literature', in Cock & Nathan, *War and Society*, 1988.

Kotze, H, 'Adapting or Dyeing: parliamentary political parties, reform and reaction in South Africa', in D J van Vuuren, N J Wiehahn & M Wiechers (eds.), *South Africa: The Challenge of Reform*, Owen Burgess Publishers, Pinetown (SA), 1988.

Kreplak, H & George, W, 'La stratégie conventionelle', in C-P David, *Les études stratégiques: approches et concepts*, Éditions du Méridien, Montréal, 1989.

Krikler, J, 'Problems of a Transition to Socialist Agriculture in South Africa', *South African Labour Bulletin*, vol. 12, no. 5, July 1987.

Krüger, D W (ed.), *South African Parties and Policies, 1910-1960: A Select Source Book*, Human & Rousseau, Cape Town, 1960.

Krüger, D W & Beyers, C J (eds.), *Dictionary of South African Biography*, vol. 3, Human Sciences Research Council/Tafelberg, Cape Town, 1975.

Kuper, L, *Passive Resistance in South Africa*, Yale University Press, New Haven, 1957.

Laclau, E, *Politics and Ideology in Marxist Theory*, New Left Books, London, 1977.

Laclau, E & Mouffe, C, *Hegemony and Socialist Strategy: Towards a Radical Democratic Politics*, Verso, London, 1985.

Landman, J P, Nel P & van Niekerk, A, *Wat Kom Na Apartheid? Jong Afrikaners aan die Word*, Southern, Johannesburg, 1988.

Lategan, B & Muller H (eds.), *Afrikaners Tussen die Tye*, Taurus, Bramley (SA), 1990.

Lazar, J, 'Conformity and Conflict: Afrikaner Nationalist Politics in South Africa, 1948-1961', D Phil dissertation, Oxford University, 1987.

le Roux, N J, *W.A. Hofmeyr: Sy Werk en Waarde*, Nasionale Boekhandel, Cape Town, 1953.

Lee, R, 'The Role of the Private Sector as a Catalyst for Social Change in South Africa', *African Affairs*, vol. 82, no. 329, October 1983.

Lee, R & Schlemmer, L, *Transition to Democracy: Policy Perspectives 1991*, Oxford University Press, Cape Town, 1991.

Legassick, M, 'Legislation, Ideology and Economy in Post-1948 South Africa', *Journal of Southern African Studies*, vol. 1, no. 1, October 1974.

Lever, H & Wagner, O J M, 'Urbanisation and the Afrikaner', *Race*, vol. XI, no. 2, October 1969.

Lewis, G, 'Moving a Rock: Business and Change in South Africa', *South Africa International*, vol. XX, no. 2, October 1989.

Lipietz, A, 'Towards Global Fordism', *New Left Review*, no. 132, 1982.

— 'New Tendencies in the International Division of Labour: Regimes of Accumulation and Modes of Regulation', in A Scott & M Stoper (eds.), *Production, Work, Territory*, Allen & Unwin, London, 1986.

— *Mirages and Miracles: The Crisis of Global Fordism*, Verso, London 1987.

Lipton, M, *Capitalism and Apartheid: South Africa, 1910-84*, Rowman & Allanheld, Totowa, N J, 1985.

— *Sanctions Against South Africa: the dynamics of economic isolation*, The Economist Intelligence Unit, Special Report No. 1119, London, 1988.

Lodge, T, 'People's War or Negotiation: African National Congress Strategies in the 1980s', in G Moss & I Obery (eds), *South African Review 5*, Ravan Press, Johannesburg, 1989.

Lombard, J A (ed.), *Die Ekonomiese Politiek van Suid Afrika*, HAUM, Pretoria, 1967.

— 'South Africa Looks Inward for Economic Growth', *Business Day*, 9 July 1986.

Lombard, J A (ed.) & Stadler J, 'Focus on Economic Issues', *Mercabank*, no. 31, 1982.

Loubser, J J, 'Moderne Afrikaneridentiteit en die Onmoontlikheid van Afrikaner Nasionalisme', address to Student Current Affairs Circle, Stellenbosch University, 27 April 1972 (mimeo).

Louw, C, 'Die SAP en die Pyn van Oorgang', *Die Suid-Afrikaan*, no. 24, Dec. 1989.

Louw, L, *Dawie, 1946-1964. 'n Bloemlesing uit die geskrifte van Die Burger se politieke komentaar*, Tafelberg, Cape Town, 1965.

Louw, N P van Wyk, *Loyale Verset: kritiese gedagtes oor ons Afrikaanse kultuurstrewe en ons literêre beweging*, Nasionale Boekhandel, Cape Town, 1939.

— *Liberale Nasionalisme: Gedagtes Oor die Nasionalisme, Liberalisme en Tradisie vir Suid-Afrikaners met 'n Kulturele Nadrup*, Tafelberg, Cape Town, 1958.

Luckhardt, K & Wall, B, *Working for Freedom*, World Council of Churches, Geneva, 1981.

Luckhöff, A H, *Cottesloe*, Tafelberg, Cape Town, 1978.

Mabin, A, 'The Struggle for the City: Urbanisation and Political Strategies of the South African State', paper to the Annual Conference of the Canadian Association of African Studies, Kingston, 11-14 May 1988

Malan, D F, *Afrikaner-volkseenheid en my ervarings op die pad daarheen*, Nasionale Boekhandel, Cape Town, 1959.

Malan, M, 'Die Aanslag teen Suid-Afrika', *ISSUP Strategic Review*, November 1980.

Malan, M P A, *Die Nasionale Party van Suid Afrika: Sy Stryd en Prestasies, 1914-1964*. Federale Raad van die Nasionale Pary, n.p.,1964.

Malan, R, *My Traitor's Heart*, Atlantic Monthly Press, New York, 1990.

Manby, B, 'South Africa: The impact of sanctions', *Journal of International Affairs*, vol. 46, no. 1, Summer 1992.

Manicom, L, 'Ruling Relations: Rethinking State and Gender in South African History', *Journal of African History*, vol. 33, no. 3, 1992.

Mann, M, 'The Giant Stirs: South African Business in the Age of Reform', in Frankel *et al., State, Resistance and Change,* 1988.

Mann, M[ichael], 'Autonomous Power of the State', *Archives européennes de sociologie*, no. 25, 1984.

— *The Sources of Social Power*, Cambridge University Press, Cambridge, 1986.

Manzo, K A, *Domination, Resistance and Social Change in South Africa: The Local Effects of Global Power*, Praeger, Westport (Conn.) & London, 1992.

Manzo, K A & McGowan, P, 'Is Apartheid Dying or is it Just Smelling Bad?', mimeo, 1991.

— 'Afrikaner Fears and the Politics of Despair: Understanding Change in South Africa',

International Studies Quarterly, vol. 36, no.1, March 1992.

Marais, A H, *Die Stryd om outonomie en spesialisasie in die mieliebedryf, 1966-1980*, SAMPI, 1991.

Marks, S, & Trapido S, 'Lord Milner and the South African State', *History Workshop 8*, Pluto Press, London, 1979.

— (eds.), *The Politics of Race, Class & Nationalism in Twentieth Century South Africa*, Longman, London, 1987.

McCuen, J J, *The Art of Counter-Revolutionary War*, Faber & Faber, London, 1966.

McGregor, R, *Investors' Handbook*, Purdey Publishing, Johannesburg, 1985.

Meiring, P, *Ons Eerste Ses Premiers: 'n persoonlike terugblik*, Tafelberg, Cape Town, 1972.

— *Tien Politieke Leiers: Manne naas ons Premiers*, Tafelberg, Cape Town, 1973.

— *Inside Information*, Tafelberg, Cape Town, 1973.

Merle, M, 'Les tribulations de l'État', in M Merle, *Les acteurs dans les relations internationales*, Économica, Paris, 1988.

Meyer, P J, *Die Stryd van die Afrikaner Werker*, Pro-Ecclesia, Stellenbosch, 1944.

Miliband, R, 'State Power and Class Interests', *New Left Review*, no. 138, 1983.

— *Divided Societies: Class Struggle in Contemporary Capitalism*, Oxford University Press, Oxford & New York, 1991.

Miller, R B, 'Science and Society in the Early Career of H F Verwoerd', *Journal of Southern African Studies*, vol. 19, no. 4, December 1993.

Mitchell, M & Russell, D, 'Militarisation and the South African State', in C Creighton & M Shaw (eds.), *The Sociology of War and Peace*, Macmillan, London, 1987.

— 'Political Impasse in South Africa: State Capacities and Crisis Management', in Brewer, *Can South Africa Survive?*, 1989.

Moodie, T D, 'The Afrikaner Stuggle for an Effective Voice in the South African Economy Prior to 1948', *South African Labour Bulletin*, vol. I, no. 7, November 1974.

— 'Dutch Reformed Churches as Vehicles of Political Legitimation in South Africa', mimeo, 1974.

— *The Rise of Afrikanerdom: Power, Apartheid and the Afrikaner Civil Religion*, University of California Press, Berkeley, 1975.

— 'The Rise of Afrikanerdom as an Immanent Critique of Marxist Theory of Social Class', in P L Bonner (ed.), *Working Papers in Southern African Studies*, African Studies Institute, University of the Witwatersrand, Johannesburg, 1977.

Morris, M, 'The development of capitalism in South African agriculture', *Economy & Society*, vol. 5. no. 3, 1976.

— 'Apartheid, Agriculture and the State', *SALDRU Working Paper No. 8*, University of Cape Town, 1977.

— 'State, capital and growth: the political economy of the national question', in S Gelb (ed.), *South Africa's Economic Crisis*, 1991.

Morris, M & Hindson, D, 'South Africa: Political Violence, Reform and Reconstruction', *Review of African Political Economy*, no. 53, 1992.

Morris, M & Padaychee V, 'State Reform Policy in South Africa', *Transformation*, no. 7, 1988.

Moss, G, 'Total Strategy', *Work in Progress*, no. 11, 1980.

Moss, G & Obery, I. (eds.), *South African Review 5*, Ravan Press, Johannesburg, 1989.

— (eds.), *South African Review 6: From 'Red Friday' to Codesa*, Ravan Press, Johannesburg, 1992.

Mouffe, C, 'Hegemony and Ideology in Gramsci', in C Mouffe (ed.), *Gramsci and Marxist Theory*, New Left Books, London, 1979.

Müller, A L, 'Ekonomiese Geskiedskrywing in Afrikaans', unpublished paper to conference on *Afrikaanse Geskiedskrywing en Letterkunde*, University of the Western Cape, 16-18 October 1991.

Munger, E, *Afrikaner and African Nationalism: South African Parallels and Parameters*, Oxford University Press, Oxford, 1967.

Nathan, L & Phillips, M, '"Cross-currents": Security Developments under F W de Klerk', in G Moss & I Obery (eds.), *South African Review 6: From 'Red Friday' to Codesa*, Ravan Press, Johannesburg, 1992.

Nattrass, J, *The South African Economy: Its growth and change*, Oxford University Press, Cape Town, 1981.

Nattrass, N, 'Profitability: The Soft Underbelly of South African Regulation/SSA Analysis', *Review of Radical Political Economy*, vol. 24, no. 1, 1992.

Naudé, L, *see* Schoeman, B M

Nolutshungu, S, *Changing South Africa*, David Philip, Cape Town, 1982.

O'Donnell, G & Schmitter, P, *Transitions from Authoritarian Rule: Tentative Conclusions about Uncertain Democracies*, Johns Hopkins University Press, Baltimore, 1986.

Oelofse, J C, *Die Nederduitsch Hervormde Kerk en die Afrikaner Broederbond*, NHK Pers, Krugersdorp, 1964.

Offe, C & Ronge, V, 'Theses on the Theory of the State', in A Giddens & D Held (eds.), *Classes, Power and Conflict: Classic and Contemporary Debates*, University of California Press, Berkeley & Los Angeles, 1982.

Olivier, G, 'N P van Wyk Low and R F A Hoernlé: Notes on Liberal and Nationalist Discourse in South Africa, 1933-1939', paper to Institute for Advanced Social Research, University of the Witwatersrand, 30 May 1994.

Olivier, L, 'Michel Foucault: théorie et pratique. Réflixion sur l'expérience politique', *Revue québécoise de science politique*, no. 25, hiver 1994.

Olivier, N, 'The Head of Government and the Party', in R Schrire (ed.), *Leadership and the Apartheid State: From Malan to De Klerk*, Oxford University Press, Cape Town, 1994.

O'Meara, D, 'Class & Nationalism in African Resistance: Secondary Industrialisation & the Development of Mass Nationalism in South Africa', unpublished M A dissertation, Sussex University, 1973.

— 'The 1946 African mineworkers' strike and the political economy of South Africa', *Journal of Commonwealth & Comparative Politics*, vol. 13, no. 2, 1975.

— 'White Trade Unionism, Political Power and Afrikaner Nationalism', *South African Labour Bulletin*, vol. 1, no. 4, April 1975.

— 'The Afrikaner Broederbond 1927-1948: Class Vanguard of Afrikaner Nationalism', *Journal of Southern African Studies*, vol. 3, no. 2, 1977.

— 'Analysing Afrikaner Nationalism: The "Christian-National" Assault on White Trade Unionism in South Africa, 1934-1948', *African Affairs*, vol. 77, no. 306, 1978.
— 'Muldergate and the Politics of Afrikaner Nationalism', *Work in Progress*, no. 22, 1982.
— *Volkskapitalisme: Class, Capital & Ideology in the Development of Afrikaner Nationalism, 1934-1948*, Cambridge University Press, Cambridge, 1983.
— 'From Muldergate to Total Strategy: The Politics of Afrikaner Nationalism and the Crisis of the Capitalist State in South Africa', Centro de Estudos Africanos, Maputo, 1984.
— 'Les couts de la déstabilisation en Afrique australe', *Afrique*, vol. 4, no.1, 1987.
— 'South Africa's Destabilisation of the Frontline States, 1980-1987', Canadian Institute for International Peace & Security, *Background Paper No. 20*, June 1988.
— 'Government Measures Against Apartheid South Africa on Areas Critical to its Economy', Report to UN Centre Against Apartheid, 1989.
— 'Changing Visions in the National Party', in D Innes, M Kentridge & H Perold (eds.), *Power and Profit: Politics, Labour and Business in South Africa*, Oxford University Press, 1992.
Opperman, D J, *Groot Verseboek* (5th edition), Tafelberg, Cape Town, 1974.
Orpen, C, 'Authoritarianism in an "Authoritarian" Culture: The Case of Afrikaans-speaking South Africa', *Journal of Social Psychology*, no. 81, 1970.
Ottaway, M, 'Liberation Movements and the Transition to Democracy: the Case of the A.N.C.', *Journal of Modern African Studies*, vol. 29, no. 1, 1991.
Ovenden, K & Cole, T, *Apartheid and International Finance: A Programme for Change*, Penguin Books, Harmondsworth, 1989.
Owen, K, 'You can't beat a system that's not supposed to work', *Cape Times*, 2 April 1988.
Palmer, B D, *Descent into Discourse: The Reification of Language and the Writing of Social History*, Temple University Press, Philadelphia, 1990.
Parpart, J L & K A Staudt (eds.), *Women and State in Africa*, Lynne Rienner Publishers, Boulder, 1989.
Patterson, S, *The Last Trek: A Study of the Boer People and Afrikaner Nation*, Routledge & Kegan Paul, London, 1957.
Pavlich, G, 'Company Lore: South African Business and its Discourse on Apartheid', unpublished MA thesis, Simon Fraser University, 1988.
— 'Company Lore: South African Capital and its Discourse on Apartheid', paper to the annual conference of the Canadian Association of African Studies, Carleton University, Ottawa, 11-13 May 1989.
Paul, M G, 'Muldergate: A Comment', *Work in Progress*, no. 23, 1983.
Pauw, J, *In the Heart of the Whore: The story of apartheid's death squads*, Southern Book Publishers, Halfway House, 1991.
Pauw, S, *Die Beroepsaarbeid van die Afrikaner in die Stad*, Stellenbosch, Pro-Ecclesia, 1946.
Pelzer, A N (ed.), *Verwoerd Speaks: Speeches 1948-1966*, Afrikaanse Persboekhandel, Johannesburg, 1966.

— *Die Afrikaner Broederbond: Eerste 50 Jaar*, Tafelberg, Cape Town, 1979.

Philip, K, 'The Private Sector and the Security Establishment', in Cock & Nathan, *War and Society*, 1989.

Pienaar, S, *Getuie van Groot Tye*, Tafelberg, Cape Town, 1978.

Piotte, J-M, 'Postmodernité et quête de sens', in *Working Papers*, Karl Polanyi Institute of Political Economy, Concordia University, Montreal, 1990.

Posel, D, 'Rethinking the "Race–Class Debate" in South African Historiography', *Social Dynamics*, vol. 9, no. 1, 1983.

— 'The Language of Domination 1978-1983', in S Marks & S Trapido (eds.), *The Politics of Race, Class & Nationalism in Twentieth Century South Africa*, Longman, London, 1987.

— 'The Meaning of Apartheid Before 1948: Conflicting Interests and Forces within the Afrikaner Nationalist Alliance', *Journal of Southern African Studies*, vol. 14, no. 1, October 1987.

— 'Influx Control Policy and the Interests of Manufacturing and Commerce in South Africa', *The Societies of Southern Africa in the 19th and 20th Centuries, Volume 15*, Collected Seminar Papers No. 38, Institute of Commonwealth Studies, University of London, 1990.

— *The Making of Apartheid: Conflict and compromise*, Clarendon Press, Oxford, 1991.

— 'Lifting the Lid on the South African State: Some Historiographical Reflections', paper to the Canadian Research Consortium on Southern Africa, McGill University, 25 November 1994.

— 'Sizing up the Population: Statistics, Statecraft and Social Transformation in South Africa', keynote address to the 23rd Annual Conference of the Canadian Association of African Studies, Trent University, Peterborough, Ontario, 13 May 1995.

— 'State, Power and Gender: Conflict over the Registration of African Customary Marriage in South Africa c. 1910-1970', *Journal of Historical Sociology* (forthcoming).

Potgieter, L J, 'Die Ekonomie van die Afrikaner en sy Aandeel in die Sakelewe', unpublished MComm. dissertation, Potchefstroom University, 1954.

Potgieter, P J J S, 'Op die Voorpunt van die Tye: Hooftrekke van die Staatkundige Denke van L.J. du Plessis', unpublished MA thesis, Potchefstroom University, 1972.

Potter, E, *The Press as Opposition: The Political Role of South African Newspapers*, Chatto & Windus, London, 1975.

Pottinger, B, *The Imperial Presidency: P W Botha – the first 10 years*, Southern Books, Johannesburg, 1988.

Poulantzas, N, *L'État, le Pouvoir, le Socialisme*, Presses universitaires de France, Paris, 1978 (English edition, Verso, London, 1980).

Pretorius, L, 'Interaction between Interest Organisations and Government in South Africa', *Politeia*, vol. 1, no. 1, 1982.

— 'The Head of Government and Organised Business', in R. Schrire (ed.), *Leadership and the Apartheid State: From Malan to De Klerk*, Oxford University Press, Cape Town. 1994.

Price, R, *The Apartheid State in Crisis: Political Transformation in South Africa*, Oxford

University Press, New York/Oxford, 1991.

Rabie, J, *Die evolusie van nasionalisme: Beskouings oor die krisis van nasionalisme in die huidige oorgangstydperk to 'n wêreldstaat*, Mishoring Pers, Cape Town, 1960.

Raper, P, *Huldigingsbundel P J Nienaber*, Tafelberg, Cape Town, 1971.

Rees, M & Day, C, *Muldergate: The story of the info scandal*. Macmillan, Johannesburg, 1980.

Rhoodie, E M, *The REAL Information Scandal*, Orbis Publishers, Pretoria (n.d, 1983?).

— *P W Botha: The Final Betrayal*, S A Politics, Melville, 1989.

Rhoodie, N J, *Apartheid and Racial Partnership in South Africa*, Academica, Pretoria, 1969.

Rhoodie, N J & Venter, H J, *A Socio-Historical Exposition of the Apartheid Idea*, Human en Rousseau, Cape Town, 1960.

Rich, P, 'The Allocation of Labour and the Evolution of Apartheid Ideology in South Africa, 1939-1960', paper to the Conference on South African Labour History, University of the Witwatersrand, 8-10 April 1976.

Ries, A & Dommisse E, *Broedertwis: die verhaal van die 1982-skeuring in die Nasionale Party*, Tafelberg, Cape Town, 1982.

— *Leierstryd: die dramas rondom die uittrede van pres. P W Botha*, Tafelberg, Cape Town, 1990.

Rioux, J-F, Keenes, E & Légaré, G, 'Le néo-réalisme ou la reformulation du paradigme hégémonique', *Études internationales*, vol. XIX, no.1, mars 1988.

Rissik, G, 'Die Monetêre Politiek', in J A Lombard (ed.), *Die Ekonomiese Politiek van Suid Afrika*, HAUM, Pretoria, 1967.

Roberts, M & Trollip, A E G, *The South African Opposition 1939-1945*, Longmans, Cape Town, 1947.

Rosenau, P, 'Once Again into the Fray: International Relations Confronts the Humanities', *Millenium*, vol. 19, no. 1, Spring 1990.

— *Post Modernism in the Social Sciences*, Princeton University Press, Princeton, 1992.

Roux, M C, 'The Elasticity of Ideology and the Instrumental Role of the *Volks* University in this Regard', mimeo, 1975.

Ruitgers, G & Niddrie, D, 'Curbing Union Power', *Work in Progress*, no. 57, December 1988.

Sadie, J L, *Die Afrikaner in die Landsekonomie*, SAUK, Johannesburg, 1958.

— 'The White Labour Force of South Africa', *South African Journal of Economics*, vol. 28, no. 2, June 1960.

— 'The Afrikaner in the South African economy', mimeo, n.d. (1974?).

— 'Die Ekonomiese Faktor in die Afrikaner-gemeenskap', in H van der Merwe (ed.), *Identiteit en Verandering*, Tafelberg, Cape Town, 1975.

Salamon, L, 'The Economic Background to Afrikaner Nationalism', in J Butler (ed.), *Boston University Papers in African History.* vol I, Boston, 1964.

Santos, A, *Afrique du Sud; une stratégie dans l'impasse*, École des hautes études en sciences sociales, Cahiers d'études stratégiques, Paris, n.d. (1988?).

Sarakinsky, I, 'State, Strategy and Transition in South Africa', mimeo, August 1988.

— 'The Impulse to Reform: The South African State from Vorster to Botha', unpublished paper presented to the Department of Political Studies, Rand Afrikaans University, 4 September 1990.

— 'F W De Klerk Crossed the Rubicon: The Politics of Negotiation in South Africa', *Capital and Class*, no. 42, 1990.

— 'From Total Strategy to Negotiation: The Vicissitudes of Politics and the Politics of Vicissitudes in South Africa', mimeo, 1991.

Sarkesian, S C, 'Low-Intensity Conflict: Concepts, Principles, and Policy Guidelines', *Air Univeristy Review*, vol. 26, no. 2, 1985.

Saul, J S, 'South Africa: Between "Barbarism" and "Structural Reform"', *New Left Review*, no. 188, July-August 1991.

— *Recolonisation and Resistance: Southern Africa in the 1990s*, Between the Lines, Toronto, 1993.

Saul, J S & Gelb, S, *The Crisis in South Africa*, Monthly Review Press, New York, 1981.

Scannel, J P, *Keeromstraat 50: Gedenkbundel vir die vyftigste verjaarsdag van Die Burger*, Nasional Boekhandel, Cape Town, 1965.

Schlemmer, L, 'South Africa's National Party government', in P Berger & R Godsell (eds.), *A Future South Africa: Visions, Strategies and Realities*, Westview, Boulder, 1988.

Schoeman, B[eaumont] M, *Dr Albert Hertzog, Die Nasionale Party en die Mynwerker*, Nasionale Raad van Trustees, Pretoria, 1969. [This book was written under the pseudonym of Louis Naudé.]

— *Van Malan tot Verwoerd*, Human en Rousseau, Cape Town, 1973.

— *Vorster se 1000 Dae*, Human en Rousseau, Cape Town, 1974.

— *Die Sluipmoord op dr Verwoerd*, Strydpers, Pretoria, 1975.

— *Die Geldmag: Suid-Afrika se Onsigbare Regering*, Aktuele Publikasies, Pretoria, 1980.

— *Die Broederbond in die Afrikaner-politiek*, Aktuele Publikasies, Pretoria, 1982.

Schoeman, B[en], *My Lewe in die Politiek*, Perskor, Johannesburg, 1978.

Scholtz, G D, *Dr Hendrik Frensch Verwoerd, 1901-1966* (2 vols.), Perskor, Johannesburg, 1974.

Scholtz, J J (comp.), *Fighter and Reformer: Extracts from the speeches of P W Botha*, Bureau for Information, Pretoria, 1989.

Schrire, R (ed.), *Leadership in the Apartheid State: From Malan to De Klerk*, Oxford University Press, Cape Town, 1994.

Schüler, G, 'Stellenbosch en Sabra Jare', in P Hugo, *South African Perspectives,* 1989.

Seegers, A, 'The Government's perception and handling of South Africa's security needs', in D J van Vuuren *et al.* (eds.), *South Africa: The Challenge of Reform*, Owen Burgess Publishers, Pinetown (SA), 1988.

— 'Institutionalising a Cultural Style of Management? Afrikaners, the National Security Management System, and State Power', paper to the Conference of the Association of Sociologists of South Africa, University of the Witwatersrand, 2-5 July 1989.

— 'The South African Security Establishment: Theorietical and Comparative Impressions', in M Swilling (ed.), *Views of the South African State*, HSRC Publishers, Pretoria, 1990.

— 'South Africa's National Security Managament System', *Journal of Modern African*

Studies, vol. 29, no. 2, 1991.

— 'The Head of Government and the Executive', in R Schrire (ed.), *Leadership and the Apartheid State: From Malan to De Klerk*, Oxford University Press, Cape Town, 1994.

Seekings, J, 'What was the United Democratic Front?', in D O'Meara (ed.), *The Politics of Change in Southern Africa*, Collected Seminar Papers, Vol. 1, Canadian Research Consortium on Southern Africa, Montreal, 1995.

Seiler, J, 'The South African Security Establishment: rationalisation to what ends?', mimeo, Yale University, 1983.

Selfe, J, 'South Africa's National Security Managment System', in J Cock & L Nathan (eds.), *War and Society: The Militarisation of South Africa*, David Philip, Cape Town, 1989.

Senghaas, D, 'Formes et types de conflits dans la société internationale contemporain', in Hentsch *et al., Le système mondial.*

Serfontein, P H, *Die Verkrampte Aanslag*, Human en Rousseau, Cape Town, 1970.

   Brotherhood of Power, Rex Collings, London, 1979.

Shingler, J, 'Education and Political Order in South Africa, 1902-1960', unpublished PhD dissertation, Yale University, 1973.

— 'Nationalism and Apartheid, 1948-1989: The growth of dissent within the Afrikaner intelligentsia', in D O'Meara (ed.), *The Politics of Change in Southern Africa*, Collected Seminar Papers, Vol. 1, Canadian Research Consortium on Southern Africa, Montreal, 1994.

Simkins, C, 'Employment, Unemployment and Growth in South Africa, 1961-1979', *SALDRU Working Paper No. 4*, University of Cape Town, 1979.

Simson, H, *The Social Origins of Afrikaner Fascism and its Apartheid Policy*, Almqvist & Wikselt International, Stockholm, 1980.

Skocpol, T, *States and Social Revolutions: A Comparative Analysis of France, Russia and China*, Cambridge University Press, Cambridge, London & New York, 1979.

— 'Political Responses to Capitalist Crisis: Neo-Marxist Theories of the New Deal', *Politics and Society*, vol. 10, no. 2, 1980.

— 'Bringing the State Back In: Strategies of Analysis in Current Research', in P B Evans, D Rueschemeyer, and T Skocpol (eds.), *Bringing the State Back In*, Cambridge University Press, New York, 1987.

Skocpol, T & Trimberger, E K, 'Revolutions and the World-Historical Development of Capitalism', in B H Kaplan (ed.), *Social Change in the Capitalist World Economy*, Sage, Beverly Hills, 1978.

Slabbert, F van Zyl, 'Cultural and Ethnic Politics in Apartheid Ideology', in *Towards Social Change: Report of the Social Commission of the Study Project on Christianity in Apartheid Society*, Sprocas, Johannesburg, 1971.

— 'Afrikaner Nationalism, White Politics and Political Change in South Africa', mimeo, 1974.

— 'South Africa: Beginning at the End of the Road', *Transformation*, no. 11, 1990.

— 'The Causes of Transition in South Africa', IDASA *Occasional Papers*, no. 32, 1990.

— 'The basis and challenges of transition in South Africa: A review and a preview', in R Lee & L Schlemmer (eds.), *Transition to Democracy: Policy perspectives 1991*, Oxford University Press, Cape Town, 1991.

Bibliography

— *Quest for Democracy: South Africa in Transition*, Penguin (Case Series), Johannesburg, 1992.

Southall, R, 'African Capitalism in Contemporary South Africa', *Journal of Southern African Studies*, vol. 7, no. 1, 1980.

Sparks, A, *The Mind of South Africa*, Alfred Knopf, New York, 1990.

Stadler, A, 'The Party System in South African, 1910-1948', unpublished D Phil dissertation, University of the Witwatersrand, 1970.

— *The Political Economy of South Africa*, Croom Helm, London, 1987.

— 'The Conditions for Democracy in South Africa', *Transformation*, no. 11, 1990.

Steenkamp, W F J, 'Bantu Wages', *South African Journal of Economics*, vol. 30, no. 2, 1962.

Stockwell, J, *In Search of Enemies*, W W Norton, New York, 1978.

Stokes, R G, 'The Afrikaner Entrepreneur and Afrikaner Nationalism', *Economic Development & Culture Change*, vol. 22, no. 4, July 1974.

Stultz, N M, *Afrikaner Politics in South Africa, 1934-1948*, University of California Press, Berkeley/Los Angeles/London, 1974.

— 'Who Goes to Parliament', Institute of Social & Economic Research, Occasional Papers No. 19, Rhodes University, Grahamstown, 1975.

— 'Interpreting Constitutional Changes in South Africa', *Journal of Modern African Studies*, vol. 22, no. 3, 1984.

Sunter, C, *South Africa and the World in the 1990s*, Human & Rousseau/Tafelberg, Cape Town, 1987.

Suzman, H, *In No Uncertain Terms: A South African Memoir*, Alfred A. Knopf, New York, 1993.

Swilling, M, 'The politics of negotiation', *Work in Progress*, Oct./Nov. 1987.

— 'Introduction: The Politics of Stalemate', in P Frankel, N Pines & M Swilling (eds.), *State, Resistance and Change in South Africa*, Southern Books, Johannesburg, 1988.

— (ed.), *Views on the South African State*, HSRC Publishers, Pretoria, 1990.

Swilling, M & Phillips, M, 'The Politics of State Power in the 1980s', mimeo, Centre for Policy Studies, University of the Witwatersrand, 1988.

— 'Reform, Security and White Power: Rethinking State Strategies in the 1980s', paper to the Annual Conference of the Association of Sociology of South Africa, University of Durban-Westville, July 1988.

— 'The Emergency State: Its Structure, Power & Limits', in G Moss & I Obery (eds.) *South African Review 5*, Ravan Press, Johannesburg, 1989.

— 'The Powers of the Thunderbird: Decision-making Structures and Policy Strategies in the South African State', in Centre for Policy Studies, *Policy Perspectives 1989: South Africa at the end of the Eighties*, Johannesburg, 1989.

Taylor R, 'Between Apartheid and Democracy: The South African Election of 1989', in G Moss & I Obery (eds.), *South African Review 5*, Ravan Press, Johannesburg, 1989.

Terray, E (ed.), *L'État contemporain en Afrique*, Éditions L'Harmattan, Paris, 1987.

Terreblanche, S J, 'The Dream Fades', *Leadership South Africa*, vol. 7, no. 3, 1988.

— 'Corruption and the National Party', IDASA lecture at the University of Cape Town, 12 April 1989.

— 'My Stellenbosse sprong na vryheid', in Lategan & Muller, *Afrikaners Tussen die Tye*, 1990.

— 'F W de Klerk verspeel sy kans om ware staatsman te word', *Vrye Weekblad*, February 1994.

Terreblanche, S J & Nattrass, N, 'A periodization of the political economy from 1910', in N Nattrass & E Arlington (eds.), *The Political Economy of South Africa*, Oxford University Press, Cape Town, 1990.

Therbon, 'What Does the Ruling Class do When it Rules?', *Insurgent Sociologist*, vol. 6, no. 3, 1970.

— 'Neo-Marxist, Pluralist, Corporatist, Statist Theories and the Welfare State', in A Kazancigil (ed.), *The State in Global Perspective*, UNESCO Publications, Paris, 1986.

Theron, E, *H F Verwoerd as Welsynbeplanner*, Stellenbosch, Pro-Ecclesia, 1970.

— *Sonder Hoed of Handskoen*, Tafelberg, Cape Town, 1983.

Thom, H B, *D F Malan*, Tafelberg, Cape Town, 1980.

Thompson, L M, 'Afrikaner Nationalist Historiography and the Policy of Apartheid', *Journal of African History*, vol. III, no. 1, 1962.

— *Politics in the Republic of South Africa*, Little, Brown, Boston, 1966.

— *The Political Mythology of Apartheid*, Yale University Press, New Haven, 1985.

Torchia, A, 'The Business of Business: An Analysis of the Political Behaviour of the South African Manufacturing Sector under the Nationalists', *Journal of Southern African Studies*, vol. 14, no. 3, April 1988.

Trapido, S, 'Political Institutions and Afrikaner Social Structure in the Republic of South Africa', *American Political Science Review*, vol. LVII, no. 1, March 1963.

Tyriakian, E, 'Apartheid and Politics in South Africa', *Journal of Politics*, vol. 22, no. 4, 1960.

van der Merwe, C, 'Die Landbou Politiek', in J A Lombard (ed.), *Die Ekonomiese Politiek van Suid Afrika*, HAUM, Pretoria, 1967.

van der Merwe, H W, *Identiteit en Verandering: Sewe Opstelle Oor die Afrikaner Vandag*, Tafelberg, Cape Town, 1975.

— *Looking at the Afrikaner Today*, Cape Town, Tafelberg, 1975.

van der Merwe, H W, Ashby, M J, Charlton, N C J & Burber, B J, *White South, African Elites: A study of the incumbents of top positions in the Republic of South Africa*, Juta & Co, Cape Town, 1974.

van der Merwe, H W & Liebenberg, I, 'Transition Politics in South Africa: Pact forming for negotiation and the role of new political leadership styles', paper to the Congress of the Political Science Association of South Africa, Rustenburg, October 1991.

van der Merwe, P J, 'The Economic Influence of the Bantu Labour Bureau System on Bantu Labour', *South African Journal of Economics*, vol. 37, no. 1, March 1969.

van Jaarsveld, F A, *The Afrikaner's Interpretation of South African History*, Simondium Publishers, Cape Town, 1964.

— *Wie en wat is die Afrikaner?* Tafelberg, Cape Town, 1981.

— 'Afrikanergeskiedskrywing, Verlede, Hede en Toekoms', unpublished paper to conference on *Afrikaanse Geskiedskrywing en Letterkunde*, University of the Western Cape, 16-18 October 1991.

van Loggerenberg, K, 'Strukture van Oorlewing veg lustig voort', *Democracy in Action*, vol. 6, no. 2, 30 April 1992.

van Rensburg, A P J, 'Strijdom. Johannes Gerhardus', in D W Krüger & C J Beyers (eds.), *Dictionary of South African Biography,* vol. 3, Tafelberg for the HSRC, Cape Town, 1977.

van Rooyen, J J, *Die Nasionale Party: Sy Opkoms en Oorwinning – Kaapland se Aandeel,* Hoofraad van die Kaaplandse Nasionale Party, Cape Town, 1956.

— *Ons Politiek van Naby,* Tafelberg, Cape Town, 1971.

van Vuuren, D J, Wiehahn, N J & Wiechers, M (eds), *South Africa: The Challenge of Reform,* Owen Burgess Publishers, Pinetown (SA), 1988.

van Vuuren, W, 'Transition Theory – Guidelines for a new Politics in South Africa', paper to Research Colloqium organised by the Political Science Association of South Africa, Broederstroom, October 1990.

van Wyk, K & Geldenhuys, D, *Die Groepsgebod in P W Botha's se Politieke Oortuigings,* Rand Afrikaanse Universiteit, Johannesburg, 1987.

van Wyk, S, *Die Afrikaner in die Beroepslewe van die Stad,* Academica, Pretoria & Cape Town, 1968.

Vatcher, W H, *White Laager: The Rise of Afrikaner Nationalism,* Pall Mall Press, London, 1965.

Vergopoulos, K, 'Ajustement, instabilité, déséquilibre: Le retour de l'économie-nation?', *Interventions économiques,* no. 22-23, 1989.

Vieux, S, 'Containing the Class Struggle: Skocpol on Revolution', *Studies in Political Economy,* no. 27, Autumn 1988.

Vorster, B J, *Select Speeches* (edited by Dr O Geyser), Institute for Contemporary History, Bloemfontein, 1977.

Waite, B, *A Land Divided Against Itself: a map of South Africa showing the African Homelands and some of the mass removals of people which have taken place, also conditions in some of the resettlement areas,* Black Sash, Johannesburg, 1977.

Wassenaar, A D, *Assault on Private Enterprise The Freeway to Communism,* Tafelberg, Cape Town, 1977.

— *Squandered Assets,* Tafelberg, Cape Town, 1989.

Weisskopf, T, 'Marxian Crisis Theory and the Contradictions of Late Twentieth-Century Capitalism', *Rethinking Marxism,* vol. 4, no. 4, Winter 1991.

Welsh, D, 'Urbanisation and the Solidarity of Afrikaner Nationalism', *Journal of Modern African Studies,* vol. VII, no. 2, July 1969.

— 'The Political Economy of Afrikaner Nationalism', in A Leftwich (ed.), *South Africa: Economic Growth and Political Change,* St. Martin's Press, New York, 1974.

— 'The Executive and the African Population', in R Schrire (ed.), *Leadership and the Apartheid State: From Malan to De Klerk,* Oxford University Press, Cape Town, 1994.

Weschler, L, 'Profile: an Afrikaner Dante', *The New Yorker,* 8 November 1993.

Wilkins, I & Strydom H, *The Super Afrikaners: Inside the Afrikaner Broederbond,* Jonathan Ball, Johannesburg, 1978.

Williams, M (pseud.), *South Africa: Crisis of World Capitalism and the Apartheid Economy,* Winstanley Publications, London, 1977.

Williams, R, 'De Klerk and the security establishment: Partner or hostage?', *Work in*

Progress, no. 83, July 1992.

Wilson, F, 'Farming, 1866-1966', in M Wilson & L M Thompsons (eds.), *The Oxford History of South Africa,* Volume II, Clarendon Press, Oxford, 1971.

Wilson, F & Ramphele, M, *Uprooting Poverty: The South African Challenge*, Norton, New York, 1989.

Winter, G, *Inside BOSS*, Penguin, Harmondsworth, 1981.

Wolpe, H, 'Towards an Analysis of the South African State', *International Journal of the Sociology of Law*, vol. 8, no. 4, November 1980.

— *Class, Race and the Apartheid State*, UNESCO, 1987.

Worrall, D J (ed.), *South Africa: Government and Politics*, J L van Schaik, Pretoria, 1971.

— 'Afrikaner Nationalism: A Contemporary Analysis', in C P Potholm & R Dale (eds.), *Southern Africa in Perspective*, Free Press, New York, 1972.

Zillie, H, 'The right wing in South African politics', in Berger & Godsell, *A Future South Africa,* 1988.

INDEX

Abrahamse, Len 385, 386
Action Save White South Africa 299
AECI 386
Africa Confidential 408
African Mineworkers' Union (AMWU) 28
African National Congress of South Africa
  (ANC) xxviii, xxxvii, 3-8, 10, 15, 26-7,
  152, 173, 181, 192, 211, 259, 265-6, 324-
  6, 328, 330-4, 336-7, 340-2, 346, 359,
  361, 362, 369, 370, 374-5, 379, 386, 401-
  17, 445, 464, 482, 483; armed propaganda
  5, 324; Youth League 26
African trade unions 25, 30, 183, 328, 428
Afrika Instituut 128
Afrikaanse Calviniestiese Beweging (ACB)
  198
Afrikaanse Handelsinstituut (AHI) 31, 122-4,
  142, 183-4, 186, 295, 328, 331-2, 360,
  361, 363, 365
Afrikaanse Pers 127, 129
Afrikaanse Protestantse Kerk (APK) 314, 337
Afrikaner Broederbond, *see* Broederbond
  (AB)
Afrikaner business 11, 42, 47, 122, 124, 139-
  40, 142, 144-5, 147, 157, 159, 183, 187,
  202, 248, 268, 313, 331-2, 385, 387;
  changing relationship with Afrikaner
  farmers & workers 140; reaction to
  'Rubicon' 331; share of economic
  ownership 139
Afrikaner nationalism, *see also* Christian-
  nationalism; xxix, xxxii, xxxv, 10-11, 13-
  15, 23, 39, 40-8, 116-17, 120-1, 125, 127,
  129-31, 136, 141, 144-5, 147, 151, 165,
  167, 168-9, 230, 232, 244-6, 248, 251,
  256, 265, 295-7, 300, 305, 307-8, 311,
  313-15, 352, 370-1, 376, 400, 406, 421,
  446, 449, 472, 476; calvinistic character
  41; cultural dimensions 124; end of 312;
  impact of Republic on 11; *volkseie* 41, 181
Afrikaner Orde (AO) xxx, 118-19, 165
Afrikaner Party (AP) xxix-xxx, xxxiii, xxxvi,
  xxxviii, 22, 32, 40, 151, 163, 310, 484
Afrikaner 'press war' 129-30, 314

Afrikaner Volkswag (AV) 313-15
Afrikaner Weerstand Beweging (AWB) 299,
  307, 337, 404
Afrikaner workers 34, 37, 136, 140-1, 165,
  295, 310-11
Agliotti affair 231
AIDS 8, 371
Akademie vir Wetenskap en Kuns, *see* Suid-
  Afrikaanse vir Wetenskap en Kuns
Aksie Eie Toekoms (AET) 298-300
Algeria 225
Allison, Graham 440, 481, 483-5
Althusser, Louis 425, 430, 446, 450
Anglo American Corporation (AAC) xxxiv,
  120, 140, 174, 179, 184, 227, 358-9, 361-
  3, 365
Anglo-Boer War, *see* South African War
Anglovaal 224
Angola xxxiii, xxxv, xxxviii, 170, 179, 180,
  181, 182, 192-3, 199, 217, 219-24, 228,
  247-9, 258, 263, 281, 292, 345-6, 348,
  372, 377-9, 381, 385, 398, 439, 463;
  Cuban role 221; first SADF intervention
  229; FAPLA 377; FNLA 220, 222; MPLA
  221; UNITA 377, 407
apartheid, *see also* bantustans; xxvii, xxix,
  xxxi-xxxii, xxxviii, 3-10, 13-15, 23, 33-5,
  41, 116-18, 133, 137, 143-4, 164, 170,
  171, 172, 173, 174-6, 178-81, 183-8, 189,
  192-202, 215, 217, 223-4, 226, 227, 231,
  246, 248-9, 254, 255, 257, 259, 265, 272-
  6, 277, 279, 280, 296, 298, 301, 308-9,
  317, 320-3, 325-8, 331, 336-7, 341, 342,
  347, 348, 353, 358, 360, 362, 364, 365,
  368, 377, 381, 399, 400-2, 405, 408, 415-
  17, 419, 421-6, 428, 431, 432, 437-8, 441,
  442, 451, 452, 454-6, 457, 459, 460, 463,
  466, 472, 475-8, 480, 482, 486, 489;
  'Grand apartheid', theory & practice 64-
  74; influx control 25, 30-1, 35, 175, 196-7,
  273, 301, 309, 322, 327, 376; job
  reservation xxviii, 172, 175, 178, 183,
  188, 193, 197, 273, 292, 310; labour
  bureaux 33-4, 322; pass laws 25-7, 30-1,

183, 193, 273, 322, 331, 335; petty
  apartheid 186, 192-3, 197, 215, 308
Argus Newspapers 247
Armaments Development and Production
  Corporation (Armscor) 226-7
Aron, Raymond 435-6
Ashforth, Adam 441, 443-5
Associated Chambers of Commerce
  (Assocom) 30, 183, 195, 201, 295, 320,
  328, 331-2, 357, 361, 364
Auditor-General 212, 230-3, 244-5

Ball, Chris 48, 116, 361, 386, 410
Bantu Education 183, 446
Bantustans 118, 175, 194, 198-9, 201, 273,
  275, 276, 279, 322, 327, 348, 351, 369,
  420
Barber, Lord Anthony 340
Barclays Bank 358, 361, 386
Barlow Rand 226, 284, 294, 301, 358, 361
Barnard, Professor Neil 283
Barrie, Gerald 212, 233, 245
Barrow, Dame Nita 340
Barthes, Roland 440
Beaufre, General André 259-66, 272, 278,
  321-2, 334, 344, 366, 396-7, 412, 478
Beeld xxxv, 130, 198, 239, 315
Bierman, Admiral HH 221, 245
Biko, Steven Bantu xxxii, xxxvii, 170, 193,
  237, 272
Black Consciousness Movement (BCM) 170,
  173, 180, 181, 193, 237, 370
Black Local Authority (BLS[s]): 276-7, 325-
  6, 347
black middle class, see also petty bourgeoisie,
  black; 184-6, 201, 274, 277, 322-4, 326,
  334, 415
Bloom, Tony 133, 331, 361
Blum, Peter 126
Bonuskor 123, 140
Bophutatswana 214
Borraine, Dr Alex 335
Boshoff, Prof. Carel Willem Hendrik 199,
  300, 313, 314
Bosnia 4
Botha, General Louis xxx, xxxvi, 254, 255,
  421
Botha, MC 202, 210

Botha, Pieter Willem xxvii-xxviii, xxx, xxxii-
  xxxv, xxxvii-xxxix, 4, 15, 130, 151-2, 159,
  161, 192, 194, 198-9, 207, 210, 212-13,
  215-16, 219-20, 225, 227, 230, 232, 234-
  41, 239, 242, 243-5, 248-9, 251, 254-8,
  263, 267, 278, 280, 283, 287, 290-1, 294,
  296-9, 301-2, 307-8, 312, 314-15, 320-21,
  328, 330, 333-6, 338-42, 345, 349, 351,
  354-5, 357-8, 360-1, 364, 365-6, 374-5,
  377-8, 380-1, 383-5, 388-93, 396, 397-9,
  402, 404, 406, 408, 422, 427, 431-2, 458,
  463, 465, 480, 482, 484, 486; election as
  Hoofleier 234; fall from power 388-90; in
  Cape NP 257; reforms 272; relationship
  with SADF 216, 254; role in first Angola
  intervention 219; Rubicon speech 329;
  State of Emergency 341
Botha, Roelof Frederik ('Pik') 193, 200, 235-
  41, 243, 246, 251, 263, 320, 329, 332-3,
  335, 340-1, 350, 384, 388-90, 393, 397,
  402-3, 407, 414
Botha, Stephanus P ('Fanie') xxxvii, 202,
  236, 238, 279, 291, 292, 296, 302, 303,
  310
Bothma, Boet 388
Bozzoli, Belinda 424, 446
Brazzaville Protocol 378, 403
Bretton Woods 474-5
Breytenbach, Breyten xxvii, 126-7, 203-4,
  278, 334, 370-1
Breytenbach, Prof. Willie 334
Brink, André xxvii, 127-8, 156
Britain 20-1, 41, 116, 174, 182, 258, 287, 340,
  373, 419, 437, 471
Broederbond, Afrikaner (AB) xxix-xxxviii,
  22, 31, 40-8, 118-19, 121, 122, 125-6,
  128, 140-1, 144-7, 155, 157-64, 195-6,
  199-200, 210, 216, 227, 254, 280, 283-4,
  292, 295-6, 299, 300, 307, 311, 313-15,
  336, 352, 371, 384-5, 388, 398, 400, 404-
  5, 410, 449; class strategies 42;
  composition & membership 46, 144;
  history, structure & role in Afrikaner
  nationalism 43; relationship with NP 45;
  struggle for control of 159; weight in
  different provinces 47
Bureau for State Security (BOSS) xxxiv-xxxv,
  xxxvii, 159, 179, 192, 196, 205, 207, 210-

11, 213, 215, 217-19, 221-3, 228, 232, 234-5, 237, 243, 247, 267, 281, 283, 332-3, 343, 484; conflict with Military Intelligence 217
Burgers, President TF 255
Bush, George Herbert 266, 378
Business Week 329
Buthelezi, Chief Mangosutho Gatsha 9, 348, 400, 409, 412, 414

Cabinet xxvii-xxxviii, 23, 27, 32, 43, 46-7, 116-20, 127, 141-2, 146, 151-2, 154, 160, 166, 194, 197-200, 202, 210, 216, 219, 223, 221, 206-7, 210, 212-13, 215, 219, 221, 233-4, 236, 238-43, 247-9, 254, 257, 258, 267, 276, 278-83, 286-7, 290-4, 296, 298, 300-3, 307, 313, 327, 334, 336-7, 340-2, 348, 349-51, 365, 374, 375, 377, 391, 392, 397, 398, 402-4, 406, 408, 412, 414, 419, 431, 482, 484
calvinism 163
Cambridge University 11, 21, 23, 36, 434, 436
Canada 258, 340, 354, 405, 431
Cape Times 193, 204, 391, 404
Cape Wine Distillers 309
capitalism 13-14, 121, 143, 145, 171, 173, 174, 177, 181-2, 184-7, 225, 386, 422-5, 428, 437, 442, 471, 473, 475
capitalist class 30, 173 174, 176, 178, 182, 185, 187-8, 258, 332, 362, 472, 481; politics of 27, 173, 175, 178, 182, 294, 328, 360, 385, 472
'Carlton' Conference 294
Carnegie Commission on 'Poor White Problem' 93
Carter, Jimmy 182, 184, 258
Castro, Fidel 378
census 136
Chamber of Mines (CoM) 28, 183, 328, 363, 365, 472
Chapman, Neal 386
Christelike Kultuuraksie (CKA) 128
Christian-nationalism, *see also* Afrikaner nationalism; 11, 40-3, 147
Churchill, Winston 21
CIA xxxvii, 221-2, 247, 477
Cillié, Pieter J ('Piet'- *nom de plume*,

'Dawie') xxxv, 103, 106, 120, 204, 373
Ciskei 275, 409, 412
civil service 22, 44, 61-3, 146, 232, 278, 283-4, 294, 310, 309, 337, 344, 351, 416; NP purge & Afrikanerisation of 61-3
civil society 44-5, 48, 116, 125, 146, 434, 439, 445, 459, 462, 472, 478-2, 485
Civilian Cooperation Bureau (CCB) 407
Clark, General Matt 20
class 147-8, 164, 166, 178, 180, 182, 200, 242, 244, 248, 258, 274, 277, 308, 310-11, 312, 315, 322-4, 326-7, 332, 334, 376, 388, 399, 401, 415, 421, 423, 425, 427, 428, 430, 431, 442, 448, 455-6, 458, 467-9, 468, 471-3, 478, 480-1, 485
Clausewitz, Carl von 220, 261, 436
Coetzee, Blaar 120, 198, 396
Coetzee, General Johan 326, 333, 341, 343
Cold War 8
Coloureds' Representative Council (CRC) 194
Commonwealth (formerly, British Commonwealth) xxxviii, 20, 21, 329, 338, 340, 341, 355, 379, 401, 419, 468; Foreign Ministers Committee 355
Communism 6, 34, 120, 124, 422
Communist Party 3, 8, 27, 121, 151, 211, 173, 328, 404, 411, 482
Congress of South African Trade Unions (Cosatu) 328, 362-4, 380, 415, 428
Conservative Party, *see* Konserwatiewe Party
Conservative Workers' Party 108
Consolidated Goldfields 359
Consolidation Commission 275
Consultative Business Movement (CBM) 386, 387
Convention for a Democratic South Africa (Codesa) 410-11
corruption 156, 215, 230-2, 242, 246, 248, 258, 351-2, 397
Côte d'Ivoire 206, 214
Cottesloe Declaration xxxvii, 106-7, 111, 292
Crocker, Chester 333
Cuba 482, 481
Cuito Cuanavale, battle of xxxiii, 377, 379, 398, 477

Dagbreek xxxv, 120, 129-30

'Dawie', *see* Cillié, PJ
de Beer, Dr Zac 362-4, 386-7
de Klerk, Frederick Willem xxvii-xxviii,
    xxxvii, 3-5, 10, 197, 236, 243, 283, 297,
    302-3, 312, 330, 335, 347, 350, 366, 375-
    7, 381, 384, 389-93, 395-407, 409-11,
    414-17, 428, 431, 439, 464, 465, 482-4;
    leadership style 395
de Klerk, Jan xxviii-xxix, 154, 197, 303, 398
de Klerk, Marike 390
de Klerk, Willem ('Wimpie') xxviii, 156, 197,
    235, 243, 315, 349, 374, 387, 396, 414
de Lange, Prof. Jan Pieter 313
de Villiers, Adv. DP ('Lang Dawid') 373, 375
de Villiers, Dr Dawid Jacobus ('Dawie') 392
de Wet, Dr Carel 231
de Wet, General Christian 255
de Wet Nel, MC ('Daan') 307
death squads 346, 372, 407
Defence Advisory Committee 301
Defence Manpower Liaison Committee 295
Dellums Bill 355, 379
Democratic Party (DP) xxviii, xxxii, 188, 364,
    378, 387-8, 398-401, 409, 416
Department of Agriculture 21, 144, 177
Department of Bantu Affairs (later,
    Deparment of Bantu Administration) xxxi,
    280, 364
Department of Constitutional Development
    280, 326-7
Department of Cooperation and Development
    (later, and Planning) 364
Department of Defence 207, 213-14, 218,
    220-1, 245
Department of Foreign Affairs 207, 213, 215,
    219, 221, 284
Department of Information xxxii, xxxiv,
    xxxvii, 129, 151, 192, 207, 210, 212, 213-
    14, 217, 223, 230-5, 238, 240-1, 245-8,
    386-7, 484; Operation Senekal xxxv, 212,
    213-16, 223, 232, 245
Department of Labour 26, 193, 227
Department of National Security (DONS) 283
Department of Native Affairs 25, 30, 33, 441
Department of Plural Relations 194
Derby-Lewis, Clive 411
Derrida, Jacques 442
Development Bank of Southern Africa 357

Die Beeld xxxv, 130
Die Burger xxviii, xxxi-xxxii, 34, 120, 129,
    157, 198, 204, 391, 234-5, 239, 291, 297,
    373, 389, 391
Die Kerkbode xxxvii, 125
Die Patriot 311
Die Suid-Afrikaan 372
Die Transvaler xxviii, xxxviii, 47, 120, 129,
    145, 151, 197-8, 235, 237, 303, 315
Die Vaderland xxxvi, 123, 129-30, 153, 239,
    296, 331, 336
Die Volksblad 129
Die Vrye Weekblad 372
Diederichs, Dr Nicolaas ('Nic') xxix, xxxi,
    xxxiv-xxxv, 123, 212-13, 234, 241, 290
Dominion Party 32
dompas 193, 197-
Dönges, Dr Theophilus Ebenhaezer (Eben)
    xxviii-xxix, xxxviii, 122, 152, 154, 160,
    162, 216, 240, 257, 303, 374, 482
Draft Republican Constitution xxix, xxxi, 84,
    95, 96
du Plessis, Barend Jacobus 236, 356, 384,
    385, 390, 397, 412
du Plessis, Prof. Lodewickus Johannes
    ('Wickus') xxviii-xxix, 84-6, 96-7, 129
du Preez, Max 280
Dubow, Saul 441
Dukakis, Michael 378
Dutch Reformed Churches, *see also*
    Gereformeerde Kerk, Nederduitsch
    Hervormde Kerke & Nederduitse
    Gereformeerde Kerk; 314, 336; divisions
    in and among 314; internal ferment 336

economic movement, Afrikaner xxxv, 11, 42,
    54, 76, 79, 87, 120-4, 141, 145, 159, 187,
    177; impact on Afrikaner class structure
    136; struggles within 120-4
economy xxviii, 3, 8, 21, 23-4, 28, 33, 42,
    116, 121, 123, 136, 139-40, 143-4, 167,
    170-4, 176-8, 183, 185, 195, 226, 274,
    286, 320, 331, 348, 353-6, 358-60, 365,
    381, 386, 412, 415, 422-4, 428-30, 442,
    438, 458, 470, 475-6, 478, 487; Afrikaner
    share of 139; agriculture 21, 28-31, 34, 37,
    41, 138, 141-4, 171, 176, 177, 178, 182,
    183, 197, 273, 297-8, 301, 309, 337, 357,

362, 421, 471, 476, 478; boom of the
1960s 171, 173; capital export/capital
flight 329-30, 358; debt 329, 340, 355;
deregulation/privatisation 272, 331, 349,
364, 386; disinvestment 357-8;
diversification 173; employment 24-5, 35,
175, 183-4, 226, 274, 309, 351, 475, 428;
exchange rate 172, 173, 340, 351, 354-5,
365; external trade 172, 354; foreign
investment 329; foreign reserves 329, 356;
GDP 171, 173, 329, 354-6; Gini
coefficient 8; GNP 21, 352, 365; gold
price 267, 324, 354; growth 21, 176, 177,
267, 320, 324, 354, 356, 386;
industrialisation 171; labour supply 24;
manufacturing 21, 24, 27-8, 139-40, 171-
7, 226, 273, 310, 356, 358, 446; military-
industrial complex 224; mining xxxiv, 21,
24, 28-30, 36, 120-1, 123-4, 137-41, 161-
2, 171-4, 179, 183, 199, 225, 298, 358-9,
361, 362, 387, 412; monopolies 121, 144,
167, 185-6, 188, 274, 294, 295, 301, 308,
309, 311, 358; National Income 21;
recession 176, 178, 324; sanctions 170,
182, 300, 330, 332, 335, 337, 340-2, 355-
6, 358-9, 365, 373, 378-9, 402, 405, 407,
410; state employment 75; unemployment
175; wages 13, 24-6, 28, 30, 143, 178-9,
186, 201, 231, 274, 362, 428
Eglin, Colin 374, 387
Eiselen, Dr WMM 68, 73
Eiselen Education Commision 72
Ekonomiese Instituut (EI) 122
Ekonomiese Volkskongres (EVK) 121, 122,
136, 145, 159, 162
elections 118, 121, 136, 145, 150-1, 154, 159,
162, 164, 165, 167, 170, 188, 194, 196,
200, 202-3, 205, 210, 214, 231, 233-5,
237, 239-42, 248, 276, 287, 291, 293, 297-
9, 310, 312, 320, 325, 347, 349, 351, 364,
373, 375-8, 380, 384-5, 387, 389, 390-2,
397-402, 403, 408, 412, 413-16, 420, 422,
462, 471-2, 483; general, 1943 44;
general, 1948 22-37, 472; general, 1953
64; general, 1958 64; general, 1961 149;
general, 1966 150; general, 1970 164, 167;
general, 1974 188; general, 1977 188, 202,
233; general, 1981 276, 320; general, 1987
372, 375; general, 1989 399; general, 1994

3-10, 413-14; municipal 380, 388;
referenda 277, 312, 320, 405, 410-11, 419;
referendum, 1960 64, 116; referendum,
1983 320, 295; referendum, 1992 312, 410
Eminent Persons' Group (Commonwealth —
EPG) 338, 340-1, 350
Erasmus Commission 211, 216, 233, 235,
237, 242-3, 245
Erasmus, FC ('Frans') 62
Erasmus, Judge Rudolph 240, 242-3
Esselen, Louis 32
Esterhuys, Prof. Willie 412
Ethiopia 20, 150
ethnicity 11, 421-3, 455
Eybers, Elizabeth 126

Fagan Commission, see Native Laws
Commission of Enquiry
FAPLA 377
far right xxxi, xxxiii, 9, 48, 153, 298-9, 305-
16, 337, 373, 384, 405, 410-11, 413-14;
social basis & divisions 305
Federale Mynbou 120, 120-1, 123, 140, 161,
388
Federale Volksbeleggings (FVB) 120-3, 140,
332
Federasie van Afrikaanse Kultuurverenigings
(FAK) 45, 122, 139, 142, 162
Federated Chambers of Industry (FCI) 27, 30,
183, 328, 331-2, 360-1, 364
Ferreira, Natie 196
Financial Mail 183-5, 188, 195, 224, 226,
258, 294, 300-1, 320, 328-30, 332, 348,
362, 365-6, 384, 387
Five Freedoms Forum 366
FNLA 220, 222
Ford, Gerald 214
Ford Motor Corporation 358
Fortune 358
Foucault, Michel 432, 442-3, 447-51, 458-9,
485
Fouché, JJ ('Jim') xxix, 104, 107, 146, 154,
160
France 258, 260, 434, 437, 470
Frankel, Philip H 228
Fraser, Malcom 340, 341
Free Market Foundation 184
Freedom Charter 403, 446
Freedom Front 350, 414

FRELIMO 182
Friedman, Steven 432
Front Line States 486
'fusion' xxx, xxxii, xxxvi-xxxvii, 33, 36, 40,
    45, 47, 153

GATT 475
Gaullism 14, 470
Geertz, Clifford 11, 421
Gelb, Stephen 185, 428, 487
Geldenhuys, Dr Boy
Geldenhuys, Deon 221
Gencor xxxiv, 120-1, 123-4, 140, 161, 183,
    225, 315, 387, 388, 412
General Mining & Finance corporation, see
    Gencor
George VI, King 21
Gereformeerde Kerk (GK) 43, 314, 336
Germany xxxvi, 21, 23, 33, 40, 126, 258, 436,
    475
Gersony Report 378
Giddens, Anthony 434, 439, 465
Giliomee, Hermann 46, 139, 201
Gilpin, Robert 436
Gini coefficient 8
globalisation 8, 417, 474-5
Gold Standard crisis xxx, 27
'Good Hope' conference 301
Gordimer, Nadine 127
Government of National Unity xxvii-xxviii, 5,
    7, 9, 413, 464
Governor-General xxx, xxxi, 86, 89, 105, 419
Graaff, Sir de Villiers 103, 104
Gramsci, Antonio 171, 428, 445, 448-9, 487-8
Great depression 21, 27
Greenberg, Stanley B 432, 441-2
Greyling, Cas 200, 306
Groote Schuur Minutes 405
Gwala, Harry 8

Habermas, Jurgen 442
Halderman, Bob 278
Hall, Stuart 487
Hammerskjald, Dag 104
Hani, Chris 8, 411
Harare Declaration 401
Hartzenberg, Dr Ferdinand ('Ferdi') 302, 303
Harvard University 263

Havenga, Nicolaas Christiaan ('Klaas') xxix-
    xxx, xxxiii, xxxvi-xxxviii, 32, 40, 54, 85,
    89-90, 129
Heard, Kenneth 22, 36, 37, 118, 129, 150,
    152, 231, 239, 243, 276, 292, 337, 341,
    417
Heath, Edward 170, 340
hegemonic project 178, 184, 195, 429, 488-9
Hendrickse, Rev. Helenard Joe ('Alan') 342,
    366
Hentsch, Tierry 467
Herstigte Nasionale Party (HNP) xxx, xxxiii,
    xxxvi-xxxvii, 40, 118, 153, 164, 165, 167,
    205, 256, 298-300, 306-16, 373, 401;
    social base and difference from KP 310
Herzov, Basil 224
Hertzog, Dr Albert xxxiii-xxxiv, xxxvi, 46,
    116-19, 121, 153, 155, 160, 162-3, 165,
    202, 236, 298, 311, 393, 477, 496
Hertzog, General James Barry Munnik xxix-
    xxx, xxxii, xxxvi, 33, 40, 42, 44-5, 48,
    166, 117, 129, 153, 216, 255, 306
Hertzog group xxvii-xxviii, xxxi, xxxiii, xxxv,
    xxxvii-xxxviii, 118-20, 130-1, 153, 155,
    159-63, 167, 205, 306
Hertzog Prize xxxii, 124, 128, 153
Het Volk xxxvi
Heunis, Jan Christiaan (Chris) xxx, xxxii,
    239, 280, 287, 326-7, 334-5, 341-4, 350,
    363, 375, 384, 388-90, 392, 397, 400, 403,
    465
Hill, Christopher 241
Hobbes, Thomas 436-7
Hofmeyr, Jan Hendrik ('Jannie') 27, 32, 34
Hofmeyr, William Angus ('Willie') xxxi, 93-
    4, 257
Hoggenheimer 34, 120, 122, 142, 201, 257,
    310, 311, 342, 347
'Homelands', see Bantustans
Hoofstad xxxvi-xxxvii, 130, 156, 163, 296-7,
    306
Hoon, Jan 298
Horwood, Prof. Owen PF xxxi, 213, 238, 242,
    293, 385
Houphouët-Boigny, Felix 206
Hugo, Colonel Gert 409
Human, CF ('Kerneels') 332, 363
Huntington, Samuel P 263-4, 267, 277-8, 327-

8, 345, 405
Hyslop, Jonathan 431

IBM 358
imperialism xxx, 34, 40-2, 136, 144, 164, 255
Independent Electoral Commission (IEC) 413
Independent Movement 373-4, 376
Independent Party (IP) 374, 387
India 32
Industrial Development Corporation (IDC) 79
influx control 25, 30-1, 35, 175, 196-7, 273, 301, 309, 322, 327, 376
Inkatha Freedom Party (IFP) 9, 407, 409, 412, 414
Institute for Christian-national Education 71
Institute for Democratic Alternatives in South Africa (IDASA) 352, 374-5, 386
International Monetary Fund (IMF) 21, 213, 238, 415, 477
Iran 320
Iscor 79
Israel 126, 206, 214, 379, 475

Jansen, Dr EG xxxii, 51, 61-2, 67, 88, 89
Jansen, Mrs MM 86
job reservation xxviii, 172, 175, 178, 183, 188, 193, 197, 273, 292, 310,
Johannesburg Consolidated Investments (JCI) 361
Johannesburg Stock Exchange (JSE) 170, 177, 301, 329, 358, 359
Johanneskerkorrel 251, 368-9
Johnson, Mark 433
Joint Management Centre(s) 286, 344, 350-1
Jonker, Dr Abraham xxxi, 115
Jonker, Ingrid xxxi, 115, 127-8, 180
Jooste, Dr CJ 311
Jooste, Marius 314

Kasrils, Ronnie 411-12
Katzen, Kitt 245
Kaunda, Kenneth 192
Keeler, Christine 230
Keeromstraat, see Nasionale Pers
Kennedy, Bobby 482
Kennedy, Senator Ted 328
Kenya 483, 486
Keynesianism 474-5

Keys, Derek 412
King, Mervyn 386
Kirsch, Olga 17, 126
Kissinger, Dr Henry 170, 221-2
Kitching, Gavin 483, 485
Klopper, General HB 20
Klopper, Henning 307
Kohl, Helmut 272
Konserwatiewe Party (KP) xxvii, xxxii-xxxv, xxxvii, xxxix, 214, 306-16, 337, 340, 369, 373, 375-7, 384-5, 388, 391, 398, 400-2, 404, 406, 409-10, 411
Koornhof, Dr Pieter Gehardus Jacobus ('Piet') xxxi-xxxii, 161, 198-200, 202, 219, 241-2, 273, 276, 279, 280, 283, 296, 312, 322, 364, 378
Korean War 37
Kriegler, Judge Johan 413
Krige, Uys xxxii, 126, 128, 153
Krog, Antje 317
Kruger, Jimmy 193, 199, 204, 292, 307
Krüger, Paul ('Oom Paul') 126
kultuurpolitiek 124-5
KwaNdebele 275
KwaZulu 8-9, 348
KwaZulu/Natal 8-9

Labour Party (British), see also Labour Party (Coloured) and Labour Party (South African, SALP); 83, 170, 214, 258
Labour Party (Coloured), see also Labour Party (British) and Labour Party (South African, SALP); 194, 277, 376
Labour Party (South African, SALP), see also Labour Party (British) and Labour Party (Coloured); xxx, 22, 31-2, 34, 36, 40
Laclau, Ernesto 442
Lakoff, George 433
Land Bank 143
Langenhoven, Senator CJ 369
Langley, Tom 298
Landman, Willem 71
Lategan, Dr Ester 336, 373, 374
le Grange, Louis 286
le Roux, Frank 193
le Roux, PMK 96, 108
le Roux, SP xxxii, 127
legislation: Agricultural Marketing Act 29-31,

77; Advocate-General Bill 291; Bantu Authorities Act 67-8; Group Areas Act 187, 274, 277, 349, 372, 376-7; Immorality Act 197; Labour Relations Act 273; Labour Relations Bill 363, 386; Mixed Marriages Act 197; Natives (Abolition of Passes & Coordination of Documents Act) 69; Natives Land and Trust Act 29, 68; Native Laws Amendment Act 69; Official Secrets Act 227; Physical Planning Act 175, 183; Population Registration Act 408; Prevention of Illegal Squatting Act 68; Political Interference Act 335; Riotous Assemblies Act 63; Security Intelligence and State Security Act 218, 280; Separate University Education Act 96; Suppression of Communism Act 63; Urban Areas Act 25, 69; War Measure 145 26
Leipold, C Louis 370
Lenin, VI 261
Leroux, Etienne 124, 127-8
Lesotho 150, 346
Letoit, André 369, 371
Liberia 150
Lipietz, Alain 428, 430-1
Lipton, Merle 422
Lloyd, General Charles 345, 350
local authorities 25, 33, 325, 438
Lombard, Ivan 145
Louw, Eric H xxxii, 46, 89, 90, 107
Louw, MS 122
Louw, Prof. NP van Wyk 111, 126, 128, 370
low intensity conflict 344, 345
Luthuli, Chief Albert John 63
Luyt, Louis xxxii, 233, 387

Machel, Samora Moises 320
Macmillan, Harold 230
Maharaj, Mac 410-12
Malan, Adolphus Gysbert ('Sailor') 20, 62
Malan, Avril 293
Malan, Dr Avril I 292-3, 398
Malan, Dr Daniel François ('Die Doktor') xxx-xxxi,xxxii, xxxv-xxxvi, 23, 32, 40, 216, 254-5, 299, 313, 374, 376, 484; conflict with Strijdom 85-90
Malan, General Magnus de Merindol xxx,

263, 267-8, 281, 292, 302, 329, 333-4, 343-4, 346-7, 360, 379, 385, 398, 407, 463
Malan, PA 154
Malan, Wynand Charl 373-4, 387
Malaya 225
Mandela, Nelson Rolihlahla ('Madiba') xxvii-xxviii, 3-4, 6-7, 9-10, 63, 211, 330-2, 334, 340, 348, 404, 411, 412, 414, 415, 417, 423, 458, 464, 483, 485
Mandela, Nomzamo Winnie 8, 333, 408, 464
Manicom, Linzi 441, 443, 451-60
Mann, Michael 434, 439, 465
Manzo, Kathryn A 441, 446, 448
Marais, Eugene 125
Marais, Jacobus Albertus ('Jaap') xxxvii, 121, 153, 164, 298-9, 306
Marais, Jan 331
Marais, Judge JF 'Kowie' 196
Maree, Johan 226
Marx, Karl 7, 205, 428, 433, 467, 481
marxism 6, 14, 225, 258, 265-6, 277, 320, 378, 421-6, 428, 434, 442, 447, 450, 454, 457, 467, 480
Mass Democratic Movement (MDM) 380, 398-9, 401, 403
Mbeki, Thabo 407
McCuen, Colonel John J 345
McNamara, Robert 482
Mearsheimer, John 436
Merle, Marcel 468
Meyer, Dr PJ ('Piet') 121, 145, 156-7, 160-1
Mfecane 9
Military Intelligence (MIS) 133, 217-18; conflict with BOSS 217
Milner, Lord Alfred 75, 111
Mine Workers' Union (MWU) 36, 165, 310
Mobutu, General Sese Seko 221
Mondale, Walter 182
Monopoly Commission 309
Moore, Barrington 453
Morris, Michael L 185, 323, 429, 430, 488
Mostert, Judge Anton 232, 239, 242-3, 386
Mouffe, Chantal 442
Mozambique 170, 179, 182, 192, 199, 219, 258, 266, 320, 325, 329, 332-4, 345-6, 378, 408; FRELIMO 179, 303, 345; Pretoria Declaration 333; Renamo 329, 332-4, 345, 378, 407

MPLA 220-2
Mulder, Dr Cornelius Petrus ('Connie') xxvii,
  xxxi-xxxii, xxxiv-xxxv, xxxvii, 194, 199,
  201-2, 207, 210, 212-13, 215-16, 219,
  223-4, 230-45, 247-8, 258, 290-1, 295-7,
  298, 307, 389, 484-5
'Muldergate': xxvii-xxix, xxxii, xxxv, 15,
  171, 228, 229-31, 237, 242, 244-8, 283,
  313, 332, 351-2, 386-7, 403; political
  significance 244
Muller, Hanlie 290
Muller, Dr Hilgard 118, 213
Muller, S Louwrens 241, 290-1, 307
Muller, Tom 216
Munnik Commission 361

Naidoo, Jay 415, 464
Namibia 49, 142, 150, 170, 179, 182, 184,
  219, 241, 247, 257, 286, 293, 296, 299,
  314-15, 320, 345-6, 351, 372, 373, 388,
  390, 402-3; 1966 World Court decision
  150
Nasionale Pers xxviii, xxxi, xxxii, xxxv,,
  xxxviii, 47, 120, 129-30, 131, 141, 154,
  198, 216, 257
Nat 80 302
National African Federated Chambers of
  Commerce (Nafcoc) 186, 274, 328, 331-2
National Conservative Party (NCP) xxxiv,
  298, 307
National Democratic Movement (NDM) 374,
  387
National Intelligence Service 281, 283, 284,
  343, 349
National Maize Producers' Organisation
  (NAMPO) 309, 337
National Management and Development
  Foundation 227
National Manpower Commission 295
National Party (NP) xxvii-xxxviii, 3-11, 13-
  15, 22-3, 28-9, 33-7, 39-40, 42-9, 116-22,
  125-31, 136-48, 150-5, 157-67, 170, 178,
  179, 181, 182, 186-8, 193-206, 210, 213-
  16, 224, 226-8, 230, 232-49, 254, 256-8,
  263, 265, 268, 272-4, 276-7, 279-84, 287,
  293, 290-6, 298-303, 306-10, 312-16, 320-
  2, 324, 326-7, 320-2, 336-7, 342, 347-52,
  358, 362, 364, 366, 368-9, 372-7, 380-1,
  384, 387-92, 396-417, 419-23, 431-2, 444,
  472, 474-6, 478, 480-5; achievement of
  Republic 105-9; [and] Afrikaner press
  129; Afrikaner favouritism 74-80;
  Afrikanerisation of civil service 76-7;
  [and] Afrikaner workers 76-8; apartheid
  policies, see under apartheid; as party of
  big business 308; [and] Broederbond 46;
  Cape NP xxxi-xxxii, xxxviii, 122, 141,
  152, 159, 161, 194, 195, 210, 215, 223,
  227, 240, 257-8, 309, 373-5, 392; caucus
  xxxi, 29, 118, 151, 199, 210, 235-6, 241,
  274, 290, 302, 307, 336, 372, 374-5, 381,
  388, 399-400, 405, 409; class base 54-6,
  308, 376; constitutional reform 194;
  corruption 230-2, 242, 244, 246, 248, 258,
  351-2, 397; economic programme(s) 34;
  electoral base 35; [and] English-speakers
  116, 167, 202; Federal Congress 327;
  Federal Council 392; gesuiwerde xxxii,
  xxxv, 45; herenigde 40-1; history of 39;
  Hoofleier xxvii-xxx, xxxii, xxxiv-xxxv,
  xxxvii-xxxviii, 119, 123, 129-30, 142,
  145, 150-2, 154-5, 157, 158, 159, 161,
  163, 195, 204, 206, 207, 218, 232, 234,
  236-7, 240-3, 248, 249, 254, 257-9, 268-9,
  290, 291, 293, 295, 297-8, 302, 303, 307,
  308, 314-15, 335-6, 348, 360, 368, 380-1,
  384-5, 388-92, 395-400, 402, 404, 406-8,
  410, 412, 414, 415, 421, 422, 432, 459,
  484; impact of Republic on 116, 236, 295;
  'Information' scandal, see Muldergate;
  internal conflicts 118, 155, 196, 234, 239,
  241, 295, 296, 298; management of the
  economy 80-2; membership 48;
  'Muldergate' xxxiv, xxxvii-xxxviii, 230;
  Natal NP xxxi, 160, 193, 213, 256, 293,
  330, 380; OFS NP xxxv, xxxvii, 129, 154,
  160, 194, 232, 236, 238, 240; provincial
  leaders xxxiii, xxxvii, 40, 129-30, 154,
  163, 199, 202, 210, 212, 213, 215-18, 223,
  235, 236, 238-41, 243, 247, 257-8, 291,
  299, 302-3, 307, 315, 330, 335, 347, 373,
  377, 384, 389-92, 398, 484;
  provincialism/regionalism 123, 129, 130,
  216, 291-2, 397; reformism 201; split
  1982 300, 313; [and] stratification of
  Afrikaners 136; structure & role in

Index

Afrikaner nationalism 48; study groups (caucus) 165, 297-8; succession struggles xxix, 154, 195-6, 209-10, 234-5, 241, 258, 377, 380-1, 383-5, 388, 398, 407, 484; Transvaal NP xxv, xxvii-xxix, xxxiii-xxxviii, 44, 47, 117, 119, 129-30, 150, 152, 154, 159, 163, 196, 199-202, 210, 234-7, 239-41, 243, 247, 256-8, 290-2, 295-6, 298-9, 302-3, 307, 312, 315, 330, 335, 347, 373-6, 380, 384, 387, 389-91, 396, 398, 484; Twelve Point Plan 491

National Security Management System (NSMS) 281-6, 344, 376, 344, 346, 350, 377, 399, 402-3, 407

National Union 286, 363

National Union of Mineworkers (NUM) 363

Native Affairs Commission 68

Native Laws Commission of Enquiry (Fagan Commission) 24, 32-4, 197, 198, 273, 376, 444

Natives Representative Council (NRC) 27

Nattrass, Nicoli 429

Naudé, Dr Christiaan Frederick Beyers 107

Naudé, Louis (pseud.), *see* Schoeman, Beaumont M

Naudé, Tom 96, 107

Nederduitsch Hervormde Kerk (NHK)

Nederduitse Gereformeerde Kerk (NGK) xxxvii, 37, 43, 103, 106-7, 292, 314, 336-7

Nel, Christo 386

Nel, Daniel Jacobus Louis 333

Netherlands, the 126

New Republic Party (NRP) 188, 202, 373

New York Times 378

Nienaber, Prof. PJ 125

Nixon, Richard, M 170, 182, 278

Nkomati Accord 266, 320-1, 325, 328-9, 332-3, 350, 486

Nobel Peace Prize 321

Noodhulpliga 45

Nuwe Orde 40, 84

Nye, Joseph S 180, 436, 477

Obasanjo, General Olusegun 340

occupational structure 136-7, 144-5; changing place of Afrikaners 136; of Broederbond members 144

O'Donnell, Guillermo 461-6

O'Dowd thesis 424

Old Mutual, *see also* SA Mutual; 140, 174, 284, 365

Olivier, Prof. Nic 34, 71, 96, 107, 108

oorstroming 34, 196, 376, 414

Operation Senekal, *see* Department of Information

Oppenheimer, Harry F xxxiv-xxxv, 120-1, 124, 161, 184-5, 187, 231, 294-5, 358, 387-8, 459

Opperman, DJ 133, 156

Oranje Unie xxx

Organisation of African Unity (OAU) 193, 206, 223, 401

Orwell, George 320

Ossewa Brandwag (OB) xxix, xxxii, xxxiv, xxxvii-xxxviii, 40, 47, 119, 129, 151, 153-4, 159, 161-3, 205, 211

oud-smelters, see *smelters*

Pact government 471

Pakendorf, Harald 336

Palmer, Bryan 451

Pan Africanist Congress of Azania (PAC) 152, 173, 259, 370, 404

pass laws, *see also* dompas *and* influx control; 183, 193, 273, 322, 331, 335

Pattle, Sqdn-Leader MT ('Pat') 20

Paulus, Arrie 310

Perskor 127, 129, 232, 247, 314-15

Petersen, Hector 223

Petersen, SV 126

petty bourgeoisie 11, 42, 202, 248, 312, 323, 472; Afrikaner 42, 54, 55, 65, 78-9, 82; black 186, 277

Phillips, Mark 345

Pick & Pay 364

Pienaar, Schalk 179, 198

Pirow, Oswald 40

poor white problem xxxviii, 24, 76, 93

populism 268, 310, 311

Portugal 225; colonial collapse 219, 222

Posel, Deborah 432, 441, 452-7, 459-60, 486-7

post-modernism/post-structuralism 442, 443, 449, 455, 458, 467

Potgieter Commission 218

Pottinger, Brian 311
Poulantzas, Nicos 425, 430, 443
Premier Milling 361
President's Council 276, 279-80, 286-7, 302, 327, 349, 373-4, 405, 407, 420
Pretoria Minutes 405
Prime Minister xxvii, xxx-xxxi, xxxiii-xxxiv, xxxvi-xxxviii, 20, 21, 23, 27, 32, 34-5, 40, 44, 47, 48, 118-19, 142, 146, 150-3, 158-63, 166-7, 170, 180, 182, 192, 194-7, 201, 203-7, 210-12, 216-20, 226, 230, 232-5, 237-8, 240-3, 245, 247-8, 254-9, 263, 265, 266, 275, 278-9, 281-2, 284, 290-2, 294-5, 297-303, 307-9, 320, 331, 340, 341, 351, 361, 391, 392, 421; Economic Advisory Council 295; Office of 278, 281
Private Eye 151
Profumo, John 230
Progressive Party (PP), *see* Progressive Federal Party (PFP); xxxiv, 150-1, 187-8, 204, 276, 387
Progressive Federal Party (PFP) xxxiv, 187-8, 196, 222, 295, 320, 335, 364, 366, 369, 373-6, 385, 387, 397, 401
Progressive Reform Party (PRP), *see* Progressive Federal Party (PFP); 188
Project Orange 311
Provincial Councils 350, 375, 419
Portugal 179
Public service, *see* Civil service
Public Service Commission 212, 232, 284

Quail Commission 275
Quebec 431

Rabie, Jan 126-7
Rabie, Ralph, *see* Johanneskerkorrel
Rajbansi, Amichand 342
Ramaphosa, Matamela Cyril 412
Rand Daily Mail 48, 183, 185, 193, 213, 230-1, 233, 235, 237, 242, 244-7
Rapport xxviii, 243, 258, 308
Rapportryers 297
Raubenheimer, Braam 199, 292
Raw, Wyatt Vause 245, 403
Reagan, Ronald 266, 272, 378
Reconstruction and Development Programme (RDP) 5, 415, 464

Reddingsdaadbeweging, see Economic movement, Afrikaner
Reddingsdaadbond (RDB) xxix, 123, 142, 162, 187
Rees, Merwyn 235, 245
Regional Services Council(s) (RSC[s]) 347, 351
Relly, Gavin 361
Rembrandt Group xxxv, 140, 167, 177, 184, 196, 301, 309, 315, 358
repression 63, 109-10, 322, 345
Republican Intelligence (RI), *see also* Bureau for State Security; xxxvii, 159, 217
Republican Party 118
republicanism xxxiii, 55, 62, 86-9, 104; 1960 campaign 105-9
Reserves ('Native') 24-5, 27, 33, 35, 280, 329, 356, 379, 471
Reynders Commission 178
Reynders, Louw ('Loot') 235, 343
Rhodesia 158, 170, 182, 192, 195, 219, 258, 419
Rhoodie, Deneys 233
Rhoodie, Dr Eschel: xxxiv-xxxv, 156, 192, 205-6, 210, 212-16, 219, 221, 223, 230, 232-3, 235, 237, 239, 242-7, 477
Richards, Dirk 120, 130
Riekert Commission 33, 193, 273, 322, 324
Riekert Commission 33, 193, 273, 322, 324
Roberto, Holden 220-1
Rockman, Lt Gregory 401
Roos, Tielman 216
Rousseau, Dr Etienne 195
Roux, Dr Jannie ('JR') 278
'Rubicon' 317, 329, 330-3, 343, 355, 358, 403
Ruiterwag 45-6
Rupert, Anton xxxv, 140, 184, 187, 301, 315, 358
Rwanda 4

SA Mutual, *see also* Old Mutual 177, 284
sanctions, *see also* Economy, disinvestment; 170, 182, 300, 330, 332, 335, 337, 340-2, 355-6, 358-9, 365, 373, 378-9, 402, 405, 407, 410; Dellums Bill 355, 379
Sander, Mike 386
Sanlam xxxi, xxxiv, xxxix, 120-4, 140-2, 154, 160, 167, 174, 177, 195-6, 224, 225, 227,

257-8, 284, 300, 308-9, 311, 315-16, 331, 363, 365, 385
Sarakinsky, Ivor 439
Sasol 266, 272
Sauer Commission xxxv, 34-5, 64-5, 67
Sauer, Paul O xxxv, 46, 50, 68, 94, 96, 103-4, 112, 141, 152, 482; 'Old book' speech xxxv, 104
Saul, John S 487
Savimbi, Jonas 377
Schlebusch, Alwyn xxxv, 194, 232, 238-41, 276, 279, 283, 286, 308
Schlebusch Commission 276, 286
Schmitter, Philippe 461-6
Schoeman, Beaumont M 118, 119, 121, 130, 153, 162; as Louis Naudé xxxvi, 165
Schoeman, Ben J ('Oom Ben') xxxv, 46, 130, 152-3, 159, 163, 199, 207, 210, 243, 257, 307, 315, 482
Schoeman, Hendrik Stephanus Johannes 197, 297, 303
Schumann, Prof. CGW 122
Scott, Archbishop Edward 340
Security Police (SP), see South African Police Force (SAP)
securocrats 283, 287, 334, 339, 343, 349, 402-3, 406, 407, 409, 427, 432
Seegers, Annnette 52, 282
segregation 24-5, 32, 33-4, 37, 186, 307; theory & practice 24
Senegal 206, 214, 374
Senghor, Leopold 206
Serfontein, JHP ('Hennie') 45, 48, 118-19, 146, 163, 196, 210, 246
Sestigers 127-8, 130, 370-1
Sewe Dae by die Silbersteins xxxii, 124-5
Seychelles, The 214
Shaka, King 9
Sharpeville xxxv, 3, 178, 123, 140, 174, 180, 196, 203, 206, 273, 325, 482
Singh, Sardar Swaran 340
Sisulu, Walter Max Ulyate 26, 63
Sisulu, Zwelakhe 335
Skocpol, Theda 433-5, 437-41, 465, 473, 485
Slabbert, Dr Frederik van Zyl 335, 374, 387
Slovo, Joe 6, 464
Small Business Development Corporation 187
smelters xxxv, xxxvi, 41, 46, 153, 307

Smit, Bartho 127
Smit, Dr Robert 214
Smuts, Field Marshal Jan Christian xxx-xxxi, xxxvi, 20-4, 27, 29, 31-7, 40, 42, 145-6, 192, 231, 254-5, 421
Snyman Commission 274
Snyman, Willie 298
Somalia 3
South Africa Foundation 123, 144, 183, 224, 273, 301, 365, 385
South African Agricultural Union 29, 31, 144, 331
South African Air Force (SAAF) 20, 222, 378
South African Associated Newspapers 233
South African Breweries 188, 284
South African Broadcasting Corporation (SABC) xxxiv, 121, 146, 150, 162, 275, 336, 352, 388
South African Chambers of Business (Sacob) 361
South African Communist Party (SACP), see Communist Party
South African Confederation of Labour (Sacol) 310
South African Defence Force (SADF) xxxiii, xxxv, 180, 192, 216-28, 245, 255, 259, 262-4, 267, 281, 284, 286, 292, 322-3, 325, 329, 332-5, 341, 343-7, 349, 356, 360, 366, 372, 377-9, 385, 398, 403, 406-7, 409, 413-14; in Angola 179, 219; Special Forces Command 333, 406-7; Total Strategy 224
South African Employers Consultative Committee 183
South African Indian Council 194, 277
South African Institute of Race Relations 185
South African Maize Specialists' Organisation (SAMPO) 309
South African Party (SAP) xxx, xxxvi, 33, 36, 202
South African Permanent Building Society 364
South African Police (SAP) xxxvi, 180, 211, 217, 224, 334, 403, 405, 411, 492; policemen in Broederbond 145; Security Police xxxvii, 146, 159, 196, 211, 283, 334, 343-4, 403; Special Branch, see SAP, Security Police

South African Political Science Association 263

South African Reserve Bank 172, 176, 272, 329, 359, 379

South African Students' Organisation (SASO) 185

South African War (Anglo-Boer War) xxx, xxxvi, 23, 36, 41, 404

South West Africa, see Namibia

South West Africa Peoples Organisation (SWAPO) 170, 402-3

Southern Life 386

Soviet Union 222, 265, 272, 333, 378-9, 399, 463, 476, 482

Soweto uprising xxxii, xxxvii, 180, 183, 188-9, 193, 196, 222, 325, 355, 422

Sparks, Allistair 246

sport xxxi, 137, 138, 158, 164, 170, 199, 200, 202, 347

Stalin, Joseph 129, 162, 222

Stallard formula 25

state corporations: Armscor (see Armscor); Industrial Development Corporation (IDC) 79; Iscor 79; SAR&H 79; Sasol 79, 266, 272

state, the xxvii, xxxi, xxxiv, 14, 23, 27, 29-30, 33, 35-6, 43, 46, 48, 143, 146, 155, 160, 166, 170-1, 177, 179, 186, 192, 203, 215, 223, 225-7, 230-2, 241, 244, 262-4, 267-8, 272, 273, 276, 278, 280-4, 287, 290-1, 293, 300, 309, 322, 325-7, 331-2, 334, 340-1, 343-4, 346-52, 357, 359-62, 364, 366, 378, 380-1, 389, 398, 416, 425, 427, 429, 428, 430-2, 434-43, 442-5, 451-5, 457, 459, 462, 465-6, 468-74, 477-89, 492; employees 76-8; reorganisation 277-87

State of Emergency 325, 331, 340-1, 343-4, 348-50, 360, 379, 380, 386, 408

State President xxvii-xxix, xxxvii-xxxix, 5, 146, 213, 234, 243-4, 270, 276, 278, 287, 343-4, 349-51, 389-92, 401, 414, 419, 427, 484; Office of 278, 287, 343-4, 349, 420

State Security Council (SSC) 218, 223, 280-4, 286-7, 393, 334, 341, 343-7, 349-50, 384, 398-9, 403, 427

Steel and Engineering Industries Federation of

South Africa (Seifsa) 183, 328, 364

Steyl, Jack 130

Steytler, Dr Jan 276, 387

Stofberg, Louis 373

stormjaers 47

Strijdom, Johannes Gerhardus ('Hans') xxviii-xxx, xxxii-xxxiii, xxxv-xxxviii, 44, 46-8, 118-19, 129, 142, 210, 216, 255, 257, 297, 299-300, 303, 308, 348, 391, 398, 400, 484; conflict with Malan 85-90; election & leadership 89-90; relationship with Verwoerd 92-4

strikes 26, 34, 129, 179, 346, 362-3, 411, 471

structural adjustment 8, 417

Suid-Afrikaanse Akademie vir Wetenskap en Kuns 124-5, 128

Suid-Afrikaanse Buro vir Rasse-aangeleenthede (SABRA) xxxiv, 66-7, 70-2, 85, 96, 107-8, 128, 199, 300, 311; Verwoerd purge 108

Suid-Afrikaanse Mielieprodusente Instituut (SAMPI) 144, 309

Suid-Kunene (Suid-Wes Afrika) 142

Sunday Express 245, 301

Sunday Times 119, 125, 130, 231, 241, 246

Suzman, Helen 150-1, 204, 335

Swart, Charles Robert ('Blackie') xxix-xxx, xxxvii-xxxviii, 369, 371

Swaziland 320, 329

Swilling, Mark 342, 345

Syfrets 385

Taiwan 255, 379, 475

Tambo, Oliver Reginald 333, 340

Terreblanche, Prof. Sampie 352, 388, 411

Thatcher, Margaret 236, 266, 272, 340, 385, 399

The Citizen xxxii, 214, 233-4, 243, 246, 362, 387

Theron Commission 193

Thorpe, Jeremy 211

Thucydides 436-7

To the Point 214

Tomlinson Commission 70-1, 444, 445, 467

Torch Commando 62-3

Torlage, Henry 307

Total Strategy xxvii, xxxiii, 4, 224 225, 227, 245, 253, 258-69, 272, 274, 277-8, 281,

292-4, 310, 316, 319, 321-4, 327-31, 334,
338, 351-2, 358, 368, 381, 396, 399, 491;
intellectual sources 259-64; reform
ideology 264; 'total onslaught' 256, 259-
60, 265-8, 272, 344, 379; Twelve Point
Plan 267; unravels 319
Tradegro 386
Transitional Executive Council 413
Transkei 118, 198, 214, 275
Treaty of Westphalia 437
Trek Investments Limited 142
Treurnicht, Dr Andries Petrus xxvii, xxxiii-
xxxiv, xxxvii, 156, 163-4, 181, 196-7, 199,
240, 256, 258, 290-2, 295-303, 306-8,
312-14, 316, 320, 337, 376, 388, 399-400
Trollip, Alf 117, 293
Trotsky, Leon 162
Trudeau, Pierre Elliot 258
Trust Bank 386
Tsafendas, Dimitrio 150-1
Tucker, Bob 364
Twelve Point Plan 491

Union Corporation 140, 315
UNITA 219-20, 222
United Democratic Front (UDF) 324, 334-5,
350, 380
United Nations (UN) xxvii, xxxvi,, xxxvi, 21,
20-2, 32, 170, 182, 193, 213, 236, 241,
263, 299, 357, 378, 379, 401, 474-5, 477,
482
United Party (UP) xxix-xxxii, xxxiv, xxxvi, 4,
6, 9-10, 12-13, 22-3, 27-37, 40, 42, 44,
47-8, 63-5, 95, 103, 117, 150, 188, 202,
246, 277, 381, 387, 472; dissolves 188;
during Sharpeville crisis 103
United States of America (USA) xxvii, xxxiii,
5, 20, 21 ,32, 45, 117, 123, 126, 130, 143,
154, 170, 174, 182, 187, 192, 206, 211,
214, 221-2, 255, 258, 264-5, 280, 296,
320, 329, 333, 345, 354-5, 373, 378-9,
378-9, 389, 396, 402, 407, 410, 412, 421,
423, 440, 444-5, 460, 463, 468, 475-7, 491
uprisings/revolts/rebellions, see also Soweto
uprising; xxxii, xxxvii, 4-5, 25, 180, 183,
188-9, 193, 196, 222, 276, 325-6, 328-9,
332-5, 337, 342, 346-7, 355, 360, 362,
368, 422; 1984-86 24, 26-8, 30-1, 33, 35,

37, 41, 325
Urban Foundation (UF) xxxv, 184-6, 188,
323, 331-2
urbanisation 24, 26-8, 30-1, 33, 35, 37, 41,
126, 139, 146-7, 196, 198, 200-1, 263,
327, 331, 365, 376, 478
Uys, Casper 298

van den Bergh, General Hendrik xxxiv-xxxv,
xxxvii-xxxviii, 159, 163, 205-6, 210-13,
215-19, 221-3, 233-5, 237, 242-3, 246-7,
283, 484; role in first Angola intervention
219
van der Merwe, Dr AJ 107, 292
van der Merwe, Prof. CF 118
van der Merwe, Daan 298
van der Merwe, IW ('Boerneef') 370
van der Merwe, JG ('Kaalkop') 122
van der Merwe, Koos 302
van der Merwe, Stoffel 348
van der Walt, Hennie 275
van der Walt, Prof. Tjaart 198
van der Westhuizen, Lt General 345
van Deventer, Lt General André 345
van Eck, Jan 409
van Niekerk, Sybrand 307
van Rensburg, Basie 160
van Rooy, Prof. JC 45
van Rooyen, Retief xxxvii, 233, 237-8, 246
van Wyk, Chris 386
van Zyl, Jan 298
Venda 275
verkrampte/verligte xxvii-xxviii, xxx-xxxii,
xxxv, xxxvii-xxxviii, 48, 116, 118, 120-1,
124-5, 128-31, 141, 144, 149, 153, 154-8,
160-4, 166, 195-202, 204, 210, 227, 236,
240-1, 246, 255-6, 258, 268, 277, 290,
292-93, 296, 300, 302, 306, 311-14, 316,
372-3, 384, 390
Verwoerd, Dr Hendrik Frensch (Die
Hollander, Die Rots: xxxi, xxxv, xxxvii-
xxxviii, 47-8, 117-19, 123-4, 128-9, 142,
150, 152-154, 157, 158, 161-2, 164, 200,
203-4, 206, 255, 266, 275, 279-80, 290,
302, 306-8, 312, 323, 351, 399, 402, 416,
482; and Broederbond 47; appeal to
English-speakers 116; assassination, 1966
150; clash with SABRA 70-1, 108;

leadership style 111-13; rejects Cottesloe 106-7, 111; rejects Tomlinson Commission 70-1; relationship with Strijdom 92-4; *Transvaler* editor 93

Verwoerd, Elizabeth (Betsie) 93

Vietnam 225

vigilantes 334, 346

Viljoen, General Constand 9, 332-3, 350, 403

Viljoen, Dr Gerrit van Niekerk 196, 200, 292, 296, 300, 385, 405

Viljoen, Marais 210, 291

Visser, Dr AJ 124

Vlok, Adriaan 344, 380, 402, 407, 465

volk 14, 41, 116, 121-2, 137, 141, 256, 311, 316

volksbeweging 43, 116, 164, 166

volkseenheid 131, 136, 289, 294, 313, 315

volkseie 41, 43, 73, 118, 156, 181

volksgebondenheid 41

Volkshandel 124, 139, 162, 183, 332

volkskapitalisme 11, 14, 120-1, 155

Volkskas xxxiii, 140, 167, 292, 315, 398

Volksparty 40-1

Volkstaat 9

Voortrekker Pers xxxi, 129

Vorster, Baltazar Johannes ('John') xxvii-xxxv, xxxvii-xxxix, 48, 116, 118-19, 125, 128-30, 133, 142, 145-6, 151-5, 157-67, 170, 180, 188, 191-6, 201-7, 210-12, 214, 216-21, 223-24, 227-28, 230, 232-5, 237-9, 241-7, 249, 257-9, 265, 268, 278-81, 283, 290-1, 293, 295, 297, 300, 306-8, 313, 315, 348, 351, 361, 366, 375, 380, 381, 393, 484; appeal to English-speakers 167; attack on Assocom 195; forced out of Presidency 243; role in first Angola intervention 219; leadership style 154, 164, 203; resignation from Premiership 234; vacillation 194

Vorster, Dr Koot 159

Waddell, Gordon 361

Wallerstein, Immanuel 437

Wandrag, Major-General 346

Waring, Frank 117, 152

Wassenaar, Dr Andries xxxix, 195, 258, 385

Watermeyer, GA 75-6

Weber, Max 431-2, 442, 479, 485

Weekly Mail 401

Weiss, Prof. PFD 128-9

Wessels, Leon 344

White Paper on Defence 265

Wiehahn Commission 193, 273, 323

Williamson, Craig 333

Wilson, Harold 170

Winnipeg Free Press 431

Winter, Gordon 125, 179, 192, 211, 217, 223, 247, 436

Wit Komando 299

Wool Board 101

World Council of Churches 340, 477

World War II xxx, 20-1, 161, 173, 219, 300, 472, 477; impact on SA 20

Worrall, Dr Denis 287, 373-4, 387, 400

Yale University 263, 468

Yugoslavia 3

Zaire 482

Zambia 192, 320, 392

ZANU 170, 182, 266

ZAPU 170

Zimbabwe 158, 170, 184, 266, 419